The West Stole Africa's Wealth

The West Stole Africa's Wealth

Khoza Mduduzi

Library of Congress Control Number:		2015907779
ISBN:	Hardcover	978-1-5035-7059-7
	Softcover	978-1-5035-7060-3
	eBook	978-1-5035-7061-0

Print information available on the last page.

Rev. date: 10/11/2016

To order additional copies of this book, contact:
Xlibris
1-888-795-4274
www.Xlibris.com
Orders@Xlibris.com
637868

CONTENTS

LIST OF ABBREVIATIONS

5 B – Fifth Brigade

ADFL – Alliance des Forces Démocratiques pour la Libération du Congo-Zaïre

ANC – African National Congress

ANCYL – African National Congress Youth League

APLA – Azanian People's Liberation Army (armed wing of PAC)

AZAPO – Azanian People's Organization (South Africa)

BBBEE – Broad-Based Black Economic Empowerment

BCM – Black Consciousness Movement

BEE – Black Economic Empowerment

BSAC – British South Africa Company

CODESA – Convention for a Democratic South Africa

COSATU – Congress of South African Trade Unions

DA – Democratic Alliance

DEIC – Dutch East India Company

EFF – Economic Freedom Fighters

FRELIMO – Frente de Libertaçào de Moçambique

GNU – Government of National Unity (Zimbabwe)

GPA – Global Political Agreement (Zimbabwe)

ID – Independent Democrats

IFP – Inkatha Freedom Party (South Africa)

IFRS – International Financial Reporting Standards

IMF – International Monetary Fund

ISIL – Islamic State of Iraq and the Levant

ISIS – Islamic State of Iraq and Syria

LRP – Land Reform Program

MDC-M – Movement for Democratic Change led by then professor Arthur Mutambara

MDC-T – Movement for Democratic Change led by Morgan Tsvangirai

MK – Umkhonto We Sizwe (the armed wing of the ANC)

NATO – North Atlantic Treaty Organization

NDP – National Development Plan

NEPAD – New Partnership for Africa's Development

OAU – Organization of African Unity

PAC – Pan-African Congress

RDP – Reconstruction and Development Programme (ANC-South Africa)

RENAMO – Resistência Nacional Moçambicana (Mozambican National Resistance)

SACP – South African Communist Party

SADC – Southern African Development Community

SANDF – South African National Defence Force

SARS – South African Revenue Service

UANC—United African National Council

UDF – United Democratic Front (South Africa)

Unisa – University of South Africa

UNWFP – United Nations World Food Programme

WB – World Bank

ZANLA – Zimbabwe African National Liberation Army (armed wing of ZANU)

ZANU – Zimbabwe African National Union

ZANU-PF – Zimbabwe African National Union–Patriotic Front

ZAPU – Zimbabwe African People's Union

ZIPRA – Zimbabwe People's Revolutionary Army (armed wing of ZAPU)

ZRP – Zimbabwe Republic Police

ZWVA – Zimbabwe War Veterans Association

PREFACE

We Africans can't understand the present without thoroughly comprehending the past. It's also true that we Africans can't comprehend thoroughly the future without comprehending thoroughly the present. The future is a derivative of the present, and the present is the derivative of the past. The African continent is not free politically, and the dearth of political freedom is attributed to the dearth of the proper interpretation of political freedom. Political freedom doesn't necessarily translate to financial freedom. We Africans have come to the point of realization that since political freedom doesn't translate to financial freedom and economic freedom, why then do we Africans continue to cling or cleave to this illusion that we are politically free even if we are in a financial and economic bondage? The preliberation political ideologies we had in the past were abandoned in the process of Africa's liberation struggle. Africa's preliberation political ideologies were altered in the process of Africa's liberation struggle in order to acquire the political Pyrrhic victory. The Western settlers came to Africa without anything in their hands, and not only did they colonize Africa but also they have stolen Africa's wealth. Africa today is a laughingstock all over the world; it is branded as the hopeless continent, the disease-stricken continent, the Dark Continent, and the poverty-stricken continent. My hypothesis is this: the West stole Africa's wealth, polluted the air, polluted the water, and destroyed Africa's natural environment and left the African people with incurable diseases. The endless infighting among African countries especially in Central Africa is attributed to the direct interest that the West has in Africa's mineral deposits. The political unrest and dearth of peace and tranquility among African countries engender the unaccountable squandering of Africa's wealth by the Western agents who come to Africa under the pretext of foreign investors. Political unrest and the dearth of political stability engender economic instability; consequentially, foreign investments and economic opportunities eventually dwindle. The political unrest engenders economic uncertainty and cripples both African investors' and foreign investors' confidence. The one-million-dollar question is this: Are we African people politically free, and are we ever going to be politically free, and what is the use of political freedom without the ownership of the means of production? In every African war and African conflict, there is a Western interest and intervention that comes disguised as an arbitrator or a mediator among the warring groups. Not only will the Western mediator ensure that both African warring groups reach an amicable consensus, but also the mediator will bring his foreign investors into the negotiation table to give them the opportunity to continue to do business with African countries as faithful partner. The theory that says African problems need African solutions is sheer madness. African people don't trust each other to engage in a business relationship. Most African countries prefer to do business with their former colonizers instead of their African brothers, attesting to the old saying that says "The better the devil you know than the devil you don't know." It is possible that African liberation movements along the way were spiritually diluted, and they realized that political freedom and economic freedom can't be achieved simultaneously and opted for the easy route that wind up in the economic wilderness than the long route of political freedom coupled with economic freedom that might have taken forever to attain. It's also possible that during Africa's liberation struggle, African liberation movements realized that achieving a wholesale economic freedom coupled with political freedom was impractical. African liberation movements believed that it was possible to achieve political freedom without economic freedom, and once they had achieved political freedom without economic freedom, then economic freedom was going to follow later. It is after a careful and thorough political assessment of the African liberation struggle that ordinary Africans began to question the preliberation political and economic ideology and the economic plan of African liberation movements. The African liberation struggle is long over, but most African people are still poor, overworked, and underpaid, and all the promises that were made by African liberation movements prior to Africa's political independence have not been fulfilled. The West continues to siphon Africa's wealth in broad daylight through foreign investments, and a vast tract of land still remains in the hands of the Western settlers. The landless Africans continue to be ravaged by poverty even to this day. African sons and daughters continue to school in the mud schools, and African women and African men still work in the farms where they receive a slave wage. This begs the question, what is political freedom without economic freedom? In church they taught me from the law of liberty that faith without work is dead. Then can I surmise that political freedom without economic freedom is like a body without a spirit? We are also taught from the law of liberty that it is the spirit that gives life and the flesh profits nothing. The body without the spirit is dead; therefore, faith without works is dead, consequently political freedom without economic freedom. Just as the spirit gives life to the body, so does economic freedom to political freedom. The dearth of economic freedom from political freedom is like the body without the spirit, so is our political freedom without economic freedom. It's abundantly clear over time that the African liberation movements altered their original political and economic agenda in order to attain political freedom without economic freedom. The political rationale behind pursuing political freedom first, then economic freedom later, was simply based on the assumption that once these African liberation movements have managed to free African people politically, then automatically economic freedom will follow suit. African liberation movements committed a grave political miscalculation by conceding to the demands of the West in order to attain political independence and political freedom from the political prison of the West. When African countries gained their political independence from the West, there was excitement and jubilation in the African continent. Finally the African people were going to live free in the land of their forefathers, but little did the African people know that they were not economically free although they were only politically free. Political freedom and economic freedom—they both go hand in hand. Attaining political freedom at the expense of economic freedom is sheer madness. It's logically sound and politically correct to make political concessions during any political talks. The main problem with most of the African liberation movements during the political talks and political discussions, due to political pressure from the West, is that they made significant political and economic concessions that were not in the interest of the African people but that were in the interest of the West. African liberation movements opted for foreign aid and foreign donations rather than to apply land and economic reform across the board. Until this day and age in the African continent, there is still poverty and unemployment, even though the African continent is the richest continent on the face of the earth as far as mineral resources are concerned. The West stole Africa's wealth and buried that wealth in the World Bank and IMF and European Central Bank, and that is why the West is too hasty to disperse foreign aid to African countries with pleasure because the West is giving only the interest of the whole African wealth to the same African countries that it took from through colonization and pillaging. African poverty and wars are the Western inventions, and the West stands to prosper economically as long as the African continent is in flames of fire owing to the endless wars.

CHAPTER 1

PYRRHIC VICTORY

The *Oxford Advanced Learner's Dictionary* defines a Pyrrhic victory in this way: "a victory that is not worth winning because the winner has suffered or lost so much in winning it." Africa is for Africans, Europe is for the Europeans, and America is for Americans. We read in the law of liberty that in the beginning, God created the heavens and the earth. The earth was without form and void, and darkness was on the face of the deep. Then God said, "*Let us make man in our own image, according to our likeness; let them have dominion over the fish of the sea, over all the earth and over every creeping thing that creeps on the earth.*"[1]

Archaeologists agreed that there was a place called the Garden of Eden. While they concurred on this notion that this Garden of Eden existed, they also concluded that they can't locate this place on planet Earth. Since this place can't be clearly located on planet Earth, it compelled archeologists to abandon the search. It's highly probably that since the archeologists could not locate the Garden of Eden in Middle East that the Garden of Eden was located in Africa. The African continent has seen more bloodshed than any other continent on the face of the earth. God created Africa and placed African people in the midst of the African continent to have dominion over the mineral resources, land and livestock, and every creeping thing that creeps on the earth. African people were living in the abundance of peace and tranquility and needed nothing, and they lacked nothing because they had more than enough. Africa was a continent of peace and tranquility until the arrival of the Western settlers; they brought disunity, wars, and covetousness among African people. African sons and daughters today—they are in endless wars over their mineral resources, land, and property that were given to them by God in the beginning of time before the arrival of the Western settlers. We should understand African history if we are to understand where we Africans come from, and we should understand the liberation struggle against colonization if we are to understand where we Africans are going politically and economically. It is inevitable that we Africans will never change our past, and we will never reverse the injustices of our past that have been committed to us by the West, but we can ponder the future and ensure that the gross injustices of the past won't repeat themselves in the near future. We African people can't reverse the injustices of the past does not necessarily mean that the mistakes of the past can't be corrected. It's also important that we revisit the mistakes of the past in order to gain valuable lessons and experiences in order to ensure that the future generation does not fall in the same bottomless pit that we, the current African generation, currently find ourselves in. History is the best teacher, but only reliable history is the best teacher, and those who ignore the valuable lessons that history teaches are likely to repeat the same mistakes that have been committed by the previous African generation even in the near future. African history should to be read thoroughly, and when we read African history, we should be brutally honest with ourselves, and we Africans should also ask the right questions in order to get the right answers. While we read African history, we should also write our own African history for the future generation because it's futile to read African history only without writing it for the future generation. South Africa is a democratic country led by a democratically elected government, and in the process, it is also sheltering anecdotal five million Zimbabweans that came to seek refuge because of the political unrest in Zimbabwe and the lack of economic opportunities. The sub-Saharan African political history is interrelated, and when one reads the South African history in order to understand the South African political landscape, it would be a great injustice if one does not appreciate the fact that Africans are children of a single mother. The whole point of reading history is not to open old wounds and dig the old graves but to learn about our historical past and shape our future based on the knowledge that we would have learned from our past history. It's sheer gibberish to blame Pres. Robert Mugabe for all of Zimbabwe's economic and political problems. Indisputably he is the president of Zimbabwe, but he was elected democratically by the sober Zimbabweans. The one-million-dollar question is this: Where did things go wrong in Zimbabwe? The majority of the African liberation movements' history was written by Western scholars writing African history about Africa, and some of these Western scholars have never ever set foot in Africa or visited Africa for that matter. And the greatest danger about writing African history without sufficient knowledge about Africa is the following: Westerners scholars consequentially formulated weird perceptions about Africa that was based on the Western propaganda and prejudice about Africa. On the other hand, majority of African scholars read African history from the Western textbooks owing to the fact that majority of African knowledge is not from Africa but is from the West. It becomes easy for the West to continue corrupting Africans through Western propaganda and prejudice. My main goal is not to rewrite the African history, and having said that, it will be disingenuous for me to divorce the notion of interrelatedness of the African history between South Africa, Mozambique, Zambia, and Zimbabwe. Zimbabwe's history came from the South African history; Zambia's history is interrelated with the Zimbabwean history; and Democratic Republic of Congo's history is related to the Zimbabwean history and also related to the South African history in a way. The Mozambican history is also related to Zimbabwe's history, and the most common denominator among these African countries that I have mentioned above is their liberation struggle and their liberation movements. It will be a futile exercise then to attempt to understand Zimbabwe's history in the isolation of the other African countries, since there is an element of interrelatedness. It will be unjust and unfair to conclude that Zimbabwe's crisis purely and squarely falls on the shoulders of Pres. Robert Mugabe alone as if he is a demigod. I am not a Pres. Robert Mugabe proponent, and I am also not a Pres. Robert Mugabe critic. There are multiple versions of Zimbabwe's history and what led to the West to impose illegal economic sanctions on Zimbabwe's economy. Some people have concocted Zimbabwe's political and economic version of events to suit their own personal agenda and interests. To every problem there is a solution; therefore, problems present us with opportunities to think and map a way forward. People don't see problems in the same light. Some people, through the midst of the problem, become the greatest critics, and some become the greatest proponents of the person whom they think is in the center of the problem. I was in church one Sunday when a preacher said, "Most people only use 5 percent of their brains." That is why many people try to run away from all forms of problems by all means, whether they are political or economic, because they only use 5 percent of their brains to solve problems, leaving the 95 percent of their brains idling.

African democracy is still very young, and already the African masses are running out of patience attributed to the lack of the fulfillment of the promises that were made by the African liberation movements prior to Africa's independence. Most African liberation movements made humongous promises to the African masses. African liberation movements promised the African people a better life. African liberation movements said you will get your fertile land back, and the natural resources of our country will be owned by your democratically elected government, and your natural resources will be utilized for the benefit of the African people; African children will no longer go to bed with hungry stomachs; and the democratically elected government will ensure that every child gets a decent education that will make him or her an economically active citizen and an active participant in the reconstruction of the African continent. In South Africa, prior to the April 27, 1994, national election, the ANC (African National Congress) compiled a very long and logically sound document that was overloaded with humongous promises that detailed how the government of the ANC was going to change the lives of the masses should the ANC win the April 27, 1994, national election. There was a very powerful catchphrase that accompanied this document, and it went like this: "Now is the time, and the time is now." Nelson Mandela writes in his autobiography, *Long Walk to Freedom*:

Sometimes there is nothing one can do to save something that must die.[2]

Nelson Mandela knew without a shadow of any doubt, even to himself, that he was born of a woman, and his life was managed and controlled not by the circumstances in which he lived in but by the invisible world, which he will only see if he departs from the visible world. Therefore, death is a way to a permanent home. The unfortunate part is this: there is nothing that the whole world can do to save something that must die even if that person who must die was Nelson Mandela. The ANC won the April 27, 1994, national election, and Nelson Mandela became the first democratically elected black president of South Africa, and the people of South Africa were very happy. They were very happy because the promises that have been contained in the document titled RDP (Reconstruction Development Program) were supposed to come to pass, and the people were happy because the land that was taken from them illegally and forcefully by the apartheid government was going to be given back to them. The African liberation movements all over the continent of Africa made humongous promises to the people that were practically impossible to fulfill, and not only did African liberation movements lack the intellectual capital to bring these humongous promises to pass, but also they lacked the financial muscle. ZANU-PF (Zimbabwean African Union–Patriotic Front) led by Robert Mugabe made humongous political and economic promises to the people of Zimbabwe—promises that were very difficult to fulfill, including the distribution of lands that have become a thorn in the flesh of most Zimbabwean people. Zimbabwe's economic crisis gets worse day by day than ever before, and the international community has decided to fold its arms and ignored the Zimbabwean economic crisis. The notion says that as soon as Pres. Robert Mugabe dies, the international community will intervene to lift off the masses from the self-imposed pain and poverty owing to the irrational and foolish political action of invading the farms in the year 2000. History is the best teacher, but we Africans will only learn from history if we are ready to read and understand the lessons that history is trying to teach us. The majority of the African people, specifically the youth, know nothing about economic sanctions except from reading definitions from the Western dictionary. Zimbabwe is the quintessence of what economic sanctions can do to the economy of a country; it's also the quintessence where one can see the cruelty and taste the brunt of the Western powers. Economic sanctions are the cancer of any economy; they paralyze the economy of a country from all angles and in many ways. The economy of Zimbabwe is suffering from swine flu, and swine flu is an economic sanction. I made a conscious decision that before I can write a book about how the West stole Africa's wealth, I will visit Zimbabwe to see for myself the effects of economic sanctions and the devastation they caused in the economy of Zimbabwe. I also wanted to understand the power grip that the West has over Africa. The fact of the matter is this: Africa is very far from being economically independent from the West. The decolonization of Africa from the Western powers still needs to be redefined, and we Africans should coin for ourselves the African interpretation of Africa's decolonization from the Western powers and Western forces. I told a Zimbabwean friend of mine that I have an important assignment that I must undertake, and as a result of this important assignment, I will be required to visit Zimbabwe. Without any hesitation, he quickly agreed that we can go together to Zimbabwe. One day prior to our trip to Zimbabwe, he began to panic. He came to me to complain about the political unrest in Zimbabwe, suggesting that the country is the fertile ground for the impending political intolerance that eventually will lead to political violence. He said, "I don't want you to be caught in the crossfire of the political violence." The fact of the matter is this: Zimbabwe is a free country, and the government of ZANU-PF was democratically elected by the masses. Now when he talks about political violence, what is he talking about? I spoke to my other Zimbabwean friend Mr. Milkshake, who suggested to me that Zimbabwe is a free country, and once I visit Zimbabwe, I will fall in love with it. He went on to criticize the media that what the majority of people are reading in the newspapers about Zimbabwe is not true. The political intolerance and the political violence that is widely reported about in the media is pure fiction about Zimbabwe. I pinned down all my hopes on most of the things that Mr. Milkshake said, but I am also surprised because Mr. Milkshake seems to hold a different view about Zimbabwe. Is it possible that two different people from the same country can have diverse views about the same country that they were both born in, grew up in, and went to school in? I had to make another conscious decision in the midst of these conflicting opinions about Zimbabwe. By the way, I am an African. I doubt that the ZRP (Zimbabwean Republic Police) can just assault me without a serious cause. I am not going to Zimbabwe to form a new political party, and I am also not going there to engage in a political campaign. I went to buy a bus ticket, and the following day, I went to the bank to change my money from South African currency to US dollars. The reason I was changing my money from South African currency to US dollars is that Zimbabwe does not have its own currency in circulation right now. The economy had collapsed to the point that the governor of the Zimbabwe Reserve Bank, Gideon Gono, decided that the bank must no longer print Zimbabwean dollars. The US dollar is currently Zimbabwe's currency with the sole purpose to streamline trade and lift the economy to its current bad position. The introduction of the US dollar makes it possible for the trade relation among African countries. Like one bus driver said, "When you are using US dollars, you will never go wrong." I was in Pretoria station in the bus terminal. I was waiting for the bus that was supposed to depart exactly at 2:30 p.m. to pick me up, and I waited until 3:30 p.m. Eventually the bus company sent us an SMS that the bus was delayed in Johannesburg by an hour; therefore, it meant we will leave at exactly 3:30 p.m. from Pretoria to Harare, Zimbabwe. Finally the bus came. The driver checked my passport and my bus ticket, and I boarded inside the bus to Harare, Zimbabwe, with my doubtful friend Mr. Brown, who believes that I will perhaps come back to South Africa with bruises from the assaults of the

ZRP (Zimbabwe Republic Police). My mind was wandering in the political wilderness, and I was trying to enjoy the journey and yet afraid that maybe I was seeing South Africa for the very last time. Most South Africans are cynics. I had a conversation with a security guard called Steve about my journey to Zimbabwe. He asked me a stupid question, and he said, "Have you been vaccinated?" People like Steve, when they think about other African countries other than South Africa, only think about diseases like malaria, AIDS, and TB as if, while they are living in South Africa, they are immune from such diseases. My seat number in the bus was 4C, meaning I will be next to the window and I will have the luxury to see outside through the window from South Africa all the way to Harare, Zimbabwe. On seat 4A sat a certain Zimbabwean lady, brown in complexion. She looked like she got it altogether as if she has planned for this journey for a very long time. By just a mere glance, I could tell that she was going to Harare to see her husband that has been waiting for her for quite some time now. I could also see from her face that she missed him so much to the point that she can't wait to get to Harare, Zimbabwe. As if I am a prophet, she called him and said, "We are leaving Pretoria right now. We will be in Harare, Zimbabwe, in the morning." On the second seat was a gentleman from Zimbabwe who was also quiet, who could not talk to me until it was dark in the bus and was forced by the circumstances to have a dialogue with me. Our dialogue was about the light in the bus that was pointing straight to our seat. Our conversation started. He said to me his name is Craig, and he was going to Harare, Zimbabwe, to a place called Chinhoyi, which is far away from the capital city, Harare. I jokingly said to Craig in the bus, "If Zimbabwe is under economic sanctions, how come this lady seated next to you has an iPad and BlackBerry at the same time?" He said, "I think this iPad can cost US$1,000 and the BlackBerry US$300." Economic sanctions don't mean the same thing to the same people. Some families, when the country is under economic sanctions, thrive economically; while other families, if a country is under economic sanctions, starve to death, specifically people who are not educated. Those are the ones that will be hit hard by the economic sanctions because they are on the bottom of the quadrant. University professors and high school teachers from the economic-sanctioned country will immigrate to other countries where they can find decent high-paying jobs. There are a many Zimbabwean teachers in South Africa that are teaching math, physics, and science, and they can work in diabolic working conditions. They work in the rural areas and in locations where most of the learners come from dysfunctional families and have serious learning barriers. Majority of South African graduates, when they complete their degrees in the universities, don't prefer to teach in the locations and in the villages because that is where they grew up. The other reason is that the South African government has abolished corporal punishment; therefore, there is a high rate of ill discipline in the public schools in the locations and in the public schools in the villages. We arrived at the Beitbridge border, which is the border that separates South Africa and Zimbabwe. Clearly it began to dawn on me that within a short space of time, I will be in Zimbabwe. I began to have goose bumps. We arrived at Beitbridge at exactly midnight. I went through the South African immigration offices for the stamping of my passport, and that took us almost an hour. As we went to the Zimbabwean immigration offices, the first thing I laid my eyes on was the poster that was on the electric pole that was cautioning visitors how to prevent the spread of cholera. I began to realize that right now I am going to Zimbabwe, and cholera is a reality in Zimbabwe. I am beginning to have real Zimbabwean experience firsthand. Zimbabwe's immigration offices are totally different from the South African immigration offices. Their architectural styles are not the same. Even the immigration officers are not having the same attitude. We stood for five long hours at the Zimbabwean immigration offices to get our bus cleared and pay the custom duties for those who had items that were beyond US$300 in value. We left Beitbridge border at exactly 5:00 a.m. All of a sudden, the bus driver was ordered to pull over by the traffic officer. The traffic officer didn't waste too much of our time, and we got back to our long journey to Harare. From Beitbridge to Harare, we passed through almost seventeen police roadblocks. This was very strange to me because I come from South Africa; I am not used to these endless roadblocks. I was told by the doubtful Mr. Brown that since the year 2004, Zimbabwe's security system has changed drastically and is attributed to the mercenaries that were going to Equatorial Guinea that were arrested in Zimbabwe International Airport in 2004. Since then, the Zimbabwean government is always alert of any security risk that might pose a danger on the safety of the country. Most of the time from Beitbridge to Harare, I was awake. I never wanted to miss any action, and I also wanted to see the proverbial Zimbabwe that has been economically sanctioned by the West because of its Land Reform Program (LRP). I wanted to see the farms that were taken away from the British sons and daughters. On our way to Harare, we took a break in a small town called Masvingo. Most passengers went to the toilets, and some bought some drinks right next to the small shop where we packed our bus. Mr. Brown—I hope you know him by now—points to the heap of gold like mountains and said, "This was a gold mine a long time ago." The Western settlers came to Africa with nothing and found Africa overflowing with gold, milk, and honey. Not only did they steal our gold and diamonds, but also they left bottomless halls that today pose a risk to the current African generation and the future generation. Most people who worked in these mines for quite a long period of time have nothing to show for their long hours in the belly of the earth drilling all day long in order to feed their families. Most of our African brothers, the only thing they came back with from these mines are STD (sexually transmitted diseases), AIDS (acquired immune deficiency syndrome), TB (tuberculosis), and silicosis. Gold and diamond are gone, but we are left with broken bones to bury and sick people that need our medical attention and financial assistance, and that is all what we are left with in Africa. My quest is how much wealth was stolen from the African soil, and is it possible that it can be quantified, and are there any reliable records that can paint a perfect financial picture for our generation and the future generation? The West stole Africa's wealth, but the one-million-dollar question that is in my mind is, how much has the West stolen from Africa? When there is a cataclysmic change in the livelihood of people, most of the relevant and reliable documents normally get stolen and misplaced for that matter, and relevant and reliable information either get washed away by the natural disasters like floods or disappear. Because of the paramount importance of information to the point and to the degree of revealing corrupt activities, financial embezzlements, and atrocities that have been committed in the past by the previous regimes, therefore some people decide to shrug off crucial information to ensure that it doesn't see the light of day because of the sensitivity of the information, as at some point it might be incriminating to others. I saw farms that were once owned by the Western settlers. Zimbabwe was known as the breadbasket of Africa, but today Zimbabwe is the basket case of Africa, importing everything including the toothpaste. I think before this era is over, Zimbabwe should construct a national museum that will only house the pictures and the memorabilia of this era of economic sanctions and poverty. African scholars all over the world should be invited to Zimbabwe to document this era, the economic sanctions era, and it's also Pres. Robert Mugabe's era, and this era must go down in history as the most painful era for the people of Zimbabwe. The greatest mistake that the Israelites did when they were in captivity in Egypt is that they didn't document their plight properly in a perfect way.

In the book titled *Walking the Bible*, by Bruce Feiler, he writes:

> *Dr. Abdel Halim Nur el-Din, professor of Egyptology, head of the Department of Egypt, Cairo University, and Giza once said, "We don't have any evidence that they left Egypt. We don't have any evidence of Joseph or Moses. When we don't have evidence, it's just too hard."*[3]

Prof. Dr. Abdel Halim Nur el-Din was disputing the fact that Pharaoh of the olden days once existed, and while he was a king in Egypt, he suppressed and oppressed the Israelites that were in Egypt, and he disputed the fact that Moses and Joseph were in Egypt. He also disputed the fact that Israelites were in Egypt and attributed that assertion to the lack of evidence and historical records that are plausible. The second bone of contention was about the pyramids—who builds the pyramids anyway? The late Libyan leader, Muammar Gaddafi, once said, "Pyramids were built by the Libyans,"[4] and the black Americans known as African Americans said, "These are our pyramids."[5] The fact of the matter is this: in the cataclysmic change of things, historical records are lost, and the relevant and reliable documents disappear, and what is left behind is oral history that should tell us old tales that are very flimsy to believe. To avoid the repeat of the case I have cited above, it's important in our African history to document these injustices that have been committed to us Africans by the West. It's important for our next generation to realize that Africa is rich not only in mineral resources only but also in livestock. African people were capable of plowing and feeding themselves before the arrival of the Western settlers with their guns and bullets that eventually became the precursor of wars and the displacement for a lot of African people.

Professor Nur el-Din went on to say:

> *"And if you take the Jews, or the Libyans, or the Americans, if they're so smart, why didn't they build the pyramids in their country?"*[6]

The point Professor Nur el-Din was making is this: pyramids were built by Egyptians, since there is neither oral evidence nor circumstantial evidence to the contrary to prove the theory of black Americans, Israelites, and Libyans. It therefore should be accepted that the Egyptians are smart because they built pyramids for themselves, and the Libyans, black Americans, and Israelites are not smart because if they were smart, they should have replicated the same pyramids in their countries of birth, since they claim they built pyramids in Egypt. If Zimbabwe's crisis is not captured on camera, it's possible that the next generation including the current generation will be easily misled to believe that Zimbabwe's economic sanctions were invited by Pres. Robert Mugabe alone and the Western powers have nothing to do with it. The Western powers can simple say, "We gave ZANU-PF a country that was African breadbasket, and they turned it into a basket case." These assertions will distort the main cause to the imposition of economic sanction to the economy of Zimbabwe and the leading chain of events that triggered the imposition of economic sanctions including the role of the Western powers in the whole process of economic sanctions. It's 2:00 p.m. I was in Harare finally, and Mr. Brown's wife had arrived to collect us in the bus terminal with her white car, which is an import from Japan. Mr. Brown told me that since Zimbabwe is in the self-imposed financial crisis attributed to the Land Redistribution Program and the political unrest that engender political violence, most car plants in Zimbabwe have shut down, and some decided to leave Zimbabwe completely. It therefore means that there are no car plants in Zimbabwe right now, and if there are any, they are very few. It would have taken Mr. Brown a considerable amount of money to purchase a car in Zimbabwe. When he decided that he wanted a car, he went straight to the South African harbor in Durban and bought a Japanese secondhand car, and it had cost him US$2,000, which is equivalent to R20,000 in South African currency, and couriered it to Zimbabwe. He said to me, "If these types of cars were to be allowed in South Africa, they were going to kill the South African automobile industry." We drove around town before I went to the hotel where I was supposed to sleep in for the night. He took me to the Zimbabwe Reserve Bank, and we went to different universities including the University of Zimbabwe, which is very smaller than I had imagined in the past. We also went to the South African embassy in Harare, and we went to rest in Nando's to have some lunch. Since we left South Africa the previous day, one never had a decent meal. At least I will have a decent meal, and Mr. Brown decided to foot the bill. Across to our table was a mother with her two daughters. The older daughter looked at me straight in the eye as if she was saying, "I can see you are not from Zimbabwe, and what do you want here—are you a terrorist?" She and her mother including her other sibling completed eating their lunch, and they left. In the parking lot of Nando's, there were all types of cars—BMW, Mercedes Benz, you name them. It didn't appear to me that we were in Zimbabwe; it's as if we were in South Africa or some European country. The music that they were playing in the Nando's restaurant was not Zimbabwean music but was DRC (Democratic Republic of Congo) music. I enjoyed the rhyme of the music, though I didn't know what the lyrics meant; it sounded like Latino music to me. Since Africans are people of music and rhythm. I was driven to the hotel where I was supposed to spend the night, and the first thing I saw in the reception was the picture of the president of the country, Robert Mugabe. I quickly learned that the Zimbabweans adore and love their president contrary to what is being reported on in the mainstream media. Zimbabweans love Pres. Robert Mugabe, and they don't perceive him the way the Western media perceive him. When I was reflecting alone in my hotel room about the events of the day, while I was in the bus, it just dawned on me that there has been deafening silence in the bus from South Africa to Zimbabwe, and even while I was in Harare, there was no political debate at all. It appeared to me that majority of Zimbabweans are not interested in any political debate, and there is a reason to that problem. In Zimbabwe, you are not allowed to disparage Pres. Robert Mugabe publicly. Though there is no declaration to back up this claim, you can only see it from the faces of the people and via the conversation that ordinary people hold. The main reason to that is this: there are many government spies in Zimbabwe than anywhere in the world. Some of the government spies are planted in the buses, and some are planted in the shopping centers. The prevailing of this deafening silence is attributed to the ever presence of these spies everywhere. In case you don't know, Zimbabwean police don't carry guns. Most of the time they carry batons, and a dangerous criminal who is carrying an AK-47 can be arrested by a police without a gun in Zimbabwe, and that is fact. While I was in my hotel room, I took a shower and watched TV a little bit. I went out to buy a newspaper few blocks away from the hotel. I could not travel much that day, since the political atmosphere in the country was very tense owing to the national elections that were going to be held on July 31, 2013. The following morning I was going to Bulawayo known as Matabeleland. I woke up early in the morning, took a shower, and went straight to the dining room. The waiter had already prepared a tea for a certain couple. This couple was very surprising to me because the boyfriend was an Indian and the girlfriend was a black

Zimbabwean, Ndebele lady for that matter. I overhead them talking about the boyfriend relocating to stay in Zimbabwe, and I could tell that they were madly in love. I completed drinking my tea quickly. The receptionist called the cab for me, and I was driven to the bus station where I would get the bus that will take me straight to Bulawayo, the second-largest city in Zimbabwe. In the bus from Harare to Bulawayo, I sat next to an old man as usual. Guess what! From my entire round trip from South Africa to Zimbabwe and from Zimbabwe to South Africa, I never sat next to a lady of my age, and that was very surprising, and anyway maybe if I ended up sitting next to a lady of my age, possibilities are I would lose focus and end up diverting from my journey and my purpose of my visit to Zimbabwe. This old man had two newspapers that contained conflicting reports. He gave me one newspaper. I went through it, and I quickly smelled the rat that I was now reading the state newspaper. I could see the unfair and unjust level of reporting that was contained in that newspaper. Having read the newspaper, I kept my mouth shut, or it might happen that the very same man who is reading these newspapers is the government spy planted by the government and he is in a search for the opposing voices of the MDC (Movement for Democratic Change) that are in this bus. My eyes were glued outside while the bus was moving. I began to see a considerable amount of land, and I could tell intuitively that these are the farms that were taken by the war veterans from the white commercial farmers, and now this vast tract of land lies in waste. This vast tract of land in the past was farms that were feeding families and the country. People all over the world said Zimbabwe was a breadbasket of Africa. They were referring to this vast tract of land that is no longer looked after, and there is no agricultural activity that is taking place here anymore. The Zimbabwean economic crisis is attributed to the farm chaos. If it wasn't for farm invasion, the political crisis that has become the cause of economic sanctions ax wouldn't have fallen on the Zimbabwean economy. I guess the white commercial farmers are saying wherever they are, "You took our farms away from us because you said you wanted to farm. Not only are you not farming, but you are also starving to death inside our farms." Zimbabwe is a beautiful country with a very gorgeous land that is conducive to farming and grazing for livestock. The Zimbabwean roads are very small, and the road maintenance is nonexistent. Zimbabwe's monkeys lack respect; they were all over the road. Maybe they are not from Zimbabwe; perhaps they were from Britain. When war veterans took the farms from the white commercial farmers, the Zimbabwean monkeys were left stranded as to where to go, and now they were wondering on the main road to Bulawayo, disrupting traffic. It's abundantly clear that when a country is in a political crisis that engender economic crisis, not only will the economic crisis affect the livelihood of average people, but it will also affect the wildlife. This is clearly pictorial on the faces of these monkeys; they are hungry, and there is no food to eat because agricultural activities are no longer taking place. There is a song that is sung by Stevie Wonder; in that song, the lyrics say, "Now that we've found love, what are we gonna do with it?" Now that we have found farms and our land back, what are we are going to do with it? The land and the farms have been deserted for almost thirteen years, and it seems as if there is no political will and a political plan that have been put in place to utilize this beautiful land for agricultural purpose. Are the people of Zimbabwe going to wait forever until this land is utilized for the benefit of the Zimbabwean people and the African continent? In Zimbabwe right now, there is another problem: it is the problem of Zanufication of the land and the Zanufication of companies. Any foreign incorporated company that will be coming from the West and from the continent of Africa, the powers that be made it crystal clear and straightforward that you should give to the state 51 percent shares, and the company remains with 49 percent shares in a company that have been incorporated by an individual not by the government. Bearing in mind the following: that if you have incorporated a mining company in Zimbabwe you will still have to pay company tax to the government, the very same government that you have already given 51 percent stake in your company, that is not a good business investment, and any investor would not prefer to inject a considerable amount of resources in an investment where there are high possibilities of a financial loss. Most investors will probably say, "Keep your mines, and we will keep our money." Our bus pulled over in small towns called Kwekwe and later Gweru. My Zimbabwean friend Mr. Milkshake and told me that "these two towns are mining towns, and they are pregnant with mineral resources that still remain untouched for a very long time. Even if in these two towns there were mining operations taking place for gold and diamond for the next one hundred years, they would never finish the gold and the diamonds in this area because these towns are very rich in mineral resources." The big question then is, where are the African mining moguls, and where are the African entrepreneurs to do mining in these towns and create employment for the African people? In South Africa, there are few mining moguls, but we have an excess of entrepreneurs who are staunch converts to the gospel of tenders and became tenderpreneurs.

We Africans are no longer exploiting the ground. There are no longer young brilliant minds. We are all waiting like the old Lazarus in the Bible, waiting for anything that will fall from the master's table, and unfortunately in South Africa, the master's table is the government. The crumbs that fall from the master's table are the government grants that choke and destroy your brains from functioning. When I was in Bulawayo in the bus terminal, a certain gentleman from Zambia told me a very sad story. He said, "South Africans are very lazy, and the government of South Africa builds houses for people for free and gives women money when they get pregnant." Since I am a South African, I became very offended. Part of what he said is true, but part of it is complete nonsense. South African population is dominated by women and children. South African men don't have tender care once they impregnate a woman; they will leave a pregnant woman to struggle alone. Most of our fathers who came from the villages to work in the mines of Johannesburg, the city of gold, ended up not going back home because of the beauty of Johannesburg. The men from the villages were saturated in the beauty of women from Johannesburg, and the only time when they will remember home where they came from will be when sicknesses and diseases would have long destroyed their lungs and broken all bones in their body, not to mention the spinal cord for that matter. The government of South Africa realized that the African culture sometimes marginalized women, and most women were struggling financially to raise children on their own; therefore, the South African government came up with social grants to alleviate poverty, but social grants are not a long-term solution to the problem of poverty, and they won't last forever in South Africa. When the president of South Africa, Jacob Zuma, delivered his state of the nation address in Parliament in 2012, he said, "South Africa is not a welfare state," meaning that our democracy is not based on social grants and building houses for free for people. Men and women should become economically activity and contribute to the country by providing skills to assist in building the economy and eventually earn a living out of their skills. I searched for a decent hotel for the night in Bulawayo. After going up and down searching for a decent hotel, I eventually found a hotel room for the night. I went to my room and unpacked my bags that I was carrying and went out of the hotel to look for food, since the hotel where I was going to sleep only provided breakfast only, not lunch. I passed through different streets before I could find a restaurant, and when I found it, it was owned by a white person, not a black person, and all of the waiters and waitresses were black, and there was a certain group of gentlemen seated in a round table drinking beers and chatting while watching soccer on TV. I ordered rice, half chicken, and cold drink and quickly departed. I was just thinking alone that is it possible that among these men that were in the round table that some of them might be government spies? Zimbabwean government is always alert about social security. Just think about it—how did it manage to arrest the mercenaries that were going to Equatorial Guinea? Zimbabwe has one of the strongest intelligence in the world; perhaps someone was watching me that I am not from this place. I went to my room and opened the takeaway. I couldn't finish that half chicken; it was full of the Indian spices and inedible. Trust me, that chicken was badly cooked, and the rice was mess. I drank the cold drink.

CAPITALISM

The *Oxford Paperback Dictionary and Thesaurus* explains capitalism in this way: "a system in which a country's trade and industry are controlled by private owners for profit." Colonization gave birth to capitalism. You will never have colonization unless you have capitalism that is running parallel at full speed. All Western economies were built upon capitalism. No wonder the list of the rich is dominated by Westerners and few African American like Oprah Winfrey who quickly learned the American system of capitalism and penetrated American market. The colonial project was to colonize first. Then African countries that have been colonized are forever debtors, and they must pay to their colonizers with their mineral resources until the ground where these mineral resources are coming from run empty, while the people that will be working to drill the ground are underpaid and overworked to pay the West the debt that they will never ever finish paying earning peanuts for monkeys. Or sometimes they will get beaten so that they will work harder to pay the West the debt that they didn't help to create. That had been the frame of the picture about colonization. It's just pure satanic. When most African countries became liberated politically, they thought they were politically free, but little did they know that capitalism wheels were already in motion, and it will take concerted effort to grind them to a screeching halt. The Western capitalists are bluntly saying to the African leaders, "If you ever intend to grind to a screeching halt our capitalist wheels, we will do to you what we did to Zimbabwe." South Africans are mum about the nationalizations of mines, and they are also mum about the expropriation of land without compensation attributed to the Hollywood movie that we South Africans are watching playing in

Zimbabwean soil. The Westerns are sipping coffee and tea in Europe and North America, saying to South Africa, "Don't take our land and our mines because if you do, economic sanctions are upon you." The next thing that follows, African countries enter into very long bilateral agreements with the Western countries, and the Western countries continue to provide Africa with foreign aid. Any African country that is relying on a Western foreign aid, that country is still under colonial bondage. Western foreign aid cripples Africa's potential to exploit business opportunities. Western foreign aid stifles Africa's economic potential. Africa claims to be politically free and economically free, while the European and the US governments have to cater for most African countries in their national budgets. If we Africans claim to have attained political freedom, why are we not using our political freedom to attain our economic freedom? The fact of the matter is this: we Africans are politically free, but we are still in the financial prison of the West. Most African leaders know this, but there is nothing that they can do about it. These are wheels of capitalism. Once they are in motion, they are very difficult to grind them to a screeching halt. Pres. Robert Mugabe was trying to stop them; he learned the hard lesson the hard way. Most African countries are afraid to reform their economies because they have structured their economies after the economic models of the West. African countries enter into bilateral agreements with the same countries that have colonized them. It's morning. I woke up, and I went straight to shower and prepared myself for the very long day in Bulawayo. I rushed to the dining room for tea. While I was in the dining room, Jacob, my driver whom I met the previous day, called me and said, "I am outside waiting for you." Jacob is a Shona, and he is from a place called Masvingo. He moved to Bulawayo for greener pastures. He speaks Shona and Ndebele fluently, and he has been a cab driver in Bulawayo for the past sixteen years. He tells me that "the Ndebeles are coming from South Africa and they left Bulawayo, and everyone in Bulawayo right now is a Shona." I could tell from the tone of his voice that he hated Ndebeles with passion while he speaks Ndebele fluently because he is a cab driver, but deep down in the center of his heart, I could sense an engraved hatred toward the Ndebele people, and that was what I had picked up in my journey as I traveled. I was in Bulawayo to see Matopos National Park, where the famous Cecil John Rhodes was buried and where the plot that he owned is located, including his house.

In his book titled *A History of the African People of South Africa: From the Early Iron Age to the 1970s,* Paul Maylam writes:

> *During the Zulu-Ndwandwe conflict, Mzilikazi had switched his allegiance from Zwide to Shaka, whom he came to serve as a military commander. But after conducting a successful military campaign, Mzilikazi incurred Shaka's wrath by refusing to hand over to him a sufficient proportion of captured cattle. To escape punishment by Shaka, Mzilikazi in 1821 led a band of refugees across the Drakensberg into the eastern Transvaal.*[7]

Shaka Zulu, or Shaka ka Senzangakhona as I prefer to call him, was a son of Senzangakhona, who was a head of a small Zulu chiefdom, and Senzangakhona gave birth to a son called Shaka, and he was also known as Shaka Zulu. While Shaka was a little boy, his mother, Nandi, they were both kicked out of the chiefdom by Senzangakhona, and it's clear from here henceforth that Shaka had a troubled upbringing, possible angry because his mother was no longer part of the Zulu chiefdom. Shaka grew up an angry man and full of resentment and bitterness. While he was in his youth, Shaka served under Dingiswayo and trained to be a Zulu warrior. There are many things that have been said about Shaka Zulu especially about his cruelty, which is pure Western propaganda to brainwash African children into believing that black people are not smart like white people. Some of the things that have been said about Shaka are just pure gibberish—for example, it is said Shaka Zulu once took a spear, plunged it into womb of a pregnant woman, opening wide the womb of the pregnant woman, to see how the baby sits in the womb of a pregnant woman. That is a Western propaganda and a Western doctrine about African people that is purely intended to tarnish and destroying the reputation of Shaka Zulu's legacy and the incredible history that he left behind for the Zulu people. It's also said that during Shaka's era as a king, if you were short, he was going to kill you on the spot. He didn't believe that short people could win a war. Shaka Zulu arose to power after the death of Dingiswayo, and Mzilikazi was part of Shaka's headman.[8]

Mzilikazi went to Zimbabwe to form his own chiefdom, since he could no longer be in good terms with Shaka Zulu owing to the herd of cattle that he couldn't give back to Shaka Zulu. He had more than enough to establish his own chiefdom in Zimbabwe in Bulawayo, and that is where

I was. When Mzilikazi got to Zimbabwe in Bulawayo, he gave birth to a son named Lobengula, who succeeded him after his death. Already at this time, Mzilikazi had a chiefdom, and a new language had already been established known as Ndebele, and the people call themselves Matabele today in Zimbabwe. The IsiNdebele that is spoken in Zimbabwe is totally different to the IsiNdebele that is spoken in South Africa. Also in South Africa there are Ndebele people who call themselves amaNdebele. These are not the same people. Zimbabwe's IsiNdebele is a totally different thing from the Ndebele that is spoken in South Africa. South Africa Ndebele borrows words sometimes from Tswana and sometimes from other Nguni languages (Zulu, Xhosa, Ndebele, and Swati), while Zimbabwe's Ndebele is purely different from the South African Ndebele. The Zimbabwean Ndebeles speak almost like Xhosa. They have a certain common click when they pronounce words. Lobengula became the king of Matabele people and succeeded his father, Mzilikazi, who fled from Shaka Zulu. Lobengula settled in Bulawayo, and the word "Bulawayo" is derived from Ndebele, which means "the place of slaughter."[9]

While His Majesty, King Lobengula, was the king of the Ndebele, people in Bulawayo befriended many of the white missionaries and hunters who arrived in his kingdom, allowing missionary society to establish centers near his capital, Bulawayo. Since Lobengula allowed white missionaries in Bulawayo and many foreign visitors, the majority of his foreign visitors began to covet the land of His Majesty and began to develop keen interest in mining in Bulawayo. Already at this time, Cecil John Rhodes was in South Africa in the Cape Colony reigning as the governor. During this time, Cecil John Rhodes had already established BSAC (British South Africa Company), which was responsible for mining South Africa's gold and diamond. These gold and diamonds that Cecil John Rhodes were mining was a South African inheritance that was given to black people by God, but at the same time he was mining it carelessly, and the majority of his employees were black that were underpaid while overworked. The mining of South Africa's gold and diamond depleted South Africa's wealth and at the same time expanded the British wealth. The fact of the matter is this: almost all the financial records that are available today can't actually give us an unbiased and reliable financial information about the exact amount of African wealth that Cecil John Rhodes through his BSAC siphoned to the West. It's possible that the exact African wealth that has been siphoned by Cecil John Rhodes to the West is worth half of the Western wealth that has been invested in the World Bank and IMF combined. The main reason I reached that conclusion is that, the West has tremendous amount of influence on these financial institutions, though it's not only the West that invests in the IMF and World Bank alone, but the West has lion share of the investments than any other country in the world. During the discovering of Kimberly mine when Cecil John Rhodes shot to fame and became wealthy and crafted his grand plan to expand the British colony from Cape to Cairo, most governments of the world at that time were not aware of the internal financial control procedures that are available today. The financial statements were not prepared according to the generally accepted accounting principles (GAAP). Most of the financial information that is available is just purely unreliable and fabricated. My main intention is to prove that the Western governments through Africa's gold and diamonds became very wealthy and grew rapidly through wealth that belongs to Africa. This wealth managed to build the Western skyscrapers and prestigious universities; pardon me to say that some of the biggest universities and buildings in the West today have been built through Africa's ill-gotten wealth. Africans have been forever working for their colonizers, and the gold and diamonds that they were mining were eventually taken to the West. And it's public knowledge that this African wealth and riches that the West stole from Africa via the colonial project, some of that money were invested in European banks and some of that money in the World Bank, Africa's money, Africa's gold and diamond.[10] Africa had been impoverished by the West and its capitalists. Africa was not supposed to be a continent of poverty, sickness, and diseases, but it was supposed to be a continent of abundance and more than enough. The Western settlers came to Africa and took away what rightfully belongs to Africans. Cecil John Rhodes was born in the United Kingdom on July 5, 1853. His father was Rev. Francis William Rhodes, and the mother of Cecil Rhodes was Louisa Rhodes, and he had nine siblings. While he was the prime minister in the Cape Colony, his obsession grew rapidly of annexing and conquering Africa from Cape to Cairo. He sent his delegation to His Majesty, King Lobengula the Lion. The delegation that was sent by Cecil John Rhodes to His Majesty, King Lobengula, was led by Charles Rudd, a member of the DeBeers and an expert in sorting out mining claims. The party arrived in Bulawayo in September 1888. Charles Rudd clearly stated to King Lobengula that Cecil John Rhodes was requesting the mining rights in Zimbabwe, and Cecil John Rhodes had the total support of the British government, and the British government will ensure the total protection of the Matabeleland from the European.[11]

King Lobengula vehemently rejected the proposal to give mining rights to Cecil John Rhodes. It was the British commissioner to Botswana, Sir Sidney Shippard, who convinced the king with the other trusted missionary, Charles Helm, that he should give Cecil John Rhodes the right to mine in Bulawayo and that would perhaps deter the precarious ambitions of the majority of Europeans, which is clearly exhibited from their endless visits in Bulawayo. On October 30, 1888, King Lobengula signed the letter that was believed to have come from Queen Victoria after discovering that he has been tricked by Cecil John Rhodes. King Lobengula dispatched his delegation to Queen Victoria, but too little too late. The country was taken, and the land, gold, and diamond were given to the British young man by the name of Cecil John Rhodes. It's true that the intentions of Cecil John Rhodes were evil from the beginning. He was not satisfied by the gold and diamonds that he was mining in South Africa. The more gold and diamonds he got from South Africa's mines, the more gold and diamonds he wanted, a typical Englishman. His Majesty, King Lobengula, had signed his death warrant and had sold the country to the Western capitalist. I was in Bulawayo. Jacob and I began our lovely day with a visit to the museum in Bulawayo. The museum opened at 8:00 a.m., but I was there a little bit late. The museum clerk explained to me that if you are a foreigner, you will have to pay ten US dollars as entrance fee. The first thing I saw on the walls of the museum was the face of Pres. Robert Mugabe. I got the message quickly: president Robert Mugabe is a darling of the Zimbabweans, and they love him and respect their political leader wholeheartedly. I began moving around in the museum. There were different carats of diamonds that were not real but pure imitations. I understand the main reason behind is that the museum is not a mine or stock exchange where they sell shares, stocks, and bonds, but it's an educational place. Those carats of diamonds were meant for educational purposes, not trading like in the stock exchange. Inside the museum there is a mine chapel. The mine chapel is also not real but was designed with a sole purpose of teaching people how a real mine chapel looks like in real life. The museum official and I entered the mine chapel. He began explaining to me the mine chapel and the different technological equipment that they are using in the mines today to drill the rocks, including those technological equipment that Cecil John Rhodes used to steal Africa's gold and diamond with it. The museum official showed me around the whole museum. He worked in the museum for a considerable amount of time, and he knew what he was talking about. He showed me a technique that was used in the past to assess whether a place had gold or not. There is an African bowl that they will use. They will put top soil on that bowl and sift the top soil until the top soil is sifted away until gold dust particles remain, and then the remaining gold dust will be an indication that there is gold in that area. Then mining operation will commence. This system is no longer used because of the new technology that is currently being used in the mines. I understood thoroughly the mineral resources that are available in the mines. Most people when they are thinking about the mines are only thinking about mining diamonds and gold only. Electricity that we are using in our households comes from coals, and coals come from the mines. South African electricity comes from coals, and since the government of South Africa does not own coal mines, therefore the state-owned electricity generator Eskom had to buy coals from private companies that are mining coals in South Africa. The government, through its state parastatal Eskom, the electricity generator, burns the coals to generate electricity, and that is how electricity is generated. The more the price of coals increase, the more the price of the electricity increases, bearing in mind that coals are a natural resources. These Western companies that are mining coals in South Africa and even in other African countries, when they cease their mining operation, they don't pay for bottomless pit that they leave in the ground after their mining operations have ceased. These Western mining companies came from the West and applied for the mining license, and after they have been granted the mining license to conduct their mining operation in Africa, they begin their mining operation in the land of our forefathers. And the land where they are conducting their mining operation belongs to the African people, but after they have mined the coals on the ground, they sell it back to the very same African government at a hefty price. When the African people complain about the electricity hikes, and the state-owned electricity companies complain about the increase in the price of coals, the Western companies themselves also complain about their wage bill—that it has arisen. As if that is not enough, they also say, "We are paying company's tax to the African governments." When foreign companies pay tax to the African governments, they think that that gives them the legal rights to double their costs for their final products simply because they are paying tax to the African governments. These Western mining companies hike their costs of their final products simply because they have a mining license in their hands as if they are saying, "Since your government gave us a mining license, we have the right to kill for profits." Mining companies, specifically Western companies, mine in the African land free of charge to a land that belongs to the African people and make huge profits and leave bottomless pit on the ground and destroy the natural environment. These mining companies have a tendency of hiring migrant, specifically African migrants from war-ridden countries, simply because they know very well that they will accept slave wages without complaining. These Western mining companies pay these migrants "peanuts for monkeys." When these Western mines have finished mining the African minerals resources, they evaporate in thin air. They shed jobs and retrench a considerable amount of people living the gaping holes on the ground and take big profits and migrate to another African country where there are still sufficient mineral resources in the ground and continue with the same practice again and again. These Western mining companies continue their evil practice of hiring migrants who come from countries that are war-ridden or where there is political instability and political violence, paying them peanuts for monkeys and placing them in the belly of the earth, letting them to mine gold and diamonds for the investors that are sitting in Europe and in the North America who are sipping whiskey and smoking Cuban cigar and enjoying life to the fullest while African people are working hard in the belly of the earth. My point is this: there are many mineral resources that are found in the mine that are used to manufacture different mineral products. Iron is used for stainless steel machines—meaning most of the car parts that are used in assembling together a car come from iron, and this iron is found in the mines. Platinum is also used in the manufacturing of fiberglass, since most African countries don't own mines. It therefore means that majority of the mining products should be bought from foreign companies that are conducting their mining operation in Africa. When all the mineral resources have been extracted from the African soil one day, these Western companies will say, "Africa is the hopeless continent ravaged by malaria, TB, AIDS, and silicosis," forgetting that when they came to Africa, Africa didn't have the gaping holes that they helped to create through conducting mining in the African continent. South Africa established what is known as the IODSA (Institute of Directorate of Southern Africa) that compelled companies in South Africa to take into consideration the environmental effects that the mining operations have on the African continent, and in their preparation of their financial statements, companies should comply with Marvin King's commission report on corporate governance and also comply with the Companies Act 71 of 2008.[13] I finally left the museum, heading straight to Matopos National Park, and Jacob told me Matopos National Park is just a few kilometers away from the Bulawayo city center. He began to show me the plot that belonged to Cecil John Rhodes, a very huge land I must say, and right then and there it began to dawn on my mind that Cecil John Rhodes was too greedy to the extreme. Since Cecil John Rhodes didn't have a wife and children for that matter. What was he doing with such a vast amount of land, and was he not satisfied with the gold and diamonds that he was extracting from South African mines? When Cecil John Rhodes came to Bulawayo and hoodwinked His Majesty, King Lobengula, of the Matabele people, he was already a millionaire from the company that he assembled in South Africa known as BSACO. While we were on our way to Matopos National Park, we encountered a police roadblock. There were four police officers wearing gray trousers and on their shoulders had badges with the abbreviation ZRP (Zimbabwe Republic Police). One police came to the car and greeted us, and he asked Jacob where he was going, and Jacob told him that he was taking a tourist to Matopos National Park to see the grave of Cecil John Rhodes. The police officer began to look inside the car, and he saw a table knife that was on the dashboard of the car. The police officer called his other colleague to come to take a look at the table knife. The second police officer said, "This is a weapon," referring to a table knife. Jacob persuaded them to the point where they believed in him that he never intended to use the table knife to cause harm to anybody, and eventually we were allowed to leave. Two kilometers down the road just after the roadblock, we were instructed to pull over by a female police officer who was going toward the direction of Matopos National Park, and gladly so, Jacob gave her a lift and dropped her on the way. Jacob told me that every time he was transporting tourists to Matopos National Park, he normally encounters these police roadblocks, and sometimes the police officers accuse him of smuggling gold and diamonds from the mines. Zimbabwe's police can stop you anytime of the day in town and outside of town. If Zimbabwean government wants to lift the country out of poverty, it should downsize their police force. The Zimbabwean government is wasting a considerable amount of money by attempting to maintain order and law in Zimbabwe while knowing full well that Zimbabwean people themselves are afraid of stealing because of the horrible living conditions in the Zimbabwean prisons. In South Africa, if you get arrested and sent to the maximum prison, you will sleep on the bed and watch DStv. You also have schools inside most South African prisons. If you get arrested while you have a grade-twelve certificate, you are likely to come out of the South African prisons with a PhD in quantum physics. Zimbabwean prisons are hell on earth, and nobody dares to think about breaking the law in Zimbabwe. There is a video that I watched on YouTube; it's about a man who stole a meat in Zimbabwe and got arrested and sentenced to three months in prison. While he was in Zimbabwe's prison, he began to shed off weight drastically, and since the government could not afford to provide food to the prisoners, the wife of this convict would come to offer him food, and the problem is she must leave the food to the prison warders and it's the prison warders who should give the food to the convict. The wife complained in that You Tube video that while she leaves the food with the prison warders, the husband always complained about hunger to the surprise of the wife, as she was always bringing food for him in prison. The problem is she was leaving the food with the prison warders with the belief that the prison officials will give the food to the husband, who has been convicted of stealing meat from his neighbors, but the food was not reaching the convict; the prison warders were eating the food themselves. The prisons in Zimbabwe were a complete living hell especially in 2003 to 2008. Zimbabwe's national election of 2008 was riddled with political violence and political intolerance, and Morgan Tsvangirai was arrested in a process and not only was incarcerated only but also was smacked before his incarceration. When he was released from prison, he flew to South Africa for medical treatment. The national election results were a mess, since both MDC-T and ZANU-PF could not win the national election fair and square. There was election rerun. And political violence ensued, compelling the international community to see the bad and the ugly of Zimbabwe's politics that has never been seen before. There was political rhetoric that people would rather go back to the bush instead of giving a country that they fought for very hard to somebody who has grade 5/standard 3. On the entrance of Matopos National Park, we came across the securities of Matopos National Park, two ladies and one a gentleman. The gentleman had an R5 rifle on his hand and was wearing green uniform. Jacob told them that I was a tourist from South Africa; I was here to see the grave of Cecil John Rhodes. The three securities told him that he is not allowed to enter with me, since he is not registered with Matopos National Park to transport tourists inside the park, but they will call a registered cab driver who is registered with Matopos National Park to transport tourists around the park. These three securities speak Ndebele, and I can hear Ndebele very well, but not all of them are Ndebeles. The first lady speaks Ndebele fluently, but she is a Shona from Mashonaland; and the second security lady is a Shona, but she can speak Ndebele fluently; and the gentleman, Mr. R5 Rifle, is quiet and he is not doing a lot of talking, but the two ladies were doing a lot of talking. I was given a phone by the security lady who speaks Ndebele fluently but who is a Shona from Mashonaland to talk to the gentleman who is a registered cab driver. The registered cab driver told me that to drive from the entrance of Matopos National Park to Cecil John Rhodes's grave, it will cost me fifty US dollars, and that is equivalent to R500 according to South African currency, bearing in mind that I wanted to see a grave of a person who died a long time ago in 1902. Besides, I was not going to see a living, breathing Cecil John Rhodes. And by the way, the person that I was going to see his grave was a British mafia who hoodwinked his way to Zimbabwe, and the very land that he is buried on it, he acquired it through unscrupulous means. The amount that I must pay to the Matopos National Park as an entrance fee was twelve US dollars, which is equivalent to R120 according to the South African currency; coupled with the amount that I should pay to the cab driver, fifty US dollars, the total will be sixty-two US dollars, which is equivalent to R620 according to South African currency. The fact of the matter is this: Cecil John Rhodes's grave is not similar to the grave of Jesus Christ, and Cecil John Rhodes is not an African hero who fought for the liberation of African people from colonial oppression. In fact Cecil John Rhodes himself was an oppressor and the mastermind behind the incorporation of BSAC. Why am I paying such a huge amount of money to see a grave of a person who stole a land, mines, diamond, gold, and platinum from the African people? I told the cab driver and the Matopos National Park's security guards that I don't need to pay such a huge amount of money to see the grave of Cecil John Rhodes, therefore I was leaving. I was no longer interested in seeing Cecil John Rhodes's grave. Cecil John Rhodes was not Jesus Christ; therefore, whether I see his grave or not, that won't save my spirit from hell. We left Matopos National Park, and then we went straight to NASA (National University of Science And Technology), which is in Bulawayo. We were going to talk to Mr. White, who is a lecturer in NASA. Unfortunately, we couldn't find him that day, and in the Commerce faculty, they referred us to Dr. Coffee, who was dean of Faculty of Commerce in NASA University. Dr. Coffee was present in his office, and we spoke to his secretary, and we explained ourselves who we were, and the lady personal assistant called him on the phone, and he blatantly refused to talk to us including seeing my face, citing lame reasons that he was very busy and we should make an appointment or come tomorrow. We were also referred to Mr. Hirambi, who is lecturing on Conflict and Resolution, and he was nowhere to be found. The fact of the matter is this: Zimbabweans are afraid to voice their political opinions about the political situation in their country. They think that maybe you are a government spy who is in the mission to sift the MDC-T members from ZANU-PF. They think we were doing a pre-election survey about the ZANU-PF prospects of winning the national election, and should they give us an unbiased and fair political opinion about the political situation in the country, they might find themselves unemployed. Most people are afraid to have a political dialogue simply because of the government spies that are everywhere. We left NASA, and we went to another university in Bulawayo called Lupane University. Jacob was a very helpful and enthusiastic man, and he went in and introduced himself and me and requested someone whom I can talk to about my visit. I was referred to a certain lady by the name of Ms. Khorombi. She was marking her exam scripts, and I introduced myself, and I began explaining the purpose of my visit in Zimbabwe, and eventually she said, "I am sorry. I don't have time. I am leaving right now. I have to pick up my baby in town," and she referred me to Mr. Khorombi, who is a lecturer in Lupane University and who is teaching Urban Management. I explained myself again and told him that I am from South Africa and explained the purpose of my visit including the reason I was looking for his help. I asked him about the standard of education in Zimbabwe, specifically the grade-twelve pass rate. He said, "Zimbabwe is doing very well in literacy, mathematics, and science compared to other African countries." I have a very big problem with this notion that Zimbabwe's education is better than South African education. South African government spends a considerable amount of money on education, but I should also say South African government also does not deliver textbooks and workbooks to schools on time, but we all know that that is an isolated incidence; it does not happen every year. This matter of non-delivery of textbooks and workbooks in Limpopo on time was a Limpopo Province saga. The non-delivery of textbooks in Limpopo Province was tantamount to intellectual genocide, and the unfortunate part was there were no culprits that were apprehended, and there was no one who was charged for misconduct or dereliction of duties. This matter was pushed under the carpet. The point is South Africa spends more on education than Zimbabwe. Mr. Khorombi said, "Since the political crisis of 2000 that had been caused by farm invasion, the grade-twelve pass rate dwindled, and that is attributed to the shortage of textbooks in schools, infrastructure collapse, and most teachers are not paid their salaries on time." I asked him this question: "How much is the average teacher earning is Zimbabwe?" He said, "An average teacher in Zimbabwe is earning US$500," and that amount, according to South African currency, is equivalent to R5,000. Zimbabwean teachers are underpaid by the government, and this amount cuts across the board; whether you are teaching in high school or in primary school, the salary is the same. We began to talk about the thorny issue—the real crisis of all Zimbabwean crisis, what I call the "the chronic Zimbabwean disease," economic sanction, and the farm invasion. He began to panic just like all Zimbabweans who are afraid to speak out. He said, "I made a mistake by talking to you without requesting to see your identity document." I quickly stood up and brandished my South African identity document and my passport. He was now at ease that he was not talking to some government spy that had been sent by the government to frame him as to whether he is a proponent of Zimbabwe's government policies or not. When I asked him about farm invasion, I became emotional, and tears began to gather on my eyes, and he said to me, "People who were behind the farm invasion were war veterans, and some of the people during the farm invasion were given more land than the others." Let me put it in a different way: during the Land Redistribution Program (LRP), some people were given unfairly and unjustly too much land than they ought to get, and they didn't need or deserve the very vast tract of land that they were given. He said to me, "There was no structure that was responsible for the Land Redistribution Program." Land Redistribution Program made Pres. Robert Mugabe's face a screen saver on the phones of many people. Most people in South Africa think that the farm invasion was just a fairy tale. They don't understand the ramification of the farm invasion. While I was in Mr. Khorombi's office, a phone rang. A lady said,

"I am waiting for you. You said you will be here in five minutes. Where you are right now?"

Mr. Khorombi responded, "I am on the way."

I quickly realized that there are many people who are like Cecil John Rhodes anyway. I said I will e-mail him a questionnaire. I took his e-mail address, and I appreciated him giving me an opportunity to interview him, and I bade him good-bye, and Jacob was already beginning to be impatient in the car, and we drove back to the hotel. That was it for the day. I had already bought a bus ticket. Before I boarded into a bus to South Africa, I went to talk to different car dealers in Bulawayo. These different car dealers were not far away from the hotel where I was staying. One car dealer told me that the cars that he is selling are imported from Japan, and they get ferried to Zimbabwe through an airplane. All the cars that were in his garage were secondhand cars.There was a green Lexus that cost US$6,000, and that is equivalent to R60,000 according to South African currency, and there was another blue Mini Cooper at the price of US$14,000, and that is equivalent to R140,000 according to South African currency. When the Japanese buy brand-new cars and drive them for five years, when they're sick and tired of driving their cars, they load them into an airplane and send them to Zimbabwe. Most of the Zimbabweans are driving secondhand cars that have been driven by the Japanese, Chinese, or Korean citizens before. Zimbabwe now is the dumping ground for China, Japan, and Korea. In Bulawayo, there is no car plant, and since there is no car plant, most people, if they want to buy a brand-new car, have to rely only on the foreign secondhand cars that are imported from Asia. The other option that Zimbabweans have to follow is to come to South Africa and purchase a brand-new spanking car and courier it to Zimbabwe. There is a considerable amount of business opportunities right now in Zimbabwe, but the only problem that is deterring and weakening investors' confidence is the government policy that requires 51 percent stakes in the company that have been incorporated by another person. Capitalism is multifarious and multifaceted in its nature. Sometimes it's hidden through wars and lucrative business deals, and sometimes it's hidden in foreign products that are consumed by Africans. If African countries are importing more foreign goods and export less goods to the Western countries, it simply means that Africa is consuming a considerable amount of foreign products that are assembled and manufactured in the West. The balance of payment in macroeconomics deals with this topic at length. The consumption of more Western products by Africa is more dangerous because it means that Africans are politically liberated and politically independent, but since most of the products that Africans consume are foreign manufactured, that makes Africa to be economically dependent on the West, and that makes Africa to be an economic parasite of the West. True political liberation is economic liberation, and it's also true that the other can't be achieved in the absence of the other. Let me put it differently. It will be a waste of energy, passion, and time to achieve political freedom without economic freedom. I also want to re-emphasize that economic freedom can't be sustained in a country where there is no political stability and political tolerance. Africa needs political freedom and economic freedom. These two should be combined together to be enjoyed simultaneously. When Africa is exporting less and importing more from the West, it simply means that the West is independent economically from Africa and Africa is dependent on the West. Most computers are manufactured in the West and imported to Africa, while most of the tobacco and tea are from Africa and exported to Europe. Technology is evolving and advancing at the same time; Africa can't keep on exporting tea and tobacco to the West. Africa needs to start assembling its own computers and iPods and export them to the West. The one-million-dollar question is this: Can Africa imposes economic sanction to the West, or is the West the only one who has the power and dominion to impose economic sanctions to African countries like Zimbabwe? If Africa is exporting computers to the West, can the West continue to run its big companies without Africa's products? The answer to this question is a resounding no. Since Africa is exporting tobacco and tea, can the Westerners continue with their normal lives without our tobacco and tea? A resounding yes. African exports should be overhauled. Gone are the days of exporting tobacco and tea. Africa needs to export iPods and laptops. Africa needs to manufacture airplanes and sell them to the West instead of our tobacco, flowers, and tea that we Africans brag about. Imagine a situation where Africa is manufacturing its own airplanes, cars, laptops, and iPods and then the West threatens Zimbabwe with economic sanctions. Africa is going to tell the West that from now on Africa is no longer going to sell airplanes, cars, laptops, and iPods, therefore kiss your Facebook account and Twitter account good-bye. The truth of the matter is this: Africa is still dependent on the West for everything. The West gave Africa Twitter and Face book, and trust me, if the West can take all their Western gadgets, all African children are going to cry all night long. Imagine if the West doesn't sell to Africa its airplanes anymore. We Africans will be back to a donkey cart or sledge for that matter. Africa is not economically liberated, and we Africans are not economically free, and the West knows this, and our political leaders know it also. African liberation movements are no longer pursuing their original political agenda. The just course and the just struggle became contaminated along the way by African capitalism. It's apparently clear right now that there is a political paradigm shift in most African liberation movements. After political liberation, the genuine struggle of economic freedom was abandoned for the pursuit of capitalism. The factionalism and infighting to most African liberation movements are attributed to the pursuit of capitalism. The politics of the stomach is reigning high in Africa. The collective political ideology was abandoned for the individual interest. He was born in United Kingdom, yet he died in South Africa and he was buried in Bulawayo, miles away from home, just for the love of mineral resources. It's true "that the love of money is the root of all evil." It's also true that the lack of it can be the root of all evil, as Robert Kiyosaki puts it. Political factionalism is attributed to the lack of the collective effort in pursuing a single goal and single political ideology. The multiplicity of goals and multiplicity of diverse political ideologies are indicative of liberation movements that have elements of capitalism in their midst. The spirit of selflessness and long suffering for the masses in African liberation movements have been replaced by selfishness and self-enrichment, which is capitalism in its highest form. Capitalism—it's about enslaving people. Capitalism—it's about owning a vast tract of land and multiple mining companies alone. Capitalism—it's about degrading and debasing people by ensuring that they rely on you for their own survival. African liberation movements have become the new oppressor in this new democratic dispensation, though unconsciously so, but the modus operandi indicates that. Africa's political liberation was not attained in order for black people to occupy state houses and state offices. Africa's political liberation was fought for and sacrificed for, for the liberation of the masses from Western political oppression. Most of the African liberation movements have the elite groups in their ranks. The proceeds of the mineral resources and the mining rights don't trickle down to the average people; they disappear in the hands of these African liberation movements who are now in government. The African masses are told that they should continue to vote for their liberation movements, since they were liberated from colonial oppression by these African liberation movements. Whether it's in Zimbabwe or in South Africa, the mantra is the same: vote for ZANU-PF. After I completed talking to different car dealers in Bulawayo, I went to my room and prepared myself to leave the country and go back home to South Africa. I have never felt so heavy on my shoulders like when I was in Zimbabwe. Part of this heaviness is attributed to the political climate in Zimbabwe. The fear of being arrested was always present in my mind, knowing full well that justice is nonexistent in this country. The violation of human rights is the order of the day. The international community is aware of it, but each country has its own sovereignty, and that sovereignty should be respected and upheld by the rest of the world. I packed my bag and ensured that I was not leaving anything behind. There were three things that were very important to me when I was packing my bag: passport, ID document and the bus ticket, and last but not least, my phone for that matter. I locked the room and ensured that all windows were closed, switched off the lights and switched off the TV, and went straight to the reception desk to hand over the keys. I went straight to the dining room where the breakfast was served, and I indulged myself. I met three gentlemen in the dining room. Two of them were Indians, and one of them was a black person. I am sure without any shadow of doubt that he was a Shona. I could hear their conversation—that it was centered around investment and business opportunities, and apparently it appeared as if this Zimbabwean gentleman is a business broker who knows Zimbabwe well and the business channels that one should follow in order to get a lease agreement in Bulawayo. I was not interested in this lease agreement that they were talking about because I missed home. I quickly finished my breakfast, and I bade good-bye to the waitresses. One waitress said to me, "Sir, why are you leaving?" I said, "I will come back." I wondered whether that concerned waitress was talking from her mind or from her heart. On my way to the bus station, I got lost, and I met a police officer who was wearing a gray uniform and had a badge on his shoulder with abbreviation ZRP. I asked him what ZRP stands for. He told me, "Zimbabwean Republic Police." I told him that I was lost and I was going to the bus station. He took me straight to the bus station with pleasure, smiling all the way, and I also realized that I can get some information from this police officer. I asked him whether or not it's true that there are lots of government agents in Zimbabwe. He laughed and said, "But that is another department." He said that "South Africa is not safe like Zimbabwe, and you can see I can walk in Zimbabwe without a gun, but in South Africa you can't do that—you always need a police van and a gun." He said to me, "I can go to pick up a suspect with my feet without using a car." In other words, in Zimbabwe, a police without a gun has the same power as a police who is holding an AK-47. He gave me his name. I jotted it down then he began to panic, and he asked me why I was taking his name down. I explained to him the purpose of my visit in Zimbabwe. He began to tell me that next time I will need papers. I said I have my ID document and passport, and he said, "Not a passport and ID document." I went straight to the bus terminal, and inside the bus terminal

I came across a certain gentleman who was seated on the chair talking to certain lady. I dropped my bag, and I went outside to get a fresh air. I took some pictures while I was outside the bus terminal. A certain Ndebele woman asked me a question and said, "Are you a journalist?" I said no, or maybe I should have said, "Yes, I am a journalist." The dialogue began now between me and this gentleman and a certain lady, and now it appeared as if this gentleman and this lady have something deeper than I think that is going on or is about to happen. Whatever this gentleman had in his mind about this lady, I really didn't care, but I joined in their conversation anyway. I became the uninvited guest and a gate crasher. I raised my concerns about the US dollar being used in Zimbabwe—that the US$1 can be easily forged. The gentleman began by introducing himself—that he is from Zambia, and he was going to use the same bus that I was going to board in, and he was going to Johannesburg. I asked him how he came to Bulawayo. He said,

"I came to Bulawayo through Livingstone border."

He began to complain about Zambia—that there were a lot of Congolese nationalities in Lusaka, which is the capital city of Zambia, and most of the Congolese are crooks and robbers. The bus came, and we went outside the waiting room to pack our bags inside the bus and also in the trailer for the big luggage. The bus left Bulawayo, and next to me was a certain married woman who came to Zimbabwe to see her husband. I was now stuck with a married woman for almost for almost fifteen hours from Bulawayo to Pretoria. I asked her a question, "Do you know that here in Zimbabwe you are not supposed to talk bad about the president Robert Mugabe?" She said, "My husband told me that I must not say anything about the president of the country, even about politics," and I took a nap. We arrived in South Africa in the early hours of the morning. I went straight to bed and slept like a little baby. I woke up the following day and went to the University of South Africa to collect different books in the library that talk about farm invasion in Zimbabwe. I saw a notice that says there is a new political party that is being launched. Since I am a politically inclined person and interested in the political matters that affect South Africa and the rest of the African continent, I saw this launch of the political party as a perfect opportunity for me to understand the underlying polices of this political party. I had a keen interest in understanding the stance of this political party about the mining crisis that South Africa finds itself in, and I also had a keen interest in understanding the land issue. The question that I had in mind was, Since the West stole Africa's land and mines, what are we going to do right now? The launch of the party was going to take place in Pretoria Show Ground at exactly 9:00 a.m. I arrived in the stadium one hour late and took seat on the grandstand. I asked myself this question: How much does political parties spend on their launch? The answer to this question is millions of rands. There was a variety of things that were going on inside the stadium: T-shirts were being distributed for free, and there was food for people that came from far. The master of ceremonies was one of the South African comedians who were a regular on a certain TV channel. The MC was a comedian, a clown. The MC/comedian had a partner who was also hosting the whole event with him. She is an actress for different South African drama series and a singer at the same time. One thing that I remember vividly about this actress is this: she looks like a professional model. This is a launch of a political party. We are going talk about serious business. We are going to talk about our land that was taken from our forefathers and the mines that are continuing to enrich the Western investors. I wonder whether the MC/clown thought we were in the stadium for a beauty contest or some silly TV awards. The launch of a political party to me is a serious business. The leader of this political party emerged with bodyguards—they were wearing black suits—and she began addressing the crowd. The security in the stadium was very tight. Quite frankly this political party had hired a security company that was going to ensure that there was no disruption in the stadium. We were told Dr. Mamphela Ramphele is about to deliver her speech. We all sat down, but since I was on the stand, I could see her quite well even if there were speakers all over, but I wanted to be close to the stage. I went straight to the ground and very close to the stage. She began addressing us. While she was addressing us, everything that she said she was not reading it from the paper, but she was speaking from her mind. Since I had a camera phone, I took a video of her speech, and one thing that stood out in the whole speech was that we South Africans should *vote for the future not for the past.* My biggest question still remained unanswered: Are we going to continue to allow our minerals resources to be extracted from the ground by foreign-owned mining companies? Instead of getting answers for this question, all I heard was that the government of the ANC is corrupt, and textbooks and workbooks are not delivered on time at schools, referring to Limpopo and Eastern Cape Province. Many people are not politically clued up, specifically the youth and even most South African adults. Most

African liberation movements were launched with an overall objective of emancipating the African masses from political oppression and economic oppression, and along the way their just cause was contaminated by the divergence of political ideologies. South Africa has many political parties, and all of them are fighting among each other. Is it possible then to have one political party? Is it possible that all these political parties can unite for a political convention and agree on important matters that are affecting the country and fuse these political ideas and establish a strong country that can manufacture its own airplanes, computers, iPods, and cell phones? All of the South African political parties are on Twitter and Face book. These are not South African inventions, but these are Western inventions. Are we Africans going to continue receiving US foreign aid forever? When are we going to be politically free, and when is Africa's economic liberation coming to the people of South Africa and the continent of Africa at large? I love the future, but if the future will mean that we Africans are going to receive the US foreign aid and continue to rely on the West for our survival, then the future is not something that we Africans can proudly desire for. Our future should be shaped by our invention and creativity, not by the Western inventions. Our future should be dominated by us assembling and manufacturing our own technological equipments that we are exporting to the West. In the future, the West must seek our ICT (Information and Communication Technology). In the future, Africa must be self-sufficient to the point that Africa will no longer import anything from the West, but it will export almost everything to the West primarily because we Africans are self-sufficient and extremely productive. Multiple political parties in one country simply means that the people of that country have multiple visions and multiple objectives, and these objectives can't be coordinated and properly structured in order to be achieved and addressed in a sequential order. Division is attributed to multiple visions, which are not coherent. This is an African political landscape; one political party will say, "Let's nationalize the mines," and another political party will say, "Let's nationalize the wine." One political party will say, "Let's legalize prostitution," and another political party will say, "Let's eat sushi on the bodies of naked women." South Africa, and Africa at large, does not need new political parties, but it needs a renewed, collective, concerted effort and a political will to fight our economic challenges together. African liberation movements need to stop accusing the West and colonization and work toward a common goal of uplifting African people out of the depth of poverty that had been caused by colonial oppression. We have seen that capitalism divides nations and is the biggest recipe for disaster. Almost all African wars are attributed to capitalism and the West. Political parties are launched behind the notion of capitalism; everybody wants the share of the spoils of the political liberation, and there is nobody right now who is thinking about the future but only about his stomach and the next meal. The questions that we Africans must ask the leaders of African liberation movements are these: Where are the land and the mines that you fought for very hard, and who owns the African mineral resources now? Why did the African liberation movements abandon its initial political objective for a mere political freedom that is not accompanied by economic freedom? Why does Africa still rely on the World Bank to fund it to carry out Africa's infrastructural programs? Why do we buy more imported goods and computer gadgets from the West? What do we Africans mean when we say we are politically liberated while we depend on foreign aid from the West? These are the questions that we Africans should ask ourselves time and again. African crisis is continually perpetuated by the Western forces. Every time there is a civil war in Africa, there will always be a Western interference supporting one party. This evil practice by the West destabilizes the African continent and creates division among people of same color, culture, and religious belief. Africa's liberation struggles have been fought and won by many African countries, and delivering on the promises made before Africa's liberation struggle remains a mammoth task to many African liberation movements. The emergence of new political parties will not in any way solve this problem, but it will worsen it more and more. There is no political space for political struggle to be fought right now, but there is space for economic struggle to be fought. The current African struggle is poverty and lack of job opportunities that are caused by the lack of creativity and innovation. Spending too much time in exile can be dangerous to a person's mind and to his creativity. The political struggle costs many of our dear brothers and sisters a lot, and right now they are suffering from psychological trauma and dementia. Capitalism will always manifest itself in different shapes, sizes, and forms. Sometimes it appears as new political idea that will save the whole country from the political banishment. Africa's economic struggle and African liberation movements have been contaminated and diluted by money and the Western influence, especially foreign investments. There is no purity and wholeness in African liberation movements. In each and every African country, you will always encounter media reports about corruption that has been committed by the members of African liberation movements that have liberated the very country and the people that they are stealing from. It's also true that the foreign media is also the instigator in the political unrest that prevails in the African continent. Most African stories are told by the foreign media. Foreign correspondents are stationed in the African continent to report daily about the African corruption that is committed by the very political leaders who have spent a considerable amount of their lives in exile for the liberation of the African masses from colonial oppression. Is it possible then that the moment you make a conscious decision to sacrifice your whole life for the emancipation of your people along the way, this unselfish conscious decision can be contaminated and altered along the way by capitalism? The political struggle was not about self-enrichment and personal gain; it was purely about the liberation of the spirits and the liberation of the souls of African people. The worst form of political oppression that we Africans are suffering from right now is the political oppression by black capitalists. Most African liberation movements for that matter claim to be core socialists and Marxists at heart. If you look at the cars that they are driving and the houses where they live in, you get a different picture. It begs this question: Are the African liberation movements still holding to the Karl Max theory, or has African liberation movements changed their original political ideologies that was worth sacrificing for? Capitalism is another form of political oppression, and having said that, capitalism does not originate in Africa, but it originates in the West. Capitalism in politics is a virus without a nevirapine. It becomes forever difficult to bifurcate the difference between communists and the capitalists. And there is no one right now in the whole of the African continent that can clearly stand up and be counted in the midst of the masses as a capitalist. Everybody subscribes to the notion of socialism and communism, and when you ask the question, "Do you have shares in the foreign controlled company?" most of the African leaders become mum and unresponsive. Socialism is a proponent of the political liberation of the masses; however, socialism subscribes to the notion of the community involvement and community ownership. Socialism advocates that land, mines, and other form of industries should be controlled and owned by the people. This notion resonates well with the masses and underpins Africa's struggle against colonial oppression and capitalism. Most of the socialists in this new democratic dispensation are pure capitalists at heart; they are wearing sheepskin while they are raving wolves inside. Most of the former socialists are now new converts to the gospel of capitalism. They hide their wealth through foreign banks and foreign investments. These African capitalists are everywhere; there are those who are in South African liberation movements, and some are in Zimbabwean liberation movements. They follow the direction of the masses while carefully monitoring political climate and economic opportunities where they can invest their capital and generate massive returns. The purity and the wholesomeness in the politics of the African continent are of paramount importance. Africa will never achieve economic liberation collectively if Africa ignores the thorns and thistles among us that have been left behind by our colonial masters. The majority of the youth in most African countries are suffering from information deficit, which is attributed to a long political and colonial oppression. When African countries were colonized by the West, colonization never meant slavery and peasantry per se, but it also meant that Africans were not allowed to think, since nothing seriously and innovative can be produced by African brain. This is very true if one has to look at Africa's knowledge production. In almost all bookstores, the majority of the books that are in the shelves are Western books that were written by Western scholars. These Western scholars are now colonizing Africans intellectually, bearing the following in mind: colonization or oppression is purely about Africa's dependency to the West, and this dependency engenders dependency syndrome. This dependency syndrome compels Africans to believe that the West did Africa a huge favor by colonizing it. Some people go on to say even if the West had not stolen Africa's mineral resources, what were Africans going to do about these mineral resources anyway? The greatest mistake that have been committed by most of our African liberation movements was the failure to acknowledge the brain damage that has been caused by the West. Most former freedom fighters are suffering from post-traumatic stress disorder, which is attributed to staying in the bush for a very long time without hope of being integrated to a vibrant community and live a normal life. Most of the former freedom fighters from the bush went straight to occupy government facilities and government buildings, and they even forgot the main reasons for the political struggle. I have said it before that Africa's political struggle was not fought for the occupation of state houses and utilization of state facilities, but it was fought for the political liberation and economic liberation of the African people, not only liberating them politically but also liberating them from the shackles of poverty that were exacerbated by economic oppression. The dependency syndrome creates mistrust and divisions among Africans, and this is the main reason most African countries still rely on foreign aid from the West while bragging that Africa is politically liberated. The mistrusts and divisions are also epitomized in the formation of new political parties, which are meant to rescue the masses from the old African liberation movements that have become the new oppressor. The formation of this new political parties are not underpinned by new economic principles and policies that are predestined to redress the imbalances of the past, but the policies of these newly formed political parties are purely to curb the mistakes that have been committed by Africa's old liberation movements that are now in charge of the government. The formation of these new political parties is always driven by rage, anger and resentment, and the desire to get the fair share of the political pie. To prove that this is true, there is a strong emphasis on curbing corruption and fraud by these newly formed political parties. It's true that money is power, and power corrupts. How possible is it that people who have been outside the country for quite a long period of time fighting endless guerilla wars have suddenly been corrupt? It therefore requires one to look no further to get an answer to this question. I squarely put the entire blame on capitalism and because capitalists will always ask you this question: What will I get for my family at the end of this just cause? Capitalism does support the idea of economic independency from the West. It's capitalism that continues to advocate for social grants and foreign aid. It's abundantly clear that the current Africa's struggle is economic oppression and economic injustice, and in the midst we have a very diabolic element of the Western inventions that is capitalism. Africa's problems cannot be solved only through African dialogue, and the endless wars that are permeating the African continent are underpinned by capitalism, which is a Western invention to suppress and oppress African people in this beautiful land that we have come to love and relish. Capitalism humiliates the mind and corrupts the human brain. It makes you believe that there are no sufficient resources for everybody, therefore get as much as you can for yourself. Capitalism threatens Africans' livelihood and makes Africans debtors who are paying debts that they don't owe, and neither are they aware when they are going to finish paying. It's capitalism that says we should continue to respect the rule of law and bury the hatchet—forget about what happened in the past because you were not even born yet when colonization took place. It's capitalism that says go to school and get a job and marry a curvaceous lady and take a loan from the bank and buy a beautiful German car and take another loan and buy a house for your lovely wife and start a family. It's capitalism that says forget about the past and focus purely on the future because you can't change the past, but you can influence the future. It's capitalism that says you don't need economic freedom, since you have political freedom, and is political freedom not enough for you? Capitalism is the enemy of democracy and economic liberation. Capitalism is the new political and economic tool that the West is currently employing in Africa right now to control and manipulate Africa's wealth and natural resources. The West is not the greatest proponent of peace and tranquility, and every now and then, when Africa is singing from a same hymn book and singing in unison, the West will sow the destructive seed of division and instability. Africans are people of love and peace. Africans love music and peace, and they love dancing to the African rhythms and lyrics. Africans are people of love, peace, and tranquility. African wars, all of them in general, have a lowest common denominator. African wars were either funded by the West or supported and perpetuated from the West. Since most African countries are in a dire poverty, where do they get the know-how and the technique to manufacture deadly weapons that they are using in their civil wars? The fact of the matter is this: these military weapons are manufactured in the West and then shipped straight to the African continent where there is peace and tranquility, and eventually they are used in instigating civil wars. Every African country that is in a civil war, the bone of contention is Africa's mineral resources. What is it that is appealing about African mineral resources? Are there no mineral resources in North America and Europe? Why are we Africans the poaching ground for the West? Every time Western capitalists think about maximizing their wealth, they think of Africa. Capitalists are the enemies of peace and tranquility, and they triumph tremendously in the midst of civil wars and conflicts. The precarious trend that has emerged in post-Africa's liberation struggle is that most members of these African liberation movements have become black capitalists; they have adopted the *modus operandi* of the master. These African capitalists disguised themselves in different shapes, sizes, and forms. In South Africa these black capitalists disguised themselves in BBBEE (Broad-Based Black Economic Empowerment) and pretend to be pro-government in the idea of eradicating poverty and uplifting the masses from the depth of poverty while underpaying their employees and buying the collections of German cars. This is still capitalism, but now it appears in a different form, size, and shape. No wonder certain members of African liberation movements want to stay in power and occupy state houses and use the ministerial handbooks as long as they have breath. They can't imagine life without the government funding their opulent lifestyle of buying clothes in London and New York. These are the symptoms and effects of a black capitalism. Capitalism feeds itself through the poor of the poorest, and capitalism is self-enrichment and self-gratification. African capitalists learned the ways of sustaining capitalism through the Western modus operandi of oppressing African people while stealing from them at the same time. Capitalism is the violation of the human rights and spiritual rights of a person. Capitalists don't care about the aftermath of their actions and the consequences thereof. Capitalism is purely about my family, my relatives, and my in-laws only, and rest of the people will follow after. There is no spirit of Ubuntu, the spirit of sharing, anymore. The spirit of sharing has been replaced by the spirit of glutton, lust, and greed. Africa's political struggle was not fought by an individual but was fought by the collective. Africa's liberation struggle was a collective sacrifice of both women and men who never had their personal agenda in mind to achieve self-enrichment and self-gratification, but they fought with the Western powers in order to lift the whole masses from the depth of poverty. Capitalism was not on their minds, but the inevitable happened. When the armed struggle was over, African liberation movements, most of their members, wanted to be repaid for the good life that they lost while they were in exile. The African liberation struggle was not a contractual agreement that contained fringe benefits, the thirteenth-month check and the performance bonus, but the African liberation struggle was a war against the Western imperialists and Western powers. The greatest danger of being in political oppression for quite a long period of time is that even if you can be politically liberated, you eventually don't enjoy the very political freedom that you fought very hard for and very long to attain. The same is true with a bachelor's degree the day you graduate—it becomes a short burst of ecstasy and in the twinkling of an eye, you revert to the former self or the old person. Capitalism and oppression both brainwash a person's psyche to the point that it becomes very difficult to believe and trust other people. The underlying notion about capitalism is this: I must eat everything before anyone arrives in here. African capitalists are also suffering from the fear of the unknown. They think that should they not steal enough for tomorrow, possibly there won't be enough food to eat tomorrow for themselves. This notion is crystal clear from the Western capitalists. Most of the Western capitalists are still crying from the pain of Africa's political independence. They regret why they granted Africa political liberation because they had not stolen enough wealth to sustain themselves for a very long time. The same fear that Western capitalists have is the same fear that the current African liberation movements who are in governments are confronted with. There is a very growing heading in most African liberation movements that should they make a stupid political mistake and lose political power, Africa's colonizers will re-colonize Africa. This notion creates fear, and this fear can be numbed through black capitalism and looting. This is the main reason most of the African leaders insist on staying in power for a very long time even if they are sick to the point of death. African leaders will still want to stay in power and enjoy the state facilities and state benefits without paying a dime of a dollar for these benefits. The rationale is, should they vacate early from their political empires that they have built through political sacrifice and long suffering, possibly the new incumbents might sell the political gains of the struggle and the country to their former colonial masters. This fear is attributed to severe harsh living conditions at the hands of the Western oppressors. Colonization and oppression take away self-confidence and self-respect and indoctrinate a person to believe that the "big brother is watching you." This notion that the big brother is watching you creates worry and anxiety about the future. Whenever there is worry, anxiety and fear and finally uncalculated errors will come into play. Past fears are oppressing African people. Africans are still living in fear of political oppression, and that is the main reason many people even in South Africa are no longer enthusiastic and energetic about the idea of economic freedom because they see it highly impossible and unachievable for that matter. The status quo remains, and people go on with their daily lives as usual while knowing deep down that we are in the midst of serious economic problem. Most people suggest that it's better now since "we black people are in government, and we are the majority that is ruling our own African countries." Majority rule is another conundrum of democracy. Capitalism feeds itself through democracy. As long as there is democracy, there will be capitalism. Capitalism supports democracy. Democracy is political freedom. Democracy is not economic freedom. There is a very wide deepening confusion that I see. Capitalism supports democracy because in democratic states there are a lot of socialists who are wearing sheepskin at day while raving wolves at night. These are the representatives of the masses; they speak for the poorest of the poor and support the political ideologies of the poor, while the same proponents of the poor are the sellouts at night. They dine and eat with the Western capitalists under the disguise of discussing economic liberation while knowing full well that they were only lining up their pockets. One preacher said, "Samson was sent to kill the enemy, but Samson ended up sleeping with the enemy"—that is a great tragedy. African liberation movements liberated Africa, and that is appreciated. But these African liberation movements are now sleeping with the enemy that they fought with for a very long time through mining rights and acquisition of shares in the Western companies, and they became black capitalists unconsciously. Black capitalism occurs when the former freedom fighters and political leaders of the African liberation movements gain unfettered access from the West through the directorships in the Western companies in exchange of political clout and political protection. Capitalism and democracy can simply coexist, but capitalism and economic freedom can't coexist. The general definition of democracy is "the government of the people, for the people, by the people." Let me put it differently—democracy is the government of the people, meaning the people selected and chose their representatives to represent them in government. The process of choosing these representatives, which can be called the people's choice, is called election. The representatives that assume their positions in government are chosen by the people, and these representatives have the interests and aspirations of people at heart. In this information age, there are no government representatives that are having the interest of people at heart even if they have been chosen and selected by the people to promote and fulfill the promises of the people—that is no longer happening in Africa. The main reason these government representatives are no longer having the interest of people at heart is black capitalism. The moment they are in government, they will ensure that they amass a considerable amount of wealth for themselves and their families. Should the state become flat broke, they will still have butter on both slices of the bread. Capitalism thrives well in the midst of democracy. The will of the people is no longer the will of the people, but the will of the people is the will of the capitalists, whether Western capitalist or African capitalist. The truth of the matter is this: there is no political campaign for all African liberation movements who are now the government, which is wholly funded in the African continent. Most of the African liberation movements get a considerable amount of money from China and Russia. China is the emerging superpower of the world and hard-core capitalist at heart. China also wants nothing from Africa other than Africa's natural minerals resources. China wants to sell its cheap clothes from Hong Kong in Africa. The only way China can succeed in achieving its dream of selling its massive production of goods and getting the mining rights from the African continent is through funding Africa's old liberation movements that are currently the governing parties. Most people think that in democracy there is no capitalism, since in democracy the will of the people take precedence. Democracy is not the will of the people, and the government is not the government of the people by the people for the people. The government is controlled by capitalists, not by the people, and the decisions that are made are not intended to address the plight of the people but to maximize the wealth of the capitalists. Democracy is not holy and sanctified but unholy and impure. The dent that defiles the will of the people is black capitalism, and in South Africa, black capitalists are called tenderpreneurs. The frame, size, and shape of capitalism keep changing to the point that tracing its roots becomes very difficult. The point is the changing of the frame, picture, and the size of capitalism does not alter the main objectives of capitalism. The underlying objective about Western capitalists and its long-term goals are to impoverish Africa as a continent and its people. African people must work hard in the belly of the earth drilling gold and diamonds that will not benefit the future African generation but impoverish the future African generation while enriching the Europeans and the North Americans as a whole. The future African generations will be heavily in debt if our current political plan and economic plan do not change to redress the imbalances of the past in a positive and constructive way. Short-term solutions for long-term problems are precarious because they don't address the root of the problem but the symptoms thereof. Black capitalism is a short solution for a long-term problem, and the reason I am saying that is the following: when an individual amasses a considerable amount of wealth only for his family, relatives, and in-laws and impoverishes the masses, that wealth can't last long, since it's ill gotten or blood money. The will of the people in politics can easily be trampled upon by capitalists. The voices of poor people normally are not given considerable consideration, and their demands are normally on the bottom of the list of things that need to be given attention. Our Pyrrhic victory is that Africa's democracy is purely hinged upon the will of the people. We Africans still don't have land, as we didn't have land before our political liberation. African liberation movements have done a very great job by liberating Africa politically, but that is not what we Africans envisaged. It's true that we Africans can right now achieve the total independence that does not lack economic substance. Democracy without economic freedom is economic oppression of a different shape, size, and frame, but the picture remains the same, which is we Africans are still in the economic prison of the West while politically free. Before the arrival of the Western settlers to disturb our peace and tranquility, we

Africans lived and sang in harmony. We didn't covet one another, for we knew as a people that what my neighbor eats, he will share it with me also. The spirit of *Ubuntu* took precedence then, but that has changed right now—it is every man for himself, the law of the jungle reign supreme. The South African constitution contained *the bill of rights.* The bill of rights contains different types of freedom: the freedom of movement and residence; the freedom of trade, occupation, and profession; the freedom of expression; and the list goes on and on.[18] Freedom of movement can't exist alone without freedom to trade, occupation, and profession. Economic freedom should be pursued vigorously just as Africans fought and attained political freedom. Freedom of movement and freedom of expression will not suffice if there is no economic freedom. The fact of the matter is this: African liberation movements have sacrificed economic freedom for the freedom of expression. If I was given an opportunity to choose between economic freedom and the freedom of expression, I would choose the economic freedom instead of freedom of expression. The majority of people don't realize that a person who has a freedom of trade automatically has the entire package of the freedom of expression and residence combined in the economic freedom and the freedom of trade, occupation, and profession. A person who has a freedom of movement only, that person does not have even the very freedom of movement that he/she claims to possess. The main reason I am saying that is the following: freedom of trade, occupation, and profession and economic freedom ultimately give a person a freedom of movement and residence. Freedom of movement and residence without freedom of trade, occupation, and profession is another Pyrrhic victory; it's like having a body without a spirit. What is freedom of movement and residence without economic freedom? How will one survive with the freedom of movement and residence without economic freedom? For trade to occur, there needs to be a seller and the buyer in a market where both of these parties will meet and engage in the process of trade. It's also true that since we live in the information age, trade can occur through a click of a mouse without people meeting face-to-face, but the fact remains: there will still be a person that needs to deliver the goods that have been bought via eBay. As soon as people come into play automatically, the movement will take place. There can't be freedom of trade, occupation, and profession without the freedom of movement and residence. But with the freedom of movement and residence, you can still possess this freedom without enjoying the benefits of freedom of trade, occupation, and profession. People who have freedom of movements and residence without economic freedom don't have freedom at all. It's like having a car without wheels to move with; even if you have wheels, without a car, it is still useless anyway because either the one who has wheels without a car or the one who has a car without wheels won't go anywhere anyway. Whichever way you look at it, they are still stuck in the same place. Freedom of movement and residence is like political freedom, while freedom of trade, occupation, and profession is like economic freedom. In South Africa, we all know the political freedom does not pay the bills. Africans need economic freedom because it pays the bills and children will sleep with full stomachs. Political freedom sends children to bed early, and their nights become filled with nightmares. Capitalism and democracy can coexist in the absence of economic freedom. Capitalism and democracy coupled with economic freedom, the three can't exist. Economic liberation in democracy will also put capitalism in a precarious position; therefore, as long as democracy can accommodate capitalism, their so-called "will of the people" is not wholly the will of the people but the will of the capitalist. Capitalists support democracy but not economic freedom because as long as the people are poor and rely on government handouts, government grants, and foreign donors, then capitalism has a fertile ground to thrive on. Economic oppression is spiritual also. Many people don't realize that they are poor because to be poor is associated with being unemployed. Unemployment and poverty are two different economic derivatives. Many people attribute poverty to high rate of unemployment, and the solution to the problem of unemployment becomes massive jobs creation. Poverty and the creation of job opportunities are two different economic derivates. You can have a job for a very long time while living in abject poverty. Therefore, massive employments opportunities do not necessary solve the problem of poverty, which capitalists claim to solve. Capitalism does not create sustainable jobs, but it only creates temporary jobs within short space of time and pays the majority of people a slave wage. To rub salt to the wound, majority of people decide to augment their slave wage with a long-term loan that further deepens the level of poverty for many African families. Capitalists create massive temporary employment that is unsustainable; capitalism does provide the economic space of shareholding in Western companies. It advocates for the theory of retirement package and lump sum. Capitalism suggests that as long as you work for me, until you age, I will give you a lump sum and retirement package, but don't ever think of owning shares in this company—that is none of your business. Many people are not concerned about their company's wealth, meaning the turnover that the company makes at the end of the year including the dividends that are declared to the shareholders. Many people are just concerned about the salary increment and the thirteenth-month check that they will get at the end of the year. Capitalism is the only available instrument of the modern century that the Western powers are using to continue to dominate and control African countries; we Africans are paying dearly for it. For how long will our land continue to enrich the Western generation, and how long will Africans stay in abject poverty while drilling our own natural mineral resources and transporting them to the West? Are we Africans ever going to be financially free? Many African people quite frankly will say we are already free—which freedom are you talking about? Many people will say, "I have a job, family, house that had been financed by the bank, and I am enjoying life because they day I retire I will get a lump sum and the retirement package from my employer." What about your children then? They also need to work hard and buy a house through the mortgage loan and wait until they reach sixty-five years of age, and then they will get the lump sum and the retirement package—is this life that we Africans are envisaging for our future African generations to come? The African continent is trapped between a rock and a wall, and the wall is political freedom and its democracy, while the hard place is capitalism. Africa's democracy has not yielded much dividends, and our political freedom has not yielded dividends either. We Africans are politically liberated but poorer than ever before. We continue to vote, hoping that things will change for the better, but the fact of the matter is this: things are moving from bad to worse. In the past it was Western capitalists, but right now it is the Western capitalists and African capitalists combined together forming their own cartel. A cartel is when two companies come together to fix prices, but it's also true that when a Western capitalist and an African capitalist come together to enrich themselves through African mineral resources, it's also a cartel of a different shape, size, and form. Political freedom and democracy do not bring economic freedom, but they further plunge the masses into the depth of poverty.

CHAPTER 2

THE FATAL ERROR OF TRIAL AND ERROR

The fatal error of trial and error. The *Oxford Advanced Learner's Dictionary of Current English* defines the word "fatal" to mean this: "causing or ending in death or causing a disaster or failure." The trial and error is the idiom meaning solving the problem by trying various methods until you find a method that is successful. The theory of trial and error is also used in cost management accounting by cost accountants to find out a point where the company will reach a breakeven point. This breakeven point is known as a point where the company won't be making a profit or a loss. The main reason the cost accountants should find out earlier where the breakeven point will be is that so they can readjust the operating expenses to avoid the breakeven point. The fact is investors don't want to hear anything about a breakeven point. The breakeven point means that the company is not generating profit, and if the company is not generating profit, therefore there won't be dividends to be declared at the end of the year. The simple basic accounting theory says that "the main aim of establishing a business is to a make profit." The investors invest their capital, known as capital contribution, to a reputable company with a belief that the company will maximize their wealth and generate sufficient revenue to pay the dividends to the shareholders and also pay its creditors and continue to function as a going concern. The moment a company reaches this point of breakeven point, it goes without saying that the management of the company should convene to chant a way forward about the impeding financial disaster. The breakeven point is red light of bad things to come. The cost accountants must now apply the trial and error to ensure that this impending financial catastrophe does not come into existence. The trial and error method simply means that the cost accountant must look at the organization expenses totally and find a place where he/she can trim down certain operating expenses in order to avoid this breakeven point. The concept of company restructuring is sometimes used in order to avoid the breakeven point. Restructuring it means firing people, though this is not a concept that companies will prefer to use. But the fact of the matter is sometimes company restructuring simply means getting rid of certain employees. It's apparently clear that cost accountants of large corporations would desire a situation where there is no breakeven point in their large corporations' balance sheets. If a situation like that arises as a result, they will try to gamble with the lives of their poor employees in order to stay afloat and have a big, fat balance sheet at the expense of the employees. The investors or the shareholders are not interested as to whether or not people will go hungry and they won't have money to pay the school fees for the children. What the shareholders are worried about is not the interest of the employees but the dividends from the capital they injected in a company. The fatal error of trial and error is that it takes a considerable amount of time to find the optimum solution for a problem. The greatest danger about that is this: a lot people would have died and the damage would have been done, and the costs would have been incurred, and the consequences of the trial and error would be irreversible. HIV/AIDS killed a considerable amount of people all over the world, while scientists were lazing around in the laboratory using different trial and error techniques to find the exact cause of the virus and the optimum way to curtail the scourge of it. The African liberation movements have utilized trial and error unconsciously and gambled with the lives of people. Since I came back from Zimbabwe, I conducted a thorough introspection and realized that my overall objective has not been fulfilled. I never managed to see the grave of Cecil John Rhodes, and I could not conduct sufficient amount of interviews inside Zimbabwe because of the political climate in Zimbabwe, bearing in mind that it was just few weeks before the national election. The national security was even tighter than ever before; it was roadblocks after roadblocks. The fact of the matter is the government of Robert Mugabe and Morgan Tsvangirai employed a considerable amount of police, and the wage bill is invariable, hitting hard on the state's coffers. Mr. Khorombi from Lupane University said that I must send him questionnaires to be able to provide me with certain important information and to answer certain question that

I raised with him. I sent him the questions according to our agreement, and guess what! He never responded. I am aware of the political conditions right now in Zimbabwe. I won't blame him for not responding back to my e-mail. He believes like all Zimbabweans that possibly I am Baba Jukwa. This Baba Jukwa is known as an antigovernment spy who was working for the CIO (Central intelligence Organization) who later resigned and is now working against the government to disseminate classified information to the opposition parties. The fact of the matter is this: Baba Jukwa is not a real person; he exists in cyberspace and in Facebook only. Baba Jukwa is a body without a spirit. I suddenly realized that the first leg of my trip was not successful as I would have wanted it to be. I was back in South Africa, and my eyes were glued to Zimbabwe's national election from the beginning until the end. I reached a conclusion within myself that after the national election, I will go back to Zimbabwe and finish what I have started. I had a considerable amount of burden in my spirit, and I had an assignment to complete, which is writing a book. When I came back from Zimbabwe from my first trip, I discovered that South African political landscape has changed dramatically. I read that the EFF (Economic Freedom Fighters) have convened in Soweto, and they were pondering the idea of entering the South African political landscape. The South African political arena is littered with a multitude of political parties that have diverse political ideologies. These political ideologies are not in the interest of the South African people. Some of these political ideologies are reactionary political ideologies that seek to reverse the political gain that have been attained by the South African liberation movements through CODESA and the armed struggle. I have a serious problem with a multitude of political parties in one country because that is the microcosm of the diverse political thinking in most of the South Africans' mind. It seems as if we South Africans have resigned to the fact that our current national problems can be solved through establishing a new political party, even if many newly formed political parties are pursuing the politics of the stomach. The leaders of these newly formed political parties, some were members of the South African liberation movements, and when their narrow minded views could not be taken seriously, they became disgruntled and frustrated. The masses in South Africa don't need a new political party that will recycle our daily problems and promise the masses new houses and clean water. Clean water and sanitation are our basic human rights. I don't have to vote for clean water and sanitation. The coalition government in Zimbabwe had run its cause, and the political parties were now supposed to start campaigning and present their manifestos that are full of promises and lies. The fact of the matter is this: politics itself is a game of words. The whole ground of politics depends on who can tell an old lie in a truthful way. If you can lie to the point of appeasing the electorate; the masses will vote for you. If you tell an old lie in an untruthful way to the point that the electorate can see that you are lying, they will not vote for you. Politicians who speak the truth normally won't be voted for by the electorate, and politicians who speak lies, those are the ones that normally end up in government offices, which have big flat screens at the expense of the state. The former president of France, Nicolas Sarkozy, once said, "The former president of South Africa, Thabo Mbeki, does not understand Africa."[1] The context of this statement was about the so-called Second DRC War. France troops were in CAR (Central African Republic) and in DRC (Democratic Republic of Congo). France took it upon itself to maintain peace and security in DRC and CAR without the approval of the OAU (Organization of African Unity). The same attitude that France has about Africa is the same attitude that the United States of America has about the Middle East. The fact of the matter is this: former president of South Africa, Thabo Mbeki, does understand Africa very well and has been involved in the DRC peace process for a considerable amount of time. The former president of South Africa, Thabo Mbeki, has been instrumental in the establishment of the coalition government in Zimbabwe where we saw three different political parties coming together to form a coalition government. The GPA (Global Political Agreement), as it is known, was former president Thabo Mbeki's initiative under the auspices of SADC. To suggest that former president Thabo Mbeki does not understand Africa simply means that Africans who were born and bred in Africa don't understand Africa at all. Is this the main reason African leaders more often than not will seek foreign aid and foreign handouts to sustain their people from the West? There is a bit of truth in what Nicolas Sarkozy said. The main problem with most Africans is that they don't travel that much. It's also true that there are other Africans that travel the world in search of better business opportunities and just seeing the world in general. But the majority of Africans don't travel at all, and if they do travel, it's only to nearby places. The day I read that statement uttered by Nicolas Sarkozy, I was provoked to the extreme. I felt very embarrassed as to how can a French tell Africans about Africa? It's Friday morning in South Africa. It's a spring day. Everybody in Pretoria is welcoming spring, and everybody is wearing casual clothes in order to welcome spring in style. I am in Maropeng, the so-called *Cradle of Humankind*. The word "cradle" means a place or a period in which something originated. The cradle of humankind therefore is the place where humankind originated. It's better to be lectured by an African about Africa than to be lectured by French about Africa. The fact of the matter is this: if you refuse to be lectured about Africa by an African, you will likely fall victim of French education about Africa. I am an African, and I was going to be lectured about the Cradle of Humankind at least this time by an African. We disembarked from our buses, and a black South African gentleman approached us, wearing a red T-shirt "Maropeng" printed on it. He told us from the start that we needed to be careful of the snakes, and everybody was now having their eyes looking around as if we lost something. A South African gentleman approached us again also wearing a red T-shirt with "Maropeng" written on his chest. They began to say, "Guys, welcome to Maropeng, the Cradle of Humankind. We will be your tour guides today." They showed us the toilets and the place where we need to get our tickets, and since this was a college trip, the college had already paid for everything. We were given our tags, and we were told that we will now go to the exhibition center and the first tour guide will be conducting the whole tour before the entrance to the exhibition center and inside the exhibition center. On our way to the exhibition center, the serious tour started, but at least this was a black South African lecturing other black South Africans; this was not Nicolas Sarkozy lecturing us about our own African history. Our tour guide began to say, "Welcome to Maropeng, the Cradle of Humankind. The word 'Maropeng' in Setswana word means returning home." He began to talk about the formation of Earth, and I was literally getting lost and I hoped I was not alone. The formation of Earth theory from the scientific school of thought differs invariably with the theory of Christianity school of thought. The geophysicists and geologists have different confusing theories about the formation of planet Earth, and I was at the receiving end of that confusion. Our tour guide began to explain how Earth was formed. "Earth was born in a ball of fire in the bright, hot, early solar system about 4.6 million years ago." Then he went on to talk about Gondwana and Laurasia. There are multiple theories about the formation of planet Earth or how planet Earth was born. The Christianity school of thought recounts that "in the beginning God created the heavens and the earth, and the earth was without form and void, and darkness was on the face of the deep."[2] Elmer L. Towns, the cofounder of the Liberty University, writes in his book titled *The Bible Answers for Almost All Your Questions*:

> *The first heaven is atmospheric, the second comprised of stellar universe, and the third is the unique dwelling place of God.*[3]

There are three heavens according to Elmer L. Towns; however, the geologists and the geophysicists don't recognize the fact that there are three heavens. While I was confused about the formation of planet Earth, our tour guide pointed his fingers to a fossil that is known as "little food." This little food was found more than three million years ago, He fell into the cave. We finally entered the exhibition center, and we began our tour inside the exhibition center with a little tour ride on the shallow water. We saw water falling on us, and one of my colleague said we were going to be wet when we leave here. The moment we approached the point where there was a waterfall, eventually the water stopped. Our tour on the water was over, and another tour guide came to help us out of the little boat, and we went into the second part of the exhibition center, which contained a collection of fossils. The tour in the exhibition center was over, and we had to get to the restaurant to get our lunch. By the way, we were now very hungry, and a hungry man is an angry man. Our lunch was hot dogs and cold drinks. We finally bade farewell to our lovely tour guide who said, "I don't mind you guys taking me pictures and posting them on Face book. I love publicity." We went straight to the caves; the caves are at Sterkfontein. My colleague, Mr. Amarula, which is not his real name, went to the receptionist desk, and the receptionist gave him rules and regulations that he needs to read to the students. He came back with these rules, and he read them, and after he completed to read them, he summoned the whole group of students to follow him. Before we could go straight to the caves, we had to pass through the toilets to answer the call of nature before we can shoot straight to the caves. We were welcomed by a black female tour guide. Before we can shoot straight to the caves, there was a little museum that we had to visit and see that ball of fire that was hot and out of it came planet Earth. The museum was stuffy for me. Inside the museum we met other nationalities; I believe those were from France. Our tour guide told us that we were now going to the caves. The first instruction she gave us before we entered the cave was "Follow me, and if you misbehave inside the cave, you will be lost, and it will take three million years to find you." We thought, *Are you kidding?* But everybody laughed and thought she was scaring the hell out of us. She started to tell us about the mouth of the cave and said, "This opening is not a natural opening, but it was blasted by miners when they were mining." We went into the cave slowly, and it was becoming darker inside the cave. The further we went into the cave, the cooler the cave became until we reached a point where all our cell phones lost network. Inside the cave was cold and stuffy. In actual fact, I became very depressed inside the cave. We were shown a cliff that looked like an elephant and another cliff that looked like Mary holding Jesus. We reached the end of the cave, not necessarily the actual end of the cave in a natural sense, but it's the point of limit, and if we were to continue inside the cave, we were going to get lost and discovered after three million years as she said. "This is the end of the cave," she said, "and three students once attempted to find out how long was this cave. They managed to see the end of the cave, but one of the students could not make it back to the natural opening of the cave. A rock fell on his way, and he was trapped inside the cave for six long weeks. He died inside the cave." We were depressed already by hearing this bad news that somebody died inside this cave; it further plunged us back to panic mode. What everybody was thinking at that point in time was how to make it to the mouth opening of the cave alive, bearing in mind that our entrance point was a superficial opening and now we will exit through a natural opening. The natural opening was tiny and convoluted in a way. We had to bend, crawl, and squat in order to make it to the surface. Obesity is a serious problem. People that are morbidly obese stand an advantage to remain at home should you decide to invite them in excursions and academic tours of this nature. The main reason the majority of people are fat is that they eat a lot and do not exercise at all. People that have flexible bodies could easily make it to the surface through this natural opening, but people that are morbidly obese will find it very hard to bend, crawl, and squat because for the simple reason that they are morbidly obese and they can't bend. Behind me was a French citizen, and ahead of me was another French citizen. These are two old men. The old French nationality who was ahead of me was struggling with his weight. He eventually made it to the ground. The old French citizen who was behind me was slim in size, and he and I made it to the ground with ease, since I made it a norm to do push-ups each and every morning before I go to work. An old friend of mine once said to me, "You can't be lost in Africa." The fact of the matter is this: you can be lost in Africa. Most Africans don't understand Africa, and that's a reason these European fellows come and steal our gold, diamonds, and rhino horns—they know our continent more than us. Since I came from Zimbabwe from my first trip, I felt very tired; my spirit and my mind were tired, and by visiting the cave, it made it further worse. I went to the doctor for the checkups, and he said that I was very tired, and he booked me off for two days. I went to different libraries in Pretoria to borrow books. I studied enough to the point where I realized that I made a lot of mistakes in my first leg of my journey. I was determined to correct those mistakes I made and eventually went back to Zimbabwe to gather empirical evidence to support my hypothesis. The West stole Africa's wealth, and I will prove it. In the first leg of my trip, the whole of Zimbabwe was gearing itself for the national election. The problem about the national election date was the MDC-T and the MDC-M requested SADC in the meeting that was held in Maputo, Mozambique, to intervene in ensuring that the July 31, 2013, elections were free and fair. The other problem that was simmering was the election date itself. The July 31, 2013, national election was strategically planned to favor ZANU-PF at the expense of MDC-T and MDC-M. The person who had legal rights to extend or change the day of the national election was Pres. Robert Mugabe as the state president of the country and the head of the executive. Since it was initially announced that the national election was going to be held on July 31, 2013, there was nothing that SADC could have done but only to ensure that there is no violence and the national election was conducted free and fair. The political parties wanted further extension so they can be able to criss-cross the country in order to meet their supporters and present their manifestos. Since Prime Minister Morgan Tsvangirai of MDC-T decided to be part and parcel of the Government of National Unity (GNU), he lost touch with his supporters. This reality came to haunt him prior to the national election. The GPA (Global Political Agreement) saw Prime Minister Morgan Tsvangirai assuming the position of prime minister. Since he was Prime Minister of Zimbabwe, some of the ministries were given to MDC-T. These meant that not only was Morgan Tsvangirai Prime Minister of Zimbabwe but he was also still the president of the MDC (Movement for Democratic Change). Prime Minister Morgan Tsvangirai had to wear two hats at the same time, balancing the responsibilities of being the Prime Minister of the country with the responsibilities of carrying the second-largest political party in the country on his shoulders. The fact of the matter is this: you can't worship two masters at the same time; you will love the other and despise the other. There is no way he could have managed to pull both of these demanding positions together. Pres. Robert Mugabe of ZANU-PF was not moving an inch; he was cool, calm, and collected as if he knew that he has already won the elections. Pres. Robert Mugabe made a startling statement that shocked the world before the national election. He said, "If I lose this election, I will quit politics." Quite frankly a person who does not trust himself can't make such audacious political remarks. It was apparently clear from this quotation that Pres. Robert Mugabe was going to win the July 31, 2013, national election by hook or by crook.

THE CONTINENT OF PROPAGANDA

The *Oxford Advanced Learner's Dictionary* defines the word "propaganda" in this way: "ideas or statements that may be false or exaggerated and that are used in order to gain support for a political leader, party." Propaganda is also known as misinformation. There would not be political parties and political movements if there was no misinformation. Political parties prey on the ignorance of the masses. If the masses were clued up about what is happening in our world, probably there would not be fertile ground for politicians to propagate their propaganda. I bought two different newspapers from Zimbabwe and crossed the Beitbridge with them. Both of these newspapers reported on two different political topics. The other newspaper talked about the squabble that broke out in Mozambique between the Minister of Finance, Tendai Biti, and the Prime Minister, Morgan Tsvangirai. The newspaper claimed that Mr. Tendai Biti of MDC-T arrived in Mozambique and checked into the suite. This suite was booked for the Prime Minister, Morgan Tsvangirai, and all hell broke loose because the Finance Minister, Tendai Biti, refused to vacate the Prime Minister's suite and quoted to have said, "The suite is mine, and I am not going anywhere." The media houses and newsrooms are often misleading the masses because they are partly propagating a certain view. I have come to the realization that it will continue to be very difficult to find the truth in the print media. The print media is used by the political parties to win votes. Whenever I am reading a newspaper in South Africa or in Zimbabwe, it becomes apparently clear to me that I am now reading misleading information or I am lied to, to the point of believing that a certain political party is going to lose election or a certain political party is going to win election. The state print media will never report on a matter that will tarnish the reputation of the government. The private-owned print media that is funded and controlled by the West will try by all means to portray African liberation movements as political parties that are in a leadership crisis. There is no longer objective reporting. Journalists themselves report according to their political affiliations. The fact of the matter is this: journalists are people, and they are part and parcel of our political global village. Since journalists are part and parcel of this global political village, they too have their preferred candidates that they would like to see winning the national elections. The Western media will by no means attempt to report objectively about African politics and African leaders. The Western media more often than not portray African leaders as leaders that are ruling their countries through dictatorship. This worldview that African leaders are dictators is the Western propaganda to misinform African people. The Western media is also used by Western capitalists to destabilize, confuse and cause strife among Africans. The stealing of African mineral resources only takes place during this period of political instability and political uncertainty. When people heavily rely on the print media or media in general, as their reliable source of information, they are likely to be misled and misinformed. The state print media in Zimbabwe published the results of the research that was conducted by the Zimbabwe Statistics prior to the national election. The Zimstats states that:

> *"only 7.7 percent of economically active Zimbabweans are unemployed. This is interesting when read in comparison to the latest African statistics that peg the rate of unemployment in Namibia at 51.2 percent, 48 percent for Senegalese, Kenya 40 percent, Nigeria 23.9 percent, South Africa 22.7 percent, Tunisia 18.8 percent, Botswana 17.8, and 10 percent Algeria."*[5]

This report had been conducted by the state institution painting a rosy picture about the state of unemployment in Zimbabwe, implying that the South African economy is performing badly and the unemployment rate in South Africa is higher when compared with the unemployment rate in Zimbabwe. If the unemployment rate is higher in South Africa, how come the anecdotal five million Zimbabweans crossed the Beitbridge border, legally or illegally, in search for job opportunities in a country that has higher unemployment rate than Zimbabwe, their country of birth? This is electioneering and the manipulation of state institutions to misinform the masses. I have a serious problem with the so-called state institutions conducting their own research, which is not approved or confirmed by independent and external experts. Government reports are frequently than not littered with exaggerations and misinformation for that matter. This form of research, understandably so, was conducted by the government to inform the public about the progress of Zimbabwe's economy. State institutions are run by people with emotions and political ambitions, just like the privately owned print media are run by people that have political ambitions to see their preferred political party winning the elections. The fact of the matter is this: these media companies, if they report well about the government, are also likely to share the spoils of the election victory. State media will always report well about the government even if there are serious corrupt activities going on in the government; they will perform a window dressing. Private-owned print media scrap the barrel to find any corrupt activities and anything useful to tarnish the reputation of the government officials and the leaders of the African liberation movements, whether it be drinking red wine or sleeping in an expensive hotel. There is no longer objective reporting in the media. The state's institutions are used as a political instrument to campaign for the ruling party through propagating the state misinformation. The private-owned print media is used by the oppositional party to perpetuate the political idea that the state is failing and the leadership of the ruling party is corrupt and the government officials are looting the state resources in broad daylight. An average person who will continue to rely on print media, whether state owned or private owned, is likely to be misled and misinformed for a very long time. The print media, specifically private owned, is likely to find an accused guilty of crime that is based on hearsay and sentence that person to life imprisonment in a court of public opinion. This trend of finding people guilty in the court of public opinion fueled the wildcat strikes that were seen in South Africa in 2012. The private-owed print media usually portrays municipal officials as corrupt fat cats who are misusing and misspending public funds with impunity. If the truth be told, there are municipal officials that are misspending and misusing public funds to buy wines and expensive suits in India for their own girlfriends and concubines at the expense of the state funds. It's also true that there are municipal officials and government officials that are working hard to ensure that the state delivers quality services to the people. The ANC was pondering establishing the media tribunal that will hold the print media in South Africa accountable should they report defamatory report that seeks to tarnish the reputation of innocent people in South Africa. The idea of media tribunal was eventually abandoned at the expense of secrecy bill. The secrecy bill deals with the classification of the information. The classified information can't be disseminated to the public for public consumption; simply put, the public can consume information to the point that, that information is not classified. The state suggests that you are deemed to read what the state deemed ought to be read which unclassified information is. Classified information is not for public consumption, and therefore it's toxic for the public to read and consume classified information. It's possible that you can read unclassified information believing that, that is there only thing to know. While people who have an access to classified information might be a little bit ahead of a person who always reads unclassified information. The point that I am trying to drive home is this: classified information is for a certain class of people, and unclassified information is also for a certain class of people. If I was given an opportunity to choose between reading classified information and unclassified information, I would prefer to read the classified information. Classified information contains top secrets. The unclassified information contains public knowledge and general information, and there are no top secrets in unclassified information. The fatal error of trial and error is to use state institution as a mechanism to get votes from the electorate. State institutions were not supposed to be used to fight political battles of political parties. The state institutions were supposed to be guided and influenced by the constitution of South Africa, and the state institutions in the Republic of Zimbabwe were supposed to be guided and influenced by the constitution of Zimbabwe. The politicians utilized trial and error method to find a political solution specifically to solve complex political problems. The greatest dangers about the trial and error method when it comes to political matter is that the lives of people are at stake, and by the time an appropriate solution is found, a lot of people would have lost their lives and families would have been broken into pieces by the system of trial and error. I met a gentleman by the name of Mr. Silverton; by the way, Mr. Silverton is not his real name. Whenever you are talking to a person from Zimbabwe and asking questions about politics in Zimbabwe, people normally begin to show signs of withdrawal from the political dialogue. The main reason a lot of people don't want to discuss Zimbabwean politics is that they believe that probably you are a government agent that is out there to collect information about the views of people on the ground. Even those that are living in South Africa behave as if South Africa is Zimbabwe. Former president of South Africa, Thabo Mbeki, once said that:

> "*South Africa is not Zimbabwe.*"[6]

Our discussion with Mr. Silverton revolved around the national elections that were about to take place in Zimbabwe. Mr. Silverton said to me, "MDC-T or MDC-M will never win national election." The majority of novice politicians think that you win elections because the majority of people voted for you or because you have a political manifesto that is spot-on. In politics, the manifestos, billboards, and Face book messages can't win you the national election; neither will campaigning hard win you elections. It goes beyond the manifestos and billboard messages. It's about the counting of the votes. Who will count the votes after the electorate has completed voting? The elections are won and lost on the counting of the votes, not on the number of people that have voted for a certain political party. As long as this system of vote counting is not properly addressed, the MDC-T and the MDC-M supporters can vote with their chickens and their pigs; together combined they will never win Zimbabwean national election. You probable heard this saying that "it's not over until the fat lady sings." It means that a situation might still change. This saying is also used in a soccer match to encourage the trailing team that they need to still play with a belief that something extraordinary might still happen, some form of a miracle. The one-million-dollar question is, what if the fat lady is Pres. Robert Mugabe and MDC-T or MDC-M is playing against ZANU-PF? Elections can be won before even the electorate cast their ballot papers in the ballot box. Some people were suggesting that in African elections, we need to have two sets of system of counting the votes. We need a manual counting and the electronic counting to ensure that there is no rigging of votes. The one-million-dollar question that remains is this: Who will do this electronic counting and this manual counting? As long as this manual counting and electronic counting is done by certain individuals of certain political party, it's possible that the results might not be free and fair even if the political conditions were summarily peaceful. The point I am re-emphasizing is that the electorate won't win you the national elections because the national elections are not won on the ballot box; national elections are won on vote counting.

It's Wednesday afternoon in Pretoria. I was going to a buy a bus ticket for my long journey to Zimbabwe (Harare). The cashier at Pretoria station said to me, "How can I help you, sir?" I said, "One ticket to Zimbabwe (Harare)," and she said to me, "When are you leaving?" I said, "Friday afternoon." She printed the ticket for me, and I paid R380. It's written in my ticket that the departure time is 2:30 p.m., and the arrival time in

Zimbabwe (Harare) is 5:30 a.m., Friday. The following day I went to the bank with my South Africa currency to buy US dollars, since Zimbabwe is using US dollars. The bank broker requested my passport and my South African identity document and the bus ticket, which I gladly provided her with. She took her time back and forth. She went and finally gave me my squeaky clean US dollars. The bank won't allow me to buy US dollars if I am not going to the United States of America or in a country where the US dollar is their functional currency. The IAS 21 defines the functional currency in this way:

> *"Functional currency is the currency of the primary economic environment in which the entity operates."*[7]

It therefore means that if a company is operating in a country where the US dollar is the functional currency, the company itself will have to pay the salaries of their employees in US dollars, since the US dollar is the functional currency. In a country like Zimbabwe where they are using the multicurrency system, you are allowed to use South African currency to buy anything in Zimbabwe. I have a very serious problem with this idea of changing South African currency to US dollars. The problem starts when you cross the border and you are in Zimbabwe because all goods in Zimbabwe are priced in US dollars. The bank broker gave me my receipts, which indicate the VAT (Value-Added Tax) and the commission that I paid the bank. The fact of the matter is this: when I buy US dollars using South African currency, the bank makes a commission through me. The question is, What do I get when I change my money from South African currency to Zimbabwean currency? The truth is I get nothing except my US dollars, which are now reduced because of the VAT that I paid to the bank and the commission that the bank has deducted from my money. This multi-currency system that Zimbabwe is using is killing my pocket. When I went into the bank, I was smiling, all the way to the bank; but the truth is when I left the bank, I was crying. I took my money, ticket, passport, and my identity document. I spoke to Mr. Brown, and I assured him that tomorrow afternoon, he and I will be in the same bus that was leaving South Africa, Pretoria, at exactly 2:30 p.m. to Zimbabwe. I informed my mother in the evening telephonically and assured her that I won't take a considerable amount of days in Zimbabwe. I told her that she must not worry—Pres. Robert Mugabe won't arrest me. Besides Pres. Robert Mugabe was not in Zimbabwe; he was in the United States of America attending the UNGA meeting. Friday morning I pulled my bag and put it on my right shoulder and all the necessary documents that I will need, and I went straight to the bus station. I have to meet Mr. Brown and ensure that we are in the same bus. Mr. Brown was a crucial player in my trip. The whole of my trip hinged on him. I arrived at the bus terminal. I looked around as if I was mad. Guess what! I don't see Mr. Brown, and out of the blue, Mr. Brown appeared wearing new brown shoes that don't match his trouser and a green jacket that does not match his shoes. While we were waiting, his phone rang. He received a call from his phone; I thought that was his wife. When he finished talking, he said to me, "Do you know who was calling me?" I said no. He said, "The person who was calling me is Mr. Milkshake. Mr. Milkshake is my colleague and is currently doing PhD in the University of Kwazulu Natal." Mr. Milkshake said, "You need to give that man a farm in Zimbabwe." I thought for me to get a farm in Zimbabwe, I had to be a war veteran. The truth is you can get a farm in Zimbabwe even if you are not a war veteran. Our bus did not get delayed this time. At around 2: 20 p.m., the bus was already waiting and we were checked in by the driver and we had already put our bags in the luggage trailer. I went straight to my seat and sat next to a dark old man who looks like he is in his late forties. I greeted him, and I relaxed a little bit. The next thing you know here comes a morbidly obese lady coming straight to sit next to me. I was sitting in the middle now. Our seat is a three-seater, meaning I was stuck in between this old man who is in his forties and this morbidly obese lady. It seemed as if I was not going to enjoy my journey today. The bus departed. Since the bus was not full to the brim, she decided to look for another empty seat in the bus. Zimbabwe is under economic sanctions, and that is not the only problem that Zimbabwe has. The other problem that Zimbabwe has is morbidly obese people. South Africa has a problem of morbid obesity too. Morbid obesity means you are now overweight in an unhealthy way. The problem of morbid obesity in Africa is caused by the West. The majority of people will say Africans blame the West for all their self-made problems. The fact of the matter is this: most of the African problems originated from the West. It's the West that is importing fat to the African continent through fast food; it's the West that is exporting calorie-rich, fatty foods to Africa. Most African women can't cook anymore because of the takeaways. The scourge of morbid obesity cuts across all spectrums of life. Most African politicians are suffering from the same disease—obesity. Africans are dying, and they are not dying because of hunger and food shortages this time, but too much food and less exercise. It simply means Africans eat too much fatty foods, which are full of calories, and drink too much Coke, which is full of caffeine, and we watch TV for more than five hours, specifically during the weekend. The morbidly obese lady eventually found a seat where she sat comfortably. She had a big bag, and the only thing that I saw clearly was a burger. She was prepared not to starve herself. I began a dialogue with this old gentleman who was in his late forties. He told me that he is a teacher. He is teaching mathematics in Carletonville. He told me that his name was Simon and he studied in Cuba. There are many Zimbabwean teachers in South Africa that are teaching mathematics, physics, and biology, and the reason there are many Zimbabwean teachers in South Africa that are teaching physics, mathematics, and biology is that most South African students don't prefer teaching as a good profession. Teaching itself is a stressful and challenging career. It requires people who have patience and love for the learners, which are the reasons why the majority of South African students don't prefer to do teaching in the South African universities. It's because most teachers are underpaid while overworked. The abolition of corporal punishment makes it easy for learners to disrespect their teachers with impunity, and there is nothing that a teacher can do about it. There are many reasons why South Africa lacks teachers that can teach mathematics, physics, biology, and accounting. It's because teaching is not paying. Teachers are public servants, and they have to strike year in and year out to get a salary raise. When learners see their teachers in the streets marching just for 7 percent salary adjustment, they become despondent and loathe teaching with the rest of their hearts. Teaching as a career is no longer appeasing. You can only teach a person who aspires to be like you, and you can only teach a person who values your presence before him or her. You can only teach a respecting child. The majority of students don't choose teaching because they know very well that if you become a teacher, you will have to march going up and down with placards and boards before you can get the mere 7 percent salary increment. Most of the young people of South Africa who were supposed to the teachers of tomorrow decide to divert to other professions. There is no shortage of lawyers in South Africa, and there is no shortage of nurses in South Africa; however, there is a shortage of doctors. Let me sound paradoxical: there is no shortage of doctors in South Africa. When South African students graduate from medical schools, they go to the private sector instead of practicing in the public sector. The private sector caters to the rich, and the public sector caters to the poor and the underprivileged. There is a theory that says Zimbabwean education is better than South African education—I have great difficulties in believing that. First of all, Zimbabwe is a small country compared to South Africa; and, second, Zimbabwe is under economic sanctions and South Africa is not under economic sanctions. How can you compare a country that is so small like Zimbabwe to South Africa, which is known as "Saudi Arabia of mineral resources"?[8] From now on, when you hear a person suggesting that the Zimbabwean education system is better than the South African education system, I suggest you keep quiet to avoid unnecessary headache. We need to compare an apple with an apple; we need to compare the like with the like. Zimbabwe became an independent democratic country with a democratically elected government in 1980, and South Africa became an independent democratic country with a democratically elected government in 1994. The South African elections were held on April 27, 1994. I still remember vividly because my lovely mother and my lovely father came from voting in the tribal office, and we sat under the tree and they told me they voted for Nelson Mandela. The whole elections of 1994 were not about the ANC quite frankly; it was purely about Nelson Mandela with his eternal smile. The late president Nelson Mandela is still the center of attraction in the ANC, and truth be told, the majority of people cared much about the late president Nelson Mandela, not the politics of the ANC. I am not implying that the ANC is insignificant in comparison to the late president Nelson Mandela as an individual. The point I am driving home is this: the ANC is the political home of the late president Nelson Mandela, and there would not be Nelson Mandela if it wasn't because of the ANC, and on the same breath, the ANC would have not been where it is today if it wasn't for the contribution of Nelson Mandela and others. The point I am driving home is we can't compare Zimbabwe and South Africa because these two countries vary invariably in many respects. Zimbabwe was liberated first, and South Africa followed fourteen years later. The truth is Zimbabwe was supposed to be very far, infrastructural and otherwise, in comparison to South Africa. Unfortunately it drifted back to the depth of poverty attributed to economic sanctions, which have been caused by the farm invasion. Simon and I began a political dialogue and the reasons why he is working in South Africa and not working in his home country. He said to me, "I studied in Cuba through a government program, and it took me five years to complete the program because I had to study Spanish first and eventually complete my degree." In Cuba they speak Spanish, and since in Cuba they speak Spanish, he too had to study and understand Spanish before he can commence with his program. He told me that he was not the only one that was studying in Cuba. Pres. Robert Mugabe's government made it possible for him to study in Cuba at the government's expense; all fees were paid for by the government, and that was 1988. The main reason the government of Pres. Robert Mugabe decided to send their students in Cuba to study mathematics, biology, medicine, and physics was to build state capacity in the country, ensuring that teaching and learning take place but at an accelerated pace. As long as they continued to invest in their education, the Zimbabwean education got better and better; but bear in mind that at this time, black South Africans were not allowed even to come to Pretoria to buy bread. Black South Africans had to carry an ID book and stay in the villages where there is no newspaper. Simon had to work in the government after completing his studies in Cuba. He came back from Cuba in 1992. He began working in government schools and never thought of working elsewhere other than home, which is Zimbabwe. The 2000 farm invasion took place while he was in Zimbabwe and the economic sanctions after that. I asked him why he decided to come and work in South Africa, and he said to me, "It's because of Tendai Biti." Tendai Biti is the then Finance Minister of Zimbabwe, and he is from the MDC-T. When the coalition government was formed, some of the ministries had to be given to the MDC-T and the ministry of finance was given to MDC-T, and it was headed by Finance Minister Tendai Biti, the lawyer. Simon said, "Since Tendai Biti assumed his position as the Minister of Finance of Zimbabwe, he never increased the salaries of the civil servants, and he used to say government does not have money, while he was buying government ministers Mercedes Benz with our money," Simon said. Due to the economic sanctions and the failure of the government to increase the salaries of civil servants, Simon had no choice but to cross the Beitbridge border to come to the "Saudi Arabia of mineral resources," which is South Africa, to look for a job. His wife is a teacher, but she is not teaching in a government school, since in government schools, the salary that teachers get is too little to cater for the two daughters that they have, so she decided to work in a private school, and the private schools in Zimbabwe are paying better salaries compared to the public schools, which are run and funded by the government. We were on our way to Zimbabwe when a certain gentleman stood up in the bus, and he took a Bible and opened the book of Luke 18:18- 23. It's about a young rich ruler who came to Jesus to ask him what he should do to enter the kingdom of God. Jesus said to him, "You still lack one thing: sell all that you have and distribute to the poor, and you will have treasure in heaven; and come, follow me."[9] He started talking about what he called the eternal life and his definition of eternal life, "the life with no beginning and no end," but he said for you to enter the eternal life, you need to die to your political ideas and political views. He said one of the things that prevented the younger ruler to follow Jesus was his wealth, and he didn't die to his material wealth. I sat in my seat, and I was pondering this eternal life theory. The life with no beginning and with no end—this statement struck me to the core of my spirit, which means in the eternal life, there are no economic sanctions that can be imposed by the West to Africa, and there is no stealing of our African mineral resources by the West. Surely the thieves can't enter eternal life, and big countries that are stealing mineral resources from small countries can't enter eternal life. I began to ask myself about the number of Iraqi people that died at the hands of the American soldiers under the pretext of liberating them from Saddam Hussein. And I asked myself this question: will the American soldiers that killed countless number of people in Iraq enter this eternal life? Eternal life does have a beginning, and eternal life does not have an end. If there is a life that I will prefer to live, it is this eternal life that the gentleman in the bus was talking about. The problem that I have about entering this eternal life that he was talking about is that I also need to die to my political ideas; I have a problem with dying to my political ideas. I believe that the West stole Africa's wealth and we Africans should be compensated for our gold and diamond that the West had stolen from Africa. The West must give us, Africans, our money, which they have invested in the World Bank, IMF, and European Central Bank. I am not going to die to my political ideas because I believe the West didn't die to its political ideas of colonizing our forefathers and grandparents, beating them and kicking our forefathers in the ass for their land that was given to them by God. I am not ready to die to my political ideas, but I also want the eternal life where Britain and the United States of America can't police the whole world. Britain and the United States of America have kept the whole world on their radar. In case they don't see you in their radars, they will just accuse you of manufacturing weapons of mass destructions, even a small country like Zimbabwe. I was flabbergasted the other day when I heard that the British newspaper suggested that Zimbabwe in the near future will manufacture weapons of mass destruction because Zimbabwe has signed a trade agreement with Iran to trade with uranium. Zimbabwe can't manufacture weapons of mass destruction because it does not have the wherewithal and know-how to manufacture weapons of mass destructions. Besides the fact that Zimbabwe does not have the wherewithal and the know-how, Zimbabwe is under the swine flu of economic sanctions. How can a country that is under the swine flu of economic sanctions sneeze and manufacture weapons of mass destructions at the same time? I once asked a friend of mine from Nigeria about his views into this matter that Zimbabwe is contemplating to manufacture weapons of mass destruction. He just began to laugh and said, "I think when they are talking about Zimbabwe contemplating to manufacture weapons of mass destruction, they are referring to witchcraft." I then said it means Zimbabwe will use their African magic to strike the United States and Britain with lightning. The gentleman who was preaching in the bus finally said, "If you want to enter into this eternal life, the life with no beginning and no end, raise up your hand." Two women raised their hands in the air, and he prayed for them and he sat down. The main reason I didn't raise my hand is that I don't like the idea of dying to my political ideas. To die to your political ideas simply means to forget about your political belief and political stance. It also means that we Africans need to forgive the West for the atrocities they have caused in Mozambique, Angola, Kenya, and South Africa. It also means that we should continue to accept the foreign donations and the social grants that are coming from the West to sustain Africans. The West taught African leaders to rely on foreign aid and donations. If African countries are not receiving donations from Britain and the United States of America, African countries are borrowing money from the IMF or World Bank. All African massive infrastructural programs are funded by the World Bank and IMF. These two biggest financial institutions are controlled and influenced by the West. The World Bank is in the United States of America; the International Monetary Fund is in the United States of America; the United Nations headquarters are in the United States of America—what else is not in the United States of America? We finally arrived at the Beitbridge border. In the border it was very hot that evening. Underneath the Beitbridge border is the Limpopo River.This Limpopo River comes straight from Mozambique, passes through South Africa, and passes through Zimbabwe. The Limpopo River is very dangerous and is brimming with crocodiles. Zimbabweans who don't have valid passports and formal documents to enter South Africa legally cross through the Limpopo River to South Africa illegally. After they have crossed the Limpopo River, they normally find a group called AMAGUMA GUMA waiting for them on the other side of the Beitbridge border. The AMAGUMA GUMA is a group that consists of men who took it upon themselves to rob and rape Zimbabweans that were crossing the Limpopo

River at night or even during the day. The AMAGUMA GUMA will normally rob the Zimbabweans of their belongings and rape women. There are Zimbabwean women who have been impregnated by AMAGUMA GUMA. The AMAGUMA GUMA are mostly young men that are angry at the government, and they can't be easily arrested because their modus operandi changes every day. When there are floods in Mozambique, the Limpopo River will be overflowing, causing cholera in Beitbridge. There is still a message on the Zimbabwean immigrations offices warning people about the danger of cholera and ways to prevent it. There was no cholera in South Africa; there is only cholera at the Beitbridge border, which is caused by the overflowing of the Limpopo River and the Mozambican floods. I am not implying that there is cholera in Zimbabwe or Zimbabwean waters are not purified. The point I am making is there is cholera at the Beitbridge border, and next time you are visiting Zimbabwe, be aware of cholera. In 2008 and early 2009, cholera killed a lot of people in the Beitbridge border. The main reason why people were dying like flies was that the Limpopo River was overflowing and the river caused the cholera breakout. Our bus pulled over, and we disembarked from the bus and took our passports and headed straight to the South African immigrations offices to get South African stamps. Under good conditions, it will take one hour to get my passport stamped from the South African immigrations offices. Then after that, we will have to cross the Beitbridge border and we will arrive at Zimbabwe's immigration offices, where the problem will start. On this day in question, we spent almost an hour in the South African immigrations offices, and we went back to the bus. On the queue outside the bus, I spoke to the gentleman who was preaching in the bus about the theory of eternal life and the life with no beginning and no end. I expressed to him my deepest gratitude about the word of God that he had just shared with us in the bus. We began to talk about life in general. He said to me that he was Pastor Sithole. He was also teaching physics in South Africa, but he is based in Durban. He showed me his passport; the man has traveled in Africa extensively, and he has been in Zambia, Swaziland, and Kenya. He said the reason the Beitbridge border is hot is that it is the lowest point of the river. He began to lecture me and Simon about the river and the reason the Beitbridge border is hot. He finally concluded his lecture, and we went back to the bus. When we were in the bus, there was this strange man who was lost and was of Tanzanian nationality. He was old and bald. He was speaking English, but you can tell that the man was not educated. Pastor Sithole suggested that he should speak to the driver; he might agree to give him a ride to Zimbabwe, and then he can connect to the bus that can take him to Zambia and finally Tanzania, which is his destination place. Some people suggested he must disembark from the bus and sort himself out. What was on my mind at that point in time was what if this man is not lost but a terrorist who planned to bomb this bus? He finally disembarked from our bus, and we were not even interested in whether he will get to Zimbabwe alive or not. By the way, we just met this man at Beitbridge, and we can't be held responsible for him getting lost—it's none of our business. I whispered to Simon, who was very quiet. I said to Simon, "A person must travel the world while he is still young and get his PhD as soon as possible to avoid to end up getting lost in the Beitbridge." He said to me, "You are right." There is one question that Simon asked me that I can't get out of my mind about Julius Malema. He said, "I hear that Julius Malema's political party is covering a lot of ground, specifically to the youth." I said to Simon, "Julius Malema's EFF will win, get some votes, and possibly get parliamentary seats. The main problem with South African parliament is this: South African parliament is the unforgiving grave of South African oppositional parties." The point I was making is this: once an oppositional party to the ANC wins a handful of parliamentary seats, most oppositional parties will prefer to get to Cape Town where the South African parliament is situated. A parliamentarian gross annual salary was beyond R900,000 as of the writing of this book, which will likely change if you take into consideration the salary adjustment that needs to be effected each and every year. Once an oppositional party is in parliament in those comfortable seats, the members of the oppositional party normally forget that they are an opposition; they begin to focus on the Secrecy Bill and the Arms Deal. The next thing you know they will begin to discuss those long and convoluted bills and fall asleep in those comfortable seats, trust me, if EFF will win a handful of parliamentary seats. The problem with most politicians in South African politics is that they worry more about the policies of the ANC than developing their own policies. South African parliamentary seats are irresistible and inviting; most parliamentarians can't help but to fall asleep in those seats. There is too much drudgery in South African parliament. Simon, since he studied in Cuba, has developed a socialist mentality; he seems to support the idea of social grants. He said to me, "At least the South African government is doing something for its people because it offers South Africans social grants." The problem about staying five years in a socialist country is that you end up thinking like the socialist. If you study in Cuba, you will be begin to speak Spanish. If you begin to speak Spanish, you will think like a socialist." He went on say, "There are no social grants in Zimbabwe, and Zimbabwe's government is not doing enough to alleviate poverty." Social grants don't alleviate poverty; they compound poverty. Pres. Jacob Zuma in his state of the nation address to parliament in 2012 said:

> *South Africa is not a welfare state.*[10]

The fact of the matter is this: these social grants cripple the psyche of economically active people. The social grants discourage people to think straight and be innovative; eventually people depend on the government for everything just because they voted for the government. The initial objective of government was to alleviate poverty; it was a good idea. But South African citizens are now milking the government. Hence, the president said, "South Africa is not a welfare state." What the president was basically saying is this: there will come a point in time where the state will not have the financial muscle to distribute social grants to all South Africans. I am not the spin doctor of the president; that is what he was implying by that statement. Social grants have run their cause; the state must rethink about a new program to alleviate poverty. Simon said to me, "In Cuba a family was given government vouchers, and in the morning this family would go to a grocery shop to collect limited number of breads for that day only." I asked Simon to tell me why Cubans are good in science. He said, "Its economic sanctions. Sanctions force people to think." I have a very big problem with his line of thinking, but partly what he was saying is true. If economic sanctions make people think, it therefore means that social grants make people to be lazy. The main reason Simon came to work in South Africa was his two daughters that are studying in a private school in Zimbabwe. He decided to take his two daughters to a private school because he realized that the public education system was collapsing, the very same public education system that the majority of people say is better than the South African education system. The fatal error of trial and error is to test different systems of education in order to find the optimum system that will serve people well. We arrived in the immigrations offices of the Republic of Zimbabwe. There were long queues of trucks that were going to Zambia and long queues of trucks that were going to DRC (Democratic Republic of Congo). We disembarked from the bus, and we took our passport and went to Zimbabwe's immigration offices to get the stamps.

Because I am a South African, I should shoot straight to the immigration officer who administers visitors and non-Zimbabweans. I went to a lady immigration officer who gave me a form to fill. The form required an address where I am going and the amount of money I have in my pocket. I didn't complete the block that required me to provide the amount of money I have in my pocket. She took the form and looked at me and said, "How much money do you have in your pocket?" I said, "US$700." She wrote the amount on the empty box or empty space, and she stamped my passport—period, end of the story. I went back to the bus, and I reunited with Simon and Mr. Brown. The standard procedure that was supposed to be followed from then onward was to get our bags searched, and after the process of searching our bags was over then we will proceed with our journey until the capital city, Harare, known as the worst city on earth. In my first trip, we spent five hours in the Beitbridge border purely on the Zimbabwean immigration offices. I wondered how many hours were we going to spend on that day; I was ready to wait to get what I wanted. Good things come to those who wait, and bad things come to those who rush, right? We were instructed to take our bags from the luggage trailer so they can be searched by Zimbabwe's immigration officers. While we were waiting, here comes a disabled person—one of his legs was amputated all the way to the knee; the other leg is healthy. He asked for money. I was standing next to Simon, and out of guilty conscience, Simon took his wallet, opened it up, and gave him some coins. He said, "Thanks." I now understood why Simon is the greatest proponent of social grants. I suspended my judgments about social grants; I guess we need them more than ever before. Every coin has two sides, the tail and the head. The head is the progressive society, economically able people who find jobs and establish their own families. The tail is the other side of the coin; on this side of the coin, people here are crippled because of diseases and wars that have left them paralyzed forever. The tail is the side of the coin where social grants should be distributed to the people because you are talking about people who have never been to school due to unforeseen circumstances. Social grants can be distributed to people that are crippled and paralyzed. They can also be distributed to people who are mentally handicapped, not to people who fake being sick while dancing all night long after earning their disability grants with hot chicks and claiming to be sick the next day. If you die in South Africa and you are a Zimbabwean, you will have to queue in the Beitbridge border just like a normal breathing person. Mr. Brown took me to this line, which I will call "the queue of the dead." All these cars that you see they are caring people who died in South Africa Mr. Brown said. The fact of the matter is this: queues are not avoidable. If you cross the Beitbridge border alive, you will have to queue, and if you cross the Beitbridge border dead, that won't help either. These queues are everywhere; it's like paperwork. There is paperwork everywhere: there is paperwork in the bank, there is paperwork in the furniture shop, and there is even paperwork at the cemetery. There is also paperwork at church. When are we going to leave a free life, a life without paperwork? The reason why children are failing at school is because of paperwork and there is less teaching taking place. There is too much paperwork. The main reason patients are dying in hospitals is paperwork. Doctors are buried under the files of patients, trying to read the reports of other doctors about the same patient who is before them dying. All these paperwork are happening under the concept of standard procedure that needs to be followed. It took almost two hours for the Zimbabwean immigration officers to search out luggage, and finally we were given the bus clearance. The bus clearance is the confirmation that the bus has been searched and there are no goods that were not declared by the passengers. If you have goods that are beyond US$300, you are supposed to pay custom duty levy. This custom duty levy is paid to the Zimbabwean immigration officers. Some of these monies do not reach Zimbabwe's government coffers; some of these monies vanish in thin air. I met some South African ladies in the bus who were going to Zimbabwe to meet their prophet. They told me they were going to see a certain prophet in Zimbabwe. When I looked at their ring fingers, they were not wearing their rings. That simply tells me that probably these women have been heartbroken many times by South African men and now they were looking for a Zimbabwean prophet who will tell them exactly whom they should marry. In South Africa, men are few and women are many. Because of this unevenness in gender, women are more than men because most South African men are in prison. Women are left alone and lonely at home, and they end up falling for the bad guys. The predators prey on the vulnerable and weak women, especially those that are desperate for love and comfort. We left the Beitbridge border at around midnight, and it will normally takes seven hours to get to Harare, if the driver is driving well and if the road is clear. Zimbabwean government is obsessed with national security to the point that they have traffic officers even in the middle of the night that are on duty. This is madness of epic proportion. While you are preparing yourself to sleep, the next thing you know the traffic cop is instructing the bus driver to pull over. This is the aftermath of national election. I was going to see what Morgan Tsvangirai calls "the monumental rigging."[11] There was a serious outcry out there about the results of the national elections. The outcry comes from the ordinary people on the streets and even from the international community. The US secretary of state, John Kerry, said, "The Zimbabwe election results are not a reflection of the will of the people." How is it possible that somebody in the United States of America can clearly know the will of the people of Zimbabwe? I don't know the will of the people of Zimbabwe. That is why I was going to Harare to possibly see this monumental rigging that the international community was talking about. Simon complained to me about working in South Africa—that he is sleeping alone, and a man of his age was supposed to work at home and sleep next to his wife on a daily basis. I understand Simon's complaints, but he is going home now. And whatever he could not do to his wife because of the distance in between, he will be able to do it now. "Stop rambling, Simon, you are going to see your wife and your two daughters," I said. At least Simon has a wife. What about a man who has been sleeping alone since birth because of lack of money to appease women with? Surely that is a pain that the majority of men can't withstand. Just few months away from his wife, Simon is crying like a baby. The bus driver started driving at high speed, and the next question that was on my mind was, does this man have a family like Simon? If he has a family like Simon, why is he driving at a high speed? The truth of the matter is this: we are going to get to Harare even if we get to Harare in the afternoon. But it's better to be late than to be dead. I began asking myself endless questions such as, what have I done to die in a bus accident? I began to panic, and part of me thought to stand up and tell the driver straight to his face, "Chief, slow down, OK?" The whole time from South Africa to Beitbridge, he was driving very well. All of sudden, once we crossed the Beitbridge border, he began to fly as if somebody was chasing him. I sat there in my seat full of discontentment and fear. I was afraid of dying in a foreign land. I was afraid of dying in Zimbabwe, of all places. If you die in Zimbabwe, the process of bringing the dead body from Zimbabwe to South Africa will be more expensive than transporting a dead body from South Africa to Zimbabwe. If you are a South African, it's better to die at home than to die outside the country because of the foreign expenses that your family might incur.

Chapter 3

JUSTICE

"*Fiat justitia ruat caelum*" is a Latin legal phrase meaning "Let justice be done though the heavens fall." This phrase is attributed to Charles Sumner. Justice must be done though the economic sanctions fall. Sometimes through the pursuit of justice many people might die. It's imperative that when Africans pursue justice, they must also take into consideration the consequences of justice. Justice is not free. Justice is costly, and sometimes justice can cause a country to incur unnecessary economic sanctions from the international community. We Africans have been granted political liberation by our colonial masters, but we have realized late that actually we are not liberated because political liberation does not mean anything if that political liberation does not amount to economic liberation. We Africans are still dependent on the West like never before. In fact we call the West our business partners. When I was at the Beitbridge border, there was something that happened that was worth my attention and my focus. There was a notice on an electric pole, and it stated, "Crossing the border with table potatoes and eggs is a criminal offence." I read the notice. I did not digest the notice that much because, above all, I was not carrying table potatoes and eggs; it was purely my clothes that were in my bag. We arrived in Harare at exactly 7:30 a.m. Simon was dropped off at Masvingo. When we arrived in Harare, it was already hot, since it was summer. We disembarked from the bus, and we had to wait for the bus driver to open the luggage trailer to be able to take our luggage. While we were collecting our luggage from the trailer, Pastor Sithole came to me as I was standing next to Mr. Brown. He said he needed a lift that can take him straight to the taxi rank. After Mr. Brown had collected his luggage from the luggage trailer, he phoned his wife and informed her that we had already arrived and she must come and pick us up. The normal routine that will be followed today will be as follows: since we have Pastor Sithole with us, we should drive him to the taxi rank, and then I must be driven to the hotel, and Mr. Brown and his wife can now drive home. I saw Pastor Sithole with a bag full of eggs. I said, "Did you see the notice that was on the electric pole at the Beitbridge border?" He said, "I didn't see it." The notice on the electric pole stated that crossing the Beitbridge border with eggs and table potatoes is a criminal offence. It's legal to buy eggs in Zimbabwe if you are a Zimbabwean, and the South African law does not prohibit a person from another country not to cross the border with eggs to South Africa. The Zimbabwean government does not allow its citizens who are outside the country to buy eggs and transport them to Zimbabwe—that is a criminal offence, and you can be arrested just for buying eggs in South Africa and cross with them all the way to Harare. The problem with this law is that there are no police who are policing this law. Perhaps Pastor Sithole was lucky because the Beitbridge border police could not detect the eggs in his bag. He said, "I think they don't want us to buy eggs from South Africa because they are cheap and they want us to buy eggs and potatoes from their farms." The fact of the matter is this: if Zimbabweans who work in South Africa earn a salary and they don't buy goods in South Africa and buy goods in Zimbabwe, the economy of Zimbabwe will improve. To ensure that Zimbabweans don't buy eggs and table potatoes in South Africa, the Zimbabwean government decided to pass a law that prevents an average individual to buy eggs and table potatoes in South Africa and transport them to Zimbabwe. The question is this: If Zimbabweans who are working in South Africa buy a lot of goods from South Africa and transport them to Zimbabwe, who will buy those table potatoes and eggs from Zimbabwe's markets? If you want to enter eternal life, it's better for you not buy eggs and table potatoes in South Africa and transport them to Zimbabwe. Buying eggs and table potatoes in South Africa and crossing the Beitbridge border with them to Zimbabwe is an act of defiance of the laws; not only will that act of defiance of the law cost you a jail term but also it will cost you eternal life. Eternal life is the life without a beginning and without an end. The fact of the matter is this: you don't need table potatoes and eggs once you enter the eternal life. I wonder whether or not Pastor Sithole was telling the truth when he said, "I didn't see the notice on the electric pole." Maybe he didn't see the notice on the electric pole, but maybe he also never wanted to see it, knowing full well that he had carried illegal goods in his bag. I wonder, how did he manage to cross the Beitbridge border with his stuff without being caught by the police? Maybe God shielded him from the Beitbridge border police. From my perspective, I really don't see something serious wrong about crossing the Beitbridge border with eggs and table potatoes to Zimbabwe. I really don't see a major violation of the law. The problem is: the law is the law, and all Zimbabweans must abide by the law that had been enacted by Zimbabwe's government. Once those parliamentarians who sit in the parliament of Zimbabwe pass a bill into an act, signed by the president of the country, Zimbabweans better respect the law of the country to avoid staying in Chikurubi Prison. The wife of Mr. Brown came with a car, which is a Japanese import. I had a very heated argument in the first leg of my trip in Bulawayo with a car dealer. The reason I got myself into the heated argument was about these Japanese cars. The car dealer I spoke to was running a car dealer in Bulawayo in the city center—meaning he was selling cars from Japan. The cars were manufactured and sold in Japan by Japanese companies. The Japanese citizens buy these cars brand new from the Japanese cars dealers and drive them until they get sick and tired of driving these cars. When the Japanese citizens are sick and tired of driving their cars, they eventually airlift their old and used cars to Zimbabwe and sell them to the Zimbabwean car dealers. This car dealer's explanation is "these Japanese cars are new because Zimbabweans who will buy these old used Japanese cars will be the first one to drive these cars in Zimbabwe." He seemed to mean that if you are driving an import from Japan, even if the car was used by a Japanese citizen, the car still remains new. That is sheer madness. The fact that somebody drove this car before, it does no longer make it new. I don't care whether or not Japanese economy is doing well; I surely don't care whether or not the infrastructure of Japan is better than the infrastructure of Zimbabwe. Once a car has been driven by someone for a certain amount of time, it does not make the car new anymore. This weird belief still exists even in South Africa. An average person who is a first-time car buyer will normally say, "I bought a brand-new car from a white person, and the car hasn't been driven that much." If a car is new, why was it sitting in somebody's garage? A car is new to the point that it hasn't been driven by somebody else before; a car is not new if it has been driven by someone else before. This weird ideology about Western products and Western cars runs deep to the veins of the majority of Africans. No wonder Africa is still in the financial prison of the West. The West studied Africa's weaknesses and then exploited Africa's weaknesses. Japanese know very well that the majority of Zimbabweans don't have a problem driving the secondhand Japanese cars under the pretext that these cars are new because they were owned and driven by Japanese citizens. G8 countries and their citizens think that they are better than countries that are not on the G8 league. That is why they can sell their secondhand cars to countries like Zimbabwe and claim that these cars are still new just because they have been driven by Japanese citizens in Asia, not by an African on African soil. One wonders, how many secondhand goods are we Africans consuming and buying from Europe, Asia and North America that are not new, but they are sold to us under pretext of being new? Mr. Brown's wife opened the boot, and we loaded the eggs that were bought from South Africa by Pastor Sithole, and we got into the car and we drove off. She drove all the way to the taxi rank or taxi station. Pastor Sithole got out of the car, and Mr. Brown opened the boot and offloaded the eggs and the luggage of Pastor Sithole. Mr. Brown got back to the car, and we drove to the hotel where I was going to sleep for the night. The same hotel I had used on the previous occasion is the same hotel that I was going to use even at this time around. We arrived at the hotel, and Mr. Brown and I went out of the car and we went straight to the reception section, and I asked for accommodation, and the receptionist gladly gave the keys at a price of forty-seven US dollars, which is equivalent to R470 according to South African currency at a foreign exchange rate of one dollar to ten rands. The reason why it is very vital that Mr. Brown should come with me and see where I will spend the night is that should something happen to me, then he will be the responsible person to account to the South African government and to my parents. I went to my room, which was situated at the first floor at the corner. I quickly realized that it was still early in the morning at that time, and I was very tired, since I didn't get sufficient sleep in the bus, talking all night long, and the driver of the bus was flying as if there was no tomorrow. It's very dangerous to drive people from South Africa to Zimbabwe who have families while you don't have a family as a bus driver because you might end up driving a bus as if you are carrying a bag of potatoes, though you are not allowed to buy table potatoes and cross the border with them to Zimbabwe. The point is people who don't have families normally live a chaotic lifestyle, and they are normally bad when it comes to driving. This is true even with children who come from dysfunctional families; they normally act wildly around children who come from good families. The same goes with a bus driver; a bus driver who is going through a divorce probably thinks that the whole world is against him and therefore ends up punishing innocent people for the sins that they have not committed. I took a shower and changed my clothes. I could not drink tea in the hotel because I realized that probably that will take me time. I went to the receptionist and requested him to organize for me a cab or taxi. He said to me, “Don’t worry, I will call one for you.” My phone needed to be charged, and I requested the receptionist to charge the phone for me. He said, “There is a plug, sir, in your room. You can charge it.” I went back to my room and plugged the phone to the plug and charged it. I was charging the phone while waiting for the receptionist to come and inform me about the arrival of the taxi. He came to my room after a few minutes to inform me that the taxi had arrived, and I went to the reception desk and went outside to meet the taxi driver. The taxi driver asked me, “Where do you want me to take you to?” I told him that I wanted to him to take me to Heroes’ Acre. The main problem about Heroes’ Acre is I really don’t know where it is, whether it’s far or just around the corner. One thing that I know about Heroes’ Acre is this: Joshua Nkomo was buried in Heroes’ Acre—that is one thing that at least I know, and I have to see his grave. This Joshua Nkomo that I want to see his grave was a founder of the political party Zimbabwe African People’s Union (ZAPU).[1] He was a Kalanga, not Ndebele as many people suggested. He was present in Lancaster when the Lancaster House Agreement was signed. If then he was present in Lancaster when the Lancaster House Agreement was signed, then he is the crucial player in Zimbabwe’s history whether you like or not. Political events define political parties, and political parties define their political leaders. The apartheid defined the ANC, and the ANC gave birth to Nelson Mandela. If we were to remove apartheid from the equation, there would not be an ANC, and if we were to remove the ANC, there wouldn’t be Nelson Mandela. The fish can only swim in the water; if you take out a fish from the water, it will eventually die. The best way to kill a fish is to take it out from the water; it will slowly but surely die. Some young politicians, if you want to kill their political potential, take them out of their political pond; they won’t swim, and just like a fish, they will slowly but surely die a political death. My driver looked cool, calm, and collected. He said, “OK, let’s go to Heroes’ Acre.” He said to me it will take us around three to four kilometers from the city center to get to Heroes’ Acre. He drove to another cab driver, and he asked him whether or not Heroes’ Acre was open on Saturday. The cab drivers confirmed to my cab driver that Heroes’ Acre opens also on Saturday, and I was delighted. The other reason I wanted to see Heroes’ Acre is I read that, that’s where the heroes of

Zimbabwe are buried. Once I am able to see Heroes' Acre, I will probably be able to get the whole Zimbabwean picture in a few minutes. There is a great difference between reading about a country without having visited it and reading about a country and visit it thereafter. We are in chapter 3 of this book now, right? I normally don't write before I travel; I travel, thereafter I come back home from my long trip, and I write thereafter. It's easy when you are talking about buildings and people that you have seen—that they really exist or not, not some Internet stuff that you are not even sure whether it's a computer-generated image or it's true. One thing that Mr. Brown's wife said when she was picking us up from the bus terminal in Harare is there is a minister who is alleged to have received a bribe to the tune of US$6 million. Evil is the greatest traveler; rumors are also a greatest traveler especially in a country that is under economic sanctions. The more people are unemployed, the more frustrated they become, and anything that is reported in the media about government corrupt activities, they are likely to believe it and act irrationally upon untested and unverified media reports. African leaders need to take stoke of the effects and the ramifications of African wars and economic sanctions in Zimbabwe. Just like an abused child who was raised in a dysfunctional family by an abusive parents is likely to suffer from posttraumatic stress disorders, so are the Zimbabweans whose country have been under economic sanctions who will also suffer from some form of post-traumatic stress disorder. The majority of Zimbabweans have deep-seated angers and rage within them, and some of them fail to express it to the point that they die angry and bitter. They are bitter because of the political liberation that never translated into economic liberation; above all, they are bitter because they are still living in the depth of abject poverty. The same goes also in most of the township dwellers; they are angry at service delivery, and they are angry at the promises that were never fulfilled. They are angry that their brothers went to exile and died in exile for a noble and just cause, but until today some of them are still living in tin houses, or matchbox houses as they call them in South Africa. This is the anger that is brewing in many South Africans and in many Zimbabweans. In Zimbabwe there is no political tolerance, since there is no political tolerance that itself makes it difficult for people to express their political views and their dissatisfaction about the government thereof. In South Africa, since there is freedom of speech and freedom of movement, township dwellers and informal settlement dwellers express their resentment and anger through wildcat endless strike. There is a new method of protesting that has been developed in Cape

Town; it's called poo protest. The poo protest occurs when the protesting shack dwellers barricade the Cape Town Highway with poo. The protestors also scatter human waste on the national highways to register their concerns. It simply means there is a serious problem about Africa's interpretation of Africa's political liberation. There are possibilities that Africans misinterpreted or misunderstood the concept of political liberation to mean financial freedom. We Africans assumed that since we are politically free, all our financial problems will go away just like that. We Africans assumed that since we are politically free, we will receive the daily manna from African liberation movements. It's also true that African liberation movements made a lot of promises that couldn't be logical and economically achieved. They were not wrong; the people needed to hear a positive message about the future. The people needed to hear that the future they have been waiting for, for quite a long period of time has final arrived. The people needed to hear that they will not suffer anymore at the hands of the cruel and brutal regime of apartheid and Ian Smith. The people needed to hear that things will get better; they had to be told in advance what they were entitled to. They had to be told that the previous regimes gave them nothing compared to what they were going to receive. The leaders of African liberation movements were not lying; they were telling the truth, but the main problem was to translate their promises into reality. These African liberation movements have not failed yet; the crux of the matter is the pace at which these promises were being fulfilled. There is a need to expedite the pace at which these promises were being fulfilled. It's also true that Africa needs an infallible blueprint to pull out its people from the man-made poverty of the West. Poverty was created by man through his own ingenuity. Just like man manufactured weapons of mass destruction, also men created poverty. The poverty that is in Africa was created by our colonial masters, and it has deepened its ugly roots to the African ground. Africa is not the poorest continent on the face of the whole world; the West made it possible that they impoverish Africa systematically and methodically to continue to stay afloat. We Africans continue to remain financial slaves of the West, and the West is loving it. We Africans are the faithful slaves; the West knows very well that they need to allocate us certain amount of money from their budget through foreign aids and donation. When the West announced its economic sanctions on February 18, 2002, after the farm invasion, Zimbabweans began to feel the heat. Most Zimbabwean did not understand the consequences of their actions; they thought that economic sanction was a game of monopoly. Mr. Brown once said to me, "Never ever mess around with economic sanctions." Pres. Robert Mugabe and ZANU-PF messed around with white farmers, and they messed around with the West, and the ax of economic sanctions fell on the innocent people. The effects of economic sanctions affected even the neighboring countries. Before the farm invasion of 2000, most South Africans didn't know how Zimbabweans look like, except the few Zimbabweans who chose to study in South Africa. Zimbabweans generally were very comfortable prior to the farm invasion predominantly because there was political stability and economic stability, which were attributed to their trading partner, Great Britain. Terry and I were going to Heroes' Acre, and it was beginning to be hot in Harare. I asked my driver Terry why there is no electricity outside the city center. Terry said to me, "Since the ZANU-PF won elections, things have moved from bad to worse." He said it was better during the coalition government because there was always electricity and water. The government attributed the lack of electricity to electricity plant maintenance. We drove and passed the main gate of Heroes' Acre, and part of me thought probably it was closed since it was a weekend. If they had closed, it therefore meant that I had to wait until Monday morning, which will have a serious impact on my budget. I had a very long and winding road to travel. I can't leave South Africa and spend a considerable amount of hours for nothing; I should find what I came here to look for. We stopped adjacent to Heroes' Acre and asked a certain old woman whether or not they had opened at Heroes' Acre. She told Terry that she was a visitor and she knew nothing about Heroes' Acre. We parked the car next to the road to Heroes' Acre, and Terry went out of the car to speak to a soldier that was safeguarding Heroes' Acre. The first thing that I saw Terry doing was he took off his hat from his head to show a sign of respect and humility. He greeted the soldier, and while they were talking, I was inside the car looking at Terry trying to explain himself. I saw the soldier and Terry finally approaching the car, and Terry opened the back door for the soldier to sit and closed it, and he came and opened the driver's door, got in, and closed it. We were now in the car—me, Terry, and the soldier. The soldier looked very young but physically fit. Unlike soldiers of other countries who are addicted to doughnuts, South African soldiers are fit too, just like Zimbabwean soldiers. That is why South African soldiers were deployed in DRC to fight the M23 in 2013. The soldier shook my hand, and he said, "Welcome to Zimbabwe." I was at ease and lay back on the front seat. Terry drove us now, me and the soldier, to the main gate that we passed and avoided to use. We entered Heroes' Acre, and Terry parked the car at the parking lot. Terry went out of the car, and the soldier and I followed suit. Terry's phone rang, and I saw Terry again requesting the permission from the soldiers to receive the call. The soldier said, "Go ahead, and receive the call." Surely Zimbabwe and South Africa are two different countries with two different laws. The Zimbabwean people are people of respect and humility. They respect the law and order. It also depends how people define respect and order. Some people might interpret respect and order as oppression and violation of human rights. Some might say it's the spirit of Ubuntu to respect the national shrine. After Terry was through with his one-minute call, he came back to me, and we went straight to the admin offices. There was a blue Mercedes-Benz parked there at the parking lot, and I wondered who was driving that car. There were two ladies inside the administration office, and Terry did the talking, and the officials of Heroes' Acre said I must pay ten US dollars, and Terry will not pay anything, since he is a Zimbabwean and a cab driver. I thought we will just walk and see the graves and off we go. A lady by the name of Princess came out of the admin offices and said, "Do you need a tour guide?" I said yes. She came to the car and opened the backseat, and I went back to the front seat, and Terry drove for some minutes, and there we were in the national shrine of Zimbabwe. The atmosphere began to change, and I never felt like this before, the way I felt that moment in my entire life. If it wasn't for the fact that I was trying to write a book, probably I wouldn't have set my foot in this place that is rich in history. Terry pulled over, and we all went out of the car. We walked a little bit, and Princess said, "Let's begin the tour." I said, "OK." She said to me, "These are the mirrors." And I said, "What mirrors?" She pointed to the statues that indicate different periods in Zimbabweans' history. The first mirror indicates black people getting kicked and dogs set on them by the Western settlers. That was how our land, farms, and our livestock were taken from us by Western settlers through guns and dogs as if black people were animals. I had to contain myself mainly because I am in Heroes' Acre to learn not to seek vengeance and retaliation to the Western settlers. I had to make sure that I understand the struggle against apartheid from a South African context and understand the Zimbabwean struggle from the Zimbabwean context. The political struggles of these two countries are inseparable, and they are intertwined. It's imperative for an African child to understand where we Africans come from; it's also important to read the African liberation struggle very well. If we don't understand Africa's political struggle, we are likely to lose the political gains that have been achieved by the fallen African heroes of African liberation movements. The second mirror depicts people coming together to form political parties. It's this time where Joshua Nkomo returned to Zimbabwe from South Africa and became heavily involved in a political struggle and became president of National Democratic Party in 1960.[2] Joshua Nkomo was detained in 1964 with his fellow rebels, Ndabaningi Sithole, Edgar Tekere, Maurice Nyagumbo, and Robert Mugabe, until 1974 when they were released by the government of Ian Smith. The mirror depicts people carrying guns and throwing stones to the police. Joshua Nkomo went to Zambia and continued to oppose the government of Ian Smith.[3] The third mirror portrays the guerilla fighters waging war against the government of Ian Smith. The guerilla fighters were being fed by African women who were spying for them. There were brave women in the African political struggle; these brave women were not afraid of the consequences of being loyal to the just cause, though a few of them do get the national recognitions that they deserve. These were the women who were feeding the guerillas. It began to dawn on me that the African political struggle was not fought by a group of people that was only belonging to a single political party. There armed struggle was fought by different people from different sectors of life. Those who were not able to go to exile fought the political struggle through various means. The theory that says political struggle was only fought by guerillas only, therefore they deserve the spoils of democracy and government tenders themselves alone, does not hold water. What became abundantly clear is this: during the liberation struggle, Chimurenga, as they call it in Zimbabwe, there were many brave men and brave women that we will never know about just because there were no political records to record their brave deeds and their contributions to the African liberation struggle against the government of Ian Smith and apartheid. The fourth mirror depicts the political parties engaging into a peace agreement. It's through this peace agreement where things went horribly wrong. African liberation movements made a lot of concessions to the West in order to end the guerilla warfare. I am not implying that the guerilla warfare should start again. Clearly our generation is not a generation of wars but a generation of Face book and Twitter, the "born-free generation" as they call them in South Africa. Our generation is also called the "HIV-free generation." In 1979 it became abundantly clear that the guerilla war had to come to an end. During this period, Zimbabwe was under economic sanctions that have been imposed by Great Britain. The main reason the government of Ian Smith managed to survive the first wave of economic sanctions is because of apartheid South Africa. The fifth mirror depicts the national election, and ZANU-PF won that national election and Robert Mugabe became the first prime minister of Zimbabwe who was elected democratically. The sixth mirror depicts the people building a national flag of Zimbabwe, and that is how the current national flag was born. Princess gave me a long lecture. She showed me a woman giving the guerillas food, and she said that during the Bush War, guerillas were struggling, and they had to rely on the ordinary village women for food to survive. We began to look for the graves. There are many graves in Heroes' Acre, roughly to the tune of 177. The majority of those graves are for heroes and heroines that were unsung. The question that I asked myself is this: If these African liberation movements had the audacity, zeal, and the zest to fight for what they believe was a just cause, can our current generation continue the economic struggle and finish where the fallen heroes and heroines have stopped? The point of the matter is this: we Africans all know that we are not economically free, though we are free politically, but the majority of African people are still poor and staying in uninhabitable conditions. Heroes' Acre is the national shrine and is well protected and safeguarded by soldiers. I have never seen a national shrine so protected and heavily safeguarded like Heroes' Acre. In fact there is a base for soldiers in Heroes' Acre that are protecting the graves from extremists that can desecrate the graves of the heroes and heroines of the political struggle. I asked princess why there are so many soldiers protecting Heroes' Acre. She pointed to the stones that had been used to build the tombs. She said, "This stone that had been used to build these graves is very expensive." Joshua Nkomo was buried next to his wife, Johanna Mafuyana. The Nkomos were buried in their own descending order. The simple test that you need to pass in order for you to be buried in Heroes' Acre is this: you should have participated in the armed struggle during Zimbabwe's Bush War, but you need to be a member of ZANU-PF also. One question that comes into my mind is, will Morgan Tsvangirai be buried in Heroes' Acre should he pass on? The perfect person who can answer that question is Pres. Robert Mugabe and the war veterans. Pres. Robert Mugabe's late wife, Sally Mugabe, was also buried in Heroes' Acre, including the sister of Robert Mugabe. The other sister of Robert Mugabe was in a hospital in Harare who was very sick and later passed on, but she was not buried in Heroes' Acre. There are two graves that I actually came to see in Heroes' Acre, the grave of Chenjerai "Hitler" Hunzvi and the grave of Joshua Nkomo. These graves are very important to me in order to understand the Zimbabwean struggle and their political role to Zimbabwe's political struggle. These two individuals are crucial in the political struggle of Zimbabwe to the point that even the Zimbabwean government saw it befitting that they should be honored and be buried in the national shrine of the country. Princess said to me that the families of most of the people that are buried in Heroes' Acre continue to receive financial support from the Zimbabwean government as a way to recognize their contribution to the liberation struggle. We climbed the steps to see the whole of the capital city of Harare from Heroes' Acre worldview. I began to realize that the capital city of Zimbabwe, Harare, is beautiful and big for that matter, though some call it the worst city on earth. It wouldn't have been possible for me to see the whole city from the hotel where I was staying. When the night falls, there are lights that need to be turned on at Heroes' Acre. I asked Princess why these lights are turned on at night—since this is a grave site? She said the lights had to be turned on in order to provide lights to the souls that are sleeping at Heroes' Acre. I said to Princess, "Please show me the grave of Chenjerai "Hitler" Hunzvi." She began laughing, and I said, "Why are you laughing?" She said the majority of people all over the world, when they come to Heroes' Acre, want to see the grave of Chenjerai "Hitler" Hunzvi. Heroes' Acre for me as an individual was an eye-opener, and it made it possible for me to understand the political distance that had been traveled by the Zimbabweans as a nation. Political events define political party, and a political party defines a political leader, and a political leader defines the economic and political direction that the country will take. Political events, though harsh and excruciatingly painful they might be, test the strength of the nation and the strength of the people. Political events bring people together. I have come to realize that most of the Africans, whether Zimbabweans or South Africans, are easily united by the struggle against oppression and suppression. We bade farewell to Princess and Heroes' Acre, including the soldier that directed us to Heroes' Acre, and we drove back to Harare. We were now going to Chikurubi Prison. While we were on the way to Chikurubi prison, my driver Terry was showing me the city, including the ZRB (Zimbabwe Reserve Bank) and the Constitutional Court and the office of Pres. Robert Mugabe. Terry began to complain, saying that the majority of people that are buried in Heroes' Acre are not heroes. He said the majority of people that are buried in Heroes' Acre had good relationship with Pres. Robert Mugabe. People that were not in good books of Pres. Robert Mugabe are not buried in Heroes' Acre. The grave of Solomon Mujuru, the late husband of Joyce Mujuru, the deputy president of Zimbabwe, is also in Heroes' Acre, and Solomon Mujuru was a hero and deserved to be buried in Heroes' Acre. Terry is a former truck driver who was transporting heavy consignments from South Africa to DRC. He fell sick around 2010 and was compelled to resigned and started driving a cab. He complained that the traffic cops from DRC are all corrupt, and they needed bribes for him to pass with heavy consignment. Terry's brother was working in the mine that was shut down before national election of July 31, 2013. The mine was not yet open even after the national election. The management of the mine instructed miners to wait for the national election results, and after the national election results have been announced then they will resume the mining operation. Terry's father worked in that very mine for quite a long period of time, and even Terry's brother worked in that very mine for a considerable amount of time. Since the mine has suspended its mining operation, Terry's brother is panicking because he doesn't know exactly when the mine will resume mining operation. We were on our way to Chikurubi Prison, the Guantanamo Bay of the Republic of Zimbabwe. This is Ian Smith's prison. The majority of politicians in Zimbabwe have been in Chikurubi. George W. Bush said that in Guantanamo Bay, prisoners were reading *Harry Potter*. The fact of the matter is this: in the Guantanamo Bay of Zimbabwe, there is no way you can even get hold of a book. There are many people that died in this prison. If you are arrested and taken into Chikurubi prison, you are likely to come out blind or dead for that matter. After we drove for some few hours, we finally arrived at the Guantanamo Bay detention center of Zimbabwe, hell in a cell. The main reason the majority of Zimbabweans obey the law is that they are afraid of Chikurubi Prison; it's not that they respect the law but it's the fear and trepidation of the prison. This is the place where boys become men and political dreams are shattered. People that oppose the government of Pres. Robert Mugabe are aware of the appalling living conditions in Chikurubi Prison. The living conditions are so appalling to the point that prisoners are not getting enough food. During the year 2007, most prisoners died because Zimbabwe's economy crumbled, and the majority of prisoners could not be provided with nutritional food at all. Prisoners that were sick could not be taken to hospitals because there were no sufficient medical facilities in the country to cater for prisoners. The prison is located outside Harare. There is a farm that belongs to the prison, and there are compounds that are used by the prison officials. We drove from the beginning until the end of the prison, and we came to the gate of the prison. Terry told me that he normally comes here to the prison on a daily basis to collect prison employees who stay in town but work in Chikurubi Prison. Terry said, "Let's get inside the prison." I thought to myself it's not prudent to come all the way from South Africa, Pretoria, and try to enter a dangerous prison like Chikurubi Prison where the majority of MDC-T members were serving their sentences for the crimes they didn't commit. To respect the human rights of political activists and the danger that it might pose unto me as a South African in foreign soil, I deemed it improper and unbefitting to enter Chikurubi Prison. We saw children playing at the prison complex that was built for the prison staff. The media reports that the prisoners are forever complaining about food and the essential goods like toothpaste and clothes. Apparently a certain NGO donated goods to the prisoners as Christmas presents, but these goods, which include underwear, toothpaste, and clothes, didn't reach the inmates; they disappeared at the hands of the prison officials. The prison officials are disputing this claim. The living conditions at Chikurubi Prison were so bad to the point that during 2007 inmates were not getting food at all. During late 2007, the whole country was under the swine flu of economic sanctions, and the currency of Zimbabwe lost value rapidly. When we were driving coming from Chikurubi Prison, there were posters of the recent national election that were still visible on the electricity poles and on the walls beside the road. Terry was complaining all the way. He complained about the Marange diamond fields—that they were only enriching politicians and their families, not ordinary individuals. The Marange diamond fields is the largest diamond project in the world; it's estimated to produce 16.9 million carats in 2013.[4] The Marange diamond fields are currently managed by the Zimbabwean Mining Development Corporation (ZMDC) in conjunction with Anjin Investments (a joint venture with China's Anhui Foreign Economic Construction Group), Diamonds Mining Corporation, and Mbada Resources.[5] This Chinese company also built the College of Intelligence for the government of Zimbabwe. The political version of events according to Terry is somewhat very vague, but I understand that the majority of people, even in South Africa, are not clued up about what is happening in their country. If you can ask an average South African what happened in Marikana, you can be really shocked about the divergence in the sequence of political events. The fact of the matter is this: the Marange diamond proceeds don't improve the lives of the Marange people or the lives of ordinary Zimbabweans, but the proceeds enrich people who are connected to the elite club of a certain political party. There are a lot of people who died in Marange because of the diamonds. Zimbabwe's mineral deposits were supposed to improve the lives of indigenous people, but in Marange the diamonds were killing the Marange people. Terry said, "You know what happened in Marange? The government realized that there were diamonds in Marange and evicted the people and gave the Marange diamond fields to a Chinese company. This Chinese company, in return, as an act of gratuity, built for Zimbabwe's government a National Defense College." Zimbabwe is heavenly dependent on China for survival. China is the fastest-growing superpower in the whole world. China will eventually control the daily lives of Zimbabweans through the electronic products. The more a country depends on the other for survival, and then it gives away its mineral resources and political power to the superpower, which is the sign of economic weakness. When are we Africans going to have our big black banks that we will manage and support our small business cooperation without "looking to the East," as Pres. Robert Mugabe often said? When are we Africans going to control and manage our mineral deposits without the help from the West? China has a firm grip on the Zimbabwean economy. During the national election campaign of July 31, 2013, there were iPads that were sold on the streets of Zimbabwe at lesser market price. The selling of these iPads was the ZANU-PF strategy to lure voters to vote for ZANU-PF. The truth of the matter is this: those iPads were not assembled and manufactured in Zimbabwe, but they were manufactured and assembled in China. China is everywhere all the time. Africa will have to dig deep to become economically liberated. We Africans are politically liberated, but will we ever be economically liberated from the economic prison of the West? Zimbabwe is in the self-made economic prison of China. Zimbabwe is the province of China. Terry said, "I want to show you where the leader of MDC-T (Movement for Democratic Change) is staying." We drove to the up market suburb of Harare, and you can quickly tell that people that are staying in this up market suburb are filthy stinking rich. The moment we passed through the gate of Morgan Tsvangirai's house, we stopped, and Terry said, "This is the house of Morgan Tsvangirai." I quickly realized that even if Morgan Tsvangirai does not have sufficient formal education, at least the guy is living large. Morgan Tsvangirai probably lives a better life than your average professor who is lecturing in the University of Zimbabwe. He is living large, and you can take this to the bank—politics pay. We drove past the government complex; this is where the majority of the government departments are located. This is also where there is a presidential compound. The presidential compound is heavily guarded by the soldiers. I have never seen such presidential compound heavily guarded like the presidential compound of Pres. Robert Mugabe. There is a gate on the road next to the presidential compound and a curfew. The curfew states that the road will be closed from 6:00 p.m. and will be open at 6:00 a.m. Terry said to me, referring to the soldiers, "They are guarding the presidential compound 24/7, and they change shifts after every four hours." They were wearing helmets and carrying big guns as if they were prepared for the war. Terry said, "If this truck"—referring to the oncoming truck going to the opposite direction—"will have a breakdown, the driver of this truck will have to push the truck alone. If you are extremely thirsty to the point of death and request water from these soldiers, they will not give you. You are not allowed to make a call around the presidential compound even if you are on the road. If the soldiers see you receiving a call, you will be arrested." I have never seen something like this since I was born. Politicians are inaccessible, but during the time of elections, they will break the very same rules that they have created. The former president of South Africa, Thabo Mbeki, while he was in office, there were numerous complaints that he was inaccessible and would not even attend a funeral of an ordinary person. It's very difficult sometimes to strike the balance between a state president who is busy to the point that he can't visit his people and the state president who can't mingle with ordinary people because probably he thinks he is the super citizen because he holds the senior office in the country. I really don't think that former president Thabo Mbeki was inaccessible to the ordinary people; perhaps he was very busy trying to solve the Zimbabwean crisis that had been created by the West. Terry took me to Nando's in Harare, but not in the city center, just outside the city center a little bit. He dropped me there and said he was coming. I ordered a half chicken, breaking my stiff diet. A brother needs to eat a half chicken once in a while. The best way to lose weight is to eat a lot and train afterward. The reason the majority of people are overweight is that they eat and sit all day long watching TV on the couch without exercising. I am extremely surprised that there is no McDonald's or Wimpy in Zimbabwe; by the way, Wimpy and McDonald's are American franchises. After I ordered my meal, I went to take a seat inside Nando's. There were two white men on the opposite table who had already ordered before me. They were served with pleasure. I am not a racist, and I will never be one in a million years. Zimbabweans of European descent behave differently when they are in Zimbabwe compared to the South Africans of European descent when they are in South Africa. South Africans of European origin look at black

South Africa with a contemptuous look in South Africa even if they know full well that they are a minority. In Zimbabwe, Zimbabweans of European descent are very few since Pres. Robert Mugabe kicked most of them out of the country during the farm invasion all the way to the Beitbridge border. The majority of the Zimbabweans of European descent didn't go back to Great Britain but immigrated to South Africa without necessary documents, and they are not even called illegal immigrants because of their skin color but black Zimbabweans when they come to South Africa,without necessary legal documents, they have to queue in the Home Affairs offices for the work permits and necessary documents to live in the Republic of South Africa. I once asked myself this question: What happened in actual fact to the Zimbabweans of European descent that was living in Zimbabwe before the economic meltdown attributed to the farm invasion? Did they go back to Europe where they came from? I realized that they crossed the border to South Africa because most of the Zimbabweans of European descent did not come straight from Europe per se, but they came from South Africa. There is symbiotic connection between Zimbabwe and South Africa. The Ndebeles that are living in Zimbabwe are from South Africa who came to Zimbabwe with their rebellious king Mzilikazi, who later gave birth to Lobengula, the son of Mzilikazi. This Mzilikazi was buried outside Matopos National Park. I quickly hammered the half chicken, and those two Zimbabweans from European descent were busy taking pictures with their cameras. I could tell from their body language that they probably thought I was working for the Zimbabwean government. Zimbabwe's government is full of spies. Nobody knows who the spy is and who is not a spy; everyone is afraid of everybody. While Terry was talking about the corruption that is spreading like octopus in Zimbabwe, part of me thought that if I make stupid comments about Zimbabwe's government, I will probably wind up in Chikurubi. The fact is even Terry is afraid of government spies himself. He complained that the government has hired a lot of spies that are doing the intelligent work, and they are paid good money to collect information on behalf of the government. After I had completed my half chicken at Nando's, I had already paid for the half chicken then Terry came back. I offered Terry ten US dollars to buy himself a drink and food; he surprisingly refused my offer. Maybe he wanted to prove to me that since the country is under economic sanctions, it does not necessarily mean that he is struggling financially. Maybe he knew that I was writing a book and probably thought I will write about him. I stood up and bade farewell to the waitresses and the waiters, and we went straight to the car, and I had just completed part of my journey in the long journey that I have to still travel. When I arrived at the hotel, I quickly switched on the plasma screen. Both Al Jazeera and BBC were talking about Kenya's Westgate mall that was under siege from the terrorist group Al-Shabaab, which is affiliated to the Al-Qaeda of the late Osama bin Laden. Africa is a very fragile and dangerous continent. I thought Osama Bin Laden was shot dead by the US SEALs. The one-million-dollar question is how many Osama Bin Ladens are on this planet? If Osama Bin Laden is dead, then where are these terrorist groups coming from? Terrorist groups are also filthy stinking rich. They have properties and expensive cars and money in the Swiss banks. The funding for these groups is wide and very difficult to trace. The undeniable reality about terrorists is they are everywhere, and they can strike when average people least expect. I imagine the situation that I was currently in right now: I was outside the border of South Africa, and the terrorists struck the Westgate mall in Kenya. My head was spinning and I had many questions that I can't answer. The question that I asked myself many times was this: How safe am I in Zimbabwe? I took a nap, it was roughly at around 3:00 p.m., and I woke up at around 5:00 p.m. I took a shower and went to buy newspaper a few blocks away from my hotel room. I was quite familiar now with some of the streets in Harare; I can't get lost. Harare is a quiet city, and the people love to chill on weekends and play music, and some are roaming around the streets as if they are headless chickens. While I was on my way to the shop two streets away from the hotel, a certain gentleman came running behind me, and I turned back, and he passed. I quickly got scared primarily because I am not a Zimbabwean; maybe this is the normal occurrence here in Harare, but I am not used to it. I bought a lot of newspapers, and I prayed that the lady on the till won't be shocked about one person buying a lot of newspapers. The newspapers were not expensive. I paid three dollars for three newspapers. The speculation on the newspapers was rife. The state-owned media claimed that Morgan Tsvangirai of MDC-T is losing grip of the MDC-T. The MDC-T itself blames Morgan Tsvangirai for all the problems that the party is experiencing including losing the national election.[6] The other state-owned newspaper reports that the MDC-T is already searching for a new replacement for Morgan Tsvangarai.[7] The previous day Morgan Tsvangirai of MDC-T was in Mutare celebrating what is termed "elections defeat." Morgan Tsvangirai complained and quibbled as usual to his supporters, attributing the overall election loss to "massive rigging." The question that I normally ask myself is, If ZANU-PF rigged the national election results of July 31, 2013, why is it that the MDC-T didn't ensure that there was no massive rigging this time around? Both of these political parties have been at each other's throat since the formation of MDC-T in 2000. Surely it's sheer madness for the MDC-T to forever complain about election results if they are not in its favor. The other question that can't be avoidable is whether or not the MDC-T is ready to govern the country under these circumstances. From the political standpoint, it seems as if MDC-T has not learned from its previous national election of 2002 because it continues to make the same political mistakes ever since its formation. You can't be beaten by the same man over and over again in a boxing match—you rather change a trainer or change your fighting tactics, but politics is not a boxing match. The same is true in South Africa. The ANC is continuing to thump DA (Democratic Alliance) on its head. The South African political landscape has fundamentally changed since we have Agang SA for Dr. Mamphela Ramphele, who later resigned from politics, and EFF (Economic Freedom Fighters) for Julius Malema, the expelled president of the ANC Youth League. When the DA (Democratic Alliance) loses national election against the ANC, it doesn't complain; it welcomes the national election results as if it knew it was not going to win the national election anyway. The crux of the matter about MDC-T is this: it placed heavy emphasis on winning national election without proper plan. By proper plan, I mean the formidable structure to run the country. If rigging national election helped the ZANU-PF to win elections, how come MDC-T didn't rig the national election results first before the ZANU-PF rigged the national election results? Mr. Brown said to me there are thirty-four ways to rig the election results and ZANU-PF up to so far has used only three. The whole allegation of rigging the election results surfaced after the Zimbabwean government has hired an Israeli company to print the national election ballot papers. It is alleged that there were one hundred thousand voters who were ninety years old on the voters' registers roll. The MDC-T claimed that they have evidence to prove that there was massive rigging on the national election day. The international observer led by the SADC (Southern African Development Community) endorsed the national election results as free, fair, and summarily peaceful. If the national election results were free, fair, and peaceful, this happened because the Israeli company that was hired by the Zimbabwean government. The Israeli company got the job done. The ZANU-PF was happy, and the SADC was happy—then where is the problem? The only party that has a problem with the national election results was MDC-T alone. The SADC didn't display displeasure on the national election results. The Israeli company was happy, Pres. Robert Mugabe was happy, and the SADC was happy—the July 31, 2013, national election was good for the country. Whether there was massive rigging or not, but by the mere fact that the majority of people didn't die, that was good for the country, and it was good for business. The Israeli company did what was good for business and what was good for the country, which is to deliver free, fair, and summarily peaceful elections. There were grave concerns about the national election of 2008 because they mirrored political intolerance and the gross violation of human rights, which saw innocent civilians to the tune of two hundred people dying due to political violence. The international community and the SADC were extremely concerned prior to the July 31, 2013, national election about the possibility of political instability that could engender political violence. To the dismay of the international community, there was no incidence of violence that was reported. Terry said something to me that I found very hilarious on our way from Chikurubi Prison. He said, "Do you know why ZANU-PF until today hasn't yet celebrated its election victory? It's because it rigged national election results." Terry said to me, "You can ask people in buses and in taxis who voted for ZANU-PF. Everybody will tell you that they voted for MDC-T. "But how come then the ZANU-PF won the national election?" I asked Terry. If ZANU-PF rigged the national election result, what is it that the MDC-T didn't do to ensure that there is no rigging? This theory of the national election results being rigged had been the strategy of MDC-T to shift the blame to others and divert the international focus to the ZANU-PF for quite a long period of time now, and it's sickening. You either lost or you won the match, period. The other problem that seems to always engulf MDC-T is its failure to accept and embrace elections defeat. MDC-T has never embraced elections defeat ever since; this also is a problem. It's highly unlikely that the ZANU-PF had been rigging national election results all along. If the July 31, 2013, national election results have been rigged diametrically, then the MDC-T should also be blamed for allowing that monumental rigging to occur under its nose. It's Sunday morning. As usual, I woke up, took a shower, and went straight to the kitchen and ate breakfast. The breakfast was cornflakes and milk. I also ordered tea with white bread and beans including fried eggs. I was already bracing myself for the long journey that I had to take. The distance that I needed to travel from Harare to Bulawayo is almost 366 kilometers with a bus. This distance is very long, and it actually takes me the whole day since I have been coming to Zimbabwe. I went back to my hotel room after I had completed drinking my tea to collect my bag, and I dropped the keys to the receptionist. Quite frankly my night was not that bad in Harare this time around, considering the fact that the national election went well. If the national election went against ZANU-PF, probably hell was going to break loose. There are multiple theories about Zimbabwe's politics. Some say the day MDC-T will win national election, there will be Gukurahundi. The majority of South Africans don't know Gukurahundi. To simplify Gukurahundi for all South Africans, Gukurahundi is Marikana massacre. The whole of Zimbabweans are afraid of the second coming of Gukurahundi, "the rain that washes away the chaff from the last harvest." The receptionist called a cab for me, and within a few minutes, the cab arrived. I greeted the cab driver, and I opened the door and put my bag on the backseat. I told the cab driver that I was heading to Bulawayo; therefore it means that he must drop me straight on the main road. He drove me to the main road very quickly, and the he dropped me not on the main road but close to the main road out of fear of police, since there was heavy police presence. I took out my bag from the backseat and walked a stone's throw distance. There was a bus that was waiting on the main road that was heading to Bulawayo. I boarded the bus quickly. I sat next to a young gentleman who looked like he was bruised and battered by the University of Zimbabwe's final examinations. I paid an amount of fifteen US dollars to the ticket examiner, not to the bus driver, unlike in the case of South Africa. The transport fee has not gone up since I went to Zimbabwe on my first trip; at least there is one thing that is stable in Zimbabwe, and that is the transport price. There was no electricity even that morning when I left Harare for Bulawayo. Harare was very hot even if it was still the early hours of the morning. Some traffic lights were out of order or not working at all. I looked through the window as we were traveling from Harare to Bulawayo. The farms still lie in waste. I am not a greedy person, and greediness is one of the deadly sins. When I looked at the farms that until now lie in waste, I asked myself many questions: Is it possible and true that Africans are destructive in their nature? Is it possible that everything that Africans touch falls apart? If it is not true that Africans are destructive in nature, how come after Africa's political independence, we Africans can't govern and run our countries effectively and efficiently? The fact that the Zimbabwean government during the coalition government and after the coalition government failed decimally to put together a national plan that sought to address this inordinate amount of land that lies in waste is a testament that Africans can't govern and run their own domestic political and financial affairs effectively and efficiently. I have a friend by the name of Joseph. He is of a Nigerian nationality, and he is studying in South Africa. He said something completely strange to me one day. He said Nigeria needs a white president to end Nigerian squabbles between the insurgent group Boko Haram and the Nigerian government. What Joseph was saying is this: African leaders are struggling to run their domestic affairs with integrity and transparency. There are few African countries, since their political independence of Africa are running their domestic political and financial affairs with transparency and integrity. Everywhere in the African continent, there are reports of maladministration and corruption, which are on a rampage whether in churches, in schools, or even in universities. Are we Africans failing to govern and rule ourselves? If we are really ineptitude in governing and running ourselves, then the one-million-dollar question is, what will happen to us the day the West will decide to cut off the foreign aid supply? One of the things that place Zimbabwe's government on the international stage was the inordinate death of people. During the early 2007, it was estimated that 2,500 people were dying per week in Zimbabwe. The main reason a lot of people died in Zimbabwe during this period was not only the absence of nongovernmental organization but also the fact that Zimbabwean government became very cruel to the international nongovernmental organization—those that were based in Zimbabwe. The Zimbabwean government chased all the nongovernmental organizations out of the country. The medical supplies ceased, and the people began to be sick partly because of drought and the economic sanctions that were imposed by the United States of America and the European Union. Most of the medical supplies that most Zimbabweans were receiving prior to the farm invasion were coming from the West. To prove that this theory is true that the majority of medical supplies that Zimbabweans were receiving were not coming from the national government but were coming from the West, look at the impact on the ground after the withdrawal of the international nongovernmental organizations. There is an inescapable reality that stares all of us in the face. Joseph's assertion that Nigeria needs a white president in order to solve the Nigerian's crisis between government and Boko Haram is partly true, but I don't wholeheartedly agree with him. I believe that Africans can govern and run their political and financial affairs with integrity and honesty, but we Africans will need to be honest with ourselves before we reach that level where we can run and govern our political and financial affairs with honesty and integrity. We will need a change of hearts and a change of attitudes. African liberation movements spend too much time in the bush not learning how to run and govern people but how to kill the enemy, which was the West at that time. Even after the liberation struggle was over, most of the guerillas that were part and parcel of the armed struggle still used the old vocabulary of the political struggle. Whenever there is a problem, the former freedom fighters will say, "We will make this city ungovernable." This concept of making a place ungovernable is still running deep in the veins of most former freedom fighters. Our greatest enemy right now in the whole of Africa is not the West but the poverty that continues to claim the lives of innocent children and women on the streets of Harare and Bulawayo.

In his book titled *Rhodesia: Ending an Era,* Major General H. P. Hutson writes,

> "*No one could contest the belief that we must honor our trusteeship of the welfare of the people of Rhodesia, but if majority rule is to lead to the replacement of a proved and stable government by a body of wholly inexperienced African 'nationalist' of whom even their won people are apprehensive, and then we are giving blind adherence to an ideology which utterly overrides commonsense.*"[08]

It's an inescapable reality that perhaps Africa's political freedom came and found most African countries unprepared and not even intellectually ready to run and govern over the political and economic affairs of the continent. The fact that Africans were inexperienced was not a reasonable excuse to further oppress Africans in their own land that had been given to them by God free of charge. The majority of Zimbabweans from European descent undermined and underrated the liberation struggle. They miscalculated and underrated the undying desire of African people to rule and run their political and economic affairs.

General H. P. Hutson went further and said, "*In Rhodesia, whites and blacks have lived together without conflict since 1897. The much-publicized idea that discontent is widespread is wholly erroneous.*"[09]

The idea that whites and blacks have lived together without conflict since 1897 is erroneous and misleading to the extreme. This notion was widely shared among many South Africans of European descent during the apartheid era in South Africa, and it was also shared widely in Zimbabwe while it was still called Rhodesia. From the arrival of Cecil John Rhodes to the era of Ian Smith, black people in Zimbabwe knew it wholeheartedly that they were living under the white man's rule in the land of their ancestors.

Nelson Mandela writes in his book *Long Walk to Freedom,*

> *The premise of apartheid was that whites were superior to Africans, coloreds, and Indians, and the function of it was to entrench the white supremacy forever. As the nationalist put it, "Die wet man moet altyd baas wees" (The white man must always remain the boss).*[10]

When Hutson said whites and blacks have lived together without conflict since 1897, he meant a situation where a black person was dwelling in a squatter camp with no running water and no electricity and enrolled his children in a government school that is dysfunctional and earned peanuts at the end of the month, while the boss (white man) was making millions of US dollars through the power and energy of a black person who was overworked and underpaid. Acquiescence does not necessarily mean happiness and satisfaction at all times. Majority of the peasants knew very well that they were working very hard for their bosses, but they were paid less than what they were entitled to. The same is true also in the mining industry in South Africa and elsewhere in the African continent. The salary gap between black people and white people remains a huge challenge. To strike the balance and bring both blacks and whites at par will forever remain a challenge for a century to come. Since the majority of black people can read and write, it's no longer possible to hide the truth from them through books and numbers. I know that numbers don't lie, but I also know that numbers can be doctored to give a misleading picture. It will be very difficult for blacks and whites to live together in harmony without a conflict, as pointed out by Major Hutson, whether in South Africa or in Zimbabwe, if the same conditions were to continue to prevail. There was another misconception that was prevalent among Africans of European descent prior to Zimbabwe and South Africa attaining their political independence—the idea that black people were living a better life in Zimbabwe and in South Africa compared to other black people in

Zambia and in any other African country. This view is shared by both H. P. W. Hutson and Tony Koenderman.

Koenderman in his book *Sanctions* writes:

> *White South Africans often seem to find it difficult to understand why the country's blacks should be discontented when there are so many people elsewhere in Africa who are economically worse off, and even some politically in the same boat. Prime Minister Ian Smith once confidently asserted that his country housed "the happiest Africans in the world."*[11]

This notion that blacks were not suffering, as most of the Western scholars suggested, is misleading and erroneous. If we are to follow this line of thinking, then it simply means therefore there was no need for a political transformation for Africans in Rhodesia and in South Africa, since Zimbabwe housed the happiest Africans in Africa who were better off than any other Africans in the whole of Africa. If black people were happy, then why would they risk their lives and cross the Lebombo Mountains to go to Mozambique to acquire military training from FRELIMO under the auspices of Samora Machel? If black people were happy, why would they cross the border and go to Zambia to acquire military training under the auspices of Pres. Kenneth Kaunda? It simply means that the majority of black people were not happy contrary to Prime Minister Ian Douglas Smith's assertion. The Rhodesian government under Ian Smith underrated and miscalculated the resentment and anger that were brewing on a daily basis within the black African masses. This is also true with the current state of political and economic affairs in Angola, Malawi, and elsewhere in the African continent; people are not happy, and they will soon get tired of bottling up their resentment and their dissatisfactions. The same view is shared by most of the Zimbabweans that there is a lot of corruption in the Zimbabwean government. This theory of undermining and underrating people from the ground is very dangerous. That is why in the majority of the African countries, the ordinary citizens reached a stage where they no longer respect and obey government institutions and even the rule of law because they believe that everybody is corrupt. Even those who went to fight in the armed struggle were not really fighting for the people, but they were fighting for their families. The main cause of the Second DRC War was the high level of dissatisfaction from people on the ground, and exclude

M23 for a time being. The people know that they are living in a rich soil, which is endowed with mineral resources, while they continue to go to bed with empty stomachs. The people know very well that their government can do more than what their government is currently doing right now. In Zimbabwe the ordinary people are not allowed to express their grievances through protest and barricading main roads and highways. In fact during the national election campaign, members of the MDC-T were told by the Zimbabwe Republic Police (ZRP) that they can attend a rally in the stadium, but there should be "no singing and dancing." The MDC-T members were singing and dancing, violating the order that had been given by the ZRP. Our bus normally will stop at Kwekwe, a small town in the Midlands Province. Some passengers disembarked from the bus at Kwekwe, and some passengers went to the public urinary to relieve themselves. I decided to remain in the bus alone. In the twinkling of an eye, our bus was full to the brim with blind, deaf, and handicapped people. All of them when they came to the bus were singing songs while carrying empty cups on their hands begging for money. There was a blind woman within this group of disabled Zimbabweans who came inside the bus. This woman was carrying a baby at her back and holding a child with her left hand. What I want you to know is this: she was blind. There is something fundamentally wrong in our African society today. Is it morally right that an economically active man can impregnate a blind woman and abandon her while she does not have education and can't even be able to support herself and her children financially? Is it legal to make love to a blind woman who is mentally unstable and who can't differentiate between what is right or wrong? What is the law saying about this situation? Common sense dictates that an economically active man who is working can't make love to a blind woman and impregnate her and abandon her thereafter without providing any financial support to this pregnant woman. It's also true that common sense is not common anymore. In the court of public opinion, a man who impregnates a blind woman who is mentally unstable was supposed to be incarcerated without bail. It's highly improbable that a mentally unstable blind woman can consent to a sexual intercourse with an economically active man who is mentally stable. Clearly there is something wrong in the morals of the African society. Normal people don't have moral values anymore. The role of the church is to inculcate morals and values to communities, and I wonder whether or not the church is still pursuing this agenda. If an economically active man impregnates a disabled woman, and eventually this disabled blind woman had to ask money from strangers to support her children who were born through a consensual intercourse, it simply tells us that there is something wrong somewhere in the African society. In South Africa we talk about the spirit of Ubuntu. The spirit of Ubuntu says, "I am therefore you are" It's also the spirit of Ubuntu that teaches us not to steal and rob other people. It's the spirit of Ubuntu that teaches the youth to respect the elders. It's the spirit of Ubuntu that teaches Africans not to covet what other people have, since we don't know how they acquired their possessions and their belongings. Not all Africans have this spirit of Ubuntu. Frankly speaking, an economically active man who has the spirit of Ubuntu can't impregnate a blind woman and renounce the pregnancy and abandon the mother who is blind and the little baby. I need to make myself clear: I am not implying that a blind woman can't make love to an economically active man who is mentally stable, nor am I saying that all blind women are mentally unstable. The point I am making is this: I find it inappropriate that a mentally stable man can make love to a mentally unstable woman and claim that the intercourse was consensual. It's highly improbable that a mentally unstable person can consent to intercourse with a mentally stable person with full understanding of the ramifications of the consensual intercourse itself. The fact of the matter is a mentally unstable person can't tell the difference between what is right or wrong; therefore, judgment of a mentally unstable person can't be trusted. Therefore an argument from a mentally stable man claiming that the mentally unstable woman consented to intercourse is misleading, and it is difficult to ascertain the veracity of that statement. In a nutshell, a mentally stable man who impregnates a mentally unstable woman, or has sexual intercourse with a mentally unstable woman, should be classified as a rapist. After the begging process was over from the group of beggars at Kwekwe, our bus was back on the road, and our next stop was a small town called Gweru. It's imperative to understand that what they call a town in Zimbabwe might not qualify to be called a town in South Africa. Gweru is a small town with a lot of business activities going on. From now henceforth, the day economic sanctions are going to be lifted off from Zimbabwe's economy, Gweru will be a beautiful marketplace with a lot of malls and American franchises. I have an adventurous spirit within me; I like new experiences and exposure. The trip from Harare to Bulawayo, in addition to the police roadblocks that I had to endure, zapped that adventurous spirit in me. Part of being me began to have misgivings about my journey, and the theory of arrive alive just flew out of the window. In Gweru a hawker with a lot of body lotion came inside the bus. He started praying for us so that our journey could be safe. He rebuked all the evil spirits that are normally on the roads that cause accidents. When he was through with his prayer, he began selling his products. The Zimbabwean government is losing a considerable amount of millions of US dollars through negligence and weak government institutions. When a hawker sells goods inside the bus to passengers, the profit that a hawker makes is tax-free, since there is no system in place that ensures that the hawkers pay tax to the government. The same is true in South Africa. In South Africa, street vendors need to register with SARS if their turnover reached a certain threshold, and the threshold changes each and every year since it is determined by SARS. There is also compulsory registration. With compulsory registration, as long as your turnover exceeded the threshold that has been determined by SARS, you are compelled to register as vendor by law. Failure to register, there are penalties that SARS will impose on a vendor who failed to register as a VAT vendor. Registering as a VAT vendor is better than SARS finding out that you were violating the VAT Act. SARS can rip off your financial house wide open if you don't pay tax. It's deadly difficult to come back to the financial life of business after SARS has ripped your financial house wide open. SARS puts businessmen and businesswomen who don't pay tax to financial sleep. The point that I making is this: the Zimbabwean government is losing a lot of millions of US dollars through this laissez-faire approach to hawkers who are selling their products in buses. The theory of Zimbabwe's hawkers is this: sell everything in the bus including lowering the prices to ensure that at the end of the day your stocks are gone when you disembark from the bus. The hawker who was selling in our bus from Gweru was selling both aloe vera moisturizers and perfumes. He came straight to my seat and gave the aloe vera Vest line to a certain lady without her asking for it. The lady just kept quiet as if she does not see what was going on. The product prices of the hawker were not static; they can fluctuate like Zimbabwe's inflation in the early 2007. The product prices of this hawker can drop from ten US dollars within a minute to two US dollars. Since the lady who was seated next to me had already determined in her heart that she was not going to buy this aloe vera, I decided to help my African brother and bought it for two US dollars. This aloe vera initially had cost ten US dollars. After realizing that people were not interested, the hawker had no choice but lower his prices to the point where consumers can afford to buy his product. The fact of the matter is this: there is no way this hawker was determined to disembark from the bus with a stock on hand. He wanted to make sure that all of his stocks were bought by the passengers. This aloe vera that I bought from Zimbabwe is not a Zimbabwean product but was an import from Tanzania in a place called Tanga. It has been manufactured by Tanga Pharmaceutical & Plastics Ltd. Because of the weak economy of Zimbabwe to manufacture products like aloe vera, Tanzanian products find their way into the economy of Zimbabwe, and these products are now in circulation. The damage that is caused by economic sanctions is countless and wide to the point that pinpointing the exact amount of billions of US dollars that the Zimbabwean government is losing every day is deadly difficult and a mammoth task to embark on. The truth of the matter is another man's meat is another man's poison, or another man's trash is another man's treasure. Not all African countries are crying foul about the economic sanctions that are in place right now in Zimbabwe. The main reason I say that is that economic sanctions favor certain neighboring countries while at the same time they don't favor certain neighboring countries. Frankly speaking, economic sanctions have some gains and losses. A sanctioned country will normally lose most of its skilled labor force and semiskilled labor force to the neighboring countries, while economic sanctions can also put the neighboring country under severe pressure because of migration of people from the sanctioned country to the neighboring countries. Zimbabwe lost most of its intellectual capital to its neighboring countries because of the economic sanctions, and it will take a considerable amount of time, investment, and undying spirit of young people to replace the entire class of intelligentsias who emigrated from Zimbabwe to the neighboring countries because of economic sanctions. After an excruciatingly painful journey from Harare to Bulawayo, finally we arrived in Bulawayo. It was around 4:00 p.m. By this time I was extremely tired, and the town was sizzling hot. I collected my bag from my seat and disembarked from the bus. The moment my feet hit the ground, a certain gentleman from the bus company that I was using requested to see my bus ticked to determine whether I was a legitimate passenger or I boarded the bus without paying. I quickly pulled the ticket from my brown leather jacket and gave it to him. He took the ticket, and that was the end of my journey—it means right now my journey with this bus had ended, but I had to start another journey. The moment I disembarked from the bus, I casted my eyes wide open, thinking perhaps that I can see Jacob, my driver from my first trip. I went to the cabs that were parked next to the road, and I asked the cab drivers that were standing next to their cabs about Jacob, the cab driver. One cab driver indicated to me that he knows Jacob and pointed to the cab and said,

"This is his cab, and he is no longer driving the cab." "If he is no longer driving the cab, what is he driving right now?" The cab driver told me that he is driving trucks that transport goods from South Africa to DRC because the salary is better compared to what he was getting when he was driving a cab. That was a slap in the face for me. My grand plan was falling apart. I thought I can walk until I reach the hotel where I slept last time I was in Bulawayo. Besides, I think I know this small town; I can't get lost in Africa. I walked for quite a distance, and my intuition began to talk to me. I knew that I was getting lost. It's better getting lost on a Monday morning than getting lost on a Sunday afternoon because on Sunday afternoon many people are already at home watching TV with their families while I am in the middle of nowhere trying to navigate my way to the hotel. Some African countries have themselves to blame about their current economic conditions that they find themselves in right now. I accepted the message that my feet were sending to my mind. The message was loud and clear: please let's take a cab to the nearest hotel. I quickly listened to the voice within me and went straight to the cab that was parked next to the road. I knocked at the window of the cab, and the cab driver who seemed glued to his cell phone as if he was talking to his girlfriend quickly responded. He opened the door of the cab, and I greeted him, and he drove me to the hotel where I slept the previous time I was in Zimbabwe (Bulawayo). I couldn't make a hotel booking in advance to the hotel where I slept in the previous time I was in Zimbabwe (Bulawayo), since most of the time, my journey is determined by external factors that I have no control over. What I mean is this: booking can restrict and control my movements. But making a hotel booking in advance is the best thing that a wise person should always do. We arrived at the hotel entrance, and I informed the driver that he should not worry—I was just going to get a room and pay for the room then afterward he will drive me to Nando's to buy half chicken just like I did in Harare the previous day. The entrance to the hotel was wide open, and I moved in and approached the receptionist. I told the receptionist that I was looking for a room. He said to me, "Did you make a booking, sir?" I said no. He took out his book, paging through it a number of times, and eventually looked at me eyeball to eyeball and said, "I am sorry, sir, there is no room that is available." My grand plan was literally falling apart indeed; I lost my first cab driver Jacob, and now the hotel is full to the brim. What else could go wrong on this Sunday? I didn't panic; I have been in many bad situations before, and God helped me to get through them. This too shall pass, I said. I asked the receptionist what are the other nearest hotels that I can visit in order to find a room for the night? He referred me to a new hotel called Inning's Place. My new driver knows the hotel very well, and he drove me there. Upon arrival in the new hotel, which is next to the main road, I had very serious concerns in my mind while he was driving to this new hotel that I don't have sufficient knowledge about, and my main concerns were the following: Let me assume that I find a room in this new hotel for the night to sleep, where will the room be located? If the room where I will sleep on is located next to the main road, is it possible then to fall asleep next to a busy road while cars are moving up and down all night long? My driver pulled over, and I disembarked from the cab. I went straight to the hotel entrance as if I had booked the room in advance. I approached the receptionist and asked her about the availability of an empty room for the night. She said there are empty rooms that are available. I requested to see the rooms in order to make a perfect choice. A man must have options to choose from; you can't be presented with one option and then you have to make a choice from one option. A man must have multiple options to choose from. I am still talking about the rooms, not women. Majority of men don't have a luxury of choosing in life. They only have one option to choose from; no wonder most men are living unhappy lives before marriage, even inside marriage. If there are no options, you must create options for yourself. Remember, you are a man, and a man is a head, not tail. I had two options to choose from. There were two empty rooms. The first room was a suite, and the second room was small and affordable; but the problem with the second room was it was close to the busy main road, and I could not have a quiet night had I chosen the second room. I chose the suite, which was the first room. The suite was expensive compared to the smaller room, but at least it was not next to the busy main road. The receptionist and I agreed that the room that I was taking was the suite. I went downstairs with the receptionist to pay, and I took my slip. I went back to the cab to inform my patient cab driver that I will spend the night at Inning's Place. I went back to the room again to put my bag and went back to the driver again. He drove me to the nearest Nando's, and I bought a half chicken. Because Nando's was not that far, I told the cab driver that I will walk back to the hotel alone; he can leave. He drove off and left me inside Nando's all by myself, after I paid him of course. I ordered a half chicken. I sat down alone, extremely tired and disappointed with many things that have gone horribly wrong that day. My mind was rushing fast. I had to eat and complete my lunch as soon as possible. I had to buy newspapers to read about what is happening in the country. I had to understand what Mr. Brown's wife was talking about when she said there is a minister who received US$6 million from a Ghanaian company as a bribe for Marange diamonds. I quickly finished eating, and I had already paid. My challenge was to look for an open shop that was selling newspaper. I moved around the streets of Bulawayo until I met a gentleman who was selling newspapers. I bought different newspapers that covered a variety of issues. State-owned newspapers normally can't report about the rot of corruption that is taking place in government ministries and government departments. The main reason the state-owned print media can't report about the rot of corruption in government ministries and departments is that the government state-owned print media is part and parcel of the government. After I bought a variety of newspapers, I went straight to the hotel. I arrived in my hotel room, and the first thing that I had to do was to take a shower. I opened the bathroom tap and checked the water whether the water was hot or cold. I quickly discovered that the water was very cold, and it seemed as if the situation I was in was not going to change for the better. I went back to the receptionist to inform her that the water in my hotel room was very cold. She said I must run the tap for a considerable amount time and eventually the water will be hot. The fact is I had been running this tap for a considerable amount of time, but the water was not getting any warmer. I accepted that I no longer have options but to take a cold shower in my suite. After I completed taking a shower, I started reading my newspapers. The US$6 million was about a former ZMDC chairperson, Godwills Masimirembwa. Essien had a stake of 24 percent in the US$100 million. Essien is a businessman who is also involved in other joint ventures like First Capital plus Zimbabwe, a microfinance institution. Essien on a certain day paid US$6 million to the former ZMDC chairperson, Godwills Masimirembwa. The controversy surrounding this amount is, where did the money go to? Essien suggested that the amount of US$6 million was not a commitment fee but for his stake in the US$100 million deal. Mr. Masimirembwa suggested that the amount of US$6 million was a commitment fee and was utilized in the first phase of the mine. The US$100 million deal is made up of different investors: the ZMDC owns 50 percent; Zimbabwe Republic Police Trust, 20 percent; Essien, 24 percent; and Dantor, 6 percent, a company representing the interest of local shareholders. Essien is from Ghana. In 2012, Essien's friend Mr. Kingsley Attah Ghansah was arrested in Zimbabwe for being in possession of seven kilograms of gold. The gold was taken from him and later on he appealed the court's judgment. He was acquitted, and the gold was not given back to him.[12] The merits and the demerits of this claim are hard to verify or confirm, but what is abundantly clear is this: there is no smoke without fire. After I have read extensively the newspapers, I had to sleep early, since my day was going to be very long the following day. Pres. Robert Mugabe was in the United States of America attending the United Nations General Assembly meeting. He went to the United States with his wife, Grace Mugabe, and his children. When I arrived in Zimbabwe for the second time, parliament had just been opened since ZANU-PF won the national election, and it meant that all the government ministries were going to be headed by the members of ZANU-PF because the GPA had come and gone, and the people of Zimbabwe were stuck for another five years of pain with Pres. Robert Mugabe, whether they voted for him or not. Pres. Robert Mugabe had to appoint ministers to head these ministries that were previously headed by the MDC-T members because of the Global Political Agreement (GPA). The burning issue about the new ministers that were appointed was about the new fleet of cars that they were supposed to receive upon their appointments. These new cars were bought by the government for both the old ministers and even the new ministers. The Zimbabwean government had spent to the tune of US$20 million to purchase the fleet of cars for both the new ministers and their deputies. In other words, ministers had to receive two sets of cars, and the deputy ministers should also have two sets of cars. The way the Zimbabwe government runs its affairs is totally different compared to the way the South African government runs its affair. In South Africa the government does not buy cars for the minister, but the ministers choose cars for themselves and pay for the cars through government's money. In Zimbabwe the government purchases cars for the ministers and pays for the cars also using the government's money, but the ministers in Zimbabwe don't choose the cars but; the state chooses for the ministers, unlike in South Africa where the ministers choose their own cars. The fleet of cars that Zimbabwe's government bought includes Mercedes-Benz E350, Land Rover Discovery SUV, and Ford Ranger. It was widely reported that there are roughly 2.2 million people in Zimbabwe who are facing starvation because of drought. The United Nations World Food Programme (UNWFP) attributes the starvation to a poor harvest realized in the last cropping season.[13] The point is new ministers and their deputies will be driving brand-new cars, while the people that they claim to represent will be swimming in a pool of starvation and hunger. This fleet of cars is bought under the pretext of expediting the pace of service delivering to the people. Simply put, the fleet of cars was not bought to the benefit of the ministers and their deputies, but they were bought to service the masses. This notion is dangerous and misleading. It seems as if politicians can get away with murder easily when it comes to the idea of expediting service delivery to the masses then buying expensive cars for themselves, claiming that the cars belong to the people. After I completed reading the variety of newspapers, I went to bed to sleep. My hotel room was on the first floor, and above my hotel room, there is a second floor. The second floor also has rooms just like the first floor. The window of the room that is on the second floor just above my hotel room was not closed all night long, and the window was banging itself. I had to contend with the noise all night long until 4:00 a.m., which is when I fell asleep. There are many things that can make a person fail to sleep especially in a foreign country. There are many vile conflicting theories about the hotels themselves. I asked myself many questions—whether I will wake up alive here in the morning or I will be visited by strange people who will attempt to rob me in the middle of the night, since I am a tourist. There is another theory about tourists, which is tourists are rich and they carry large sums of money with them. This theory places me in a center of a potential robbery; in fact it portrays me as a person who has a large sum of money. The fact of the matter is tourists don't have large sums of money with them, since they would have paid for the flights, bus tickets, and accommodation for their stay in the Zimbabwean hotel. I woke up in the morning the following day. It was a lovely Monday, and Bulawayo was jam packed with people going up and down. I quickly ran the bathroom tap for a considerable amount of time, and eventually the water began to be warmer on this day. I took a long shower, bearing in mind that today I am going back home to South Africa, "the Saudi Arabia of mineral resources." Most South Africans don't know that South Africa is the Saudi Arabia of mineral resources; they think they are living in the lion's dungeon. My hotel fee was inclusive of breakfast; therefore, I will not pay additional amount for the breakfast, since my hotel price is inclusive of a breakfast. After my long shower, I then applied the aloe vera that I bought in a bus. My aloe vera had cost me two US dollars. It was manufactured in Tanzania in Tanga. I quickly packed my bag, and I made sure that I was leaving nothing behind, since from here I am no longer coming back to this hotel room. I locked the room, and my bag was already on my right shoulder, and I went straight to the reception desk to drop my bag and quickly went to the kitchen, as the breakfast was waiting for me. The waitress greeted me with a smile, and she said her name was Betty. I asked her who the owner of the hotel was. She said the owner of the hotel was Mr. Naidoo, an Indian. Zake's Place is owned by an Indian, and Inning's Place is owned by an Indian. What is it that black Zimbabweans own if all these hotels are owned by Indians? Let me make myself clear: Indians are not black people in Zimbabwe, just like coloreds are not black people in Zimbabwe. When you are talking about a black person from Zimbabwe's perspective, you are talking about Morgan Tsvangirai and Robert Mugabe; these two gentlemen are black people with black skin. However, from the South African perspective, the whole situation will be totally different, since South Africa is a rainbow nation with different people with different colors, creeds, and ethnicities. In South Africa, Indians and coloreds are classified as blacks. I recently read about the case that involved Chinese people claiming that they should be classified as black so they can qualify for BEE status. The constitutional court ruled in their favor. Chinese in South Africa do qualify for the BEE status if they incorporate a company in South Africa; they can therefore get a tender. I hate to address the issue of race personally because people can eventually draw a wrong inference about my opinion. Imagine a situation where I immigrate to China and claim to be a Chinese. I think Chinese from China can simply say to me, "You are out of your mind. Go back to the African jungle where you came from." I am not a racist; I am being brutally honest. Betty said to me that she has been working in Inning's Place for almost two years now. I asked her about her educational level. She said she didn't complete A level. She had completed O level, which is the ordinary level, and A level is the advanced level. If you have completed A level, you will qualify to commence your studies in the university. The main problem with A level is this: not all government schools in Zimbabwe can afford to offer A level because it is extensive and tense. It requires teachers with specialized subjects. The majority of pupils complete O level, but because of lack of these specialized teachers who can teach specialized subjects, they eventually have to relocate to high schools that can offer A level, and that does not come cheap to the parents. I ate cornflakes and afterward drank a cup of tea with some slices of bread, and that was it. I bade good-bye to Betty and shot straight to the reception and requested the receptionist to call a cab for me. I relaxed in a little bit in the reception while waiting for a cab. After a few minutes, a cab came, and I went to the driver and explained myself and the places where I wanted him to take me to. The driver was an old man in his late forties, and he was Shona-speaking person, not Ndebele-speaking person.

During Gukurahundi, most Ndebeles left Bulawayo; some went back to South Africa, and some went to Botswana. I opened the passenger door and put my bag in the backseat and told him that I needed to go to Cecil John Rhodes's grave, and finally if time allows us, he must drive me to the late Joshua Nkomo's house. I also needed to go and buy a bus ticket, as I was leaving for South Africa in the afternoon. We went to the Greyhound offices in Bulawayo and bought a bus ticket for the bus that was going to leave for South Africa at exactly 4:00 p.m. He said he wanted to change the car because in Matopos National Park they might have a problem with the car that he was driving. We drove for a few kilometers and arrived in certain house on the outskirts of the town, and he changed the car and drove back to town with a different car altogether. While passing Joshua Nkomo Street in Bulawayo, I saw the statue that was still being built for the late Joshua Nkomo. It was covered with a black plastic, indicating construction was still under way. While I was in Bulawayo for the first time, Joshua Nkomo statue was only on the concrete slab level. But at this time around, construction had progressed amazingly so. We began an unavoidable dialogue, since we were together and probably we will spend the rest of the day together. He said to me that his name is Joseph and he is a cab driver. He has been driving a cab for a considerable amount of years. He is literally a Shona from Masvingo. We talked politics and economics at the same time. We are approaching Matopos National Park, which is the park where the Englishman Cecil John Rhodes was buried. Previously I was denied entrance to Matopos National Park because of the car that Jacob was using. For an ordinary cab driver to enter Matopos National Park and drive tourists inside and around the park, he should register with the park first. If the cab driver is registered, then it gives him an allowance to enter the park with his own tourists without any problem. If the cab driver is not registered with the park, he won't be allowed to enter with his own tourists in the park, since he is not a registered. I was very frustrated in my first visit to this park because of the escalation of costs. I am from South Africa; I am not used to the hyperinflationary economy. Everything is very expensive; it's expensive to sleep in a hotel, and it's expensive for a cab driver to drive you around. We arrived at the entrance of the Matopos National Park. On our way from the park, we were lucky because we didn't meet the ZRP (Zimbabwe Republic Police). It was a beautiful morning in Bulawayo. There were two security guards at the gate, a man and a woman. The male security guard opened the gate for us without hesitation, and we entered the Matopos National Park and parked the car inside the park. We then went back to the female security who was seated on top of a chair in an office that had an open window facing the main gate. Since I am a South African, I had to pay an amount of eighteen US dollars; this amount included my entrance fee, the car, and the cab driver who was going to drive me around. I paid the amount of eighteen US dollars with a smile, and we drove off. We were given a map at the main gate by the male security. The area that I wanted to see wholeheartedly was the grave of Cecil John Rhodes. We arrived at the graveside. The next thing you know, I see a gentleman under a tree. He claimed that before we can climb the mountain and be able to see the grave, we need to pay an additional ten US dollars. I am becoming frustrated with these additional unavoidable costs but because I am in another country which is under economic sanctions unfortunately I should follow their rules and regulations. I paid the required amount of ten US dollars. We climbed the mountain with my cab driver, Joseph. We walked a distance before we can see the graves. My assumption all along was that Cecil John Rhodes was buried alone on top of the mountain. I was not under the impression that there could be other graves that have surrounded Cecil John Rhodes's grave. We stood on top of the mountain and saw the whole of Bulawayo from the mountain. I wonder why they normally say, in Bulawayo, when you stand on top of that mountain where Cecil John Rhodes was buried, you will have a Cecil John Rhodes worldview of Bulawayo. It appears as if they worship Cecil John Rhodes in a way. There are multiple endless theories about Cecil John Rhodes, and some of these theories emanated from the fact that Cecil John Rhodes was not married for fear that he couldn't be a good father. The other theory is this: Cecil John Rhodes was not a heterosexual but a homosexual—that is why he was not married. Some of these theories can't be validated with certainty. I asked the Matopos National Park's official who was under the tree why there isn't an inscription on Cecil John Rhodes's grave as to when he was born and when he died. He simply said that the autobiography of Cecil John Rhodes was taken by Zimbabwe's government in order to be edited. We were with two other white gentlemen who were also taking pictures on top of the mountain. I began to follow these gentlemen on top of the mountain. While my eyes were fixated on the grave of Cecil John Rhodes, I soon discovered that there are other graves around Cecil John Rhodes. There are additional two graves that are in Matopos National Park next to Cecil John Rhodes' grave, the grave of Dr. Leander Starr Jameson, who was an administrator, and the grave of Sir Charles Coghlan, the premier. I was not wholly satisfied with my adventure. We went back to ask the Matopos National Park's official about the caves that we can visit before exiting the park. The Matopos National Park's official told us that there are caves that are called Ntswatugi Cave and Pomongwe Cave that are twenty kilometers away from Cecil John Rhodes's grave. These were caves where the indigenous people were living in prior to the arrival of black people from Central Africa. We drove almost twenty-five kilometers searching for these caves. I am not an anthropologist, and apparently it seemed as if I lost my main goal of coming to this park. I came to Matopos National Park to look for Cecil John Rhodes's grave. I didn't come here to look for archeological evidence and the inscriptions on the caves to confirm that the Son people came to Zimbabwe before the indigenous people. I took this decision while we were on top of the mountain at Silozwane searching for a cave. Quite frankly, if a lion would have appeared while we were on top of the mountain, it was going to devour us alive, and our bones were not going to be discovered even after three million years. One thing that Joseph did that frightened me to the core was allowing me to lead the search. The man is older than me, with a considerable amount of experience and knowledge, yet he is afraid to lead. We got to the point where I said, "You know I think for us to find this cave, we should have woken up earlier in the morning and came here to start searching. It was also not advisable to search for caves without a gun because you might not know what could be waiting for you ahead." We went back to the car and drove off. I asked the Matopos National Park's official about the grave of King Mzilikazi. He said to me that King Mzilikazi was buried outside the Matopos National Park, and his grave is looked after by the Khumalo family. I couldn't search around for King Mzilikazi's grave, who is known as "the Cattle Raider," because of time and the fact that I had already bought the ticket for the bus. Before we drove back to the bus terminal, we had to pass through Joshua Nkomo's house. The late Joshua Nkomo's house is in the suburb of Bulawayo. We searched for the house until we found it. It is right on the end of the road. It's a beautiful house surrounded by a white wall and the red main gate that was wide open. Joseph suggested that we enter. I couldn't find it logically appropriate to visit the children of the late Joshua Nkomo and possibly ask them questions about their father who passed on a long time ago. I found it inappropriate and logically unsound specifically if the children lost both the mother and the father. We drove off straight to the bus terminal where I was going to catch my bus to South Africa. Joseph warned me that morning and said, "You must tell that gentleman Julius Malema that he must not nationalize the mines and expropriate land without compensation because South Africans will suffer." I am not a friend of Julius Malema, and I don't see Julius Malema taking an advice from a cab driver like Joseph. He said, "I don't want our brothers to suffer as we are suffering here in Zimbabwe." I never said I will pass the message for him. The fact of the matter is the president of EFF (Economic Freedom Fighter), Julius Malema, is damn popular in Zimbabwe, and most Zimbabweans think that he is going to be the president of South Africa one day. I bade farewell to Joseph and paid him his exuberant fee, and he drove off in peace. I went to the waiting room and sat for quite some time. I realized that it was very hot, and I needed something to drink. I went to the shop nearby the bus terminal where I bought water and some snacks. I had left my bag in the waiting room with some women and the security guard. The bus came, and we were ordered to produce our tickets, and we then loaded our bags on the luggage trailer. While we were loading our bags in the luggage trailer, a certain lady came to me and said, "How you are?" I said, "I am fine." I didn't think too much about her, since I was not in Zimbabwe to look for love but for the truth. It's the truth that sets a nation free, not lies. I was searching for the truth about Africa's wealth that was stolen from our forefathers by the West. I was searching for the truth about the source of the current Zimbabwe's problems. There are many men in Zimbabwe. I hope that she will get somebody who is going to propose love to her. She looked very professional. She was holding car keys on her right hand. She knew that I was from South African. I went inside the bus and sat next to a young lady by the name of Bajabulile. She is a Zimbabwean, and she has been working in South Africa for almost four years now. Bajabulile is a Ndebele-speaking person, and she speaks English with a South African accent. She is working in Johannesburg and staying in Hillbrow. Inside the bus I began to reflect about the events of the day and my journey from South Africa to Zimbabwe. When I was in Heroes' Acre, my mind was racing fast. I had a lot of questions without answers: What really happened in Zimbabwe? Was Zimbabwe's crisis purely about the farm invasion or there is something else to it? Is it possible that the leaders of African liberation movements stayed long enough in the bush to the point that they now struggle to cope with the mounting challenges that come with running their countries? If the main objective of African liberation movements was to achieve total political independence from Africa's colonial masters, and the total political independence was achieved, why then are these political leaders of African liberation movements struggling to run their own countries successfully? Is it possible then that if the late Joshua Nkomo won the national election in 1980, possibly the Zimbabwe I see today would have been invariably different from the Zimbabwe that Joshua Nkomo envisaged? The fact of the matter is we can't dwell in the past forever, and what happened in 1980 is irreversible. Crying foul does not help anymore. The July 31, 2013, national election has come and gone whether we like it or not. The fact is Pres. Robert Mugabe of ZANU-PF won the election, and Morgan Tsvangirai of MDC-T lost the national election, and SADC went on to authorize the election as free, fair, and summarily peaceful. It seems unlikely that Pres. Robert Mugabe can get sick to the point of resigning from the presidency before his political tenure is over. It seems unlikely also that the Movement for Democratic Change (MDC) has any options available on the table to use without waiting and praying that perhaps in the next election probably things will get better. That is politics; it is the cruelest game of them all. Elections are not won on newspapers but are won after the vote counting has been completed. I have learned something powerful about politics, specifically the African politics. The G7 countries are worried about the political stability in the African continent because that is where the majority of mineral wealth is coming from. The superpower countries like China, the United States of America, and Britain are fighting their financial wars through the African continent. If the Zimbabwean national election went in favor MDC-T, the United States of America and Britain were going to be happy and eventually lift off the economic sanctions from the economy of Zimbabwe. Since the national election went in favor of ZANU-PF, China is happy because it will continue to mine the Marange diamond fields until there is nothing left on the ground for the future Zimbabwean generation. When China has finished mining all the Marange diamonds, it will eventually leave a bottomless pit on the ground just like all Western companies who came to Africa before. Western companies come to Africa to extract the African mineral resources, generate exuberant amount of profits, pay their labor force peanuts, and eventually leave the country in taters and chaos, and go back to the West. The African story is the painful story. It's the story about rich people who are poor. It's the story about rich people who don't have wealth. We Africans have nobody to blame but ourselves. We are addicted to the Western foreign aid and the food parcels from the West. We Africans are addicted to Western products and addicted to the Western culture and we are even addicted to the Western churches including their songs. If an African man can visit the United States of America or Britain, once that

African man comes back to the African soil, that African man will be extremely happy as if he was in heaven. I wonder whether or not Americans, when they visit Africa, feel very happy as Africans feel when they visit the United States of America or Britain? The West has hypnotized Africans. We Africans have been hypnotized to the point of madness with American music and American movies. We Africans love the Western shows, *The Real Housewives of Beverly Hills* and *The Real Housewives of Miami*. We read too much of their books, and they don't read any of our books. Some Africans regret why they were not bought as slaves during slave trade age. The main reason the majority of Africans feel like that is that the majority of African countries are forever in political crisis that translates to economic crisis and that engenders abject poverty. The poverty that we Africans find ourselves in is not divine but carnal. African poverty is man-made and is largely orchestrated by the West through political influence and economic influence in Africa. The West has a strong grip on Africa's wealth. Our African leaders are also largely to be blamed for the economic crisis that we find ourselves in. Why is it that until this point in African history, we are still largely dependent on the West for foreign aid? Why is it that until this point in African history, we allowed the West to extract diamonds in African soil and ferry them all the way to the West to cut them and polish them? Is it possible that we really don't understand the value of our wealth and that is why we behave like we are poor though we are rich as far as mineral resources is concerned?

Guy Arnold writes,

> *Pres. Julius Nyerere, speaking at the state in Beijing on a visit to China in February 1965, said, "Those who give us loans . . . must do so because they wish to take part in man's human development, not because they wish to control our young state."*[14]

This statement came from what now is known as Arusha Declaration, which was later published in 1967. The second part of the Arusha Declaration deals with the self-reliance.

> *Independence cannot be real if a nation depends upon gifts and loans from another country for its development. Even if there was a nation, or nations, prepared to give us all the money we*

> *need for our development, it would be improper for us to accept such assistance without asking ourselves how this would affect our independence and our very survival as a nation.*[15]

One of the greatest hindrances for Africa's total economic emancipation is the loans and foreign aid. These two economic traps keep Africa on Western financial prison. We Africans can never be a superpower continent and form part and parcel of the G7 countries as long as we are a continent of consumers not producers. I began to monitor everything that I was purchasing, and I discovered something shocking about many products. I discovered that my belt that is on my waist was made in China, and I also discovered that my sneakers that I am wearing were made in China. I went to buy a calculator, and to my dismay, the calculator was made in China also. This is real: China's invasion in Africa is a living reality. Just like the West invaded Africa, China is sitting on Africa's neck. China is controlling Zimbabwe, and its influence I am feeling right here in South Africa. I began to notice in Pretoria, South Africa, that if a shop is not owned by a Bangladeshi, it is owned by an Italian, Portuguese, Chinese, or Japanese. There are very few shops in Pretoria that are owned by a black South African. I need to make this point clear: when I say owned, I don't necessarily mean owning title deeds of the property, but I mean trading through buying the stock and selling the stock to customers.

When Prof. Arthur Mutambara was a deputy prime minister of Zimbabwe, he addressed the Zimbabwe National Chamber of Commerce (ZNCC) annual congress on June 13, 2013. He said:

> "*Competitiveness refers to the ability of a firm or a nation to offer products and services that meet the quality standards of the local and world markets at prices that are lower than those of rival entities and provide adequate returns on the resources employed or consumed in producing them.*"

He went further to talk about productivity and national competitiveness. And he said:

> "*National competitiveness is defined by the productivity with which a nation utilizes its human, capital, technology, and natural resources.*"[16]

For Africa to achieve average competitiveness, it will need to utilize our natural resources, not receiving loans and foreign aid from the West. It simply means that when the West donates food parcels and cheap T-shirts to African people, it proves that the West is competitive because not only can it support its citizens and invest some of their reserves in the World Bank and IMF, but also it can even donate food parcels to the poor African people. When I was in Zimbabwe, I was extremely shocked to learn that the West was sending its investigators into Kenya, Nairobi, to assist in conducting the forensic investigation when the Westgate mall was under siege from the Al-Shabaab terrorist group. This is an African tragedy happening in African soil, how come African forensic investigators are folding hands and waiting for the FBI or CIA or the British forensic experts? On second thought, Africa does not possess the wherewithal to investigate complex cases and tragedies like the Westgate mall fiasco. Maybe we are not yet competitive to the point where we can run our own forensic investigation without any help from FBI, CIA, or British forensic experts. It makes logical sense then that we are not near to achieve average competitiveness Prof. Arthur Mutambara talked about.

The World Bank senior economist John Robertson said:

> *Zimbabwe requires more than US$33 billion for infrastructure projects over the next twenty years to turn around its economic fortunes.*[17]

US$33 billion—it's not peanuts; it's a lot of money. The one-million-dollar question then is, Where will the Zimbabwean government, which is forever embroiled in never-ending political squabbles, get such a gigantic amount of money? Perhaps the answer lies in the offices of the World Bank. For the World Bank to lend a country an exuberant amount of money comes with heavy restrictions. The World Bank is situated in the United States of America and is controlled and influenced by the West. I don't mean that the World Bank is owned by the United States of America, but truth be told, all the employees of the World Bank drink US water and breathe US oxygen, somehow they are thinking like US citizens. Since the government of Pres. Robert Mugabe is always against the West, it's not possible that the World Bank can approve a loan of such magnitude without serious political and economic reforms. Structural and political economic reforms simply mean that the country should have the political leadership that is representative of the wishes of the people. The political representatives must have been chosen by the people, and in the process of choosing these political representatives, the country in question should have put measures in place that seek to protect and prevent lawlessness. Economic reforms mean that the current national economic targets and the trade agreements that are in place should be such that they address the pressing needs of the economy. The World Bank now and then watched Zimbabwe's politics unfolding day in and out and realized the monumental vote rigging that took place on July 31, 2013. It's abundantly clear that such political profile of Zimbabwe's politics is an economic hindrance. This is Zimbabwe's politics. Election results sometimes can be withheld for almost five long weeks, just like what happened in 2008 in the election rerun. But for July 31, 2013, it took almost three days to count the votes. The Israeli company that was hired got the job done quickly, and it delivered the election results to Pres. Robert Mugabe on a silver platter with pleasure, end of the story. Where to from here? This is the question that most Zimbabweans asked themselves, and we discussed this question with Mr. Silverton, and he confided to me that things will remain the same forever. He said Pres. Robert Mugabe is not that much bad; there are very hotheaded people in the ranks of ZANU-PF. Guy Arnold writes:

> *Africa is a rich continent but her riches are unevenly distributed. So long as her states remain separate political units, most of them will not be poor, but will have little prospect of escaping poverty. This is because most of them depend on the sale abroad of primary products and as far as one can see into the future the terms of trade will move against them.*[18]

It's now common knowledge that Africa relies on the West for military weapons and military training. It's also common knowledge that Africa relies on the West for electrical products and cutting-edge gadgets. As long as Africa continues to rely on the West for everything, then Africa's liberation struggle is not over. We Africans need to accept the fact that Africa's liberation struggle was in multiple phases. The first phase of Africa's liberation struggle had been achieved, which was emancipating the African people from the shackles of the political bondage and Western-orchestrated slavery. The second phase of Africa's liberation struggle is the economic struggle, which is about lifting the masses from the depth of Western-made abject poverty. Political event defines political party, and political party defines a political leader, and political leader defines, shapes, and directs the political profile and economic profile of a country. The young African generation is a totally different generation compared to the generation that liberated Africa both in Zimbabwe and in South Africa. The current young African generation is the postliberation generation; sometimes political history is not relevant in the day-to-day lives of this generation. What this young African generation needs is the creation of employment opportunities and massive investment on Africa's capital projects. The blame game on the West will not hold enough water to convince this African young generation. South African population is growing in leaps and bounds, so is Zimbabwe population. South Africa is the home of the homeless and the home of the destitute. Central African wars are weighing heavily on the South African government and on the South African economic targets to eradicate poverty for its people. The Zimbabwean economic sanctions are directly and indirectly affecting South Africa's financial muscle to do more for its citizens. It's also true that South African economy is diverse and can withstand the test of time. But the main problem is the number of illegal immigrants that is now living in South Africa because of the political unrest and political intolerance in the Central African region. The xenophobic attacks in the late 2007 and earlier 2008 were exacerbated by the illegal migrants that were occupying new RDP houses without following due process. This trend of illegal migrants occupying RDP houses was prevalent in Gauteng Province, not in any other province, since Gauteng is the hotbed of South Africa's economy. The other trend that emerged after South Africa achieved its own political independence in 1994 is the high volume of foreign nationalities migrating to South Africa as if South Africa was Miami of the United States of America. This influx of foreign nationalities altered South African culture and motto. South Africans began to see the high level of drug supply for the first time and the ever-growing slumps within a rapid amount of time. The pace of South African government to provide social services to South Africans fall short not because the government of South African is incapable and corrupt, but because of the rapid population growth and the influx of foreign nationalities. This problem of influx of foreign nationalities is deadly serious and is costing the South African government a considerable amount of money. There are two sides of the coin when it comes to dealing with foreign nationalities. It's true that since South Africa was under apartheid for a considerable amount of time, it's now experiencing fundamental skills shortage in crucial sectors. It's also true that South Africa's knowledge production is low compared to other countries. It's also true that South Africa's literacy rate is poor on average when compared to the literacy rate of other developing countries. Most of these problems can be attributed to apartheid and its oppressive educational policies that were applied to black South African people by the oppressive and cruel apartheid government. Some will say, "But you cannot continue to blame apartheid forever—you have to accept the blame." Most of the new South African government policies to address the crisis in education, which are in place right now, were nonexistent during the apartheid era. The level of financial transparency that is currently being practiced by the government of South Africa was nonexistent during the apartheid era. During the apartheid era, there was abject financial maladministration by the apartheid government, but those incidences were not reported, since there was no freedom of expression and freedom of speech. The print media was always sympathetic to the government of the day. Since the dawn of Africa's democracy, we Africans are normally bombarded daily by the foreign-owned media about the corrupt activities of African leaders as if the Western leaders are not corrupt. We Africans have come to know that the greatest weakness of them all for a black person is money. We have accepted the theory that says a black man is corrupt, and he can't govern and run his country successfully. The West has deepened its corrupt roots on the psyche of the black person. Most African countries are afraid of the second coming of colonization; no wonder there is too much looting on the state resources by the very same African leaders who liberated Africa. We Africans are politically free, but it's also true that some of us doubt and wonder and ask ourselves this question: How long will our freedom last? As a result of this fear, we degenerate to glutton and greed. We eat too much of what is already ours, and we steal what we already legally own. We Africans destroy our own infrastructure that is meant for our own good because we believe that the world-class infrastructure epitomizes a white man, and poverty epitomizes the permanent state of a black person. The fact of the matter is this: the white man is gone, and he is no longer going to come back to control us politically, then why do we destroy our own schools, municipal buildings, and clinics during our own protest? There are multiple ways in which fear exhibits itself. The fear of recolonization exhibits itself through mistrust. When I was in Zimbabwe, I asked Terry this question: What if MDC-T of Morgan Tsvangirai one day wins the national election and sell the country to the West? Terry said, "We will vote him out of office." The current political gospel that is being preached in Zimbabwean churches is that you must defend your country with everything. Why do you need to defend your country with everything since Zimbabweans have attained their political independence and got their land back? Who wants to take our own country from us? Surely the West can no longer control and tell Africa how to run its political affairs as long as Africa displays political maturity and governs itself successfully. The only time the West can jump into the African affairs is when we Africans continue to fight each other like cat and mouse. Then we are placing ourselves on a global political arena, and the West will claim that they want to save us from us. That is exactly what happened in the Second DRC (Democratic of Republic of Congo) War. The Congolese were fighting each other like mouse and cat, and by so doing, they were inviting global attention. They were inviting the global attention of the United Nations. Whenever there is a war, there are causalities of war; these are innocent civilians who are struck by rockets and shelling. There are also profits to be made within every war. Tshinga Dube once said,

> *"There are fortunes to be made in Congo," said Col. Tshinga Dube on television. "They import everything there, even potatoes and cooking oil," he added. "Why rush to conquer the rebels?"*[19]

The fact is Western companies that are manufacturing military weapons normally generate a considerable amount of revenues during the war. It's therefore not in the interests of the Western companies that are manufacturing military weapons and fighter jets to have peace and political tranquility on the African continent. If political peace and tranquility can prevail on the African continent, these Western companies will have to close shop. To continue generating massive profits, blood needs to continue dripping, and it must be dripping on African soil. It's a sad story, but that's how the game of politics and money works. It's the survival of the fittest, and the lame and the weak get eaten by the strong. Most of the time the lame and the weak are the African people who get eaten by the West. The West will never ever destroy Africa completely partly because it will have no one to brag on. The West can't brag on Asia because Asia and the West are enemies. Asia is another emerging superpower that is trying by all means to impose itself on the world. Therefore, as long as the West lives, Africa will live. In fact some of the Western nationalities think that we Africans live and eat with lions on a daily basis. Some people have an illusion about Africa, and this illusion about Africa has gotten the better of them. That is why you will hear most of the Western-educated African scholars say, "I studied in the United States," as if when a person studied in an African university, that person did not get good education. The West has bewitched Africa by indoctrinating African people and African leaders to believe the lie that you can never accomplish anything on your own, therefore you need us more than we need you. Most Africans therefore agree with this theory that says we need the West more than the West needs Africa. When the West steals from Africa, most Africans don't see that as stealing, but they see that as helping Africa anyway. If a person is extracting diamond on your ground and take it to his home country, cut them and polish them, and sell them with a higher price, tell me, how is that benefiting the owner of the land where these diamonds were taken from? Not only will the owner of the land lose the very diamonds that were given to him by God, but he will also lose and miss the valuable opportunity of knowing how to mine diamonds, cut them and polish them, and above all he will lose the profits that he would have generated had he mined the diamonds and sold them himself. I also don't think that God can be happy with such a person, and that person is Africa. The Marange diamond financial scandal will forever hang over the heads of Zimbabwe's government. And it's the perfect example to illustrate my point.

> *The committee headed by Edward Chindori-Chiniga, a vocal ZANU-PF MP and former mining minister, visited four mining companies operating in Marange: Anjin, Diamond Mining Corporation (DMC), Mbada Diamonds, and Marange Resources. The report quoted Mbada Diamonds as saying that it had paid US$293 million to the government since it started mining in 2009, including US$117 million in 2011–2012. But it pointed out that that the finance minister Tendai Biti said in his 2013 budget statement that the government received a total of only US$41 million in diamond revenues in the previous year.*[20]

As long as we Africans continue to rely on the West for everything, this picture of plundering of Africa's wealth will continue to bedevil Africa even in the times to come. As the world population grows, so are the needs and wants of the people. The growth in the world population is partly a good sign of good things to come in the near future because the main reason

God created Adam and Eve was for them to have dominion over the earth and partly to procreate. The problem that comes with procreation is sustaining what you have given birth to. By sustaining, I mean providing and protecting what you have given birth to. Sustaining can only happen if there are sufficient resources to provide and protect what people have given birth to. Children and women will forever need serious protection from men. For men to continue to play their crucial societal and moral role, they will need resources to be able to support their families—which means men must wake up in the morning and go to work and earn a living. It also means that there must be sufficient employment opportunities to cater to almost all men in order for these families to survive and thrive. Children will have to go to school, and they will also need a strong roof over their heads, and the women also will expect to have money to do shopping. I really understand that in some parts of the world women are no longer dependent on men but on their academic ability to earn a living. The fact is, in some parts of the world, the majority of women still rely heavily on men, since this has been a culture time immemorial. Since the world population is growing and growing very faster than expected, it also poses a serious challenge on the world resources. It means that there should be a continual trend of creating employment opportunities, and companies must grow at rapid speed to cater to the future generations and pay even the retirement benefits to the current labor force that they currently have on their payroll. This is a serious challenge, and the Arab Spring bears a testament to that. If the majority of people can complete their post-grade-twelve qualifications within a set time and expect to enter the job market, but they can't find employment, they will cause a revolution. Africa's population as a global village is growing, just like the world population is growing. To prevent and divert the Arab uprising wave to heat the shores of sub-Saharan Africa, African leaders must strategize and think decisively as to how to create jobs and meet the citizens' expectations. I heard a certain story when I was in Zimbabwe that a certain Zimbabwean gentleman was arrested because he was always following the news about the Arab Spring, and the police accused him of planning to mobilize the youth of Zimbabwe to revolt against government using the same Arab uprising technique that was used in the Middle East. The fact is anything is possible in Zimbabwe. By the way, you are not allowed to talk bad about Pres. Robert Mugabe. Even writing disparaging statements about him might wind you up in Chikurubi Prison. Terry said to me, "All people who are incarcerated in Chikurubi Prison eventually come out as pastors and prophets and no longer interested in politics but in spreading the word of God." Chikurubi Prison is the cathedral where political dreams are shattered and where aspiring young politicians are politically circumcised. Chikurubi is Zimbabwe's Guantanamo Bay detention center. Unfortunately you don't read *Harry Potter* books in Chikurubi Prison unlike in the real Guantanamo Bay.

Chapter 4

LIFETIME ERROR

Jan Van Riebeeck arrived in the Cape Colony in 1652. He established what was termed Dutch East Indian Company. Since the arrival of Jan Van Riebeeck in 1652 until 1994, the indigenous people of South Africans were living their lives under the white rule, and they were oppressed from left right and center. Indigenous people and Bantu people for that matter lived under the white rule for a period of 342 years. There has never been a black rule that was governing South Africa prior to 1994. The black rule that was in existence was happening under the TBVC (Transkei, Bophuthatswana, Venda, and Ciskei). Bophuthatswana was under Prime Minister Lucas Mangope.Kaiser Matanzima was the Prime Minister of Transkei, and Chief Mphephu was the Prime Minister of Venda.[1] These four Bantu homelands (Transkei, Bophuthatswana, Venda, and Ciskei) were eventually merged through CODESA talks. These homelands ended up forming part and parcel of the new South Africa. It's imperative to mention the fact that these homelands were divided by the apartheid government with a sole intention to segregate and thwart black people to visit and work in places where there were only white people of European descent. The apartheid government succeeded through this political tool to contain and control South Africa as long as the chiefs were running their homelands. Mpumalanga was called Kangwane, and the majority of people who were living at Kangwane were siSwati-speaking people. During this period, the majority of South Africans were not worried about the land. The government of the day was dispossessing the indigenous people of their land indiscriminately without even black people complaining and murmuring. Even the very land that was under the chiefs, the apartheid government would dispossess it whenever it wanted, and the indigenous people would not have recourse for their plight. The ANC (African National Congress) was formed in 1912. The ANC was going to be the voice of the voiceless and the voice of the oppressed by the government system of the day. Black South African people were very rich in culture, livestock, and land. Prior to the arrival of the Europeans in Africa, Africans were living their lives in peace and tranquility with no wars and no proliferation of weapons of mass destruction. There was a serious cataclysm change after the arrival of the Europeans in South Africa and in Africa in general. There Europeans began to take what does not belong to them using guns and horses, killing South Africans who were resisting their rule and control. The Europeans not only took the farms and livestock that black people had but also took the wives of the Nguni people. When the Europeans came to South Africa, they were flat broke without food and decent clothes to wear. The only thing that they had was guns and bullets. The old theory goes that the Europeans were not really coming to settle in South Africa, but they were thirsty from their long voyage that was heading toward India. The old theory says they were going to sell species to Vasco da Gama of India. South Africa was a resting place after their long winding journey from Europe. The notion says the Europeans were only looking for clean water, and the resting place in the Cape is another political propaganda that was manufactured by the Western scholars when they were running out of ideas as to why and how Africa, in particular South Africa, was colonized. There is no way that a person can travel from Europe to the Cape Point and rest at the Cape Point and eventually wind up in Johannesburg digging gold in Witwatersrand mine. If the Europeans were only looking for clean water, why didn't they collect clean water at the Cape Point and leave the indigenous people of South Africa alone and continue with their journey to sell spices to Vasco da Gama of India? Were these spices that the Europeans were selling worth a billion of pounds? The land of the indigenous people was taken, and since 1652 until recently, black people began to realize that the Europeans came from Europe with absolutely nothing, and unfortunately now they have everything that was once owned by black South Africans. Today South Africans of European descent owned the vast tract of land, livestock, and farms. After they have owned almost everything, as if that was not enough, they compounded the problem of black South African people with apartheid and dompas. The main focus of the liberation struggle has been predominantly channeled to end the white rule and the painful apartheid system. The multiplicity of the political theories about how to end apartheid became the main source of variety of political parties that exist today in South Africa. Most of the political parties that are in the process of formation are very irrelevant and useless. The reason I say they are irrelevant and useless is that they never dare to challenge apartheid when it was raising its ugly head back then, but they went straight to their cocoons to hide. Now that apartheid had been decimated and dismantled diametrically, they emerge like penguins in the sea to check the political cost. The next thing you know, everybody right now is a politician with an infallible plan that can save South Africa from political hyenas that are plundering South African resources. There are a lot of people today in South Africa who had an abundant opportunity to join the South African liberation movements and join the political struggle then, but they couldn't, since in the liberation struggle there were no guarantees. Some of these people waited at the corner somewhere until the political dust has settled, and when all is well, they emerged with the new blueprint about the future of South Africa. The question that I asked myself is, where the hell have these folks been when the sons of the soil were fighting the Ian Smith regime in Zimbabwe? Where the hell have these folks been when the sons of the soil were fighting the apartheid agents in Mozambique? Where the hell have these folks been when the sons of the soil where fighting in Angola, Uganda, Namibia, and Zambia? In Zimbabwe it is said you can never run the country if you were not part of the liberation struggle. The point is, if during the liberation struggle you couldn't join any other young men who were part and parcel of the liberation struggle, there is no way now you can pop up like a grasshopper and attempt to run the country. The rationale is simple: you were afraid then to die for your country—what makes you think that you can run the country that you couldn't sacrifice your whole life for? This is where the former freedom fighters and the African academics are at loggerheads. It makes logical sense that if a person couldn't sacrifice his youth and his sex life in the pursuit of a just cause, then when that just cause has been achieved, the very fearful and cowardice person can't come to the table to share the spoils of the freedom that have been achieved and attained through the barrel of a gun. That is why the Zimbabwean war veterans vow that they would rather take the arms and go back to the bush to fight rather than be ruled by a person who has never been in exile, like Morgan Tsvangirai of MDC-T. Most of the war veterans are old and physically frail; I don't think that they meant what they said. The point they were making is simple and straightforward: you will lead the country provided that you were with us in the bush fighting the war against the Western imperialists. If you were working in the mines and dating women as if there is no tomorrow while the sons of the soil were fighting in the bush, you can't lead the former freedom fighters if you were not a freedom fighter before, therefore continue dating women as you did before. I don't mean that men who were not part and parcel of the liberation struggle fighting in the bushes were necessarily chasing after women in the streets of Soweto and Harare. The fact is some men had an opportunity to join the liberation struggle, but after weighing the political cost price that they had to pay and losing the luxury of sleeping next to a woman on a daily basis, they found out that the political cost price of the armed struggle was too high when compared to the luxury of staying at home, sleeping next to a woman on a daily basis. The same is true even today. The majority of the youth, when they compared the cost that they have to pay for studying all night in comparison to pursuing the forbidden fruit, they opt for pleasure than education and knowledge. Nelson Mandela became the first black president of South Africa who was democratically elected after April 27, 1994. The national election of South Africa was held on April 27, 1994. South African black people who have never voted since time immemorial voted for the first time on April 27, 1994. On April 27, 1994, finally the apartheid of Hendrik Verwoerd was finally put to rest forever. Cyril Ramaphosa, the deputy president of the ANC, once said, "If all South Africans don't vote, we will regress. The Boers will come back to control us."[2] What is abundantly clear is that the deputy president of the ANC who is now the deputy president of South Africa knows very well the unforgiving shackle of apartheid. It's possible that the deputy president of the ANC does toss and turn in the middle of the night when he is thinking about living life under the apartheid rule. The fact is apartheid is gone, and it will never come back again in a thousand years, if I may use the expression of Ian Smith. However, there is another form of apartheid in South Africa—the apartheid of corruption. This form of apartheid is insidious and is spreading like octopus. The problem with corruption in South Africa is everybody is accusing everybody of being corrupt. The genuine question is, who is corrupt and who is not corrupt? If we were to follow the precepts and the definition of what corruption is to the latter we will soon discover that even the man of the white cloth is corrupt? I heard a Russian comedian saying that there is nothing wrong about being corrupt; there is corruption even in Russia. But the problem with corruption in South Africa is that the government officials who are at the forefront of committing corruption eat too much steak of meat alone without providing services to the people. The Russian government officials are corrupt, but at least they start by providing services to the people; thereafter they eat the remainder of the steak of meat alone. The people are happy because they got services, and the Russian government officials are happy because they ate from the public purse. The message of this comedian was simple and straightforward: if you are a government official, you must eat, but don't eat too much—provide the people with services. Then after all is said and done, you can now eat after the masses have eaten. The problem with Africa is this: the government officials are eating the whole slice of the pie, and the people are not getting anything at all. Nelson Mandela didn't spend a considerable amount of time in government. He is the founding father of peace and forgiveness. He taught South Africans not to retaliate but to forgive your enemies and stay with them. Archbishop Desmond Tutu is the founding father of Truth and Reconciliation Commission. He chaired the Truth and Reconciliation Commission, which was instituted by Pres. Nelson Mandela in 1995, and eventually it overlapped to 1996. The point is, at this point in South African history, there was no sufficient time that was dedicated to the fundamental issues of land. The main reason South Africa until today has not made significant strides in the issue of land is partly the lack of focus and attempt to achieve everything at once, which is also impossible. The late Nelson Mandela resigned in government, since he was old, and most of his life had been already spent in Robben Island, the Chikurubi Prison of South Africa. Robben Island was a theater of dreams where the political dreams of young politicians who were thinking of governing South Africa one day were dashed before their very eyes by the apartheid South African government. The leaders of African liberation movements were in prison, but the prison was not in them—that was a difference maker. Thabo Mbeki, the son of Govan Mbeki, who was also a former prisoner with Nelson Mandela in Robben Island, became the second South African president in 1999, succeeding Nelson Mandela. Pres. Thabo Mbeki was given a leeway by the ANC, since his father was a former prisoner in Robben Island. He is educated from the West and was groomed and mentored by the late president of the ANC, Oliver Tambo. Former president Thabo Mbeki, while in the United Kingdom, stayed at some point with the late Oliver Tambo's family. His master in economics came very handy, since he was the president of a country that has just been politically liberated from the shackles of apartheid and long oppression. There is no university that can prepare a political leader to run a country.

Education is important, but education alone can't help a political leader to run a country effectively and efficiently. Running a country is much more challenging than staying in class before a professor who is regurgitating something that he has never been put to practice. The point I am making is this: it's easy to acquire a degree in record time, but that does not necessarily mean that you can run a country effectively and efficiently. There are three things that former president Thabo Mbeki is famous for: he is revered as the man of principles, and he does everything according to a textbook. During his tenure, he established a corruption fighting unit called Scorpion. A friend of mine complained to me and said, "Out of all names, why name a corruption fighting unit Scorpion?" He said the Scorpion is cruel in its nature. The Scorpion was effective in fighting organized crime, but its main problem was busting black people who were in exile during the apartheid era and now working for the South African government. It was largely dominated by the former apartheid intelligent agents. The ANC members were forever crying foul, and in 2007, after Pres. Thabo Mbeki's defeat in Polokwane, the Scorpion was given a decent burial with an expensive casket. The second thing that former president Thabo Mbeki did was the establishment of BEE (Black Economic Empowerment). There are multiple derivates of BEE. BEE was a government program to empower black South Africans who were excluded from the mainstream economy by the apartheid government from the beginning. The government of former president Thabo Mbeki was going to uplift black South Africans by empowering them economically by ensuring that they were getting tenders from government projects to partake and participate in the economy of the country. The majority of people who benefited from BEE were former freedom fighters and former members of the South African liberation movements. There are other people who benefited who were not part and parcel of the liberation struggle. The second group of people who benefited significantly from the BEE was the black diamonds. These are South Africans who were studying very hard inside South Africa, and some even went to study abroad while the guerillas where fighting in the bush. The black diamonds have postgraduate degrees, and they can negotiate and break a serious deal that is worth multimillion rands. The black diamonds are the greatest travelers, and they can incorporate a company in the twinkling of an eye. Most of the black diamonds, just like the former freedom fighters, relocated from the townships to the suburbs, and they became neighbors to white folks. They left their fellow Africans languishing in poverty in the location. Both of these groups became known as tenderpreneurs. The reason they are called tenderpreneurs is that partly they do nothing besides waiting for *Tender Bulletin,* which is gazetted and published by the government, and that is how they survive, and they survive through government tenders. They eat from government programs, they feed themselves through government tenders, and they will do anything possible, including falsifying tax clearance certificate to get a tender that is worth millions of rands including eliminating people who stand in their way to their financial success. The third group of people is still continuing to benefit from the BEE. These are people who are akin to the educated black diamonds, but this group of people believes heavily on the power of prayer. They believe that if a famous pastor can lay a hand on them, they will get a tender worth multimillion rands. The ministers of the word are also involved in spreading the gospel of tenders. Instead of the minister of the word preaching the word of God, they preach the gospel of winning government contracts that are worth millions of rands. This is a dangerous spiritual trajectory. Former president Thabo Mbeki incorporated New Partnership for Africa's Development (NEPAD), and the general secretary of NEPAD was a wise black scholar by the name of Prof. Wiseman Nkuhlu. Former president Thabo Mbeki facilitated the cease-fire agreement between M23 and the government of Joseph Kabila of DRC (Democratic Republic of Congo). The DRC War, I termed it the never-ending war of mineral resources. When I came from Zimbabwe in July 2013, there were media reports that the war between the DRC government and the rebels M23 will soon resume. The DRC War is a never-ending war. The main problem with the DRC War is the myriad of internal and external players in it. The DRC War is the war of mineral resources, and the West loves this war. The more the DRC War continues to claim lives of innocent women and children, the more looting and plundering of mineral resources continues. The fact of the matters is this: some players of this war have been accustomed to the profits that go hand in hand with the shedding of blood. The day the DRC War will invariably come to an end, there are a lot of businesses that will have to close shop, since their survivals depends heavily on the continuation of the DRC War. Most political analysts saw former president Thabo Mbeki's role in the DRC conflict not as a mediator but as an associate of Joseph Kabila, the son of the late Laurent Kabila who was shot by his bodyguard on January 16, 2001.[3] Even if there is no plausible evidence to attest to some of the claims that were made about former president Thabo Mbeki, however there are some claims that were really absurd to the extreme. For example, in South Africa former president Thabo Mbeki was accused of not attending funerals of ordinary people, and he was extremely disengaged with the masses on the ground. His inability to sing and dance like Pres. Jacob Zuma was another contributing factor to such claims. There is one accusation that stands out in all accusations that has been leveled against former president Thabo Mbeki. It was the accusation about AIDS/HIV. There is a video clip that the South African media will frequently flash to our faces now and then. In this video clip, former president Thabo Mbeki said, "How can a virus cause a syndrome?" The other interpretation of this statement is this HIV does not cause AIDS, and hence he earned the name "AIDS denialist." The fact of the matter is former president Thabo Mbeki is not a medical doctor by profession, and there is no way he could have known whether HIV does cause AIDS or not. It's also imperative that I mention at this stage that the majority of medical discoveries normally originate from the West, since it is in the West where AIDS originated, not from Africa as many Western scholars suggest. Africans are honest people with a culture that is too rich to be questioned. African culture does not promote a man to sleep around just like the Western culture does. The fact that the African culture promotes polygamy that does not necessarily mean that the African culture promotes promiscuity. The fact that an African man has many wives, it does not mean therefore he will be sleeping with whomever except his wives. An African man in a polygamous marriage will forever have sexual relations within the confines of his polygamous marriage. The fact of the matter is there is no such thing as cheating in Africa because cheating is Western, not African. The reason I say an African man can't cheat and does not cheat is that if an African man sees a beautiful woman, normally he will propose without hesitation and marry the woman after all cultural practices have been fulfilled, including paying the dowry for the bride to the bride's parents. In the West you are not allowed to take more than one wife even if you can afford to have many wives. Pres. Robert Mugabe of Zimbabwe said something strange about homosexuals. He said he will allow gays to get married, and he will give them a period of a year to make a baby, and if they fail to make a baby, they will be arrested.[4] The point that Pres. Robert Mugabe was making is this: homosexuality is not African but Western. Since we have been taking the foreign aid from the West for a long period of time until now, it makes no logical sense to refuse the Western culture. Most African countries have accepted Western culture not because they really appreciate its values and ethos but purely on the basis of foreign aid that goes with it. Africans listen to Western music a lot compared to African music that is recorded and produced in Africa. When I was in Zimbabwe, Rihanna was also in Zimbabwe and eventually came to South Africa, and the tickets were sold out even before the show started. This is how a culture of nations can be stolen in broad daylight. Give them endless foreign aid then supply them with Western products and Western music, and eventually they will lose their identity and their sense of worth. Our rich African culture has been eroded by the pervasive Western culture that is widely spreading like a wildfire. The fact is all the shows today that we are watching in South Africa even when I was in Zimbabwe are predominantly produced in the West. Even the news that we are watching originated from the West. If we are not watching BBC, it's CNN, and the latest is Al Jazeera, which is from the Middle East. The West controls what we eat and what we drink, and the West controls what we read and what we don't read. The West supplies Africa with all sorts of drugs that are wiping the African youth away in a split second. Most of the African youth will not live longer if the speed and the velocity of the drugs supplied accelerate. I am not talking about ARVs; surely the supply of ARVs needs to be accelerated. But I am referring to the drugs that cut short the lives of the African youth on the prime of their lives. Drugs like cocaine and meth are widely supplied to Africa by the Western drug lords. When slave trade was abolished, the majority of the Western countries went to ICU because they were no longer going to enjoy the luxury of having a maid who was going to make tea and cook for them free of charge without paying a dime of a dollar. The Western agents invented human trafficking, and it is partly responsible for the widespread of women abuse and children that are above the age of ten years old. Human trafficking feeds itself through poverty-ridden countries and dysfunctional families. The velocity of human trafficking has overlapped the speed of rhino's horn and elephant's ivory poaching in Africa. The poaching game is not coming to an end now until Africa is an empty case. The fact of the matter is most African countries are now hollow underneath. The mineral resources have been extracted, and they have nothing practically tangible to show for these gaping holes that have been left behind by the Western companies. The brain drainage is the last on the list of the damages that have been caused by the West on the African soil. The Southern Times reports:

> *"Physician Emigration from Sub-Saharan African to the United States: Analysis of the 2011 AMA Physician Masterfile"—this study says 77 percent of Liberians are in the United States.*[5]

While the average Liberian patients are languishing in hospitals without doctors' care, Liberia's doctors that were supposed to look after Liberia's patients are looking after US patients, and this is a sad African story. Liberia is the US smallest town situated in Africa, just like Zimbabwe is smallest province of China situated in Africa. The capital city of Liberia is called Monrovia, named after the US president Joseph Munroe. Former president Thabo Mbeki's tenure came to an end in September 2008. He was the first state president in the democratic South Africa to be recalled by the ANC. Some people began to question the approach that was used by the ANC to recall the state president of South Africa. South African electoral system is different from the electoral system in the United States of America. In South Africa the electorates vote for the political party of their choice then the political party will appoint a candidate that will serve as a head of state on behalf of the political party that won elections. The electorate doesn't have a say on who is to head the state machinery, while in the United States of America political parties choose their preferred presidential candidates that will head the government should the political party in question win election. The difference is in US politics, the electorate chooses its own preferred candidate, while in South Africa you don't choose the candidate, but you choose a political party then the victorious political party chooses an individual of their choice to head the government. The problem with the South African system is this: what if the electorate doesn't like the person who has been chosen by the victorious political party to head the government? What if the person who is heading the government is not political savvy and lacks intellectual depth? The point is the electorate's role ends after casting the ballot paper on the ballot box; from henceforth the victorious political party decides on behalf of the electorate. It's important then to understand the power of the pen and the power of voting for a political party. It's also important to understand the political power that is entrusted to a political party by the electorate. South African electoral system is not going to change soon. The recalling of former president Thabo Mbeki in 2008 was very shattering, and truth be told, there are many people even today who are still in political ICU from that tragic event of 2008. The question that a lot of people asked themselves was, what did he do wrong? There were multiple responses that came from the ANC National Executive Committee (NEC). Some said it was political management, and some said the recalling of the state president was to unify the polarized ANC. There were two poles that emerged after the Polokwane policy conference in December 2007. These two poles were also called two centers of powers. The two centers of powers were invariably unavoidable, since the incumbent state president lost in a party presidential race to a candidate who was not the president of the country. Let me simplify it for you: Pres. Thabo Mbeki the president of South Africa, and the president of the ANC at that point lost the ANC presidential elections. It meant therefore that the South African president was no longer the president of the ruling party. This political defeat created a leadership vacuum in the government of South Africa and also created a vacuum in the ANC. It meant that Luthuli House could not implement its economic policies in government, since the state president was no longer the president of the ANC. I need to make this point clear: I am not discussing the politics of the ANC and the political decision of the ANC.Whether the recalling of the former president of South Africa Thabo Mbeki was part of the ANC political management or not, that is not my baby to nurse. The main reason I need to lay concrete political foundation is that I will not able to strike the balance between the current economic sanctions that are in place in Zimbabwe if I don't lay a concrete political foundation about the political storms that were prevailing in the South African politics at that time. It's sheer madness to the extreme to separate Zimbabwean politics from the South African politics even though South Africa is not Zimbabwe, but there are almost anecdotal five million Zimbabweans that are currently living and working in South Africa without legal documents. Therefore Zimbabwean political crisis and economic crisis directly and indirectly affect South Africa whether South Africans like it or not. Former president Thabo Mbeki is still the loyal member of the ANC, and even after he was recalled in September 2008, he remained the loyal member of the ANC, and he never uttered a word that sought to sow division and put the ANC in disrepute. Former president Thabo Mbeki is a scholar of a rare reputable character. His humility and respect of the principles and values of the ANC speak volume of his behavior. The point I am driving home is this: there are many accusations that were leveled against former president Thabo Mbeki that were very debasing and degrading. It's also worth mentioning that the tripartite alliance marriage was on the rocky ground during Pres. Thabo Mbeki's tenure as the president of South Africa. The tripartite alliance is made up of the ANC, COSATU, and the SACP. The writer of the book *Eight Days in September*, the former director general in the presidency of Frank Chikane, likened former president Thabo Mbeki's recalling by the ANC to a coup d'état.[6] It's imperative to understand that until this point, there was no strong political will and political attention that was directed toward the issue of land and the nationalization of mines in South Africa. Even Pres. Robert Mugabe of Zimbabwe was running around the whole of Zimbabwe seizing the land from the white commercial farmers. South Africans were not even close to start talking about the expropriation of land without compensation and the nationalization of mines. When the late colonel Muammar Gaddafi of Libya came to Zimbabwe, he said, "White farmers need to leave Zimbabwe." These are some of the statements that infuriated the West about Maummar Gaddafi and cost him his life and his political career. Libya is currently up in smokes; there are currently multiple insurgent groups in Libya. The current prime minister of Libya was recently abducted and released afterward by these insurgent groups. There are four main things that former president Thabo Mbeki established: Scorpion, NEPAD, peace agreement in DRC, and BEE. The list is not exhaustive, but surely the ones that have been mentioned above top the list. He was also instrumental in ensuring that South Africa hosts a spectacular 2010 FIFA World Cup event. He was instrumental in the 2010 FIFA World Cup because his decision to resign from the government without using any legal avenue to delay his departure expedited the program of the South African government to host the FIFA World Cup with ease. Kgalema Petrus Motlanthe was selected as deputy president of the ANC in Polokwane conference of 2007, and the general secretary of the ANC was Gwede Mantashe, who is still the general secretary of the ANC, and Pres. Jacob Zuma became the ANC president, and he still remains the president of the ANC after his reelection at Mangaung conference 2013 until the writing of this book. Kgalema Petrus Motlanthe was quickly rushed into parliament and sworn in as member of the parliament and became the acting president of the Republic of South Africa. Kgalema Petrus Motlanthe was the acting president of South Africa for a period of nine months. It's possible that during this period he aspired to be the full-fledged president of South Africa someday in his life. It will be disingenuous to say that he never envisaged himself holding the respectable position in the South African political arena one day. There is one thing that the former acting president Kgalema Petrus Motlanthe did that has worked against his leadership aspirations to become the full-fledged president of the ANC and the president of South Africa while he was in office. He used to invite the former president Thabo Mbeki to many government functions. To many ANC supporters, it was very shocking, since they dealt with former president Thabo Mbeki during Polokwane policy conference period. Former president Thabo Mbeki started attending government functions via the acting president Kgalema Petrus Motlanthe. In 2009 South Africa went to the polls, and the ANC won the national election free and fair, and the national election was entirely peaceful. Pres. Jacob Zuma became the president of South Africa, and former acting president Kgalema Petrus Motlanthe became the deputy president of the South Africa. Migrating from being the acting president of South Africa to being the deputy president of South Africa quite frankly sounds like a demotion to me. South African politics had changed dramatically, and the politics of the sub-Saharan region had also changed drastically. Pres. Robert Mugabe was now sick now and then, and he was frequently in Dubai for his medical checkups. When Pres. Robert Mugabe is sick, he does not go to a Zimbabwe's hospital, but he is air-transported to Dubai to see his cardiologist; sometimes he goes to Malaysia. The late president of DRC, Mobutu Sese Seko, it is said, used to drink water from France while he was staying in DRC. His son was attending school in France on a daily basis while staying in DRC. Pres. Mobutu Sese Seko legalized kleptomania while he was president of DRC. In June 2013, Dali Tambo, the son of Oliver Tambo, the late president of the ANC, interviewed Grace Mugabe in a program called *People of the South* about the relationship between Gideon Gono and her. She vehemently denied the existence of relationship, and she went on to say that even Robert Mugabe believed her.[7] Grace Mugabe told the supporter of ZANU-PF in Marondera that Morgan Tsvangirai courted one hundred women before he settled with his current wife, Elizabeth Macheka[8]. While the ANC was involved in their own political battles, the ANC Youth League had its own policy conference in Free State, and the new president of the ANC Youth League that was elected was Julius Malema. The ANC Youth League president shot to fame with a speed of lightning. The print media of South Africa was waiting with bated breath to hear the president of ANC Youth League, Julius Malema, open his mouth. I should mention the fact that all this time in South Africa, there was no discussion about the nationalization of mines and the expropriation of land without compensation. The reason there was no sufficient political will and sufficient national attention directed toward these two crucial issues is partly what a lot of people saw in Zimbabwe. The farm invasion of 2000 in Zimbabwe sent South Africans and the

South African government to a panic mood. You will often hear people on the streets saying, "If we take the farms, the people will die with hunger just like they died in Zimbabwe. It's better to leave the farms in the hands of South Africans who are of European descent than to take them." The land crisis has been dragging for quite some time in South Africa, and postponing it will not help any longer. My younger brother had an excruciating pain in his tooth, and I took him to a dentist, and the tooth was quickly removed without any hassle. South Africa had an excruciating pain on its teeth, and the pain had been avoided for quite a long period of time. The arrival of the ANC Youth League president Julius Malema woke many people from their political slumbering that was prevailing in South African politics. The print media and the newsrooms came alive, and the annual turnover for many print media companies shot up astronomically. South Africans comedians could easily crack a lousy joke using Julius Malema's punch lines. It became easy to switch on the television again. The ANCYL president Julius Malema brought the ANC and the ANC Youth League to life again. There are many awards that Julius Malema won while he was the president of the ANC Youth League, and there are many books that have been written about Julius Malema. He was the big thing in South African political circles and the hottest property in the political market. Credit must be given where credit is due. The president of the ANCYL Julius Malema was the microcosm of the "young lion" that Oliver Tambo talked about. The expelled ANC Youth League president Julius Malema was not really the young lion but a wild young lion. There is a difference between a calm young lion and a wild young lion. A wild young lion is deadly and can cause serious harm at its early age, and it needs to be tamed as soon as possible. The ANC had a serious problem, and the ANC problem was the ANCYL. The problem of the ANC was the young lions that it has given birth to. It became apparently clear that the ANC had given birth to a seriously dangerous wild young lion. We are told that the ANC does not devour its own children because the ANC is an elephant, and the elephant protects its own calves. There were two options that were on the table of the ANC, and the first option was to allow this young wild lion it has given birth to, to grow, and the ANC risks being devoured itself by the young lion as the mother body, or the ANC devours this uncontrollable, unbridled wild young lion and save itself and the tripartite alliance, which consists of COSATU, SACP, and the ANC. Even if there is no tangible and hard evidence that suggests that there was ever such a debate about the ANCYL, the people of South Africa asked themselves this question: Is the ANC afraid of the ANCYL? The general secretary of the ANC, Gwede Mantashe, was asked, "Is the ANC afraid of the ANCYL?" He said the ANC is like a sea that cleans itself over time. Whether the ANC is the sea that cleanses itself over time or an elephant that is very slow but acts decisively when it moves, the fact is the ANC was further incurring financial debts through legal costs because of the ANCYL. If it wasn't "Dubula Ibhunu" (shoot the Boer), it was an expropriation of land without compensation coupled with nationalization of mines. The government of South Africa and the ANC general secretary made it clear over a number of occasions that nationalization of mines and expropriation of land without compensation was not an ANC policy and South African government policy. The ANC Youth League wanted nationalization of mines and the expropriation of land without compensation to be an ANC policy and a South African government policy. The question was asked by a lecturer in one of my accounting lectures, How do you eat an elephant?—and the answer was one butt at a time. The question that the ANC had to answer was, How do you eat a wild young lion?—and the answer was one butt at a time. There are many ways to kill a cat, but the problem with a cat is that it has nine lives. A wild young lion does not have nine lives like a cat. The ANC political oven was turned 360 degrees when the expelled ANC Youth League president visited Zimbabwe on April 3, 2010.[9] Zimbabwe was under the care of the South African government. It is the South African government that made it possible for Zimbabwe to have a coalition government and put to an end to political violence that was destroying the country and its economic reputation. There is no prudent investor that can inject a considerable amount of financial resources in a country that is teetering in the brink of political collapse. Political instability stifles economic opportunities, and that is the main cause of disinvestment and economic sanctions. Any country will never rise above its political profile and economic profile. This is also true about Zimbabwe because it became a very dangerous country where investors could not entertain a notion of investing in it. The Zimbabwean economic policy made it impossible for any foreign investors to invest in its economy. There are many people that have been killed by the HIV/AIDS in Zimbabwe compared to the number of the people that have been killed by the West in Iraq or in Afghanistan. Even the number of US citizens that were killed by the late Osama Bin Laden on 9/11 can never match the number of people that have been killed by HIV/AIDS in Zimbabwe. Richard Brown and Christopher Saunders both record in the book called *Africa South of the Sahara 2005* that six thousand people were dying each and every week in Zimbabwe. This number emerged from the UN Human Development Index.[10] The population of Zimbabwe had dropped drastically. If South Africa, through the government of the ANC, had not intervened Zimbabwe, Zimbabwe was going to be Somali of the sub-Saharan Africa. Former president Thabo Mbeki, through his intervention, had stabilized Zimbabwe politically, even if he was removed from the presidency haphazardly by the ANC in September 2008. Zimbabwe managed to dollarize its currency in 2009 after the formation of the coalition government or the Government of National Unity. I was told when I was in Zimbabwe in my first visit that even if you were to rob a bank, you still would not afford to buy one egg. The currency of Zimbabwe had depreciated to the point that ordinary people decided to immigrate to South Africa and some to Botswana. My driver Joseph who was driving me around Bulawayo in my second visit to Zimbabwe said to me, before he became a driver, he was working in a factory, and he will go to work early in the morning. When he knocks off from work, the transport fair would have increased astronomically. Zimbabwe's national inflation is still very high; it needs to be reduced to an acceptable level. This is the country where the ANCYL was going to learn how to nationalize the mines and expropriate land without compensation. During the ANCYL visit to Zimbabwe, the ANCYL described the then Prime Minister Morgan Tsvangirai as a Western imperialist and a Western puppet.[11] The ANC Youth League intensified its political stance toward nationalization of mines and expropriation of land without compensation greatly after the ANCYL members visited Zimbabwe. The national debate about expropriation of land without compensation and nationalization of mines was upon us all in South Africa. Ordinary people were asking themselves many questions that could not be answered. How can the government of South Africa nationalize the mines and expropriate land without compensation effectively and efficiently without any bloodshed if the South African government can't deliver textbooks in time in Limpopo Province and in Eastern Cape Province? Who can then run these mines, since the state lacks the capacity and the know-how to run the mines? These were part of many questions that average people were asking themselves. The ANC had to act, and the time to postpone the nationalization of mines and expropriation of land without compensation issue was over. The fact of the matter is this: South Africans were divided in between about these two issues. The majority of the youth were for the nationalization of mines and expropriation of land without compensation. The main problem about this notion of nationalization of mines and expropriation of land without compensation was the following: it was contained in the ANC freedom charter, which is the ANC document. The ANC Youth League was merely exploiting the ANC using the ANC freedom charter. The freedom charter stated unequivocally, the people shall govern! The freedom charter advocates for the nationalization of mines and the expropriation of land without compensation.

> Under the subtitle *"The People Shall Share in the Country's Wealth!"*
>
> *The national wealth of our country, the heritage of South Africans, shall be restored to the people;*
>
> *The minerals wealth beneath the soil, the banks and monopoly industry shall be transferred to the ownership of the people as a whole;*
>
> *All other industry and trade shall be controlled to assist the well-being of the people;*
>
> *All the people shall have equal rights to trade where they choose, to manufacturer and to enter all trades, crafts, and professions.*
>
> *The land shall be shared among those who work it!*
>
> *Restrictions of land ownership on a racial basis shall be ended, and all the land redivided among those who work on it to banish famine and land hunger;*
>
> *The state shall help the peasants with implements, seed, tractors, and dams to save the soil and assist the tillers;*
>
> *Freedom of movements shall be guaranteed to all who work on the land;*
>
> *All shall have right to occupy land wherever they choose;*

> *People shall not be robbed of their cattle, and forced labor and farm prisons shall be abolished.*[12]

The freedom charter was officially adopted on June 26, 1955, in Kliptown. The ANC Youth League under the expelled president Julius Malema advocated strongly for the notion of nationalization of mines and expropriation of land without compensation and placed heavy reliance on the freedom charter as the document of the ANC. The ANCYL visit to Venezuela in April 2010 further bolstered its stance on the issue of nationalization of mines and expropriation of land without compensation. It's imperative to understand history as Koenderman writes:

It may be true that those who ignore the lessons of history are condemned to repeat them, but the trouble is that history is subjected to such a variety of interpretations that is impossible to determine precisely which is the correct lesson to be learned.[13]

We must read history, and we must understand history from the South African perspective. We South Africans need to differentiate the current political era we live in and the political era of the writing of the freedom charter. The fact of the matter is this: most people who contributed into the writing of the freedom charter are gone. The political climate that was prevailing in South Africa at that time and the current political climate that is prevailing in South Africa under the ANC government vary invariably. The point is since the writing of the freedom charter in 1955 until today in 2013, there is a fifty-eight-year gap in between, and a lot has happened. People who wrote the freedom charter were from a different political era, and the majority of them were the victims of apartheid. It's possible that their political views were clouded by the oppression of the government of the day. It's also possible that their political views were influenced and induced by the oppression and suppression that the apartheid government was dispensing at that time. It means therefore that we, the youth of South Africa, need to read the freedom charter with an understanding of the political era under which the freedom charter was written. We need to understand that some of the assertions contained in the freedom charter are inapplicable in the current democratic dispensation, since the government of the day is the government of the ANC, which was elected democratically by the people of South Africa. The freedom charter was written in order to fight the enemy, and the enemy is gone. Then why do we South Africans use the same political tool to destroy ourselves? There is no longer a need to carry a dompas when you travel today in South Africa. It therefore remains crucial then to look at South Africa through democratic lens not through the lens of the freedom charter. It does not therefore necessarily mean that everything that is contained in the freedom charter can be implemented today in the current political dispensation we live in. It's important to look at a political matter with a helicopter view and extricate the truth from facts. The truth does not change, but facts change with time, and the truth shall set us free as Jesus said. Many people say political facts die but the political truth remains. Political facts consist of emotions, resentment, anger, and insanity; while political truth consists of long-sightedness, sanity, and proactive thinking. Since the ANCYL had developed its own document, the ANC had nothing on the table to defend and deter the ANCYL to give it what it wanted, which was the nationalization of mines and expropriation of land without compensation, eventually kicking and driving the entire South Africans of European descent to the sea. Even if the ANCYL never mentioned it publicly, the notion of driving South Africans of European descent to the sea, one can suspect that such notion was existing somewhere and somehow in the minds of the ANCYL members. The ANC quickly scrambled for world-class researches, and these researches were going to visit different countries and assess the success and the failure of nationalization of mines. The researchers incorporated their report and submitted it to the national office of the ANC in Johannesburg known as Luthuli House. What was made public is this: the report suggested multiple ways of nationalization of mines. The ANC Youth League knew for sure that the ZANU-PF approach will not win them any political points in the South African politics and invented a new modus operandi of making their political points. They began to disrespect the mother body, which is the ANC, and the alliance partners of the ANC, COSATU and SACP. The ANC Youth League began to publicly lambast government ministers who did not support the ANC Youth League policy. It became public knowledge through the ANC Youth League that some government ministers were drinking red wine excessively and some government ministers were only good in buying flowers for their girlfriends only. The skeletons of government ministers were tumbling out of the closet, and the person responsible for opening the closets was the ANCYL. It became apparently clear that the elephant had been very slow, and the time for the elephant to move was at hand. The problem with the elephant when it moves is the carnage that it leaves behind, and the ANC is that elephant. The wild young lion was even unbridled and wilder than ever before, and it had gained some muscle. The ANC Youth League had to be dismantled and decimated in broad daylight while the whole of South Africa was watching; the elephant had to dismantle, decimate, and eventually devour its child. The wild young lion was eaten alive. The sea was cleansing itself again and again.

THE CLOSING OF THE EYES

There is nothing so powerful like being alive within an era of writing history or when history unravels before your very eyes. It's Thursday evening in South Africa, and the state president of South Africa, Mr. Jacob Zuma, who is the president of the ANC, delivered bad news to the nation of South Africa and the nations of the world that the former president of South Africa, Nelson Rolihlahla Mandela, had passed on at around 8:50 p.m. in his Houghton home in Sandton, and he passed on in the midst of his family. The news of the passing of former president Nelson Rolihlahla Mandela began to spread around the globe. Each and every news media was scrambling to tell their side of the story about the former president Nelson Mandela. The biggest news network in the world had to change their normal programs and dedicate their daily programs just to cover this historic moment in the history of South Africa and in the history of the world. When I left South Africa for my Zimbabwean first trip, former president Nelson Mandela was in a hospital in Pretoria, and he celebrated his ninety-fifth birthday in a hospital in Pretoria. The statement then that was coming from South African government was "former president Nelson Mandela is in a critical condition yet stable." There are no perfect or lofty and poetic words to describe the emotional roller coaster ride that the majority of South Africans were going through that day. The whole world was mourning, and the continent of Africa had lost its father, and the whole world had lost a great hero and the father of peace and democracy. All print media and some international news networks hijacked the moment as if former president Nelson Mandela was a British icon or United States icon. The fact of the matter is former president Nelson Mandela was a South African child and groomed and natured by the ANC and eventually given to the nations of the world. Whichever news media I turned my TV to; it was paying its tribute to former president Nelson Mandela. CNN reported that the British flag was going to be lowered half-mast in honoring the world icon, former president Nelson Mandela. The South African president Jacob Zuma announced that "former president

Nelson Mandela is now resting and he is now at peace. The nation has lost a father." As the nations of the world mourned for the passing of former president Nelson Mandela and his political legacy that he has left behind, it's important to understand that he left behind the united South Africa that was once divided and broken apart by apartheid. It's important to understand that the current Syrian crisis and the endless suffering of women and children in the Central African Republic is the product of human ingenuity. Human beings have created chaos and endless suffering on earth. The world is no longer a better place because of human-made catastrophe. Archbishop Emeritus Desmond Tutu of the Anglican Church in Cape Town, in the prayer meeting that was held on December 5, 2013, the day of the passing of former president Nelson Mandela, said something that was very profound and striking to the core to the congregation that had gathered in Cape Town. He said, "Jesus said to his disciples, this is my command—love one another as I have loved you." He prayed and thanked God for this wonderful gift that has been given by heavens to the world, which was the former president Nelson Mandela. Former president Nelson Mandela not only taught South Africans to forgive and forget about the pains of past that have been inflicted on the South African people by the apartheid government but also taught the whole world that it's possible to forgive your worst enemy and live with your worst enemy in peace even if your worst enemy has stolen your land and your mines. The idea of forgiving and forgetting what your worst enemy has done to you, even if you're worst enemy has stolen your land and your mines, is the bitter pill for Pres. Robert Mugabe and the war veterans to swallow. The failure to forgive and to forget has been proven over and over again that it is the victim that usually suffers more than the perpetrator. The enormous amount of pain that have been inflicted in the souls and spirits of South Africans by the apartheid government is more frequent than not understated and underrated properly. South Africa needed a political leader that was going to unite both whites and blacks and further propel the nation forward in the spirit of caring and building the prosperous, nonsexist, and democratic free South Africa. Former president Nelson Mandela managed to save South Africa from that sinking ship called apartheid. It's also true that the current poverty that the majority of South Africans find themselves in is a direct result of apartheid. Hendrik Verwoerd's government treated black South Africans as aliens in the land of our forefathers. Patricia De Lille of Democratic Alliance and the mayor of Cape Town made a profound statement, and she said former president Nelson Mandela would come in the Kempton Park where the CODESA talks were held, and he would say, "Both parties need to find the common ground because these talks are for building the nations." Patricia De Lille made it clear that she was also very angry because of what apartheid has done to black South Africans, yet in the former president Nelson Mandela, she saw a man who arose above the resentment, anger, and hatred that have been inflicted by apartheid in the spirits and souls of many South Africans. The Zimbabweans have not risen above hatred, bitterness, and resentments that have been inflicted by the Ian Smith regime. The main reason why most Zimbabweans are still bitter is, because, Zimbabweans never went through the truth and reconciliation period of their own. The fact of the matter is this: Pres. Robert Mugabe as leader of Zimbabwe's people should have learned from former president Nelson Mandela to forgive and forget about the enormous amount of pain that have been inflicted on innocent people by the Ian Smith regime and Great Britain. The opportunity that the people of Zimbabwe afforded Pres. Robert Mugabe in 1980 when he was elected as the first black prime minister of the country should have been used effectively and efficiently to heal the wounds of the past and unite the nation of Zimbabwe like never before. Instead of uniting the nation and healing the wounds of the past, Gukurahundi was unleashed to the people of Matabeleland. Gukurahundi pushed the Zimbabwean masses further into the shell and cocoon of pain and misery. The already fragmented souls of people were further silenced by the death of many innocent people in Matabeleland. The ANC needed Nelson Mandela more than ever before. The 2014 national election would have been totally different had former president Nelson Mandela not died. Perhaps the death of former president Nelson Mandela will teach the whole world to look at the world with a different view. The endless killing of innocent people in Syria, Central African Republic, and DRC is the human ingenuity. It's possible to make the world a better place. When Archbishop Desmond Tutu was addressing the congregation that had gathered in Cape Town to pray in the memorial service of former president Nelson Mandela, he related a story of how he got the news of the passing of former president Nelson Mandela. He said that he was called by the assistant of former president Nelson Mandela under the instruction of Graca Machel, the former wife of the late president Samora Machel of Mozambique, that former president Nelson Mandela was nearing his end. Many people suggested that you can't mention former president Nelson Mandela's name and Pres. Robert Mugabe's name in the same line, since these two different individuals epitomize different things. Pres. Robert Mugabe presumably embodied the spirit of resentment and revenge, while former president Nelson Mandela embodied the spirit of democracy and freedom. It should be said that Pres. Robert Mugabe of Zimbabwe is currently eighty-nine years old and physically frail. The age difference between Pres. Robert Mugabe and the late former president of South Africa, Nelson Mandela, is six years. The late president of South Africa, Nelson Mandela, resigned from government at the age of eighty-one, while Pres. Robert Mugabe of Zimbabwe is eighty-nine years old and still in office. Pres. Robert of Mugabe of Zimbabwe will eventually give in to his medical problems and body ailment, but he sees resigning from government as a victory for MDC-T. Dali Tambo, the son of the late president of the ANC, Oliver Tambo, when he interviewed Pres. Robert Mugabe of Zimbabwe in June 2013, Pres. Robert Mugabe looked frail and fragile compared to the president Robert Mugabe that many people know. As people of the world and the leaders of the world came to South Africa to join South Africans to lay to rest the wonderful gift from the heavens, if there is one thing that we must all remember is the love that we need to have for one another. If we love one another, there is no nation that can send drones to strike another nation. If we love one another, we can't support the insurgent groups to continue to cause violence and rape innocent women and young girls. If we love one another, we won't steal gold and diamonds from one another, but we will support one another and we will make the world a better place. As people of the world closed their eyes and prayed for South Africa, we must also remember that former president Nelson Mandela was a disciplined person who never used unbecoming ways to make political points. Above all that, former president Nelson Mandela loved—he loved children, and this notion of loving children and loving people was also echoed by Patricia De Lille of Democratic Alliance, the mayor of Cape Town, that former president Nelson Mandela contributed R150,000 from his salary to start the Nelson Mandela Foundation, which is currently estimated to have an amount to the tune of R2 billion. I have said in the past that it's political events that define political party and it's a political party that defines a political leader. The apartheid system and the apartheid government defined the ANC, and the ANC defined Nelson Mandela. A political party can groom a political leader to be a leader just like former president Nelson Mandela, or a political party can also crush a leader. The point I am driving home is this: the onus of raising a principled and disciplined political leader lies on the shoulders of a political party. As the whole world was mourning and remembering the passing of former president Nelson Mandela, one counts himself among the fortunate people alive on earth to find himself born and bred in this country, South Africa, that is very rich not only in mineral resources but also in history and world icons. It's soothing to the souls and healing to the bones to find myself in the midst of this wonderful history that is unraveling before my very eyes. The greatest challenge that will lie on the shoulders of the Twitter and Face book generation is to preserve and protect the freedom that our forefathers and our political leaders fought hard to attain. I have said it many times that perhaps the main reason most African leaders would not want to vacate their political office as soon as possible is that partly when they look around in the current pool of African leaders, they can't find young African leaders with high morals and reputable character. The same notion is being shared by many political commentators of the world. Since former president of South Africa Nelson Mandela is gone, then who will lead South Africa to the political Promised Land? This question does not necessarily mean that South Africa does not have a sitting president right now. The point is, can South Africa and ANC ever produce again a political leader of the likes of former president Nelson Mandela who will be disciplined and principled to the point of spending twenty-seven years in prison for the love of his people? The best people who can answer this question are our political leaders in the continent of Africa. It's also important to mention that former president Nelson Mandela did not seek personal glory or self-enrichment in everything that he did, but rather he fought for the just cause for all people. His greatest wish was to see both black people and white people living together in harmony. He did not subscribe to the theory of driving white people to the sea or expropriation of land without compensation. He understood that white people of South Africa cannot live alone and triumph economically in the absence of black people, and black people cannot live alone and triumph economically in the absence of white people. Black people need white, and white people need black people, period. The rainbow nation where people will respect the culture of one another and the religion of one another requires both black people of South Africa and white people of South Africa to continue to join hands and work together in order to build the prosperous, nonsexist, and nonracial South Africa where all persons live together in harmony. As we closed our eyes and prayed, many questions were asked as to who will lead South Africans forward in this never-ending journey of discovering ourselves as nation and country of peace and political tranquility. South Africa had two heroes: one is former president Nelson Mandela, and the second one is Archbishop Desmond Tutu. As Archbishop Desmond Tutu continues to lead South Africa in this period of great loss, it's also imperative to remember that to be a leader of people; one does not need necessarily to be a leader with a political office. A political leader can lead even if that leader is no longer in office. Leaders teach and train and therefore pass on. The illusion that a leader must stay in office forever until he falls from his office chair is madness to the extreme. Any leader who will attempt to rule his country forever and stay in power because of the fear of what might happen should he vacate his leadership position has failed decimally in an attempt to transfer his leadership skills to the future generation. Leaders come and go, and leaders are born each and every day. As we closed our eyes and prayed, and as we continued to mourn for what has befallen us, we had to remember that South Africa is a country that is looking after many nationalities of the world. These nationalities of the world continue to look at South African leadership in the midst of their political crisis and economic crisis. The Zimbabweans that are living in South Africa continue to rely on the South African government for their economic survival and political direction for their country. The Congolese that are living in South Africa continue to look to the South African government for their economic survival and political direction in the DRC. It's sheer madness then that since former president Nelson Mandela has passed on, then South Africa will drift into flames fire and chaos. South Africa is not Zimbabwe, and South Africa is not DRC or Central African Republic. The reason former president Nelson Mandela resigned after spending almost five years in government is he had trained and taught sufficiently enough his successor, former president Thabo Mbeki, how to run and lead a country. The leadership role and leadership influence that have been exemplified by former president Thabo Mbeki through solving the variety of African conflicts can be easily attributed to the leadership style and values of former president Nelson Mandela. It's also true that former president Nelson Mandela was what he was merely because of the ANC. The ANC made former president Nelson Mandela, not the other way around. Former president Nelson Mandela did not make the ANC, but the ANC made him. My point is this: since former president Nelson Mandela is gone, it does not necessarily mean that the ANC is also gone. The ANC remains, therefore the potter is still intact even if the pot has fallen; but the potter still remains, and that potter is the ANC. It's important to get accustomed to a leader, but we need to also bear in mind that leaders come and go, for what is born by woman surely must die one day. The main problem with many people is this: many people want to be led while they fold their arms and point to the mistakes of their leader. Many people are afraid to take an initiative of leading a church and leading a country. The majority of people on this planet are followers, and they never even dare to lead because they are afraid of criticism and negativity. That is why perhaps when the likes of former president Nelson Mandela pass on, they cry as if there is no tomorrow. Archbishop Desmond Tutu said, "The sun will rise tomorrow and even the next day." It's a fact that the sun will rise again in South Africa tomorrow and even the next day. The world has not come to an end, and life will continue as usual after the burial of former president Nelson Mandela. South Africans knew that the day will come where former president Nelson Mandela will have to depart from us, but the majority of South Africans could not fathom to live their lives without the presence of former president Nelson Mandela even if they knew well that former president Nelson Mandela was old. It's also imperative to mention the fact that former president Nelson Mandela lived long enough to see the finals of the World Cup in 2010 that was organized and hosted by South Africa. It's important also to mention the fact that former president Nelson Mandela was very instrumental in ensuring that South Africa emerge as a winner in Zurich to host the World Cup 2010. When the motorcade carrying former president Nelson Mandela and Graca Machel entered the FNB Stadium in Soweto, the football commentators said that the World Cup was now sealed, since the former president Nelson Mandela was driven around the pitch, waving his hands on the football spectators that had filled the stadium to capacity in Soweto on July 9, 2010. The match between Spain and Holland ended with Spain winning the World Cup, beating Holland with a goal to nil. It will be sheer madness to assume that life has come to a standstill just because former president Nelson Mandela had passed on. It will also make logical sense to continue to promote and advocate for legacy of former president Nelson Mandela and make each and every day a Mandela day. It's also true that South Africans need to accept the fact that life should continue after the burial of former president Nelson Mandela. Former president Nelson Mandela writes in his book *Long Walk to Freedom*:

> *Education is the great engine of personal development. It is through education that the daughter of a peasant can become a doctor, that the son of a mine worker can become the head of the mine, that the child of a farmworker can become the president*

of a great nation. It is what we make out of what we have, not what we are given, that separates one person from another.[14]

There is inescapable reality about former president Nelson Mandela: he was a greatest advocate of lifelong learning. He believed that education can open the eyes of a nation.

He continued and said the following about Bantu education:

The discussions were fierce, and both sides had forceful advocates. The argument for an indefinite boycott was that Bantu education was a poison one could not drink even at the point of death from thirst.[15]

I have heard a lot of black people who became successful through Bantu education, saying that Bantu was even better than the current educational system that the South African government is providing to South Africans. If Bantu education was poisonous, one could not drink even at the point of death from thirst. No wonder a lot of black people remained untrained and uneducated until this day and age even if there are greatest proponents of Bantu education and people who are the greatest critics of Bantu education. People who completed their grade twelve through the Bantu education system simply support the Bantu education merely on the basis that they succeeded in completing their high school education under the Bantu education. But people who could not complete their grade twelve under Bantu education system clearly hold a different view about the system. This is not surprising given the fact that in each system in any country, there will be people who will oppose it and there are people who will be in favor of it. There are Zimbabweans who continue to see Pres. Robert Mugabe as their hero who went to jail for them for almost eleven years, and there are Zimbabweans who see Pres. Robert Mugabe as a dictator. I have often wondered why the same groups of people who live in the same country, governed by the same rules and regulations, hold different political views completely about the same political issue. The same is true even in South Africa today. There are people who believe that living life under the apartheid government was better compared to living life under a democratically elected government. Most of these people who support this notion that says living life under apartheid government was better compared to living life under the democratically elected government are those who are not educated and had stable jobs under the apartheid government without proper qualifications. In the apartheid system, the importance of education was not that much required as it is now in this democratic dispensation. The same is true about farm invasion in Zimbabwe; people who benefited from the farm invasion of 2000 saw the illegal occupation of the farms as an appropriate move by the War veterans. The peasants, who were working in the farms, staying with their white bosses in the farms, could not agree with same idea of taking the farms from white commercial farmers, since it meant that they will lose their jobs if the commercial farms were taken from the white commercial farmers.

CHAPTER 5

THE LAND CRISIS

The lifetime error that has been committed by the ANC Youth League was to use ZANU-PF style in order to address the fundamental issues of land and nationalization of mines in South Africa. From the hindsight, the ANC Youth League had put forward a compelling argument. The main problem with these key political issues that the ANC Youth League had raised is this: they required urgent national attention, and the ANC Youth League was not prepared to lose these two key national issues that had a potential to alter South African political and economic profile altogether in a global stage. South Africa is not an island that can function on its own without taking into consideration what is happening in the global market. Simply put, each and every country all over the world should, as a matter of must, in taking national decisions and developing economic targets, take into consideration what is happening in this global village—meaning, there is no country that can function independently, though a country might have its own constitution and credible legal framework; but when it comes to trade, it's a different ball game altogether. The other reason there is no country that can function as an island is the multilateral agreements and bilateral agreements. These bilateral agreements and multilateral agreements join all countries of the world together. Just like a baby is joined to her mother through an umbilical cord, all countries of the world are also joined to each other through this umbilical cord of multilateral agreements. South Africa's national economic decisions could affect directly or indirectly somebody who is in Europe and China. It therefore compels South Africa to ponder the imponderable and predict the unpredictable in its national economic decision process. It's also imperative to comprehend the complexity of running a mixed economy just like the South African economy, which consists of state-owned entities and private-owned entities. The crux of the matter is this: most of the private-owned entities are foreign controlled while stationed and located in South Africa. Private-owned entities are the conduit pipe for the West to continue to siphon Africa's wealth to the West. The other problem with these private-owned entities that are foreign controlled is this: they were established during the colonial era, and when most African countries gained their political liberation and political independence, these foreign-controlled entities had already deepened their economic roots in African soil and had employed considerable number of Africans. Most African leaders, even the leaders of African liberation movements, had a growing headache because they had fought hard for political liberation, but they quickly realized that the war was not far from over, and in actual fact, they lost the war against the West. The West had always beaten Africa in all these games of politics and economics. The ANC Youth League was full of young people who had never run and headed complex economic system. Most of them were not even members of parliament, yet they wanted the South African government to change its economic system in the twinkling of an eye. The ANC Youth League were very close to the youth of South Africa, which is made up of people who are young and unemployed who are between the age of twenty-two and thirty-six years old. The ANC Youth League in a way was the voice of the voiceless and the advocate of the poor. It's also true that most of the African liberation movements, after they have attained political power and political independence, began to slumber economically as if all was well. There is a growing chasm between most of the African liberation movements and the very people that these liberation movements claim to represent. I have seen this in Zimbabwe. Most people have just divorced politics completely because they believe that African politics is brimming with corruption and votes rigging. They believe that African politics have become the politics of the stomach—me, my family, and my friends first, and the rest of the people last. When I was in Zimbabwe and the scandal of US$6 million was the talk of the town, ZANU-PF had to respond to the public about the scandal.

Dr. Tafataona Mahoso writes:

> *From the point of view of persons, it may be useful to isolate two types of corruption:*

> *Primary corruption includes the corruption of mind and character through propaganda of corrupt ideas and beliefs.*
>
> *Secondary corruption refers to the particular consequences of a corrupt character and corrupt mind—the lies, the cheating, the dishonesty, and the self-justification and alibis, which are used in particular cases of bribery, deceit, theft, and unfair or immoral self-promotion.*[1]

Whether corruption is committed by an individual at a lower level or it is committed by state institution, the fact of the matter is this: it's still corruption. The net effect of corruption is this: it affects innocent people that were supposed to receive pivotal services from government. Whether it's a wholesale corruption or microcorruption, but in the end, lives of innocent people will be negatively affected. Assume a person who is a drug dealer smuggling drugs in and out of the African continent with ease, paying his way out of the busiest airport and paying his way into the African continent through the busiest airport, eventually makes a fabulous profit of US$200 million. The fact of the matter is this: no one will be hurt from the face value, but when you begin to pay an undivided attention of the flow of these drugs, they end up hurting innocent communities and innocent families because their loved ones have become drug addicts. Drugs make life even tougher compared to what it is right now. Drugs pull out children from schools and compound the problem of poverty to many impoverished families. The point is the drug dealer does not realize the net effect of his corrupt activities. The same is true with the government officials and politicians that are corrupt. It's simply impossible to quantify the adverse effect that is caused by the corrupt government officials and corrupt politicians. It's also another form of corruption to slander a person's name who is not corrupt just because you hate him or her. It's also corruption when a couple or lovers make love and at the end of the love encounter, one party lays charges of rape to the police just because the male partner could not yield to the financial demands of the female partner. Corruption in a simple form involves financial or emotional gain at the end. The Western view about corruption is this: Africans are all corrupt. The West is responsible for all the corrupt activities that are happening in the African continent today. Most of the researches that are carried out all over the world today are carried by corrupt scholars that seek to please certain group of Western countries to provide justification of killing innocent people and to showcase their military powers to the whole world. In the movie of Bruce Lee called *Enter the Dragon,* a Chinese master once said, "We are in the business of corruption, and the business of corruption is a lucrative business."

The business of corruption is a lucrative business, and it yields a considerable amount of revenue compared to any other business. The business of corruption is tax-free, and in the payroll of most of the drug lords, there are many senior police officials who are paid double to what the state can afford to pay them. It becomes very difficult then to arrest the velocity and the speed of corruption. Corruption itself more frequent than not continues to change its shape and form.Dr. Tafataona Mahoso argued that the West is responsible for corruption that is happening in Africa. Simply put, when an official receives money that was supposed to be paid to the government and puts it on his back pocket, we cannot blame the person but blame it on the West. The next question that comes to mind is this: Are we Africans ever going to take responsibility for our actions? Surely we cannot continue to blame the West for everything that is going wrong in African soil now and then. We need to pause and ponder. We need to accept the fact that it's possible to be corrupt even if you are a political leader with an impeccable struggle credentials. Corruption is a spirit that ceases and controls anyone. It's possible to be a person of high morals and good character when you are poor and you are too far away from money and lack political influence. But once you are appointed into a senior position in government or in a political party and occupy a position of significant influence, you might change the tune. In my previous chapter, I meticulously expatiated expansively the beginning of the land crisis in South Africa until the period in time where it appeared crystal clear that there was a political boredom until the ANC Youth League came into the picture to attempt to hijack the ANC and South African land issue using the Zimbabwean war veterans' style. The ANCYL failed to hijack the ANC and the government of South Africa. It made its intention clear from the beginning, and it made its plan plain too early. The president of South Africa, Jacob Zuma, admitted in his state of the nation address in parliament in February 2013 that the willing buyer, willing seller policy was ineffective, and the state had to find an effective way to address the issue of land. He indicated that the state was going to appoint a state land auditor. A state land auditor was going to audit the land and compile a report as to who owns a vast tract of land in South Africa. Until this point, the South African way of handling the issue of land was through a willing seller and willing buyer principle. The willing buyer and willing seller principle is effective if there is a market value for the land that is in question. Market value is the fair value of the land. Land, according to International Financial Reporting Standards (IFRS), is non-depreciable asset. It simply means that land does not lose value over a period of time, unlike a car. If land does not lose value, therefore it means that the fair value or the market value of the land appreciates. What it simply means is this: if you bought two hundred hectares of land in 2000 for R200 million, if you decide to sell these two hundred hectares of land in 2020, you might sell it at a price of R600 million provided that there is a market for it. This scenario that I have mentioned above is only applicable provided that the owner of the land bought the land legitimately. We all know that when the Western settlers came to South Africa, they did not carry land with them in their ships. They found land in South Africa and claimed that this land now belongs to them because the government of Hendrik Verwoerd gave them the land free of charge. The mistakes that happened in the past and injustices are also happening now. Indigenous people of South Africa were evicted from their land that was given to them by God by the apartheid government, and the Western settlers kicked indigenous people all the way to the mountains where there is neither life nor a river and occupied the fertile land with pleasure without any hassle or problem. The Western settlers began to farm and breed herds of cattle. The Western settlers thought that all is well, and that is where they miscalculated the black power. The fact that black people were working in the farms of these Western settlers did not make the peasants happy. How would you feel if I came to your house and took your lovely gorgeous wife at gunpoint and pimp her back to you again? Most people would say, but that is not fair. I, a pimp, have your wife, and I continue to derive money from you anytime you want to make love to your wife. The point is I have your wife, and since your wife is mine, I don't pay to make love to her, since she is mine. In your case, you lost your wife and you have to pay me as a pimp to make love to the wife that was previously yours. This is injustice of epic proportion. The question then is, how do you address this kind of monumental mistakes that happen in 1937? Problems present us with opportunities to learn and grow. We must not hate solving problems; they are part of life. There are multiple avenues that can be utilized. You can choose to take the land using the ZANU-PF style and incur the wrath of the international community. It's also barbaric to apply a system that has failed in one country to another country. This perhaps could be the reason the South African government has been very reluctant and patient in dealing with the land issue. The state land auditor made public his land audit reports.and it stated the following:

> *Seventy-nine percent of land in South Africa is privately owned, 7 percent of land in South Africa is unaccounted for, and the state owned 14 percent of land.*[2]

The question then is, does it mean that all along since the dawn of democracy there wasn't any research or audit that was conducted about the land? If 79 percent of this land is privately owned, who owns this vast amount of land, and the owners of this land, where did they get this vast amount of fertile land? My friend and I were driving one day in one of the game reserves in Pretoria. We went to a certain game reserve just a few kilometers outside Pretoria. In this game reserve, there is a vast amount of land that lies idle, and there is not even a single animal there. I had to drive a considerable amount of kilometers until we began to see a few rhinos. The rhinos that were there were only two to be precise. We then stopped with different tourists that were there, and we got outside the car and watched these gigantic animals eating grass. I said to my friend, "Why won't the owners of this game reserve take these few animals, sell it to the Kruger National Park, and sell this land to the government to resettle black communities here that are cramped into a small area in Alexandra and Diepsloot? My friend said to me, "This place is very clean. Once they give this land to black people, they will mess it up." The idea that when black people are given a beautiful land they will mess it up did not sit well with me, and in fact I thought my friend was a racist. What do you expect from a person who has been living in the shack for a long time? The only thing that this person knows is pit toilet and unclean water. Your social environment shapes and changes your view and your belief. People more often than not behave directly or indirectly according to their social environment and their upbringing. It goes without saying that a person who grew up in a chaotic environment will have a tough time to cope in a structured and organized environment. This was the point my friend was trying to drive home. It therefore does not necessarily mean that black people are uncivilized and backward, but it simply means, given their social environment that they have been exposed to for a considerable amount of years, they might replicate and duplicate a consistent behavior even in a different social environment. The old saying goes, you can't teach an old dog new tricks. Black people are not dogs, and given an opportunity, I have no doubt in my mind that black people can change and adapt even in new social environment where there are running water and flushing toilets. The tenderpreneurs and black diamonds bear evidence of what I am talking about. They have relocated from their locations and resettled in posh suburbs where there are flushing toilets and clean water, and they are doing just fine. Human beings are the species of learned behavior, meaning that if you grow up in a loving and warm family that is brimming with love, you will surely, without any shadow of doubt, duplicate that behavior even if you are in a different social setting because that is the only thing you know. Poverty-stricken families normally produce poverty-stricken children or children with poverty mentality. This is also true with countries that are always in endless wars. I have seen these with Congolese that are living in South Africa; they are very violent and bitter because of what is happening in their country. This is not to say that we are mocking them because black South Africans are also angry, bitter, and resentful at other black people who are now tenderpreneurs who are residing in Sandton. I was very shocked to hear a black South African man expressing his hatred toward tenderpreneurs and black diamonds saying, "They come to the location to flaunt their instant wealth and throw a party out of nowhere and take all the beautiful girls."

THE THIRD CHIMURENGA

"Chimurenga" is a word in the Shona language that roughly means "revolutionary struggle." This word's modern interpretation broadly denotes a struggle for human rights, political dignity, and social justice.[3] There are three Chimurengas in Zimbabwean political history. The First Chimurenga was in 1896–1897. This First Chimurenga was led by the Shona-Ndebele against the British South African Company's administrator leader, Starr Jameson, who was buried in Matopos National Park next to Cecil John Rhodes. The Second Chimurenga was between 1966 and 1979. The Second Chimurenga is also called the Bush War, or the Zimbabwe Liberation War, refers to the guerilla war of 1966–1979.[4] The Second Chimurenga came to an end when the Lancaster House Agreement was signed in 1979 in Great Britain, which eventually brought to an end the Bush War as some might call it. The Third Chimurenga was the farm invasion of 2000 where white commercial farmers were dispossessed of their farms by the ZANU-PF war veterans, and the farm invasion was orchestrated and led by the war veterans of ZANU-PF who were part and parcel of the Second Chimurenga of 1966–1979. Pres. Robert Mugabe of ZANU-PF was not famous until the farm invasion of 2000 in Africa. All along the people of the world and South Africans in general did not follow the national politics of Zimbabwe simply because there was no one famous and politically attractive in Zimbabwe. The point is, had it not been for the farm invasion of 2000, God knows surely there would not be any reason for me personally to visit Zimbabwe. What we knew all along was that Zimbabwe was a beautiful country, and food in Zimbabwe was in abundance. What I also knew was that Zimbabweans were very educated people because their system of education was similar to British education system. In fact Zimbabweans were writing exams that were set by the Cambridge University. It's also true even today that most Zimbabweans are very educated, and this is seen in the quality of the mathematics teachers that Zimbabwe's system of education continues to produce. Most of the teachers that are teaching mathematics and physical science and biology in South Africa are from Zimbabwe. What went wrong then in this country that I grew up hearing fairy tales that the country was the breadbasket of Africa that now became the basket case? What happened to this country that was good in mathematics, biology, and physical science? Where is this food that was feeding the whole of Africa? I wanted to see this breadbasket that was able to feed the whole of Africa. There is great difference between reading about a country on history textbooks and visiting the country and seeing it for yourself. I was about to receive my salary from my part-time Job. I have a secular job, but sometimes to supplement my salary and be able to buy things that I want, I decided to work part time. I went to church one Sunday. I could hear that the Holy Spirit was talking to me about the money that I had not received yet. I could hear from within that if I receive my salary from my part-time job I should not use it but contribute to the building fund of the church. I tossed and turned about giving this exuberant amount of money that I had worked hard for. Finally I yielded to the voice that was originating within me. I gave away the money to the building fund of the church. It was a couple of thousands, and I mourned for my hard-earned money a little bit. This is straight talk, if you know what I mean. Where your money is, is where your heart will be as well, Jesus said. It's almost nine months after I had given that money, but there is nothing divine happening in my life. I began to doubt and question myself why I gave away my money anyway. Maybe that was not the Holy Spirit that instructed me to give that money anyway. I began to collect my thoughts and pondered my purpose in this drama of life. Surely one cannot live his life by waking up every morning and going to work from Monday to Friday to scream at the spoiled brat children and at the end of the day go home to an empty room and watch the same old news on TV. Surely this thing called life should be lived to the maximum. It's possible to live and die without having lived life. Life is not about making a lot of children and making love to a woman and buying expensive cars and residing in a posh suburb; there is more to it than that. I have to find myself and the main reason I am here in this planet. It became abundantly clear to me that I am just like all these Africans who are in Africa but who really don't know anything about Africa. They watch too much CNN and BBC News, and they believe what they see on TV about Africa while living in Africa and don't even dare to take a step of faith to search the truth for themselves about their own continent. It's a fact that Africans listened to the West to hear the West telling and reporting about African stories. It's like waiting for somebody who is in Atlanta and Dubai to report to you what is happening in Zimbabwe while you are in Harare. We tune to big news networks to report to us about what is happening in our backyard. Perhaps we trust too many of our former colonizers to the point that even if we are politically liberated, we still want to watch their TV and their news. When you are a slave even if you are liberated, you are likely to envy your master and the very chains that kept you in one area for quite a long period of time. Trust me when I tell you this: there are a lot of people in South Africa who still envy apartheid wholeheartedly. I have heard a lot of people saying that under apartheid this was not happening. The problem is we Africans have been in political bondage for quite a long period of time, and now slavery is in our DNA. In the villages of South Africa, poverty had been naturalized. In fact more villagers are more comfortable with being poor than being rich. If you are rich, people are likely to accuse you of practicing witchcraft. I have also heard people in the villages saying, people that are rich don't sleep at night. People that are poor have a peaceful sleep because they have nothing to worry about; by the way, they don't have money to think about. I have also heard that when you are educated man and marry a wife who is educated, you won't have peace in your marriage. This is a product of the painful system that twisted and bewitched the mind of a black person. I had a very heated debate at one point with a certain gentleman who was in favor of the municipality. He argued that the municipality was doing an appropriate thing by supplying water to the communities once a week. I argued that this is not normal in Pretoria and Johannesburg. There is water every day in Pretoria in the city center, and if there is no water, perhaps there is a serious maintenance that is going on. He seemed to suggest that it was normal for the villagers not to have water, and I believe that he felt very offended, and he eventually said, "This is not Pretoria." His name is Goodwill, and he became extremely accustomed to a village to the point that he accepted the status quo. He assimilated the idea of poverty and mediocrity. It's a norm to be poor and uneducated. It's a norm to have children out of wedlock, and it's also a norm to have children that you can't afford to support, clothe, and provide shelter for them. This is the apartheid story. The worst form of oppression is the fear of the unknown. The worst form of oppression is to stay in one area for the rest of your life simply because you are afraid of what awaits you out there. We need to live life. We must not be afraid of making mistakes. Many children live their lives trying to impress their failed parents—parents who did not achieve anything in life not because of the system of education of the time but because of fear, the fear to leave the village and resettle in a new place, and greatest fear of all fears is the fear of the unknown, the fear of what life might bring to you. This kind of fear is permeating Africa. We Africans are forever afraid that our former colonizers might come back to take back this political freedom that we have attained through the shedding of blood. We Africans are afraid that should we cut the relationship with our former colonizers, we might starve to death with hunger. That is why there is no African country in the whole of African history that is not a recipient of foreign aid from the West. The West now and then boasts about distributing foreign aid to Africa. We Africans gladly take the Western handouts and eat them in peace. Poverty and handouts are our reality. It's like being born in prison and the only thing that you ever knew was prison and prison becomes your reality. Even if you can be freed from prison, you will struggle to live life outside of prison, since what you know all of your life was prison. In fact when you are free, you feel oppressed, and when you are in prison, you feel free, therefore prison became your reality. What is a reality to one person is not a reality to another person, and what is common sense to one person might not be common sense to another person, and that I understand. There are three types of slavery in African history: there is slavery of the mind/soul, slavery of the body, and slavery of the spirit. The slavery of the body is better than the slavery of the mind/soul, but the slavery of the spirit is the worst form of slavery. Africans have been decolonized mentally and physically, but she (Africa) and her children are still in the depth of the pit of colonization spiritually. The colonization of the spirit came through religion and music. The colonization of the spirit came through belief system, Western products, and Western science. Africa will forever look for help from the West until and unless she conducts a thorough introspection.

Nelson Mandela in his *Long Walk to Freedom* writes:

> *We are tenants on our own soil. We have no strength, no power, no control over our own destiny in the land of our birth.*[5]

It's this Africanness in me that rise up time and again, and it's this Africanness in me that compelled me to go to see Zimbabwe and the farms that were once productive and fruitful. When I went to Zimbabwe for the first time, what struck me was the vast tract of land that remains underutilized and lies in waste. I have said before that I nearly broke down in tears when I was in Bulawayo talking to one of the lecturers in Lupane University. Almost everybody in Zimbabwe points fingers to the war veterans saying they were responsible for the farm invasion of 2000. If this is true, then it therefore means that the war veterans are responsible for the death of six thousand people that were killed by HIV/AIDS according to United Nations Population Index. If this is true, it also means that the war veterans are responsible for the economic sanctions that are currently in place in Zimbabwe right now. If this is true, it means that the economic downturn that happened in early 2000 was as a result of the war veterans. It therefore means that the main problem in Zimbabwe is the war veterans. This can be interpreted in this way: had it not been for the war veterans, Zimbabwe today was still going to be a beautiful country as it was in the past and was still going to be a breadbasket of Southern Africa, not a basket case as they (economic experts and political experts) call it. When you watch the program *Seconds from Disaster* on a National Geographic channel, you will often hear these words "Disasters—they don't just happen. There are critical chains of events that lead to the final moments." It simply means it will be sheer madness to point the fingers to the war veterans and Pres. Robert Mugabe only. There should be critical chains of events that led to the final moment, and those are exactly what I want to find out. I want to find out those critical chains of events that led to the final moment of the farm invasion. There are multiple divergences in the account of farm invasion. African history in general has been largely written by Western scholars. There are very few African scholars who have contributed to the writing of an African story. That is not surprising, since the majority of African scholars are also pro-Western in their thinking and belief system. They believe that the West is the economic savior of the masses of the world. They also believe that the West is the spiritual savior of the masses of the world who are on their way to hell where the worms don't die and the fire cannot be quenched. The West is there to save these doomed souls that are going to hell through drone strikes and endless wars. We Africans are now and then are told that certain leaders of certain countries need to be eliminated because they have violated human rights, and they are responsible for the death of many people. We are also told that certain leaders of certain countries harbor terrorists, and they are manufacturing weapons of mass destruction to destroy the world. Therefore, they need to be bombed, and when it is discovered later that there was no evidence of manufacturing weapons of mass destruction, the case is closed. No one gets prosecuted, and there is no suspect and there is no culprit. But disasters don't just happen; there are critical chains of events that lead to the final moment. If we can follow the clues very well, we can find truth. We must write African history from the truth, not from facts, because facts change, but the truth will forever remain.

Yamkela Fortune Spengane writes in Southern Times:

> *Freedom is a holistic entity. It is achieved as is and not in compartments. You are either free or you are not, and there's nothing in between. A prisoner in solitary confinement eating crumbs and sleeping on the floor with no blankets and a prisoner who has a nutritious menu, good mattress, and even time for television and gym are both prisoners; yes, one might have better conditions to live under, but they are both prisoners nonetheless.*[6]

Freedom is a holistic entity, but surely it will be sheer madness to achieve wholesale freedom without breaking it down into compartments. The main problem with African liberation struggle and African liberation movement is this: most of African liberation movements were trained by the Russians and the Chinese to fight the Western imperialism, but these African liberation movements were not trained to run their economies. Had the Russians and the Chinese trained African liberation movements on how to run their economies well, most of the African problems today that are under developing the African continent will be gone. There is some bit of truth in that statement; the Russians and the Chinese were not really helping the African liberation movements in actual fact, but they were helping themselves to continue where the West left off after Africa has attained its political independence. That is why now and then you will hear African leaders say, "We will continue look to the East"—the East is where China is. As long as Africa continues to look to the East, then Africa will end up thinking like the Asians, and the East is only worried about owning and controlling Africa again as the West did for quite a long period of time. I have heard many South African academics conceding to the fact that the economic powers are now shifting to the East. It's true that China wants to control the world by hook or by crook. It's also true that Russia wants to control the whole of Middle East, possibly even extend its control even to Africa. No wonder when the opportunity like BRICS came to Russia's door, Russia came running, knowing full well that such an arrangement dovetails very well in the Russian master plan to regain the control of Africa from the West. The fact of the matter is this: the West is not happy to see Russian and Chinese footprints in African soil because the West knows full well what the ramification is of the presence of China and Russia in Africa. The whole world is conspiring against Africa. We are being tossed to and fro like a baby. We are tossed to and fro like a wave of a sea tossed by the wind of the sea. The East is now conspiring against Africa. The word "conspire" in Latin means "*breathe together.*" But as long as young Africans continue to spend a considerable amount of time in Face book, Twitter, and WhatsApp, the East will eventually oppress Africa just like the West did. It will be very difficult to be politically liberated from the East once the East gets hold of Africa's mineral resources. No wonder after our political liberation, we began to see the Chinese and the Russians coming to Africa to set up businesses. Now and then I get a sick feeling when I see a bus full to the brim with Chinese touring Pretoria as if they are watching animals in Pretoria zoo. I wonder whether or not we Africans can fill the bus to the brim and tour the city of Hong Kong. I also wonder whether or not we Africans can fill the bus to the brim and tour the city of Moscow. It makes logical business sense that you can only invest in a country that you know its economy and politics very well. The Chinese read more about Africa than we Africans read about China, and the Russians read more about Africa than we Africans read about Russia. It is of essential importance then to read about the East before the East penetrates Africa in a painful way. The only way to stop this Eastern wave from penetrating Africa is to counterattack the East in its own economic power house. The time has come for African investors to search for business opportunities in the East in order to prevent the Eastern investors to come and invest in Africa with their ulterior motive of further colonizing Africa as the West did in the past. The majority of African scholars don't see the East as a potential colonizer of Africa in the near future, but from my perspective, I do see the East as a possible future colonizer of Africa. The problem with colonization is it does not have to be political, but it can be economic also. Keep the picture but change the frame. Let political power remain in the hands of the African liberation movements and black people, but let economic power be with us, the West says, and that is what the West is doing right now in Africa. After I have learned that most of the things that I claim that I own were manufactured in China, I became very worried. I became very worried because I am shooting myself in the foot if I continue in my dangerous path to criticize China while the very belt that holds my trousers tight in my waist had been manufactured in China. I had a very serious problem the other day; in fact cockroaches were penetrating my kitchen from left, right, and center, and I wanted to bring the cockroaches' invasion to an end. I went to buy an ant-killing bait, and to my surprise, I discovered that it was manufactured in China. Simply put, if it wasn't for China, my kitchen would have been annexed by cockroaches. The Russians, Chinese, and Koreans didn't have the interest of Africa at heart when they were helping the African liberation movements; they had their eyes fixed on the big prices. They knew very well that when Africa is politically free, they will expand their economic influence through these skewed multilateral agreements where Africa is the recipient and they being the providers of everything. Political freedom without economic freedom is useless and fruitless. There is nothing that African countries can boast about if the means of production still rest in the hands of the former colonizers. After I gave that sum of thousands to the church for a building, I had been tossing and turning on my bed to hear that divine voice that should guide me to the still waters, as the writer of Psalm David put it. I could hear very clearly within me that I need to write a book about Zimbabwe. The problem is I have never been in Zimbabwe and I don't even know how far it is from Pretoria. In actual fact, I knew from within me that the wars that are ravaging Africa have originated from the West. The main problem with these complex African wars is this: sometimes they emerge as insurgent groups that are dissatisfied with the government, and sometimes they emerge through coups that are bankrolled and funded by the West. If you would cast your eyes wide open and observe what is happening in Central African Republic, you would quickly understand what I am talking about. If you would cast your eyes further to Democratic Republic of Congo, you would quickly understand that Africa is stuck between a rock and a wall. There are more African leaders focused on solving the problems of poverty, inequality, and lack of sanitation. The very infrastructure that has been built it gets destroyed through endless wars. The African economy and Africa's infrastructure would have been extremely advanced had it not been for the wars and the coups that are funded by the West. The West is using Africa as a training ground to exhibit its military power and its IT innovations. Everything that is produced in the West, frankly speaking, is produced for Africa. Africa produced nothing, and the West produced everything and sends it to Africa at quadruple price. It seems as if everybody in the whole world is saying, how can I benefit from this rich African continent that is blessed with mineral resources and with gorgeous arable land? What is it that one needs to do to ensure that the Western citizens benefit from Africa through exploitation and pillaging? François Bozizé was sponsored by Chad's president Idriss Derby in 2003 to get to power. Since François Bozizé came to power through a coup, the Seleka rebels also removed him from power through another coup. He went to hide in France and cried foul—that he was the president of CAR in exile and he was still the legitimate president elected democratically by the people. It therefore means that former president of CAR, François Bozizé, had been in power for almost eleven years. In the process of being in power for eleven years, he forgot completely how he ascended to the throne of power. Since the Seleka rebels ascended to the echelon of power through a coup also, there has never been peace in CAR for almost ten months right now. The United Nations Security Council sent additional one thousand troops to CAR to further provide stability and peace. The main problem with the United Nations Security Council is this: it heeded the calls of sending additional troops to CAR because of France, which was a former colonizer of CAR. It seems as if France wants to ensure that CAR is safe; this is not for the goodwill of CAR people but for France's own good. Simply put, France understands Africa more than Africans themselves. In CAR that is where fourteen soldiers from South Africa were killed on a combat with the Seleka rebels. May the departed souls of those fallen soldiers in CAR rest in peace. Africa is the breeding ground for coups. In fact the only continent where coups have been legitimized is in Africa. Where there is a war, there are mineral resources and where there are mineral resources, there are coups and mercenaries from the West. The problem with mercenaries is they are not classified as terrorist simply because they are on a special mission to kill and get paid and go home. Mercenaries are on assigned mission, and when the mission is over, the assignment is over. Former president of CAR, François Bozizé, claimed that the Seleka rebels have hired mercenaries to topple him from power.[7] There is no country in the world that can be economically viable if there is no political stability and respect for the rule of the law. The so-called constitution, which is classified as the supreme law of a country, normally flies outside the window during the time of mayhem. Human rights violation in a political unstable environment is normally endemic. There is no intellectually sound investor who can inject massive amounts of US dollars in a country like CAR where there is no rule of law. Political instability is succeeded by economic instability, and prowling and kleptomania then follow. This political crisis in Central Africa, meaning Central African Republic and DRC, has robbed the Central African region a vast amount of economic opportunity to grow and flourish economically. While Central African region is busy engaged in the endless civil wars, the majority of the world is moving ahead with new innovations and scientific discoveries. It's an open secret that it takes a country quadruple amount of effort to resuscitate the economic engine of a country after the war is over. It will more frequent than not require massive foreign investment to change and alter the CAR crisis. Irrespective of how rich a country is in terms of its mineral deposits, as long as it would degenerate to a civil war for a long a period of time, the price to resuscitate the economic engine of that country will by far exceed the cost incurred to go to war. It's also an open secret that wars are very expensive to bankroll. The Iran-Iraq War in 1980 to 1988 had cost both the Iraqi and Iranian governments an average of US$1.2 billion. The next question is this: What kind of economic benefit could be received had both countries decided to take this considerable amount of money and invested in Technology and in Education? The truth is the results and the ramifications of investing in education and technology are perennial. The West stole Africa's wealth and further labeled Africa as a continent that is hopeless and backward in everything. Africa is the dumping ground of the West. There is no democracy in war, and there is no will of the people in war. The rule of law in any war is traversed to the extreme and innocent children and women die haphazardly. In a war, looting is the order of the day. In fact it is very difficult to steal in an organized environment, since everybody is alert and security is tight. We all know that the thief comes to steal, kill, and destroy, but I have come so you may have life in abundance to the full until it overflows, and that is according to John 10 verse 10. Presumably you were not skipping your Sunday school classes, you should have been taught that scripture in your Sunday school. Some of us, when we have an opportunity to learn, we take an advantage of it; while some folks, when they have an opportunity to learn, they squander it. Squandering your time to learn is like eating your investments and expecting an interest in the near future. The reason Africa is where it is today is partly the West, but apart from that, there is no massive investment that is injected into Africa's economies. We invest in buying military weapons that are further used to start unnecessary endless wars. Africa must buy military weapons for security reasons, but it must also make a considerable amount of investment into its own economy. Africa needs to build roads, dams, and universities. There is no complex political narrative like Zimbabwe's farm invasion of 2000. The record of account of what happened in 2000 causes confusion to almost everybody who is a Zimbabwean, even to people who are not Zimbabweans, like South Africans. The slow pace of land reform in South Africa has been grinded to a screeching halt partly because of what happened in Zimbabwe in 2000. What you don't understand normally you will fear it. Fear originates from uncertainty and lack of trust. Confusion and misunderstanding send a person into panic mood. My assignment then is to understand the conundrum of farm invasion of 2000 after fourteen years since the farms have been taken. I will understand the farm invasion from the South African perspective. I have interviewed a considerable amount of people who are Zimbabweans who are living in Zimbabwe and Zimbabweans who are living in South Africa. At one point, I have interviewed one person at different times, asking this person the same question, and he gave me very conflicting versions of events. At one stage, this gentleman told me an account of events that was squarely putting the blame on the shoulders of the government of ZANU-PF; but at a different time, the very same person gave me the account of events that puts the blame on the shoulders of MDC-T. What the hell is happening in here? It's also possible that some Zimbabweans really don't even know what happened in 2000. They are like most South Africans who are disinterested and clueless about what happened in Zimbabwe. The fact of the matter is this: Zimbabwe is very close to South Africa. If Zimbabwe's crisis is not solved with an immediate effect directly or indirectly, it affects South Africa and its citizens. It affects South Africa simply because Zimbabweans would not stay in Zimbabwe if there are no job opportunities in Zimbabwe. It therefore means that Zimbabweans will cross the Beitbridge border legally or illegally and come to South Africa and compete in the job market with South Africans for the same job opportunities, which are not even enough to cater for South Africans alone. It also means that the Zimbabweans citizens will also ensure that they seek the same economic benefits that were supposed to be enjoyed by South Africans alone, further more complicating the South Africans' problems. South Africa has its fair amount of problems just like any other country. With that being said, there is no need for South Africa to accommodate a considerable amount of people that lack semi -skills and scarce skills that can turn the tide on the economy of South Africa. The point is South Africa is not the United States of America that can accommodate the Venezuelans, Hondurans, and Mexicans. South Africa has been politically liberated for barely nineteen years now. That does not necessarily mean that South Africa does not need to accommodate immigrants from other African countries, since South African immigrants were also accommodated by Zimbabwe's government during the time of apartheid. The fact of the matter is, at some point, whether we agree or disagree, there should come a point where Zimbabweans who are displaced all over the world take conscious decision to go back home and solve their national problems. It's true that this statement will cause the blood pressure of many people to shoot up given the political intolerance that is currently prevailing in Zimbabwe, but political problems give ordinary people an opportunity to alter the course of history. If one takes stoke of Morgan Tsvangirai's life, one will understand that sometimes to live, one must die. It took Christ to the crucifixion to save the whole world from its own sins. It will also take some Zimbabweans to bite the bullet in order to change the situation of their country and eventually save the future generation of Zimbabwe. One thing you must be rest assured about is this: Pres. Robert Mugabe is eighty-nine years old, and he is physically fragile and weak, and the Zimbabweans can build on that foundation. Running around like headless chickens and staying in different countries cannot solve the political and economic challenges that are facing the country. It's true that during the time of war and political mayhem, people will be displaced all over the world; but when the war is over, people will need to come back home and rebuild their country from scratch. There are many South Africans who were displaced and living in different countries during the apartheid era, but when sanity kicked in, they realized that they had to come to South Africa and face apartheid head-on. It's also true that at some point Zimbabweans will need to go back home and rebuild their country that had been destroyed by economic sanctions that have been imposed to Zimbabwe as a result of political misbehavior. Zimbabwean problems can be solved by Zimbabweans alone. The international community can lend a helping hand to Zimbabweans when a pressing need arises. Political problems sometimes don't require a political solution. I had already made up my mind that I would dare take a complex political issue of them all and demystify it. It's a complex challenge riddled with lies and half truths, and some people speaking from their own emotional understanding miss the bigger picture and point fingers and criticize the government partly because their loved ones died during Gukurahundi. Victims of political mistakes are not good storytellers simply because they were in the midst of the action, and it is highly impossible that there could be sanity and logic in what they are saying. I met a gentleman in Johannesburg who was a victim of the Gukurahundi. He criticized the government of ZANU-PF from the get-go. There is no point in time where he credited the government of ZANU-PF for defeating the Ian Smith regime, not even once. I have also met some Zimbabweans who are pro-President Mugabe and ZANU-PF even if they are living in South Africa partly because of the political decisions that ZANU-PF took, which were childish and illogical. If you live in a glass house, don't throw stones to your neighbor because if the very same neighbor can throw the same stone to you, your glass house will come down crumbling. What is the net gain that has been achieved by taking the commercial farms from the commercial white farmers? Was it because there was no other viable option that could have been explored to reach a mutual beneficiary solution? Not only did the war veterans plunge a considerable amount of people in the depth of poverty, but due to its weird economic policy, Zimbabwe also incurred unnecessary economic sanctions that could have been avoided had they used their brains to think with them. Pres. Robert Mugabe is very educated, and in fact most senior members of ZANU-PF are very educated. Pres. Robert Mugabe has seven hard-earned degrees, and one expects that such a political leader and the leader of the country will use his education to solve complex problems that are facing the country. Many people summarily conclude that because a person has seven hard-earned degrees, therefore he is an intellectual or a genius. It's possible to have education while you remain dumb. Education is good, but education alone is not enough in real life. Life is real; therefore, political decision should be made based on political experience and economic experience. Political decisions and economic decisions that will plunge a considerable amount of people in the depth of poverty, even if they might look good at a face value, should either be deferred or put on hold until certain conditions warrant such decisions to be taken. There was no need to take the commercial farms in 2000 from the white commercial farmers irrespective of what the ZANU-PF war veterans said. Political power at the expense of many people is useless. There is no honor and pride to govern and rule a few people who are poor and sick at the expense of the masses who are skilled and trained just to remain in power until one falls and faints on the floor from the chair. It's true that African leaders, once they ascend to political power, can't let go of the luxury of the state facilities and flying all over the world. South Africa's late world icon Dr. Nelson Mandela has set a very good example for many African leaders, and they need to learn from him. My point is simple: the whole world has no business sticking its long nose to Zimbabwe's problem. There should come a point in their lives where Zimbabweans who are living abroad in the United States of America and even in the United Kingdom need to decide to come back home and solve their national political crisis. Former president of South Africa, Thabo Mbeki, had been living in the United Kingdom for quite some time during the apartheid era, but it dawned on him that he should come and solve the apartheid problems that the country was facing then, and he was part and parcel of the delegation that negotiated in CODESA. Short-term solutions for long-term problems are unsustainable and unworthy of taking.

In the beginning, Cecil John Rhodes annexed Zimbabwe using his delegation that consisted of Charles Rudd and Queen Victoria's name in the process.[8] The country at that point in time was in the hands of Lobengula, the king of Matabeleland. This king called King Lobengula was a son of King Mzilikazi, who fled from Shaka Zulu from the Zulu Kingdom of Kwazulu Natal. King Mzilikazi felt King Shaka was greedy and a bully then he wanted his own freedom. He wanted freedom from the oppression of Shaka Zulu ka Senzangakhona. The Zulus liked cattle raiding, and by the way, Zulus like meat wholeheartedly, even today. Zulus and Swatis won't serve supper or dinner in case the relish is meat. They will wait until the visitors are gone then they will serve supper. This is still happening even today in South Africa. They have inculcated stinginess in their culture, but with Tsongas, it's a different story. In fact Tsongas are happy to serve supper or dinner in the presence of their visitors just because they are not stingy, unlike the Zulus and Swatis. I hope that my

Zulu friends and Swati friends will still love me even after reading this book. Whether or not it is the wrong interpreter that interpreted the whole mining rights incorrectly to King Lobengula, it does not matter anymore. The net effect of King Lobengula of the Matabeleland to sign that mining treaty gave Cecil John Rhodes the rights to mine, and it also meant the British invasion in Zimbabwe. It's therefore irrelevant and useless to continue to blame King Lobengula. King Lobengula's father, King Mzilikazi, himself walked away with what did not belong to him from South Africa to Zimbabwe. The Matabele people were cattle raiders, and they were raiding the kraals of Shona people, and in the process, the Shonas became very poor simply because all what they had was taken by King Mzilikazi. The fact of the matter is this: Gukurahundi of 1983 to 1986 was partly a revenge for the Shona people to what happened in the 1880s. It's politically correct that in 1983 to 1986 the ZAPU ex-combatants did not hand over all their weapons to the government after the political independence and after the signing of the Lancaster House Agreement, but it's also politically correct to suggest that the Shonas were still fuming with anger because of what happened in the 1880s. It's possible that the Shonas wanted this opportunity for quite a long period of time to revenge for their herds of cattle that was taken forcefully from them by King Lobengula of the Matabele people. When the 1983 to 1986 window of opportunity opened, the Shona people seized the moment and unleashed their anger on the Matabele people who are partly responsible for selling of the country to Cecil John Rhodes. The end was inevitable even if Cecil John Rhodes did not hoodwink King Lobengula in signing the treaty. The fact of the matter is this: somebody could have come to give King Lobengula a different treaty and eventually Zimbabwe could have been annexed in any way by either the Boers of South Africa, the Germans who were in Namibia, or the Portuguese who were in Angola and Mozambique. The point is give King Lobengula a break—it was not all his fault.

Alexander Kanengoni writes:

> *It was a document that Cecil Rhodes used to obtain the backing of Queen Victoria to occupy the country, and the circumstances surrounding its creation and signature left, for me, an enduring scar.*[9]

The enduring scar that still remains in Zimbabwe's people is the lack of herds of cattle that they once owned and the land that they once plowed in. The land is gone, and the herd of cattle is gone partly because of King Lobengula's signature on the mining treaty. We should not cry over spilled milk; what happened is now water under the bridge. Cecil John Rhode then brought his British South Africa Company and began mining. There is a new theory that says Cecil John Rhodes did not find enough gold and diamonds in Zimbabwe.

Richard Brown writes:

> *The mineral deposits found there proved much more limited than Rhodes hoped, but within a decade large areas of agricultural land had been seized from the Shona and Ndebele people and occupied by white farmers, mainly from Britain and South Africa.*[10]

Some people argued that if there were no gold and diamonds, why then did Cecil John Rhodes stay in Zimbabwe until his death? Some even suggested that he probably would have moved to Democratic Republic of Congo that is rich in mineral resources. Since I have been in Zimbabwe for quite some time, now I have seen with my naked eyes the vast tract of land that lies underutilized. The arable land of Zimbabwe is an irresistible temptation even to me. It's possible that Cecil John Rhodes went to Zimbabwe purely for mining gold and diamonds only, but in the process he got tempted by the land that he never saw since he was born, and he lost his original mission of searching for gold and diamonds and eventually went for the land instead of the gold and diamonds, and it's also possible that perhaps he was tired of traveling. It does not necessarily mean that there were no gold and diamonds in Zimbabwe as many people suggest. It's like a married man walking with his beautiful wife, holding hands, and all of a sudden he meets a deadly gorgeous lady. The next thing you know, there is a polygamous marriage, and that's how polygamy came into existence. It's not black people's culture; it's the irresistible beauty of women, and married men can't let go of it. There is no man right now who is in a polygamous marriage who intended to be in a polygamous marriage in the first place; it is the irresistible beauty of women that married men can't wrap their heads around that created polygamy. I have made my point, period. All along the people of Zimbabwe were very angry at their land

and their herds of cattle that were taken away from them through the guns and dogs. They bottled up this resentment, anger, and hatred for quite a long period of time. The people began to revolt against government, but then the BSAC was very strong, and the native people were conquered, and they even surrendered to the Pioneer Colum. Zimbabwe was under Britain for quite a long period of time. The political history of Zimbabwe was altered by the wind of change that was sweeping Africa in a speed of lightning. The West had contained Africa for quite a long period of time. The main problem came when the majority of African people started reading and writing and their minds began to be opened, and they realized that the Western settlers had stolen their land and mineral resources, and they were starving in the land of their forefathers. The missionary schools taught the sons and daughters of farmworkers about Christian values, like thou should not kill, thou should not steal, thou should not commit adultery, thou should not envy the donkey of thy neighbor, and thou should worship thy Lord only. During this time in African history, there wasn't enough reading material; even the Bible itself came with the missionaries, but this does not mean that Africans did not know God. Africans all along knew that there was a supernatural being with higher power. Africans did not know about Western medicine, since they had their own African science and African medicine. The arrival of the missionaries was the Western political instrument to ensure that Africans are brainwashed politically, economically, and religiously. They were indoctrinated to believe that the Satan/Lucifer was a black person and Jesus was a white person. African indigenous knowledge was trampled upon simply because there were no laboratories to prove African science. The Western settlers think that they have a better IQ compared to the Africans who have been living in the African continent since time immemorial. I often asked myself this question: Why would someone come from Europe to Africa and find people living in Africa in peace and harmony then start a war and then change the street names and go as far as naming the very place where the native people were living unpronounceable names? When Cecil John Rhodes arrived in Zimbabwe, he found King Lobengula, and he imposed himself to the native people by changing the name to Rhodesia, taken from his surname, Rhodes. When the Boers came to Tshwane in South Africa and came across the native people of the land, they decided to change the name from Tshwane to Pretoria. They also changed the names of the streets into their own heroes' names, like Paul Kruger and Jacob Maree. This was a well-orchestrated plan by the West to make native Africans believe that they (The Anglo- Saxons) were superior intellectually to normal native African people. The missionaries succeeded in carrying out the grand plan of the West. The biggest mistakes of the Western missionaries were failing to understand that the very sons and daughters of the farm workers will revolt one day. They (Western missionaries) underestimated the power of education and the power of knowledge. There is a great difference between knowledge and wisdom. It's possible to have knowledge without wisdom. Knowledge is not wisdom, and wisdom is not knowledge. Knowledge is information, and wisdom is the prudence and astuteness to use the information that you have. Knowledge predominantly comes from written material, but wisdom does not come from written material, but it comes from your faculty of thinking called intelligence. African people knew that there was a higher power called God, and they had different names for him that they were using to refer to God, and in South Africa, even today, there are many names that are used to refer to God. Some call him God, Mvelingqangi, Modimo, Nkulunkulu, Sonini nanini, and the list is endless. The notion that African people were worshiping idols and trees is sheer gibberish. During the Dark Age, there was no sufficient reading material that native African people could read and understand the ways of God. The native people only knew that the only way to communicate with God was through your ancestors. Simply put, when your father passed on, he did not just die completely, but he went into the spirit world and became close to God. Native Africans then thought that by communicating with their forefathers, their needs and their concerns will be heard quickly, since the message will be carried to God, who is a spirit by their forefathers. This does not necessarily mean that native Africans believed that when a person dies, he becomes a God to them. The Buddhists believe that when a person dies, he will reincarnate into a pig or a goat, but native Africans didn't believe that. The Muslims believe that when a person dies in fighting a war against the West, he will automatically enter heaven and will be given a great reward by Allah. The West promoted and advocated for their religion, which was far superior to an African religion. Traditional medicine became unholy to use. By the way, it became an abomination and a sin to God to use a tree that was created by God. Western scientists use trees to manufacture the Western medicine that they claim is holy and unblemished. African culture and values were wiped away by the missionaries, and the eventuality of that is the arrival of the homosexuality. It's quite amazing that the Western governments are presumed to be the most advanced governments in the world, and yet in the process they democratize homosexuality. The constitution of the West is advanced compared to any other African constitution in the world, yet they (Western governments) legalized abortion and same-sex marriage. Many African scholars don't agree with Pres. Robert Mugabe of Zimbabwe in many things, but when it comes to the issue of homosexuality, they normally see eye to eye with Uncle Bob. The institution of marriage was established by God for procreation, and there were no sperm banks and surrogate mothers that were created by God. The point is, in the beginning, God created Adam and Eve, not Adam and James. The Dark Age came to an end. Even before the Dark Age came to an end, the children of the peasants were not happy about the living conditions of their parents. Some thought that the liberation struggle against the Western imperialists was insurmountable, and whoever dares to change the cause of history was doomed to fail. The sons and daughters of the farm workers had already gone to the United States of America and met the late Dr. Martin Luther King. They have already heard him saying, "I have a dream." The six mirrors that I talked about in the previous chapters then followed. The war of the people started, which is known as the First Chimurenga, and then the Second Chimurenga followed, and eventually the Third Chimurenga in 2000. It's imperative to question the connection between the Third Chimurenga and the First Chimurenga. I find it very difficult to associate the farm invasion with the word "Chimurenga." Pres. Robert Mugabe came to study in South Africa in Fort Hare University. It is in Fort Hare University where he met the likes of the late Oliver Tambo and Nelson Mandela, but at this point in time, he was not politically savvy and cruel as he is today. South Africa was still in the hands of the Western settlers, and apartheid became very rife in South Africa, and native South Africans had to carry a dompas just to move from one area to another, specifically if you were black trying to get to a white area. The fact of the matter is black South Africans were not allowed into a white man's area. It will be fruitless exercise to rewrite what has been already covered by different scholars, like rewriting about the biography of Nelson Mandela or rewriting the biography of Joshua Nkomo or the biography of Pres. Robert Mugabe. There are many books that could be read for such topics, but for this topic, I will only look at the political component of their contribution to their African liberation struggle, not their personal lives. When I was in Zimbabwe in a place called Heroes' Acre, I began to realize that there is lot about African history that has not been written about yet. People who should rewrite African history should be the "the born-free generation." As long as the born-free generation is stuck on their Twitter, Facebook, and WhatsApp accounts, then the one-million-dollar question is, who will rewrite the African history? The formation of the political parties in Zimbabwe and in South Africa happened at different intervals. The political influence of the formation of these liberation movements came from Kwame Nkrumah and Julius Nyerere.

Patrice Lumumba of Congo writes: "*The day will come when history will speak . . . Africa will write its own history . . . it will be a history of glory and dignity.*"[11]

That history of glory and history is being written today in South Africa. The death of former president Nelson Mandela had changed the face of the African continent, and I need to say this: the late former president Nelson Mandela was not an African American but was a Nguni of South Africa. The West was hijacking the former president Nelson Mandela's memorial service as if the West is the one that helped liberate South Africa. If there is one thing that the West needed to draw from former president Nelson Mandela's memorial services is this: ensure that the world is a better place. The West must stop supporting the insurgent groups in Syria. There is a fable that is told by Jomo Kenyatta of Kenya in an attempt to explain the Pan-Africanism and he said:

> *A simple interpretation of the fable shows that the man is the African and the hut is Africa, while the animals are the colonialists who invaded every corner of the continent as dictated by the 1884 scramble for Africa, which is the commission. Every colonialist used violence to scare, torment, exterminate, destroy, and control the African who in most cases was a docile believer and follower.*[12]

It took the sons and the daughters of the African peasants to study very hard and realized that education alone will not liberate the nation. Education alone would have not liberated the African continent alone without a radical liberation struggle. The point is this: there will be many people who have been hailed as heroes today had they seized the moment and joined the liberation movements and went outside their comfort zones and acquired military training to fight the enemy. But many saw the liberation struggle as something that was extremely costly and risky and that can't be wholeheartedly relied upon. Some people were accustomed to the system of oppression. They were only worried about the stomach and not even daring to think about the future, since the future looked very bleak and doomed in that moment. There are many black people in South Africa and all over the continent of Africa who knew very well that political oppression was a heinous crime to humanity, yet they murmur, quibble, and whine and did nothing about it. The very same thing is happening in Zimbabwe today. Complaining does not help at all while people are dying and a considerable amount of people are living under oppression. The question I have been asking most Zimbabweans I have met is, where to from here? They all say the same thing: there is no way out. We are stuck with ZANU-PF forever. When Pres. Robert Mugabe came from Ghana where he met his late wife Sally Mugabe, he discovered that there was already ZANU (Zimbabwe African National Union) as a political party in existence. This information was confirmed and affirmed by His Highness, Pres. Robert Mugabe, when he was talking to the son of the late Oliver Tambo, Dali Tambo, on a program called *The People of the South,* which was aired in South Africa on September 25, 2013. Joshua Nkomo had already formed his ZAPU (Zimbabwe African People's Union). Many scholars hold different political views about the formation of ZANU and ZAPU. According to Major General Hutson, ZANU was formed by Rev. Ndabaningi Sithole and Leopold Takawira and others while Robert Mugabe was in Ghana teaching there.[13] However, because of the political intolerance in Rhodesia at that time, political parties were banned by Ian Smith. It became very difficult to publicly announce that a certain person was a leader of a political party, since that meant imminent arrest. A political party would not have succeeded to bring the necessary change that was required to bring the government of Ian Smith in the negotiating table. ZANU (Zimbabwe African National Union) was led by Robert Mugabe, and ZAPU (Zimbabwe African People's Union) was led by Joshua Nkomo. ZANU formed their armed wing called ZANLA (Zimbabwe African National Liberation Army), and ZAPU's armed wing was called ZIPRA (Zimbabwe People's Revolutionary Army). It's of fundamental importance that I lay down on this political ground a concrete political foundation because these armed wings will later fight against each other even after independence in Matabeleland. Both ZIPRA and ZANLA were supported by the Republic of China and Russia. ZIPRA was stationed in Zambia and Angola, and ZANLA was based in Mozambique.[14] The ANC (African

National Congress) was also based in Mozambique. Even if the ANC had an office in Lusaka, Zambia, its members were also receiving training in Mozambique in Maputo under the leadership of the late president Samora Machel of Mozambique. Rhodesia was under economic sanctions that have been imposed by Great Britain, since Ian Smith decided to declare Rhodesia as the UDI (Unilateral Declaration of Independence) in 1965.[15] Great Britain had been enjoying the luxury of running Zimbabwe all along, since it was in control of Zimbabwe through its administrators. The UDI not only precipitated the fall of the Ian Smith regime but also brought about the most awaited change in Zimbabwean politics. Russia and China were funding the armed wings for both ZANU and ZAPU. These armed wings were infiltrating Zimbabwe from left, right, and center, and since Zimbabwe was under economic sanctions, it meant that Zimbabwe (Rhodesia) then didn't have sufficient financial muscle to defend itself. Apartheid South Africa became a crucial player in Zimbabwe's political drama. I have often argued that most of the Zimbabwean problems have been caused by apartheid South Africa, and they have to be solved by democratic South Africa. But South Africa too had its fair share of its political drama. The apartheid South Africa could not contain the infiltration of the armed wing of the ANC, Umkhonto We Sizwe, the MK. The apartheid government attempted to shut down the ANC by incarcerating the leaders of the ANC into the South African Chikurubi Prison know as the Robben Island. This prison known as Robben Island was later called the University of Robben Island simply because many inmates who were arrested at that time were educated and were teaching each other inside the prison. The fact of the matter is this: while these leaders of the ANC, PAC, ZANU, and ZAPU were languishing in prisons, the West was digging more holes in the African continent, and gold and diamonds were extracted like never before in the African soil. It becomes very difficult to split your focus between an economic issue and apolitical issue if you have to spend the rest of your time contemplating more about the political issue alone at the expense of economic issues. The point is during the liberation struggle, most African liberation movements were worried about voting than owning their mineral resources. Africans were worried about laws that were preventing them from commuting from one area to the other, and they did not pay sufficient attention to the economic issues of the time. It is of late where you begin to see the African people talking about economic freedom in our lifetime. Economic freedom should have been discussed in Lancaster House Agreement in 1979 in the case of Zimbabwe, and economic freedom should have been discussed in CODESA at Cape Town and Kempton Park in the case of South Africa. From 1966 to 1979, prior to the signing of the Lancaster House Agreement, Zimbabwe was surviving through the financial support from apartheid South Africa. If apartheid South Africa did not provide financial support and military support to the government of Ian Douglas Smith, then Zimbabwe could have attained its independence earlier than it did in 1980. The government of Ian Smith applied the same military strategy that was used by apartheid South Africa of using military power to quell the political violence that was engulfing the country. The Ian Smith government decided to arrest leaders of ZANU and ZAPU in 1964 and released them in 1974. The apartheid government decided to arrest the leadership of the PAC, AZAPO, UDF, and ANC in 1965. The incarceration of these political leaders of these political movements did not quell political violence that was going in Zimbabwe and in South Africa; in fact violence escalated out of control. It should be mentioned that during the liberation struggle, there were myriad of political ideologies at play in political circles. Some people suggested that the liberation struggle could not overcome well-orchestrated government machinery like that of South Africa, while some decided to form their splitter parties that did not make a significant impact after the democratic dispensation. PAC (Pan-African Congress), which is a splitter party from the ANC and was led by Robert Sobukwe, who later died in Robben Island in solitary confinement, is the case in point. The PAC did not make significant political impact in a democratic South Africa just like the Black Consciousness Movement (BCM). Most of the members of these political parties were disintegrated, and their political ideologies leave a lot to be desired. Nine months away before the South African national election, there were almost three political parties that have been formed. One should ask himself this critical question: How political correct is it to target voters as if voters are shares that are traded in Johannesburg Stock Exchange? The divergence in political ideologies between the ANC and the PAC was seen in the Sharpeville Massacre. The Sharpeville Massacre was succeeded by the Soweto uprising of June 16, 1976. The Sharpeville Massacre came to haunt South Africa again in 2013 in the Farlam Commission. There were comparisons that were drawn by advocate George Bizos in the Marikana inquiry—that the way the Marikina massacre victims were shot was exactly the same way as the Sharpeville Massacre victims were shot. The point is, had the ANC and PAC did not have political differences that emanated from varying political ideologies; Sharpeville Massacre could have been avoided. Had ZANU and ZAPU not had political differences that emanated from varying political ideologies, Gukurahundi of 1983 to1986 could have been avoided. During the liberation struggle, everybody was trying to be a political savior of the masses. In South African politics, everybody is trying to save South Africa from the depth of corruption that is ravaging South Africa like cancer. Some of our political leaders that are trying to save South Africa from the depth of corruption are already sitting on top of corruption charges. Some of these political leaders have already served their time in prison already for fraud and corruption. The apartheid system was a heinous crime against humanity, and its time had come to be abolished, and indeed it was abolished, but today we are confronted with another system that is facing us—the apartheid of poverty and corruption. The Palestinians have been marching in Palestine holding the picture of former president Nelson Mandela and calling the Israeli wall that had been erected by the Israeli government to separate Israel from Palestine "Apartheid Wall." The Palestinians likened themselves to black people who were living in oppression for quite a long period of time under the apartheid system of Hendrik Verwoerd and P. W. Botha. The Israeli government was in support of apartheid in South Africa, hence Prime Minister Benjamin Netanyahu could not attend the former president Nelson Mandela's memorial services, citing a lame excuses. The Zimbabwean economy was purely dependent on South African economy after Great Britain imposed economic sanctions on Zimbabwe. I have often said that Zimbabwe is addicted to economic sanctions, and economic sanctions are addicted to Zimbabwe. It seems as if Zimbabweans, even today, really don't worry about economic sanctions anymore. By the way, economic sanctions don't bother them any longer. The main aim of Britain to impose economic sanctions to the Zimbabwean government was to compel the government of Ian Smith to rethink the possibility of renegotiating a political agreement that would possibly bring to an end the political impasse that was crippling the economy of Zimbabwe. Prime Minister Ian Smith was a strong man, and he did not mince his words when he said, "A black man will never govern Zimbabwe in a thousand years." Simply put, there is no way a black person can lead white persons and govern white people as long as he lived. He miscalculated the black power, and he realized later that such statements were further destabilizing the country to the extreme. South Africa eventually withdrew its financial support from Rhodesia, and that made the regime of Ian Smith further weak and financially unsustainable.

During this period, the ANC armed wing known as Umkhonto We Sizwe worked closely with the armed wing of ZANU, since both armed wings were based in Mozambique fighting against RENAMO.Samora Michael of Mozambique became the first democratically elected president to head Mozambique that had been under the Portuguese rule since time immemorial. Samora Machel was instrumental in ensuring that the armed wing of the ANC, Umkhonto We Sizwe, and the armed wing of ZANU were getting proper military training. The political and military assistance that was provided by Samora Machel didn't sit well with the apartheid South African government. The apartheid South Africa wanted to make sure that the ANC armed wing was not getting a military support from the Mozambican government, and the Komati accord was signed.

David Hoile writes:

> *The resultant civil war in Mozambique had been one of the longest-running conflicts in Africa, socially and economically devastating the country: 90 percent of Mozambicans are said to live in poverty, 60 percent in conditions of absolute poverty.*[16]

The Mozambican war was the deadliest war in the sub-Saharan African region. The apartheid South Africa was providing military support to RENAMO of Afonso Dhlakama. There are many reasons why the apartheid government was supporting RENAMO militarily. First and foremost, RENAMO was fighting against FRELIMO, and in the thick of things, FRELIMO will provide military training to the armed wing of the ANC and the armed wing of ZANU known as ZANLA. The political instability in Mozambique was destroying the economy of Mozambique, and Mozambique became the shooting range for the ANC armed wing and the ZANU armed wing. The Mozambican war forced a lot of Mozambican immigrants to cross the border legally and illegally to settle in South Africa in the parts of Mpumalanga. The majority of us thought that the Mozambican war was going to spill over to South Africa. David Hoile continues:

> *On October 19, 1986, Samora Machel, the president of Mozambique, died when his Soviet-crewed Tupolev airliner crashed in South Africa on the mountains of Mbuzini.*[17]

There are multiple theories about the death of Samora Machel. Some suggest that Samora Machel did not die instantly when the plane crashed, but he was injected with a lethal injection that eventually killed him. It's undesirable to delve into the depth of speculation, since hearsay and speculation under serious scrutiny will not survive the legal test. What I do know personally as an individual is this: Samora Machel died on October 19, 1986; whether or not he was shot by the apartheid South African agents that could not be verified. The Soviet-crewed Tupolev was quickly transported to the police station in Tonga by the apartheid government. The commission of inquiry that was instituted by the Mozambican government attributed the crash to the engine failure, and that was the end of the story. The South African government under the late president Nelson Mandela erected a Samora Machel memorial, which is still celebrated by both South Africans citizens and the Mozambican citizens in Mbuzini in Mpumalanga where the airplane crashed. What was a contributing factor in the late president of Mozambique Samora Machel's death was to provide military training and military support to both the armed wing of the ANC and the armed wing of ZANU. The rationale behind providing military support to the armed wing of ZANU and the army of the ANC was this: when these armed wings of these liberation movements have been trained, they will launch a war in South Africa against the apartheid government and a war against the government of Ian Smith. It's also true that the Ian Smith government began to slowly but surely crumble piece by piece because of strong infiltrations that were coming from the guerillas who were based in Mozambique and those who were based in Zambia and Angola. The end of an era had come. The wave of political independence had come, and most of the leaders of the African liberation movements were not economically ready to turn their complex economies of their countries around. Political freedom is not more important than economic freedom. Economic freedom gives power to make economic choices, while political freedom gives power to make political choices, but it does not give you power to make economic choices. A rich man has absolute power to choose his breakfast whether he prefers cornflakes and milk or bacon and eggs. A poor man does not have a choice, but he eats whatever is available and whatever is given by his rich master. Do you still remember the story of Lazarus in the Holy Bible? The rich man in the Bible story of Lazarus represents a black person and Africa, but the rich man and his wealth represent the West and the Western settlers. Some people say the former president of South Africa, Nelson Mandela, represented Moses of the Bible days, and Egypt was the apartheid South Africa. The children of Israel were the black people that were living under the pathetic and inhumane condition of apartheid system. The death of Samora Machel was the biggest blow to the master plan of the African liberation movements that were based in Mozambique. Afonso Dhlakama of RENAMO released a press statement on the death of Samora Machel.

David Hoile writes:

> *"The struggle for national liberation in Mozambique does not end with Machel's death," and he went to say that "RENAMO struggle is to institute a political democracy and a system of constitutional government. Restoration of individual liberties is basic to redressing the economic ills and human rights atrocities of the FRELIMO regime." President Dhlakama ended by declaring that "the end of the long night of suffering of our people draws nearer."*[18]

It became apparently clear that the white rule in the land of our forefathers will be a thing of the past, but ushering this new political dispensation required the shedding of blood. It's the blood of the lamp that washes the sins of the people, but sometimes it's the blood of the brave people that can liberate the masses from political oppression. The African soil has soaked in a considerable amount of blood for innocent children and innocent women, and this African soil continues to soak in a considerable amount of blood of innocent children and innocent women in the Central African Republic even today. The end was near, but the problem was the end will catch the leaders of the African liberation movements flatfooted. African political independence caught everybody by surprise. South African political liberation came very late, and many black people had already assimilated apartheid in their DNA. The fact is even today in South Africa many black people have an apartheid DNA, and some black South African, to appease their white bosses, decided to study Afrikaans as their first language. These are the people who have given up their political ambitions to achieve their dreams of a democratic-free South Africa. Ian Smith and his UDI government eventually conceded to the idea of political settlement. The political solution to Zimbabwe's debacle will ensure that the country will go back and standstill with its economic feed. Economic sanctions have never been good since time immemorial. I have already said that some people think that an economic-sanctioned county will be creative if it is under perennial economic sanctions, while some people believe that economic sanctions can neutralize the political power of a robust and radical regime. In 1979 the British government invited leaders of the patriotic front to a constitutional conference at the Lancaster House. The Lancaster House Agreement had to ensure that there was a constitution that will ensure that free and fair elections are held. The Lancaster House Agreement had to also ensure that the Republic of Zimbabwe is led by the democratic government that have been elected by the people free and fair.[19] Lord Carrington, Foreign and Common wealth secretary of the United Kingdom, chaired the meeting. The conference took place from September 10 to December 15, 1979, with forty-seven plenary sessions.[20] These are the agreements that were reached by the conference:

- an outline of the Independence Constitution;
- arrangement for the pre-independence period; and
- a cease-fire agreement signed by all the parties.

In concluding this agreement and signing its report, the parties undertook

- to accept the authority of the governor;
- to abide by the Independent Constitution;
- to comply with the pre-independence arrangements;
- to abide by the cease-fire agreement;
- to campaign peacefully and without intimidation;
- to renounce the use of force for political ends; and
- to accept the outcome of the elections and instruct any forces under their authority to do the same.

Lord Carrington and Sir Ian Gilmour signed the report for the United Kingdom; Bishop Abel Muzorewa and Dr. Silas Mundawarara signed for Zimbabwe/Rhodesia; and Robert Mugabe and Joshua Nkomo for the Patriotic Front.[21]

The land crisis was a stumbling block in the Lancaster House Agreement, but eventually Robert Mugabe and Joshua Nkomo of ZANU-PF finally signed that they will not institute land reforms until the period of ten years has elapsed. Simply put, in Zimbabwe, even if Robert Mugabe would have won national election in 1980 for which he won, there wouldn't be a land distribution program that will be instituted until the ten years' period has elapsed. The truth of the matter is this: that is where things went horribly wrong in that Lancaster House Agreement. Why would you sign such a binding document that prevents and hinders the implementation of Land Redistribution Program? The whole idea behind this waiting period was this: the United States of America and Britain would fund the Land Redistribution Program. The question that springs forth in my mind is this: Where would the US government and British government get the money to fund such a costly program? The West had already amassed a considerable amount of wealth in their banks through enslaving the African people for quite a long period of time. Britain was already fabulously rich through the BSAC or BSACO, which was an amalgamation of Cecil Rhodes's Central Search Association and the London-based Exploring Company Ltd., which originally competed to exploit the expected mineral wealth of Mashonaland but united because of economic interests and to secure British government backing.[22] The annual revenue of BSAC or BSACO in 1937 was £311,000.[23] There was a considerable amount of pressure from both the United States of America and Britain for the African nationalists to yield to the United States of America and Britain's demands, and the land reform agreement could not have been reached if it was not for the intervention of some of the African leaders.

The British and the Americans, without putting pen to paper, promised the nationalists US$2.5 billion for the purpose of land reform within the first ten years.[24]

Simply put, this gigantic amount was going to be paid in installments to Zimbabwe's government provided that the nationalists would stick to the agreements that were enshrined in the Lancaster House Agreement. It's also true that the West never wanted their grandchildren to suffer in a situation where the Land Reform Program is implemented haphazardly. It was a wise move from the West to derail and delay the process of land reform because the West in that process would end up being the winners, not the losers. The game of politics is the cruelest sport ever, and the problem with it is this: the losers, most of the time, lose unfairly, and they normally die without recourse. There is abundant evidence that we see normally every day. Take for example the late Libyan president Maummar Gaddafi; he was killed by the militia groups, and no one was arrested. It is possible that the West knew very well that there were possibilities that the amount of US$2.5 billion might not materialize to be paid completely to the Zimbabwean government, since Africans are disorganized and they don't even keep proper financial records. The 1980 national elections went fairly well, and ZANU-PF won elections free, fair, and square. The following is the speech that was delivered by Prime Minister Robert Mugabe after ZANU-PF victory in 1980:

> *We will ensure that there is a place for everyone in this country. We want to ensure a sense of security for both the winners and losers . . . I urge you, whether you are black or white, to join me in a new pledge to forget our grim past, forgive others and join hands in a new amity and together, as Zimbabweans, trample upon racism.*[25]

It was apparently clear that the majority of Zimbabweans did not vote according to their political allegiances, but they voted along their ethnic lines. The reason why this is crucial is the following: there were many Nguni groups in Zimbabwe. There were coloreds, whites, Shonas, Ndebeles, Vendas, Tsongas, and other small groups that are not relevant for the purpose of my discussion. Ndebeles and Shonas were different people from different ancestral background, and they are both worlds apart from each other. The majority of people that are living in Zimbabwe today are Shonas. The number of Ndebeles has diminished drastically attributed to the mass killing of Ndebeles in Matabeleland. It's of critical importance to mention that Ndebeles are not Zimbabweans by origin because they came from South Africa. The argument of cataclysm change is also not relevant, since that will send us back in time. It's not relevant for the purpose of my discussion who got to Zimbabwe first between the Shonas and the Ndebeles. What is now public knowledge is this: the first people to advance to Zimbabwe were the Beja Tonga. These were Negroid. The rest of the groups followed after that. The debate and the discussion of who got to Zimbabwe are irrelevant and do not provide practical solutions to the economic problems that the country is currently facing. I find it stale and disinteresting, specifically to the youth of today. I am the greatest proponent of African history, but the problem with African history is much of it was written by Western scholars who were paid by the Western governments to write about Africa, which they don't understand. The irrelevance and the relevance of African politics will also depend upon the current political leaders that are leading African liberation movements.

Perhaps this is the reason there is a huge chasm between the political leaders of African liberation movements and the African youth today. This chasm emanates from the fact that the generation of the African liberation movement is old and pale. Most of the political dialogue hinges on the liberation struggle and the way the West annexed Africa. The African youth has great difficulty to juxtapose the current political and economic problems and the annexation of Africa by the West. It's imperative to make mention of the fact that most of the current political problems date back to the beginning of the eighteenth century. These problems were not solved then, and even today they are recurring to the future generation. It's my responsibility then to set the record straight that postponing a problem for the future is deadly dangerous. It's better to solve problems then and there when they emerge than to postpone them for the future. This theory that political problems will be solved by the next generation is sheer madness. African leaders of the twenty-first century should not think like the African leaders of the eighteenth century. African leaders of the past were confronted with a different set of political problems at their time. The next generation of African leaders should solve their political problems of their time also. The two distinct and unique political problems of different generations can't be married and be compared and contrasted, since they occurred in different times and different seasons. There is an African theory that says Africans problems need an African solution, but in the case of the Lancaster House Agreement, it was a totally different story altogether. The political defeat that the Ndebeles suffered at the hands of Shonas did not sit well with many Ndebeles, and they revolted.

Luke Zunga writes:

> *ZANU won fifty-seven seats, and ZAPU won twenty seats, and Bishop Muzorewa won three seats—a total of eighty seats out of one hundred; twenty seats were reserved for the whites.*[26]

I often wondered what could have happened had Joshua Nkomo won the national elections. I often wonder whether or not the current political problems that the government of Pres. Robert Mugabe is grappling with are going to be solved differently. I often wondered whether or not the killing of Ndebeles by the Fifth Brigade in Matabeleland could have happened. The same question can be asked in South Africa that had Chris Hani lived and succeeded former president Nelson Mandela after

1999, was South Africa going to be different compared to the South Africa we see today? In the case of South Africa, many people suggest that South Africa could have been better off with Chris Hani at the helm of South African government. These entire questions spring forth from the infinite intelligence of my subconscious mind and out of my curiosity. Curiosity killed the cat. Prime Minister Robert Mugabe of Zimbabwe did not institute the Land Redistribution Program per Lancaster House Agreement until the period of ten years had elapsed. When I was in Zimbabwe, I saw some of the farms that were bought by the Zimbabwean government and the current communities that have been resettled in those farms. I need to say this: part of my reasons to embark on such a back breaking journey is South Africa is currently dealing with the problem of land redistribution, and the person who brought back this land issue is the expelled ANCYL president Julius Malema. I have written extensively and expansively about the ANC Youth League including the expelled ANC Youth president. I have no desire then to continue the very same discussion even in the next chapters about the ANC Youth League. The amount of US$2.5 billion was paid in tranches, and as it is expected, there was corruption taking place. Where there is money, there is corruption, and where there is corruption, there is money. The greatest destroyer of all radical politicians is money; in fact it is money that got Jesus killed. The love of money is the root of all evil, as the apostle Paul said in one of his epistles. Money divides and destroys political parties, and money steals textbooks from classes. The love of money compels a couple that is deeply in love to divorce just because of money. The old saying goes, "Money makes the world to go round," and more money more problems, so they say. The Land Redistribution Program of Zimbabwe was not immune from corruption and nepotism just like any other land distribution program. The more I write about Zimbabwe's Land Redistribution Program, which in actual fact is the land redistribution problem, the more I become very frustrated and angry, and I will tell you why. My maternal grandparents were living in an area known as Komatipoort today. Komatipoort is very close to the Lebombo border, which is a border that separates South Africa and Mozambique. During the reign of Shaka Zulu ka Senzangakhona, there was a cataclysmic change in the lives of indigenous people. The head men of Shaka Zulu became rebellious and could not respect Shaka anymore, and in the process many people were scattered all over South Africa. What is critical at this juncture is this: even if indigenous people were not educated in Western methods and Western science, they could still detect and discover a place where there was life in it. Simply put, the South African indigenous people knew whether there was life in an area or not. After they have detected that there is life in a particular area, they will eventually settle in there. Let me give you this nugget: if there is life in an area, that area must be able to feed your livestock and feed your family. It's imperative that we bear this in mind: communicable diseases that are spreading like octopus today could be restrained and contained through African science even if the indigenous people were not educated in Western methods and Western science. My maternal grandparents settled in Mjejane in 1900. My maternal grandfather is still alive even today—his name is Joseph—and my maternal grandmother's name is Julia. They were both born 1937 in this place called Mjejane. My maternal grandfather's surname is Mazibuko, Mwelase. My maternal grandfather is a Zulu. In 1951 my maternal grandparents were awakened in the middle of the night by the apartheid regime agents, and they were supposed to collect all their belongings because the government of the day had realized that Mjejane was a very fertile land and there was enough water to support their irrigation system. My maternal grandparents were dumped in a bushy area in the middle of nowhere. There was a big fig tree is that area. You must bear in mind now that there was no water in that place and there was no school at all. By the way, there are no businesses around that can provide jobs for the community of my paternal grandparents. The apartheid government decided to name the area Fig Tree just because there was a big fig tree next to the main road where they were dumped. This fig tree community, which my paternal grandparents are now part of, was required to clear the land. They were also required to build mud houses, since at that time there were no modern houses of today that are built through bricks and roofed with heavy tiles. I am the product of that community, and I have often realized that the people of my community were angry at what happened to them in 1951. The people of my community are angry at the apartheid system that dispossessed them of their land without reasonable causes. They are the first one who discovered Komatipoort, but the Western settlers came to put their lousy inscriptions, claiming that they discovered Komatipoort and built a big sugarcane company, which is making millions of rands per year, while the indigenous people of the land are starving and suffering in the land of their forefathers. I was born in that area called Fig Tree just because of the big fig tree that was next to the main tar road. For the children of this village to be able to attend school in another village called Madadeni, they had to cross the Nkomazi River, which is always full of crocodiles and hippos. The majority of people were discouraged to study, and they opted to go work in the farms of the Boers in a place called Komatipoort. Simply put, the apartheid government would dispossess the indigenous people of their land and dump them in a deserted and far area where there is no life and come back with pickup trucks to pick them up again and give these indigenous people employment again. The sad part is this: you will now be working in the farms of the Western settlers that were once yours and head the herd of cattle that was once yours. It's like somebody taking your wife and pimping her back to you, and now you are paying double for your trouble. The majority members of this community have apartheid mentality, and some of them even today were wired to believe that a black person is inferior compared to a white person. That is why now and then I will hear members of my community say, "My white boss loves me," and the fact of the matter is this: your white boss does not love you. If he loves you, why can't he build a house for you next to his house? Bingo. The main reason your white boss loves you is now and then you look after his flock of pigs. It would take you three hours' walk to get to the bus station where there is a tar road. Their bus back then would move once a day, in the morning at five thirty and in the evening at five o'clock, obviously dropping people that were coming from work. My grandmother, who is still alive even to this day, was working for Mr. John, and her responsibility was to clean and cook and do the laundry and babysit the spoiled brat children for Mr. John. Sometimes in the evening my grandmother will come home with rice that Mr. John and his spoiled brat children were eating, and I would seize an opportunity and eat the leftovers of what Mr. John and his nasty children were eating. When I am full, I will drink water and relax. One day my grandmother came home with a white puppy; this puppy was given to him by Mr. John. The fact of the matter is this: whatever Mr. John would give my grandmother, it does not change the fact that Mr. John and his government of Hendrik Verwoerd and P. W. Botha have taken our land and are now enjoying the benefits of our fertile land. Fast forward to former president Nelson Mandela, after being realized in 1990 from prison, the change became imminent, and change became inevitable, and apartheid had run its course, and it had to get a decent burial, and indeed apartheid was given a decent burial. The release of Nelson Mandela meant that things were going to change politically. It meant that the ANC will take over the government from the apartheid government, and it meant that the land that was once dispossessed by the apartheid government will be given back to these communities that once owned the land and cultivate it. The apartheid government had provided financial support to these Western settlers to do farming in the land of our forefathers. When Nelson Mandela was released from his Chikurubi Prison known as Victor Verster Prison, the Western settlers were already filthy stinking rich. They had control over the economy of South Africa, and they have already established companies that were manufacturing their products and selling their products to the local market in South Africa even to the international market. The sugarcane industry is a big industry, and the majority of sugar in South Africa comes from two provinces, which is Mpumalanga and Kwazulu Natal. The sugarcane farms were already there from Nelspruit all the way to the Lebombo border, where there is a border that separates South Africa and Mozambique. These sugarcane farms also stretched from Komatipoort all the way to the border that separates Swaziland and South Africa. The point is the Western settlers had already covered a lot of ground economically, and there is nothing that could have been done economically to reverse the imbalances of the past. The majority of the means of production was in the hands of the Western settlers, and South Africans had sustainable jobs, and people had forgotten about the past, and they wanted to move forward with their lives. They had forgiven and forgotten. The fact of the matter is this: forgiving and forgetting does not change your balance sheet, but it changes your heart, and the fact remains—you will still be poor and broke, while your enemy is enjoying what was rightful yours. We are told that in the Bible, Jesus was invited by certain man by the name of Zacchaeus, a certified thief who was cheating people of their monies. Zacchaeus knew the tax system of the time, and the ordinary people did not know the tax system. He was cheating the people to the point that he became fabulously rich. Zacchaeus at one point invited Jesus, the Son of the living God, and hosted him in his gallery dinner that was probably funded through his ill-gotten wealth. Zacchaeus, out of nowhere, confessed that he cheated people their monies and pledged that he will give half of his wealth to the poor and he will eventually repay people that he cheated in fourfold. At least Zacchaeus would give half of his wealth to the poor, but the West has not given Africa anything except foreign aid that is slowly shrinking because of the financial crisis. The West is very rich—no wonder it can afford anything for its people—while Africans and our cheap political independence are languishing in poverty. The democratic government that was elected by the people of South Africa established a department known as the Department of Land and Rural Development. Through this department, South Africans of whom their land was dispossessed by the apartheid government would submit the land claims, and these land claims will be processed by the Department of Rural Development and Land Reform. My community also submitted their land claim and, the Department of Rural Development and Land Reform processed their claim of my community as soon as possible. There is a monumental mistake that I have seen happening under the sun. There are very few people in South Africa's land debacle that are resettling on the same land that was dispossessed from them by the apartheid government. Most of the communities opt for what they call "vouchers." Some communities have opted for the amount of R30,000 per family than returning back to the land that was dispossessed from them by the apartheid government. The fact is in South African communities, if their land was dispossessed, they don't return to their land, but they sell their land through vouchers. The community of my grandparents decided just like all communities did—they opted for money rather than returning to the original land of their forefathers. The politics of land is unfair and unjust. The winners take all, and the losers lose everything. They remain poor partly because of their stupidity. It's unfair and unjust to ask a poor person to choose between R30,000 and the land that he once owned. It's like asking a drug addict to choose between going to rehabilitation center and the next fix. We all know that most drug addicts won't prefer to take the rehab route; they would rather settle for the next fix. My grandparents' community settled for the large sums of money, which was not disclosed, and all what we know is that the money was invested in a bank, and it's generating interest each and every month. Each of my grandparents receive R10,000 at the end of each year, which is the interest of the original principal amount that is not known to the community. The fact is the exact amount is known by certain members of the community, and certain members of the community are not allowed to know. Prior to the establishment of this investment scheme that is generating interests and distributed to the community that once owned the land, there was another project that was very dubious and complex to understand. In the mid-1996 to 1998, people of my community began to submit names to the tribal office, and it was reported that these names will then be used for the allocation of farm for the people that were evicted and their land was dispossessed by the apartheid government in Mjejani. I have not seen the list, but what I do know is this: my late uncle by the name of Isaac did submit his name, and he was allocated a piece of land. I guess my late uncle was not kissed by the angel of luck. He sold back that land that was supposed to be his inheritance for life. My lovely uncle passed on as a humble pauper. My community members began to get eight hectares of land, and some even got twenty hectares of land. There was no scientific formula that followed that justifies the allocation of this land, which later became sugarcane farms. The Mozambican war that saw the late president of Mozambique, Samora Machel, dying at Mbuzini Mountains in South Africa caused a considerable number of people to immigrate to the Republic of South Africa. Some of the Mozambicans came to settle in my community. Since my community speaks SiSwati, and in Mozambique they speak Tsonga and Portuguese, the Mozambican Tsonga did not have a tough time to learn and understand the language that is being spoken in my community. The Mozambicans learned our language with ease and blended into our community, but the fact of the matter is we knew who Mozambicans were and who were the real South African people who came from Mjejane. We were shocked to the extreme to see that the people whom we knew very well are Mozambican migrants getting sugarcane farms at the expense of the native people of my community. The point is South Africans, just like my late uncle, got the land, and the process of farming started, and the Mozambicans also got the land, and the farming process also continue even in their farms. This was very bizarre to me and even to some people of our area. Is this Land Redistribution Program? If this is Land Redistribution Program, what system was used to separate South Africans from the Mozambican immigrants, or should I say illegal Mozambican immigrants? During Zimbabwe's election of July 31, 2013, it was reported that the Mozambicans were bused into Zimbabwe to vote for ZANU-PF, and that is why the elections of Zimbabwe were not free, fair, and peaceful. Some of the people who got the farms in my community who are Mozambicans are still staying in my area even today. They became rich instantaneously, and one man began to date all the women of my community. This man is from Mozambique, and he came to South Africa not even long ago; but all of a sudden, he now owned a farm, and he became rich in the twinkling of an eye. He bought a Rough Rider Toyota and was dating a schoolteacher. Majority of people who are educated would not prefer to date an uneducated person, particularly if this uneducated person is poor at most. But with this Mozambican rich man who is now a farm owner, those rules did not apply to him at all. The guy was the hottest property of the community. He was dating educated women and uneducated women at the same time. Since this man did not have a valid driving license, he destroyed the gear box of his Toyota Rough Rider in the twinkling of an eye. He eventually impregnated the schoolteacher, and they had a baby girl. The point is the Land Redistribution Program is dubious and complex to understand. Sometimes it becomes the breeding ground for corruption to happen. All systems somehow are bound to have sufficient cracks and loopholes that opportunists can utilize and take advantage of. South African municipalities are selling land to the property developers and make exuberant amount of millions, and the people of South Africa are still cramped in Alexandra and Diepsloot. I am surprised to hear people talking about expropriation of land without compensation because the very same people who are now landless, when they get their land, sell it through vouchers for R30,000. The West stole Africa's wealth and purely because of Africans' stupidity. I hope you know by now that land is a non-depreciable asset. Land does not depreciate but appreciates only; it therefore means that land is a precious commodity, and therefore there is no need for a person to sell his land just for a mere voucher of R30,000, and that is sheer madness of epic proportion. I have difficulties in understanding why a group of people would choose to take money instead of their land that was forcefully taken away from them by the apartheid government. I have great difficulty in understanding why my community decided to take money instead of their fertile land that was taken from them by the apartheid government. The idea of expropriation of land without compensation is not a viable option and can plunge a country like South Africa in the depth of poverty and in the process incur unnecessary economic sanctions that are perennial. I have argued that the impact of economic sanctions by far outweighs the impact of drone strikes. The reason I say that is the following: drone strikes will occur probably for a period of a week, while economic sanctions will hit the sanctioned country for quite a long period of time. The expropriation of land without compensation is a brutal system. It's fair to say that the Western settlers indeed took what belong to Africans. The approach that should be used to redress the imbalance of the past should be carefully thought through. There must be a national system that intends to address specific objectives that we are quite sure that they will contribute to the economy of the country positively. This is not the nineteenth century but the twenty-first century. Therefore, an approach of the twenty-first century should be different compared to the approach of the nineteenth century. It's imperative to understand that all problems present us with opportunities. This African generation has an opportunity to learn and the opportunity to grow economically and otherwise. It does not make logical sense to utilize the same method in South Africa; we know very well that it has failed Zimbabweans decimally. It's important then to study the Zimbabwean mistakes and learn from them in moving forward. It's also common knowledge that doing the same thing over and over again, expecting different results, is an incurable mental disorder. It's better not to implement an economic system if you don't understand it rather than to implement an economic system that you don't understand and create perennial problems that will have to be solved by the future generation.

> *In 1979 Zimbabwean whites made up 5 percent of the population and, counting only 4,500 farmers, owned 70 percent of the most fertile land.*[27]

We cannot blame the white Zimbabweans for owning such a vast tract of land because the nationalists signed in the dotted line in the Lancaster House Agreement that the land reform will not be implemented until the end of ten years. The point is, why would you sign a self-defeating document like that? I have often asked myself this question over and over again: Did the African liberation movements understand the economic trajectory of their economic policies, or they just apply trial and error now and then, killing innocent people through policies that have not be thoroughly researched and tested? It's easy to develop a policy that is heavily worded with political, grandiloquent, and unheard-of economics jargon, but the question is, will this policy address the pressing challenges that are affecting the masses on the grounds? An economic policy that is not well thought off will affect the masses on the ground in a negative way and therefore frustrate everybody including the foreign investors. Foreign investors hate chaos and mayhem because in a chaotic environment, there is no order and peace. Political stability provides economic environment for businesses to grow. Political stability is a fertile ground to establish perennial government institution that can stand even in the test of time. The lack of strong government institutions that can hold government accountable is more frequent than not the microcosm of political instability. There are many ways to measure political stability of any country. We can measure economic stability of a country through economic development and the level of financial resources that are dedicated to infrastructure projects. We can also measure economic stability through the strength of government institutions that can hold government officials accountable. There are three government institutions in South Africa that can hold government departments and their officials accountable. I don't mean that these are the only three government institutions in South Africa that can hold government departments and the government officials accountable. The Public Protector, the Auditor General, and the Judiciary Service Commission—all of these South African institutions are very critical in creating a perennial political stability in South Africa. It becomes very important then to ensure that these institutions maintain their independence and are led by people of higher integrity who can't be implicated in sex scandals and political scandals. I have discussed in depth that the Lancaster House Agreement did usher the dawn of democracy in Zimbabwe, but it ended violence that had ravaged and destroyed the country for quite a long period of time. Many people had lost their lives in the Second Chimurenga. I was shown a bowl while I was in Heroes' Acre in Zimbabwe. That bowl represented the spirits of people who died outside of Zimbabwe while fighting for the political liberation of Zimbabwe. In the case of South Africa, there are many graves that have been identified after 1994 that belong to the sons and daughters of the soil. The concept of the sons of the soil is also used to refer to people who were fighting for the political liberation of both South Africa and Zimbabwe. It's also used to refer to freedom fighters not only in South Africa and Zimbabwe only but also in any other country in the African continent. The dangerous clause that was contained in the Lancaster House Agreement was "willing buyer, willing seller" principle. Who is the willing buyer, and who is the willing seller? The willing buyer are the Zimbabweans of whom their land was taken by the government of Cecil John Rhodes, and the willing sellers is the Western settlers who were given the land free of charge on their silver platter by Cecil John Rhodes and his friends, the likes of Leander Jameson. Leander Jameson was also buried in Matopos National Park not far away from his friend Cecil John Rhodes. Cecil John Rhodes, Leander Jameson, and Coghlan breathed together. They were mafias of Britain. They came to Africa purely for gold and diamonds. They didn't come to Africa to enrich Africa, but they came to Africa to impoverish Africa; after all, they are not

Africans, and they didn't have Africa's interests at heart. They did colonize Africa, and they did impoverish Africa. Little did they know that they would not see Britain anymore because eventually they died in Africa. The love of gold and diamonds is the root of all evil. The love of Zimbabwe's diamonds and gold is even the worst root of all evil, or should I say the love of mineral resources is the real root of all evil. Gold and diamonds are very addictive precious metals. Once you start smuggling diamonds and gold, it's extremely difficult to stop. Even the people of Marange struggled to let go of their precious stones just because gold and diamonds are the most addictive mineral sources ever. Gold and diamonds are addictive just like cocaine and tick. Unfortunately there are no rehabilitation centers for people that are addicted to diamonds and gold, but there is help for those people who are addicted to drugs. I have often heard people saying that drug addicts can sleep while standing. I thought they were lying until I saw it for myself in Pretoria. It's a scientific fact that you can sleep while standing under the influence of drugs.

> *Between 1980 and 2000, Britain provided a total of £44million to the government for land resettlement.*[28]

Different people have different view about this amount of money. Some say, look, the Zimbabwean government was not buying the land from the white commercial farmers to resettle destitute and displaced communities, but the government was using this money for the benefit of ministers not for the benefit of the poor people of Zimbabwe. Simply, put the large chunk of money that was paid by Britain to the Zimbabwean government did not go to the purchasing of farms for the purpose of resettling destitute and landless communities. Some of this money grew legs and disappeared, just like the late Osama Bin Laden, who disappeared in Afghanistan for years, only to be found later in Pakistan.

> *In 1981 the new government organized the Zimbabwe Conference on Reconstruction and Development in which more than £630 million of aid was pledged. Only a small share of this amount was used to finance land resettlement. Despite lobbying by the British government, no other donor was willing to help finance the purchase of land, and only the African Development Bank, EU, and Kuwait Fund paid for other investments required by the new settlers.*[29]

If the amount of £630 million was not used entirely for the benefit of the people on the ground, then what was is used for? When I was in Johannesburg interviewing a certain Zimbabwean gentleman who said to me, "I don't blame the British—they have played their role. I blame our leaders—they have misused the money that was designated for the purchasing of land," I have often wondered when I was in Zimbabwe which communities were given these farms, since there was a vast tract of land that was empty. The answer to that question is this: quite frankly people who occupied the farms in 2000 were not organized communities but a group of young boys who were supposed to be at school, but they occupied land that they don't even understand a thing about.

> *British contribution in terms of aid to Zimbabwe stood at half-billion pounds since independence. Of this total, £47 million was targeted for land reform, and approximately £100 million was budgetary support, which could have used for land reform. Britain's initial £44 million resettlement grant, which ran out by 1988, formally expired in 1996.*[30]

Under normal circumstances when financial transactions take place, there are relevant documents that need to be kept. These source documents become important in the case of dispute. The lack of financial record keeping becomes a problem when the disputes ensue because everybody will be pointing fingers at everybody trying to protect themselves. I have heard conflicting stories about Zimbabwe's farm invasion of 2000. Some people seemed to put the whole blame on Britain, while some people put the whole blame on the government of Zimbabwe. Some African scholars seemed to have varying views about Zimbabwe's crisis. Some African scholars have emphasized the fact that the whole farm invasion problem was not necessarily a serious problem that warranted the rapid response that it received. The main problem was the formation of the MDC (Movement for Democratic Change). The MDC-T, as is known today, was formed almost in 2000. ZANU-PF had been enjoying the political leeway all along, and in the process, it became politically lazy and ignorant of the people. The people of Zimbabwe became sick and tired of the draconian laws of the government of the day. The people wanted change, and the MDC-T came at the right time at the right place. The main problem with the MDC-T, as it is known right now, is it had a backing of white commercial farmers. The white commercial farmers believed that by joining the MDC-T, they will outvote ZANU-PF through the national elections and take over government from the ZANU-PF. Corruption in Zimbabwe prior to the invasion of 2000 reigned supreme in the government. Prior to the formation of MDC-T, as it is known today, there was a DRC War. DRC (Democratic Republic of Congo) had been in the civil war for quite a long period of time. Most people say there is an intricate connection between the farm invasion of 2000 and Zimbabwe's troops that were sent to Democratic Republic of Congo in 1998. The Zimbabwean troops that were sent to the Democratic Republic of Congo in 1998 cost the Zimbabwean government a considerable amount money that was not even budgeted for. The fact that a considerable amount of money was spent in sending the Zimbabwean troops to DRC also meant that the majority of government services to the Zimbabweans had to suffer. Wars have become very expensive to fund over the years. There is no country in the world, maybe excluding the G7 countries, that can send its troops to a war zone to carry out peacekeeping missions out of the blue without proper financial plan. The DRC War nearly brought the government of Laurent Kabila to a standstill. The DRC War saw the president of DRC, Laurent Kabila, being murdered by one of his bodyguards. I have asked Mr. Silverton about the DRC War. Mr. Silverton, who was part of the six thousand troops that were sent to DRC in 1998, said to me, "Listen, the Congolese were behaving like animals, and they are not even educated, most of them." Mr. Silverton said to me that the Congolese from Katanga believed that if they die in Katanga, they will resurface in Kinshasa. He went on to say, by the time the Zimbabwean troops got into the capital city of DRC, Kinshasa, the M23 had already advanced, but they had not yet taken control of the city. The Zimbabwean troops managed to push back the rebel group M23 and got control of the capital city, Kinshasa. The sending of Zimbabwean troops to DRC in 1998 was partly a business decisions due to the business opportunities that were existing in DRC. There are business opportunities in each and every war. Please don't get me wrong; there are economic gains in each and every war to be made. The Zimbabwean government saw the DRC as a good business opportunity to make up for the shortfall it had suffered over the years. The sending of the Zimbabwean troops to DRC was not purely for humanitarian reasons—who cares nowadays about innocent people dying anyway! Political leaders and heads of states of the world are only concerned about lining up their pockets, not providing humanitarian aid to innocent women and children. Providing humanitarian aid is the last thing on the list of many good economic opportunities that need to be seized and maximized. I don't enjoy the game of war, and I am not an advocate of a considerable amount of people dying just because someone or somebody wants to make a profit. The farm invasion of 2000 was an indictment specifically to South Africa and all other countries that are still battling with the issue of land. There are many lessons that need to be learned out of Zimbabwe's Land Redistribution Program, which I prefer to call land redistribution problem. It's possible that South Africa can learn from Zimbabwe's Land Redistribution Program and not repeat the same mistakes in the future.

Chapter 6

THE END OF AN ERA

Each and every generation will have its own challenges and problems that it should solve. Each and every generation is unique in its own way. Generations come and go, and a new generation will be born. Within each and every generation, there are leaders that have potential and capability to outdo and outsmart the brave works of the previous generations. The main problem of the new generation will be wasting time glorifying the brave works that have been achieved by the previous generation. Political problem defines a political party, and political party defines a political leader, and political leader shapes, changes, and builds a political profile of a country. This is exactly what apartheid did to the people of South Africa and to the ANC. There would not be Nelson Mandela without apartheid, and there would not be an ANC without apartheid; therefore, apartheid was necessary at that time to elevate the ANC and the leadership of the ANC to the level where they begin to attract the world's attention. The political conditions of that time warranted that some brave people had to confront the system head-on, and the brave generation of that time did exactly that. The Mandela generation clearly cannot be duplicated or replicated; in fact there is no need to try and mimic or imitate the Mandela generation, since the current economic conditions that we are facing today in South Africa and in the continent of Africa are totally different from the conditions of that time. Our economic challenges that are facing South Africa and the rest of the world are totally different from the economic challenges that were facing the Mandela generation. It's worth noting that not all African countries have reached the political milestone that has been traveled by South Africa. There are other African countries that still need to produce their own Nelson Mandela, just like the Republic of Zimbabwe, Central African Republic, and DRC (Democratic Republic of Congo), which are still under political quagmire. There are a lot of books that have been written about former president Nelson Mandela, and Nelson Mandela himself has written extensively about the liberation struggle and the political challenges of his time. He has written extensively and expansively about his own belief and the reason he believed that the South African political problems could be solved through establishing the armed wing of the ANC, which was known as Umkhonto We Sizwe (the spear of the nation). I have no desire or interest to duplicate and rewrite what already is in the public domain about either the ANC or Nelson Mandela because that would not serve any purpose anyway. What is critical about the life of the late Nelson Mandela is the political trend and political standard that he has set for all political leaders all over the world. He has set a very high political standard that made the United States president Barack Obama say, "He makes me want to be a better man." The fact of the matter is this: somewhere, somehow, deep down in the center of his heart, Barack Obama probably thinks that he is Nelson Mandela of the United States of America, since he is the first black president of the United States of America who was democratically elected by the people. Let's just say there are minor similarities between Barack Obama and the late president of South Africa, Nelson Mandela, simply because both of them are black and they are the first democratically elected presidents to head countries that were previously led by the white political leaders. Though the president of the United States of America would compare the late former president of South Africa to President Lincoln or Roosevelt, the fact of the matter is political leaders are incomparable. You cannot compare Weston Churchill Sr. to Nelson Mandela, and you can't compare Roosevelt to Nelson Mandela simply because some of these people have committed the most despicable atrocities against humanity. I have never heard people worshiping Adolf Hitler of Germany simply because of the considerable number of Jews that died at his hands. Nelson Mandela was in a class of his own, and nothing can be compared to him, and there is no need to attempt to duplicate and replicate his bravery deeds simply because the same challenges that were facing South Africa then are not the same challenges that are facing South Africa today. The current responsibility that is facing South Africa is to ensure that South Africa, specifically the current leadership of the ANC, conducts itself in a manner that would have pleased former president Nelson Mandela if he was still alive. The Mandela generation has marked the end of an era.

The Nelson Mandela era had come and gone, and right now we are in the new era—the era of the weapons of mass destruction and the era of social networks, and Zimbabweans are in the era of economic sanctions. This new era has many challenges that are facing this generation compared to the challenges that were facing the previous generation. The Nelson Mandela generation dealt with the political impasse that was facing the country then. They (the Nelson Mandela generation) confronted the political problems of that time and conquered them, and we are now in the second transition, as they call it in the ANC. This new South African generation is confronted with the apartheid of poverty and unemployment. This new generation is confronted with the apartheid of AIDS/HIV and economic challenges. This new generation has been confronted with the apartheid of corruption and land that is still a very serious problem in South Africa, and it's likely to remain unsolved partly because of the confusion around this problem. This new generation is confronted with the apartheid of lack of clean water and electricity, and poor sanitation. Since the Mandela generation had solved the political problems of that time, which were purely political, now we must solve the economic problems of our time, which are not purely political but purely economic. Our economic problems are much more complex, but they are also not insurmountable. Times, seasons, and challenges define leaders, and these leaders are more frequent than not defined not only by their acts of bravery but also their decisiveness in the midst of those economic challenges. The end of an era marks the beginning of new things that are about to come. The end of an era simply means that the past is gone, and we have overcome the past through the bravery deeds of the previous generation. The previous generation, or the Nelson Mandela generation, had taught us South Africans and the rest of the world that there is no problem and there are no challenges that can withstand the zeal, zest, and gusto of the human spirit. There are no mountains that are too high enough not to be climbed, and there are no rivers that are wide enough not to be crossed. There is no system, whether it's a political system or an economic system, that has been created by a stubborn person like Hendrik Verwoerd that can withstand the collective zeal, zest, and gusto of people when the people themselves are united in their own diversity and they are determined that they will confront the same problem collectively as one. The problem that is likely to make this new African generation perhaps not to rise above the political trend that had been set by the generation of Nelson Mandela is partly because everybody is trying to be a hero. Instead of confronting our economic challenges of our time as a unit and a collective, we confront our economic challenges as individuals seeking self-glory. There is one piece of information that has been missed in the whole Nelson Mandela generation—the fact that the Nelson Mandela generation was not functioning as an individual but as a unit and a collective. This new generation will not achieve what the Nelson Mandela generation had achieved unless otherwise we conduct a thorough introspection within and begin to understand that unit is power, and united we stand but divided we fall. This new generation has a considerable amount of ammunition to strike the enemy in the head should we come together and work as a unit, not in silos in an attempt to become Superman. I have learned something profound when working with a group or studying with a group. I have often discovered that in a group there are people who listen very carefully, and they are very good in listening to a good idea and can listen to a good idea and then refine it and fit it straight where it should be fitted. Then there are people who like talking all the time, and these are people that are very destructive, and more often than not they usually seek their own ideas to be the adopted as if they are the genius of the geniuses. These groups of people in politics, when their political ideas of expropriation of land without compensation and nationalization of mines are not adopted, normally break away and start their own thing. They start their own political party in order to prove that their political ideas are always right. The Nelson Mandela generation could not have achieved the political victory that we are celebrating today in South Africa had they failed to work as a collective and a unit. It's important to mention the fact that behind the success of the Nelson Mandela generation, there were many people that were not even mentioned, and their names could not be written in the history books, but the contribution that they made was very important in ensuring that the political objectives of that generation were achieved. Those who worked behind the political scenes to ensure that the political objectives of that time were achieved understood it clearly that every product should have a face. The face of every product represents the product itself; therefore, the generation of Nelson Mandela chose Nelson Mandela as the face of the product. When the product sells, the whole company will make good revenue, and everybody will be happy. But that does not mean that the face of the product is better than the people who manufactured the product. There are people that you will not read about in the history books of the ANC, but they were very crucial in the construction and in the crafting of the ANC policy document called RDP (Reconstruction Development

Programme). This is the very document that was used by the ANC in 1994 to campaign for the national elections, and in that national elections, the ANC had to have a face, and Nelson Mandela was the face of the RDP, but that does not necessarily mean that Nelson Mandela single-handedly crafted that document that saw the ANC assuming the state power. My point is this: our generation is more obsessed with self-enrichment and self-gratification to the point that it would have been very difficult to achieve the same amount of success, or even more in comparison to the Nelson Mandela generation if we were given the same political conditions the previous generation was operating under. The difference between the Nelson Mandela generation and my generation is not the political conditions but the political approach to a political problem. Our economic approach today is primarily dominated by individual ideas and individual philosophy. When a person becomes rich, he normally thinks that the best way to flaunt his wealth is to establish a political party. The political party becomes the political vehicle to flaunt his massive amount of money that he has attained through unscrupulous means. I have seen this happening in the South African politics. Political parties that have been founded on an individual philosophy and a personal belief of a single person become very dangerous because in politics the success of a political party is based on the success of collective leadership that is unanimous in decision-making process. The decision-making process does not necessarily mean that all individuals involved in the decisions-making process should have like minds. The individuals involved in the decision-making process can have different political ideas but must allow this diversity of ideas because it's through diversity where unity can be tested and strengthened. The Nelson Mandela generation had set a political bar too high for the current generation, and we will need to work in one accord economically to perhaps reach that political bar that had been set by the Mandela generation. It's important to note that that there are no political gains right now to be achieved. The political challenges that are facing this generation are totally different to the political challenges that were facing the Nelson Mandela generation back then. Some even went to say there are many complex challenges that are facing this new African generation compared to the challenges that were facing the previous challenges. Personally I think the world keeps on evolving, and as results of that, there are many challenges that are facing the world today than ever before. The scientific inventions that are happening today are by far exceeding the scientific inventions that were ever discovered in the history of science. It therefore poses a very serious challenge to this African generation because it simply means that there is more that needs to be done with less time. India has just sent its astronauts to space, and in the African continent there is no African country that has managed to explore this scientific endeavor. We Africans still rely on the West to hear the Western scientists telling us about how is life on Mars. We are still grappling with minor issues, the issues of land and mineral resources, while our counterparts are advancing. The fact of the matter is this: we have spent a considerable amount of time reciting our political victory to the point that at the end we lost a broader picture—the broader picture that does not only end in political gain but also ends in economic gain and even in a new scientific discoveries. If I may ask, when are we (Africans) going to send our scientists to the moon and Mars? I am not talking about joining the Americans when they are going to the moon or Mars, like Mike Shuttleworth did in the past—I mean, sending our own black scientists and astronauts to the moon and to space to study that other side of the world and eventually come back with a vast amount of knowledge to disseminate among us. It therefore means that we need to change the way we think about ourselves. I really don't see any reason to keep on sending our African students to study medicine in Cuba while we claim that we are an exceptional continent that had been endowed with a vast amount of mineral resources while still sending our youth abroad to study medicine. I am looking forward to an era where different countries will come to South Africa to study medicine in our South African universities simply because we are now advanced. While we are celebrating the life and the political achievements that have been attained by the Nelson Mandela generation, we must remember that the economic and scientific challenges that are facing the world today are increasingly becoming complex each and every day. I went to buy a Samsung plasma television the other day. I discovered that this Samsung plasma was manufactured in Thailand. I became very angry simply because everybody right now in South Africa almost owns a Samsung plasma flat screen, and the painful part is this: these products are not manufactured by my African brothers and sisters. Whenever South Africans buy a Samsung plasma screen that was manufactured in Thailand, it simply means that we are sending job opportunities to Thailand and we are creating unemployment in South Africa. It also means that we are participants of our own destruction because there won't be sufficient employment opportunities for the youth that are still at South African universities. We Africans need to dance and sing, but there must come a time when we must stop dancing and singing and start using our brains. The world is moving, and the world is moving fast. We need to eat, dance, and marry, but after that we must begin to plan and strategies for our future. I don't think that God created Africans and placed us in the African continent for the mere simple reasons of eating, singing, and dancing. If Africans claim to be only good in eating, singing, and dancing, that must be an insult to God. There is no way that we can be created and placed in the African continent that is rich in minerals resources while we the people of Africa don't have the know-how and the expertise to utilize these mineral deposits to our advantage. We have learned that God, through his own wisdom, normally creates the end from the beginning; simply put, he created the African continent first and then impregnated the African soil with mineral resources and eventually created Africans in his own wisdom. It therefore means we (Africans) do have the sufficient IQ to utilize our mineral deposits to lift ourselves out of poverty. It also means that we (Africans) have sufficient IQ to solve our own African problems without the help of the West. I have often heard France president François Hollande suggesting that France has a moral responsibility to solve CAR problems. I think African leaders collectively have a moral responsibility to solve CAR problems. The main reason the French president François Hollande says that France has a moral responsibility to solve CAR problems is that most African leaders are afraid to step into CAR soil partly because there is too much infighting in CAR. But the other reason France has a moral responsibility to solve CAR political problems is that partly CAR is a French colony. On July 18, 2013, it was Nelson Mandela's birthday, and it took place while he was still in the hospital, in MEDI CLINIC, in Pretoria. The majority of South Africans were now and then flocking to the MEDI CLINIC to either sing outside the hospital or put flowers and pictures on the hospital wall. There was a bit of political tranquility and peace at some point because the reports that were coming from the state spokesperson were sometimes very conflicting and confusing to follow and believe. These were the normal words that the state spokesperson will use: "The former president of South Africa Nelson Mandela's health condition is critical but stable." Some people might say, "What is this guy talking about? There is no such a thing as critical but stable." The fact of the matter is this: the late former president of South Africa Nelson Mandela was very old and frail, but the problem is most South Africans could not admit the fact that perhaps his time had come to meet his maker. The word "father" has a very deep meaning than what the normal ordinary people would think. The language of the state spokesperson was a political language. The reason the state had to come up with this complex medical statement was to ensure that South Africans don't lose focus and begin panicking. The medical language and medical jargon of being critical but stable brought about hope and courage, and it managed to diffuse the emotional pressure that a lot of people were beginning to experience. On September 1, 2013, the late president of South Africa Nelson Mandela was released from MEDI CLINIC and transported to his house in Houghton. The South African public was largely at ease partly because he was discharged from the hospital, and that makes logical and medical sense. The common assumption that average people will have is this: if you are released from hospital, it simply means that you are normally well. It does not mean that you are critical but stable, as the state spokesperson will normally suggest. If you are released from the hospital, it simply means that you are completely well, at least on the surface. We all knew that sometime there will be a time as South Africans that we will have to live our lives as a fatherless nation when former president Nelson Mandela is now gone but not forgotten, as one song says. The passing of the former president Nelson Mandela came as a shock to every South Africa, I must say. Though the former president Nelson Mandela was of age and frail physically, nobody expected him to die the way he did. It was Thursday evening, and the news that we were getting from the media was that the Mandela family had called for an urgent family meeting at their Houghton house in Johannesburg. The Mandela family has been calling family meetings now and then since the now late former president Nelson Mandela was hospitalized until the day he was discharged. There is nothing that the public of South Africa could have expected or suspected about that. It's a fact that each and every family should meet now and then to discuss their family plans and perhaps discuss even their family business. I slept little bit earlier that night, so I didn't see the South African president on TV when he was delivering the saddest news to the people of South Africa. When I got to work the next day, we were told that the former president of South Africa Nelson Mandela has passed on, and we stood up to observe a moment of silence. South Africa is an exceptional country in the whole world, though this concept of being exceptional is normally used by the US president Barack Obama when he compares the United States with other countries in the G7 league.

The president of Russia Vladimir Putin argued that the United States of America is not exceptional. He writes in the *New York Times*,

My working and personal relationship with President Obama is marked by growing trust. I appreciate this. I carefully studied the nation address on Tuesday. And I would rather disagree with a case he made on America's exceptionalism, stating that the United States' policy is "what makes America different. It's what makes us exceptional." It is extremely dangerous to encourage people to see themselves as exceptional, whatever the motivation. There are big countries and small countries, rich and poor, those with long democratic traditions and those still finding their way to democracy. Their policies differ, too. We are all different, but when we ask for the Lord's blessing, we must not forget that God created us equal.[1]

I guess when Vladimir Putin said that the United States of America is not exceptional, he meant that Russia is the exceptional country in the world. Every person is entitled to his own opinion about his or her country, and therefore that does not necessarily mean that you are a chauvinist. Pres. Barack Obama thinks the United States of America is exceptional, and Putin thinks Russia is exceptional, and I think that South Africa is exceptional. Vladimir Putin went on in his letter that he wrote to the *New York Times* that if the USA citizens think that they are exceptional, they might be opening themselves up for more attacks from terrorists in the near future. This is the statement that has been read by the South African president Jacob Zuma on December 5, 2013.

My fellow South Africans:

Our beloved Nelson Rolihlahla Mandela, the founding father president of our democratic nations, has departed.

He passed on peacefully in the company of his family around 20h50 on the 5th of December 2013.

He is now resting. He is now at peace.

Our nation has lost its greatest son. Our people have lost a father.

Although we knew that this day would come, nothing can diminish our sense of a profound and enduring loss.

His tireless for freedom earned him the respect of the world.

His humility, his compassion, and his humanity earned him their love. Our thoughts and prayers are with the Mandela family. To them we owe a debt of gratitude.

They have sacrificed much and endured much so that our people could be free.

Our thoughts are with his friends, comrades, and colleagues who fought alongside Madiba over the course of a lifetime of struggle.

Our thoughts are with the South African people who today mourn the loss of the person who, more than any other, came to embody their sense of a common nationhood.

Our thoughts are with the millions of people across the world who embraced Madiba as their own and who saw his cause as their cause.

This is the moment of our deepest sorrow.

Our nation has lost its greatest son.

Yet what made Nelson Mandela great was precisely what made him human. We saw in him what we seek in ourselves.

And in him we saw so much of ourselves.

Fellows South Africans,

Nelson Mandela brought us together, and it is together that we will bid him farewell.

Our beloved Madiba will be accorded a state funeral.

I have ordered that all flags of the Republic of South Africa be lowered to half-mast from tomorrow, 6 December, and to remain at half-mast until after the funeral.

As we gather to pay our last respects, let us conduct ourselves with the dignity and respect that Madiba personified.

Let us be mindful of his wishes and the wishes of his family.

As we gather, wherever we are in the country and wherever we are in the world, let us recall the values for which Madiba fought.

Lets us reaffirm his vision of a society in which none is exploited, oppressed, or dispossessed by another.

Lets us commit ourselves to strive together—sparing neither strength nor courage—to build a united, nonracial, nonsexist, democratic, and prosperous South Africa.

Lest us express, each in our own way, the deep gratitude we feel for a life spent in service of the people of his country and in the cause of humanity.

This is indeed the moment of our deepest sorrow.

Yet it must also be the moment of our greatest determination.

A determination to live as Madiba has lived, to strive as Madiba has strived and to not rest until we have realized his vision of truly united South Africa, a peaceful and prosperous Africa, and a better world.

We will always miss you, Madiba!

May your soul rest in peace.

God Bless Africa.

Nkosi Sikelele' iAfrika[2]

Friday, December 6, 2013, became a very long and a somber day in the Republic of South Africa. That was not the only the problem but the fact that the government of South Africa had to organize a memorial service within a short space of time, and in this memorial service, heads of states were supposed to converge in South Africa in order to pay their last respects to the late president of South Africa. The South African government managed to pull its resources together within a short space of time, and the heads of states from almost ninety-one different countries managed to attend the memorial service that was held in FNB stadium in Johannesburg. The list of the dignitaries was endless, but one person that I should not forget to mention is Pres. Robert Mugabe of the Republic of Zimbabwe with his wife, Grace Mugabe. In South Africa, since the death of the former president of Nelson Mandela, it has been raining heavily. Even on the day of the memorial service, on December 10, 2013, it was bucketing very heavily. There are many African theories about rain in African culture. Rain means a sign of good things to come, and rain also means that your ancestors are happy about you; but it can also mean that you lived a good life, and all your spiritual ways are open and clean. We were told through government agencies that the public will be given an opportunity to pay their last respects to the late former president of South Africa Nelson Mandela. The public was going to get their last opportunity to pay their last respects to the late former president Nelson Mandela in Pretoria. The public were given three days in order to pay their last respects. It's imperative to understand that the late former president of South Africa was a world icon. A world icon wants to be seen not only by South Africans but also even by people that are not South Africans. The fact of the matter is this: there were many people who wanted to pay their last respects to the late former president of South Africa Nelson Mandela, but taking into consideration the logistics and the volume of people that wanted to come and view the body of the late former South African president Nelson Mandela in the union building, only a few could manage to enter the union building without hassle. There were long queues in Pretoria to the union building, and even those who have seen the late former president of South Africa were crying afterward, and some even fainted after paying their last respects. The point is seeing somebody of the late former president Nelson Mandela's stature changes your life altogether. There is another theory that I have heard people talking about in Pretoria, though this is not even a Xhosa tradition or a belief for everyone in South Africa. Some people believe that if they can pay their last respects to an important person who was vital and instrumental in changing the political system of the country, if you can lay your eyes on a such a person, there is a bit of luck that you take away with you should you see the face of such a person. There is such a thing as Mandela magic in South Africa. This Mandela magic means that wherever the late president of South Africa would show up, there will be a change in the atmosphere and change of social environment. This theory is attributed to many events that the late president Nelson Mandela attended, and suddenly everything changed in favor of South Africa. In 2010 South Africa became the first African country in the whole world to host the FIFA World Cup, and that achievement was squarely and fairly attributed to the presence of the late former president of South Africa Nelson Mandela in Zurich. There are two crucial events that the presence of the late president Nelson Mandela changed the atmosphere. It was in 1995 when the Springbok, the South African Rugby team, won the Rugby World Cup. The second event where the presence of former president South African Nelson Mandela changed the atmosphere is when Bafana Bafana was playing against Tunisia in the final of the African Nations Cup in 1996. The South African team was full of amateur players, soccer players who never played soccer outside the boundaries South Africa. Tunisian players have been playing soccer for a considerable amount of time on an international stage. The South African soccer team appeared as underdogs. The presence of the late president of South Africa Nelson Mandela quickly changed the atmosphere, and Bafana Bafana won the African Nations Cup through this Madiba or Mandela magic, as they call it in South Africa in 1996. The same is true about paying your last respects to him. In fact one woman said she believes that paying her last respects to the late president Nelson Mandela could change her life forever, maybe even the life of her children. The theory about paying your last respects to an important person like the late president of South Africa Nelson Mandela runs very deep. I don't believe that there is enough information that has been written about the political struggle of South Africa. I have also come to the realization that had everything that happened in Robben Island was written, it would have been very difficult for South Africans, even for ordinary people, to understand the amount of knowledge that was going to be written. The point is assume that each and every inmate that was arrested and serving their prison term in Robben Island had to write his own book after being released. The one-million-dollar question is, How many books were these Robben Island ex-prisoners going to write? It's abundantly clear that there would not be enough libraries to contain and store the number of books that would have been written by the ex-prisoners who were serving their prison term in Robben Island. The point is not everything that happened in Robben Island is in the public domain. The late president Nelson Mandela had written extensively and expansively about his political struggle, including his love life. But there is less that we know about all the inmates that were in Robben Island. There is also less information that has been written about the wives of these inmates who were in Robben Island. The question that could easily spring forth to a young person's mind is this: How did these women of whom their husbands were serving their prison sentences in Robben Island survive the cold winter of Johannesburg while their husbands were away for a considerable amount of time? How did these women manage to survive a lonely life without thinking about the possibility of getting remarried to other men, since their husbands were away for quite a long period of time without any glimpse of hope that possibly one day they will come back home? I have come to the realization of the fact that there has not been enough knowledge and enough material that have been written about the beginning and the end of the African political struggle. It was 1:30 p.m. in South Africa, and everybody was glued to their TV screens, and I had already written that my Samsung plasma was manufactured in Thailand. Simply put, if it was not for the Thailand people, probably I would not have been able to enjoy the magnificent pictures that I am currently enjoying. We began to see on our TV screens the number of dignitaries that have come to witness the burial perhaps of the last world icon and the last gift of his generations. It's imperative that young and enterprising scholars should record the truth for our future generation, not the facts. I have said it before that facts normally change with time, but the truth remains even in the test of time. The list of dignitaries in the late president of South Africa Nelson Mandela's funeral was endless. But there is one person that I saw in that funeral processions that got me to think thoroughly about the future of Zimbabwe. I saw Morgan Tsvangirai, the president of MDC-T, walking with his wife. The question then that sprang forth to my mind was this: Is it possible that Morgan Tsvangirai of MDC-T was coming to take inspiration from the funeral of the late president Nelson Mandela? It is possible that the death of Nelson Mandela, as it was, does not only mark the end of an era from the South African political perspective but also marks the end of an era for the Zimbabwean people. Zimbabwe is not South Africa, and South Africa is not Zimbabwe. What happens in Zimbabwe does not happen in South Africa, and what happens in South Africa does not happen in Zimbabwe.

There is a person that I think has been ignored by history, and that is the father of the former president of South Africa Thabo Mbeki, Govern Mbeki. Nelson Mandela once said that the men that were serving their prison time with him in the Robben Island, if you can have a conversation with these prisoners, after the end of the conversation, when he was reflecting back, he normally realized that one's horizon had been enriched indeed. Govern Mbeki, the late father of former president Thabo Mbeki, was exactly that. He was very slow in speech but full of wisdom. He said in Robben Island, "They had to hope against all hope." Some of the tales of Robben Island in actual fact sound like chestnuts. Terror Lekota, the current president of COPE (Congress of the People), was arrested and sent into Robben Island. He said that in Robben Island some of the people who were serving their prison sentences there were not educated. There was a certain man who was illiterate and was serving his prison term in Robben Island. Because this man was not educated, he did not understand what ten years meant. When Terror Lekota and others began to teach this man that a year has twelve months and a month has thirty or thirty-one days, it began to dawn on him that he will be in Robben Island for a very long time. Then there was another man also who was illiterate. This second man was sentenced to twenty years in prison. He was illiterate just like the first man. He (Terror Lekota) and others, when they began teaching him how to count and write, began to understand that he will be in Robben Island for quite a long period of time, and he got a heart attack and died just like that. The late Steve Tshwete said, "The fact that you were serving your time in Robben Island, it meant that you were a dog even if you were educated like Nelson Mandela." The late Govern Mbeki said, "The warders of Robben Island cared much about their dogs than they did with the inmates that were serving their prison term in Robben Island." Each and everybody that was serving their prison term in Robben Island had their stories to tell. The more I spend a considerable amount of time focusing and reading more about Robben Island, the more it becomes clear to me that Robben Island was more than just a mere prison but a cemetery of political dreams. Robben Island is where political dreams were put to rest.

> *Former president Thabo Mbeki has called on South Africans to use Nelson Mandela's death to have a "critical review" of where the country is in terms of what Mandela and his comrades stood for.*[3]

It's important that we do a thorough review of what had been achieved by the South African government since the beginning of our democracy in 1994. It's also important to realize that the majority of the promises that were made prior to 1994 could have been achieved by the South African government provided it stayed true to its plan and long-term objectives. It's possible to set national goals that can't be achieved. The other problem that the South African people have come to accept is the fact that rural development is very slow and will perhaps remain like that for a considerable amount of time. The other problem that is facing the people of South Africa is this issue of goals. It's insanity to the extreme to set unrealistic goals. It's better not to set goals at all than to set unrealistic goals. Unrealistic goals are goals that can't be achieved at all. Then the next question is, why set goals that you know very well you can't achieve? It's like the issue of promises. There were many promises that were made prior to 1994 elections. These promises were made in the spirit of political freedom, but on hindsight and on vantage point, you begin to realize that perhaps much was expected from government and less was delivered by the government not because of lack of money but because of lack of capacity and skills. The last remaining legacy of apartheid is poverty. But we all know now that poverty is not spiritual but natural. Poverty is a product of man's ingenuity. There are multiple ways to decimate and destroy poverty. One of the ways to destroy poverty is through education. But education alone cannot solve South Africa's problems completely. But there is a need for a change of mind and a change of heart from the financial institutions like the World Bank (WB) and the International Monetary Fund (IMF) in their lending models. They have to recognize the fact that Africa has been impoverished by the West, and in the process the West invested Africa's wealth in these big financial institutions. Prof. Adam Habib writes:

> *Perhaps Graca Machel put it best to me when she said, "This is his final gift to South Africa. He could have just passed on, and we would have mourned. But he lingered on for six months and in the process got us to think about what it means to lose Madiba, what he stood for, and most of all, how to unite across the social boundaries that separate us."*[4]

We need to mourn and close the chapter of mourning; we can't mourn forever. Nelson Mandela has come, and Nelson Mandela is gone. The question that the majority of South Africans need to answer is this: Did the Nelson Mandela generation compromise their political values in exchange for instant pleasure, and did the Nelson Mandela generation stay true to their initial objectives and initial political goals, and did they achieve those political goals and political objectives? While we are answering these hard, pressing questions, we Africans must also ask ourselves fundamental questions that are relevant to our time and to our economic challenges. We must review the way we Africans set our goals and objectives, and we must now assess our economic trajectory in the African continent and compare our economy with the economies of the Western countries and then craft a long-term plan. The world is changing very fast, and African and South Africa specifically will need to change and adapt to the way the first countries do business. We (South Africans) need to mourn, but we can't mourn forever; that is a very serious mistake that we should not commit. Most African countries, after attaining their political independence, immerse themselves in the never-ending jubilation mood, and they folded their hands and said, "It's all well." It's possible to win the battle and lose the war. It's possible to declare yourself free while you remain in economic chains forever. The problem of the African liberation struggle is this: it was purely based on liberating Africa on the political level, not on the economic level. This was a very serious problem because the moment you shift your focus from the economic oppression and pay focus on a political oppression, even if you might win on a political level, but the fact of the matter is this: you lost the serious war, though you won the battle on a political level. These are the critical question that we need to keep on asking ourselves. Are we Africans really free because African children are now studying with white children, and are we free only because we are no longer carrying a dompass? Are we free while the majority of our people still live in shacks and tin houses? It will be very difficult for a person who is living in a matchbox house and tin house to concur with most South Africans who are living in the opulent suburb in Sandton, or opulent suburb in Pretoria. There could be varying views and varying responses that these two South Africans might give. The whole of Africa is suffering from a syndrome known as "dependency syndrome." It's dependency syndrome to live the rest of our lives as Africans relying on the West to provide everything for us Africans including the very same Samsung plasma screens that we are watching every day in our living rooms. I have given myself an assignment to monitor and assess most of the shops in Pretoria. I have come to the realization that Chinese citizens are invading South Africa, and they are not here to play but to make money.

I have also realized that most of the owners of most shops that are owned by Africans are not South Africans, in actual fact, but Ethiopians, Nigerians, and Cameroonians. I should make this point clear: I don't have any problems with Ethiopians, Nigerians, and Cameroonians. Most of the Internet cafés are either owned by Nigerians, Cameroonians, and Asians. It's rare that you will find a South African citizen owning an Internet café. The reason I am raising this crucial point is that partly the SMEs, small and medium enterprises, are very important in the reduction of poverty. It's also critical to mention the fact that there are other black South Africans who are owning mines and owning big businesses, the likes of Saki Macozoma, Patrice Motsepe, etc. That is not enough; that is just a handful of people that are thriving in this new democratic dispensation. I should also state that there are people who own big businesses in Sandton who are black South Africans. My point is this: there are very few South Africans today who can clearly say we are not living under the poverty line. The majority of people are living under poverty line even if they might deny it. The worst form of mental disorder is denial. The problem with being in denial is this: it will take you longer to get help than it ought to be. There is no way a sick person could get medical assistance unless that sick person acknowledges that he or she is sick. The longer the sick person takes, the worse the sickness becomes. The point is the more we prolong in Africa to solve the economic problems that are facing the African continent, the worse Africa's economic problems become. Everybody is coming to South Africa. I am not xenophobic or chauvinist for that matter. I am stating facts as they are. The Beitbridge border is the busiest port of entry to Zimbabwe. What makes this port of entry to Zimbabwe the busiest port of entry in Africa is partly because of the majority of delivery trucks that are passing through the Beitbridge border. Heavy-load trucks that are going to Zambia, Tanzania, and DRC pass through this border. Zambia, Democratic Republic of Congo, and Zimbabwe are landlocked countries. That simply means that they are not surrounded by the sea. Since these countries are landlocked countries, it simply means that their cargo that should be transported or shipped to the European countries should either be shipped through South Africa's port or at least the Namibian or Angola's port. The fact of the matter is this: most of these countries prefer the South African port Durban; the same is true with cars. The majority of cars that the majority of Zimbabweans are driving are from Japan and Korea. There are some Zimbabweans obviously who are driving cars that are manufactured in South Africa, but the majority of Zimbabweans in general are driving cars that are manufactured in Japan. The car dealers in Zimbabwe claim that the Japanese cars are new simply because they have not been driven for quite a long period of time in Japan. I beg to differ with them right then and there. The point is these Japanese cars can only reach Zimbabwe via South African port if the car dealers choose to transport them through road and even rail. The other route that the car dealers normally use to ensure that their cargo reaches their intended destination is through air transport. It's an open secret that if a cargo of goods is transported through an airplane, it will save time and complex logistically transport systems that it has to go through. But the problem with air transport is this: it is very costly, and it will still need an additional delivery truck to transport the cargo to its point of destination. Therefore, the majority of companies just decide to use the road and rail rather than following the easiest route, which is expensive and fast. Since Beitbridge border is the only route that connects most of the sub-Saharan African countries with South Africa, it becomes the busiest border in the whole of the sub-Saharan Africa. Where there is money, that is where there is corruption. Where there is corruption, it also means that there is money. Corruption is a new incurable cancer of Africa. In fact the only incurable disease that Africa is struggling with right now is corruption. Corruption is contagious and incurable. Corruption is the new leprosy for Africa, and it's also true that some people are corrupt from the womb. The question is, who is corrupt and who is not corrupt? I have often said that the main problem with the liberation struggle is this: it had denied the freedom fighters basic essential services like clean water and flushing toilets. While these freedom fighters were in the liberation struggle, they were not properly trained to run their own economies and understand the international trade after Africa has attained its political independence. There are those who chose not follow the guerilla route but went straight to Russia to study econometrics and quantum physics. Those Africans who chose to study in Russia more frequent than not lack liberation struggle credentials, and they know it deep down in their hearts. When the former freedom fighters normally argue, they argue on the basis of their personal experiences and personal challenges that they went through while they were in the bush; while the African intellectuals, when they argue, they based their arguments on what they have studied while they were in class in Russia. People who have been in the bush for quite a long period of time are inclined to be emotional and violent when they are in a robust debate rather than people who are from a class in Russia. This is critical because if political analysts will understand this principle, it will save our political analysts a lot of energy and power. This has been a case in the debate about the nationalization of mines and expropriation of land without compensation in Zimbabwe. African intellectuals who were educated abroad were defeated in this debate of expropriation of land without compensation, and eventually a considerable amount of people were plunged in the bottomless pit of poverty just because African nationalists were angry and bitter with Africa's colonizers. Joel Netshitenzhe writes,

> *When perfect balance in the middle is attained, a good leader emerges who is able to take a nation to new heights, but not necessarily remarkable in the public consciousness as "a maker of history."*[5]

South Africa managed to maintain this perfect balance in the middle; that is why leaders, the likes of the late president Nelson Mandela, emerged because there was a perfect balance in the middle. It's abundantly clear that since the majority of African countries are still in the never-ending wars, they have never attained this perfect balance that South Africa managed to attain in its political leadership. The one-million-dollar question then is, what constitutes this perfect balance in the middle? The perfect balance in the middle can only be attained in the middle only if there are varying views that seek to address the same problem. The point is there should be informed views that seek to address the common problem that will uplift the masses out of poverty. Informed views should be accompanied by the development of the economic policies, and then these policies should address the original problem that is on the table. What is abundantly clear about African leaders is they are always signing bilateral agreements after bilateral agreements, but when you observe the effect of those bilateral agreements, the only thing that is palpable is the very same poverty that was there prior to the signing of these bilateral agreements. Bilateral agreements that can't change the lives of the people should not be signed because signing a bilateral agreement and not signing the bilateral agreement won't change the lives of the masses anyway. Bilateral trade agreements were supposed to better the lives of the people, not further impoverish the lives of the people. The net gain of bilateral trade agreements can be measured through the economic perennial effect that it has in the lives of the ordinary people. The net loss of the bilateral trade agreements can be seen through the perennial appalling living economic conditions that the majority of African people are still living under. The precarious notion that the African leaders seem to follow is this: they seem to believe that the economic power is shifting from the West to the East, and as a result, they make an attempt to climb into this fast train of China. In effect most African countries right now believe that when China sneezes, the whole world is catching flu. Most African leaders feel very comfortable doing business with Asia than doing business with the West. The mere fact that China did not colonize Africa in the first place does not necessarily mean that China is a good and faithful business partner. It's possible that China will be a superpower of the world in the near future. But to be a superpower does not necessarily mean that you need to control the whole world, but it simply means this: as long as you can provide Africa with a considerable amount of foreign aid and intervene now and then in political squabbles that are crippling the African continent and pass that test, you are a superpower. The theory about being a superpower country all over the world is no longer based on your military power but on the amount of goods that you can export to Africa and the amount of money that you can offer African countries as a gratuitous gift in a form of foreign aid. Therefore, in essence, there are two tests that a superpower country needs to pass: one, manufacture a considerable amount of goods in your country and then export these goods to Africa, and, two, provide a never-ending stream of foreign aid to Africa as long as you can. Then you are a superpower country. This has been the business model of the West from time immemorial, and I have great difficulty thinking whether China is going to use the same business model in Africa or not.

The information office of China's cabinet recently published a white paper on "*China-Africa Economic and Trade Corporation*" in which it said *"the scale of China-Africa trade expanded rapidly. In 2012 the total volume of China-Africa trade reached US$198.49 billion, a year-on-year growth of 19.3 percent. Of this, US$85.319 billion consisted of China's exports to Africa, up 16.7 percent, and US$113.71 billion was contributed by China's imports from Africa, up 21.4 percent. Total China-Africa trade volume, China's import volume from Africa all reached new highs."*[6]

I beg to differ with the information office of China on this trade relation between Africa-China trade relations. What is visible to the eye even a blind person can see is this: China is exporting the majority of its goods to Africa, and Africa does not export same volume of goods to China. My point is simple: China imports less from Africa, and Africa and its citizens consume a considerable amount of products from China. I have already mentioned it before: as far as I know, the majority of the products that are used in South Africa are imported from China. I have already mentioned the fact that the majority of the cars that are driven in Zimbabwe are from Japan. The only visible way to see which continent exports more between Africa and Asia is the impact of the results, which can only be seen in the balance of trade of these continents. It will be unjust and unfair to say Africa is exporting more now compared to the previous years simply because Africa's economy is not on the same economic scale as the economy of the West. South Africa's economy is the biggest economy in the African continent, and that does not necessarily mean that South Africans are all rich in a literal sense. It's also a scientific fact that South Africa has the biggest economy in the African continent. It's possible to say that Africa is exporting more to China, while in essence; it's only South Africa that is exporting more to China compared to any other African country. My problem with China and all this statistics that people are always throwing around to make their economic points make sense is this: almost everything that I can get my hands on, except for a few products that are manufactured in South Africa, were manufactured in China. The same laptop that I am using right now to write this book was manufactured in China. The question that I need to ask those who are the proponents of Africa-China trade relations is this: Do you honestly realize that China is invading Africa just like the West invaded Africa in the past? China is invading Africa. The majority of Africans don't really see China as a political threat. They see China as a friend in need and a friend indeed. Africa has been tossed to and fro by the West in the past, and right now China is tossing Africa to and fro. The more a country imports more goods from other countries, what it means to the people of that country is this: they won't have sufficient employment, since the majority of their products are not produced locally. The more China continues to export their products to Africa, whether they are fake or McCoy, the fact of the matter is this: China will be at a better advantage compared to the importing continent or country, which in this instance is Africa. China is not a continent but a country, while Africa is a continent trading with a country that is based in Asia. But still a country that is based in Asia is sustaining a continent with its products; surely there is something wrong somewhere, somehow. Something is not right between these China-Africa trade relations. The same view is also shared by a lot of people even outside the borders of South Africa. The same view is also shared by the Namibians and the Zimbabweans. In fact the Zimbabweans have been disregarded by the British and adopted by the Chinese. The Zimbabwean's government has given freely their mineral resources to the Chinese company. In effect China is mining Zimbabwe's diamonds freely without any worry or hassle.

Dr. Tafataona Mahoso writes:

> *"In the summer of 2005, Lukas Lundin, an intrepid mining entrepreneur, rode his 12,000 cc BMW motorcycle the full length of Africa—from Cairo to Cape Town (three times the distance from New York to California) . . . At the time, 85 percent of the roads he traveled were tarred—of the highest quality, no different from the ones he rode on in California. He was astonished (considering the US media's stereotype of Africa) because this was not what he had expected at all. Along the roads, in country after country, there were clues as to how this had come about: signposts proclaiming 'this road constructed with the grateful assistance of the Government of the People's Republic of China . . .' In the last sixty years, no country has made a big impact on the political, economic, and social fabrics of Africa as China has since the millennium (that is since the year 2000)."*[7]

There is a general consensus among most African scholars, and the view expressed above it bears testament to that. It's a common view among most African scholars that Chinese investment to Africa is totally different compared to the infrastructure investment that the West made to Africa. It's a common understanding and a common consensus among African scholars that it's better to forge a partnership with China rather than to forge a partnership with the West. The rationale behind these partnerships is purely based on common interest and mutual respect. It's also a common belief that most African scholars share that China will be a friend of Africa forever. It's important to understand the international politics and also important to understand that since time immemorial, Africa has been a playing ground for the West, and now I think it's a playing ground for Asia. The West wants to own the whole world, and it is for that reason that the West will do anything in its power to ensure that it interferes in African domestic affairs either through providing political solution or partnering with African countries through forging trade partnerships like BRICS (Brazil, Russia, India, China, and South Africa). The whole rationale with these bilateral agreements and trade agreements are not really in the interest of Africa, but it is in the interest of Asia, not Africa at all. The scramble for has not ended yet, and it seems a lot of people have forgotten that the scramble for Africa has not ended yet. The day the scramble for Africa will be over will be the day Africa will be self-sufficient and self-reliant. As long as Africa relies on the East, as is the case at the moment, Africa will remain in a financial and economic bondage of the West for quite a long period of time. I am not against the China-Africa trade relations, but it's imperative that while Africa enters into these bilateral and multilateral trade agreements, it should not turn a blind eye on the net gain for these bilateral and multilateral trade agreements, which means it should not only be China, Brazil, Russia, and India that should reap in the investments rewards, but also Africa should also reap the rewards. There had been a very long cry from African people, and I have also heard about the same cry when I was in Zimbabwe. The majorities of African people normally complain about these bilateral and trade agreements, saying that these bilateral and multilateral trade agreements don't benefit the masses on the ground; they wind up in the government officials table and government officials' laps. Bilateral and multilateral trade agreements are fruitful provided that the masses on the ground will reap the long and lasting effects of these China-Africa trade relations. It's also crucial to understand China's policy concerning its labor force. I have paid an undivided attention toward Chinese businesses in Pretoria and the whole of South Africa. I have realized that the working hours in most of these Chinese retailers are very long compared to the normal working hours to the retailers that are owned by the South Africans. I have also realized that the Chinese also open their businesses very earlier in the morning and close very late at night, and that does not sit well with the majority of businesspeople in South Africa. The point I am making is simple and straightforward: Chinese businessmen and businesswomen are workaholics compared to the average South African businessmen and businesswomen. The Chinese businessmen and businesswomen normally work very long hours within a week to the point that from the South African perspective, it could even be interpreted to mean the violation of workers' rights. In other words, it's important to understand that if a Chinese company will come to run an infrastructure project in South Africa, it will have to hire the South African labor force at least to ensure that there will be a trickle-down effect on the spoils of the project. The normal working hours in South Africa is eight hours per day, and if the employee has exceeded those working hours, then it's overtime. Overtime is more expensive than normal working hours. Overtime is calculated according to the rate that has been set by the Department of Labor. Simply put, there are multiple factors that cause businesses and even investments to fly away from Africa. And part of it is a considerable amount of money that the business will have to fork out to service its wage bill. One of the reasons why the Chinese economy is growing fast than any other economy in the world is purely through the exploitation of its cheap labor; while one of the things that makes the economy of Africa not grow as fast as it should is partly because of high wage bills that are unsustainable. The Department of Economic Development led by Minister Ibrahim Patel crafted what is today known as NDP (National Development Plan). The NDP suggests that for business to flourish in South Africa, wages need to be capped. The net effect of this economic policy is this: it will create a favorable economic environment for foreign investors to invest a considerable amount of capital in the South African economy. The unions see the NDP as a deviation from all economic policies that have been set by the South African government that were not implemented properly. The trade unions themselves ask this fundamental question: If salaries will be capped, how will we the trade unions survive, since we survive through the collection of membership fees from our members that are originating from their salaries? The point is if you cap the salaries of the employees automatically, you are directly and indirectly plunging the majority of the families further into the depth of poverty. The majority of South Africans are living under the poverty line, but the majority of South African labor force is also living in denial that they are living under abject poverty line. The NDP became the hottest potato to the point that some trade unions threatened to break away from the tripartite alliance with the ANC and establish their own political party that will stand alone and contest national elections in their own right. The political idea that was mooted by certain unions in COSATU (Congress of South African Trade Union) did not materialize in practice, since it will not weaken the political power of the ANC, but it would further create more divisions in the tripartite alliance that is already teetering on the brink of splitting. The NDP did not suggest that the wages of senior government officials need to be capped. It suggested that all public servants' wages need to cap to a certain level that perhaps will be determined by the Department of Economic and Development. There are huge wage disparities in South Africa, and these wage disparities are not attributed to the level of education that one has, but it's purely attributed to the positions that one occupies. Simply put a person who has only grade twelve can occupy a position that pays him more money when compared to the person who has a degree. The wage disparities have been created by the apartheid government. The apartheid government crafted this system of wage disparities to ensure that black people don't ascend to the level of white people in terms of their economic lifestyle, and even the food they eat. Simply put, black people were poor by design, not by mistake, and there is nothing that they could have done to alter the diabolic system of wage disparities that was meant to keep the majority of black society in the depth of poverty. The wage disparities in South Africa, specifically in the mining sector, became very clear in the wildcat mining strikes on August 16, 2012, that led to the loss of lives of miners in Marikana in Rustenburg. The president of South Africa Jacob Zuma instituted the commission of inquiry to find out the causes of the Marikana massacre and the possible ways to avoid such diabolic mistakes to happen in the near future. The end of an era for South Africa has come, and that era ends with the death of Nelson Mandela. There are two new generations that have emerged now in South Africa, the "born-frees" and the millenniums. The "born-frees" are people that have been born after 1994, and the millenniums are people that have been born since 2000 going forward to be precise. The millenniums are still too young to vote, and they know absolutely nothing about the political struggle, including the scourge of apartheid. Some of the millenniums were born in double-story houses and in posh suburbs where there are flushing toilets and running water. The millenniums know nothing about the pit toilets, and they even hate the locations where other black people reside. The millenniums are always watching CNN and BBC. Most of the millenniums are white people trapped in black skin. Simply put, the millenniums are the Face book and Twitter generation. The only thing the millenniums know is living a lavish lifestyle. The millenniums know the constitution of South Africa, and they know their rights in depth. They know what the constitution says about their rights. In fact the millenniums have a right to engage in a consensual sexual relationship with their partners without being arrested; that is within their constitutional rights—they are entitled to that. The millenniums can't be spanked, since spanking is a violation of their human rights. The sad thing about the millenniums are they are too young to vote and too young to work. The majority of the millenniums are still at school, some at primary level and some at secondary level, depending when one was born. The "born-frees" are almost the same with the millenniums. They don't want to work hard for money; they believe that they are entitled to everything that is enshrined in the constitution. The fact of the matter is this: not everything that is in the constitution of South Africa can be implemented. There are budget constraints that hinder the implementation of all the constitutional rights that are enshrined in the South African constitution. I have argued in the past that some of these political documents were crafted by people that were angry, bitter, and full of resentment, and the political conditions of the day clouded their political judgment. I don't mean that the South African constitution was crafted by people who were angry, bitter, and full of resentments. It's possible that some of the people were indeed angry partly because of what the apartheid system has done to them. But on a general level, the majority of South Africans who crafted the constitution knew what they were doing, that is why they managed to produce the best constitution ever up until this day. I have heard most of the fugitives who normally come to seek refuge or asylum in South Africa professing their love to the South African constitution. They claim that the reasons why they fled from their country are partly the human rights violation and lack of democracy and political tolerance. The fact of the matter is this: some of these fugitives really don't like the South African constitution, but they see South Africa as a safe haven where they can commit blue-collar crimes and get away with it. They know that corruption in South Africa is on a rampage and it's spreading like octopus, as Guy Arnold would put it. The end of an era means that South Africa is a fatherless nation. What the majority of people forget including South Africans is this: we had two fathers. We had Nelson Mandela as an earthly father, and we have God as our heavenly father. Nelson Mandela went to be with our heavenly father, but the heavenly father is with the South African people forever. We are not going to live our lives as orphans in the orphanage home because our heavenly father is still with us even to this day. It is our heavenly father who said, "I will not leave you nor forsake you." The Western media have been saying, who is going to lead this nation to the future? The fact of the matter is this: God will lead us South Africans to the future. Many people think that we are going to be wandering in the wilderness like the children of Israel just because Nelson Mandela is no longer with us. I should say, may his soul rest in peace, and he has ended the era for his generation. We have another era ahead of us. We need to focus and recompose ourselves and move on instead of dwelling in the past and cry forever. There are times and seasons under the earth. The time had come for the Nelson Mandela generation to depart. History was made in the FNB stadium in the memorial service of the late president of South Africa Nelson Mandela. Under one roof, you had the president of Zimbabwe, "the old man" Robert Mugabe, and the former president of the United States of America George W. Bush. Tony Blair surely will blame Pres. Robert Mugabe, and Pres. Robert Mugabe will surely blame Tony Blair, or Tony B. Liar as they call him in Zimbabwe. Under the same roof, you had the former president of the United States of America George W. Bush. I wonder whether or not there is a relationship between the surname of the former president of the United States of America and his political decisions that he took while he was in office as a USA president. From a vantage point, I think there is a relationship between his surname and his political decisions that he took while he was in office. The Second Chimurenga of Zimbabwe was also called the Bush War, which took place around 1966 all the way to 1979. Therefore, the former USA president George W. Bush was always in wars now and then. In fact it was the father of George W. Bush who did not kill Saddam Hussein. George W. Bush came and did what his father could not do. There is a symbiotic relationship between the surname, name a person carries, and the decisions that will be made by that person later in his life. The late president of South Africa Nelson Rolihlahla Mandela lived up to his name. He shook the very foundation that held apartheid system together, and the apartheid system collapsed completely. In fact the majority of USA citizens are sick and tired of the USA involvements over these endless wars that are happening all over the world. The United States of America had just slipped away from going to another war which is under way in Syria. The president of the United States of America Barack Obama was determined to annihilate the walls of Damascus to the ground. I hate wars partly because there is a lot of bloodbath and unnecessary loss of lives of innocent children and women in particular. But we all know that there are monetary gains to be made in each and every war. If there were no monetary and economic gains to be made in a war, countries would not engage in wars knowing full well that there are no monetary gains to be made. After the Syrian government forces have used the chemical weapons on its people and killing almost 120 civilians in a day, which made USA president Barack Obama mad to the extreme, the USA president became very mad to the point that he wanted to use drone strikes right then and there. It was very difficult for him (USA president Barack Obama) to lodge air strikes without the approval of the USA citizens. The United Nations

Security Council could have quickly approved anything that the president of the United States wanted without even considering the net effects of the USA involvement in the Syrian War in the long run. Let me concede that Bashar al-Assad regime and his government did use chemical weapons on the Syrian people during the course of the Syrian War. The UN report on Syrian War bears testament to that effect. The question then was, What should the heads of states do, since innocent people were dying and are even dying today in Syria at the time of writing this book? The option that was on the table of the USA president and his loyal secretary of state John Kerry was a "limited strike to Bashar al-Assad regime." There was all the bickering and the whining going all over the world. Most people asked themselves this question: What is the meaning of the limited air strike? Now and then the president of the United States of America will appear on CNN to answer that question from his White House office. His argument was the limited air strike does not necessarily mean that the United States of America is going to the Syrian War—"the boots won't hit the ground," as the Americans will often put it. His argument was that unleashing the air strike to the Syrian regime will in a way deter the USA enemies, like North Korea, which have been threatening to lodge missiles to the United States of America. Simply put, to lodge limited air strikes to the Syrian government forces ultimately would have worked in favor of the USA citizens. It would have deterred North Korea to lodge its missiles to the United States of America simply because North Korean leader would have seen the military power of the USA forces through the Syrian air strikes. The North Korean's threats of lodging air missile strikes to the United States of America eventually turned cold, and life continued as normally in the United States of America and even in North Korea. The Russian president Vladimir Putin, who has close ties with Syrian president Bashar al-Assad, emerged out of nowhere and suggested that the Syrian stockpile of chemical weapons should be placed in the hands of the international organization that will monitor and eventually destroy the Syrian stockpile of chemical weapons. To this day I cannot wrap my mind around this concept of limited air strikes, which was later changed to "strategic limited air strikes" by the United States of America. The secretary of state John Kerry, when pressed hard by the US senators, will sometimes refer to this limited air strikes as "a portion of limited air strikes," and he would usually say, "The boots won't hit the ground." The fact of the matter is this: whether or not the boots would hit the ground or whether the air strikes that the United States of America were going to lodge to Syria were limited air strikes or strategic air strikes, but at the end, there was going to be a bloodbath, and the Syrian people owe their lives to the Russian president Vladimir Putin. The end of an era has come, and we did not see it coming, specifically in South Africa. The majority of South African wanted the late president of South Africa Nelson Mandela to remain with us forever. There are statements that the late president of South Africa Nelson Mandela made that will remain forever throughout the South Africans history, specifically to some of us who call ourselves young enterprising scholars. These are the statements that were made in the dark moments of the South African history; these statements were made in the midst of impending death and capital punishment. I concede that every person is a master of his or her faith, and a person can declare a thing and come to pass. A person will never rise above the level of his declaration and confession. What holds a person together is his confession and self-confidence that originate from within. If you believe that you can change a system, yes, you can change any system. And if you don't believe that you can change a system, indeed you can't change a system. It's not all in the mind as a lot of people suggest, but it's all in the heart; it's an inner voice. Nelson Mandela writes:

> *During my lifetime I have dedicated myself to this struggle of the African people. I have fought against white domination, and I have fought against black domination. I have cherished the ideal of a democratic and free society in which all persons live together in harmony and with equal opportunities. It is an ideal which I hope to live for and to achieve. But if needs be, it is an ideal for which I am prepared to die.*[8]

A political problem defines political party, and a political party defines a political leader, and the political leaders will have to change and steer the course of history and eventually build the economic profile of a country. It's apparently clear that for one to change an unjust system, one will probably need more than just faith and meditation. One will need to own and master his fate. Our lives are in the hands of God, but sometimes we do speak things in the atmosphere, and they eventually materialize in the physical realm. Failure to speak your mind and your belief is indicative of people that are living in fear and trepidation. There is nothing that can happen and change unless one speaks his mind and his belief into the future. Our fear and trepidation derail our future and our outcome. There more positive we become about the future, the more the future will look bright; but the more negative and pessimistic we become about the future, the more the future will respond to what exactly we have been hoping for. South Africans and African people can do anything as long as we set our minds on doing what we have purported in our hearts. We all want to live a good life—life that is full of happiness and joy and peace. There is no South African who can claim that the death of Nelson Mandela had not moved him or her in a way. All of us have been moved to a certain extent, but the main issue is this: What are we going to do now to change the current problems that are facing South Africa today? There are many problems that still remain unresolved and not even challenged. I have said before that South Africa and Africa have not yet sent scientists and astronauts to space, and India already had sent its scientists and astronauts to space. I am not talking about a single individual going to space out of his own pocket. I am talking about a full-fledged government project that will see our young scientists landing in space and bringing back a wealth of knowledge to the people on the ground for other inspiring young South Africans. Nelson Mandela writes:

> *I am fundamentally an optimist. Whether that comes from nature or nurture, I cannot say. Part of being optimistic is keeping one's head pointed toward the sun, one's feet moving forward. There were many dark moments when my faith in humanity was sorely tested, but I would not and could not give myself up to despair. That way* lay *defeat and death.*[9]

The Nelson Mandela generation has ended an era of an unjust and unfair system. My generation has another system that it should defeat—the unjust and unfair system of poverty. There is nothing that takes away a dignity and self-confidence of a person like poverty. Poor people normally have one thing that they lack in common, and that is self-confidence. Bear the following in mind that self-confidence comes from both within you and in your social environment. The social environment of a child dictates the social belief of that child. The social belief of that child is translated to the actions and the way that child carries himself or herself around. Poverty compels one to believe that there is possibly something wrong with me or there is something wrong that my parents did. Some people even mistake poverty as witchcraft. Witchcraft is that belief that there is a supernatural evil force that is at play in a circumstance of a person. It's very difficult to tell exactly that when a person is poor, there is witchcraft at play. It's also important to note that when you believe that something exists, it will eventually exist to you. That statement does not necessarily mean that witchcraft does not exist at all. Witchcraft exists to the point that you believe it, and witchcraft does not exist to the point that you don't believe it. Simply put, whatever you believe will eventually manifest into your life, and whatever you don't believe cannot manifest into your life. Poverty is not natural and not even divine for that matter. Poverty is a human-made disaster, and in the case of Africa, it is the West. The West is responsible for impoverishing Africa methodically and systematically. It's true that some people are so poor to the point that they can't even pay attention. It's also true that children who go to bed with empty stomachs will mostly have a long night that is filled with nightmares. My generation will have to put to an end to those long nights that are filled with nightmares from the African children. There is no system that can't be defeated; even the most difficult system in the world can be defeated. The West will probably say, "Africa had been politically liberated from colonization a long time ago. We wonder why Africans are continuing to blame us now and then for poverty and suffering that is in Africa." It's true that Africa has gained its political independence from the West for a considerable amount of time with respect to other African countries like Democratic Republic of Congo and Zimbabwe. The fact of the matter is this: political independence alone does not really guarantee economic independence and financial independence. It's possible to be politically liberated while you are still in economic slavery, and that is exactly the case with most of the African countries, and even South Africa is not an exception to this kind of slavery. There is no man who can live alone in an island, as the old saying goes. There is no country that can be self-sufficient to the point that it can't trade with other countries. It simply means that Africa should also join all other countries that are in this global village of trade, not to rely on the Western handouts and Western foreign aid as is the case now. The new era is coming, and it looks even brighter than the previous era.

Chapter 7

THE POVERTY CYCLE

There are many concepts that are used to refer to Africa as a continent. Some say Africa is the Dark Continent, and some say Africa is the hopeless continent, and some say Africa is a continent that is ridden with diseases like AIDS/HIV. In fact everyone in the West, when they are talking about malnutrition and child mortality, are talking about Africa. Even the Western ministers of the word of God, when they are called to preach, are only called to preach to Africans who desperately need God because they are going to perish anyway. Africa as continent is associated with poverty, diseases, and political instability. Africans, with no exception to African Americans in general, are associated with wars, poverty, and crime. These perceptions have been in existence for a considerable amount of time. I have seen cases in the South African courts where a non-black South African would commit a premeditated murder toward a black person, and the accused will take the stand in court and tell a presiding judge that "I am sorry, Your Honor, I had mistaken him for a monkey." Barack Obama writes:

> *How could America send men into space and still keep its black citizens in bondage?*[1]

There is still the same cry and the same complaints from different people from different African countries that were under the colonial rule of the West. Some people even suggest that poverty has now deepened in Africa compared to the colonial era. Some suggest that it was better in the colonial era compared to this political dispensation that we Africans are currently living under. I have interviewed different people of different nationalities. They still complain about the same thing that the majority of South Africans complain about, which is corruption. One newspaper reports that the sad thing is this: poverty and crime have also reached an icon status in Africa! Crime and poverty are not divine but are human-made disasters that were partly inculcated by human beings in their human behavior. A human being is a free moral agent; you make your own choices on your mind alone then you execute your choice through your actions. Our choices are influenced by our surrounding and our social environment. The great difference that existed prior to the liberation of most African countries then and now is the role of media. During the colonial era, there was less media freedom, but today there is too much media freedom to the point that this media freedom could easily be used to fuel the political turmoil through bad reporting and biased reporting. I have also noticed in our media that there is too much emphasis on reporting about corruption than on African development and investments on infrastructure projects. Some have argued that the West is now using the print media and the big media networks to prompt political instability in Africa. It's true that some of the news that we read on a daily basis are either pro-government, meaning it's a government propaganda; or antigovernment, meaning that the news themselves are a propaganda to instigate an uprising against the government. It will be unwise and unjust to muzzle and muffle the media from reporting to the people. But the print media and the media have a very daunting task to report free, fair, and unbiased news. The fact of the matter is this: our world has been shaped by the media, and some of the people can't even read along the lines that even some of the so-called editors of the print media are indeed underground agents for certain political organizations of their choice. State-owned media companies are normally pro-government in their reporting, while private-owned media companies are antigovernment in their reporting. The state-owned media companies will never ever report about the fraud and corruption that are implicating members of the government and even cabinet ministers, while private-owned media companies report about corruption all the way. I have seen journalists who do not even understand South African politics, making unfounded statements about the scourge of corruption, poverty in South Africa as if there is no corruption, and poverty in Britain and in the United States of America. The fact of the matter is this: sometimes African poverty and corruption are exaggerated to the extreme. However, that does not mean that we Africans should condone our political leaders in Africa to get away with corruption and self-enrichment as they please. We Africans must draw a line for our political leaders, and if an independent court of law finds that a person has embezzled state funds in enriching himself and his family, he should resign from government with an immediate effect. Some people might say, if every time a person commits fraud and corruption is fired, who will remain in government offices then? This question is a legitimate question, but that is not a reasonable reason to commit fraud and corruption with such an absurd rationale in mind. Corrupt officials need to be given harsh sentences that will deter and hinder the aspiring future corrupt individuals—that corruption does not pay, and it lends one in hot water. I think there is a misconception about corruption not only in South Africa but also all over the world. The misconception is this: average people normally confuse corruption to the stealing of a considerable amount of money from the bank as an act of corruption. The unilateral taking of someone's property without the consent of the owner of that property is not corruption in nature but pure theft. Generally speaking, fraud and corruption have to do with undue influence that one exerts into a situation to achieve favorable outcome. Sometimes the undue influence will mean flouting the government regulatory frameworks that have been established by the government to acquire supplies or even to pay contractors. But it's also true that what sometimes is called corruption is not corruption in the true sense of the word but pure clerical mistakes or even lack of reporting for that matter. Misspending, underspending, and overspending can't be classified as corruption from a face value; there should be through forensic investigation that should be conducted to ascertain the intentions and the motives of certain transactions that have been embarked on. However, I should also say that there is a lot of corruption that is going on all around us every day that is undetected purely because of the complexities and the sophistication of corruption itself. The more the business of corruption is booming, the more sophisticated and complicated the business of corruption becomes. The drug lords of the world have decided to shield themselves from incarceration by just putting police commissioners and station commanders in their payrolls, and that allows them to continue with their crimes unabated. This is a norm that is carried all over the world, and even the authorities know it. Fraud and corruption are the ones that are committed by big institutions like banks and construction companies. Most of these major companies commit these crimes under the pretext of soaring operating cost of doing business. The government of South Africa has established the Competition Commission to curb these kinds of crimes that are committed by big construction companies and big financial institutions.[2] When the big construction companies and big financial institutions commit fraud and corruption, either through hiking interest rates in the case of financial institution or inflating operating costs by construction companies, the executives of these companies are not arrested, but they are compelled to confess their crimes and pay hefty penalties and go home to their lovely wives and lovely husbands and continue with their lives as if nothing happened. It seems as if the governments of the world have accepted that corruption and fraud are part of human DNA. It seems as if everybody accepts that there will be corruption in one way or the other in government or even in private sectors, but the scale of corruption should not reach an extreme proportion to the point where even a blind person can see it. This message is not clearly articulated, but from the actions of most governments' pronouncement in relation to these white-collar crimes—that is the tone that the governments of the world are sending in their messages to the public. In the World Cup of 2010, South African construction companies were found to have formed cartels. These companies have inflated and fixed price in order to generate a considerable amount of profits.[3] There was a wide outcry in Zimbabwe after Zimbabwe's government had spent US$20 million to buy cars for the ministers and the deputy ministers.[4] Quite frankly the public outcry was coming from the fact that ordinary people on the ground are not working, and there are no sustainable jobs where the masses can generate income to support their households. When the reports about the average amount of money the Zimbabwean government was going to spend on ministers' and deputy ministers' cars, some people said the Zimbabweans government was corrupt. The fact that African leaders are spending too much money on vain projects, that does not amount to corruption per se but can be classified as maladministration. The former president of South Africa Thabo Mbeki delivered a paper at the Al Jazeera Center for Studies in Qatar on November 2, 2013, where he said:

> *Let us also consider the matter referred to in the PSC protocol as sustainable economic development. One of the central issues is the class stratification in all African societies as a result which all our countries face the challenge of gross and visible disparities in terms of the sharing of wealth, given the existence of a well-off and ruling elite on one side, and a desperately impoverished overwhelming majority, on the other. It's true*

> *that this is unacceptable tendency internationally translates into a very discriminatory system of wealth distribution beyond class, relating to ethnic, regional, religious and other features of our diverse societies, all of which are directly relevant to the challenge of achieving peace and stability on our continent.*[5]

While some suggest that Africa is not a poor, hopeless, and Dark Continent, there are those who argued that the problem with Africa is inequality. There is inequality in the distribution of wealth in Africa. Some eat too much of the steak, while some are languishing in abject poverty that is man-made. The law of the jungle says "eat or be eaten"—this law of the jungle seems as if most African leaders are applying it clandestinely to their people unconsciously. I have often said to myself, if my father was a renowned politician from one of the South African liberation movements, probably I would not be writing this book. Probably I will be occupying a directorship position in one of the government departments and sipping coffee with other government ministers. I would not have to join this long snaking queue for government services, but they were going to be delivered to me at my doorstep. The fact of the matter is this: it pays to be a politician from one of these African liberation movements. I have often wondered in South African politics and even in Zimbabwean politics why after the national election, most of the politicians cross the floor, as it is called in South Africa. The losing political party not only loses the national elections but also loses the members of parliament because of the floor crossing. One can quickly deduce that these folks are not really in politics because they want to serve the people, but they are in politics because they want to serve their bellies and their families. There is unequal and visible overwhelming distribution of wealth in Africa that continues unabated, and hence the public outcry is continuing unnoticed. It should be said that though members of parliaments should be given necessary working tools to a carry out their responsibilities, in the process there be should fairness and equality—meaning, that buying cars and essential working tools for ministers and including the deputy ministers must be done in accordance with legislatives frameworks that have been developed by each and every African country, and this legislative framework should be followed to the letter. South Africa over the years has developed strong and reputable public institutions that keep the checks and balances of government, and these public institutions also ensure that the rule of law rules supreme, and they could also impeach government officials and even ministers if they are found to have violated certain sections of the constitutions of South Africa or even the very legislative framework that governs the government institutions. Felix Njini writes,

> *A working paper for African Development Bank written by Cedric Achille, Mbeng Mezui, and Uche Duru reveals that African economies need not struggle at all for funding key infrastructure projects. The analysts in their paper titled "Holding Excess Foreign Reserves Versus Infrastructure Finance: What Can Africa Do?" say that financing infrastructure in Africa should not be as much of a headache as it is now for the continent. In their view, it is a problem that simply requires new thinking on financing mechanisms at a time that lack of sound infrastructure continues to hamper Africa's growth prospect and efforts at economic integration. Between 2001 and 2011, African countries held reserves of more than US$150 billion each year. The continent needs US$93 billion yearly to finance its infrastructure needs.*[6]

If the African continent has such a considerable amount of foreign reserves, then why are we suffering in Africa with such wealth that can lift a lot of African people from the bottomless pit of poverty? I have realized this even in the case of South Africa. I have learned over the years that sometimes African poverty is not caused by the lack of money and mineral resources. In fact what makes Africa to be underdeveloped for a considerable amount of time is the lack of capacity and capability of how to utilize the wealth and the mineral resources that we have. In the case of South Africa, now and then we will always read in the media about what is called wasteful and fruitless expenditures. We also read reports now and then in the media about expensive wines and Gallagher dinners that the public officials are indulging themselves in. It's abundantly clear that African problems are not caused by of lack of financial resources, but they are as a result of too much money that we Africans really don't know how to use. Having money and not knowing how to use it is as good as not having money at all. The reason I am saying that is the following: the net effect of a poor person because presumably he is without money and the net effect of a person who has more money to the point of confusion and as a result not using the money wisely is still poverty. Poverty is not the lack of money, but it's also having too much money to point of confusion and not even knowing what to do with it. There are conflicting media reports about the USA jackpot that has rolled over for much time now. Some are suggesting that lottery winning can ruin your life. Some financial experts suggest that there are many things that can befall a lottery winner. You can get sick and die immediately, and you can be assassinated by your family members, and if you are married you can be killed by a hit man who has been hired by your wife if you are a man in a heterosexual relationship. The gist of the message is this: play lottery, but when you win the lottery, you need to know that your days are numbered. The fear of not playing lottery because you are afraid that when you receive your lottery winnings, you will be assassinated and playing lottery and squandering it with women is still the same. Simply put, the fear of playing and not playing is the same just like the fear of stashing money by African leaders in the World Bank with a hope that someday things will change on the ground and that money can be utilized for the benefit of the poor communities. The fear that when money hits the bank of certain government officials, it will disappear without a trace, and therefore stashing money in the bank where it's safe rather than being used by the public is a fact indeed. One of the reasons why South Africa is having a huge backlog in housing is the squandering of money and stealing of bags of cement by the building contractors. In fact the building contractors even replace cement with ashes. Kleptomania is rife in Africa, even growing in leaps and bounds. While Mobutu Sese Seko was the president of Democratic Republic of Congo, stealing was allowed under his government. I am convinced that the Holy Bible that Mobutu Sese Seko was reading was totally different to the current Bible that is being read in churches today.The corruption and greed of Pres. Mobutu Sese Seko had been on such a scale that he and his supporters were deemed to be responsible for the new political term "state kleptocracy" or rule by theft.[7] The fundamental question that we as Africans need to ask ourselves is this: Where were we going to be economically, socially, and otherwise if the leprosy of corruption was not within our midst? Where were we going to be academically if the leprosy of corruption was not stealing the money that was meant for the feeding scheme for children that are coming from poor family background? The main problem with corruption is this: it is contagious and communicable. And the good news about it is this: it is curable. A strong government must build a strong institution, and strong institutions must ensure that there is order and justice at the end of the day. It's the responsibility of every African government to ensure that state institutions are efficient and effective in delivering services to the people.

The weaknesses in the state institution will manifest itself through wide spreading of corruption and greed, which will stall the pace of service delivery to the people. It's also true that charity begins at home. When the institution of marriage is falling apart into pieces, that is an indication that there is something wrong in our society today. A nation is made up of a society, and a society is made up of a community, and a community is made up of families, and these families are made up of two individuals who came together and professed their love to one another and took a solemn oath that they will love each other in sickness and in health. The two individuals had vowed before God and the church that they will love each other for richer and for poorer until death, not divorce, do them part. In the beginning of 2008, the divorce rate in South Africa went up astronomically simply because the majority of people lost jobs. The institution of marriage is of crucial importance and essential component of a nation building. There is no country that can be strong, economically, financially, and otherwise, if the marriage institution of that country is weak. It's also true that the institution of marriage is under a severe attack from certain minority groups that have their own perverted interest. The corruption that is happening at homes translates to the schools and eventually to the government institutions, and the whole nation is painted with the same brush. Africa is not the continent of the poor and the feeble. Africa is not the continent of wars and diseases. Africa is the continent of music and rhythm. Africa is the continent of gold and diamonds. Africa is the Garden of Eden. The poverty cycle can be broken only if there is collective effort in ensuring that the financial resources and the proceeds from the sale of Africa's mineral resources are used effectively and efficiently by those that are in the position of power, not to benefit their families but to benefit the whole of the African people.

WHAT IS THE POVERTY CYCLE?

The poverty cycle is the "set of factors or events by which poverty, once started, is likely to continue unless there is outside intervention."[8] Through the cycle of poverty, poverty-stricken families bear poverty-stricken families, and the wheel of poverty carries on nonstop. Poverty is man-made and can be overcome, but overcoming the poverty cycle simply means that the cycle needs to be broken and it will need an external intervention like government intervention and that of the private sector. The following are the causes of poverty:

- low productivity
- low salary
- poor infrastructure and government
- business failure
- ignorance, lack of skills and technology
- unhealthiness or diseases
- disaster
- inability to access resources such as land, finance, information, technical assistance, etc.
- no ongoing education

One of the factors of poverty is ignorance, which can be explained as a lack of knowledge. Ignorant people normally are argumentative and brimming with pride. Ignorant people are also cynical and arrogant. Poverty-stricken families are not only lacking education but also lacking functioning brains to think with. Arrogance and ignorance are the deadliest combination of ingredients to poverty. Arrogance and ignorance is the recipe for disaster. Ignorance and arrogance are the major contributing factors in perpetuating the cycle of poverty. As the old saying goes, "Ignorance is bliss," meaning if you don't know something, you can't worry about it. The fact of the matter is what you don't know is what makes you poor. The main difference between rich people and poor people is a thin line in the middle. Poor people don't know much, and rich people know more about poverty, even about the causes of poverty. The other crucial factor in the causes of poverty is no ongoing education. There are two types of education: a good education and a bad education. Good education encourages a spirit of entrepreneurship, while bad education encourages the idea of looking for a job and staying in the job for quite a long period of time and hoping and praying for a raise. Good education can reduce the scourge of poverty, but education alone can't erase poverty from the face of the earth. The majorities of children in Africa normally get bad education and suddenly develop a dependency syndrome to rely on the government for job opportunities, and when these job opportunities don't come by, the next thing that follows is the uprising. I am not the greatest proponent of social grants or welfare because I believe that the welfare, or social grant as we call it in South Africa, will compound the scourge of poverty. From South African perspective, there are almost 16.1 million people right now in South Africa in 2013 who are receiving social grants. These social grants can be divided into multiple categories. There is an old-age grant (pension), disability grant, and child grant. There are other social grants, but for the purpose of my study, I will just concentrate on those few that I have mentioned above. It is estimated that there are almost 16.1 million people in South Africa today who are receiving social grants—16.1 million people is a very big number. South African population now stands at 52.98 million, according to Statistics South Africa midyear reports,[9] I should also say that the average population of South Africa keeps on changing now and then, and it's possible that it will keep on growing forever. If I were to follow the current midyear report according to Statics South Africa, then it means the current population of South Africa stands at 52.98 million. According to the budget review of the National Treasury, there are almost 16.1 million people right now in South Africa who are receiving social grants. This number of 16.1 million is inclusive, meaning there is no breakdown as to who is receiving which form of social grants, as there are different forms of social grants that are administered by the government of South Africa to the people of South Africa. For argument's sake, let me assume that the population of South Africa stands at 52.98 million, according to the Statics South Africa midyear report, and the total number of people that are receiving social grants stands at 16.1 million people right now as of the writing of this book, which is likely to change overtime, since children are born each and every second, and there are multiple social grants applications that are processed each and every day for the new social grant recipients.[10] If these statistics that are mentioned above are anything to go by, it therefore means that in South Africa today 30 percent of the population is receiving social grants, and these numbers are likely to increase astronomically in the next financial year. In the Luxembourg Income Study that was conducted by Bradley and Lane Kenworthy, it has been discovered that the distribution of social grants does reduce the level of poverty in society. The comparison was made between the years 1970 and 1997 in almost fifteen countries, and it was discovered that social grants, or what other countries called welfare, do play a significant amount of contribution in reducing poverty in a society. The main problem with social grants is this: in the case of South Africa, the more social grants are distributed to the people by the government, the more people are making more babies with the rationale of receiving more social grants from government. The fact of the matter is this: social grants have created a welfare state where people do nothing when they wake up in the morning except having unprotected sex that compounds both poverty and HIV/AIDS. The welfare state creates welfare families. In a welfare state, there is high level of dependency syndrome, and the government is the golden goose that is expected to lay the golden eggs now and then. There is no sense of creativity and ownership in the welfare states. Most African countries are welfare states and are expected to lay the social grant eggs now and then for their people. The whole rationale behind the distribution of social grants is to rescue the majority of people from the depth of poverty, but in the process, people themselves are further digging themselves deep into the pit of poverty. I know people in South Africa who are making babies now and then with the rationale that says "the government will take care of me and these children and please don't worry." The fact is these social grants are costing the South African government a considerable amount of billions of rands. There is a need to review social grants rules and regulations and the whole process of applying for social grants if Africa wants to alleviate and lift majority of people out from the depth of poverty. It's either intentionally or by design that a person will make a first baby and apply for a social grant and continue to make four additional children with the idea of drawing more money from the social grant purse. It should be stated that perhaps the government can assist a family for the first time if that family has one child. But if this family continues to add more children with the hope of getting more money from government, the family in question needs to be deregistered from the state database, since it did not show remorse or repentance from its former sins. The welfare states harbor welfare families, and there is knowledge deficit and lack of creativity in communities where the majority of the people are relying on social grants or social welfare. The research that has been conducted in New Zealand, which is known as "'Life shocks' tip people into hardships," suggested that people who had more than eight life shocks in their lives are likely to live in poverty. The study lists the following life shocks that can cause a person to live in poverty:

- marriage (or similar) breakups (divorce)
- forced sale of house
- unexpected and substantial drop in income
- eviction
- bankruptcy
- substantial financial loss
- redundancy
- becoming a sole parent
- three months or more unemployed
- major damage to home

- house burgled
- victim of violence
- incarceration
- a noncustodian sentence
- illness lasting three weeks or more
- major injury or health
- unplanned pregnancy[12]

Out of all the life shocks that have been mentioned above that are coming from the study "Life shocks," I have seen only three life shocks that make the majority of people stay in "development trap" or poverty cycle, which are unplanned pregnancy, incarceration, and victim of violence. The evidence on the victim of violence is abundant, and there is no need to provide further evidence on the victim of violence. Apartheid South Africa has left indelible scars to the majority of South Africans to the point that South Africans have become a violence-ridden nation. A violence-ridden nation is likely to have multiple social ills, like high rate of crime, child abuse, and rape. The list of social ills is endless. In the process, these social ills deter communities to acquire skills that are necessary to lift themselves out of poverty and to break the poverty cycle. The second life shock, which is unplanned pregnancy, has been a daily bread even in Zimbabwe. There are multiple conflicting theories about sex, and in the midst of these conflicting theories, there are myths to top it up. There is a school of thought that suggests that if a person can't have sex for a certain period of time, that person is likely to get sick mentally, and the proponents of this school of thought see sex as an antibiotic to their sexual sickness. No wonder we have a lot of children that are born out of wedlock and marriages that are falling apart. I have learned recently that sex is a drug of choice, and it will give a person the same chemical rush that is received by the drug addict when he or she is shooting drugs into her or his skin with a syringe. The theory of understanding poverty has been explored by different scholars and even by entrepreneurs.

Donald Trump writes,

> *"Don't depend on anyone but yourself for providing your financial security."*[13]

In other words, welfare families depend on government for their survival and for their livelihood, and in the process of relying on the government, they lend their votes to politicians for more social grants or social welfare. The dependency syndrome is the microcosm of the welfare state and is succeeded by laziness and complacency.

Ruby K. Payne in her book titled *A Framework for Understanding Poverty* writes:

> *Time is something that is treated differently by the poor; they generally do not plan ahead but simply live in the moment, which keeps them from saving money, which will help their children escape poverty. One aspect of generational poverty is a learned helplessness that is passed from parents to children and on down the line. This learned helplessness can be explained as the ideology that there is no way for one to get out of poverty, and so in order to make the best of their situation, one must live in the moment and experience what they can when they can.*[14]

As the old saying goes, "Time is money, and money is time." The poor who are trapped in the poverty cycle do not value their time, and that simply means that the poor don't value money, since time is money. It's imperative to thoroughly comprehend that there is a serious need to pay undivided attention to the poor in order to eradicate poverty. The fact of the matter is this: as long as some of the people in Africa are in the fast train and the majority of people are lagging behind financially, that means that our economic freedom is incomplete. African heads of states have a serious responsibility on their shoulders, and that is to eradicate poverty completely from the face of the earth because failure to do that, their political heads will sooner than later roll. I have often wondered whether or not political leaders do understand comprehensively the enormous responsibility that is on their shoulders each and every day. The fact of the matter is this: every time university students graduate and they don't get an employment, they normally blame the government or even the university where they have studied. It's true that African leaders must take this issue of creation of job opportunities seriously, and they must act as soon as possible before the Arab Spring wave hits our shores. There are different levels of poverty, and even if there are different levels of poverty, the fact is poverty is still poverty whether you are poor or the poorest of the poor or extremely poor as some may suggest; the fact of the matter is you are still poor. The common international poverty line has in the past been roughly one US dollar a day.[15] The World Bank came out with a revised figure of US$1.25 in 2005 purchasing power parity.[16] If these standards that have been set by the World Bank are anything to go by, it therefore means that the majority of people are indeed living under the poverty line. They might not be classified as the poor of the poorest, but they are living under the poverty line. What is also crucial to take stock of is the fact that each and every country is using its own currency, and currencies differ from one country to another. What is also suggested by Ruby K. Payne is this: the poor are only worried about the now, and they don't worry about tomorrow. I often get worried about the parents, specifically those who could not complete their grade twelve. Why do you take your own child to the very same school where you yourself could not complete your grade twelve from? The school did not do any good for you—what makes you think that this school can improve and change the life of your child? The truth of the matter is poor people don't even give a damn about the education of their children, right? They just send their children to school and hope that everything will work out well, and if things don't work out well, they blame the education system and they don't bother to blame themselves. It's an inescapable reality that poor families, specifically welfare families, normally produce children that are struggling academically, and that does not necessarily mean that there are no rich families that have children that are struggling academically. The main difference between the rich families and the welfare families is this: the poor don't plan for their children, and by the way, what makes the poor remain poor is the number of children that they have. The rich have few children, and the poor have a lot of children that they can't even afford to maintain financially. China came up with a strange policy to curb rapid growth of their population by introducing one-child policy. The one-child policy was not designed necessarily to reduce poverty diametrically but to reduce and arrest the growth of China's population. The fact of the matter is this: the population of China is growing and is growing at a very alarming rate, and the Chinese government had to do something about it sooner rather than later. The other problem that is a serious contributing factor in keeping the majority of people in poverty is alcohol and drugs. There is an inseparable relationship between drugs and poverty by the way. Many people who are shooting drugs in their bodies now and then are poor except the few that are rich. The term "absolute poverty" is also sometimes used as a synonym for extreme poverty. David Gordon's paper "Indicators of Poverty and Hunger," for the United Nations, further defines absolute poverty as the absence of any two of the following eight basic needs:

- food
- safe drinking water
- sanitation facilities
- health
- shelter
- education
- information
- access to services[17]

It simply means for an individual not to live in absolute poverty, he or she should have the above-mentioned basic needs met. If I were to follow this standard that has been set by David Gordon, it therefore means that the majority of people in South Africa are living in absolute poverty. There are hundreds and hundreds of people in Africa who are dying of hunger each and every day as a result of this absolute poverty. The one-million-dollar question then is, how can Africa overcome this absolute poverty? It's true that education alone cannot overcome poverty, and education alone cannot solve all of the African problems. Though education is a vital component in changing and shaping human perspective about life and even about the choices that they make, it will not solve all of the African problems completely. It's also true that most African countries don't invest a considerable amount of money in their education system, except South Africa, which always invests a considerable amount of billions in its education system. Though the desired results are not forthcoming, but as long as South Africa continues in this path of investing a considerable amount of money in its education system, it will eventually reap the rewards. Building any system takes not only time but also commitment and willingness. Any system is likely to have glitches and mistakes that can cause an adverse effect on the system. Building an education system that will stand the test of time not only requires willpower but also requires political will to get the job done. It's critical therefore to say, African political instability had a negative effect over the years in ensuring that the education systems that are put in place in Africa by African governments are yielding the desired results that were envisaged in the beginning. Let me take for example the war that was under way in CAR (Central African Republic) as of the writing of this book. Children were losing school time.

Children from CAR were supposed to be at school, but instead of being at school, they are in the United Nations shelters fearing for their lives. The reports that were coming from the media suggested that almost one thousand people have been confirmed dead as of the writing of this book. It's also inevitable that these numbers will increase astronomically. Africa, with its own political instability and endless wars, will never reach its own millennium goal that has been set by the OAU (Organization of African Union). The African wars perpetuate the cycle of poverty. The West is responsible for most of the African wars that are going on in Africa, either through supporting a particular militia group financially to topple the democratically elected government or providing military support. I was very surprised when the Seleka rebels toppled the government of François Bozizé and the whole world turned a blind eye on CAR. First of all, it's illegal to topple the democratically elected government by either mercenaries or even by rebels. It seems as if CAR is not immune from coups and countercoups. The cycle of poverty will remain intact for quite a long period of time as long as the African wars are continuing unabated and there is no political stability. Political leaders have a crucial role to play in every society in ensuring that there is political peace and tranquility. There is no way a considerable amount of people can be lifted from the depth of poverty as long as there is no fertile ground for investors to invest in. There is no astute investor who can invest his financial resources in a country that is being ravaged by civil wars and looting. I hate the war, but as we all know, there are gains to be made in every war. The African wars are not about politics per se, but they are about mineral resources. Everybody has his eye set on the bigger price, and that price is the precious mineral resources of Africa. The African people have come to realize that the majority of African leaders don't have political ambitions to occupy the presidential palace or presidential office for the mere fact of leading the people and providing services to the people, but these African leaders are the only legal channel to steal Africa's mineral resources without being arrested by the West. Stealing is legal if you are in authority, but stealing is not legal if you are not in authority. The Seleka rebels in the case of CAR have come to that realization that as long as they were still not in control of government, there is no way we can't have access to the mineral resources of our country, and the only way to the mineral resources is through heading the government. We are now in the information age, and most African countries are free politically and are on their path to a better future, but you still have countries that are retrogressive, going back in time further, fighting one another instead of negotiating their way out of their economic problems. When the CAR war is over, the people of CAR have to pick up the pieces and start afresh to build everything that they have destroyed. The African wars not only involve children as soldiers, but these children also commit the most barbaric acts of violence during the war. When the CAR war is over, the very same children who were child soldiers are expected to go back to class and learn. Violent and rebellious children normally don't do well in school, not because they have a low IQ but purely because of the PTSD (posttraumatic stress disorder). The net effect of the war in any country is an indelible mark on the lives of the people and even on the economic profile of the country. In each and every war that is fought in the African soil, families are disintegrated and the institutions of learning become the refugee camps and everything that was once working is no longer working. Maintaining peace becomes more difficult than starting a war. The poverty cycle has multiple dimensions, and there is no one-size-fits-all solution that can be given. The complexity and multidimensional of the poverty cycle make the problem of poverty forever complicated and remain unresolved for quite a long period of time. Poor people, unlike rich people, lack patience. Poor people like quick schemes and fast cash. I have noticed two things that the majority of poor people do in South Africa, specifically those that are staying in shacks. Those who are working in medium-size factories and earn their wages every fourteen nights, after receiving their wages, will literally throw a party out of the blue. Bear in mind that these folks are not earning that much, and in this party there will be hot chicks that will be drinking expensive wines. When the morning comes, not only will this fellow who was rich yesterday be broke the next day, but also he won't have food to sustain himself until he receives his next pay. Drinking and being promiscuous are the culture of the poor. As long as the poor are obsessed with temporary pleasure, they can't be saved from their highway to hell. Many poor people believe that lifelong learning is a waste of time and a waste of money; no wonder the majority of people who are poor not only are poor intellectually but are also poor financially. The poor deprive themselves knowledge, and eventually what they don't know makes them very poor financially. The theory about alcohol through the lanes of the poor is this: alcohol numbs their poverty and their pain of being poor. In effect the poor believe that by being sober is very dangerous, since it reminds them of their poverty; however, by being intoxicated all the time makes them (the poor) forget about the state of their financial affairs. The fact of the matter is this: you can't be drunk all the time; sometimes you have to be sober and confront your self-inflicted poverty head-on. The beginning of the way to a long and lasting solution in every problem is to realize and acknowledge that you have a problem. Denying that you have a problem does not provide a long-lasting solution to your problem, but it worsens the problem you are already in. The majority of people who are poor are cocky and puffed up with pride. I have often realized this with people that have little education; they normally think that they have achieved it all just because a person has a tiny two-room house and an ugly wife who has a certificate in communication and a secondhand bakkie. When you engage this kind of people who have less education, they normally brag about their achievements that do not even amount to anything in the world of the rich people. These are people that are not rich and are not even going to be rich even in a single day of their lives. They normally claim to have money that is lying in Swiss banks gathering dust. The fact of the matter is this: the majority of people are not really rich in South Africa and even in Zimbabwe, but these people put up rich faces to look rich. The main reason the majority of poor people will never get out of the poverty cycle is they are not true to themselves and they are not even true to the people around them. The poor people normally throw big financial figures around just to intimidate other poor people and to prove that they have money, which they don't actually have. I have realized something strange in South Africa—that the national lottery is the sport of the poor. The poor love playing lottery wholeheartedly because they believe that lottery one day will change their lives for the better. There are many people in South Africa who won the lottery to the tune of R15 million and still remained in poverty. The poor families fail to realize that being rich is not about having enough money only but also having the skill of keeping the money after you have received it. The heavy drinking that is going on in the family of the poor, once they get money, will continue to perpetuate the cycle of poverty further worse. Sex is another drug of choice that the poor can't deny themselves. There are two things that the poor families have in common all over the world. They are heavy drinkers and sex addicts coupled with multiple social ills that are endless. African leaders need to save the poor. The Gauteng government in South Africa at one point mooted the idea of revoking liquor licenses for liquor outlets that were selling liquor on Sunday. There was a serious public outcry about this bill that the Gauteng government was trying to implement. The majority of the owners of liquor outlets complained that they were going to lose a considerable amount of revenue, since they generate a considerable amount of revenue over the weekends. There is a symbiotic relationship between poverty, sex, and alcohol. Sex is the drug of the poor coupled with alcohol. It's important to underscore a very crucial point about this subject. The majority of people in this planet are afraid to be alone. Some people even go as far as saying, "Sleeping alone if you are a man is not normal." The question that one needs to pose is this: When do you find time to conduct a thorough introspection if you are always in the midst of the masses? When do you find time to reflect on the events of the day when you are always in the midst of friends and family members? The truth of the matter is this: most people are too busy to even conduct introspection about their lives. The culture and set of values that the poor have developed and inculcated in their children are very bad; in fact are these set of values and set of beliefs make the majority of the poor families poor by design not by mistake. Poor families are not only poor financially but also poor mentally. Poor people have another factor that is also a common denominator among them: they make poor and bad choices all the time, which are attributed to their lack of education and lack of insight. I find it very absurd to the extreme to marry an uneducated woman if you are an educated man, and I find it very absurd to the extreme to marry an uneducated man if you are an educated woman. However, there are educated men who decide to marry an uneducated woman simply because they want to control and manipulate the woman. The other reason that is cited by educated men about not marrying educated women is this: educated women are very difficult to manage, and they are very difficult to control, and they seek attention like small children. It's very difficult to lie to an educated woman if you are an educated man. But it's easy to cheat and even to lie to an uneducated woman simply because an uneducated woman doesn't have an insight and sufficient intellect to notice the variation in the behavioral pattern of a man. Educated women are very dangerous because they can easily see the changes in the behavioral pattern of a man. The educated men prefer to marry uneducated women for the mere reasons of control and manipulation. Sometimes the educated men marry uneducated women to be able to cheat and lie as they want without the fear of being divorced. Educated women are prone to divorce, unlike uneducated women, simply because they don't have anywhere to go after the dissolution of marriage. The other reason educated men prefer to marry uneducated women is that there is no competition in the house and in the family. In fact when an educated man is married to an uneducated woman who is a housewife, she will always be at home waiting for him to come back from work, unlike an educated woman who will sometimes tell it straight to the face of a man that "I think you need to get another high-paying job because this lousy job of yours doesn't pay you enough money." Most men hate that statement that they are not making enough money even if they know it. Many poor families were not poor at some point in their lives. They were classified as middle-class families, and the main problem started when the sole breadwinner passed on, who is the father in this case. When the sole breadwinner passed on, not only should the mother now pick up the pieces and carry on supporting the family financially, but also she must now assume the leadership role that she never dared to assume while the sole breadwinner, father, was alive. It becomes a burden then for this single woman who is not educated to assume a position of leadership without necessary expertise and even knowledge to run the family. The cycle of poverty begins invading this family that was once rich and plunging this family that was once a middle-class family in the depth of poverty. I have often seen middle-class families degenerating into the poverty cycle just because the sole breadwinner, father, has passed on. The truth of the matter is this: there is no family that was supposed to rely on a single breadwinner. There should not be family members who were supposed to be lazing around all day simply because "my big brother will take care of us." Everybody was supposed to be working and doing things for themselves to deter the wave of poverty. Poverty is not divine but a man-made catastrophe. The main problem about poverty is this: more often than not people who are always in the midst of poverty are innocent women and children. Men are also caught in the middle of this wave of poverty, but the majority of people that feel the scourge of poverty are innocent women and innocent children, and this is what is happening even in any civil war. Women and children normally bear the brunt of poverty even in the first-world countries. Now since almost everybody knows that women and children are normally in the receiving end of poverty, what is it that should be done to overcome this dilemma that is affecting these innocent women and children? The no single answer could solve this problem diametrically. It's important to realize that there is serious work that needs to done about educating women and ensuring that women are not taken advantage of by men. South Africa does have programs that are designed to improve the lives of women. As a South African man, I think that the South African government is giving too much rights and too much job opportunities to women at the expense of men; there is too much black women empowerment at the expense of black men empowerment in South Africa. The fact of the matter is this: there are many women now in South Africa who are in senior positions in government compared to men. The point is, during the apartheid government, African men were not occupying senior positions; even in this democratic dispensation, African men are not occupying senior positions. Since African men are not occupying senior positions partly because the government of South Africa has decided to implement the affirmative policy, the majority of these African women who are occupying senior positions in government are beginning to disrespect African men. I have heard it many times where a woman who is occupying a senior position will say, "What is it that he has?—because he is just a mere security," referring to a man. As a result, the institution of marriage in South Africa is crumbling partly because of the affirmative action. Let me put the record straight: there is nothing wrong about the affirmative action, but the problem is with these women who suddenly come to big money and big office that they were not used to since time immemorial. They begin to think that for a man to be complete, he needs to have a lot of money. The ratio between women and men in South Africa is one is to three; simply put, for every one man, there are three women in South Africa. This ratio might change in the twinkling of an eye, since numbers change every day, but the fact of the matter is this: there are a lot of women in South Africa who are occupying senior positions who are lonely and single partly because they have a high expectation about men. There are very few men that are rich in South Africa who are married already, and there are few men in South Africa who are single and rich. Most men that are single are poor, and that is a scientific fact. In case you are single woman who is rich and you are waiting for a rich man from South Africa, you must be ready to wait patiently because the queue is very long. Most South African men, to prove that they have money and they can afford the opulent lifestyle, decided to use the BEE status to lure these rich women. Most South African men use the BEE status to attract and entice rich and demanding women. Why do you have to cheat your way to the heart of a rich woman just because you want her to fall in love with you? The fact of the matter is this: the truth has a way of coming out when you least expect it. Americans say, "The truth has a way of jumping out of the bush and biting you in the ass." What has made Africa poor for quite a long period of time is not only the long colonial rule but also the long civil wars in some instances. The African liberation struggle was also the war of destruction. After the African liberation struggle was over, now, Africa is faced with another war, which is the economic struggle and inequality that is further perpetuated by criminals that are stealing from the state coffers via leadership roles and leadership position in most African governments. There are two types of criminals in the world. There is a criminal who does not dress smart and can't even speak English. This kind of a criminal who can't speak English and does even wear a tie and is always not clean, when he commits a crime, can be easily caught. There is another criminal who works in government offices, is educated with postgraduate degrees, and steals massive amount of billions through offshore accounts and through forging signatures of ministers and even for the president. For the first criminal, it's easy for him to be arrested and taken to custody without any hassle, but the second criminal does not get arrested; he will remain guilty while walking free. Africa is full of criminals who can topple any government with coups and mercenaries. Africa is full of criminals who have postgraduate degrees from prestigious universities. The main problem with the second criminal is this: when he commits crime, it's called a white-collar crime, while the crime that is committed by the uneducated criminal is called fraud. In Africa we have a lot of criminals who are walking free; even the law, when it comes to these kinds of criminals, does not take its cause. Those of us who are from the Christian faith, we ask ourselves this question: Is this the end of the world? Is this the end times that the Holy Bible was talking about? CAR has been declared as the failed state in Africa, and there are very few African troops that are in CAR except the handful of troops that are largely from France and the UN. South Sudan has embarked on its own civil war that will surely rip the newly formed country apart. Africa is forever in crisis. The fact of the matter is this: there would not be big media organizations if there were no African wars and terrorist groups in Africa. We all know that failure to plan is planning to fail. Therefore, failure is the outcome of poor planning or lack of planning thereof. There is nothing that happens in this universe by happenstance or by chance. If planning is such a crucial component of our lives, then how can it be utilized to improve our lives and deter the scourge of poverty that is ravaging the African continent? There is no planning in most of the African countries, and as a result, there is either chaos in the government institutions or there is chaos even in families. Proper planning is crucial in any sphere of life. When there is no planning, the only thing that will be visible is chaos all over the place. I suggest that for people who are not married who are still in courtship, they need to agree on how many children they want to have even before they think about marriage itself. Planning will help these young people that are still new perhaps in love who are thinking of getting married someday. When they get married, they would already have had a plan and the blueprint as to how many children they want to have, unlike getting married and then start thinking about the number of children that you want to have while you are already inside marriage. It's also important for our sisters to ask the brothers before they even get married this question: Are you a polygamist man? or Are you a monogamist man? This will help our sisters to even prepare for the future. Polygamous marriages are not the thing of the past; there are African men who still believe in polygamous marriages, and it will help my African sisters to raise this matter as early as possible in order to find a clear answer. Nothing happens in this universe by happenstance or by chance; there should be proper planning that succeeds actions. We all know that our master God himself is not the author of confusion but the author of peace and tranquility. The reason Africa is in serious chaos is partly the lack of planning that is palpable in the running of the African governments. Africans themselves have been labeled as people that are not organized, and they don't plan earlier for everything that they do. I have often observed in this life—that planning is the most crucial and essential component of any action that should be taken. If there was thorough planning, most of the African problems that are tearing the African continent apart without any shadow of doubt could have been avoided. Since there is no planning, people just come up with an economic policy that they believe will revolutionize the economy in an unprecedented way and implement it without even thinking about the ramifications of this economic policy and without even thinking about the behavior of the international markets. The fact of the matter is this: I really don't see any necessary reason to take back the land from the white commercial farmers in South Africa unless, otherwise, we South Africans know for sure what we will do with these massive tracts of land. There was no logical reason for the Zimbabwean government to invade the commercial farms in 2000 without knowing full well what they were going to do with the farms. The information age is no longer the era of retaliation and revenge, but it's the era of thinking like intellectuals by finding a better way to solve an economic problem. I have come to the realization of taking each and every problem as a challenge that can be overcome not as a hindrance or an obstacle that needs to be removed out of the way by a barrel of a gun. Today arguments are won on the table and are also lost on the table. The ANC (African National Congress) did not take South Africa from the apartheid government by the spilling of blood and the killing of innocent women and children. The ANC and the apartheid government negotiated until they found their way out of the woods, and today in South Africa we are enjoying the benefits of CODESA negotiations. Why can't other African countries learn from South Africa—that civil wars don't solve national problems; in fact they worsen the national problems that a country has in the first place? There is one common denominator that you will find among the poor—it is lack of planning. This is a serious problem that the poor need to take note of. The poor families fail to develop an effective mechanism to counterattack poverty, and due to this failure, they wind up only poor and miserable. Poverty is man-made catastrophe; in fact there are two plans that people have. There are people that are planning to be poor, and there are people who are not planning to poor. People that are planning to be poor have their own vocabulary that they use, which is totally different from the vocabulary that is used by people who are not planning to be poor. I have often heard poor people, since I have lived among them, saying, "When are you going to get married?" This notion of marriage is grounded and rooted within the poor community. In fact there are young girls with brilliant and bright minds who drop out of school just because of marriage and sex. Most of these absurd beliefs you will normally find predominantly in poor communities. The poor have different views about life that shape and change their belief. The poor have a tendency of blaming the government and even other people. There was a point in time in South Africa where child mortality was very high, and most of the pediatricians were requested by the media to give direction to the cause of these massive deaths of children. Most of the pediatricians complained about the time in between that women take to have children. They suggested that women were not taking enough time to raise the first baby before they bring the second child to this earth. The time in between birthing the children was very little, and that was the essential contributor in child mortality, but eventually the situation was properly neutralized, and everything now is normal. Planning should not only be done at the government level but must also be done at the family level. The Western science took longer to arrive in Africa, As a result, African women were bearing children as if there was no tomorrow. A woman who was bearing a lot of children was considered a good woman, and woman who was a barren was considered a community outcast. The culture of bearing a lot of children to appease the in-laws is outdated and useless. It does not necessarily mean that women must not bear a considerable amount of children, but there are certain economic factors that need to be taken into consideration today when a woman is thinking of bearing a child. She must take into consideration the fact that there should be a functioning structure that will ensure that the child gets proper care and proper family support. Single-parent-headed families can't raise children in a proper way. There are two crucial figures that a child needs, which is a father figure and a mother figure. The presence of the mother figure without the presence of the father will cause disaster. It has become a norm that in South Africa most marriages don't last long partly because of the westernization of African marriages. The grandparents don't have any role today in the African families, and their roles have been replaced by the TV and video games. The grandparents no longer transfer knowledge that they have learned through life via their grandchildren, and as a result, indigenous knowledge is disappearing on the surface. Indigenous knowledge is that knowledge that the elders have learned and acquired through life since their arrival in this planet. This knowledge is very crucial in ensuring that marriages last forever and the institution of marriage can continue to flourish as an ongoing entity that can be sustained over time. Indigenous knowledge have been replaced by life coaches and marriage counselors who are not even married at some point and who are using the Western methods in Africa to solve African problems. It's abundantly clear that the West does not have its own culture and even its own values. Africans must desist and cease mimicking and imitating the West. The Westerners praise God in their own way, and Africans praise God in their own, and I am not talking about worshipping idols and the trees that don't have life. I am referring to the way we are shaped and wired. We all know that Africans are dancers in nature and music is part of their lives. In fact God loves music. Heaven is not a quiet place that is brimming with boredom; music is an ongoing thing night and day in heaven. I don't feel offended when a person says Africans like dancing. There is nothing wrong about loving music only if everything is done according to plan. There are different times and seasons under the sun that dictate what should be done. Africans must listen to music but at an appropriate time; you can't listen to music all day long. Too much of a thing can be dangerous sometimes. Africans must listen to music, but there should be a time to study mathematics, accounting, and psychics. We as Africans can't keep on dancing all day long as if we have arrived in Canaan. We have soon discovered that political freedom does not necessarily translate into economic freedom. This does not necessarily mean that our political victory that was attained through tough negotiations in the case of South Africa was attained with ease. The point I have been making since the beginning of this book is this: we

Africans got too excited when we were politically liberated to the point that we miss the moment to advance the economic debate. Simply put, we stayed too much on our political mountain to the point that we even forget that we were not yet in the land of milk and honey. There are some people who believe that political freedom is the land of milk and honey. I beg to differ with people who believe that political freedom is the land of milk and honey. Political freedom was the manna from heaven that the children of Israel ate in the wilderness; political freedom is not Canaan of the olden days. There is a political wind that is blowing in South African politics, and if this wind is not properly monitored, it might cause serious problems for South Africa going forward from now. I am not an advocate of multiparty in an open democracy. However, even if I am not a proponent of a multiparty democracy, that does not mean that, there shouldn't be opposing parties that are opposing the ruling party. My main problem with multiparty democracy is this: there will be divergence of political agendas that are confusing and misleading to the majority of people. There are people in South Africa even in Zimbabwe who really don't understand the economic trajectory of their countries and who don't even understand the political trajectory of their political parties. Let me be brutally honest, whether we like it or not, politics affects us all directly or indirectly. The fact that people are killing each other in CAR does concern me even if I am very far away from CAR. The fact that there is a war in South Sudan does affect me directly or indirectly. The one-million-dollar question is this: How does it affect me? Mass migration of people normally takes place when there is a civil war that is threatening the lives of the people. One thing that comes to people's minds when there is a war is, which country can we go to—where will we find jobs and live a normal life again? South African economy is the biggest economy in Africa, and the majority of people in the whole of Africa know that, which means when they think about the country where they can feel safe and sound and start to live a normal life all over again, probably they will think of South Africa. South Africa is a country with its social and economic problems that can't be solved, and when you compound the South African problems with that of CAR immigrants who would have immigrated to South Africa, the economic puzzle gets further confusing. I have noticed certain strange behavior from people that are coming from countries that have been in civil war for a long period of time. I have also noticed a strange behavior from people that have been abused for a long period of time. The behavior of people that have been in an abusive environment for quite a long period of time is consistent with the people that have been in war for quite a long period of time. These two groups of people are victims of torture and violence that have destroyed their souls and spirits. I have also realized that such people lack self-confidence and self-reliance. They won't do anything unless they are told to do it. They won't initiate anything unless they are told to initiate. Let me be brutally honest: there are many men even in South Africa who are beaten by their wives night and day, but they don't have guts and balls to speak out because they were told that "a man does not cry," and there are many men who are in an abusive relationship just because of the children—they can't end the relationship; they decide to stay in the marriage for the sake of the children. This behavior is consistent with a person who has been in an abusive relationship or an abusive social environment for a very long time, and this behavior is consistent with a person who has been in war zone for quite a long period of time. There is nothing good about war, except the fact that the people who are the victims of war will be displaced and left with scars that are indelible in their spirits and souls. I believe that a two-party democracy is better than a multiparty democracy. In a multiparty democracy there are a lot of economic policies that each political party is mooting. Let's take for example the case of South Africa: there are multiple political parties, and as a result, these political parties have divergent views about the economic policies that the government must develop and implement. The big question is this: What do you do in a situation where you are confronted with multiple economic ideologies that are emanating from different political parties? The majority of the African wars are as a result of multiparty democracy. The rationale behind the formation of these multiple political parties is simply to get control of the government, and we all know that the one who has the gold makes the rules. I have argued in the past that South Africa does not need another political savior; simply put, South Africa does not need another Nelson Mandela. We already have our Nelson Mandela who has saved us from the political shackles of apartheid, and what we need right now is economic policies that are economically sound and practically logical, not another political party on top of these political parties that we have already. It's true that the other crucial reason people opt for the formation of their political party is that purely they feel that they are not taken seriously when they are raising political issues. They also feel that the rules of engagement don't favor them, and therefore whatever they might suggest, even if there is political and intellectual soundness in what they are saying, they won't be listened to. Therefore, the formation of these political parties is not based on addressing political problems that are affecting the masses on the ground but is purely based on settling political scores with a certain group in another political party. Let me put it bluntly, many of the political parties that are existing in South Africa are the breakaway groups from the ANC that did not get sufficient support on their political ideologies that were not only toxic but also destructive even to the South African economy. It makes one to wonder then, are these political parties that are mushrooming like wild spinach for real? Do you know why it's easy to be a politician? It's because you don't need to have a serious degree to be a politician. In fact the easiest way to get rich quickly is to become a politician and incorporate your CC (Close Cooperation). Then you are filthy stinking rich with millions in the bank gathering dust. The other reason the majority of people are opting for politics is that there is free publicity in politics than in any other sphere of life. In fact women love politicians because politicians ooze a considerable amount of power. Politicians can shoot to fame within a split of a second. That is why politicians are famous than soccer players. It's true that soccer players make a lot of money compared to politicians, but politicians are very powerful in terms of influence and control. Politicians have unlimited power to screw up anything they want to screw up; they can even kill a lot of people by not giving them clean water until you vote for them. They can even release a murderer from prison if they choose to do so. During the time of Gukurahundi in Zimbabwe in Matabeleland, some of the communities were no longer getting food supplies simply because the Zimbabwean government assumed all Ndebeles were dissidents. The innocent communities of Bulawayo were now being punished for the sins that they have not committed. The same is true even today in Zimbabwe; members of MDC-T did not get the land when there was a bogus distribution of land. They were told that they must go to Britain to get their land where they get their politics. The poverty cycle can be dismantled and decimated by collective effort. It's also true that there wouldn't be poverty in Africa had the West not exploited the Africans through its slave wage policy. The poverty that is ravaging Africa today is part of the grand plan of the West to keep Africa as a begging continent. The African poverty has multifaceted components and multifarious dimensions. African poverty sometimes comes through wars and natural disasters, and sometimes it emanates through bad governance and bad political leadership that is suffering from the leprosy of corruption. African poverty is sometimes Western made and sometimes even African made as long as Africa remains as a political unstable continent that will continue to give the West a competitive advantage economically and even politically and will further place the West ahead of Africa in terms of development. It's abundantly clear that part of the African migration is fueled by economic instability and politically instability in Africa. As a result, economic instability and politically instability stifle Africa's economies and foreign investment to come to Africa. Foreign investment, even local investment for that matter, can't be a driving force behind a successful economy if there is no economic stability in the African continent. There is no amount of foreign investment and even local investment that can alter Africa's situation without political will from the politicians. It therefore suggests the following: politicians have the power to build the economy of any country or to destroy the economy of a country in a way. Political instability is another driving factor behind Africa's poverty. The West always watches Africa's politics and its endless wars closely. Sometimes if the West realizes that there is political stability and economic growth that will lift the majority of people in poverty, the West will just support the insurgent groups that will destabilize the African countries politically and economically push the African people further into the war. It's an inescapable reality that politics play a central role in ensuring that there is economic growth and job creation for that matter. It's also true that there won't be sustainable economic development, even economic growth, in a country that is constantly in a civil war. If Africa one day can succeed in sustaining the political peace for a very long time, Africa can emerge as a powerful economic force that can compete globally with the West economically and even technologically. As things stand right now, the West is supplying most of the African countries with military weapons and even military training simply because African countries can't be able to manufacture military weapons for themselves. The West not only continues to supply African countries with these cutting-edge military weapons and military equipments but also provides African countries with a considerable amount of foreign loans at very high inflated interest rate, further indebting African countries to the West like never before. When these foreign loans are received, they don't even serve the very purpose that they were requested for; they normally disappear mysteriously without even a trace. If one can take a look at the foreign loans that have been given to African countries by either the World Bank or the IMF (International Monetary Fund), if these foreign loans were utilized successfully for what they requested for, it goes without saying that the current infrastructural problems that the African continent is grappling with were supposed to be a thing of the past.

The overall aim of requesting or borrowing a loan from the World Bank and even from the IMF (International Monetary Fund) is partly because the borrowing country has pressing needs that need to addressed urgently, and these pressing needs are affecting the lives of many people in a negative way. It's a normal standard that any financial institution, before it lends money to any person, whether it be a country or even an individual, will request a borrower to provide a master plan. The borrower would have to have enough time and space to incorporate the plan in such a way that it is convincing and persuading to the lender, and eventually the main lender will see the necessity and the economic net gain that will be derived from such loan agreement. The lender more frequent than not does not even bother to further scrutinize the borrower after the borrower has received the funds as to whether or not the funds were used effectively and efficiently per the initial agreement. If one takes a closer look at the foreign loans that have been received by most African countries with the exception of South Africa, one can quickly realize that the majority of these foreign loans didn't change even an iota of the economic problems, which were there in these African countries even before the arrival of the foreign loans. Foreign loans are not used to address the economic challenges of the people, but they are used to build unnecessary swimming pools and to buy private jets and to build posh houses for the politicians, and then the leftovers and crumbs are given to the masses in the form of T-shirts, caps, and free food parcels. The greatest mistake that a poor person should not commit is to rely on the government for almost everything and for anything as if the government has all the solutions for your problems. The poor families need to be supported through varieties of grants even though personally I have my own reservations about grants to a certain extent. The other problem that I have with social grants is this: as long as the poor are receiving grants from governments and they are not in a form of skills program that will enable them be employable in the near future, then they will continue to draw social grants from the national government as long as they breathe. When the poor families receive social grants, they also need to be monitored and assessed thoroughly as to what they buy with these social grants that they receive from the government. I know that the majority of the people will probably say that is highly unconstitutional and unlawful to distribute social grants to the masses and eventually follow them behind to see what they are buying with their social grants that they have received from the government. Do you think it is constitutional and lawful to rely on the government for the rest of your life even if you are an adult? The reason I suggest that the poor families need to be monitored and watched closely by the authorities after they have received the social grants from governments as to what they buy with it is that partly the overall objective of any government to distribute social grants to the masses is to alleviate the scourge of poverty that the majority of families find themselves in. The alleviation of poverty comes in the form of receiving these social grants and utilizing them for their own intended purposes, which is to buy food and grocery. It's also true that the majority of these poor families, when they receive these social grants, don't use it for purchasing of food and grocery, but they even purchase alcohol and drugs with these social grants. The poor families, if they are left unattended and unchecked, have a potential of further harming themselves and impoverishing themselves even further. As long as the African governments continue to distribute social grants to the poor families without a proper instrument to monitor and assess the poor families, these social grants can be in a way a bait to keep the poor families in the poverty cycle. At large social grants are a crucial instrument to alleviate the scourge of poverty, since there is no other way right now that is deemed feasible to pull out the majority of people from this pit of poverty that is ravaging poor families. It's also true that there are many ways to kill the cat, but we must also accept that the very cat we are trying to kill has many lives. When you are dealing with a cat that has many lives, you need to have more than many (nine) ways at your disposal in order to put this cat of many lives where it belongs, which is in the grave. It's also true that a person who invented social grants has developed only one way of killing the cat, and as a result, almost everyone has come to acceptance that there is no other way feasible and viable that needs to be developed in order to destroy the ugly head of poverty. While we should support and rally behind the social programs that alleviate the scourge of poverty, we should also support and rally behind social programs that will create sustainable employments for the poor families and the young generation that is coming after us. This young generation that is growing very fast will not be interested in hearing the old fairy tales that the West colonized Africa and took all of Africa's mineral resources and even the land. The "born-frees" generation, as they are frequently called in South Africa, want all the rights that have been enshrined in the constitutions to be relished without even thinking about the financial muscles that will be required to make those constitutional rights a reality. There are two crucial drivers of poverty that I have just noticed recently that are common among the poor. Except the fact that the poor have their own set of values and culture that is totally different from the culture of the middle-class families and the rich families, the poor lack one of the crucial basic needs of life, which is information. We all know that information is knowledge and knowledge is power and power corrupts. Knowledge helps one to make informed decisions and even predict the unpredictable about the future; however, the poor, since they lack information, seem to believe that the only way to solve poverty is to make a lot of children and get more child grants from the national governments. This weird belief is palpable in South Africa. If one takes a closer look at the social expenditure to service these child grants in South Africa, one can get worried about the number of children that are born each and every day by people that are not even employable. The large chunk of people that are receiving these social grants in South Africa are children that are born out of wedlock and children that are born by teenagers who were supposed to be at school studying, but instead they are on top of each other making love to one another. The South African social expenditure is forever swelling out of control. I need to make this point frankly clear: I don't have a personal problem with people that are making children out of wedlock, even the teenagers that get children while they are still at school. But when you take a closer look at the subject of poverty in general, one cannot ignore crucial factors like teenage pregnancy as a fundamental driving force behind the scourge of poverty not only in South Africa but also all over the world. If the governments of the world are intending to bring the level of poverty down compared to where it is now, the governments of the world should do some serious sexual education not only to the youth but also to the ignorant adults, and this sexual education should go further even to the married couples. The fact that a man and woman are married that does not necessarily mean that they will be faithful to each other through thick and thin, and in the process of infidelity a child will be born, and this child who is born out of wedlock can't be registered for child grants, since the father is working and has a stable family. The mother of the child might be struggling financially, but that is not a reasonable reason to register the child for child grants as if the father of this child is gone. The little baby that have been born out of wedlock can't be integrated to this existing family where there is warmth and financial stability, but the little baby will be left to be raised by the child mother who is still at school and possibly coming from a struggling family financially. Under normal circumstances, the teenage mother can approach the court to compel the married father of the child to pay maintenance for the child, but a lot of young teenage mothers just opt for the child grant even if it does not cover all their essential expenses. The reason the majority of these teenage mothers opt for the child grants than maintenance of their children is that simply these married men who are educated and occupy senior positions don't pay the maintenance of their children even if they can afford the maintenance amount that has been set by the maintenance court. These married men, including celebrities, feel that paying maintenance for their children is a rip-off. The question that springs forth to one's mind is this: How can paying the maintenance for your child be a rip-off if making the child was not a rip-off? If you hate the process of paying for maintenance, I suggest that you stick to your wife if you are a married man, and if you are not a married man, then wait until you get married. We have a lot of children who were born out of wedlock—why add to the existing number? The poor families have perfected the art of sleeping. The reason a lot of people are poor is that simply they sleep a lot and they even eat a lot. The normal standard hours that an average human being needs to sleep is eight hours, and it's possible that some people sleep less hours than the normal sleeping hours. The truth of the matter is this: the poor people sleep more hours, and in the process, they consume the majority of their normal lives in bed not at work. Sleeping is not good for the body, and I mean sleeping a lot or exceeding more than eight hours. However, there is a need to sleep enough hours specifically if you were working for a very long time without getting enough sleeping time. This should be done by people who were working almost the whole year, specifically the CEO of companies, who need to sleep long hours at a certain point in time, since they have been working very hard presumably pulling big acquisitions for the company and traveling all over the world. The problem with the poor is this: they sleep more than eight hours even if they were not doing anything the previous day or night. The poor sleep more than eight hours and wake up and eat then sleep again more than eight hours. The poverty cycle continues as the sleeping habit continues. The poverty cycle is now compounded by the sleeping cycle. The poor families need to be trained about the flow of poverty and the ways to prevent poverty from flowing from one generation to the other. The previous generation has been in the pit of poverty purely because of the West, but right now the West has allowed Africa in general to be politically and economically independent, but the bad news is this: Africa is in poverty, and the cycle continues unabated with the exception of South Africa. There are two dangerous theories about poverty: the dependency syndrome and the entitlement mentality. The dependency syndrome victimizes its victims by perpetuating the idea of "you deserve to be looked after by your government because you voted." This syndrome of depending on the government for almost everything is another instigator of poverty, and it continues to claim its victims day after day. The victims of dependency syndrome are intellectually paralyzed to the point of doing absolutely nothing about their situation. The victims of the dependency syndrome are also in a serious denial about being victims of dependency syndrome. The victims of dependency syndrome normally continue with their normally lives unnoticed for a very long time. Sometimes, not always, politicians are responsible for the dependency syndrome that is palpable everywhere in the world today. Politicians perpetuate the dependency syndrome by suggesting that voting for their own political party is the ticket to great wealth and life of abundance. This idea that voting for a certain political party will change the lives of people diametrically was true while Africa was still in the shackles of the Western powers. This idea and political strategy need to be changed. The masses needs to be told that there is no way any government can have enough money to build houses for everybody; sometimes communities will have to come together to build libraries for themselves instead of waiting for the national government to do everything for the masses. The entitlement mentality is the social grants syndrome, which creates a welfare state. The main problem with entitlement mentality is this: their victims are not doing anything, since they have placed the whole of their burden on the shoulders of the national government. One pensioner told me that the money that he is receiving from government for pension is too little to cover all his expenses—by the way, he is getting that money from the government of South Africa for free without having to work for it, but on top of that, the person is quibbling and complaining like the children of Israel when they were receiving manna from God on a daily basis. Why complain if somebody is giving you a pension that you know very well you didn't work? The worst form of gift is a gift that you didn't earn because there is no effort that you have exerted in acquiring the gift. A gift should be given to a person who has performed a certain responsibility. Then after the person has completed the responsibility, then he/she can be given a gift as a token of appreciation for the work well done. This practice of giving a person a gift because the person has earned it is visible and practical in soccer. A best player in a soccer match receives what is called a "man of the match award." The man of the match award is given to the deserving player, not to Tom, Dick, and Harry, people who did absolutely nothing. The entitlement mentality is accompanied by the culture of complacency. The culture of complacency suggests that there is no need to shake yourself up, since everything is being taken care of by your national government in Pretoria—therefore relax and enjoy life, in the case of South Africa. There is no problem that is big enough not to be overcome, and there is no system that is strong enough not to be changed or destroyed completely. I have to accept the fact that the West stole Africa's wealth, and not only did the West stole Africa's wealth, but also it established a viable system to ensure that Africans don't rise to their full potential in terms of technology and science. It's not easy to understand the economy of the world system without education; therefore, it becomes very crucial to have education as a fundamental basis in order to understand the mineral resources and the utilization of these mineral resources. It's useless and nonsensical to give a considerable amount of money to somebody who does not know anything about money. It's also useless and meaningless to have a large amount of carats of diamonds if they cannot be used for the benefit of the masses. I have heard people saying, "Those who have gold make the rules." The fact of the matter is this: that is not true in South Africa, even in Africa in general. There are many people who know how to mine diamond, even gold itself, but they can't do anything about it afterward simply because they were not taught the value and the importance of gold and diamond. I need you to understand this at this point time. I have been in Zimbabwe, and I have been lectured thoroughly about diamonds and even about gold. I understand that gold, unlike diamond, is a totally different thing, and it goes through its unique process until it becomes a final product, while diamonds are just mined and eventually have to be cut and polished, and some countries in Africa are still not even aware how the whole process of their mineral resources is utilized to benefit the masses on the ground except the few that are perhaps educated about the usage of the mineral resources. The point that I making is simple and straightforward: those who have gold don't make the rules in Africa, period. It's possible that for those who have gold in the United States of America and elsewhere in the World, perhaps that statement is applicable to them—that "those who have gold make the rules." I have also heard people saying, "Money makes the world go round." What I have seen about money is this: money does not make the world go round, but politicians can make the world go round. Bill Gates might be the richest man on the face of the earth, but trust me when I tell you this: the president of the United States of America Barack Obama has more political power than Bill Gates. In 2013 the US Congress decided to shut down the government of the United States of America, and Warren Buffet and Bill Gates could not do anything to open the US government except to complain in the media like everybody else. I have to state it clearly that personally I don't have anything against Bill Gates and Warren Buffet with their billions of dollars that they have in their bank accounts. The point I am illustrating is this: money does not make the world go round, and because this is the twenty-first century, it's not like in the nineteenth century where if you had some little money in your bank account you were considered the big shot. Politicians today determine the future of people, and they even determine the schools that should be build in a particular area. Politicians decide who should die and when he should live. Politicians determine the number of jobs that have to be created in the economy, and politicians decide who should be given a presidential pardon and who should remain in prison. The fact of the matter is whether the majority of people agree or disagree, politicians run the show, not the rich people with their pockets that are full of money. The truth about money is this: it gives you a considerable amount of power to associate and mingle with people that are in authority, like the presidents of countries. There seems to exist a theory that says when you are able to make a lot of money, perhaps you are very clever and therefore whatever you say should be taken into consideration just because you have a lot of money. The fact of the matter is this: there is a bit of truth in that statement even if that is not entirely true. There are some dumb guys out there who are making a lot of money without even a decent education, but that does not change the fact that these guys are dumb. There are some clever guys who are struggling with their MBA from prestigious business schools simply because they rely a lot on what they were taught at school, and they can't use their knowledge in a new and unorganized environment, and all what they were taught at school is to control and lead people. It's very difficult to save somebody who is drowning in the sea of poverty without realizing it himself or herself. It's a universal standard that is applied all over the world right now that before any problem can be solved, there should be an admission and acceptance that there is a pressing problem that requires urgent attention. The more I pay a closer look at the poverty cycle in Africa, the more I realize that the problem of poverty in Africa had already deepened its roots in African soil to the point that solving this problem of poverty will not only require foreign aid but also require a holistic and thorough approach in order to root out the deeply entrenched roots of this poverty cycle in the African continent. The problem with the poverty cycle is the fact that it's part of the major scale of corruption. There would not be poverty if there was no corruption, and there would not be corruption if there is no poverty. Poverty and corruption are inseparable components in the master plan of impoverishing Africa by the West. The majority of people will probably ask themselves this question: How does the West feature in the corruption and in the poverty of Africa? Let me simplify it for you: the West knows very well that Africa has been in endless wars of liberation struggle for quite a long period of time, and in the process the freedom fighters themselves not only are poor, including their leaders, but have also sacrificed almost everything. The best way to control people that are poor and even expose them further that they are corrupt is to give them a considerable amount of US dollars; eventually they will start quarrelling and fighting among themselves simply because everyone will like to grasp a piece for himself or herself. The West will then establish what they call internal monitoring institution that will more frequent than not report about the corruption that is happening in Africa as if corruption does not happen in the West. Mabvuto Banda writes:

> *Malawi president Joyce Banda is facing the toughest political crisis of her career. At stake is her reelection next year and the aid the poor Southern African nation is so dependent on. The country's traditional donors, which contribute about 40 percent of the total budget, have threatened to pull the plug if she does not deal with what is known as the "Cashgate" scandal in which more than US$2.5 million is said to have been stolen by some in the civil service. The government has now shut down its payroll, delaying the salaries of over 150,000 public servants.*[18]

When the majority of your donors are originally from the West, it simply means that everything that is happening in your government must be transparent and open to the Western donors simply because they are funding your government. When the Western donors smell a rat, they will just simply pull away their resources and accuse you and your government of corruption even if there is no corruption and further stigmatize the African continent as a corrupt continent that lacks corporate governance. The more Africa relies on the West for its financial existence, then it simply means Africa is still a colony for the West even today. We all know the old English saying that says something about biting the hand that feeds you. If Africa will be critical to the West and even oppose the foreign policies of the West, whether they are appropriate or inappropriate, the West will just freeze all the foreign aid that was destined for Africa. The fact of the matter is you don't want to bite the hand that feeds you. The question that needs to be answered by African leaders is this: How long will Africa rely on the West for its financial existence? How long will the West continue to control African politics and African mineral resources? The G7 club is made up of countries that are filthy stinking rich, and these countries control not only the mineral resource of the world but also the very oxygen that we breathe. They have the rights to pollute the air that we breathe without going to jail and kill a considerable number of people with impunity, yet these countries also set standards for carbon dioxide emission.

Aristides Cabeche writes:

> *In Luanda-Norte, a province in the northeast of Angola known for its mineral wealth, a representative of another opposition party, Bloco Democratico, is reported to have been severely beaten by the police after he was arrested. Police changed tack after the latest demonstration in Luanda last Saturday by picking up the demonstrators and dropping them off in different parts of the city. The protesters have demanded that the government account for the whereabouts of Alves Kamulingue and Isaias Kassule, who were abducted on the streets of the capital in May last year by "militias" that activists connect to the Angolan secret services. They have also demanded an end to government corruption, heavy-handed police treatment of street vendors known as zungueiras, and the enrichment of Dos Santos's family and friends, especially his billionaire daughter, Isabel dos Santos. One of the youth activists is seventeen-year-old Nito Alves, who was charged with defaming Dos Santos by printing a T-shirt carrying the president's face and the slogan "When war is necessary and urgent . . ."—the title of a controversial antigovernment book by dissent journalist Domingo da Cruz.*[19]

It seems to me that everywhere in the whole of the African continent, everybody is complaining about corruption and the looting of state resources either by the civil servants or by the president of that country. It's worth noting and mentioning, for that matter, that it makes no logical sense for the family members of any president of any African country to be suddenly rich overnight just because the father is the president. It's also very difficult to demarcate the different between wealth that has been attained free and fair, and wealth that has been attained through unscrupulous ways. It's true that Isabel dos Santos is filthy stinking rich and a billionaire for that matter. Let me assume at this point in time that her wealth is hard-earned wealth and she is a self-made billionaire, and the next question will be this: If her father, Dos Santos, was not the president of the Angola, would she have made the very same money that she managed to make without the her father's political influence and political connection? This is not to suggest that families of political leaders and even the presidents of African countries must not do business and acquired wealth like everybody else, but the way in which this wealth is acquired, it makes ordinary people on the ground to question the authenticity and the credibility of this sudden and overnight hard-earned wealth. It goes without saying that if my father was a member of the ruling party occupying an influential position in the ruling party here in South Africa, I will be in a better position compared to the current economic position that I am in right now. It also means that I would have an opportunity that the majority of people don't have of meeting not only powerful people in the government of South Africa but also powerful people that are in position of power in business. The iron sharpens the iron. If you rub shoulders with the big shots now and then, you are likely to be influenced by their business dialogue around the dinner table, and not so long, you are going to incorporate a company that will generate a lot of revenue within a split second not because you are corrupt but purely because your father is a political heavyweight. This is an advantage that many children of politicians have, and this is the advantage that Isabel dos Santos had, and she used it wisely and became filthy stinking rich. I have also realized that rich people, specifically those are in position of influence, like the presidents and the kings; really don't appreciate when their children get married to a poor man. The fact of the matter is a princess and the daughter of the president can't be married to a poor man who does not have a big, fat bank balance. I know many women will say, "Not all women want a rich a man. Some women want a man who can only be able to provide for the family then that's it." What if I tell you this: you can't provide for the family as a man if you are poor. The kings and presidents, even politicians, around the dinner table teach their children that they must marry the daughters and the sons from the rich families just like them. The reason the rich families teach their children this kind of principle is quite simple. They don't want a poor person to be associated with them. They know that a poor person has a unique set of rules and belief system, and they also know that poor people normally come from poor family background with a troubled past and many unresolved problems that are ranging from domestic violence and even sexual abuse. This does not necessarily mean that rich people don't go through what poor people experience in real life. The point that I am driving home is this: poor people, most of the time, are poor because of the family background and their troubled past. It's very rare to find a poor person with good education and that poor person was brought up in a warm family environment with all the basic essential goods that a normal child should access while he /she is still young. The majority of the poor people come from families that are dysfunctional and torn apart by either divorce or alcohol. No wonder the rich families don't want to even dwell among people that are poor. I have seen something strange happening even in South Africa. Once a poor person gets good education and gets a good high-paying job, he eventually leaves the village and buys a house in a suburb where there are other rich people who are also on the same level as him or her. This poor person who is now rich will even change the church that he was attending and begin attending the church of the rich, leaving the church of the poor where they preach the poor sermon to the poor people. This rich person, or should I say this middle-class person, now listens to international speakers and even attends business dinners with the who's who of this world and listens to the world-renowned speakers who are not only preaching about being wealthy as your blessing that you are entitled to it, but (renown international speakers) also selling their books in these kinds of gatherings. The very same poor person will have a different set of belief about poverty, and this person will even go as far as hating the very same place where he/she comes from. I know people that were once poor, and after getting some little money or even some two or three tenders from the government, they disassociate themselves from their original place of birth, and now they are staying in town and even denouncing and rejecting the notion of knowing the village. This is a serious problem, and it needs serious attention. A poor man does not have a choice by the way; beggars are not choosers. It simply means that when you are poor, you have no option; you are probably going to reside in an area that is overcrowded with poor people, and crime and pick pocketing are on a rampage. Poor people normally attend schools that have poor learning facilities and lack proper sanitation and water. Poor people normally work very long hours, but when you look at their salaries that they earn, "it's peanuts for monkeys." It's true that the poor have a different set of values and different set of beliefs that are contrary to the set of beliefs that the rich have. This set of beliefs and this set of values are significant distinguishing facts between the lives of the poor people and the lives of the rich people. When I started this chapter, I never had an idea to expatiate expansively and extensively as I did, and if you feel very offended in a way, I am really sorry; my intention was not to stigmatize and label people as the poor and the rich, but the fact of the matter is there are people in our communities and our societies who are poor and who will never get out of the developmental trap known as the poverty cycle. Some of the poor families have lost the fight too early in their lives. They have embraced hate like Kane of the WWE Raw. I don't suggest that the poor must embrace hate just like Kane, but they need to work hard, and even harder, to get out of poverty. The poverty cycle is a breakable cycle, and it's possible to break the poverty cycle only if a person is committed and dedicated to withstand the heat. It's also true that a child who was born in a poor family will forever lack and be behind in most of the things, like laptops and tablets, when compared to his or her own peers. Poor families can't afford to put food on the table—then how can they purchase tablets and laptops for their children? Poor families send their children to poor schools that don't have sufficient learning facilities that can alter the life of their children. Education is a key to the success of any community and any family. The lack of good education to any community and any family is a result of poverty that is deeply entrenched in the DNA of that family. It has been widely proven all over the world that the majority of people that are coming from poor backgrounds normally become bad employees, and that is attributed to their family values that they have developed while they were young as part and parcel of their upbringing. Simply put, poor families send their children to poor schools that lack sufficient teaching facilities and sufficient teachers that are properly trained, and eventually these students, even when they complete their studies in these poor schools, are still not adequately trained because of the poor family background that compels the parents to send them (children) to the poor schools that have further committed the intellectual genocide to the already poor families of these children. When people are poor and have been living in poverty for quite a long period of time, they become desperate for success and begin to embrace hate, as Kane put it in WWE Raw. They begin to hate everybody even the government because they feel as if they are being cheated of what is rightfully theirs. Poverty is a breeding ground for crime. Poverty is also a breeding ground for drugs and all sorts of evil deeds that a poor person can think of just to get out of poverty. Recently all over Africa we have witnessed an attempt to put to an end the rhino family by poachers who are hell-bent to make sure that they make a considerable amount of millions of US dollars at the expense of these precious animals that have been given to us Africans by God. It's also abundantly clear that Asia and its citizens are hell-bent to make sure that these precious animals in the African continent are brought into extinction by hook or by crook. Some years ago the focus was on drugs. The West was supplying Africans with illegal substances that were not only destroying the lives of the African youth but also rendering the brains of the African youth useless. The whole game plan had to change, and now the focus is on these precious species of Africa. I have also realized something weird in the scheme of rhino poaching. Common sense dictates that it is highly impossible for someone who is in Asia to fly all the way from China or Vietnam to come to the African continent to poach rhino horns without proper connection on the ground from the local people. If Africa continues to have the majority of its people living below the poverty line for a very long time without paying a requisite attention to the problem of poverty in the continent, that will render the African continent dangerous and a breeding ground for poaching to thrive. There is no way poachers can find their way and even have the audacity to run their poaching business successfully in the African continent if Africans who are living in Africa were not starving to death. Africa is a soft spot for crime, and it's also the soft spot not only for poachers but also for drug lords.

> *According to the government's Tanzanian Wildlife Research Institute, Tanzania loses thirty elephants a day to poachers. Total numbers are now less than a third of what they were in 1960s. "At the end of the year, you are talking about ten thousand elephants killed," says James Lembeli, chairperson of the parliament's natural resources committee and a former parks official. "Move around this country where you have populations of elephant carcasses everywhere." In 2011 more than 65 percent of the carcasses encountered on patrols in Selous had been killed by poachers. On his visit to Tanzania last*

> *month, United States president Barack Obama pledged $10 million to curb the illegal ivory trade.*[20]

When the majority of people are stuck in the depth of poverty, they will do anything necessary to break the cycle of poverty whether the action that they will take is legal or illegal; as long as they can see themselves on the other side of the fence, that will be enough. Poverty mixed with insatiable greed in Africa will remain a serious problem if there are no necessary steps that are taken toward the people who are committing crimes. Rhino poaching is not a South African problem or even a Zimbabwean problem and Tanzania problem alone; the whole sub-Saharan African region is under siege from the poachers. The poverty cycle can be broken when all private and public stakeholders come together to work toward a common goal and common objective. If Africa wants to meet its millennium goals and millennium objective, it will be very critical to ensure that there are no children that are loitering on the streets without proper care and proper education. Trevor Manuel, the head of the South African National Planning Commission, which was situated in the presidency, delivered a paper in Kampala Uganda in 2013 at the twenty-first Joseph Mubiru memorial lecture. The paper that was delivered by Minister Trevor Manuel was broad and inclusive. Trevor Manuel not only addressed a variety of issues that are affecting the African continent but also had cast his eyes wide open even to what is happening even in the East. Trevor Manual writes:

> *This is an important time in Independent Africa's political economic history. Africa's economic performance over the past decade has been stellar, reaching levels of growth not seen in the decades. This solid performance is against the backdrop of a world economy that is now in its sixth year of crisis, with no end in sight. During the decade long boom for Africa, poverty rates have fallen, school enrolment has increased, infrastructure investment spending has quadrupled, exports have increased, and Africa is receiving a growing share of foreign direct investment.*[21]

It's true that Africa has made remarkable strides since its liberation from its colonial masters; it will be unjust and unfair to suggest that Africa is worse off today than before. What should be said is this: Africa is better off than what it was in the past. We should also accept the fact that Africa has been in crisis for a very long time, and the root of the African crisis is not yet known to many African leaders. To understand the root of the problem, we need to conduct a root analysis to be able to diagnose Africa's problems from top to bottom, not from bottom to top, which had been the approach of many African leaders since time immemorial. African leaders must also accept that Africa is a very complex continent to understand and to control, and I will prove that statement in my next chapter. There are very few African leaders who understand the politics of each African country. You can't claim to understand the African continent if you don't understand the African politics and the corruption that is spreading like wildfire and contagious for that matter. There is no way a good leader can survive politically if he is surrounded by corrupt and mentally twisted comrades. There is no way a person of good character and a person of high integrity with high morals can survive in the midst of perverted and self-serving individuals. The perverted and self-serving individuals will eventually influence the saint and holy one of Israel. We all know that bad company corrupts good character. It therefore means that in understanding the African corruption and the looting that is going on in Central African Republic, one needs to understand not only the politics but also the political cliques that are in existence in these African countries. But most African leaders seem very reluctant to act in the midst of the African conflict until the West thinks for Africa and eventually comes in with their squadrons. The response that had been given by France when it intervened recently in the war that was under way in Central African Republic between Christians and Muslims including the Seleka rebels was "We have an international responsibility to stop the loss of lives in CAR." If there is one thing that confused me was the arrival of the French troops in CAR to supplement one thousand troops that were already on the ground working together with the United Nations peacekeeping forces. The additional six hundred French troops that augmented the one thousand troops of the United Nations peacekeeping forces who were on the ground met with heavy fighting of Seleka rebels, and within two days of heavy fighting between the French troops and the Seleka rebels, when the dust settled, two French troops were on the ground, dead, killed by the Seleka rebels, and they had to be airlifted back to France. As if that was not enough, the French president François Hollande, coming from South Africa from attending the memorial service of the late president of South Africa Nelson Mandela, landed in the middle of the crisis in

CAR in the capital city, Bangui. I hope the average presidential adviser could have just said, "Mr. President, I don't think that your life will be safe in CAR because they have already killed two of our soldiers." Crisis tests the strength of a leader. The French president François Hollande exhibited to the world and to Africa at large that not only can African leaders not solve their own African conflicts, but also they can't exhibit the leadership qualities that have been exhibited by the French president François Hollande. I understand that probably most of the African leaders were concerned about their well-being and the safety of their own lives. I guess most people from CAR were saying, "Where are the African leaders when you need one?" The West stole Africa's wealth, and the West now took it upon itself to solve most of the African conflicts that are tearing the Central African region apart. It has always been my concern that Africans have been in the bush for quite a long period of time, and in the process of long fighting in the liberation struggles, not only have the African wars damaged our psyche as Africans, but also they left an indelible mark in our minds. The poverty cycle can be put to an end, and there is no system that has been designed by another person that can't be changed or destroyed diametrically as long as Africans unite together behind the scourge of poverty. Africa has presented a united front around the issue of HIV/AIDS and malaria, and Africa might not be out of the woods yet as far as AIDS/HIV issues are concerned, but Africa has turned the tide as far as distribution of ARV is concerned. If we can make such an incredible progress around the issue of AIDS/HIV, surely we can break the cycle of poverty in our continent. We all know that poverty is not natural, but it's a human-made catastrophe to keep a certain group of people in financial bondage while the few who are connected politically and otherwise are enjoying the benefit of the hard-earned spoils that have been achieved by the collective. This is how capitalism works; it oppresses a certain group of people while it allows a certain group of people to thrive at the expense of the rest of the population. Trevor Manuel writes:

> *Twenty years ago, when South Africa entered its democratic phase, the centers of power still rested solely on the West. Since then, we have experienced a shift in economic power to the East and more recently, to countries such as Brazil and Russia.*[22]

It's an inescapable reality that the centers of powers have shifted, and not only has the centers of powers shifted to the East but even the West is following the wind of change that is blowing toward the East. The theory of Africa about the centers of power all along had been to follow what others have developed and follow what others have researched and unearthed. Africa as a continent does not research and discover for its own people and for its own generation; whatever it does is to follow what the West has established as a practice, and we Africans accept it as a universal standard. The time has come for Africa to stand up and be accounted among the living. How can China have such a powerful impact and influence in the whole world while it is just a country not even a continent on its own? Africa has to wake up and smell the coffee. The future African generation will not appreciate to live their lives relying on foreign aid and social grants. We must put an end to the social grants syndrome; therefore, African leaders must replace social grants with viable social programs that will ensure that the majority of African people are living their lives to the maximum of their potential. Surely social grants recipients are not using their potential to the maximum of their ability simply because there is no proper ground to apply their skills and their potential that they have at their disposal. When I am talking about social grants, I am not referring to the social grant recipients who are disabled, but I mean those folks who are receiving social grants simply because they went to the doctor and told the doctor to his face that they will not be able to work anymore simply because they have a pain in the ass that is incurable, therefore they deserve social grants like all those folks who are disabled. In South Africa there is one funny term that they used frequently in the media that seems to be confusing, and the majority of people are getting away with murder through this term. The term that I am talking about is "terminally ill." A terminally ill person is a person who is on the verge of dying, or simply put, this patient that has a terminal disease and is staring death face-to-face. A terminally ill patient is a patient that has an incurable disease, and not only does the patient have an incurable disease, but also keeping the patient who has been convicted of a crime in the hospital will not help the patient to recover from his or her medical condition but worsen the medical condition of the patient; therefore it's better for the patient to be at home than to be in prison. Most of the South African prisoners who were supposed to be serving their long sentences of corruption have cheated the system through this term. After they have been released from the prison by the state, they are found buying newspapers while claiming to be "terminally ill." If you are really terminally ill, why are you not in bed nursing your pains? Most of these convicts who were released through the concept of being "terminally ill" are playing golf and sipping expensive wine and punching people all over. In the near future, people that have been diagnosed to be "terminally ill," when their medical conditions improve and they begin running around the golf course, they should quickly be reported to the police and get arrested and sent straight to prison to serve their long sentences that have been handed down by the courts. That is normally happening in South Africa, and I hope that, that does not happen elsewhere in the world. The fact of the matter is each and every country has its own unique set of laws. I believe that there are prisoners, who have been convicted by the state, and the courts handed down long sentences on those convicts; but these convicts are seriously sick, and they should be released simply because they are not going to get proper medical attention within the prison facilities. With those kinds of prisoners, I do agree that they should be released and sent home. But there are these kinds of prisoners who have been convicted by the courts to serve their prison sentences, but simply because they are afraid to stay behind bars, they play the sick game and eventually get released from prison under the pretext of being "terminally ill" while knowing very well that they are not terminally ill but physically fit. The West stole Africa's wealth, and the poverty cycle is the result of the mineral resources that have been taken away from our great-grandfathers through guns and dogs. There is nothing so humiliating for a man like failing to afford your family an opportunity to eat a decent meal. The fact of the matter is the reason many marriages in Africa are on the rocks is that partly most men can't afford to put a decent meal on the table, and the children are no longer having sweet dreams but their nights are filled with nightmares, as the former president of South Africa Thabo Mbeki once said. The poverty cycle is a very long subject. I understand that I could not cover all the necessary valid points and all the angles that should have been covered, but it's important to bear in mind that this book is not about the poverty cycle but about the stolen wealth by the West in Africa. If I have to cover the poverty cycle in depth, surely it will require a new book altogether that will focus on the subject of the poverty cycle diametrically. What is key and imperative to comprehend is this: the poverty cycle is breakable, and it's also possible that the majority of people can live not only in harmony but also decent lives where the majority of people will have decent jobs and decent houses. It's possible that we can all live a life that is worthy to be lived by normal human beings where the roads are all tarred and water that we Africans drink is clean and purified. It's possible for all Africans to live in the African continent where our mineral resources only benefit the West but also starve the African people, but opposite in the case—meaning, our mineral resources are used to the benefit of African people only, not to the benefit of Western settlers who have already amassed a considerable amount of wealth. I have great difficulties to let go of this chapter, and in fact the more I decide to draw a conclusion, the more I find myself coming back to the same topic again and again. Perhaps the main reason I am camping in this same chapter for a very long time is the current poverty that I see every day in my life. I hope by now you clearly comprehend that I am not pro-social grants, what they call social security in the United States of America. Though there is a countless amount of research output that suggests that social grants are the most viable tool to alleviate the scourge of poverty, I have serious difficulties with such notion, and I will tell why I beg to differ with a lot of people when it comes to this pivotal economic issue. Those who have studied economics can concur with the fact that the best way to fight poverty is sustainable employment opportunities, not social grants or social security. The more there are people who are receiving social grants, the more there will be perennial poverty in many households. Social grants and social security are the greatest deterrent to human ingenuity. Simply put, the more there is a considerable amount of people who are social grant recipients, the deeper is the scourge of poverty. The leaders of the world are fighting a losing battle if they simply think that throwing money at a problem will eventually cause the problem to disappear in a minute. It's like giving drug addicts money to pay for school fees. Drug addicts can't realize the necessity and the vital importance of taking such money to pay for school fees, since paying for school fees for the drug addict is a waste of money and a waste of impending pleasure. The poor are like the drug addicts; they can't let go of the pleasure of remaining poor, and there are even theories that are weird by the people that are poor. I have heard poor people saying, "The rich people don't sleep at night because they are always thinking about their money." We all know that, that is a red lie. Rich people do sleep at night because they have mental contentment and spiritual contentment. The poor are the ones who are not sleeping at night because they are always thinking about where the next meal will come from. The poor are living in appalling social conditions that are not conducive to human beings; even pigs themselves would not concur to live in such condition. I hope the next question is this: What can we do then to save the poor from their self-inflicted pain of poverty? Before we can conjure up any attempt to save the poor from the scourge of poverty, the poor need to be empowered first, and then they can be able to get on with their feet on the ground and start lifting themselves in this bottomless hole of poverty. There is no greater economic empowerment tool that surpasses education. In South Africa people are encouraged to become "lifelong learners." That does not necessarily mean that people should repeat the same grade for almost a decade without any meaningful academic progress. What lifelong learning means is this: the doors of learning are open for you as long as you are mentally and physically able to pursue any qualification. The quintessential example of what I am talking about is the musician Sipho Mabuse. The man has just completed his grade twelve at the age of sixty, and so what? He has grade twelve and is currently registered for a degree. The poor hate education simply because they believe that education is a waste of money and a waste of time—why not ambush this money that was meant for tuition fee with booze? The poor love temporary pleasure and it cost them their lives. One of my colleagues said something strange to me some couple of months ago. She said, "The cost of ignorance outweighs the cost of the money you would have spent if you were studying." Simply put, ignorance is the most expensive commodity in the whole world. Ignorance is also punishable. In other words, saying "I didn't know" will never save your soul during the day of trouble. The average person, once he completes a degree, doesn't study anything anymore. He normally says, "I have finished studying." The fact is you can't finish knowledge, since knowledge is always in motion. I have just learned recently that I know very little about the history of the African continent, and that is where I took it upon myself to empower myself with African literatures about Africa and even about the Middle East. It's very difficult to understand capitalism if you don't understand socialism. In other words, before you can even think about understanding capitalism, I suggest that you give yourself a considerable amount of time and study the history of socialism and its formation. On my desk right now, there is book titled *The End of the Ancient World and the Beginning of the Middle Ages*. This book was written by Ferdinand Lot and published in 1961. Without getting into the nitty-gritty of the book, it's about the establishment of the Roman Empire and the fall of it. There is nothing substantial that I can claim I am intending to extract from this book except the fact that one needs to understand socialism first before one can make politically incorrect assertions about capitalism. Dependency syndrome is on a rampage in Africa. In fact Africa is the most dependent continent in the whole world. We depend upon Europeans and Americans for our education, and we love everything that they eat. Even if what the

Europeans and Americans are eating is junk food, we still want this junk food anyway just because we are dependent upon the West. We have been brainwashed to believe that the West knows better what is good for us. We Africans can't be able to think and act independently without assistance from the West. We even define beauty from the Western dictionary, and most African women are struggling to keep up with the Western beauty. Some couple of years ago, when the Rihanna's hairstyle was on fashion, almost all African women wanted to look like Rihanna. Now the Chinese are cutting the tails of their horses and putting them in plastic and sending them to Africa and calling it extensions. I have asked several women where these extensions come from, and they said China. The West stole Africa's wealth, and now Asia is gun blazing to rub salt to the already bleeding African wounds. Africa has not healed from the wounds of colonization, and China already is comforting Africa with its products. China is Africa's best friend indeed. People that are the greatest proponent of social grants not only are supportive of the social grants idea to fight the scourge of poverty that is ravaging African people but are also supportive of the idea of foreign aid. George W. Bush writes:

> *In 2001 Africa received $14 billion in foreign aid, more than any other continent. Yet economic growth per capita was flat, even worse than it had been in the 1970s. Another problem was that the traditional model of foreign aid was paternalistic: A wealthy donor nation wrote a check and told the recipient how to spend it.*[23]

The West wrote a check and gave it to Joyce Banda and told her how to spend, and what happened in Malawi was the check disappeared, and now most of the government officials are to stand trial for stealing the foreign aid that was meant for the poor. The charge sheet is very long for the government officials who were serving under the administration Pres. Joyce Banda of Malawi. The fact is Africa's economic house was built with foreign aid, and the very donors of these foreign aid are beginning to be tired of pumping money to the bottomless pit of Africa that don't get full. In the case of Malawi, the donor countries decided to take it upon themselves to come to Malawi and hold a meeting with President Joyce Banda, even threatening to withdraw their financial support should the wheel of justice turn slow on those government officials implicated in the Cashgate scandal. It pains my heart to see most of the African countries kneeling down at the feet of the West and begging for financial assistance. It's like Africa is the orphan living in an orphanage home. Orphans don't own anything, and everything that they possess has been given to them by the donors. The clothes that they wear and even the very food that they eat have been donated by foreign donors. An orphanage home is not a conducive place to raise a child. Africa, since its political liberation until this day, I am afraid to say, is still in that orphanage home. There is nothing we Africans can do about it, since we Africans until this day depended upon the West for our well-being. I know that a lot of people will probably say that the reason I am saying this is because I am a pessimistic. Let me just be optimistic for one moment: Where in the world have you ever seen a foreign donor getting involved in the financial affairs of a sovereign state? Maybe Malawi is not a sovereign state. Where is the sovereignty of a state if that state is depended on the foreign aid, and where is the pride of that state if the large chunk of its budget is originating from the West? The one-million-dollar question that can't be answered by anybody is, where to from here? Are we destined for foreign aid even in the next century? The president of Zimbabwe Uncle "Bob" decided to expel almost all Western NGOs, and what followed was calamity and disaster. Philip Shingirai writes:

> *Research done by the United Nations Children's Fund on Africa in the past shows that countries like Sierra Leone, the world's largest producer of diamonds; the Democratic Republic of Congo, blessed with vast mineral resources; and South Sudan, an oil hub, constantly suffer from malnutrition. As if that is not curse enough, some countries in the Southern African Development Community (SADC), including Namibia, the world's fourth-largest producer of uranium; Zimbabwe, booming with platinum and diamond resources; Botswana, blessed with diamonds; and South Africa, which is by far the world's largest producer of platinum, suffer from rampant unemployment.*[24]

Sustainable employment opportunities do have necessary wherewithal to lift the majority of people from poverty, not social grants and foreign aid. If that is true, then why can't African leaders join hands together to fight the scourge of poverty by ensuring that there are sufficient sustainable employment opportunities in the African continent? People have been using the left hand to feed their mouth with it for a very long time; it becomes very difficult for such people to suddenly use their right hand to feed themselves. Different people were wired differently. There are people who don't see any problem with foreign aid just as there are people who don't see any problem with receiving social grants from government. Some people have made it their way of life to live their lives depending on somebody else as if they deserve to be looked after. Let me be brutally honest with you: in this drama called life, there are people who don't grow; even if they can be fifty years of age, they still need to be fed with a teaspoon. Most African leaders were wired that way; they don't see life continuing post–foreign aid from the West. It's like the foreign aid is the solution to all of Africa's problems. Not all problems can be solved with money; there are other problems that actually don't require money as such, but they require innovation and creativity. With that being said, money is a vital instrument to ensure that most of Africa's infrastructural projects come to fruition. We all know that you can't buy innovation and creativity with money, just like you can't buy your way out of the casket with money. There are certain projects in life that require money, while there are certain projects in life that can proceed at an accelerated speed without exuberant injection of financial resources. Everybody right now has made it their mission that whenever they are involved in a project, they want to know how much money they are going to get as the reward. This theory about money is almost everywhere; that is why there are no volunteers anymore. You have to a pay a prophet to prophesy to you, and you have to pay a preacher to preach to you. I have heard people saying, "If I had enough money, I can do a lot of things for my community or even for my country." I have also heard preachers say, "If I had enough money, I could travel the world preaching the good news." The fact of the matter is we all wish that if we had enough money, we could change the world. The fact is money can never be enough, and therefore there is no such a thing as "if I had enough money, I could change the world." You are either helping your community with what you have now, or you will remain dreaming about the future that will never come to pass. The poor don't need money to be lifted out of their poverty, but they need both formal education and informal education. Formal education alone is dangerous; it teaches you only to be an employee of a company and receive a salary for the rest of your life. The main reason the majority of our youth in Africa can't incorporate company from scratch and see it registered in US Stock Exchange is a consequence of formal education. Products of formal education are wired to earn a big, fat salary with fringe benefits. Formal education instills the mentality of statistics and inflation. Formal education teaches and instills fear and panic among its students. Most of the students are afraid of failing simply because failure has been associated with being incompetent. The fact of the matter is this: most children, when they are born, are born with a considerable amount of power to be creative and innovative, but they get crashed in the school system because they are told to follow the rules lest you fail and be dubbed a failure. Bill and Melinda Gates write:

> *We worry about the myth that aid does not work. It gives political leaders an excuse to try to cut back on it—and that would mean fewer lives are saved, and more time before countries can become self-sufficient. So we want to take on a few of the criticism you may have read. We should acknowledge up front that no program is perfect and there are ways aid can be made more effective. And aid is one of the tools for fighting poverty and disease: wealthy countries also need to make policy changes, such as opening their markets and cutting agricultural subsidies, and poor countries need to spend more on health and development for their own people.*[25]

Different people might have different views about a particular subject or topic, and that is not new and strange either. I read widely and thoroughly about foreign aid. We need to understand that the greatest recipient of foreign aid is not the West, but it's Africa. If foreign aid was working and is one of the tools for fighting poverty, how come in Africa the scourge of poverty had deepened since most of the African countries have attained their political independence? Africa has become more dependent on the West like never before. I want to give you a practical example: I have been moving to and fro between Zimbabwe and South Africa for some time now, and I can lecture you on a few things that I have seen on my journey while I was in Zimbabwe. Foreign aid should only be given to a country that has encountered some form of a natural disaster, like storms, heavy floods, landslide, and cholera outbreak. In other words, foreign aid should be a temporal intervention to assist the majority of people who are in a devastating catastrophe that is not of their own making. In other words, countries that should receive foreign aid should be countries that are in a state of helplessness and hopelessness. The gravitas of the situation should be such that it warrants an urgent intervention in order to save the lives of innocent people who are either sick or trapped under some rubble because of the devastating natural disaster that had occurred. Even if that is the case, foreign aid should not continue forever flowing into a country as if it's a way of life. Most countries have made it their way of life to depend upon the West, specifically African countries, and that makes me sick to my stomach. Foreign aid, just like social grants, destroys one's brains to function. Dependency syndrome is a result of government handouts and free food parcels. Every day when I am going to work, I normally come across a certain gentleman on my way to work. This gentleman is still at his early thirties, I suppose. There is one thing that is surprising to me now and then about him: he will be asking people to buy for him milk and white bread. When I look down at him from the bottom of his feet until the top of his hair, he looks very healthy even down there. The question then is, why would such a handsome gentleman who has all parts of his body working very well, even down there, opt to live his entire life as a beggar? I might not have an exact answer for this question, but it's possible that he might be suffering from dependency syndrome. He sees people as if they owe him something. He believes that he is fully entitled to free food parcels and handouts. This is the syndrome that the majority of African countries are suffering from; they are suffering from the dependency syndrome. In South Africa the majority of people are suffering from what I call "social grant syndrome," where the citizens of the country are holding the government responsible for almost everything. One of my neighbors is a taxi driver, and his lovely wife is not working. After receiving his second child, he decided that his wife must register for the social grant (child grant). This is a grant that is received by children who do not have parents who can afford financially. I will not even dare to expatiate expansively and extensively about the requirements of receiving this social grant (child grant), but the point that I want to drive home is this: since his wife has been receiving child grant, his family has also expanded, and guess what! He is working, and his wife is still receiving child grant for almost four children now. All the other four children are recipients of the child grant, while the father is working. The theory that the majority of people hold about defeating the demon of poverty varies from one person to the next person. Whatever your conclusion is about the way to fight poverty, I don't subscribe to the foreign aid school of thought. And I also don't subscribe to the free food parcel and handout school of thought. Though for countries that are experiencing devastations like natural disasters, those conditions that I have outlined above should be the only conditions that warrant foreign aid. There is a dangerous trend that has been set by South Africans who are receiving social grant. They expect the government to provide clean water, world-class infrastructure, child grant, old-age pension, and above all free houses. There is no way a national government of any country can be able to meet all these pressing challenges without sufficient financial muscle. The question is, If the government is doing everything for its citizens, what is it that these citizens are contributing to the sustenance of these costly national projects? And the answer is votes only. It's dangerous to raise a child in an irresponsible way. It's also dangerous for citizens of any country to live the entire of their lives depending on the national government for their livelihood. People who believe that the government must do everything for its citizens are socialists. They believe that poverty can be eradicated completely if the government owns everything including the wine farms. But if the national government can own everything, there can't be a market. Every economy, for its long-term survival and to be able to sustain itself for a very long time, should consist of both the private sector and the public sector. That does not necessarily mean that there will be a laissez-faire and capitalists will be amassing a considerable amount of wealth as they wish. There still needs to be strict rules and regulations that should govern both the private sector and the public sector in order to make sure that there is transparency and objectivity in the smooth running of their financial affairs. But the bottom line is this: nationalization of mines to the full scale can have dire consequences should something wrong happen in the international market. It's important to remember that there is no man who can live alone in an island; somewhere somehow you will get lonely if you decide to stay in the island alone. The point is we are all now living in this global village, and in this global village sometimes we even have neighbors that we can't stand. All countries now are connected to help one another whether through trade or through information. Self-sufficiency is the thing of the past. One way or the other, countries must share their know-how and their expertise in certain areas of the economy. There is a sense of guilty among parents, who have a moral obligation to provide and protect their children from poverty, if they can't be able to provide for their children. Some of these parents want to go beyond and above to ensure that their children get every little thing that they need, in the end destroying the child's mind by being overprotective. Children must be protected to a certain extent, and children must be financially provided to a certain extent. But in the process of providing for and protecting these children, there must be an open space for them to learn and experience life on their own. They must have their own space to learn that in this drama of life, for all your actions, there are consequences. But most parents deny their children this marvelous opportunity to learn and experience life on their own. Sometimes you must give your children tough love. My mother used to spank me, and that didn't kill me, and I became a better man today, and had she treated me like an egg, probably I wouldn't have amounted to anything today. Africa has been spoiled by the West by giving it foreign aid since time immemorial, and until this day many African countries are still looking at the West through the eyes of foreign aid. Whenever the president of United States of America Barack Obama comes to sub-Saharan Africa, he is expected to make some major announcement about foreign aid that the United States will give to African countries. If the US president comes to Africa and returns home without any major announcement about foreign aid, many people become very angry. You will hear people saying, "How can this guy come all the way from the United States to Africa and return without even giving us Africans something to eat?" Every time Africans see an American, they expect something from an American simply because that somebody is from the United States or United Kingdom. This is also true when you are staying in the city and visiting your relatives who are staying in the village; they will keep their eyes wide open and stare at you in the face until you feel guilty. The fact of the matter is they were taught that people that are staying in the cities are fabulously rich. It's partly true that some people who are residing in the metropolitan areas are fabulously rich, but it's also true that some of the people who are residing in these metropolitan areas are starving to death. The belief that says people who are residing in metropolitan areas are fabulously rich by the mere fact of residing in a developed area is unfounded and misleading. It costs more to reside in a metropolitan area than what you would pay provided you were residing in the village or townships. But some of the factors that one needs to contend with is the high rate of crime that is ravaging people who are residing in the townships. The main reason there is too much crime in the township is that there is high rate of unemployment and people are starving to the death. The fact that there is high rate of unemployment is not the only factor that is the greatest cause of crime; there is also high level of competition that is taking place. I have lived in the location for quite a long period of time, and one of my friends by the name of Paul lost his life in the location. Paul was a very young man who had just completed his BSc in computer science. Paul lent his homeboy an amount of R3,000, and his homeboy was supposed to repay it to him.

When the day arrived for Paul to receive his money, Paul decided to invite his other friend to accompany him to collect his money from his homeboy, and when he arrived at the apartment where his homeboy was residing, his homeboy emerged with a pistol and fired shots to Paul, and he died instantly on the scene. The eyewitness to this crime was the friend who was with Paul when all of this happened. Paul's homeboy was a police reservist and was arrested and sent to jail. May the soul of Paul rest in peace. Poverty is dangerous; not only does it affect the poor but it also affects the rich. The theory that the rich people will enjoy their money in peace while the majority of the people are eating worms is not going to work. As long as we don't solve the problem of poverty as a collective, we will all experience the effects of poverty—all of us, directly or indirectly. When I was residing in the location for some time, I use to see bitterness and anger that were brimming on the faces of the poor people who were dwelling in the location. People who are residing in the locations believe that they were on the frontline during the liberation struggle, and some of the families sent their children to exile to liberate South Africa; but when they look at their social welfare, it has not changed much from then until now. Therefore, to level the playing field, most residents of poverty-stricken communities surrounding Johannesburg decided to steal from those who are in the upper middle class in order to level the playing field. Rich people don't stay in poverty-stricken areas whether they are black or white. Even politicians themselves don't reside in poverty-stricken areas because of fear of their lives. Poverty-stricken communities like villagers and township dwellers normally resort to crimes for their survival; by the way, they don't feel guilty when they are stealing from the rich because they believe that they are repossessing what belongs to them. The BEE (Black Economic Empowerment) in South Africa has created bitterness, anger, and animosity within black people, even amongst white people. There are black people who have been trying by all means to make it through this BEE (Black Economic Empowerment) since time immemorial, but up until this day they have not made it, while some of the people who are connected in high places have been swimming in the swimming pool of tenders and they are now comfortable rich. Poverty creates envy, greedy, and lust. An average poor man can never approach a single good-looking woman who is rich and educated, even if this poor man might have genuine love for this woman, just because of his poverty; he will never even dare to open his mouth again. Poverty debases and degrades and leaves most men emotionally withdrawn, especially from relationships. Most men know that they want gorgeous women, and as a result, they don't even attempt to propose love to gorgeous women because these men are not financially stable. More often than not a rich man has a competitive advantage compared to a poor man when it comes to relationships and women. But a poor man does not have a flurry of opportunities before him. What he eats is what he does not want, and what he wants is what he can't afford. Let me be brutally honest for one moment: there are few poor men on this planet who can confidently say that the current woman that they are married to is the exact woman they could have married if they were rich. Most poor men are not only denied love but are also discriminated by women who are rich and educated. What a painful story to be a poor man. The same is true even among children. Rich families send their children to good-performing schools, while poor families send their children to poor-performing schools, and the cycle of poverty deepens even further like never before. I hope that you will understand that the poor are stuck between a rock and a hard place. The rock is poverty, and the hard place is the discrimination by the rich. It's also true that there are some people who are not rich in every sense of the word, but they are faking to be rich in order to fit in with the Andersons. As long as there is huge income inequality and huge income gap between people of the same color or even people of different color, there will be animosity and indignation among people. Income inequality is another main cause of poverty. Income inequality alone is not the only main cause of poverty; there are other factors that need to be taken into consideration when we look at the poverty crisis, and trust me when I say poverty crisis. While I was doing my first year in the university, my economics lecturer asked the class a question: How can we solve the problem of poverty, class? And one student said, "By creating sustainable jobs for the unemployed people and building schools, hospitals, constructing tarred roads, and providing poor communities with clean water." My economics lecturer said, "But we must remember that even if we can create sustainable employment opportunities, we can never have full employment." It seems as if my economics lecturer was echoing what was said by Jesus, "The poor you will always have." Sustainable employment opportunities cannot be our way out of this degrading poverty alone. There must be more to it than meets the eye. What is abundantly clear is this: there is a close symbiotic relationship between poverty and crime. There is nothing that seems to function well in a poverty-stricken community; even the people who are residing in poverty-stricken communities normally age quickly compared to people who are residing in affluent areas. South African poverty has been caused by the unequal, unfair, and unjust political system of the past. There are many South African people who are still bearing the brunt of poverty not because of the ruling party and its economic policies but because of the inherent poverty of the past that seems to bedevil us even to this day. Foreign aid and social grants are the short-term solutions to long-term problems. Many poor families are also suffering from entitlement mentality and dependency syndrome. For the poor families to be lifted out from this bottomless pit of degrading poverty, they should acknowledge that they are in a serious predicament and they need serious help. What you don't acknowledge you can't solve, and living in denial also does not help either. We all know that there are extremists everywhere, and I believe that there are also extremists even in poverty. There are people who believe that is better to be poor than to be rich because when you are poor you have less problem. The problem with being poor is you are defenseless and hopeless in the midst of any attack. Most of the people who are gone today have gone before their God-ordained time. The main reason behind their departure is that simply they could not defend themselves enough because they lack financial means to counterattack the diseases that was attacking their bodies. I am not suggesting that rich poor can't die just like poor people. But if you can observe properly, rich people live longer compared to poor people simply because they have necessary financial means to look after themselves. A poor person, when he is sick, will invariably receive poor medical care and eventually die because of lack of money and necessary resources to afford good medical care, while a rich person can afford medical care at an astronomical cost. Therefore, poverty has sent many innocent people to the grave before their God-ordained time. There are people who believe that we can't all be rich, therefore there are some members of the society who should be poor in order to be housemaids and be garden boys for those families that are rich. The fact of the matter is I hate to be a garden boy of some rich family. Poverty can also be in the mind, soul, and spirit. There are some people who have divorced the idea of pursuing wealth anymore simply because they think that living a life of abundance is not for them but it's reserved for a certain people. That is why certain people prefer cheap clothes because they believe that being cheap is the way to run away from poverty and is the way to go. We all know people who are trying to save money by being cheap; they are living an unhappy life. The fact is even the poor want to drive expensive cars and live in posh houses and have a glass swimming pool. But because of lack of money and the lack of drive to pursue wealth, they just decide to settle for less in order to get by. The poor must pursue wealth at all costs just like the rich do. I need to make this point: no one was born poor, and no one was born rich. Some of the people who are rich today were once poor, and some of the people who are poor today were once rich. Whatever your current financial position might be right now in life, you must not give up in pursuing a better life. I have often asked myself this question: Why would a lot of people settle for less under the pretext of "I love my job"? The fact of the matter is this: people who normally say "I love my job" are lying through their teeth. The main reason you often hear people say "I love my job" is that is the way to say "I don't love my job" and "I don't have anywhere to go." Most people who are working for the government normally, you will hear them bragging, saying, "I have a permanent job, and I am also contributing to my RAF (retirement annuity fund), and when I retire one day, I will receive half a million from GPF (government pension fund)." Why would a person brag about an amount that he has not received yet? And why would you bank on GPF and RAF? Does it mean that the majority of people have run out of ideas on how to make money? There is nothing wrong about joining the GPF, and there is nothing wrong about contributing certain amount of money per month to your RAF. But my problem is, why would you settle for RAF and GPF as if these are the only ways to make money? One of the greatest hindrances to financial freedom is not pension from the government but the freedom to think outside the box. As long as many of us think like our parents and grandparents, we are likely to end up where our parents and grandparents are financially. If there is one thing that I disdain with the whole fiber of my being is a person who is dependent upon another person financially for the rest of his or her life. I need to make myself clear. There is nothing wrong with a child who depends upon his parents financially while he is still at school. When this child who is dependent upon his parents financially, she or he must understand that the parents cannot be present forever to provide financial support at all times. I wonder whether or not most parents do tell their children that there must come a point where they should learn to stand with both of their feet on the ground without leaning on their parents financially. If many children were taught at home by their parents about money matters, the poverty that is in the world would not be here anymore. The main problem is most parents are poor as a result of lack of financial management and financial literacy, and they can't even dare to open their mouth and utter a word about financial planning because they are too poor to pay attention to their financial matters. Everybody has an abundance of potential to become what we want to be in this life. What is critical is our own plan and our own goals. It is important to plan, and when you plan you must pay too much attention on your strength not on your weaknesses, for we all have weaknesses within us. Focusing too much on your weaknesses will cripple your spirit and eventually destroy that firepower to divorce poverty completely. The issue of poverty is a very serious problem, and there is an urgent need for almost everybody in the world right now to pay undivided attention to the demon of poverty, which is sending young people to the grave before their God-ordained time. I have just seen some disturbing pictures about the Syrian War, and this time I am not talking about those disturbing pictures of dead bodies. These disturbing pictures I am talking about were about young children who were dying of hunger in Syria because of the Syrian War. The Western media says, "Bashar al-Assad is killing young children with hunger." Therefore, the Syrian War is the hunger war. I think that the greatest mistake that has been made by the West is this: they have paid too much attention on the weapons of mass destruction (WMD) and have forgotten that poverty and hunger can be the deadliest weapons of mass destruction ever. Hunger and poverty have a long-lasting visible impact on the lives of people compared to the WMD and chemical weapons. One thing that worries me about the subject of poverty is this: when I see an innocent child bragging about his parents' wealth without knowing full well how hard they have worked to acquire the very same wealth that he now he brags about. Money, like any other commodity, if not looked after properly, has a propensity to disappear. Money that was never worked for is likely to disappear within a short space of time. It's better to become rich out of hard work than to be given wealth by somebody else without having worked hard for it. I am not implying that parents who leave behind considerable amount of wealth for their children, therefore the children must not inherit the wealth. But the point I am making is this: wealth that was not worked for is likely to slip away from the heir or heiress with ease. It's also true that there are people even to this day who are rich not because they have worked very hard for the wealth that they have but because they inherited a considerable amount of wealth from their parents who are gone. The poor families don't save money for their children, and they don't even save money for retirement. The poor are worried about the "now," and the poor care less about tomorrow as if tomorrow will never come. The fact of the matter is this: there is a tomorrow, and the sun will rise again tomorrow. What the poor are doing today, they forget that it will affect their children's future tomorrow. The poor make more children and task them with enormous responsibility to save the whole family from the degrading poverty that they themselves helped to create purposefully. It breaks one's heart to see a young man working very hard to support his family of fifteen members with a small salary. More often than not you will even find that out of this family of fifteen members, there is a biological mother, biological father, and his siblings, and none of these family members are working or schooling; most of them rely on social grants for their livelihood. Poverty is a man-made human disaster. God never created human beings with an intention to let them starve to death with hunger and poverty. Human beings, perfected the art of starving each other in order to show dominance and power over each other. Poor people are considered powerless and weak, meanwhile the rich people are considered powerful and strong. That is why this theory that says, "We are all equal before the law" is not true. The law itself is discriminatory, and it favors the rich at the expense of the poor. If a poor person dies, there is less serious investigation that is conducted, and even if there can be any investigation that can be conducted, the outcome of that investigation cannot be made known to the public. Even if the outcome of the investigation can be made known to the public, there are no necessary follow-ups that will follow after. The poor are in a very dangerous position, and they have to think, and they have to think right now not tomorrow. The theory of believing in the national government for your survival must come to an end. People must start to think for themselves. If you will make babies like there is no tomorrow, you must understand that the onus to support these babies will rest on your shoulders alone not on the national government. The national government can intervene with social grants, but the government can do so much. The large chunk of the responsibility of raising these children will have to be carried by the man and woman of the house alone. I think that men also need to be taught about the danger of having a bigger family.This is the twenty-first century; we are no longer living under a rock and riding sledges. The idea of a bigger family and polygamy is no longer financially viable. The world has changed, and the people too need to change. Old methods of surviving are no longer working in our current economic conditions. Times have changed, and the ways of doing business have changed also. There is no longer barter trade, and there are no longer donkeys that need to be ridden on from one place to another. The mode of transport has also changed completely, so is the flow of money. There are a lot of people who are going to be stuck in the bottomless pit of poverty if they will continue to use old methods of surviving rather than conforming to the new methods of living life. Technology has taken the world by storm and by surprise. Most of the people are left with an egg on the face while the few are moving forward, and those who are left behind either play a catch up game or will decide to fall sleep and wait for tomorrow. In order to decimate and destroy completely the demon of poverty, the poor will have to conduct a thorough deep introspection and make serious decisions and take drastic steps to destroy and decimate the demon of poverty. I heard that poverty is the spirit and it has nothing to do with the material world. I have a different view; I think that poverty is the invention of a man to continue to rule and control the other. Rich people think differently compared to poor people. Poor people only think for now, and they can't even see the future impact that their current actions will have on their children. That is why poor people are not saving money for their children, and besides the fact that the poor families are sending their children to poor-performing schools, they don't even bother whether their children are performing at school or not. As long as they are sending their children to school, that is enough for them. It's important to understand that no man can live alone in an island. The rich must also come to the party, and they have been absent for quite a long period of time on this debate of poverty. Money alone can't solve the problem of poverty, neither can foreign aid. The worst form of tool to lift the masses out from the depth of poverty is foreign aid and free food parcel. It's possible to use the same method over and over again even though this method does not produce desired results. The leaders of the world have been using the old method to fight poverty even though they can clearly see that the problem of poverty does not require the old methods of foreign aid and free food parcel. Whenever most people run out of ideas, they normally revert to the old method they know to solve problems with, even if the problem is new and unique in its nature, but they will always go back to what they know and what they were taught. That is why most people resist change and new reality. New problems present us with new opportunities, the opportunity to learn new things and the opportunity to be creative and be innovative at the same time. Most people don't want to be confronted with new problems and new challenges in life simply because they fear new reality and change. It's possible to defend an old belief that is no longer true. That is what I have seen with people who are defending government handouts and free food parcel. They can clearly see that this method of free food parcel and foreign aid is no longer working, but admitting the guilty and confessing their sins, they see it as a humiliating exercise. I hope in the near future, world leaders will open their eyes and see the destruction that they have caused by supplying foreign aid and free food parcel to Africa. I hope that there will be a day where ordinary people will be given an opportunity to use their God-given talent to make a living without being a burden on any government.

Chapter 8

REFLECT

It's important as a human being to take some time off to reflect and recharge. The main purpose of reflection is ultimately to find within you the inner strength and the inner force that lie within you. While the majority of the people are busy as a bee going up and down and don't give sufficient time to themselves to conduct a thorough introspection of their lives, it's important for you and me to reflect thoroughly about the events of the year and our personal progress in life. You need to take stock of your life and assess the success and the failure that you had in the year and eventually make necessary adjustments if you should. The best place to reflect and recharge is obviously out of the hustle and bustle of the city. You need to choose a place where you will be alone and conduct a thorough unbiased internal assessment of your life and make necessary adjustments, and even reprioritize some of the goals that you had in the beginning of the year and make necessary adjustments. A year has twelve months, and in the period of these twelve months, obviously there are things that happened in your favor and there are things that happened that were against you. I am glad that I went to Zimbabwe prior to the national election of July 31, 2013, and we all know that the national elections of Zimbabwe are more frequent than not free and fair and summarily not peaceful unless there is a monumental rigging. When I take stock of what happened in the year and the progress that I have made as an individual, then I realized that there are certain things in my life that I am proud about, and surely there are certain things in my life that I am not proud about. I think it's very difficult to achieve all your dreams at once, though some people pretend as if they have achieved all of their dreams at once.

The fact of the matter is there is no way a living, breathing, normal human being can achieve all of his or her dreams in a period of a year without cheating or corrupting certain individuals in the process of achieving all of those personal dreams. I hope you are quite familiar with the phrase "Don't be too hard on yourself." You are being hard on yourself when you set your personal goals and intend to achieve all of them at once. And the main reason you could be doing that quite frankly is that you are in competition either with your neighbors or your friends at work. I have friends who are ahead of me in life, and I have friends who run to marriages in pursuit of happiness, and right now as a I am writing this book, they are in a long protracted divorce process that seems to take forever to be completed. The main reason a lot of folks are in serious debts today is that simply they don't set their own personal goals according to their own plan, but what they do is to follow the wind that is blowing at that time. The fact that the majority of your friends are getting married that is not a valid reason for you to engage in some stupid relationship with somebody that you know very well you don't love and eventually get married to him or her just for you to fit in the clique of your friends. What if I tell you this: that the majority of your friends who claim to be happily married in fact are unhappy in their marriages. The point that I am driving home here is this: don't follow a universal pattern and don't even follow what the majority of people are doing. Set your own goals and set your own plan and then follow your own plan, and at the end of the year conduct your own assessment whether or not those goals that you have set for yourself were attained, and if you could not achieve your goals depending on whatever reasons, then you need to make necessary adjustments to achieve your goals. One of my friends once told me that the reason the majority of people don't achieve their goals is that simply they set unrealistic goals. It's imperative that before you set your personal goals, you must also take into consideration the time factor. We know that time is money and money is power and power corrupts. Instead of setting long goals that can't be achieved with ease, why not break your goals into segments then achieve your goals in a piecemeal form? If I had set my goals in the past thoroughly and put an action plan that was working for me not working for my friends, trust me, right now I would probably have completed my PhD. The problems with me then, just like most of the folks, was I followed the crowd and tried to fit into the lives of the Andersons. I am not mourning, though, since there is no reason to cry over spilled milk; we just have to shake ourselves and move on. I prefer to reflect and recharge in a quiet environment simply because I am allergic to noise and hostile environment. I went to Pretoria library to submit some of the resources that I had borrowed for my research and even for this book. When I got to Pretoria library, I asked two librarians, one was white and the other one was black, whether or not they have anything that they can get for me about the life of Dr. David Livingstone. The white gentleman said, "You mean Dr. David Livingstone, the explorer?" I said, "Yes, Dr. David Livingstone, the explorer." The white gentleman said that they have books of Dr. David Livingstone that contained letters that were written by Dr. David Livingstone. There is a book that this white gentleman once recommended for me that I must read. The book was about the Rwandan Genocide that happened in 1994. The truth of the matter is this: I did take the book simply because he gave it to me to read it. But given the amount of books that I had to read then, it was highly improbable that I could read the book about the Rwandan Genocide that happened in 1994. But this time I was determined to read and know what happened in Rwanda in 1994. The white librarian with the help of his friend eventually gave me the book that was written by Paul Rusesabagina with Tom Zoellner. I took the books both of Dr. David Livingstone and the book written by Paul Rusesabagina with Tom Zoellner about the Rwandan Genocide of 1994 and left the library. I had to reflect and recharge, but in my case, I can't reflect and recharge by just staring at empty spaces like most of the people. I reflect and recharge through reading a book. In fact I reflect and recharge well when I am reading a book because that is how I was wired. I don't suggest that you must always read books in order to reflect and recharge, but you need to find something that will make your body relax and forget about your debts that are forever pilling up. Different people are wired in different ways, and also different people reflect and recharge in different areas. I find it difficult very to reflect and recharge in the city, where there are always people walking up and down as if they are selling who knows what! I prefer to reflect and recharge in a quiet place where there is perennial peace and tranquility. It's important to reflect and recharge, but in the process of reflecting and recharging, you need to stay away from the politics of the day. We all love politics, but sometimes our national politics can also give you an unnecessary headache. If you want to reflect and recharge, then you will need to stay away from the mainstream media and forget a little bit about the CAR war and the DRC War for a minute. I once saw a picture of a soccer fanatic man who went to the doctor because of stress and growing headache. The doctor conducted an assessment on him, and in the end, the doctor recommended that this soccer fanatic man must stop watching soccer because the more he watches soccer, the worse his medical condition becomes. It's like telling a morbidly obese person that he must stop eating fish and chips. We all know that most of the people who visit doctors really don't take the doctor's advice seriously because if people were taking the doctor's advice seriously, most people who are dead today would probably be alive. I have great difficulty understanding people who are working from the beginning of the year until the end of the year without taking a decent break. People need to take a break and time to reflect and recharge. Sometimes companies do give their staff members time to go on holidays, and some companies even make sure that they pay for their employees' holiday expenses. The reason you need to budget for your holiday vacation in time is that so you can be able to relax and recharge. Employees who are always working from the beginning of the year until the end of the year without proper and decent break are likely to reach a breaking point in the middle of the year. It's easy to work very hard each and every day without having meaningful results to show off for your work. The reason some companies are breaking even financially is that they are punishing their employees by keeping them at work 365 days a year without a decent break in between. The same thing is true even in soccer and in any sphere of life. One of my friends told me that pastors don't have even a break time to reflect and recharge, and that is why they end up preaching the same sermon over and over again to the same congregation that has already repented. The reason pastors are afraid of taking a decent break and stepping away from the pulpit is this: they know very well that some members of the church might hijack the church in the name of edifying the church. There is competition everywhere. And there is even competition in church. There are people who are always contemplating the aftermath of a fall of another man. I retreated from the capital city of South Africa, Pretoria, and this name Pretoria was actually a surname of a gentleman by the name of Andries Pretorius who was a Dutch and died in 1853. If you are walking in the capital city of South Africa, Pretoria, there is a statue that was built by the apartheid government in honoring Andries Pretorius, which is situated in the city hall opposite to the national museum in the street called Paul Kruger. The museum was called Transvaal Museum and later renamed Ditsong by Lulu Xingwana while she was a minister of arts and culture. The statute of Andries Pretorius is facing the Ditsong Museum, and Andries Pretorius is riding a horse and carrying a machine gun with his right hand. I retreated from this Pretoria of Andries Pretorius and went to the rolling hills of Lebombo Mountains. I wanted to see whether or not the Lebombo Mountains were probably going to whisper words of wisdom in my ears. We all know those mountains don't speak, but the fact of the matter is this: if you can take time and look at the mountains very closely, and I mean mountains that you know very well, you are likely to hear the voice of God through the mountains. We know the story of Moses—that God appeared before him through the burning bush. The reason God appeared before Moses in the burning bush was that simply through the bush Moses's spirit and soul were in peace and unison. Moses's mind was in unison with his soul and spirit. The hustle and bustle of these big cities normally corrupt the spirit and the mind. It's highly impossible to reflect, relax, and recharge if you are in the city simply because there is too much noise and a lot of movements. In the big cities there is movement of big trucks and movement of cars that do not seem to come to an end. There is no peace and tranquility in the city, therefore the spirit and the soul of a person are not in unison. The majority of rich people in South Africa normally build two houses, one house in the village where there is no movement of cars and one house in the suburb where there is always commotion of cars and the movement of people nonstop. The reason the majority of rich people build two houses, one in the village and one in the suburb, is that simply they know very well that in the city there is no peace and tranquility, and you can't even reflect, relax, and recharge well because of the social activities that are always taking place in the city. I have often wondered why Cecil John Rhodes wanted to be buried in Matopos National Park in Bulawayo not in Harare in Zimbabwe. I now know the answer to that question. He knew very well that in Matopos National Park his soul would rest in peace and his soul would be in unison with his spirit. There is no way one can have peace of mind in a place that is forever noisy and overcrowded. In the big cities it seems as if sleep eludes the majority of the people. In fact the majority of the people that are staying in the cities don't sleep properly, and no wonder a lot of people are stressed to the extreme. I should also state that in the city there is a bit of fun in a way. It's not necessary for me to discuss the pleasure and the happiness that could be found in the city. I love the city, though, with all the hustle and bustle that is going on nonstop. I once lived in the location for almost four years, and living in the location was my nightmare that I would not like to experience in the near future. When I was in Mpumalanga visiting my parents, I will wake up in the morning at look at the sky and the rolling hills of Lebombo Mountains, and the mountains bring that peace and tranquility that was in the Garden of Eden before the snake came in to screw up everything that was created by God. Lebombo Mountains are always at peace, and the more you look at them, the more they eventually transfer that peace to you. The Lebombo Mountains were once on the spotlight because they ended the life of Samora Machel, the late president of Mozambique and the late husband of Graca Machel, who later got married to the late president of South Africa Nelson Mandela. Graca Machel had been a widow twice in her live. My father said something stupid to me the other day; he said, "I think Pres. Jacob Zuma must marry Graca Machel." I really didn't agree with my father's idea that Pres. Jacob Zuma must marry Graca Machel. The main reason I beg to differ with my father's idea is that simply the president of South Africa Jacob Zuma has enough already in his plate. It's possible that my father does not see things politically the way I see things politically. When you reflect, relax, and recharge, make sure that you cut certain people away from your life in order for you to generate sufficient energy that is within you. The main purpose of reflecting, relaxing, and recharging is not only for you to generate sufficient energy but also to be able to see the future with spiritual lanes. Spiritual enlightenment comes through thorough meditation and relaxation. The more you relax, the more God can be able to give you good business deals and the best way to make money, in fact the easy way to make money, just like me. The more you worry and grumble about life, the more stressed you become, and the next thing you know, you are very sick, and the eventuality is to consult the doctor for antibiotics. It's important to read even if you are on holiday or in a place of peace and tranquility; by the way, you are likely to understand what you are reading very well when you are in a place of peace and tranquility. I have realized something strange about black people even if I am black myself. I have learned that there is a special connection between black people and fire, and I don't mean electricity. Fire represents God, and fire represents life. Making fire from the woods not only symbolizes life and God itself but also says that there is food that is being prepared in that family. Old African women would just wake up in the morning and prepare fire and boil water for the children, even for their husbands. It was the responsibility of the wives to wake up early in the morning, make fire, and prepare hot water for her own family. I am not a stereotype by saying that statement. It's possible that the husband can wake up at the same time with the wife, but the wife must make sure that the fire is burning in the kitchen. Hot water that is coming from the geyser and hot water that is coming from the fire of woods smell different. Hot water that comes from the firewood smells of life, while hot water that comes from the geyser smells of Western chemicals. Africans normally never had a problem with being overweight since time immemorial, but the arrival of the West in Africa screwed up all Africans, and everybody now is fat; even the dogs are fat. Obesity has invaded Africa, and obesity is killing Africans like flies. There is no province in South Africa where you can't find obese people. It's more difficult right now like never before to find a gentleman or a lady that is in good shape. Africans are ballooning, and they are ballooning not in a good way but in a bad way. The West is killing Africans through food, and most Africans have not come to the realization of the fact that takeaways are the main reason a lot of Africans are obese. The main reason our forefathers managed to live longer and lived healthy was purely the foods that they were eating. They were not eating fish and chips, but they were eating fruits and vegetables, not takeaways. But today everybody is feasting on takeaways and burgers that are poisonous not only to our well-being but to our brains as well. Reflect, relax, and recharge because it's necessary for your body and even for your health. It's doesn't matter when are you taking time to reflect, relax, and recharge, but what is important is this: when you are reflecting, relaxing, and recharging, make sure that you relax very well. Each and every morning I will wake up and perform my daily chores, and after I have completed with my daily chores, I will sit down facing the east, and while watching the rolling green hills of Lebombo Mountains, I will be devouring the book that was written by Paul Rusesabagina and Tom Zoellner. In the evening I will be reading letters that have been written by Dr. David Livingstone. The majority of people who don't give themselves enough time to relax are not only prone to stress and heart-related diseases but are also likely to struggle in maintaining and sustaining a successful social relationship. We need to live life, and part of living life is enjoying life. It does not help anymore to work hard for money that you will not enjoy it at the end of the day. It does not help to work hard for the rest of the year to acquire wealth while you don't a wife, even children, to enjoy that wealth with. There is nothing so painful to almost all men to work hard all day long and knock off from work and go home to an empty big house that does not have a woman inside. A woman makes a man complete, so is the man to a woman. I know that things have changed; some women have jobs that are paying them more money, and they even think that they can make it in this drama of life alone. The fact of the matter is this: sleeping alone also as a human being is not healthy not only for your mind but also for your body. There is something that I have discovered recently about this drama called life. I have discovered that the reason the majority of families are falling apart is that simply there isn't sufficient money in the family. Simply put, most men are not making enough money in order to keep the fire burning at home, and as a result, the wife eventually decides to file for divorce, as if filing for divorce is the solution to life's problems. People who see divorce as the gateway to their happiness soon discovered that in this life there is no greener pastures on the other side of the mountain. My colleague by the name of Alex once said to me, "Why do people think that the grass is always greener on the other side of the mountain?" The fact of the matter is this: even the green grass can be problematic sometimes. I am not intending to be a marriage counselor, but as far as divorce is concerned, it does not solve any of your financial problems at all. I have to admit, though, there are exceptional cases where a couple should file for divorce—in a case where there is no love anymore and their marriage can't be salvaged and it's even beyond redemption. My point is this: reflect and recharge and live life to the fullest. There are more people today who are in the graves that still wish they should have done certain things, and trust me when I tell you this: they had time, energy, and money to execute what they should have executed, but they did not get the job done and now they are dead, as they say, end of the story. We need to dream again and we need to set goals again. Even if our previous goals could not be achieved, simply put, because they were too high and unrealistic, we still need to dream again and we need to still love again. Many people who are claiming to be successful are actually failures in life. How can a man who has a big house residing in an affluent suburb claim that he is rich if every time he goes home there is nobody to kiss him good night? How can a rich man claim to be rich if there is no one to share his riches with? We came with nothing in this world and we will leave with nothing also—from the dust of the earth you were made, and eventually you will return to the dust of the earth where you came from. Enjoy life to the fullest and stop blaming other people for your mess, and we all mess up sometimes in life. One of my colleagues told me recently that he is starting a new degree altogether. He has some other degree, but he thinks sitting all year long doing absolutely nothing is a waste of time, money, and energy. I also heard that one Chinese old man who was ninety-two years old, after thorough reflection and relaxing at home, came back to his senses, and he decided to register for a master's degree in philosophy and completed it. You must understand that he was no longer studying in order to get a job, but he was studying in order to remain alive and relevant. There are people in this life that are no longer relevant, simply put, because they lost the drive and the energy of living life; some have been run over by the train of life. They have given up on their dreams and they think that yesterday is same as today and tomorrow will be no different to today I hope you know that love does not come from receiving love, but it comes from giving love. Simply put, if you want to be loved, then you must love first, and if you want a smile, you must always give a smile. It's also true that if you want a slap in the face, give somebody a slap in the face. Now you know that I will begin my mornings with Paul Rusesabagina with and Zoellner's book, and at the evening I will read the letters of the explorer Dr. David Livingstone. When I was going through the letters of Dr. David Livingstone, I discovered that Livingstone was against getting married in the beginning. He was very energetic and full of zeal at that time until loneliness caught up with him, and he had to change his mind and change his set of plans about life. It's possible that as a man you can achieve all of your dreams without a woman, and it's also possible as a woman that you can achieve all of your dreams without a man, but the fact of the matter is this: you need a man if you are a straight woman, and you need a woman if you are a straight man, and the idea of me, myself, and I is a Western idea, and it's killing more people even in the West. That is why there are surrogate mothers and sperm donors for people who don't want to have families but they want to have children. It's very difficult to understand Africa from a Western school of thought. It's also difficult to understand Africa from the monopolistic school of thought. We all know that there is no monopoly of intelligence therefore that suggests that there is no single person who can claim to understand Africa diametrically. African politics is complex to the point that even Africans who are living in Africa themselves don't understand Africa very well. I have been a victim of people who don't understand Africa very well while living in Africa, and no wonder the West is always poaching rhino horns in Africa. Let me ask you a question: When the Europeans, Americans and the Asians are through with poaching the rhino horns and the elephants' ivory, who do you think they will go after? There is no way one can understand the history of Zimbabwe without understanding the history of South Africa, and there is no way one could understand the history of South Africa without understanding the history of Mozambique. I have also realized that the majority of African wars are cross-border wars. They don't originate in one country; they are cross-border wars, and they were structured like that.

> *"Whatever happens in Burundi eventually spills over into Rwanda, and whatever happens in Rwanda will also spill into Burundi."*[1]

This is true not only into the Rwanda-Burundi situation but even into the Zimbabwe-South Africa situation. It's abundantly clear that the farm invasion of 2000 in Zimbabwe has become a South African baby to nurse now, since the majority of Zimbabweans are now residing in South Africa and have fled their homes and their country because of economic collapse. If I may use Paul Rusesabagina's phrase, I will put it this way: whatever happens in Zimbabwe eventually spills over into South Africa, and whatever happens in South Africa will also spill into Zimbabwe. The quintessential example of that statement is the issue of the farm invasion. The issue of land and farms and nationalization of mines is Zimbabwe's embargo; it's slowly but surely coming to bite South Africa in the ass, as Americans may put it. The same thing that happened in Mozambique during the Mozambican Bush War came to bite us (my father and my grandfather) in the ass, as Americans may put. When the Mozambican war was over and the Mozambicans who had come to resettle in South Africa decided to go back home to Mozambique, they did not go home empty-handed as you would imagine; they started stealing the herd of cattle from South Africans and crossed the Lebombo border fence that separates South Africa and Mozambique, and my father had a herd of cattle that was given to him by his grandfather, and it was stolen by the Mozambicans, and my grandfather also has a kraal full of herd of cattle, and it was stolen also by the Mozambicans again. I don't have anything against the Mozambicans; I am just telling my story the way I know it. Many people who had herds of cattle were suddenly poor in the twinkling of an eye. It's like going to bed rich because of the herd of cattle that you have and only to wake up in the morning poor because your wealth is gone. I believe that the Mozambicans thought that the government of South Africa had anything to do with their civil war that claimed the lives of innocent children and women. Remember that in "The Land Crisis" chapter, I wrote that Mr. Rough Rider, who is a Mozambican, got a farm even if he was not in South Africa, while my grandparents were kicked around like ball by the apartheid government in Mjejana and eventually plunged into a place called Fig Tree just because there was a big fig tree by the roadside in 1951. I met Mr. Rough Rider over Christmas, and now his South African daughter, who was born from the South African mother, is old enough to be a wife but not to be my wife for that matter. Mr. Rough Rider is now a complete South African and everything is well. The Mozambicans who were stealing the herds of cattle from South Africans eventually stopped. This is the *modus operandi* the Mozambicans were using when they came to South Africa. They will pretend to be the poor of the poorest and ask for a mere job of being a Shepherd. While they are herding your livestock of cattle, not only are they counting your livestock of cattle as to how much money they can make out of it, but they are also studying the people and the way of stealing the livestock of cattle from their employers. What the Mozambicans were doing was purely simple: they will make sure that they gain complete trust of their employers and then eventually the master will trust the servants to the point of death, and within a blink of an eye, the Mozambicans servants will clean their masters of not only the herd of cattle only but even the chickens and the goats if there are any. That was the *modus operandi* of the Mozambicans. I need to give credit where credit is due. The beautiful thing about the Mozambicans is this: they are workaholics, and even today some of them are working in the sugar plantation in Mpumalanga and they are not stealing the herd of cattle anymore, but now they are stealing the South African women from the lazy South African men who can't put meat on the table. It's sad to be a South African man and your beautiful woman is taken away by the Mozambican man. I need to make one point clear: I don't have anything wrong against the Mozambicans. As I said, I need to give credit where credit is due. Mozambicans are workaholics and they are also good builders. They know how to lay a brick; by the way, my parents hired Mozambicans to build for them the very house that my parents are living in right now. I give credit where credit is due, but that does not change the fact that the Mozambicans stole the herd of cattle from my father and the herd of cattle from my grandfather. It does not change the fact that the Mozambicans are still stealing South African women from South African men who are lazy and weak. To understand South African politics without understanding Zimbabwe's history is a sheer madness, and to understand Zimbabwe's history without understanding the Mozambican history is also dangerous because one is likely to have half truths and misinformation about either Mozambique or Zimbabwe. People who work hard for money don't really make much money, and people who work less for money in actual fact make a lot of money. This is not a lame excuse for people to be lazy, though. I have tried very hard in the past two years to work hard for the money, and I every time I worked hard, it was as if my pockets had holes that caused my money to slip away. I know a lot of people who are working very hard for money, but guess what! They will remain financially behind not because they are not getting paid but simply because the money that they make is cursed. When you earn money that is cursed, it does not last long in your hands; it just slips away before you know it. Money that is cursed is just like blood money—there is nothing that is good you can buy with it. Money that is cursed does not stay in your pocket. There are many sex workers that have been in the business of prostitution for a very long time, but until this point in life, I have never seen a prostitute topping the list of the rich, though the sex industry is worth a lot of billions of dollars. My point is sex workers make blood money, though they don't kill anybody to make their money, but the fact is they are killing marriages and relationships of innocent women and innocent men; no wonder their money does not last longer. Money that you work hard for normally does not last longer. It's like money that you make through working overtime—it does not stay and it does not change your life even a bit. There are many people who are working overtime in their secular jobs just to augment their normal salaries, but even if they work overtime, they are retrogressing now and then financially just because overtime money is blood money also. It's blood money because you sacrifice the time for your family for it, and it's blood money because there are people out there who don't have employment and they could have used your overtime had the company that you work for given them an opportunity to make money. Overtime money is blood money because it takes away your time to be with your family. I have been working very hard in 2011 by working overtime and always arriving in my place late and exhausted trying to get rich by working hard and trying to get rich through blood money, and eventually I had to make a decision. I had to make a decision that I will never work very hard in the entire of my life for blood money. The God of heaven gives you a secular job and then you eventually become greedy in the process by trying to make more money in order to beat the Johnsons financially. The greatest sins of them all is not even the love of money, but its insatiable greed that got Jesus killed by Judas. The fact of the matter is there are many Judases out there, and some of them are in politics. These Judases are not in politics to provide services to the people, but they are in politics to ensure that they are enriching themselves and their families. There are a lot of people that are opening churches right now in South Africa, and in fact opening a church has been a lucrative business in the West and even in Africa. I need to make myself clear: there are people that have been called by God to run a church for the purpose of the kingdom of God, and there are some people who are also using the name of God in vain. They are trying to be rich by becoming servants of God. I have been in a church where the pastor refused to close the morning service simply because the church could not pay him his monthly salary. I have been made aware by a colleague of mine of one pastor who told his congregation simply and straightforward that he will quit preaching and go back to his former employment if the church doesn't give the tithe. I love the servants of God, and I love God too. It's important to understand that when you receive your spiritual calling to serve in the ministry full time, you must understand that you are not serving in the ministry to live like the president of the country. You are a servant of God, remember?—meaning that you are there to serve people. I have also seen the same thing with people who study medicine. Doctors are not studying medicine in order to be rich like soccer players, but they study medicine in order to help sick people. There are many doctors in South Africa—and I repeat there are many doctors in South Africa, but the problems is once these South African doctors graduate from the school of medicine, they work in the public health system for a few years and establish their own private practice and leave the public health system to collapse. I don't have anything against doctors, but I was just making my point. It's also true that doctors in the public health system make less money compared to their counterparts in the private health system. It's important then to make sure that doctors are paid well and, in order to prescribe proper diagnosis for their patients, happy, especially those who are working in the public sector. It's impossible to conduct a thorough introspection about your life if there are things that are always vexing your mind. It's also impossible to reflect and recharge if you always feel like you are a failure. All people have certain areas in their lives where they feel that they have failed. There are certain areas of my life that I am not even proud of, but that didn't deter me to write a book or to study further. It's up to you how you view life. There are people who always see the worse out of life, and there are people who take everything that life throws at them as a challenge not as a stumbling block. Life is a good teacher, and the reason I say that life is a good teacher is this: life will always forgive you for the mistakes that you have made in the past by giving you a new opportunity now and then. It's important to learn from your past mistakes and never repeat the foolish decisions that you have made in the past. As I have said before that, it is very difficult to understand the Rwandan war and the Rwandan Genocide of 1994 without understanding the cross-border politics between Burundi and Rwanda. It's also impossible to understand the DRC (Democratic Republic of Congo) War without understanding the Burundi war and the Rwandan Genocide. When one studies the African history, one is confronted with atrocities that have been committed by the West against Africans, and at some point one is also confronted with atrocities that have been committed by the African colonizers in the process of maintaining order and political stability. The exact number of people who were killed in the Rwandan Genocide varies from one source to the other, and quite clearly I don't expect Human Rights Watch groups to give a correct number of people who were killed in the Rwandan Genocide, and for the simple reason: in a war there are causalities of war. The causalities of war are the people who are killed sometimes by stray bullets that were not aimed at them. There are also causalities of a war that are not even understanding as to what is happening at all. As I have said before, the exact number of people who were killed in the Rwandan war varies from one source to another, but that is not of paramount importance at all to me. I am not intending to get to the bottom of the Rwandan war, but the crux of the matter is this: the Rwandan war was between Hutus and Tutsis. The Human Rights Watch group estimated that the number of people who were killed in the 1994 Rwandan Genocide ranges from five hundred thousand to one million people.[2] Paul Rusesabagina estimated that the number of people who were killed in the Rwandan Genocide in 1994 was not five hundred thousand to one million, as the Human Rights Watch group have estimated. Paul Rusesabagina writes:

> *In the late spring and early summer of 1994, it meant the difference between life and death. Between April 6, when the plane of the president Juvenal Habyarimana was shot down with a missile, and July 4, when the Tutsi rebel army captured the capital of Kigali, approximately eight hundred thousand Rwandans were slaughtered. This is a number that cannot be grasped with the rational mind. It is like trying—all at once—to understand that Earth is surrounded by billions of balls of gas just like our sun across a vast blackness. You can't understand the magnitude. Just try! Eight hundred thousand lives a day. More than five lives per minute.*[3]

It's important to understand the colonial impact that has been caused by the long period of slavery and oppression in Africa. I have discovered that most of the African countries, even after political liberation, remain very angry and disgruntled inside if they didn't go through the process of reconciliation and the process of healing. The Tutsis and Hutus wars are not new in the African history, just like the wars between the Ndebeles and the Shonas in Zimbabwe. Ethnic rival wars can't come to an end in Africa soon unless otherwise special attention is given to these rival tribes and rival groups. There are certain people who hate you just because of the color of your skin, and there are some people who will hate you just because you have a long nose. I have also heard that the best way to identify an M23 member is to look at the nose. It simply means that in the DRC (Democratic Republic of Congo) war, the simplest way to see people who were fighting the government of Pres. Robert Kabila are people who had long noses. This theory of a long nose emanated from the fact that the majority of M23 members are not actually people of Congolese nationality, but they are Rwandese who fled Rwanda during the 1994 genocide and resettled in DRC. These Rwandese are now partaking in the DRC War with the belief that they will be rewarded with mineral resources when the war is over and they will be fabulously rich. It's a humbling experience to visit an area where you were born and raised, and that gives one an understanding of the right choices and the wrong choices one made. I would have never managed even to conceive a thought of writing a book had I stayed with my parents and never took the leap of faith and went to the university even though my mother was opposing the idea of going to the university. I have come to the realization of the fact that God will only communicate his vision to your spirit depending on the level of your education and depending on the insatiable desire to seek him. Many people on this planet regret why they were born simply because they can't communicate with their master who brought them on this planet. Many children follow dreams of their parents, which are not even realistic and achievable, purely because of greed and self-gratification. While you are reflecting and recharging alone in the middle of nowhere, please be brutally honest with yourself and ask yourself this question: Why are you here, and what difference are you making to this world? I have come to the realization of the fact that certain people who are alive today due to lack of plan and lack of agenda of life were better dead than alive, and I know that this is a painful statement that I have ever written probably in the entire of this book. The point I am driving home is this: the majority of people who are living on this planet are not doing what they were created for, but they are living the dreams of their friends and the dreams of their siblings. No wonder a lot of people are not happy. I always come across these unhappy faces now and then in the capital city of South Africa, Pretoria, and I also come across these unhappy faces whenever I visit my uncle in the location around Johannesburg. I have seen these unhappy faces when I was in Daveyton last year. These unhappy faces are all over the world. I have seen these unhappy faces when I was driven around in the capital city of Zimbabwe, Harare. I have also seen these unhappy faces when I was in Bulawayo in Zimbabwe. The biggest question is this: Why are the majority of people not happy? I have a groundbreaking answer for you: the main reason a lot of people are not happy is that mainly the majority of people don't respect time. There are some years even in my life that when I look back I regret how I mismanaged my greatest asset—time. At one point I spent the whole year not studying and not even doing anything at all. I know that some people will think that doing something is better than not doing anything at all. Let me be brutally honest with you: doing something that you were not supposed to do is ultimately similar to a person who was doing nothing because at the end of the day there won't be satisfactory results to show for your effort. Let me give you a practical example. There are many Zimbabweans and even South Africans who visit Zimbabwe now and then, but they don't write books about Zimbabwean economic crisis when they immigrate to the Republic of South Africa. They just go to Zimbabwe to relax and not even to recharge for that matter. Many people don't respect time, and many people are still going to waste time by being either in the wrong company that corrupts or in the wrong company that will devour that very little time that the God of heaven had given them. I have discovered something powerful about time, and please allow me the opportunity to share with you. First of all, we all know that time is money and money is time. But let me say, money is not time but time is money. Time is money to the point that you use your time to generate money, and time is not money to the point that you don't do anything with your time to generate money. At some point in my life, I will consult a doctor maybe once in a period of three months, and he will take time talking to me simply because talking to me is money to him. Simply put, when you consult your doctor, talking to your doctor puts money in his pocket while taking away money from your pocket. This is the same thing that happens in a football match; many soccer fans are paying good money to see Lionel Messi of Barcelona playing football and becoming rich before their very eyes while they are degenerating into the depth of poverty. Many people spend their time watching other people making money, while they remain in the long queue of the poor. There are people who spend their lives helping other people, building their own businesses, while they remain in poverty. I should stress this point; one needs to have mentor in order to be successful in life. But a mentor is somebody who mentors you to become what he has already become, not to become what he has not become. Imagine a situation where a young person who is not educated and is very poor now and then spends too much time with an old man who is not educated and not even rich, and he is mentored by this poor man to become rich. Let me be quite frank with you: the other reason there is too much poverty specifically in the African continent is that there are a lot of poor mentors who are mentoring young people to become rich while these mentors are poor financially. We all know that at the end of the day, the young mentee will not only become poor and uneducated just like his mentor but also have wasted his precious time and literally money by spending too much time with a failure. If you spend too much time with a failure, you will eventually develop immutable characteristics of a failure. I have a friend of mine who asked me even yesterday, "When is your book coming out?" And I realized that the guy is putting me on the spotlight. There is another group of people who waste their time in the so-called relationships, and they eventually complain, "He wasted my time." The fact of the matter is this: the main reason a lot of people are wasting your time is they have soon discovered that you don't have anything reasonable that you are doing with your time, and they came into your life to continue the destruction. There is no one who can waste my time unless I allow another person to waste my time. I am no longer in the business of wasting my time with people who are also in the business of wasting their time by wasting mine. I have taken a serious new resolution that I will always be happy and I will enjoy every opportunity that the universe has afforded me. Love life, as we say in South Africa, and enjoy life, as Jesus said to his disciplines. Time wasted can never be regained, and the biggest question is this: what possibly could be one doing that constitutes waste of time? I have just mentioned relationships—that they are the greatest time waster and friends as well. But the other greatest time waster is time itself, and I know some people will say, how can time can be a waste of time? One of my friends recently told me a story of three young boys who were incarcerated by the US police and charged with murder, and when they were asked in court why they committed murder, their response was "We had enough time and we didn't know what to do with it." We all know the famous phrase of being at the right place at the right time, and sometimes being at the wrong place at the right time. The majority of people are normally at the right place at the wrong time; that is why now and then these are the people who are always hit by a stray bullet—it is because you were simple at the right place at the wrong time. Some will probably differ with me and say, being hit by the stray bullet is because you were at the wrong place at the wrong time. If the time is wrong and the place is wrong, how come the bullet hit the innocent people? The reason these stray bullets hit an innocent person is that the person was at the wrong place at the right time; by the way, your right time might not be my right time. Take heed of your time and spend your time wisely. Remember money is not time but time is money. If money was time, therefore everybody will be rich because there are lots of people who have an abundance of time, but they simply squander their time while thinking that they are making money. Time is money but money is not time. I am not going to go further to explain myself because I could sense that this point can generate some confusion. Let me just say, a motor mechanic who is an expert in assembling a motor car, his money will come specifically from the number of cars he fixes per day, right? The more cars he fixes, the more money he makes, but you need to remember one thing: this guy is a genius, and he takes less time to fix a car than an ordinary motor mechanic will take. The point is an expert will make more money with less time, while a fool will waste more money within a short pace of time. Some people waste more money within a short space of time; others are making more money within a short space of time. Time is a crucial commodity, and in fact time is more important than money itself. You can use time to buy money, but you can't use money to buy time. Time wasted can never be regained, and time wasted can never be bought back by money. The greatest loss in life is not money, but the greatest loss in life is time because time is everything. From now on, think beforehand with whom you want to spend your time and what you will be doing. The main reason there are a lot people with long faces always is that simply they are angry with God and they are even angry with themselves for having wasted a precious commodity that is more precious than gold, which is time. Reflect and recharge in order to make the right decision about tomorrow, and remember that tomorrow starts today. If we don't plan for tomorrow today, our tomorrow will still be the same as yesterday. It's important to plan, but you can only plan for tomorrow today. The majority of people are always on the move, and as a result, they can't make sense of what is right and what is wrong. These are people who are changing jobs and changing life partners in the twinkling of an eye. My former university friend told me that he is divorcing simply because of the problems that he has encountered in marriage, and he went on to talk about the nature and character of his spouse. I cannot dwell on the negative comments that he made about his spouse. One thing that he made it clear to me is this: you will never know a person completely until you live with that person. This is true. When you are dating a lady, she will try by all means to present to you a good picture about her life to the point where you will be easily persuaded and propose marriage. When the honeymoon is over and the necessary paperwork has been completed, and what is hers is yours and what is yours is hers, then she will unwrap her anaconda behavior and place it on the table. You will never know a man also unless you are married to him. Many women get fooled easily by a man who is driving an expensive car and wearing tight jeans with a six-pack and money. Most women really don't understand this principle that when a man loves a woman, he will marry her. When a man does not love a woman, he can date as long as he lives, and he will never marry her because he does not want live with her. Simply put, when a man loves a woman he will want to spend the rest of his life with that woman, and there is no better way to spend the rest of your life with the lover of your life than in marriage. Love succeeds marriage, not the other way around. Proper planning will only happen only when a planner is in a relaxed and comfortable environment. That is why it's important to find some time alone to ponder your future and the mistakes that you have made in your own life and learn the valuable lessons that those mistakes brought into your life. There is no learning without making mistakes, and people who are afraid of making mistakes are making the biggest mistake of their lives. When I mean mistakes, I mean mistakes that emanated because the main plan could not unfold the way things were expected. Mistakes happen even though there is a well-thought plan. I think sometimes mistakes are part of life, and they are bound to happen in one way or another, but that is not an excuse not to plan. The Fukushima reactors of Japan taught the whole world how dangerous it is to rely on nuclear energy and the danger that comes with utilizing the nuclear energy as the only source of energy. Some mistakes that happen are within the natural realm and some mistakes that happen are outside the human control, and there is nothing that a normal human being can do about a certain situation simply because they are outside of the human control. Mistakes that can be controlled and be prevented from happening must be stopped from happening, while mistakes that are outside our human control must be planned for also. Planning is important, but good planning should be accompanied by good execution. It's simple to see that the majority of people are not planning because of the net results of their plan. Planning should be succeeded by good execution, and good execution must therefore yield desired results. The president of the United States of America in late 2013 attempted to implement the Obama Care, as they call it in the United States of America, and his administration could not fathom the enormous amount of people who were going to apply online for the Obama Care. The IT system that the US government was using could not cope with the volume of online applications, and the IT system shut down, and the US president had no options but to take the blame as the president of the country. The point I am driving home is this: there is no way a person can put together an effective plan that would not yield the desired results. The fact of the matter is this: if your plan does not yield desired results, it's simply because the plan itself was poor and was accompanied by poor execution. A plan and its execution should not be separable. Good plan should always be executed correctly and appropriately. Correct execution will amount to good results, but incorrect execution will amount to bad results. Sometimes irrespective how good our plans are, but at the end of the day, the effectiveness of a plan will be realized on the net results at the end of the execution process. Bad plans normally produce bad results, and good plans with bad execution will ultimately produce bad results also. It's difficult to reflect and recharge for me specifically because I always want to know what is going around the world. In 2013 South African soldiers were killed in Central African Republic. Trust me when I tell you this: most South African were not even aware that there is a country called CAR except the few that are always reading like me and the majority of scholars that are always following through the international media networks. When the news began to trickle down to South Africa that South African soldiers were killed in CAR and they have been shot by the Seleka rebels and the Seleka rebels have taken the capital city, Bangui, the whole of South Africa was mourning, and our condolences went to the families of those soldiers who lost their lives in the midst of the battle of saving innocent lives of innocent children and women. Let me be brutally honest with you: very few South Africans then understood what was going on in CAR. There were multiple theories why the South African troops were in CAR; some said the main reason South African troops were merely in CAR is to protect and secure the mining interest of certain ministers in the government of South Africa who had business with the CAR government. Little did we know then that Pres. Françoise Bozizé is a gangster who took over the government in 2003 through the support of the Chadian president Idriss Derby and remained in power until 2013. The eyes of the South African public were now wide open, and everybody was mourning the loss of the lives of the South African soldiers who died in CAR. After the chaos that happened in CAR, the SANDF withdrew their troops in CAR. We South African people were happy that at least some of our fellow countrymen did not lose their lives in the foreign land as soon the Seleka rebels took over the capital city, Bangui, and Michel Djotodia made the announcement that he is now the president of Central African Republic (CAR) without any democratic electoral process that was followed. The president of CAR Michel Djotodia imposed himself to the people of CAR without the people having any say at all. That was the end of the story, and CAR in September 2013 had a self-appointed president by the name of Michel Djotodia, who was not even known to the world, not even to his people, since they didn't vote for him. As an African living in South Africa, that struck me with fear, and I asked myself many questions, how possible is it that you can wake up one day and be told that the country has a new president by the name of Michel Djotodia and you didn't even vote for him and his instructions are to be followed as if he was elected democratically? In CAR the concept of democracy does not exist at all. After the Seleka rebels have taken over the capital, Bangui, things became a little bit normal from the international community point of view simply because many people, including South Africans, thought that the Seleka rebels got what they wanted, which was to run the government, and there was a CAR delegation that was sent to South Africa to urge the South African government to withdraw its troops that were in CAR, and the South African government gladly withdrew the South African troops who were in CAR. The then toppled president by coup François Bozizé fled with his helicopter to France with the briefcase carrying an undisclosed amount of cash. The South African media met François Bozizé in his hotel in France, and he accused the Seleka rebels of being criminals who hired mercenaries to take over the country, and he still then declared himself as the president of CAR in exile. The CAR violence began to catch the South Africans' attention and the world attention again when it was reported that the violence in the CAR is continuing and many people are dying like flies. The death toll that was reported by the media as of the writing of this book of people who died in CAR was in the tune of one thousand. It's possible that the French president François Hollande feels guilty that somehow and somewhere he has a social responsibility to save the lives of innocent children and women simply because the CAR problem had been caused by France through its colonization of CAR. Many African countries struggle to stand with both of their political feet on the ground after attaining political independence from their colonial masters, and it's as if there was no need for some African countries to be politically independent, since they are failing to govern themselves. I had great difficulty to reflect and relax while at the back of my mind I knew very well that there were people somewhere who were dying in the African continent. The United Nations Security Council admitted that CAR is a failed state where there is no government and where there is no rule of law, hence there was an urgent need to send more troops to CAR to support the current troops who were on the ground. The United States president Barack Obama sent a recorded message that was played on the national radio in CAR. In that recorded message, the US president condemned the violence and called the CAR people to stop killing each other. While the focus was mainly in CAR and its growing national problems, Africa had to still pay attention to the violence that was taking place in South Sudan. It seems as if African problems are here to stay. It seems as if Africa is the continent that is at war with itself. How do you explain to your son what is happening in CAR and in South Sudan? South Sudan broke away from Sudan in 2011.[4] Many people thought that when Sudan was divided in between, there will be perennial peace in Eastern Africa, and that has not happened. It's true that children who are born in a violent environment become violent in life. The young generation of CAR and of South Sudan will be violent in the near future when they mature simply because they were raised and even some born in a war zone. The sound of guns and bullets somehow will give these children of CAR and South Sudan a chemical rush, and they will wind up believing that war is a part of life. The Second DRC War came to an end on November 4, 2013, and the people of DRC were very happy that their lives will become normal again.[5] The main reason above all why I had a keen interest in the DRC War was that partly there were South African troops who were in DRC, and one South Africa soldier was quoted saying, "This was will never come to the end, and I have been in DRC for eight months," and the South African state television showed clips of the South African soldiers who were in DRC. The South African soldiers who were in DRC while this book was written appeared in the state television and most of them said they were missing their families and they were coming home to South Africa soon. As the DRC War came to an end on November 4, 2013, those of us who call ourselves critical rationalists breathed a sigh of relief. In fact some people went on to describe the CAR war as a genocide that is akin to the Rwandan Genocide of 1994, where eight hundred thousand innocent people lost their lives. What happened in DRC spilled over to CAR and what happened in CAR spilled over to South Sudan, if I may use Paul Rusesabagina's phrase. There is an umbilical cord that connects all African countries together, and this umbilical cord can't be ignored. It's sheer madness that what is happening in CAR does not affect a person who is living in Botswana, Namibia, and even South Africa because the late reggae singer Peter Torch once said, "As long you are black you are an African." It does not matter where you live, but as long you are black you are an African. It therefore means that you can't ignore what is happening in any African country whether in East Africa or even in North Africa because Africans have a tendency of behaving the same way whether they are from Central Africa or Eastern Africa. The SADC leadership took necessary steps to ensure that the CAR war came to an end, and the self-appointed president of CAR Michel Djotodia agreed to step down as the CAR president on January 10 2014. It was an important step to the right direction to solve the CAR debacle that has thrust African leadership's ineptitude to the international stage. SADC has been ignoring CAR people for quite a long period of time. There was no need for France president François Hollande to land in CAR in the middle of the battle had the African leaders were proactive in solving the CAR embargo. Where is this concept that says African problems need African solution? It seems as if some African problems can't be solved by African solution. Most of the African problems have been created by the West through its long and protracted illegal annexation of Africa. Even after the majority of African countries attained their political independence, they are struggling to conceptualize concepts of democracy and independence. I don't mean that most of the African countries don't understand the concept of democracy and independence, but the application and dynamics of democracy and political independence to most African countries remain a myth and fiction. The most dangerous thing in the world is to be a prison for a very long time to the point that you lose your true identity, and most of the African countries have been in political prison of the West for a very long time. Even after they are were released from the political prison of the West, they are still behaving and thinking as if they are still in the political prison of the West. The damage that has been caused by the West through long and protracted colonization of Africa can't be defined by any word in the *Oxford Advanced Dictionary*. The colonization of Africa by the West still remains a root cause of many African problems. It's true that the West will say, "We have given Africa total political independence, and please don't blame the West for your ineptitude to govern yourselves and your people." It's true that Africa is totally independent politically from the Western shackles, but is Africa really economically free from the Western shackles? The fact of the matter is this: Africa is now further in another prison that has been created by the West. The colonization of Africa had different phases and different faces. These multiple phases and multiple faces of colonization have been ignored for quite a long period of time, and they have not been addressed properly until this point in time, hence the post-independence wars have engulfed most African countries. Africa not only suffers from the leprosy of corruption that is contagious but also suffers from the leadership vacuum as a consequence of long and protracted oppression by the West. There are very few African leaders who have spent the entire of their lives in the African continent and studied the African continent dynamics. Most of the African leaders of our African liberation movements were away in exile acquiring military training to fight the enemy, which was colonization after colonization has come and gone, and some of these leaders of African liberation movements are now leading most of the African countries economically, and they are not cutting it simply because they lack the wherewithal and necessary skills to steer the economy to the direct direction in order for the economy to generate sustainable employment. I was warned in my first trip to the Republic of Zimbabwe that I should change my South African currency to US dollars, since the functioning currency in Zimbabwe is US dollars. The overall reason I had to change my South African currency from the South African bank instead of exchanging my South African rands in Zimbabwe is because I could be opening myself up for exploitation. I listened carefully and followed the advice that was given to me by Mr. Brown. I have never exchanged my South African rands in the Zimbabwe since I have been visiting Zimbabwe. One of my main concerns with the US currency was specifically the one US dollar. The one US dollar paper money that is being used in Zimbabwe baffles me to the extreme. I disembarked from the bus and I went to a shop that was already open, and I pulled out my wallet that was loaded with US dollars and I bought a drink. The teller gave me a change after I bought a drink, and when I looked at the US dollar that she gave me, it was very old and on the verge of tearing itself apart, and I became very worried. Mr. Brown came to explain to me that I need not worry about those US dollars; they will eventually purchase anything that

I would like to purchase in Harare. I took those US dollars and put them in my loaded wallet and went back straight to the bus. The Zimbabwean government introduced the US dollars in 2009 as an economic measure to resuscitate the economy that was forever in shambles. The issue of dollarization came into being when the GPA (Global Political Agreement) was reached. The GPA saw many economic changes taking place, and the economy was on its feet again. The majority of people can concur that the GPA did play an effective role in ensuring that the Zimbabwean economy does not continue on its downward spiral. During the GPA period, things were almost better simply because there were many heads in the government that could come together and hatch out a plan to source out funding from different countries and inject these funds to the Zimbabwean economy. We all know that if it wasn't for the GPA that has been initiated by SADC through its mediator, the former president of South Africa Thabo Mbeki, it was a foregone conclusion that Zimbabwe was going to be another Somalia. The GPA came to an end just before the national election of July 31, 2013. Since the GPA came to an end, it also meant that economic stability that had prevailed because of the GPA agreement had also come and gone. I know that the Zimbabwe has its own political and economic complexities, but even if it has its own political and economic intricacies, but the fact remains there are pressing problems in Zimbabwe that require necessary and urgent attention. When I was in Bulawayo in a bus terminal, I raised my concern to other passengers I was with while we were waiting for the bus about that one US dollar that is currently used—that it could easily tear itself apart. I also suggested that this one US dollar can be duplicated with ease, since the paper that it was printed on was very weak and cheap from the face value. There is nothing special about that one US dollar that they are using in Zimbabwe. While I am writing this book, Zimbabwe was in a cash liquidity crisis. What it simply means is this: there was no money in Zimbabwe sufficient enough to pay civil servants, and the situations had dire consequences to the people on the ground. While 2014 has been dubbed as the year of completion and perfection in South Africa, but trust me when I tell you this: 2014 is not the year for completion and perfection for most of the Zimbabweans who are living in the Republic of Zimbabwe. Hard times are upon the Zimbabwean people. I suggest that leaders of different church denomination from all over the world must now and then pray for the people of Zimbabwe for the current dilemma that they find themselves in. There is a theory in South Africa that suggests that apartheid was brought down to its knees by prayer. Let me just accept that theory that suggests that apartheid was brought down to its knees by prayer. Lets us now pray for the people of Zimbabwe and ask God to give them strength to overcome their own political and economic challenges. If apartheid was brought down to its knees by prayer, I suggest that people who prayed for the people of South Africa to overcome the power of the apartheid system should be the same people who are praying for Zimbabwe's economic and political problems to come to an end. After I left Zimbabwe, there were numerous reports about the poaching of elephant's ivory in Hwange National Park.[7] The scenes that were broadcasted on CNN were startling. The West stole Africa's wealth, and now the West with its partner in crime, Asia, are wiping Africa's elephants and rhinos away. The West has been saying that the biggest market for the elephant's ivory and rhino's horns is in Asia alone. It simply means that there are no Europeans, not even Americans, who are poaching rhino's horns and elephant's ivory in Africa. For the moment it appears as if it's true, but there is more to it than meets the eye in the rhino and elephant poaching debacle. Even though there are a lot of bad things that seem to happen around us, and with no end in sight, we still need to reflect and recharge. Remember we can't solve all our problems and we can't solve all Zimbabwe's problems. That is why I suggested that we need to pray for the Zimbabwean people simply because there is nothing more powerful that we can offer that could change their political and their economic situation without prayer. By the way, prayer is a free commodity, and there are no financial losses that you will experience when you are praying for the Zimbabwean people. There isn't an appropriate time and period to fast and pray for the Zimbabweans to overcome their political and economic challenges than now. While you are fasting and praying for the Zimbabwean people, in the process you will soon discover that not only will God answer your prayers about the challenges that the Zimbabwean people are facing but he will also answer your prayers of losing weight that you have been struggling with and God knows for how long. There are perennial benefits that one can reap in prayer. Reflect and recharge even though there are a lot of things that are going wrong around us, but we need to still celebrate and enjoy this gift of life that has been given to us by God. We need to enjoy life in the midst of trouble and problems. Life is too short, and when you get an opportunity to enjoy it, please don't feel guilty—enjoy life to the fullest. I am not suggesting that you must eat fatty foods from the West and kill yourself. The Western agenda about Africa and about the people of the African continent is purely self-serving and self-enriching to the West, not to the

African people. African people and African leaders who are placing their entire hope and faith on the Western governments for help are in for a big surprise. There is nothing that the West can give Africa now for free, and there are no more free handouts and food parcels. If the African leaders continue to look up to the West for financial assistance without thinking about losing anything in the process, they are also in for a big surprise. The days of free handouts and free food parcel are over; there are no more free gifts and free food parcel from the West anymore. Most of the African children grow up listening to the Western music than any other children in the world. Chinese children listen to Chinese music, and African children were supposed to listen to African music, but that is not happening, and the opposite is the case in terms of the African children. African children are forever becoming Americanized in the name of development and civilization, and those are the trade-off we African people have to make to remain a foreign aid destination for the West. It seems as if most of the African countries are strategically and systematically positioning themselves to be the perfect destination for the Western foreign aid. Everybody is doing everything possible to be the perfect recipient for the Western foreign aid. The question that I asked myself about the Western foreign aid in Africa is this: How come the Western foreign aid will only be sent to Africa during the time of wars and political mayhem? Why can't the West and its allies cancel the debt that most African countries are owing to the World Bank and International Monetary Fund?

Joseph Kay writes on *Southern Times*:

> *There are many frustrations with the UN in Goma. In November 2012, MONUSCO did not protect the city from the M23 who went on to hold if for ten days. Residents remember MONUSCO soldiers standing by as the M23 rolled into the provincial capital and then looted government offices and a hospital. Not only do locals feel MONUSCO does not protect them, but there is a perception that the members of MONUSCO are overpaid, over-sexed and over here. Whilst controversy in the past has led to tougher rules to reduce sex scandals, MONUSCO staff is still widely considered to be overpaid. Speaking to mortars over the last week, the perception is that Goma is awash with money.*[8]

When one analyzes the Second DRC War from the beginning until its end on November 4, 2013, it becomes apparently clear that each and every African war that had been fought by the militia groups against any African government is not exactly about the lack of democracy and corruption that is frequently touted on the mainstream media, but it's purely about greed and financial gain. The estimation of mineral resources that are buried in the belly of the DRC soil is estimated to be in the region of US$27 trillion. That makes DRC the wealthiest country in Africa on paper, yet this wealthiest country in the African continent has been locked in the endless civil war with its people for quite a long period of time. There are untold tails about the DRC; for example, the number of women who were raped by the militia groups were sometimes exaggerated and doctored in order to receive more funds from the international NGOs. Each and every African country will do anything necessary to acquire these foreign funds that come only if there is a war. Average people will also do anything possible in their power to acquire more funds from even their national governments. The same is true even here in South Africa. I have seen with my naked eyes people who are beggars on the streets of Pretoria while receiving money from the national government for disability grant. I then asked myself this question: Are these people really poor or are they were wired like that? Even if they can have money because of the poverty mentality that they possess, they still believe that they are poor. It's possible that some of the statistics of poverty about Africa are now and then doctored just to make sure that there is enough money that is siphoned from the UN to keep these African NGOs afloat. It's true that there is poverty in Africa, but my main concern is this: poverty should not be used as an instrument to enrich others in the process of fighting the African poverty. There are millions of US dollars contracts that are signed and sealed in the middle of these African wars. I don't want to go further with this point, but God knows how many people made millions of dollars in the Second DRC War in the name of fighting the M23. As the war in CAR came to an end, some people would have long ago made their killings in that CAR war financially. There are financial benefits that are to be made when blood is spilling like a river on the bodies of dead people. We all know that blood money is bad money because it does not stay long enough in your pocket after receiving it; eventually it disappears without a trace. The main reason there are many wars in Africa is that simply the nationalists miscalculated the political emancipation of most African countries from the political shackles of the West. There were no effective plans that were put together by the African nationalists prior to the political liberation of the African continent. When the Berlin Wall fell in Germany that was not only symbolic to the German people that political freedom has finally arrived but it was also symbolic even to the African people that not long Africa will be a politically free continent from the slavery of the West. When I was in the Cradle of Humankind in Marupeng in South Africa, one taxi driver was murmuring about working hard for money that he does not even have time to enjoy. You can't keep on amassing wealth without enjoying some of the wealth that you are making. Most parents work hard day and night for their children so that their children would not suffer when they are gone. The question that I have for you parents who are working hard for your children to enjoy your money with prostitutes when you are gone is this: How do you know that your heir or heiress will be very thrifty with the money that you are leaving him or her behind with? It's possible that you can work very hard for the rest of your life and even miss to live your life for the sake of your children who are not going to look after what you have been working for all these years; therefore, I say to you, enjoy life to the fullest, take yourself out with your group of friends or even some of your family members, and spoil them. Good ideas and good business ideas, including witty ideas, spring forth out of the minds of people who are relaxed and refreshed. I have discovered something fascinating about this drama called life. Sometimes life can be cruel to be kind, and sometimes life can just be very unfair from the beginning until the end of your days on this planet. The problem with many of us is this: we are taking too much time to learn the lessons that life is trying to teach us. Some people don't even take time to reflect and introspect their lives thoroughly for the lessons that life is trying to teach them. Some people keeping on making the same mistakes over and over again until lesson time is over. Study while you can and fall in love while you can, but bear this in mind: there are no guarantees in this life, and that is why people take life policies because they know very well that anything is possible in this life. There is a neighbor of my parents who has been living alone for quite a long period of time. This woman was divorced by her husband not because she cheated him but simply because the man has found a new love and a new wife. They had kids together. They had spent some couple of years together in their marriage, and I firmly believe that for all the years in her marriage, she believed that she has found her Prince Charming but only to discover later in life that she was very wrong about the whole thing. Her son bought her a piece of land and built for her a wonderful house; she has been living alone in that house since her marriage ended. Sometimes in this drama of life there are no happy endings. The strongest vow that the majority of people make when they get married says "Until death do us apart." They don't either mean it or honor it. I think some of the couples, when they are getting married, are getting married for sex reasons, not for love reasons, and some are getting married for material reasons, not for love reasons. There is a commercialization of marriage in recent years. It seems as if for one to find true love, one needs to have a very fat bank balance, and failure to have a fat bank balance, you will not have the woman of your dreams. Some people have been saying, if you are an educated man with a degree, you can't get married to a woman who does not have a degree because people who are not educated more frequents than not like to stir up strife and unnecessary arguments. There are also couples who are both educated and working good jobs, but they are always beating the hell out of each other as if they are not educated. There are no happy endings sometimes in this drama of life, and there are people who deserve to be in jail; unfortunately, they are walking freely in public view. There are people who were not supposed to be in prison; unfortunately, they are in prison because of some petty crimes that they have committed. There are people who are poor because of the wrong and bad contracts and bad deals that went horribly wrong. There are good men who had a dream of having a family and children, but unfortunately, these good men are sterile. There are good girls who have been playing it safe and abstaining sexually for quite a long period of time until they get married, but inside marriage not only didn't they get love but also they got the HIV/AIDS. The point that I am driving home is this: there are no guarantees in life. There is no one that has a crystal ball who knows what tomorrow holds for us. I suggest that you need to have a backup plan for yourself, not for other people. There are no guarantees in life, and there are no guarantees even in politics either. There are very few people who believed then that the people of Zimbabwe can find themselves in this current political predicament that they find themselves in right now. There are very few people in South Africa today during the apartheid era who thought that they will enjoy the life that they are enjoying right now simply because there are no guarantees in this life. The points that I am making is simple and straightforward: enjoy life to the fullest while you can because you really don't know what is going to happen tomorrow. Most of the financial advisers have been telling people the following: "Plan for the best and expect the worst." I am not subscribing to an idea like that. Though it's true that we need to plan somehow, we need to be positive about the future. We need to believe that things will change for the better. After the announcement of Zimbabwe's national election results, the majority of people were saying, "Where to from here?" Remember what Terry told me while I was in Zimbabwe on my second trip. He said the reason ZANU-PF until today, referring to September 21, 2013, has not celebrated its political victory is that it knows very well that it has rigged the national election results. If ZANU-PF won the national elections through rigging, I think it's fair and just for ZANU-PF members to write a book on how to rig elections free, fair, and peacefully without dropping even an iota of blood of an innocent people. I hope a book like that can be the best-selling book of all time. Sometimes bad things happen to good people, and sometimes good things happen to bad people. Sometimes a guy just comes out of nowhere and steals the girl of your dreams whom you thought you will spend the rest of your life with, marry her before your very eyes, and send you an invitation card to the wedding. Good things normally happen to bad people, and bad things normally happen to good people. The fact that you are a good person, that does not guarantee you that you will receive good deals now and then; sometimes you will be robbed by people whom you know. There are good people out there with good intentions, but they more frequent than not get bad deals. There is nothing that bothers me like a person who talks about a subject that he does not have sufficient knowledge about. It's like a South African person who is trying to tell me about the politics of Zimbabwe who has never been in Zimbabwe in the first place. It makes me sick to my stomach simply because most of the things you are going to tell me from the onset are lies; besides, you have never been in Zimbabwe in the first place. Should I say you will never ever visit Zimbabwe because of the fear of what might happen to you while you are in Zimbabwe? I have often heard many folks talking about the politics of Zimbabwe and going as far as speculating what has caused the economic meltdown. These folks will talk for a very long time without facts and evidence but simply basing their arguments on what is available on the mainstream media. One of my roommates at the university by the name of Steve used to say to me, "Many people have a vision without a mission," and then he will continue and say, "Some people have a mission without a vision." I always remember those words that Steve uttered a long time ago to me. The point Steve was trying to drill into my mind is this: have a vision and have a mission. Simply put, have a picture of what you want to achieve and then hatch a way to get to your final destination, which is the picture that you have in mind. For me to write a book, I had to visualize the book before even beginning to write it. Dream and eventually act upon your dream. The mistake that is made by a lot of people is this: they keep on dreaming without acting their dreams out. As long as you continue on your path of dreaming without acting your dream out, then your dream will remain a dream, and eventually it will disappear.

CHAPTER 9

THE PLUNDERING OF WEALTH

It will be very difficult, if not impossible, to attempt to understand the plundering of wealth in Africa without the necessary understanding of the scramble for Africa by the West. It's through the Berlin Conference in 1884 where the main plan was hatched that Africa should be colonized and through that Berlin Conference where the colonization of Africa by the West was regulated. Since 1884, from the Germany Berlin Conference, until very late in 1990s, African mineral resources have been enriching the West while impoverishing the African people and the continent of Africa. The West saw Africa as the playing ground, the Dark Continent and the hopeless continent. I have argued all along that the wealth of the West is blood wealth that had been stolen from the African people through guns and dogs. Through the colonial era, the West not only colonized Africa and pillaged Africa's mineral resources but also managed to enslave African people mentally for quite a long of period of time. Until this day and age, Africans they might be politically free, but they are mentally in bondage economically and financially. We Africans until this day and age want everything that the Westerners have, and we want to live the lives of the Westerns whether or not it is against God's laws and precepts; as long as it's a Western practice, we Africans also want to practice it. In order to see and understand how the future will look in the next twenty years in Africa, you have to look at the African children when they are playing with their white counterparts. That will give you an exact picture where Africa is heading to in the next twenty years. The African languages are disappearing on the surface, and English, the language of commerce and trade, is reigning supreme. African children want nothing that is associated with their African culture and African values. Africa is importing its culture from the same people who have colonized it for quite a long period of time. If Africa continues with its diabolic practice of importing everything from the West, it will be a cultureless and valueless continent in the near future. African languages are not even nourished and preserved like other countries are doing, such as Russia and China. These countries prefer to use their language often than any other country in the world, yet Africans, including African leaders, prefer to use English and do away with African languages in order to fit into the culture of the West. Colonization has three facets, which are the colonization of the body, spirit, and mind. I have argued that the colonization of the spirit is more dangerous than the colonization of the mind and body. The colonization of spirit takes away your God-given identity, while the colonization of the mind takes away your God-given mental capacity, skills, and talents. The colonization of the body is purely about restricting a person in one position without moving to a new position. That is why in South Africa apartheid laws restricted black people not to move to white areas because that was going to expose black people to new atmosphere and possibly to new circumstances, and they were going to see how their white counterparts lived and enjoyed life, and these black people were going to covet the life that was lived by white people. To keep the black race in the mental cage, black people in South Africa had to stay in the villages and locations where the standard of living is pathetic, if not dehumanizing. I have stayed in both the village and the location, and I have seen that the majority of black people have come to the point of assimilation of the location culture and location values. In the locations, what they call "the hood" in the United States, crime is normal. One day they broke into my room and pointed a gun at me and robbed me of my possession, and after they have robbed me of my belongings, I was even discouraged even to open a case because stealing and robbing people is the location's culture. In fact if you have never been robbed or pointed at with a gun, you have not been welcomed. Therefore, being robbed is part and parcel of the initiation practice. I have seen this culture, and I had to be assimilated to it as quickly as possible, and indeed I, like many people who were born and bred in the location, also acclimatized. Likewise in the villages, teenage pregnancy and school dropout are part and parcel of the village culture. These are the dynamics that have been created by the apartheid in the case of South Africa, and these are the dynamics that have been created by the Western colonizers in the African continent. Portugal colonized Mozambique and Angola. Germany colonized Namibia. Great

Britain colonized South Africa, Swaziland, Botswana, Lesotho, Zimbabwe, and Zambia. The colony of Great Britain stretches forth almost to the Caribbean Island. In fact Great Britain wanted to colonize the whole world. While colonization was purely about the demonstration of the military power and military strength on the face value, the fact is colonization was about the plundering of Africa's wealth. That is why until this day and age, most of the African liberation movements could not even come closer to the point of fathoming the gravitas of colonization, and these African liberation movements thought that colonization was purely about political power and political dominance. The fact of the matter is this: it is indeed true that on the face value, colonization was about the demonstration of military power and military strength; however, in its totality, colonization was purely about Africa's wealth. It troubles me to see the way the West has advanced in comparison to Africa economically. The West is on the cutting edge of everything that is world class. The main reason the majority of the African youth don't want to do their postgraduate degrees in African universities is simply the lack of the libraries and laboratories in Africa. While these libraries and laboratories in the West are available in large numbers, in the African continent libraries and laboratories are still rare commodity to find in Africa. The best instrument to a keep a person in mental bondage is to deny that person information forever, therefore that person will be rich in ignorance and arrogance and eventually will become a certified cynic. The West was starving Africans with knowledge and information to the point that even to this day and age, there are more people in Africa who can't read and write, and that renders these African people unemployable and irrelevant to the development of the African economy. I am by no means suggesting that people who can't read or write are irrelevant to the economy, but the point I am driving home here is this: the development of the African continent depends on the skills and expertise that the African people possess that are in the African continent. The dearth of the scarce skills in the African continent renders the continent of Africa stagnate economically and otherwise. The West knew that in order to keep the wheels of colonization lubricated and moving, there was a requisite need to starve African people with knowledge; let them not read and write, therefore they will lose their identity and their sense of worth. That is why most African women classify beauty according to the Western standard. In fact African women love weaves and extensions like never before because beauty is beauty according to the standard of the West, and should African women fail to fit into the Western beauty, they are classified as not so sexy. The word "sexy" has been refined and redefined; in fact a woman is sexy when she has curves and long hair. Even those long hairs are not originally hers, but she is sexy according the Western standard. To African men, the standard is just pathetic. First of all, when you don't have money, as a man you need to know very well that you will not get love. Money is love and love is money. The position that you occupy at work also speaks volume about you and your physical appearance. To keep African men sexy and hot, the West brought its own gyms and weights, which African men must now and then lift in order to fit into this concept of being sexy. The West brought fast food to kill Africans slowly but surely. Africans are dying like flies, and they are not dying of hunger this time, but they are dying because of eating doughnuts and burgers of the West. African women can no longer cook, and the African culture is disappearing rapid on the surface. The West got Africa where it wanted it to be. We Africans are living the lives of the West, and we Africans are being transformed every day to the image of the West. African education, still to this very day, is the microcosm of the Western education. There are more books in the African bookstores that were written from the West than books in the Western bookstores that are written in Africa. These information imbalances have to change in the future. Africa consumes the Western knowledge more than the West consumes African knowledge. The fact of the matter is this: the West does not consume any African knowledge, and if it does, it's just a little bit of it. We Africans of the African continent know more about the European history and American history than about the African history. The very African history that we know little about was not even written by African scholars but was written by Western scholars, and some of these Western scholars have never even set foot on the very Africa that they have written about extensively. These Western scholars have written African history from the Western perspective. After the West has amassed a considerable amount of wealth that was stolen from the African continent and from the Caribbean Island, then it began its own club known as the G7. The G7 countries are made up of the countries that benefited immensely during the colonial era. These G7 countries have also invested heavily on the World Bank and even in the International Monetary Fund. These G7 countries also have invested their wealth in the European Central Bank. The G7 countries are responsible for the economic sanctions that have been imposed to the economy of Zimbabwe. These G7 countries are responsible for many atrocities that have occurred in the African continent that were not even recorded in history books. It was Adolf Hitler of Germany who killed more than six million Jews, and it is Britain that tortured and killed Kenyans during the Mau Mau uprising. The Sharpeville Massacre was supported by the West. It was Britain that supported the annexation of Zimbabwe by Cecil John Rhodes. It was the United States that bought African slaves from the Gorée Island in Senegal and shipped them to the United States of America. These African slaves were not only responsible to work in the sugar plantation but also responsible for building the American dream that the United States feels proud about. Indeed the United States is the exceptional country in the whole world. It has a world-class infrastructure and good education system for its people. But if truth be told, the United States has benefited immensely through the slave trade though the United States, unlike Britain that was not on the forefront of colonization per se, but through slave trade, it benefited immensely economically and financially. The benefits of slave trade are still relished by many American people even to this day. While Africa had been robbed of its most precious mineral resources and land and livestock, the remnant of colonization even to this day is visible and permanent in the African soil. Many people will say, "Let bygones be bygones." We can't dwell in the past. What happened to Africa can't be reversed and changed for that matter. The fact of the matter is this: we need to know about the past before we Africans can even think of contemplating about the future. There is no reason that one should be positive about the future if one does not have sufficient knowledge about his past. I have come to the point of accepting that the future proceeds from the present, and the present is a result of the past. Therefore, it's imperative to comprehend thoroughly Africa's past before we can even bother ourselves to contemplate Africa's future. That is why I went to visit Zimbabwe to see for myself the grave of Cecil John Rhodes in order to comprehend thoroughly Africa's future from the lens of the past. What I mean is this: it is unfair and unjust to attempt to project and plan about Africa's future unless we Africans understand Africa's past, and that is what I am doing through this book. This book will teach Africans who are in the African continent and Africans who are in diaspora to comprehend thoroughly why things are the way they are in the African continent. The problem of Zimbabwe is not Robert Mugabe and the war veterans, but it is the economic sanctions of the West. The problem of Zimbabwe is not Pres. Robert Mugabe but the political puzzle. A puzzle is made out of different pieces, and all the pieces of the puzzle need to be fitted together in their own spaces for the puzzle to make sense. Pres. Robert Mugabe of

Zimbabwe is not the puzzle; he is just a piece of the puzzle just like any other piece in the puzzle. Therefore, puzzling out Pres. Robert Mugabe does not necessarily mean that Zimbabwe's economic puzzle will be solved. The same was true even in Libya—eliminating Muammar Gaddafi didn't solve the Libyan puzzle, but it complicated it even further. The same is true even in the case of Iraq. Since the dethroning and the death of Saddam Hussein, what emerged after the death of Saddam Hussein are ISIS (Islamic State of Iraq and Syria) and ISIL (Islamic State of Syria and the Levant). These groups are changing their names in the twinkling of an eye. I have just learned that ISIL has changed its name to ISI (Islamic State of Iraq). After the 9/11 in Nigeria, Boko Haram was born, and in 2013 and 2014 this group had been bombing shopping malls and abducting young girls like there is no tomorrow. Boko Haram had managed to abduct more than two hundred girls in Chibok. The pictures of the abducted young girls were publicized all over the world in 2014. I think the West has not applied sufficient firepower to root out terrorist groups in Africa. The power base for terrorist groups is slowly but surely shifting, and in the near future it will be very difficult to locate the origin and the source of these terrorist groups. What is abundantly clear to all Africans is this: terrorism has moved to West Africa, and it is no longer the problem of the Middle East alone; it's now the problem of the West Africa, and the African leaders need to stand up and confront these terrorist organizations head-on.

THE SCRAMBLE FOR AFRICA

Just like King Lobengula and his father, Mzilikazi, resettled in Zimbabwe at Bulawayo, therefore Cecil John Rhodes followed suit to annex Zimbabwe through the barrel of guns. The Pioneer Column was used by Cecil John Rhodes to conquer and annex Mashonaland and Matabeleland. There are many unanswered questions about the scramble of Africa by the West, and indeed there are many questions that don't have answers even to this day and age. I was told by my driver John that Britain wanted the bones of Cecil John Rhodes to be ferried back to Britain to be buried in dignity, which the Zimbabwe government vehemently refused. It's possible that had the Zimbabwean government conceded to the request of Britain, the only valuable evidence could have been stolen for the future African generation to study about the cruelty of the West. It's one thing to study a history book and formulate an opinion, but it's another thing to see the grave of a person with your naked eyes and draw a conclusion. Not only did the Berlin, Germany, conference in 1884 hatch the plan for the West to annex Africa, but it also meant African people who were opposing the Western forces were going to be eliminated. There are many African men and women who have perished at the hands of the Western forces, and some of their graves even to this day and age are not known. African leaders of that time like Joseph Mobutu Seseko of Congo and Idi Amin of Uganda were hailed by the West because they were giving the West what the West wanted, which were mineral resources and African wealth. When I come to think of the pain that the African people are going through on a daily basis, I drown in my river of tears.

Guy Arnold writes,

> *In Katanga British and Belgian capitalist interest—Union Miniere du Haut Katanga and Tanganyika Concessions—used their influence in support of Tshombe's secession. In a felicitous phrase Tshombe was described as the "darling of the imperialism of all kinds" until he was discarded by the imperialists he had served. The United Nations, dominated by the Western interests and most notably the United States, became tainted and its refusal to rescue Lumumba, who was considered by the West to be a dangerous pro-Moscow Marxist and too independent, was long seen by the Afro-Asian bloc as a black mark against the UN and its Secretary General Dag Hammarskjold.*[1]

African leaders who were seen by the West as a hindrance to the resolutions of the Berlin, Germany, conference in 1884 were eliminated on the spot. It's baffling to know that the Katanga government in 1961 announced that Lumumba was murdered by one of the tribesmen in Kolwezi.

Guy Arnold continues:

> *Given its huge resources the Congo should have become one of the richest states in the new Africa. In 1959 the GNP stood as US$1.300 million; by 1975 it had increased to US$3.695 million. The principal agricultural exports were palm oil, coffee, cotton, timber, and rubber; and the principal minerals*

> *were copper, cobalt, diamonds, tin, gold, and uranium with many more besides.*[2]

If the DRC was politically stable, it would have been economically stable, and it would have flourished economically. But due to its complex political setting and the vast amount of mineral resources that it possesses, it has become the battleground for mineral resources. The number of mercenaries that were employed in DRC Wars was just too much for the mind to fathom. During the Simba revolt, the number of mercenaries who were in DRC grew from 400 to 1,500. When the president of Central African Republic François Bozizé was ousted through a coup in 2013, he blamed the Seleka mercenaries—that they were responsible for his ousting. He went to hide in France and called himself the Central African Republic's president in exile. Though he ascended to the echelons of political power through a coup, he was very angry when he was ousted through a coup. For me, as a South African, it became an eye-opener to see how complex the African politics have become. The more I had to pay too much attention on the politics of Zimbabwe and Mozambique, and I had to monitor what was going on also in CAR. The CAR problem was not just another political problem for another African country, in the case of South Africa. There are South Africans who lost their lives in the Central African Republic just like there are South Africans who lost their lives in the Second DRC War. The African wars have been claiming lives of innocent men and women for a considerable amount of time now. When one takes a look at the political and economic trajectory of the African continent, there is nothing strange and new to expect, just more wars even in the near future. The modus operandi of the West is to cause confusion and disarray, and then mineral resources are looted and the new transitional government is formed, and the same political system and the same political problems repeat themselves again and again with no end in sight. There is no way the African children can ever match their Western counterparts at school simply because the African continent is very unstable politically and very unstable economically. There is no astute businessman who can invest his money in a country that lacks political stability and economic stability. However, the main reason the African wars don't come to an end diametrically just like the DRC Wars is the mineral resources, and that is an established truth. Therefore, the DRC mineral resources have been killing the Congolese people. There is one thing that surprises me about the West: more frequent than not the West normally claims to be the custodian of human rights. If one takes into account the number of weapons that the West has been supplying to the African people to kill each other like dogs, it baffles my mind how the West can claim to be the custodian of human rights and go as far as even daring to prosecute the war criminals while it is the West that places dangerous weapons at the hands of young children. The Central African Republic children will struggle to concentrate at school after being involved in the ethnic cleansing war. Children who are coming from violent communities normally struggle to concentrate at school owing to the fact that they are spontaneous and can't cope for a very long time in a structured learning environment. Just like the old song that says, "War, what is it good for, absolutely nothing." The winners of any war when the war is over become losers too. There is no powerful instrument that can destroy a mind of a person like a jungle. The lives of the US and British soldiers, after being involved in the Iraqi war, have fundamentally been changed completely. Soldiers of war struggle to function effectively in a structured family setting because the only thing that they know is violence. As it is norm that when you are writing a book, you should also read innumerable newspapers to keep up with what was going on in the world, I bought a newspaper, this time in South Africa, and read it thoroughly and kept it properly in case I will need it in the near future. When I went back to the shelf where I had placed innumerable amount of articles, I could not find this article that was rich in information. One morning, out of nowhere, there it was on the shelf. It's unfortunate in life that when you want something so bad, more frequent than not you normally don't get it; but if you can be patient a little bit longer, you might get it. I remember vividly one Sunday in church, the pastor of the church where I fellowship said something striking to the church. He said, "All ladies who know that they are ready for marriage and they want to get married must stand up and raise their hands to God so that I can pray for them." I was shocked to realize that almost 60 percent of the ladies stood up, and those were ladies who were ready for marriage and ready to settle down in this busy life. It was painful to me to see that there is a myriad of good ladies out there who are waiting for marriage, but there are no good gentlemen to marry these ladies. It's always the case that when you are looking for something so bad, like me when I was looking for my article that I had filed in my shelves properly, I could not get it. I hope that those ladies who were prayed for in church that day will be lucky and get their heart's desires and settle down in this busy life. The Holy Bible tells us that "When two or three are gathered in my name, I will be in their midst." I think that passage of the scripture was talking about marriage. I think God wanted to say if a husband and his wife have gathered in the dinner table in their lovely home, he will be in their midst. He also meant that when a husband and his wife with his child are gathered in the dinner table, he will be in their midst. God is a family man; he is not a bachelor. There comes a point in the life of every man to settle down and have a normal decent family. The time of visiting clubs and pubs must come to an end in the life of every man. It's true that some men don't grow up; they still remain as children even at the age of forty. Age is just a number to some men; no wonder good ladies are found in churches petitioning God for husbands who can look after them and marry them. The point that I am making is this: in this busy life, when you want something so bad, you normally don't get it, and that is the whole truth and nothing but the truth. One lady came to me one day after the church service and told me that she was leaving church because there were no brothers who were approaching her in the church. She was older than me, and there is nothing that I could do about it. There is everything wrong about getting married to a lady who is older than you. But there is nothing wrong about being a man and getting married to a lady who is younger than you. In fact most men prefer to get married to a younger woman than them than to get married to an older woman. Though in Africa it has not been crystal clear as to why a man is not encouraged to marry a woman who is older than him, there is a school of thought that suggests that if a man marries a woman who is older, that man will literally have bad luck from the day he get married henceforth. There is no scientific evidence to back up this assertion. However, what is abundantly clear is this: women normally mature earlier in life than men. Therefore, men take time to mature, and that is why it is advisable for a man to marry a lady who is younger than him simply because a woman matures earlier in life than man. Simply put, a woman might be young in terms of age, but in terms of mental capacity and the ability to reason logically she might be advanced and be fully developed. Therefore, a man must always marry a woman who is younger than him, period.

OIL AND WEALTH

"Welcome to Libya, where drugs are free and murder is on sale"—this headline appeared on the *Daily Mail* and in one of the South African newspapers.[3] After the West and NATO destabilized the tranquility and peace that had permeated the atmosphere of Libya for quite some time, the rationale behind toppling Muammar Gaddafi was to free the Libyan people from the dictatorship rule that the Libyan people have been living under for quite a long period of time, according to the West. Then as it is common knowledge now, Muammar Gaddafi was requested to step down prior to his death, which he vehemently refused. On hindsight, had Muammar Gaddafi heeded the international community call to step down, he probably would have been alive even to this day and age. What is wrong with African leaders and power, and is it true that power corrupts? Why would you decide to put your life on the line just for a swerving chair and an office? I think Muammar Gaddafi was not clever enough. Besides, Muammar Gaddafi had also amassed a considerable amount of wealth in the foreign banks, and he would not have starved had he relinquished his political power and went to exile and enjoyed life as an ordinary human being. It's human nature that once a person tastes the gratification of total power, he becomes addicted to it; it becomes very difficult to relinquish that total power and let go of the gratification that comes with being in power. That is why many soccer stars and movie stars struggle to live a normal life after they left the limelight. They normally feel as if the world is against them, since they are no longer being followed by the paparazzi. The same is true with politicians: they can't let go of the total political power and the gratification that comes with being a colonel of the country, just like Muammar Gaddafi didn't let go of the his total power. It's possible that he miscalculated the move of the West. The same warning was given to Saddam Hussein prior to his deposition, and eventually his undignified death. The same fate that befell Saddam Hussein is the same fate that the Libyan leader was awaiting him. Muammar Gaddafi of Libya died an undignified death, and a political leader and a leader of people should not have died the way he died. The West was at the center of it all, and it (the West) took credit for liberating the Libyan people from being ruled by the dictatorship regime. There is nothing that was mentioned about the price of oil that was forever escalating. When I began to contemplate the financial crisis and the role that the financial crisis has played in the whole world, it's abundantly clear that the West was somewhat trying to stabilize its economies by ousting political leaders of countries that were producing oil and selling oil to the West. The fact of the matter is if it was not for the financial crisis of 2007/8, there is no way the West could have ousted Muammar Gaddafi because he has been in power for a very long time. Somewhat the West attributed the financial crisis to countries that were supplying the whole world with oil. In fact the West was blaming countries that were supplying oil that they were responsible for the financial crisis of 2007/8, and that is why these political leaders and their countries who were supplying the whole world with oil had to be ousted through a coup or ousted through mercenaries or using terrorist organizations. Do you remember why Saddam Hussein was ousted in 2003? The rationale behind the ousting of Saddam Hussein was the fact that he was manufacturing weapons of mass destruction, and that assertion could not hold enough water, and the story goes that Saddam Hussein had harbored Osama Bin Laden. The fact of the matter is this: none of the two allegations that were made by the West in the mainstream media were true. All of the assertions and accusations that were leveled against Saddam Hussein were false, and the United Nations Security Council, as always, did absolutely nothing about the perpetrators of those crimes that were committed against the Iraqi people. The new assertion that was doing rounds on the media was this: "the world is a better place without Saddam Hussein." I don't think that the world is a better place without Saddam Hussein. I think the world is a better place without drones. The main reason behind the killing of Saddam Hussein was the Persian Gulf War and the animosity that prevailed after the Persian Gulf War. There was a high level of confusion about the Persian Gulf War. Saddam Hussein himself never thought that the West was going to unite together behind his back and try to kick him out of Kuwait. I don't intend to unpack the whole Iran-Iraq War of 1980–1988.[3] The war between Iran and Iraq was purely about the oil-rich Kazakhstan province. The West was supporting Saddam Hussein with the belief that should Saddam Hussein win the Kazakhstan province, then he will sell the oil to the West at a very low price. Though it was not explicitly stated that the war was about oil on the face value, it appeared as if the war was about the territory of Iraq that was undermined and invaded by the Iran forces. The West and its darling of that time, Saddam Hussein, could not win the Iran-Iraq War, and in the West there were even dramatic changes politically. Pres. Ronald Reagan was succeeded by Pres. George H. W. Bush, the father of George W. Bush. The relationship that existed between Pres. Ronald Reagan's administration and Saddam Hussein faded away as soon as Pres. Ronald Reagan left the White House. The West didn't buy into the theory of Saddam Hussein that Kuwait was part and parcel of Iraq. That is the theory that Saddam Hussein conjured up and relied heavily upon, and it didn't hold enough water either. He seemed to suggest that Kuwait was part and parcel of Iraq, and when he was annexing Kuwait through a war was just to extend and expand his territory, which was taken from him by Britain. The United Nations authorized coalition force from thirty-four countries led by the United States and kicked Saddam Hussein's ass out of Kuwait. There is one fascinating aspect about Saddam Hussein: he moved from the Iran-Iraq War to another war within a period of two years. The Iran-Iraq War had just ended in 1988, and in 1990 he was already fighting another war. Saddam Hussein was very stubborn, and he became enemy number one in the list of the West. The nationalization of oil made the West to be even further infuriated with the regime of Saddam Hussein. The 9/11 attack on the Twin Towers in New York introduced the whole world to the new era of terrorism. The very ground that capitalism stood on was shaken to the core. The people of the world were introduced to the devil's favorite demon, Osama Bin Laden. The irretrievable broken-down relationship between the West and Saddam Hussein placed him in a very precarious central position, and he had no place to hide. The fact that most of the Middle East countries are of Muslim religion and the hijackers in the 9/11 attack were of Muslim faith, it placed Saddam Hussein in the center of the investigation. The West searched high and low for Osama Bin Laden. The US president by then was George W. Bush, the son of the George H. W. Bush, who kicked Saddam Hussein's ass out of Kuwait. There are people who said, "Why didn't George H. W. Bush topple Saddam Hussein from political power instead of just kicking him out of Kuwait only?" The West was not prepared to annex Iraq, and in fact the overall plan was not to topple Saddam Hussein from power, but the main plan was to deny him more access to more and more oil because oil is wealth. The whole world had for the first time witnessed the cruelty of the West and its military power and including its preferred weapon—drones. The world is no longer a better place with drones from the West. The political pressure coupled with the media pressure that the West was facing from its citizens that it could not capture red-handed Osama Bin Laden brought pressure to both US president George W. Bush and Prime Minister Tony Blair of Britain. There are other events that had fueled the demise of Saddam Hussein. The administration of British Prime Minister Tony Blair brought the economic sanctions to the government of Zimbabwe that are currently in place, and I think Zimbabwe was also caught in the cross fire of the Western politics. I think the poor Zimbabwe is the victim of the circumstance. The unfortunate part about Zimbabwe is that the farm invasion happened just before the 9/11 of 2001, but the economic sanctions were imposed on February 18, 2002, and that itself tells a different story. There is no way in which the

9/11 attack can't be linked to the economic sanctions of February 18, 2002. Though I am not suggesting that the main reason the economic sanctions were imposed to the Zimbabwe economy was purely the 9/11 attack on the United States, it's possible that the US Congress and the British parliamentarians were exhausted and flabbergasted due to what happened in the United States, and the farm invasion of 2002 made matters worse also. The West didn't blink on Pres. Robert Mugabe; it crippled the Zimbabwe economy completely. In fact at one point mistakenly so in the Vatican, Pres. Robert Mugabe shook the hand of Prince Charles of Britain. The British government had to issue a statement to the press. The fact of the matter is this: Prince Charles shook Pres. Robert Mugabe's hand by mistake because Robert Mugabe was invited in Vatican, and Britain never thought that Pres. Robert Mugabe was going to be at Vatican. The economic sanctions are still in place in Zimbabwe, and I felt the venom of the economic sanctions when I was in Zimbabwe. Andrew Malone writes:

> *There are thousands of truck-mounted missile launches for sale as well as rocket-propelled grenades and antiaircraft guns. There are an estimated fifteen million Kalashnikovs in a country of just six million people. Guns are available everywhere—from dealers outside the fish market to a kiosk selling cigarettes on the street near Sammy's flat, where arms and other contraband goods are kept in cupboards below the counter.*[4]

The fact of the matter is this: Libya will literally turn into Somalia unless otherwise drastic steps are taken to curb the violence that is ravaging the country apart. The Western leaders were attacking all the political leaders of the oil-rich countries because of the financial crisis of 2007/8. There was a belief in the West that the financial crisis was a manufactured crisis and countries that were selling oil were the main cause to the financial crisis that the world was facing in 2007/8. It's important to understand how the petroleum industries played part in the financial crisis of 2007/8. The world has become a global village, and it means that what happens in South Africa, Pretoria, it affects a person who is in USA, New York; what happens in UAE, Qatar, it affects a person who is in Zimbabwe, Harare. The soaring of prices in the petroleum industry meant that trade relations were going to be stifled. There is one funny thing about inflation and the prices of goods and services: they are not controlled by the government of any country. In fact the governments of the world have nothing do to with the soaring of the prices of oil. Though the governments of the world might put measures in place to control and monitor the prices of oil, at the end of the day, it is the capitalists with their big pockets who control the inflation. There is nothing that the governments of the world can do about the private sector and the way the private sector prices its petroleum products. The South African government has introduced a commission known as the Competition Commission, and its responsibility is to make sure that there is fair and transparent competitive practice among companies and there is no company that will monopolize the market and overprice its products and make a killing out of innocent poor consumers. With that being said, it does not change the fact that inflation is not controlled by any government but purely by the capitalists. The overall reason countries who were rich in oil had to be attacked was that purely they were overpricing their petroleum products during 2007/8. The only way that the West deemed to be effective and efficient was to launch a war against countries that were selling oil to the rest of the world. There was also another fear—the fear that countries that were oil-rich were likely to use their proceeds from the sales of oil to buy more military weapons and become more powerful militarily and control the world. This fear was real in the West. There is one aspect of the war that is always startling to comprehend: every time there is a war, the first thing that the UN forces will do is they will to secure the oil tanks and the oil refineries and not protect the civilians. After the oil refineries and oil tanks have been protected, then they will ensure that they get a reporter from these big news networks and broadcast that the oil refineries and oil tanks have been secured by the NATO and UN forces. That is the modus operandi of the Western war to all oil-rich countries, specifically in the Middle East region.

THE WAR OF MINERAL RESOURCES

There is an abundance of admissible objective evidence that Africa is the richest continent on the face of the earth, yet the continent of Africa is trapped in poverty of a distinctive nature. There are African countries in the continent that can't even distribute the very same social grants that the South African government is distributing to the South African people. There are African countries that are still struggling to distribute the ARVs that are now being distributed for free in the South African hospitals. The question then is this: Why are African countries not moving and growing economically at the same pace? The answer to this question lies in the way African countries have structured their economies. It's of vital importance to comprehend the qualities of a leader. African leaders not only are supposed to lead their countries to fight the Western imperialism only but also need to lead their economies to the new economic heights. The war against the Western colonization is over, while the war against the Western economic imperialism in Africa is very far from over. In fact the West has deepened its economic grip to the African economy to the point that contemplating to break this economic grip in pieces is scaring the hell out of the African leaders. There is fear among African leaders, even among Africans themselves, that letting the West loosen its tight grip on African economy will kill the African people with hunger because companies will have to shut down. South Africa has witnessed one of the longest strikes in the mining sector since the dawn of democracy in 1994, which dragged for almost five months. The miners not only were literally flat broke but also some of them had begun to be rats. A rat is a person who goes to work secretively while his fellow coworkers are on strike fighting for wage increment and salary adjustments. When the strike was over in June 2014, which dragged for five months, everybody in South Africa breathed a sigh of relief. I have an uncle who is working in Rustenburg who began to be a thorn in my back. He could no longer even afford cold drinks for himself and his wife, let alone attend significant family events like funerals. The guy was literally broke, and due to the strike, not only he alone but also with other miners, they have begun cheating—going to work in the mines illegally without being noticed by their fellow miners in the early hours of the morning and coming back very late while it's dark without being noticed by their fellow miners. The mining strike had dragged far too long to the point that breaking the impasse of the strike appeared as if it was at some point unattainable. In fact pessimistic and cynics concluded that the South African mining strikes were going to toss the South African economy into the ground. The mines' bosses, after the end of the strike, began to count the costs, and they were throwing big figures around. Lisa Steyn writes:

> *The platinum companies estimate the strike caused a R24 billion loss in revenues and R10.7 billion in employee earnings.*[5]

The West until this day and age in Africa is making a killing through its mining companies that are based in Africa. While these mining companies are making a killing through mining in Africa, they continue to underpay and overwork their employees at the same time. There is a window of economic opportunities that had been missed by the African liberation movements, and that is to overhaul the African economy to the benefit of African people. It's public knowledge that most of the nationalists are sell-outs, and they are now lying in bed with the same enemy they were fighting in the bush for quite a long period of time. As long as the politics of the stomach does not come to an end, Africans need to be rest assured that the Western grip on Africa's economy will be perennial. It is astounding to me to see that the majority of African countries are not yet fully developed to the point that they can't even assemble their airplanes and even computers. The only times we see a new phone is when the Western companies like Apple introduce us Africans to their new phones. It's even sickening to keep up with these new phones that are made in the West. When Africans are still trying to understand the new phone that has been introduced in the market, the next thing you know there is another phone that has been introduced again. All electrical appliances and confusing phones are made in the West and sold to Africans, and yet Africa is politically free. There is no amount of justification that we Africans can put on the table for the lack of our innovation and creativity. The fact of the matter is we Africans in our nature are creative and innovative, but the political climate and political conditions in the African continent don't provide space and room for that creativity to be nourished. The political and economic roller coaster ride that we Africans find ourselves in, coupled with the stealing of Africa's mineral resources by the West, makes life to be very difficult even further. The West, through its multinational companies, is incessantly transferring Africa's wealth to the West in broad daylight. Let me give you a classic example: bank QEO is based in London, Britain, and is registered in London Stock Exchange, and this bank has offices in Pretoria, South Africa. The bank lends money to the South African citizens and makes hefty profits through its mortgage bonds and investment products. Not only should these mortgage bonds that this bank lends be paid within a period of thirty years, but also by the time the mortgage bond holder completes paying the mortgage bond, he would have paid the bond at an interest of 2,000 percent. That is exactly what is happening right now in Africa with the multinational companies—they are now stealing from Africans legally. Everything has been reduced into debt. The financial lenders have access to the phones of almost everybody and they're sending attractive messages now and then, promising people that "there is R150,000 waiting for you and call this number." I wonder whether or not it is violating someone's right by having access to his phone number and sending messages without being given the number by the owner of the phone himself. The financial lenders are now colluding with the mobile phone companies, and they are sharing numbers of innocent citizens, and these financial lenders are now using these cell phone numbers to hunt down people who are in financial trouble. This has been going on for quite some time now, and there is no one who is doing anything about it. During 2013 it emerged that one of the print media in Britain was so desperate for news to the point that the print media began hacking the phones of innocent people and even celebrities. The phone hacking scandal was so gigantic in Britain to the point that it led some print media organizations to shut down completely, and the prime minister of Britain David Cameron instituted a commission of inquiry to the phone-hacking scandal. The point that I am driving home is this: the West is using everything possible to ensure that it drains Africa financially and otherwise. When a young brilliant African soccer player emerges, the Western soccer teams come to Africa to buy the player and eventually change his citizenship to be a Western citizen completely. The World Cup of 1998 was won by France, and that French team that won the World Cup of 1998 was dominated by Africans who were then living in France and playing for the French national team. Let me put it differently: the World Cup of 1998 should have been won by an African team had the African players who were playing for the French national team were playing for their countries of birth period. This problem of African soccer players being bought by the Western teams and being given citizenship in the West is a common phenomenon. The World Cup of 2014 in Brazil saw many African teams exiting the World Cup competition early. There is no African team that managed to qualify for the quarter finals, and that puts the African continent in a very bad light in the world stage. Some of the African teams that participated in the World Cup 2014 in Brazil had financial problems. There is one funny thing that emerged out of the World Cup of 2014 in Brazil. England and the United States are not good in soccer, but they are good in fighting a war on the ground. The Argentine and the Germans are good in soccer, and they are not good in fighting a war. The West is crippling Africa in whichever way you look at it. The songs that we sing in our churches are not African songs; they are Western songs. The attires that we wear in Africa were not designed in Africa but were designed in the West. The West is now fighting tooth and nail to erode the very last thing that Africa has, which is the African culture. It's common knowledge that the West does not have culture and values. Because the West does not have culture and values, then the West wants to mess up the African culture, which has been left behind by the African forefathers to this African generation. Once the African culture has been eroded completely, therefore the whole world will now dance to the Western music. Africans are people of music and rhythm. Africans are not prone to wars and infighting, but because of living in slavery and political oppression for quite a long period of time, Africans today are the most violent people on the face of the planet. This view and this assertion are also true among children who are coming from dysfunctional and broken families. A stable family gives birth to a stable community, and a stable community gives birth to a stable society, and a stable society gives birth to a stable nation. Family values and cultural values can only be instilled to children provided that there is a stable and conducive family. Perhaps that is the main reason most African countries in terms of literacy rate are still lagging behind due to the family disintegration and high rate of divorce. Lazarus Sauit writes:

Prof. Mthuli Ncube, chief economist and vice president of the African Development Bank, agrees: "*The African continent is resource-rich. With good resource husbandry, Africa could be in a position much of its own development.*"

> *The question that haunts every caring and concerned Africans is, "With all our vast resources, why are we poor?"*

I have read such statements over and over again, and I have come to the point of realizing that the more such statements are made in the public domain, the more ordinary Africans are infuriated. It's like saying your father was the richest man who ever walked on the face of the earth. Unfortunately, that is the reason you are poor. Africans in general don't deserve to read that the African continent is resource-rich because they have nothing to draw out of that statement. In fact saying that the African continent is resource-rich while a considerable amount of Africans are languishing in poverty is a slap on the face of the poor. Though it's inevitable and true that Africa is resource-rich but Africa's riches don't trickle down to the ordinary Africans on the ground, then what is the use of saying that the African continent is resource-rich while the very people of the African continent are starving to death with hunger?

Lazarus Sauit continues and says the answer is simple: *the rape of the African continent is happening faster, more violent, and with less resistance today than at any time in history.*[6]

The African continent is being raped constantly by the West, but why are African leaders not stopping this rape that is happening in the African continent? The truth of the matter is this: some of the African leaders are accessories in the raping of the African continent by the West. Ordinary Africans themselves have joined the fray of raping the African continent just like some African leaders are raping the African continent with their fellow Western friends and Western capitalists. I was very shocked to see the number of expensive cars that are driven by Zimbabweans in 2013 while I was in Harare. It appeared to me as if Zimbabwe was not under economic sanctions; though in some part of Zimbabwe, you can really witness and attest that indeed Zimbabwe is under economic sanctions. But the overall impression that I got while I was in Harare was positive, and from the surface everything looked good. While if you take one step further and scratch the surface and take out the lid, then you will be confronted by the shocking reality of economic sanctions. The same is true even in South Africa. If you board the fastest train in South Africa known as the Gautrain, which I normally call "the train of the rich and the black middle class" simply because white people and the black middle class of South Africa normally use it, you can be fooled and think that all is well in South Africa. The South African international airport, formerly known as Jan Smuts International Airport and now called O. R. Tambo International Airport, is the busiest airport in the whole of South Africa. The very same Gautrain, which I call "the train of the rich and the black middle class," takes its passengers from Hatfield all the way to the O. R. Tambo International Airport. The airport resembles the developed world and the advanced society on the surface, and the fact is not all is well. The fact is there are still South Africans who are still languishing in the bottomless pit of poverty. Let me make my point clear: I am not implying that the South African government is not doing anything to eradicate poverty; surely the South African government and the ANC can only do so much, but in general poverty is still a pressing issue not only in South Africa but also in many parts of Africa. There is poverty in Africa just like there is poverty in the United States of America and even in Britain, therefore poverty is not an African phenomenon.

> *"Africa is well endowed with natural resources that are of finite nature. These natural resources have over the years been exploited, largely for the benefit of multinational corporations and other foreign business entities. Foreigners are getting huge profit turnovers from minerals, forests, tourist facilities, and wildlife, while the indigenous people (Africans) are benefiting nothing at all. This must stop," Pres. Robert Mugabe says.*[7]

The multinational companies don't just enter by force in Africa and start running their mining operation without following the legitimate process, but they apply for the mining licenses in the case of the mining corporation, and after they have been given these mining licenses, then they start their mining operation in Africa. The main culprit in the rape of the African continent is not only the West but also the government of the nationalists. African liberation movements did not know a lot about corruption while they were fighting the armed struggle. The moment the nationalists became in power, they learn that corruption was not only a lucrative business but also through it you could get a lot of things done within a short period of time. In fact it's a known fact right now that corruption is the new cancer of Africa, what I call the virus without nevirapine. Africa's corruption not only is unholy but also is happening at a rapid pace and on an unprecedented scale. That is why the Western leaders realized that the nationalists would be corrupt once they become in power and build a court for them. The International Criminal Court (ICC) was solely built to prosecute African leaders who are corrupt to the point that they don't share with the West in their ill-gotten proceeds from the corrupt activities. Let me put it differently: not only are the Western powers are against African leaders who are corrupt, but also the Western powers are against African leaders who are corrupt, and in their corrupt activities, they don't share with the West the spoils of corruption. As long as African leaders can have the Western capitalists as their partners in crime, then there is nothing wrong; but if the African leaders are practicing corruption without sharing it with their Western counterparts, then Hague is waiting for those African leaders who don't share with the West. Therefore, blaming the multinational corporation by African leaders is also a way of African leaders to apportion the blame but knowing full well that even these African leaders are benefiting through the corrupt activities of the West. Rhino poaching in Africa would not have occurred if African leaders have tightened the laws. But because some of these African leaders are involved in Rhino poaching, that is why now and then when Rhino poachers are arrested, the next day they are back on the street continuing with their normal life as if nothing happened. The same is true with drugs. It's common knowledge that the West is responsible for the drugs that are doing rounds in the African continent. While drug trafficking is a multibillion dollar business and there are drugs cartels all over the world, some of the African leaders now and then are getting free gifts from these drug lords. Some of the political campaigns even in the West are funded by these drug lords and drug cartels. That is why the West is not hard on the drug lords and drug cartels because these drug lords and drugs cartels are helpful during political campaigns; they can get things done easy and cheap for politicians. The war of mineral resources will never come to an end in Africa, not even now unfortunately. As long the African continent is resource-rich, and we all know that the African continent is resource-rich, then the African capitalists with their Western capitalists partners are going to make sure that they rape the African continent until the continent is a bottomless pit. Through the interviews that I have conducted in South Africa and even in Zimbabwe, I became alive to the fact that not only is the African continent rich in mineral resources, but also the rape that is committed toward Africa's mineral resources is on the rise. There are people now and then who are on the way smuggling drugs and cocaine. There are Africans who are on the way day and night transporting gold dust and diamonds. Ordinary Africans have no faith in the rule of law because even the law enforcers are also corrupt to the core. When I pause and ponder my overall objective of writing this book, I am baffled and amazed at the amount of information that I had to go through and sift through in order to select what is necessary and what is not necessary to write about. Some of the information that I came across were so dangerous to the point that I find it unfair and unjust to write about it. The fact of the matter is this: the world has changed and has changed completely than what it was in the past. There is just too much information out there to the point that collecting and digesting it takes a considerable amount of time. I have seen in the process of my journey that had I opted to proceed with my journey to Zambia and eventually DRC, not only would my life be in danger but also perhaps I would have witnessed the most atrocities that will never be removed in my memory. I do feel pity for those journalists who had to cover the DRC War and the CAR war. Sometimes witnessing people being subjected to trauma and pain for quite a long period of time can make you numb and unresponsive even when you are expected to respond quickly.

The same reaction is what is exhibited by children who are the victims of sexual abuse. Most of them go out and become abusers themselves simply because they have been abused, or for some of them, they just choose to be introvert and bottle everything up to themselves just because of fear of being judged. I have taught in a high school, and I know what I am talking about. I have seen a learner who had been raped three times by members of her family, and she became very withdrawn and aloof. The same thing that happened to rape victims is the same thing that happens in politics. There are Africans who don't even want to know what caused the African continent to be colonized by the West because they don't see the necessity of knowing about it and even the political gain and political value that come with knowing about it. It's true that the West colonized Africa, and there is no amount of reason that the West can provide to mitigate its ugly actions toward the African people. The old cliché that is normally given by the West is this: "It was not us but the previous administration," and the same thing was told to Pres. Robert Mugabe when he requested Britain to fund the Land Redistribution Program that was agreed upon in Lancaster in 1979. The world now knows Pres. Robert Mugabe as a tyrant and an incapable leader who led his people for thirty-four years without relinquishing political power. I am not Pres. Robert Mugabe's proponent as I have said before, and I am not even Pres. Robert Mugabe's critic. Though each and every political leader does make political mistakes and costly mistakes at some point, to draw an inference that says, had Pres. Robert Mugabe been out of the picture, the Zimbabwean people would be living a better life than the life that they are living right now, is pure speculation and exaggeration that can't even been substantiated with credible facts. The fact of the matter is this: Pres. Robert Mugabe will never live forever, and those of us who will still be alive after his departure should study, contrast, and compare the economic success and failures of Pres. Robert Mugabe's tenure with the would-be president of Zimbabwe at that time and then make a reliable conclusion. But drawing a conclusion based only on the farm invasion alone would not add value and even new knowledge to what is already known. I hope that through reading this book you have managed to understand the way Africa was colonized and the proceeding economic challenges that the African continent finds itself at the moment. Allow me the pleasure to use Paul Rusesabagina's statement: what happened in Mozambique spilled over to Zimbabwe, and what happened in Zimbabwe spilled over to South Africa, and that is damn true. There is no way one can attempt to understand Pres. Robert Mugabe without understanding the late Samora Machel of Mozambique, for it was Samora Machel of Mozambique who was sick and tired of his country to be infiltrated by the South African forces coupled with the Rhodesian forces. While there are many young scholars even in the future who will attempt to investigate and read through the innumerable history records to understand what happened in the past that led Africa to be the way it is today, it is important to comprehend the politics of Zimbabwe with the politics of Mozambique. One would not have done justice and favor if he isolates the South African politics from the Zimbabwean politics. The Western powers don't understand that allowing economic sanctions to remain in place in Zimbabwe for quite a long of period of time creates a perennial hatred and anger among Zimbabweans toward the West. The truth of the matter is there are Zimbabweans who don't want to buy the theory that says the economic sanctions were imposed due to the farm invasion and because of the farm invasion lives of white commercial farmers were lost as a result of the fast track of land reform, and that was tantamount to human rights violation. While the West claim to be the custodian of human rights, the champion of democracy and freedom of expression do violate the very same human rights that it claims to advocate for by killing innocent Iraqis with drone strikes. There is a sharp difference between using drones against terrorists like the Al-Shabaab and the Boko Haram versus using drone strikes toward innocent children who are at school. It is an inescapable reality that terrorism does not have a place on the face of the earth, while the West is against terrorist organizations and would stop at nothing to end terrorism diametrically; it's important also to strike the balance. Terrorism and terrorist organization should be eliminated completely on the face of the earth, but at the same time innocent people should not be sacrificed at the expense of the terrorist organizations. The West stole Africa's wealth and invested that wealth in the IMF and World Bank, and I want to make myself very clear once and for all lest people who are going to read this book will get a wrong interpretation. I am by no means implying that the West is the only investor in the IMF and World Bank, and it's true that there are other African countries that have invested their wealth in the IMF and the World Bank; in totality, the largest investments in these two financial institutions have been invested by the West. The fact is that the West is controlling the IMF and the World Bank through its appointment and preferred candidate as to who should head the IMF and World Bank, and that is attributed to the fact that the West is the majority shareholder in these financial institutions. I am not implying that the West must compensate Africa with foreign aid and more loans, as it is the status quo right now. But what I am calling for are full transparency and openness between the West and Africa. The West must come into the table of negotiations and indeed acknowledge and accept that the poverty that is ravaging the continent of Africa is because of its own making. The endless wars that are destroying the continent of Africa are funded by the West. There is no way a person who is in the United States of America can claim to comprehend thoroughly what is good for Zimbabwean people, and it's also true that there is no way a person who is in the Britain can claim to understand what is good for the Zimbabwean people. Zimbabwe's politics and Zimbabwe's economic problems including its domestic affairs can only be understood by the Zimbabweans, and they can most excellently be solved by Zimbabweans. The whole world must help when a pressing need arises not by imposing economic sanctions to a small country like Zimbabwe, which has a history of being under economic sanctions from Britain. When I arrived in South Africa from my journey, normally it will still be dark in South Africa, and I will ask myself this question: *What the hell am I doing in the middle of the night alone?* The voice within me will say, *You are doing what I have told you to do.* I believe that in each and every one of us there is that inner voice that propels and compels us to take an action, and sometimes due to fear and trepidation, we suppress that voice, and after it has been suppressed long enough and it becomes silent, it eventually dies. It's common knowledge that the West is behind all the wars that are going on in the whole world today. The main reason I suggest that the West fuels the wars that are going on in the world today unconsciously is that the West sometimes confuses money to mean power, and that is not always the case. In some instances money does not always mean power. The fact that the West has control over the World Bank and IMF does not therefore mean that it has control over everyone who is walking on the face of the earth. And that is the biggest mistake that the West is committing. Some of the wars that the West has been involved in are tribal wars, which a foreign person can't even understand simply because a foreign person does not even know the language that the warring tribes are speaking. I don't suggest that by any means if two tribes are fighting, therefore the whole world must wait until the stronger tribe kills or destroys the weaker tribe completely then the international community comes in afterward. What I mean is this: it's imperative for the West to intervene if there are two warring groups to end the killing. But to jump in the burning fire and support the strong tribe with weapons to kill the weaker tribe is a violation of human rights. Let me be practical, though I have already made mention of this issue in the past: I don't see the reason NATO with military forces took part in the dethroning of Muammar Gaddafi of Libya. The OAU had the situation under control; besides Libya is an African country, not a Middle Eastern country, and it was still under the control and the supervision of the OAU. And on hindsight it's a known fact that the OAU does not have teeth to bite—that is why NATO just circumvented the OAU and killed Muammar Gaddafi without the approval of the OAU, and again the same lies are told that Muammar Gaddafi of Libya was a dictator. The problem with lying sometimes is that even if people whom you are lying to know the whole truth, they just keep quiet and allow you to tell the same lie again and again. There are people who are patient enough to listen to a liar, while there are people who are not patient enough to listen to a liar. The death of the late president of South Africa Nelson Mandela united South Africa together like never before, and it also managed to unite not only South Africans alone but also the whole world together; there were memorial services all over the world. It has never ever happened in history that the former president of the United States of America George W. Bush and Pres. Robert Mugabe of Zimbabwe can be in the same stadium under one roof. But during the memorial service of the former president of South Africa Nelson Mandela, history was made, and it will go down into the history record as the day that will never be forgotten in the history of South Africa. The president of the United States of America Barack Obama will go down in history as one of the most visionary leaders and forward thinkers in the US history and as an example to the African community and even to the African American community. Africans, even African Americans, are classified as people who are careless and dumb in nature. Africans and African Americans in general, are seen as people who don't possess leadership skills that can warrant them a position to lead a complicated and sophisticated economy like the economy of the United States of America. But the president of the United States of America Barack Obama has displayed leadership qualities that no other African American leader has ever displayed in the history of African Americans. The fact of the matter is this: when Pres. Barack Obama became the first black president of the United States of America, historians and writers of the African history were too confused and dizzy as to where to start and how to start telling this historical event, where a black person will be leading a country of a white-dominated people. Pres. Barack Obama just did exactly that—lead the white-dominated country, and not only white-dominated only but also where even to this day a black person is still considered to be intellectually inferior to a his white counterpart. The whole of Africa was happy for Pres. Barack Obama when he was inaugurated. There was a South African singer by the name of Lira who was invited to sing during the second inauguration of Pres. Barack Obama, and I can't fail to mention Beyonce, the wife of Jay-Z, for that matter. We Africans of the continent of Africa are happy when we see our fellow African American brothers taking the leading roles in the West because that is a morale booster. Though there are African Americans who pretend as if they are not black and they never originated in Africa, the fact of the matter is this: all African Americans originated in Africa. The ancestors of these African Americans were shipped to the United States through boats, and they were required to work in the cotton fields, sugar plantation, and the mines to build the US economy and the American dream. I have heard a pastor who is black but now living in Britain saying, "I am British." I was very disappointed at him. The truth of the matter is this: he might be in possession of a British identity document and British passport, but that does not change the color of his skin. The fact of the matter is this: he is still an African who is now living in Britain. I know for a fact that pure British might be talking about him behind his back, referring to him as an African migrant. I am not a racist, and I am just a straight talker. Pres. Barack Obama tried by all means to withdraw the US troops that were deployed in Iraq, and those are the troops that were responsible for the demise of the Iraqi leader Saddam Hussein. What followed then in Iraq after the withdrawal of the US troops was chaos that the whole world is still shocked even to this day and age. When Prime Minister Nouri al-Maliki took over power and became the prime minister of Iraq while the US troops were still stationed in Iraqi, there was a bit of peace and stability in Iraq. The complete withdrawal of the US troops from Iraqi left a gaping hole on the ground to the point that the Iraqi security forces could not even maintain and sustain peace and stability in Iraq. The emergence of the extreme groups was visible all over. ISIS (Islamic States of Iraq and Syria) and ISIL (Islamic State of Iraq and the Levant) became the new government of Iraq, and the people of Iraq found comfort and safety on the shoulders of these extremist groups. There were reports in the media that ISIS and ISIL were the extremists to the extreme; even Al-Qaeda leaders were denouncing and rejecting the modus operandi of ISIS and ISIL. The ISIL mooted to turn Iraq into what they called "the caliphate state," where there will be a caliph running the government, and people will be forced to read the Qur'an and memorize it to the point of dreaming Qur'an at night. The same thing that the ISIL was mooting is what the two hundred girls who were kidnapped in Nigeria went through. There were video clips that were televised all over the world, even on You Tube, showing the kidnapped girls citing the verses from the Qur'an. The Islamic State of Iraq and Syria (ISIS) changed its name to the Islamic States of Iraq (ISI). The name of these extreme groups keeps on changing every now and then, and it won't be surprising to me if the ISI changes its name again even in the near future. During the entire tenure of Pres. Barack Obama, he never went to war, except the Syrian War, which he was determined to undertake until the president of Russia Vladimir Putin intervened. Had it not been for the president of Russia Vladimir Putin, Damascus skyscrapers should have been razed to the ground by the president of the United States Barack Obama with drone strikes. The whole world remains a volatile place with wars ravaging the earth. Perhaps politicians have run out of ideas as to how to solve political conflicts and political problems. I think a war is microcosm of political leadership vacuum. There is no need now even in the near future for any country to attack any country unless there are reasonable reasons that warrant such an attack, and an attack must be in the interest of saving lives of innocent women and children, not to kill innocent women and children.

THE SHEDDING OF INNOCENT BLOOD

The Central African Republic president Michel Djotodia attended a meeting in Bangui, which was organized by the regional leaders in 2014. The mediators of the CAR crisis included the president of Gabon and the president of the Democratic Republic of Congo. The regional summit passed a resolution that says Central African Republic president Michel Djotodia must step down with an immediate effect to allow the country and the people of CAR to establish an interim government that will ensure that there is a national election that will be free and fair that will take place on the date that will be decided upon by the interim transitional government. That was an important step toward a long and lasting peace in the Central African Republic. Michel Djotodia didn't return to CAR after the regional meeting in Bangui, but he went to exile in Benin. The regional summit appointed Mr. Alexandre-Ferdinand Nguendet as the head of the transitional government of the Central African Republic.[8] What happened in Central African Republic did affect South Africa directly or indirectly. The Rwandan Genocide of 1994 saw thousands and thousands of Rwandese exiting the country to the neighboring countries, and some Rwandese came to stay in South Africa while some went to stay in Belgium, the former colonizer of Rwanda. There was little information that was known about Rwandese who fled the country to resettle in other countries like South Africa. The whole of South Africa was very shocked to hear the news that the former Rwandan spy Col. Patrick Karegeya was found dead in a his Sandton Hotel on December 31, 2013.[9] When the news of the death of Patrick Karegeya were announced in the media, they were very sketchy and very vague for one to piece them together. The majority of people in South Africa could not make a connection between the death of Rwandan spy Col. Patrick Karegeya and the current president of Rwanda Paul Kagame. Throughout the entire Second DRC War, the name of the president of Rwanda Paul Kagame has been featured in many instances, though the Rwandan president Paul Kagame has vehemently denied his involvement in the Second DRC War, which ended on November 4, 2013. The theory about the Second DRC War says the Rwandese who were part and parcel of M23 were supported by the Rwandan government militarily and financially. This assertion that the Rwandan government was supporting the M23 militarily and financially was vehemently denied by the president of Rwanda Paul Kagame. The one-million-dollar question then is, who was supporting the M23 fighters with military equipments and financial resources if it was not the Rwandan government?

It's worth repeating the statement that Paul Rusesabagina made in his book titled *The True Story behind Hotel Rwanda*. Paul Rusesabagina writes:

> *"Whatever happens in Burundi eventually spills over into Rwanda, and whatever happens in Rwanda will also spill into Burundi."*[10]

Paul Rusesabagina was right when he wrote the above statement some years ago. What is abundantly clear is this: there are certain Rwandese who left Rwanda unhappy, and they are contemplating the possibility of going back home to Rwanda provided that there are political reforms that are made in the Rwandan government. The former prime minister of Israeli Ariel Sharon died at the age of eighty-five on January 11, 2014. The Lebanese people rejoiced on the streets of Beirut, and some were burning posters, which were depicting the face of the late prime minister of Israel Ariel

Sharon. The Lebanese people nicknamed the late Israeli prime minister Ariel Sharon "the Butcher of Beirut." The former prime minister of Israel Ariel Sharon was buried in his farm on January 13, 2014, and people all over the world had mixed reactions about the passing away of former prime minister of Israeli Ariel Sharon. It's important now and then to stay in the moment, and there is no better way to stay in the moment like reporting political events as they are unfolding before your very own eyes. There is one piece of information that I came across in the newspaper that was startling to me about the Second DRC War. Maria Hengeveld writes,

> *I had interviewed survivors of rape in eastern Congo before; a psychological element seemed to be missing in these interactions. "Before I managed to articulate the uncomfortable feeling that we had just been lied to, my Congolese colleague spit it out: Those women have been coached." The FP author supports her suspicion by visiting a local health-care professional, who tells her that during the insurgency he only treated six rape survivors. Yet when the UN came in, the number soared into hundreds. This drastic increase seemed odd at best and outright manipulative at worst. One way in which the number could have been distorted, he figured, was that the large majority of female patients were listed as rape victims, regardless of the actual cause of their injury or illness. Was the clinic purposefully cheating in numbers game, and if so, to what effect? The author suggests that fabricated high numbers will cause aid to flow disproportionately toward sexual violence to the neglect of other urgent needs.*[11]

It's abundantly clear that sometimes crimes that are reported to have taken place during the Second DRC War were sometimes not entirely true. It does not mean, though, that all the war crimes that are reported are not true in all material respect, but sometimes the war crimes have an ability to attract massive foreign financial aid from the international community even from the UN itself. First of all, what I am writing about is not a new thing altogether; perhaps what is new might be the methodology that I have used to gather my evidence and the trips that I have taken to Zimbabwe. I need to make one point very clear: my book is not about the farm invasion of 2000, though it's one of the driving factors to the current economic situation that the majority of Zimbabweans find themselves in, but I am not implying that I have exhausted the whole topic of farm invasion of 2000 through this book. I believe that the farm invasion of 2000 fiasco could have been handled totally different by Pres. Robert Mugabe and the war veterans. We all know that the Western settlers emerged from the sea with no farms and no livestock of cattle. The one-million-dollar question then is, how possible is it that a person from the West can come to Africa with absolutely nothing on his hand and in the twinkling of an eye now he owns the vast tract of land, including Africa's mineral resources? Many people will probably say that the Western settlers acquired their wealth through colonizing most of the African countries. It's an inescapable reality that the West has colonized Africa, but is that enough to simply suggest that the overall reason the Western settlers are fabulously rich is that they have amassed a lot of wealth through colonization of most Africa countries only? I beg to differ with people who suggest that the reason the Western settlers are fabulously rich today is the colonization of most African countries. There is more to it than meets the eye in this colonization conundrum of Africa by the West. I am taking a different approach than most conventional thinkers have taken before. I have great difficulty with old tales that have been told many times simply because they normally miss the crucial pieces of information. That is why we young Africans need to wake up and smell the coffee and be able to write Africa's history instead of waiting for the Western scholars who are not even aware of the African continent to write the African history for Africans. The scramble for the Southern part of Africa started in the sixteenth century, and in the case of South Africa, it was marked by the arrival of Jan van Riebeeck on April 6, 1652, in Cape Town. There are multiple theories from the Western scholars who are obviously trying to do everything in their power to ensure that they conceal the juicy details about the arrival of Jan van Riebeeck. It's of less interest to me whether Jan Van Riebeeck came to South Africa with his company DEIC (Dutch East India Company) to build waiting station in Cape Town or not. What we know and what is visible to the eye today is this: after the Dutch invasion to South Africa, eventually the entire African continent was under the control of the West. Germany colonized Namibia; Portugal colonized Mozambique and Angola. Great Britain under the auspices of Queen Victoria colonized many countries that are not even worth mentioning. Cecil John Rhodes, through the love of the African mineral resources and Zimbabwe's land, eventually died in South Africa and was buried on the peak of the mountains of Matopos National Park with his partners in crime, Dr.

Leander Starr Jameson and Charles Coghlan. These three gentlemen (Cecil Rhodes,Dr. Leander Starr Jameson, and Charles Coghlan) were the pioneers of the BSAC (British South Africa Company). The BSAC was a British company that was used a financial vehicle to siphon the African wealth to the West. It has been proven over time that the best way for the West to steal Africa's wealth was not to rob Africans on broad daylight. But the best way to steal massive amount of wealth was through incorporating a company that will be used as legal conduit pipe to siphon wealth from Africa to the West while creating employment for a lot of people yet remaining active on the ground for a long period of time. It becomes very difficult for many people to understand that the Western form of slavery is not only political oppression but also financial oppression. The nationalists miss the whole point when they were fighting for political liberation. Let me say that political oppression was not even the main issue, but the main issue on the agenda of the West was African wealth. Freedom and democracy without economic freedom is sheer madness. Democracy, as it is known today, is the government of the people, for the people, by the people. The point is there has never been the will of the people since the dawn of democracy in Africa. Let me say I am totally shocked just by watching political rallies in Africa prior to the national elections; whether in East Africa or sub-Saharan Africa, the behavior of politicians is the same. Politicians will be very accessible to the poor and the ordinary people from the ground; they will even leave their air-conditioned offices unlocked just to talk to the poor masses on the ground, making more promises on top of the previous promises that were not even fulfilled. And at the end of it all, these politicians will distribute to the poor one chicken per person, food parcel, and vouchers of three hundred rands. The poor people are told more promises on top of the previous promises that were made in the previous political campaigns, and since the poor will be having chickens in their hands, they will be completely drunk with these bags full of goodies to the point that they won't concentrate on the political manifesto. I know that poor people have poor memory and short concentration span. No wonder politicians prey on the poor. The poor people have just to perform their constitutional responsibility, which is to continue to vote for the betterment of their lives, period. All over Africa, if one can take a closer look at the behavior of political parties and the gratuitous gifts that they are showering the poor people with prior to national elections; one asks himself the fundamental question: Is this how democracy works? I thought that in a democratic state, people vote for a political party that they prefer based on the economic performance and economic achievements that the said political party managed to achieve while it was in power. I am not implying that by no means those are the only factors that we should look at closely when the electorate is choosing a political party to govern. Some political parties in South Africa, just because in 2014 there were national elections, were throwing bashes right and left and center, and some of these political parties have been building houses for the poor people just to garner votes, and when national elections were over and they have extracted the votes from the poor forcefully using their financially means and their chicken strategy, these political parties melt like ice on surface on a sunny day. The last thing that they will do for the voters is to slaughter a cow for the poor people who voted for them, and that will be the end of the story, and the poor continue to live in abject poverty, and the rich and the ruling elite go back to their air-conditioned offices and continue with their lives as usual. There is no such thing as freedom and democracy in Africa. What exists now in Africa is perhaps another version of freedom and democracy. As long as there is an undue influence to coerce and coax people to vote for a particular party, that is not democracy for me. In the politics of Zimbabwe, the electorate is told prior to national elections that should it vote for a certain political party, Gukurahundi might come back. As long there are undue influences that seek to coerced or coax people on the ground to perform a particular political act in exchange of chickens and free houses, then that is not freedom and democracy. Political freedom and democracy can only happen in an environment where there is equality and political tolerance. It's fair and just to say that South Africa has turned the tide on ensuring that there is political tolerance and gender equality in all spheres of the government. I need to state this: South Africa has not completely turned the tide on the issues of racial segregation and income disparities. The point I making is this: there are practical and visible improvements that are taking place in South Africa as far as political tolerance and gender equality are concerned. I have heard a bizarre statement about South Africa sometime ago—that South Africa is the most unequal society in the whole world.*Mail & Guardian* reports:

> *On paper, South Africans are the wealthiest people in Africa, with $11,310 (R121,941) per person; while Ethiopians are the poorest, with only $260 per person. This is according to survey released by research consultancy New World Wealth. Oil-rich Libya came in second, with a wealth per capita of $11,040,*

> *while Namibia out of the top three with a wealth per capita of $10,500. Wealth per capita is a snapshot of the net asset value of individuals, such as cash and other holdings, distributed among its population. Two South Africa's neighbors made it into the poorest five of the list: Zimbabwe had a wealth per capita of $570, while Mozambique had $430.*[12]

The wealth per capita measures the amount of assets an individual has, whether its cash or otherwise. South Africa is ranked at the top among all African countries in the whole of Africa including Nigeria with its massive oil reserves and the DRC with its vast mineral resources. This begs the following question: Out of the fifty-three million South Africans, how many people who actually posses this $11,310 (R121,941) that is mentioned by NW-Wealth.com? The fact of the matter is this: there are very few South Africans who can claim to have such assets per capita except those who are connected in high places and those who are tenderpreneurs in the name of entrepreneurs. In the case of Zimbabwe, which is listed in the poorest five countries in the African continent, there is no logical reason to dispute the claim. Since the farm invasion of 2000, the economy of Zimbabwe suffered a very serious setback due to the massive foreign investment exiting out of the country, though there are poor people in Zimbabwe and there are poor people in South Africa, and there are rich people in Zimbabwe and there are rich people in South Africa. The point is there are many rich people in South Africa in numbers compared to the rich people that are in Zimbabwe on average, though the statics do alter the fact that the majority of wealth in South Africa is in the hands of the fortunate few who are politically connected or people of Anglo-Saxon descent. The majority of people in South Africa are eating the crumbs that are falling from the table of the rich man just like in the story of Lazarus and the rich man in the Bible. I have already said that there are almost 16.1 million people that are beneficiaries of social grants in South Africa in the financial year 2012/2013, and it's apparently clear that this number will increase sharply in the next financial year 2013/2014. There are many children that are born out of wedlock each and every day by parents who are not financially able to raise them and look after their children financially. When the number of births in any country exceeds the number of deaths that is a harbinger of looming economic problem. This is why the Republic of China enacted the law of one-child policy simply because people were making more babies as if there is no tomorrow. I think that the majority of people, especially parents who have failed in life, normally make a lot of children with a belief that when these children grow up, they will be educated and lift the whole family out of poverty. It has been proven all over the world that poor families normally send their children to poor-performing schools that have teachers that are poorly trained and lazy. It has also been proven that the majority of poor families don't even bother to offer support academically to their children, since even these children's parents are poor themselves and uneducated. When the South African matric results were released by the minister of basic education Angie Motshekga, there were 549,746 who disappeared in the process when you are comparing the number of pupils who wrote matric exams in 2013. Let me give you the whole picture now: there were 1,111,858 in grade two in 2003 and there were 562,112 in 2013 who wrote matric, and out of the 562,112, only 439,779 passed grade twelve exams in 2013.[6] The fact of the matter is this: there are majority of young people who are not completing grade twelve, and the whole blame can't be apportioned to the schools and the teachers. There is a point in time where one needs to be brutally honest with himself and with herself. Many young people in South Africa have bought into the idea of getting rich quickly through tenders without going through the long route of going to school to study thick and heavy books for a period of twelve years. In order to understand the plundering of wealth by the West, one needs to understand thoroughly the African wars that have been perpetuated by the West in Africa since time immemorial. It will be extremely difficult for one to comprehend thoroughly the African wars, which are consequential of Western influence, without taking into consideration the terrorism element into the picture. We can all agree that we began to comprehend terrorism in full scale after the 9/11 attack in the United States of America. The name Osama Bin Laden became a recitation worldwide. Majority of people all around the world began to ask themselves this question: Who is this Osama Bin Laden? Prior to 9/11 too little information was known about Osama Bin Laden except the CIA, FBI, and other intelligence agencies. The one-million-dollar question that sprang up to people's mind was, why would one man kill so many innocent men and women in a single day without a reasonable reason? When 9/11 happened, the then current president of the United States was George W. Bush. Allow me to call him George W. Bush Jr., since his father, George H. W. Bush, the senior, was the president of the United States during the Gulf War of August 2, 1990–February 28, 1991. There are countless books and countless articles that have been written about the Persian Gulf War, and I will suggest that should you be interested in reading further about the Persian Gulf War, you should read those countless articles and countless books, which are also available electronically. I went to Centurion Mall in South Africa to purchase a book written by George W. Bush. When I got to CUM Books in Centurion Mall, I was shocked to hear that they don't have the book written by George W. Bush Jr. in stock. I placed an order and left in peace. After two months I received a call from CUM Books, and they indicated to me that my book has arrived. The title of the book is *Decision Point* written by George W. Bush, the former president of the United States of America and who was still in office when Osama Bin laden struck. The *Decision Point* was published in 2011 and somehow sparked controversy all over the world. George W. Bush writes:

> *The nature of history is that we know the consequences only of the action we took. But inaction would have had consequences, too. Imagine what the world would look like today with Saddam Hussein still ruling Iraq. He would still be threatening his neighbors, sponsoring terror, and piling bodies in mass graves. The rising price of oil—which jumped from just over $30 a barrel in 2003 to almost $140 five years later—would have left Saddam awash in wealth.*[13]

The question that can spring into one's mind is this: Why was Saddam Hussein's government toppled brutally and eventually Saddam Hussein hanged by his countrymen? The answer that had been given by the intelligence community then was that Saddam Hussein was manufacturing weapons of mass of destruction (WMD) and was likely to use them anytime since Osama Bin Laden had already unleashed his 9/11 attack. George W. Bush writes:

> *The left trotted the new mantra "Bush lied, people died." The charge was illogical. If I wanted to mislead the country into war, why would I pick an allegation that was certain to be disproven publicly shortly after we invaded the country? The charge was also dishonest. Members of the previous administration, John Kerry, John Edwards, and the vast majority of Congress had all read the same intelligence that I had and concluded that Iraq had WMD, so had the intelligence agencies around the world. Nobody was lying. We were all wrong.*[14]

It's surprising that the UN Security Council was quiet about the atrocities that have been committed by different countries that were part and parcel of the invasion of Iraq in 2003. Many people have also questioned the way the ICC (International Criminal Court) dispensed its justice. Some people have even gone further to label the ICC as the kangaroo court of the West, which is only responsible for prosecuting African leaders and all leaders of the world who are anti-Western. There is no justice in the ICC, since the ICC is the Western court that dispenses justice to African leaders only who are anti-West. When you do the crime, you must also be ready to do the time. The Western leaders can commit the most heinous crime on the face of the earth, but they can walk freely with impunity. There is a school of thought that suggested that the main reason Saddam Hussein was brutally toppled was simply the oil. If you take a closer look at Iraqis' sanctions, which were in place prior to the death of Saddam Hussein, it tells a different story. After the dethroning of Saddam Hussein and his cohorts, the West decided to establish a new government that was pro-Western. Since the Iraq invasion of 2003 until this day, and I mean until this day, there has never been perennial peace in Iraq, and the Iraqi people are killing each other in what has been described as a sectarian violence. This sectarian violence is the war between the Shia Muslims and the Sunis Muslims. Prior to the dethroning of the government of Saddam Hussein, there was perennial peace in Iraq even though most Western experts would probably reject this assertion. But if we all cast our eyes wide open and think outside the box, we can clearly see that the 2003 Iraq invasion by the West has ruined Middle East forever. The Iraqi invasion of 2003 brought about the Arab Spring of 2011 that saw Hosni Mubarak of Egypt overthrown by the people of Egypt. The Iraq invasion of 2003 brought about the Arab Spring, which has now created wars that are spreading like wildcat fire not only in the Middle East but also even in Africa. The CAR is the case in point. The CAR war and the Second DRC War have been fashioned after the Arab Spring. Today in the Middle East there is what is known as the "Ring of Steel." It is believed that the Middle East regional crisis will only take within this ring of steel. The fact of the matter is this: the ring of steel has been long broken, and there is no longer any ring of steel in the Middle East. If there was such a thing as a ring of steel only in the Middle East, Africa would not have had a Westgate mall in Kenya under siege in September 2013 from the Al-Shabaab terrorist group and we would not have seen the CAR war and even the South Sudan war. This simply proves that the ring of steel had been broken a long time ago. Wars can ensue any time and in any place right now in the whole world. As of the writing of this book, there were still Geneva negotiations that were under way in Switzerland, which sought to put to an end to the Syrian crisis, which has claimed innocent lives of women and children. Before the Geneva 2 convention could commence, there were forty countries that were invited by the United Nations general secretary Ban Ki-moon to Geneva 2. All these countries had sent their representatives to Geneva 2, and the representatives of these countries were given an opportunity to express their views by the UN general secretary Ban Ki-moon. The United States was represented by the secretary of state John Kerry, and as usual he was very critical of Bashar al-Assad labeling him as the "magnet of terrorists." I was extremely disappointed to the extreme about such remarks, since the Geneva 2 was convened by United Nations general secretary Ban Ki-moon, not by the United States and Russia. Though the United States and Russia were the crucial players in ensuring that such a convention comes to fruition, it was very irresponsible for the secretary of state John Kerry to make such irresponsible remarks bearing in mind that Bashar al-Assad was still the president of Syria. During the preliminary talks that were going to succeed Geneva 2, the Syrian envoy to the United Nations Bashar Jaafari said that the Syrian War was caused by terrorists. He went on to give figures and even the list of countries that were involved in the Syrian War. Bashar Jaafari said that "Tunisia was a terrorist exporting country." Tunisians and Egyptians are the inventors of the Arab Spring supported by the Western extremists. The Syrian War was made up of extremists, fundamentalists, jihadists, and sex jihadists. Iran was invited to the Geneva 2 to take part in the negotiations and was eventually uninvited at the last minute. There was no logical reason that was given by the UN general secretary Ban Ki-moon as to why did he invite Iran and later changed his mind and decided to uninvited Iran again. Many people see Iran as a central player in the Syrian crisis. Before the Geneva 2 talks could even begin, most Western news networks were already broadcasting to the whole world disturbing pictures of dead bodies which were said have been slaughtered by the Syrian government. These news networks are the same news networks that said that Saddam Hussein was manufacturing weapons of mass destruction (WMD). The same news networks that were wrong then about Saddam Hussein, what makes them right this time about Syria? The news networks have been used sometimes in these wars to perpetuate a certain political agenda. The fact of the matter is every time we are watching news, we are already watching a particular political agenda of a certain political party. There is no longer unbiased, free reporting in the media, whether it's print media or television. Why would a news network broadcast disturbing pictures of dead bodies to the whole world about a war that is still going on and claim that these dead bodies have been killed by the Syrian government? It's possible for argument's sake that those dead bodies were not killed by the Syrian government forces but they were killed the ISIL or even Hezbollah fighters. The Syrian people have to find an amicable solution to their crisis. The broadcasting of those disturbing pictures of dead bodies protruding bones as a result of starvation was the painful revelation about the Syrian War in 2013. Those pictures show Masha al-Arb'een neighborhood before the war and after the war. There are many countries who were involved in the Syrian War, and some of these countries have their eyes set on the bigger price, which is economic benefit. These economic benefits come through a form of contracts and trade agreements. As long as Bashar al-Assad remains the president of Syria, some of the countries that are anti-Bashar al-Assad won't benefit economically through Bashar al-Assad government. It follows then that for certain trade agreements to take place and certain bilateral agreements to come into fruition, Bashar al-Assad should vacate his position to make a way for the new administration that will be pro-Western and anti-Russia. I firmly believe that the Syrian War is not the war between the Syrian oppositional parties and the Syrian government, but the war between the superpowers of the world disguising themselves through the Syrian War. We all know that Russia is supporting Bashar al-Assad, and the United States and United Kingdom are supporting the oppositional parties in Syria. It was the president of the United States of America who suggested that Bashar al-Assad was using the chemical weapons against his people and killed 130,000 innocent women and children, and in the twinkling of an eye, Vladimir Putin jumped into the picture and suggested that the chemical weapons that the Syrian government have used to slaughter its people with should be disclosed and handed over to the international community. Bashar al-Assad's government, through the help of Russia, managed to disclose and declares its stockpile of chemical weapons, though the exercise of moving the stockpile of chemical weapons to the safe location has been very slow. It's important to note then that the idea of declaring and disclosing of these chemical weapons was not Bashar al-Assad's idea but was Vladimir Putin's idea. The deadline for the Syrian government that had been set in the international community for Syria to remove its stock pile of chemical weapons was January 31, 2014. Bashar al-Assad's government failed to live up to the expectation of the international community, and as always, the Russian president Vladimir Putin came into the picture again as always and said Syria should set a new of date, March 31, 2014, for the removal of all stockpile of chemical weapons. It baffled my mind when I hear the oppositions in Russian calling their president Vladimir Putin "Grandpa." The Russian citizens don't exhibit the same respect to Pres. Vladimir Putin like the whole world. Quite frankly right now in the whole world, I don't think that there is any leader of any country who has managed to save many lives of innocent women and children compared to Vladimir Putin. It was the unique wisdom of Vladimir Putin that saved the people of Syria and the government of Bashar al-Assad. If the Russian government did not support militarily and financially the government of Bashar al-Assad against the Western terrorists and the sex jihadists from Tunisia, Bashar al-Assad would have been long defeated just like Muammar Gaddafi of Libya and Saddam Hussein of Iraq. The scramble for Africa is over, and now there is a scramble for the Middle East. The West has made it its mission to take control of the Middle East, which seems easy to penetrate and control because of the lack of unity among the Arab leaders. If you can cast your eyes wide open in the Middle East, you can quickly tell that Middle East is divided like never before. No wonder there is never-ending sectarian violence that seems to not come to an end in the Middle East. This holy jihad concept is killing people in the Middle East. People are dying like flies under the notion that when they die fighting the holy jihad, they will automatically enter heaven where Allah has prepared a resting place for them. After the 9/11, the United States of America began to tighten its immigration laws specifically toward people who are from the Middle East region. The main reason the United States had to tighten its immigration laws against the people of Middle East was that simply the 9/11 hijackers were from the Middle East not from Africa. There are many people who have untold tales of how they were denied entrance into the United States of America after the 9/11 attack. The government of the United States had to do anything possible within its power to ensure that the tragic event of 9/11 does not happen anymore in the near future. The US intelligence community was partly blamed for the 9/11 tragic event. The US government not only had to overhaul their ways of conducting intelligence work around the world but also had to make sure that they nail the ass of Osama Bin Laden who was on the loose, and nobody knew then where Osama Bin Laden was and what he was thinking on his mind. Because of the fear of Osama Bin

Laden, who some suggested was killed in Afghanistan through the drone strikes, and the fear of the possible coming wave of unforeseen attack by terrorists, the US intelligence agency decided to spy on the whole world to ensure that the 9/11 tragic event would not happen anymore. Prior to the revelation of the mass spying by the United States for its citizens, the United States was also spying on everybody, not only on its citizens but also on all leaders of the world. Meaning the United States was simply controlling the whole world through its NSA program. The fact of the matter is the US citizens didn't know that the big brother was watching them every now and then. The whole world woke up to this reality that the United States was spying on the world leaders including its citizens through the whistle-blower Edward Snowden. Before I delve deep into discussing this point, I had a very troublesome night one day. It was about 4:00 a.m. I began to toss and turn trying to find answers from my own mind and trying to understand the rationale behind Richard Snowden's brave action to expose and disclose the NSA security program of mass surveillance on the world leaders including Angela Merkel of Germany. It's possible that Richard Snowden had a troubled night before he broke out the story to the public, and he knew the consequences of his action were going to cost him his life. He knew very well that his days will be numbered the moment he disclosed the NSA mass spying programs to the whole world. The one-million-dollar question then is, what could have led this young man of twenty-nine years of age to take such a bold and dangerous decision to reveal the NSA mass spying programs? Why didn't he just turn a blind eye and walk away from the Booz Allen Hamilton and got another job? The truth of the matter is he had trouble to stomach the lies about the United States. He was tired for hiding the truth about the United States. He was once and for all trying to prove to the world that the United States does not have good intention about any country but its own selfish interest only. The next thing you know, Richard Snowden was running around like a headless chicken. Some media reports were suggesting that Richard Snowden was on his way to Ecuador, and some reports said he was in a hotel in China. The guy was the next big thing. Richard Snowden shot to fame in the twinkling of an eye just like that. The fact of the matter is this: the US cat was out of the black bag, and the whole world saw it. There were contentious views in the United States; some people suggesting that Richard Snowden should be protected because he is a whistle-blower, and some suggested that the guy needs to be electrocuted because he revealed the sensitive information about the security of the United States, and that was tantamount to espionage. Bradley Manning was arrested and charged for espionage for supplying Julian Assange of WikiLeaks with thousands and thousands of documents about the NSA security programs. Bradley Manning decided not to run for his life. While all of this was happening, Vladimir Putin was not asleep; he was hatching a plan again to save the life of this young man who has defiled the orders of his master and spilled the beans to the whole world about the US corruption while playing clean before the whole world. As always Vladimir Putin came into the picture and saved Richard Snowden from his growing headache. Most of the world leaders wanted nothing to do with Richard Snowden because they thought that giving Richard Snowden an asylum would jeopardize their relationships with the US government. Imagine what could have happened to Richard Snowden if he fled to Israel or to United Kingdom—he could have been arrested on his arrival and airlifted to the United States with both of his feet and hands handcuffed. Israel is a strong ally of the United States of America. As of the writing of this book, Richard Snowden was comfortable and relaxed in Moscow, the Russian capital. The Ukraine citizens call the capital city of Russia "Mother Moscow." When the Olympic torch arrived in the Red Square in Sochi in October 2013, Vladimir Putin told the world that "the torch would show the world Russia as she is and as we love her." Russia has pulled the most expensive Olympic Games ever just to show the world that Russia has the same potential just like the United States to be the new police of the world. Russia, just like any other country, has its own problems. There is even "Osama Bin Laden of Russia." The plundering of the wealth by the West in Africa happened during the colonial era. Colonization robbed Mother Africa of her precious mineral deposits, which were given to her by the heavens to be able to support her children and take her children to school. Today African children are starving to death because of opportunistic diseases because Mother Africa cannot afford anymore to look after her children. The West stole brutally what was once hers and her children's, and took it to the West to feed the Western children. When the African children cry because of hunger and starvation, the West gives Mother Africa crumbs that have fallen from the Western table known as food parcels and foreign aid. Mother Africa was once rich and pregnant with mineral resources, and she was able to feed her children. Right now she is poor and broke, and her children are poor too; her children don't have a land to settle in, and her children don't have a place that they can call home. It's painful to know that you were once rich and now you are poor permanently. My problem that compelled me to conduct a thorough investigation about the African wealth is what I have been hearing since I was a little child. I have heard many people saying Africa is a poverty-stricken continent, ridden with diseases and malnutrition. Some Western scholars, when they are tired of researching and they are running out of ideas about the causes of certain diseases, will just say this disease is prevalent among Africans. It also believed in the West that AIDS originated in Africa even though there is no scientific evidence to back up such assertion. It seems as if African people are prone to everything that is bad. It seems as if we Africans are prone to crime and diseases like HIV/AIDS. If you look at the crime statistics of any country where an African community is residing, there will be crime, violence, and theft. Whether or not you cast your eyes wide open even in the United States today, the majority of inmates who are flooding the prisons are members of the black community. Even today in South Africa, the majority of people who are in prison are black people. The one-million-dollar question then is, what is wrong with us? Why are the majority of our people in prison? Bear in mind that those African men and women who are in prison are not in prison because of political reasons, but they are in prison because they have committed crimes against their communities. The answer to this question lies in our social environment. If you raise a child in the slums and shanty towns, that child is likely to grow and believe that life is complete if you are living in shanty towns and slums. Most African children were born in poverty-stricken environment and grew up in a poverty-stricken neighborhood. All what they were taught is to work for the white man because the white man is your boss. We Africans are always behind with technology even to this day. We are looking to the West to save us. While we Africans look to the West and China to save us, we are giving away our mineral resources in exchange for our redemption and economic salvation. The West is consistently and systematically stealing from Africa now and then. The West is now stealing from Africa in broad daylight. We Africans all know that we are giving too much of Africa's mineral resources to the West in exchange of food parcels and foreign aid. Since I have started traveling to Zimbabwe, I became alive to the fact that the majority of Africans don't know much about Africa, and even the majority of South Africans don't know much about South Africa either. How can you even dare to talk about national issues that affect your country if you don't even understand your country that you live in? If I can tell some of my friends that South Africa is the Saudi Arabia of mineral resources, they can be very shocked! Because all that they know about South Africa is this: South Africa is a poverty-stricken country and is riddled with diseases and malnutrition. They don't know much about either the South African mineral deposits or about the foreign companies that are mining South African mineral resources. We Africans should ask ourselves this question: How could our lives have been if we were not colonized by the West? The truth of the matter is our lives could have been very different compared to the current lives that we are living right now. There wouldn't be wars in Africa that are tearing the African continent apart. We Africans were going to live in peace and in harmony just like our forefathers did before the arrival of the West in Africa. We would be sharing everything, except wives of course. The spirit of *Ubuntu* was going to be our beacon of life. There wouldn't be poverty that is tearing African families apart, and there wouldn't be street kids as is the case today in any African country. We were going to live just like Adam and Eve were living in the Garden of Eden. We all know that in the Garden of Eden, the serpent came with poverty, sicknesses, and death. Before the arrival of the Western settlers in Africa, Africans were living as children of one mother, and there were no wars that were meant to bring people to extinction. There were no WMD (weapons of mass destruction); people were living in peace and in harmony. The arrival of the West with its quasi-civilization brought to an end the peace and harmony that existed in the African continent. Today we learn that Africans are migrating to Europe in search of a better life. There is mass migration of people from Africa to the West because of political instability and economic uncertainty in Africa. Africans are now and forever in the run like never before. Africans are always running from endless wars and Africa's dictatorship governments, which are oppressive and repressive. Africans are always on the run because there is perpetual hunger that is meant to bring the majority of African people into extinction, just like rhinos. When I pause and ponder and begin to analyze the African story, I begin to realize that Africa is in a very serious predicament. It's a serious predicament that has been systematically hatched from the West that is meant to keep the African continent on the Western radar. There has never been a point in history where people are extremely stressed and economically uncertain as they are right now in Africa. I remember in my first trip to Zimbabwe. While our passports were being stamped, we saw a large crowd of people running toward to the main road, and within that crowd there were women and children. I remember asking Mr. Brown this question: "Why are these people running?" I remember him vividly saying to me, "These are the hikers." They were going to the main road in order to hike big trucks that are going to South Africa because they believe that once they get to South Africa, their economic problems would be solved. This is the same theory that is held by the majority of Africans about Europe. Most Africans believe that if they were living in the United States of America, their financial problems would be gone. The truth of the matter is this: there is poverty also in the United States of America. When GM (General Motors) shut down one of its plants in California, the majority of people in the United States were unemployed. The same belief is widely held in Zimbabwe that if they can jump the border and come to Johannesburg or Pretoria, their lives will be better off. It's true that South African economy is not on the same footing just like the Zimbabwean economy; however, South Africa has its own economic problems like corruption and unemployment also. Many people hold different views about unemployment. Unemployment might not necessarily mean that there are no jobs at all in the market. What it might mean sometimes is this: there are no permanent and high-paying jobs that are available at that time in the job market. If you are looking for a job at that time, you need to lower your expectation because if you raise them too high, you might be disappointed. We all know that most Africans don't understand what the meaning of political freedom is, and they normally equate political freedom to economic freedom. Political freedom is a totally different animal from economic freedom. The fact that you are now allowed to cast a vote for your preferred political party, that does not necessarily mean that your life will ultimately, in the twinkling of an eye, take a U-turn just like that. It does not mean that you will now have clean water and electricity that is not paid for just because you voted for a particular political party. It means that the status quo will still remain to some of the people. There are people who will progress financially in democratic dispensation, and there are people who will be left behind even during a democratic dispensation. Those who will be left behind financially in the democratic state are those who don't understand how democracy works. It does not mean that in democracy everything is free, and it does not mean that in a democratic state there won't be cronyism and cabals. In case you don't know, corruption is part and parcel of democracy, and cronyism is part of a developmental state. I am not suggesting that there should be corruption in order to reinforce the foundation of democracy, but the point I am making is this: the theory says there won't be corruption in democratic dispensation because certain politicians are in power is also unfounded and untrue.

Among people all over the world, there is a general moral decay and character flaws. People don't seem to care about what is happening to their neighbors anymore. People will go as far as saying, "A good fence makes good neighbors." There are high walls that have been erected by almost everybody in South Africa, even in Zimbabwean suburb. People don't want to share anymore; they are now locking themselves up in their homes that are surrounded by high walls. The only thing you will hear is the smell that they are grilling meat next door. Unfortunately, there is nothing that you can do about it if you are not invited. High walls really don't stop all the nonsense that you are running away from. As long as we Africans are not exercising our collective wisdom to solve our common problems, we are likely to drown together as fools. Even those who have erected high walls to stop other people from seeing why they are eating will finally realize that the best way to deal with a problem is not to build a high wall around yourselves and place a security guard on the gate and install CCTV cameras but it's to confront our hard-pressing problems together. Divided we fall and united we stand. Our economic and political problems in Africa are originating from the West, and we Africans are also afraid to divorce and distance ourselves from the West. We have relied on the West for quite a long period of time, and all what we know is the West just like the Ukraine citizens calling the capital city of Russia "Mother Russia." By the way, Vladimir Putin has turned his back from Ukraine once and for all now, suggesting that if the Ukraine government can't be able to repay its debt, there won't be any future financial assistance from the Russian government. George W. Bush writes:

> *In February 2008, Lauara and I returned to sub-Saharan Africa. The trip was my second and her fifth. We viewed the visit as a chance to showcase some of Africa's best leaders, who were serving their people with integrity and tackling problems like poverty, corruption, and diseases. Their good example stood in stark contrast to the African leader dominating the headlines, Robert Mugabe of Zimbabwe. Mugabe has stifled democracy, subjected his people to hyperinflation, and turned the country from a net food exporter to a net importer. His disgraceful record was proof that one man could ruin a country.*[15]

Zimbabweans problems don't entirely rest on the shoulders of Pres. Robert Mugabe alone. There are a lot of people in Zimbabwe who contributed to

Zimbabwe's problems, and they don't get their names mentioned simply because they are not in the forefront. Corruption does not happen on the front, but it happens behind the stage when the lights are off and the room is dark—that is the perfect time and space for corruption to take place. That is why it's possible for a minister to use his wife, children, and even his siblings to shield millions and millions of dollars through their names and still remain as a minister without any form of wealth under his name, while his siblings, wife, and children are filthy stinking rich. This is the new way most of Africa's leaders use to plunder the little wealth that still remains in Africa. The Western agents also work hand in hand with Africa's elected political leaders to plunder the little wealth that remains in the African continent. When I pause and ponder what Terry said in my second trip while I was in Zimbabwe, I could quickly sense the level of frustration spewing out of Terry's heart. In case you have forgotten who Terry is, he was my driver that I hired to drive me around in my second trip while I was in Harare. I believe there are many people in the world who are like Terry who are complaining, but they only complain behind closed doors because of fear of reprisal. It's disingenuous to suggest that Pres. Robert Mugabe alone is solely responsible for the economic mess that is tearing Zimbabwe apart. It's also impossible to rig the entire national election results if there are no people who voted for you. The fact of the matter is this: there are Zimbabweans who love Pres. Robert Mugabe and his ZANU-PF wholeheartedly and they see the West as the enemy of Zimbabwe. They are too loyal to their master to the point that they can't even see if their master is making a costly mistake. African liberation movements have become oppressive and corrupt in nature. These African liberation movements have inherited the practices of the former colonizers and picked up where the former colonizer left off. What do you expect from a person who has been in the bush for quite a long period of time without knowledge of running an economy? The moment former freedom fighters had to come into their community and be integrated and live the very same normal life they have been running away from, these ex-combatants often now and then brandished their struggle credentials and sought compensation through tenders and contracts in an unscrupulous way from the state. Because these ex-combatants fought in the armed struggle, they perceive themselves superior than a normal people who had never participated in the armed struggle. Everybody knows now that politics pays, and there is no better-paying job like a politician's. In politics that is where the majority of serious economic decisions are made. Tenders are not awarded based on your company profile or work experience, but they are awarded based on who you know and how much you will donate after receiving the tender to a certain political party. In Africa for you to be a good businessman and good businesswoman and continue to get more and more contracts from the state, you must know the right people in high places. As long as you are doing business in a scrupulous and honest way, you are likely to remain poor for a very long time. Even the establishment of post in most of the companies, whether it's parastatal or private sector, there is corruption of epic proportion that is taking place. The question then is, why are we Africans still so poor and backward even after receiving our political liberation from our colonial masters? The answer to this question is obvious: corruption has been legitimatized, and even the so-called "state-independent institutions" have become dependent. I think the greatest mistake that have been committed by most African liberation movements in Africa is the deployment of ex-combatants who became the state man and state woman while they knew nothing about either the very mineral resources that they always make noise about now and then or even running the very government that they were deployed to run. There is a great difference between holding an AK-47 and firing at an enemy, and crafting a yearlong plan for a country. The fact that a person is a terminator in a Bush War does not make him a terminator in an office. The point that I am making is this: good ex-combatants normally don't make good ministers. Most of the ex-combatants after the liberation struggle had nothing to show off for their youthful time that they have spent in the bush, and their families that they have left behind went even further into the depth of poverty that have been caused by the skewed economic system of that time. In an attempt to even the playing field, most of these ex-combatants, to appease them by the African liberation movements, were absorbed by the newly formed African governments, and they were also allowed to incorporate companies and tender to do work for government. Though in the case of South Africa, there are very strict rules and principles when it comes to government officials to conduct business with the state. The majority of government officials can just register their companies through their siblings and even their wives, and that is the end of the story. Wealth doesn't trickle down to the poor, and that is why the poor will remain poor as long as the system remains the same. It's painful to see a big, fat financial figure and not lay your hands on it. Most people often hear about big, fat numbers, even in parliament, but they never get an opportunity to lay hold of those monies. We all know how rich Africa is, but the truth of the matter is the majority of the African people on the ground are very poor. The West has perfected the art of corruption and then exported it to Africa. Most of the ex-combatants are financially fragile, and they are emotionally fragile even today; that is why they can't wrap their heads around a big, fat financial figure. The only thing that the ex-combatants who are now in government are thinking about is to loot the state resources for themselves and their families. The plundering of Africa resources will not end soon. The end is still far, and guesses what! This is just a beginning of a long winding road. Corruption does get to the nerves of ordinary people at some point. When corruption gets to the nerves of people, there is nothing, I mean nothing, that can stop them to overthrow the very political leaders that they have legally elected. That is exactly what is happing in the Middle East and even in Asia; ordinary people are extremely exhausted with grinding poverty and unemployment. It's also true that some of these African leaders have used military power to stay in office long enough even if the masses are no longer happy with their services. Magome Mogomotsi writes:

> *The tragic cohabitation of capital flight and poverty in African oil-rich countries is a result of occult management of natural resources and external borrowing by African governments on the one hand, and a global banking system plagued by perverse incentives as well as the primacy of African leaders accumulate wealth, the African people are saddled with debts and watch helplessly as their natural resource reserves are depleted with little to show for in return. On the other side, Western bankers and governments turn a blind eye to the plunder of African resources and the illicit accumulation of wealth by the continent's elites.*[16]

The Western governments have become accomplices to the plundering of Africa's resources with Africa's elite. As long Africa's elite continue their never-ending relationships with the Western criminals, their ill-gotten wealth cannot be questioned. As long as Africa's elite partners with the West in their corruption, there is nothing wrong; but as soon as that corrupt relationship is threatened, suddenly everything changes. Most of Africa's elites are Western puppets, and they're used by the West to plunder Africa's wealth in exchange of expensive houses in the West. One thing that most Africa's elites forget is that there is no honor among thieves. A relationship that is based on money is destined to fail. African leaders have been accused of staying in power as long as they can breathe and enriching their families and their cronies. I have interviewed different people of different African countries; all of them have one common complaint—our leaders are enriching themselves at the expense of the masses. Why can't they be removed then if they are enriching themselves and their families at the expense of the masses? They can't be removed simply because they are Africa's liberators who have become oppressors. And the worst part of this oppression is this: black people are now oppressing black people just like in the colonial days. Most of these African leaders are using the power of the military to terrorize the very masses that elected them democratically. Most of the African intellectuals are not involved in Africa's domestic politics and even in African affairs. The reason this is happening is that simply these African intellectuals have realized that in African politics there is no fairness and transparency. When most of the African intellectuals see the unfairness and injustices that happened before their very eyes, they just decide to emigrate from the African continent and use their hard-earned knowledge somewhere in the world. Africa is struggling to retain its intellectuals and even to educate and develop its youth. When Africa's young intellectuals travel to study abroad after completing their studies, they normally don't come back to Africa to apply their hard-earned Western knowledge. That is why Africa is a continent of intellectual bankruptcy and information deficit. The majority of books that are read in most African libraries were written in the West. It seems as if the West has not only colonized Africa politically only but also colonized Africa intellectually. With intellectual colonization, you are told what to think and what not to think. Our definition of democracy is Western not African. We African people are the people of culture, values, and traditions, but the West, through its quasi-democracy, has indoctrinated us to believe that we need to disregard our cultures, traditions, and values because they are satanic and follow its footsteps. There is nowhere in African culture where an unborn child can be aborted willy-nilly. A human being is a superior being than animals, and he or she does not deserve to be aborted just like that. Democracy and freedom will only happen the day the West will decide to admit and accept that their empires have been built by African slaves and migrants who were abducted from Africa from the Gorée Island in Senegal and shipped to the West. That is the day the West will admit to slice some of that cake that has been invested in the World Bank and IMF. The fact of the matter is after the West has completed its colonization exercise and robbed Africa its wealth, it invested that money in the World Bank and IMF. The majority of people think that IMF and the World Bank's wealth have been contributed by the world's richest countries only. Little is told even today of what the West did with the considerable amount of wealth that was stolen from Africa through slavery and long years of colonization. The answer to that question is simple: the West invested Africa's wealth in the World Bank and IMF, and now the West is reaping the benefits of that wealth like never before, and the interest of that wealth is given back to most struggling African countries as foreign aid and to some African countries, if they are lucky, as loans at a weird astronomical high interest rate. The West is now stealing from the poor African countries through these loans from the World Bank and IMF. Most of our infrastructure projects in most African countries have been funded by either the Western financial institutions like the World Bank and IMF. Most of the African countries, even those with mineral deposits, are not able, even to this day and age, to raise sufficient capital to finance their infrastructure projects. My personal problem with South Africa is this: it has allowed a considerable amount of foreign immigrants to reside in South Africa illegally; some of these illegal immigrants are from Zimbabwe, Zambia, and DRC. When a country has a considerable amount of migrants who are some even unregistered and undocumented, it's easy for these migrants to commit a crime and get away with it without being caught. Bear in mind that the majority of these African migrants are not in possession of legal documents to reside in South Africa. What happens then is the high level of lawlessness and crime that is deadly difficult to solve, since the majority of these foreign immigrants did not enter South Africa legally. There are anecdotal five million Zimbabweans who are living in South Africa both legally and illegally simply because of the political and economic problems that have engulfed Zimbabwe until today. The sooner the political solution of Zimbabwe's conundrum is found, the better. As long as the Zimbabwean government continues to hold its economic stance about the economy of Zimbabwe, the worse can be expected. South African government is feeling the pitch because of the considerable amount of Zimbabweans who are living in South Africa legally and illegally. There are more Zimbabweans who are residing in South Africa illegally than there are Zimbabweans who are living in South Africa legally. There more South Africa continues to be benevolent and generous toward non-South Africans who are coming from war-ridden countries, the more money South Africa must spend to ensure the rule of law is being observed and to ensure that these foreign immigrants get jobs in order to survive. South Africans who are living in posh suburbs don't care much about these political issues because they say it doesn't affect them. It's only when they are hijacked in the middle of the night on their way home—that is the day when they will realize that the problem of allowing foreign immigrants to dwell in South Africa without being documented or registered is a serious problem. The one-million-dollar question is this: How do you ensure that illegal foreign immigrants are integrated into a country like South Africa lawfully without these foreign immigrants turning to crime in an attempt to provide for their families? There is no single answer to that question. Some of the legal and illegal foreign immigrants have requisite skills that the South African economy requires, and some of these legal or illegal foreign immigrants don't have necessary requisite skills that can earn them sustainable employment in the South African economy. It follows then that housing a lot of illegal foreign immigrants who don't have requisite skills that can be used in the economy of South Africa is an accident that is about to happen soon. South African economy is the biggest economy in Africa; having said that, that does not necessarily mean that South African economy can solve Africa's problems alone. The United Kingdom and Australia are countries that are very strict on their immigration laws. The UK and Australian government don't want even to see African migrants except when those African migrants are entering these countries as students to study in their universities. Except the above-mentioned reason like looking for a job, African migrants who are found in the United Kingdom and Australia will be deported back to their home country. There are hotheaded Africans who like to reside in the United Kingdom and Australia, some legally and some stay even illegally, so risking their lives to be deported to their country of birth on a daily basis. But in general, the United Kingdom and Australia are not hospitable countries in terms of African migrants, even to the Middle Eastern migrants. The Northern African migrants who were sailing to the island of Lampedusa to look for greener pastures often now and then are mistreated, and at some point they have to be stripped naked and be sprayed with horse pipe as the cleansing process for the alleged diseases that they are carrying in their bodies from Africa. South Africa is a mother of the motherless and a father of the fatherless and an orphanage home for African orphans that have been left behind by the DRC War and Zimbabwe's crisis. Though there are net gains that South Africa can make through these African migrants through its (EPWP) Expanded Public Works Programme, there is nothing wrong about people immigrating to another country provided that they have requisite skills that they can utilize to survive in the country that they are immigrating to. There are Zimbabweans who are making a positive contribution to the South African economy, and there are some Zimbabweans who are costing South Africa more money because they still need to be fed and deported to Zimbabwe. Though the issue of migration of people is a sensitive issue, more often than not one risks to be called xenophobic or chauvinist if he raises these issues. It's also true that there are economic net gains that can be made through migration of people from one country to another provided that this migration process is properly monitored and properly coordinated. South Africa is reaping the rewards economically through the Mozambican migrants who are working in the sugar plantations in Mpumalanga. The biggest problem about people who are immigrating to South Africa and even elsewhere in the world is when they don't possess the requisite economic skills that are required by the economy to grow. More often than not many people are afraid to recognize and acknowledge this financial burden that should be borne by countries who are housing a considerable amount of migrants who don't have requisite skills that are required by the economy. Let me give you a practical example: the Mozambicans migrants are hard workers in nature, and as far as I know, even until this day, the majority of the workforce in the sugar plantation in Mpumalanga, South Africa, is dominated by the Mozambicans. Simply put, any honest sugarcane farmer will tell you straightaway that the Mozambican migrants are workaholics and they are the backbones of the South African sugar Industry. Simply put, any country is likely to benefit immensely economically if it can utilize the excess labor force that is provide by the migration of people from one country to another. South Africa has benefited immensely through Zimbabwe's crisis because the majority of Zimbabwean intellectuals immigrated to South Africa to look for employment. The truth of the matter is this: once Zimbabwe's debacle is over, they will have to migrate back to Zimbabwe and leave South Africa again struggling with teachers who can teach math, physics, and science. In another words, while migration can contribute positively to the economy of any country where the majority of people are immigrating to, it's also likely to create tensions among the citizens of that country. It's also worth noting that some of the foreign migrants do have a weird attitude toward South African people. Just because South African people are hospitable to foreign migrants, that does not necessarily mean that they are not clever enough. It's true that the South African population does not possess sufficient requisite skills that are necessary to grow the economy in leaps and bounds. Therefore, as a result of the shortages of these requisite and scarce skills in South Africa, which has been caused by the apartheid system with its policies that were unfair and satanic, the majority of South Africans don't possess those skills that could be utilized in the South African economy. Importing foreign scarce skills becomes very important and necessary to keep the economy growing in leaps and bounds. However, that is not a reasonable excuse not to provide necessary training within the country to the South African citizens. I need to make this point clear unless otherwise someone might misinterpret me. What I am saying is this: South Africans must be hospitable to African migrants because some of them have necessary requisite scarce skills to grow the South African economy, but at the same time these African migrants need to start showing some respect to the people of South Africa, since they are living in South Africa not elsewhere. I have often discovered something wonderful about the Zimbabweans: most of them are very humble and down-to-earth, but I can't say the same thing about other foreign immigrants who are living in South Africa. The plundering of wealth in Africa will continue unabated unless otherwise someone who is brave can grind to a screeching halt Africa's train of corruption, which is carrying the heavy weights of the world. Whenever there is political peace and tranquility in Africa, the Western agents will form a political party through citizens of that country and shower the newly formed oppositional political party with financial resources and even with cars to ensure that this oppositional political party eventually topples the ruling party, which is the governing party. When these Western agents have managed to topple the ruling party, which is the governing party in this case, they will come back through a back door and pretend to be foreign investors who are sympathetic to the newly formed political party that now is in government. If these Western agents fail to succeed in their well-crafted plan to topple the ruling party, which is the governing party, they will make sure that they hire mercenaries to topple the government right away to parachute their preferred candidate to the position of presidency and start looting natural resources legally with impunity. Mr. Silverton once said to me, "Do you know why when I was posted in DRC during the 1998 war DRC was the busiest airport?" I said no. He said to me, "It's because there was a lot of looting taking place in Congo." Rodney Walter writes:

> *The imperialist carved up Asia, Africa, and Latin America for themselves. Nowhere was this more apparent than in Africa. King Leopold of Belgium, literally, claimed personal possession of the Congo, as if it were his own backyard. Different imperialists occupied different parts of Africa to directly manage the transfer of resources and labor from Africa to the Imperialist countries.*[17]

Even though DRC has been under the colony of Belgium for quite a long period of time, but even after it has gained its own independence from the Western powers, it is still trapped in endless wars. Most of the DRC wars were funding by the West even until today. DRC government will forever need military support to either to defend itself against the defunct M23 or the ADFL rebel groups. It's important to understand the Western agenda about Africa. There is no point in history where the West has allowed any African country to be self-reliant, self-sufficient, and self-governing. All African countries owe their being and existence to the West. Zimbabwe owes its existence to China, and Zimbabwe is the province of China in Africa. As long as Africa will forever follow the Western culture and Western civilization to the letter, Africa will be forever in the economic prison of the West. Africa has been emancipated from the political prison of the West and transferred to another prison known as economic prison. Most of the African countries are in this economic prison, and they have been blindfolded to realize that they are still in prison, though to be in economic prison is better than to be in political prison because there are social grants, free food parcel, and foreign aid in economic prison; but the fact remains—the economic prison is still a prison. Residing in the rich neighborhood does not necessarily make you rich. Residing in a white-dominated neighborhood does not make you white if you are black. Black people who have migrated from their shanty towns and their locations where the sewerage is spewing all the way to the streets are also trapped in the same economic prison where the majority of the African countries are. These black middle class have misinterpreted the concept of political freedom to mean economic freedom, and they have also misinterpreted the concept of political freedom to mean residing next to white folks. Just like many African countries have misinterpreted the concept of political freedom to mean foreign aid and free food parcel and cheap free blankets from the UN, so are the middle-class families. I am not therefore implying that there is something wrong about residing in the white neighborhood with white folks if you are black and sending your children to a multiracial school is a sin. We all know that most of the black middle-class folks prefer to fellowship in the white churches with white folks than fellowshipping in black churches where there are a lot of black folks who are poor and uneducated. It's important to know your roots, and it's important to know where you come from as an African woman and an African man. I know that if you have been reading this book carefully, you probably have made very wrong conclusions about me that are not factual based. We, the young African generation, need to learn about our forefathers and the causes of myriad African problems that we have in the African continent. If we, the young African generation, can't spend time to find out and open the history records and read them thoroughly, we are likely to be mercenaries of the West to destroy the very African continent that had been fought for very hard by our forefathers. Opening the history records does not necessarily mean that you want to reverse everything that went horribly wrong in the past. It means you are seeking to understand the presence by first understanding the past in order to plan properly for the future. It does not mean that you want to drive all the Western settlers to the sea and send them packing back to Europe. But what it means is this: any other bilateral agreements that Africa will enter into with the West will be based on mutual benefit, unlike in the past where Africa was a beggar and the West was a giver. It will also curtail and prevent most African countries to be exploited by the West under the pretext of trade partnerships that most of the African leaders don't even understand because they work in favor of the West than they work in favor of the African continent. Mutual agreements should be mutually beneficial, and trade partnerships mean this: both trade partners will receive equal proportion of their capital injection. Simply put, we all know that in any partnership there should be a capital contribution that both partners should make. It also means that both partners, if not all partners, involved into this partnership have a fair share of the revenues that will be generated by the partnership during the course of trade. There is no partner who has more power than the other unless otherwise he can contribute more than the other. The problem with many African countries is this: they have been giving too much love to the West only to be cheated on by the West. The West has been an unfaithful partner to Africa, and until this point in time, Africa is still a faithful sleeping partner with the West even though the West has been cheating on Africa for quite a long period of time. When is the time to end a bad relationship if the faithful partner has been cheated on for quite a long period of time by the unloving and unfaithful partner? Even in real life it's like that—faithful partners are normally cheated on and taken advantage of by the unloving, uncommitted, and unfaithful partner. Most people can see that they have been losing by giving too much love to the unfaithful partner, but they still stay anyway, hoping that things will get better someday only to be worse than ever before. Africa has been giving mineral resources to the West to sustain its shaky and fragile relationship with the West, and the West has been an abusive partner to Mother Africa. She (Mother Africa) has been endowed with mineral resources and has been highly favored by her parents (God). The one-million-dollar question that still baffles my mind even to this day is this: How much mineral resources have been under the belly of the African soil prior to the arrival of the West, and what was the value of these mineral resources? Since we all know that the West has been extracting mineral resources from this African soil until this day, how much mineral resources have been extracted, and what is the value of these mineral resources? The so-called experts have been telling us that DRC mineral resources are worth US$27 trillion; quite frankly that is not relevant to me. What I will like to know is this: How much mineral resources have been buried under the DRC soil before the arrival of King Leopold of Belgium, and what was the value of these mineral resources before the arrival of the King Leopold of Belgium in DRC? To suggest that the current mineral resources of DRC are worth US$27 trillion is useless to me and irrelevant, since until this day we Africans really don't know how much was taken from us Africans by the West. There will never be forgiveness of sins unless otherwise there is confession of sins. In fact sins that are not confessed are sins that are not forgiven. I normally hear people, when they are about to deliver an announcement of some sort, say, "I don't know where to start." I normally say its simple start from the beginning and then continue until the end. Before the West and Africa could even begin to talking about the Western doughnut of foreign aid and free food parcel including their cheap blankets of UN, they should first assess the root of the problem and the total costs therefore and begin from there. The damage has been done to Mother Africa and her children, including her mineral resources, which were given to her by her parent and have been taken from her by the West. There are contentious views about Africa's wealth, which was stolen away by the West; some Africans do acknowledge the fact the West indeed is rich purely because of Africa's wealth that was stolen from Africa through the idea of developing Africa and creating sustainable jobs for Africans. If we all agree then that the West indeed is rich, as is the status quo today simply through ill-gotten wealth from Africa, why can't the West meet African leaders halfway at least by reimbursing Africans for the wealth that was stolen from Africa? The fact of the matter is this: the West can't acknowledge the fact that its wealth is purely ill- gotten that has been taken away from Africa. What the West would rather prefer to do is to provide African countries with loans from the World Bank and IMF at an astronomical high interest rate even though the very money that had been invested in these financial institutions was clearly generated through the colonization of Africa. Instead of the West coming to the party and putting concerted effort to solve the financial impasse that most African countries are struggling with right now, the West just seeks regime change and provides more funds to the opposition parties, which are not going to challenge the status quo and go with the flow. That is why the Zimbabwean debacle is the way it is. The majority of the people in the whole world, even in Africa, hate Pres. Robert Mugabe with passion simply because they don't see him as a solution to the Zimbabwean problem but purely the instigator of the current economic crisis that the Zimbabwean people find themselves in. African leaders who are opposed to the Western agenda are normally classified as corrupt by their countrymen and dictators, and they can even be dubbed to be responsible for the human rights violation. The gross violator of human rights is the West and its allies. The West trains mercenaries and funds the extremist groups, while the Middle East trains jihadists and sex jihadists. The Western leaders, when they violate the human rights laws, are not called to account in the ICC (International Criminal Court), while African leaders, even those who are currently serving as presidents of their countries, have charges that they still need to answer to in Hague. When one takes a closer look at the cases of human rights violation committed by African leaders, it's possible for one to quickly realize that the majority of the cases that are faced by African leaders in Hague are not genuine but are politically motivated charges. There has never been a point in history where the ICC Court has ever indicted a Western leader to appear in Hague because of the charges of human rights violation. It simply means that the West practices democracy to the letter, while in Africa there is no democracy, only human rights violation. While Africa is considered as a continent of poverty, which needs to be rescued through foreign aid and the free food parcels, the West forgets that the majority of problems that are in Africa are as the consequence of a long and protracted period of colonization and the pillaging of Africa's mineral deposits by the West. Even after Africa has gained its own political independence from the West, there is nothing that seemed to have changed, since the majority of Africa's wealth is still in the hands of the Western settlers even today. In fact Africa has become the trading partner of the West. Since Africa's has gained its political independence but not economic independence, the Western leaders have been traveling to Africa with their delegation of businessmen to look for business opportunities. Are there no business opportunities in Iraq or Syria? The same thing also happens when African leaders are visiting the West; African leaders will be luring the Western investors to come to Africa to invest even though the current composition of Africa's economy means that the Westerners still hold the majority of Africa's wealth in their hands. What is the point then? The point is this: surely a normal person can never invite the very thief that stole his property in the past to be his business partner in the near future. The leopard does not change its spots, and once a snake always a snake. One of the reasons that made it difficult for the MDC-T to win the national election in Zimbabwe on July 31, 2013, was that simply MDC-T aligned itself with the Western countries that had imposed economic sanctions to Zimbabwe. It became very difficult then for ordinary people to decide as to which political party to believe between MDC-T and ZANU-PF. It's possible that the majority of people are sick and tired of the economic sanctions that have been imposed to the economy of Zimbabwe, but the ordinary people also don't trust MDC-T simply because of the Western factor in MDC-T. Pres. Robert Mugabe of ZANU-PF then exploited that Western element in MDC-T and snatched the national election before the very eyes of the world and even before the very eyes of the West because of the involvement of the West in the Zimbabwean domestic politics. As long as the West keeps embroiling itself in Zimbabwean domestic politics and seeks a political outcome that will suit its economic interest, Zimbabwe's economic conundrum will forever spiral out of control and with no end in sight. As much as Syrians need to solve their own economic and political problem, so should Zimbabweans solve their own domestic political and economic problems. There is no better person who understands Zimbabwe's political and economic problems in the whole world like the Zimbabweans themselves. It therefore goes without saying that Zimbabwe's political and economic dilemma can be solved perfectly well by the Zimbabweans themselves with the help of SADC and OAU only. As long the MDC-T continues to realign itself with its Western allies, it can be guaranteed to lose the national election even in 2018. The bigger picture is this: the West has imposed what Pres. Robert Mugabe calls "illegal economic sanctions" on Zimbabwe, and now the very same countries that failed to make sure that the Land Redistribution Program was successful funded are the very same countries who are sponsoring the MDC-T financially to dethrone and unseat the government of ZANU-PF. I find this very political episode very bizarre and worrisome in a way. The one-million-dollar question is this: Can the leopard change its spots? The answer is simple and straightforward: the leopard can't change its spot even at nighttime. The West has been plundering African mineral deposits for quite a long period of time, and when the time came for Africa to be politically liberated, some of these Western countries lost a considerable amount of political power in Africa. We all know that the West is obsessed with enormous political and economic power in Africa. This political and economic power sometimes was misused and abused by the West to its own favor. I have often seen most Africans who are trying by all means to keep up with the Western technology and the Western culture, spending too much money on unnecessary gadgets just to look Western and advanced. Most Africans have lost their African identity in pursuit of Western identity that is costly and financial unsustainable. The West is still controlling Africa through commercializing women's beauty. Things that were once free today, they now have a price tag. It's extremely expensive today to bury your loved one than the way it was in the past. Decent funerals are very expensive, and when one cannot afford a (expensive) decent funeral, one is classified as uncivilized and backward. Laying your loved one to rest through African way is not expensive, but laying your loved one to rest through what many people consider a decent burial, which is Western and perpetuated by capitalism, is deadly expensive. There is normally a scramble and even stampede in many retailers the day before Valentine's Day. We are all coaxed through the Western media to buy our loved ones a Valentine's card and even a Valentine's underwear just to fit in with the rest of the world. It seems as if the whole world is suffering from the Western swine flu of capitalism and greed to the extreme. We African men even go as far as borrowing money from the banks to finance what is called "white wedding," what I call Western wedding, just to fit in with the crowd. Love has become a commercial commodity, and death has become a commercial commodity also. People whose financial houses are not in order are not likely to be loved, and people whose financial houses are in order are going to receive more love. Africans have yielded to the Western call, which says everything has a price; even wars have a price.

While Africans were not people of greed and covetousness, recently most of the African families went as far as commercializing even the dowry. The dowry was paid in the past by the bridegroom's family according to what they have, not according to what the woman is worth. In other words, it's costly to marry an African woman who has a PhD than to marry a woman who is uneducated. Simply put, women too have a commercial value, which can be bought with a commercial price. Not only have we Africans lost our moral compass in pursuit to be a democratic society, but we also lost our values and culture in an attempt to follow the Western society that does have neither morals nor deep cultural values. There are many guns that are floating in the hands of the Western society under the principle of democracy and freedom. The commercialization of women in Africa is an indictment to all African societies. In other words, a person who does not have money not only does not deserve to love but does not deserve to be loved back too. There is even commercialization of birthday parties. Parents go as far as taking a loan from the bank to finance a mere twenty-first birthday party just because of what they see happening in the West. The West controls Africa through its media networks because that is how information can get disseminated easily without borders and boundaries. There are many street kids in Africa today than there have ever been street kids in an African history before. Most of the so-called "street kids" are children who have parents who don't subscribe to the principle of discipline and respect. Most of these street kids subscribe to the Western notion of free-for-all society. It's deadly difficult today to raise children who will understand African values and culture. Children that are born out of wedlock are growing in leaps and bounds because of African culture and values that have been eroded by the West. I am not blaming the West for everything. Bear in mind it is the West that colonized Africa and stole Africa's wealth, not vice versa. It makes logical sense and sound argument to attribute most of Africa's problems to the West. Even most of our political leaders have also been bought into this Western culture of opulent birthday parties at the expense of the poor masses.

> *"His majesty's government has the honour to announce to the nation that the king has received a gift of a DC-9 aircraft from development partners and friends of the king, to be used by their majesties for travels abroad," Dlamini said.*

> *Mswati celebrated his birthday on April 19, 2013, with R3 million ($386,000), partly paid by the state.*
>
> *He is rated by Forbes magazine as the world's fifteenth-richest monarch with a personal fortune of US$100 million, but he reins over one of the world's poorest nations.*[18]

His Majesty Mswati III will use his DC-9 twin-engine with his thirteen wives alone, not with the masses. Living a lavish lifestyle by most African leaders at the expense of their poor people has become a norm. I have been in one wedding where the bridegroom and the bride had hired a small aircraft just to fly them around as a gesture to flaunt their wealth. It was embarrassing to me because an average person can't afford to hire a small aircraft to fly himself around during his wedding day. An average person can't even afford to get decent food. Then you have South African entrepreneurs who have made it the through the BEE who eat sushi on the body of models during their birthday parties. I need to say this: there is nothing wrong about throwing a party that costs R700,000 as long as you can afford it. But in the process, you need to remember that there are many children whose lives can be altered completely with that kind of money. Eating sushi on the body of a female model by a man or eating sushi on the body of a male model by a female is anti-African and is practiced by both women and men in South Africa. Africa is indeed a continent of the extremist and extravagance. I believe that is one of the reasons why most of the African leaders who were involved in the liberation struggle of Africa are reluctant to vacate their political position when they look at Africa's youth, who are a replica of the US youth, who are obsessed with guns and video games. There is no way in the world where a person who is a heavy whiskey drinker can become the president of a country. Because if that happens that a heavy whisky drinker becomes the president of a country, it means that the country will be in chaos because the president of that country himself will be a living a chaotic lifestyle. Leadership position is not a popularity contest; one needs to be of sober mind and be dedicated to the course of leadership role as if it's a service to the lord. Africa is slowly but surely losing its moral and cultural compass because of the Western culture fused in an African culture. Simply put, times and seasons come and go, but a culture of a nation must remain. There is nothing that will be left behind for Africans to proud ourselves with if the very culture that our forefathers have left for us has been decimated and destroyed by the

Western culture, which changes over time and which is propelled and controlled by democracy. There is a great difference between culture and democracy. Democracy is what people vote for, while culture is what people were born into; you can't change culture completely, but you can only modify it to fit the times and the seasons and the people of that time. The West does not have a culture, but it has democracy, and the Western democracy is now decimating and dismantling the African culture, which dates back almost to the fifteenth century. Africans had values and ethics before the arrival of the Western education. Africans knew then before the arrival of the Dutch Law and the Roman Law that stealing someone's property was anti-African values and anti-Ubuntu. When the Westerners came into Africa, many of them suggest that Africans were worshipping gods and idols. The fact of the matter is this: African knew the Almighty God before the arrival of the Western missionaries and Western theologists. When an African man says to a woman "I love you," he literally means that I want to take you to my parents and introduce you to them so that they can know you for real. When all the necessary cultural processes have unfolded, the two will eventually get married and bear children. The West came into the picture with its own democracy of guns and video games and said, "A man can love another man, and they can even get married," but when Africans say this is not allowed in Africa, we Africans are branded as undemocratic and violating human rights. African culture has not been derived from the United Nations charter; it dated back as far as the fifteenth century even before the inception of the United Nations Security Council. There is no way then that the West and its UN can dictate what Africans should do and what they should not do. As Pres. Robert Mugabe said, "Keep your British and I will keep my Zimbabwean." On February 14 each year, every young man and young woman flocked into commercial stores to acquire cards and expensive gifts for their loved ones as a gesture and a token of love. The problem with this kind of practice is this: What happens to Mr. John who is unemployed and flat broke? What will happen to the masses who have just lost their jobs but who are still in love with the lifetime partners? The point I making is this: love is a matter of heart. We all know that most of these men who are buying gifts and Valentine's cards for their wives are professional cheaters who say one thing to their wives in public and do another thing when the lights are off. The West has put a price tag on love. In other words, if you love a person and you don't have money, rather get into debts by borrowing money from the bank and buy expensive roses and cards just to prove to your loved one that you love her. Most Africans are in serious trouble by trying to fit into the Western culture. Africans knew love and the meaning of love before the arrival of the West with their Valentine's card and expensive bag of roses. During the Valentine's Day in South Africa, almost all the Western commercial restaurants were jam-packed owing to the fact that the majority of people were eating out and some buying takeaways as a gesture of expressing their love to their loved ones. We all know that eating out is costly and the prices of food are forever increasing now and then. It's also true that the majority of Africans are also struggling with obesity because of eating out and drinking too much soft drink, which are full of caffeine. Valentine's Day, or the V-day as some call it in South Africa, is a commercialized day. The poor are meant to spend the very last money that they have to buy things like V-day cards instead of buying food that has vitamins and proteins. When you question this V-day, you are likely to be label uncivilized and backward. The same thing that happens during Valentine's Day is the same thing that is happening during a funeral. Death has been commercialized, and there is apartheid even in the cemeteries. There are cemeteries of the poor and the cemeteries of the rich, just like there are churches of the poor and churches of the rich. There are schools of the poor and the schools of the rich. The Western culture teaches the whole world to segregate and discriminate poor people. In the cemetery of the rich, there are tombstones, and in the cemetery of the poor, there are no tombstones. In the school of the poor, there are no libraries and sufficient books, while in the school of the rich, there is almost everything necessary for effective teaching and learning to take place. The school of the poor was meant for poor families and their poor children, while the school of the rich was meant for the rich families and their rich children so they can become rich businessmen and rich businesswomen and employ the poor children from the poor schools. The poor schools were meant for black people, and the rich schools were meant for white people—get it into your skull; even after the political liberation of many African countries, the status quo has not changed. One man said to me during Valentine's Day, "There is great change if you choose to see it, but there is no great change if you choose not to see it." Let me choose to see the great change, but the fact remains: there are cemeteries of the poor and there are cemeteries of the rich whether you choose to see the great change or not. It's true that there are schools of the poor and schools of the rich whether you choose to see it or not. One of my problems with most Africans is to choose to turn a blind eye on serious issues and pretend as if these serious issues are insignificant and irrelevant. The West is keeping Africa systematically poor for a reason. Africa must remain a beggar and technologically behind to the West, while the West and its allies continue to parade their stolen wealth from Africa through donation and foreign aid. My point of view about life now has changed dramatically, and every time I enter into a building, I will size up the building and look at the design, even the architectural design, though I am not an architect by profession, and I will eventually reach a conclusion. It's possible to see if a structure or building was built by the Anglo-Saxons for themselves during the colonial era or not. It's also possible to see if a building was built by the post-1994 government. If a building was built by the pre-1994 government, even if that is a church building, you will normally find statues of the Anglo-Saxon heroes and heroines. That will be a striking difference, though there could be many another distinctive distinguishing features like the architectural style; but in the end, I can see with an ease a building that was built by the pre-1994 government in the twinkling of an eye, in the case of South Africa. I have also seen the same thing when I got into Cecil John Rhodes's grave side in Zimbabwe Matopos National Park. Cecil John Rhodes's grave has been designed and built on a strong and permanent rock in a very unique way compared to most graves that I have seen when I was in Zimbabwe. It's easy to see the grave of the poor and the grave of the rich, as I have said it before, and it's not a matter of choosing not see the grave of the poor and choosing to see the grave of the rich. It's like spotting a rich neighborhood from the poor neighborhood; it's just that simple, and it has nothing to do with turning a blind eye on the poor neighborhood at the expense of the rich neighborhood. There is Sandton and there is Alexandra, and these two residential areas are not far away from each other in terms of distance, but they are far way from each other economically. They resemble the exact tale of two cities of Charles Dickens. It's possible to choose to see these areas on the same level, though we South African know it very well that these two areas are not on the same economic level. Sandton is the microcosm of the rich and the opulent, while Alexandra is the microcosm of the poor, angry, and unhappy community. I suggest that if you will decide to remain poor, choose to stay away from the rich folks rather than to be poor among the rich folks because they will make you quickly acknowledge that you are not like them but you are poor. When there is a funeral, it's easy to see whether the deceased who is going to be buried was poor or rich, and one of the yardsticks that is user-friendly to tell the difference between the poor and the rich deceased is the funeral procession and the cars that has formed part and parcel of the funeral procession. One of my friends who was a security guard passed on in 2013, and I joined the masses to go and lay him to rest. The funeral procession speaks volume about the financial position of a person. It's disrespectful and anti-African to discuss about the deceased, specifically if he was an elder not a child. The fact remains: you can tell the difference between the rich deceased and the poor deceased with your naked eyes by looking at the number of cars in the funeral procession. Funeral procession has become a big thing in Africa just like marriage. Africans will do everything in their power to make sure that they bury their loved one with dignity by preparing a decent burial for the deceased. Africans may rather go to the bank to get a loan just for the mere funeral in order to look rich outwardly even if the family is poor financially. The one-million-dollar question is this: Why would a person go all out to the point of borrowing money from the bank just to fund a mere funeral? The rationale about laying your loved one to rest is all about dignity and honor. To capture the essence of dignity and honor, the masses will source exorbitant funds from the financial institution just to fund a funeral and even borrow cars to decorate and glamorize the funeral. At the end of the funeral, reality kicks in because bills need to be paid thereafter. A colleague of mine one day showed me his wedding pictures, and I was happy for him, and as always, I asked him how much money he spent on his wedding. To my surprise, he couldn't disclose with certainty the exact amount of money that he had spent on his wedding simply because he was still paying back the loan for his wedding. Why would you borrow money from the bank to throw a wedding? The rationale behind this white wedding is to show off and to prove to the masses that you are not poor like everybody and you can afford a white wedding even if there is nothing white in that wedding. This "white weddings" are impoverishing the majority of the African youth. The reason I say that is this: when the wedding is over, the bridegroom and bride must go to the honeymoon, which is another Western concept to further impoverish African people even further. In the honeymoon, this couple is supposed to spend more money than the money that they have already spent before in putting together the wedding. The next thing you know, when the honeymoon is over, misery and pain will follow because of the heap of debts that this young family will be confronted with. The Westernization of our lives as Africans is costing us money and is costing us dearly. I know that a lot of people will probably say, why would you follow the West if you can't afford financially? No one wants to look poor and uncivilized, and everybody would like to look like the Anderson family and the Smith family who are staying in Sandton though in essence they are poor financially. In order to keep with the rest of the people and to avoid being talked about as the poor family in the neighborhood that could not even afford a decent funeral or the white wedding, people will go to the extreme just fit into the masses. I have written extensively about the poor and the poverty cycle in chapter 7, and I believe that one should read that chapter with clarity and understanding and make necessary financially adjustment if the need warrants it. A white wedding is not a white wedding in the true sense of the word in most African families. A white wedding is a wedding within weddings. Let me explain it in this way: a white wedding is an umbrella of two weddings. Within a white wedding, there is a white wedding and there is a traditional wedding. Bear in mind that the concept of a white wedding takes precedence and is ranked high compared to the traditional wedding. In other words, a couple will have to fork out money for both weddings, the traditional wedding, let me call it the African wedding, and the white wedding (Western wedding), and all the operating costs for both of these weddings are incurred for by this young couple who is still expected to fork out thousands of rands to buy a house and to even buy a car. It's possible that one of the parties in this couple might not be working and might not even have a job, and therefore if that is the case, it means that the working spouse will have to carry all the financial burden alone without the help of the other spouse. Africa is a stress-ridden continent because of trying to keep up with the West. Why follow the West if we can't afford and the West is not even our God? The West should not dictate the music we listen to and even the clothes we wear. The same thing that is happening on the ground level is what is happening on the political level. Our political leaders are living large, while the average people that they are serving are eating crumbs. The working spouse will have to enjoy enduring the pain that comes with servicing a heap of debts all by himself without the help of the other spouse. That is why in Africa there are "street kids." These are children of whom their mother is a street and their father is also a street. A Street cannot conceive a child and a street cannot raise a child. The reason streets are having children is that the average people cannot afford to raise children financially. When these young families cannot raise children financially, they send the children to "Mother Street." Children who were raised by the street are heartless and brutal in nature, and most of them turn to crime as the source of making money. Heroin and meth become a tranquilizer of the pain that they find themselves in during the middle of the night. Keeping up with the West costs money and it can even cost you your life. The African culture is simple and cheap, and the West has branded our culture as demonic and backward. We Africans therefore look up to the West for cultural inspiration, and the next thing you know, there is nothing forthcoming because there is no culture in the West; there is only democracy, which is not consistent and perennial. It's about how people feel about you in democracy. In the so-called democracy, you must convince people in order for them to vote for you. The marijuana addicts from Colorado will ask you this question: Will you allow us to smoke marijuana for free if we vote for you, Mr. President? Surely you won't shoot straightaway and say, "When I become president, I will allow you to smoke marijuana as you like." You will try to modify your answer to suit your crowd. The fact of the matter is this: you will eventually agree to their demands and legalize the smoking of marijuana even though deep down in the bottom of your heart you know you disagree with their demands. In democracy if you disagree with the masses, you are voted out, and you might find yourself jobless and loitering on the streets. To avoid the cold that is existing outside the political blanket, the majority of politicians just goes with the flow and allows everything that the majority of people want. I hope that these politicians are not telling their children the opposite of what they are allowing the masses to practice. The fact of the matter is this: what is morally and culturally wrong should be viewed wrong, and there is no need to philosophize and rationalize something that is wrong. In democracy anything can happen and everything is possible, and one hopes in the near future that our African leaders will advocate for laws and policies that are meant to unite the African people and that will take the African values and culture into consideration. The obsession about political power can also be a dangerous thing because it compels one to follow the masses even though you disagree with the masses. The fact that the majority of people approve a particular behavior that does not necessarily mean that what they approve is correct just because they are many. It's possible that the masses can approve something that is wrong in order to continue in their pervasive way of self-destruction. What the masses are looking for is the legal affirmation that what they are doing is right provided that the state legalizes their behavior and they will vote for you. Most of the leaders of the world, because of the warmth and the heavy perks that come with holding a public office, would rather swallow their pride and even denounce what they believe to be right and follow the crowd just to remain in office and use the public funds as they want. But deep down in their hearts, when they are with their families and children, I believe that they do sometimes tell their children that marijuana is not good for a young person who aspires to continue with his studies and become an economically active member of the society not a beggar on the streets begging money and food from everyone who is passing. The greatest danger that is currently facing Africa is the erosion of Africa's identity. The identity of a nation is the microcosm of the culture, value, and philosophy. There is no African history without African identity because history speaks directly to the African identity, which is slowly but surely being eroded by the democracy of the West, which is the Western culture. The most probable conclusion that an average person is likely to draw is this: Africans have been blaming the West for a very long time even after Africa has gained its own political independence. The fact of the matter is this: Africa has never been independent from the West, and even what the majority of people call political independence was not sufficient enough to allow Africa to be able to take off from the ground economically. Africa's political independence has been a mess since the beginning. There is no way you can claim to be politically free if you are not economically free unless otherwise you are schizophrenic. Africa is free politically, but Africa is not economically free, since until this day most of the African countries are heavily reliant on foreign aid. I have come to think of foreign aid as social grant in this way; money that is given to you without you having have to work for it is dangerous, and the reason I say that is that it does not allow you to grow intellectually and even to apply your skills and be able to make a living out of your own skills. The fact of the matter is this: African countries that are the greatest recipients of foreign aid are not growing economically. And instead of these African countries to grow economically and explore variety of economic avenues in their economies, they normally fold their hands and close their eyes and continue to expect the manna from the Western heaven to fall on their lap without putting any concerted effort at work. The West then gets an opportunity to further exploit the African mineral deposits because the very people who are living in Africa can't utilize the mineral deposits of their land. I think we Africans must blame ourselves about some of the things that are happening in the African continent. If one takes a closer look at the number of the foreign banks that are in Africa, it's easy to see why the majority of African governments are still in financial trouble even today. I know a situation where a government institution will run out of money and will request funds from a Western bank for the overdrafts in order to be able to pay their operating expenses like wages to their employees. It simply tells you that the majority of African economies are heavily reliant on the West. The West now controls Africa through its financial grip. We all know that there is nothing that you can do without financial muscle; you can speak politics all you want, but at the end of the day, you are supposed to eat and drink water, and without financial muscle, all your aspirations of seeing your stomach full of chicken and rice are not going to materialize. The point is financial muscles are the cornerstone of any economy, and the lack of financial muscles thereof can be the biggest impediment for any economy to expand and to grow to the level where it can even create sustainable employment opportunities for its people. Any superpower country with the biggest economy in the world could not just take off without some failure and even some form of foreign investment by another country in its economy. Simply put, there cannot be a strong African country economically without foreign investment into these African countries. Foreign investment has tremendous effect on the economy of any country. The dearth of foreign investment can have devastating consequences even on the power of currency of any country in the world. Part of Zimbabwe's problem is the dearth of the foreign investment into its economy. There is no way in the whole world you would incorporate a company as an investor and take it to the country like Zimbabwe only to be told by the government that you need to give 51 percent of your shareholding to the government as a way of compliance with the government policy. Whoever came up with this draconian Zimbabwe's economic policy of indigenization and for private companies to give away 51 percent of their shareholding to Zimbabwe's government has destroyed the economy of Zimbabwe deliberately and systematically. Foreign companies and foreign investors are looking for tax breaks and flexible labor laws, and not political quagmire and economic laws that are not thought through thoroughly. The main reason Zimbabwe's economy is still likely to take some serious knock even in the near future is the political dissatisfaction in the country, which is emanating from the way the July 31, 2013, national elections were conducted and the outcome thereof. It's important that the national result should be reflective of the people's aspirations and dreams. What I do know for a fact through visiting Zimbabwe and talking to different people is that people want jobs and they want to continue with their lives. Average people are not interested in domestic politics whether the president of the country is Morgan Tsvangirai or Robert Mugabe; the only thing that the average person is worried about is food. What is the use of having a president who cannot put food on your table? Zimbabwe's politicians are killing their people with hunger deliberately because of the obsession with political power and political greed. The Dark Age has come and gone, but some African leaders are still holding grudges against the West about political mistreatments they received at the hands of the Western powers. It's true that time is everything and political wounds sometimes take time to heal. It's easy to break someone's heart within a short space of time, but mending that heart takes a long period of time. In case you are in love with someone, it will take you a long period of time to gain the trust of that person should you break the heart of that person once. Even after you have repented, you are not likely to receive the forgiveness of sins soon and gain the old trust and the old love back. I believe that the main reason and the main cause for divorce is the trust that is lost, and that can never be revived and resuscitated again to its former glory. I know that experts in this field will probably cite variety of reasons like money, sex, and communication. But the fact of the matter is this: once trust is broken, it's deadly difficult to win it back. That is what exactly happened during the colonization of Africa by the West. Even today majority of African people don't trust the West; even if the West can come into the negotiation table in good faith to negotiate any business deal, there will be suspicions already in the room. The main reason above all that makes most of the African people not trust the West is what is happening in the Middle East and the Western intervention in the Middle East crisis. How can the West support the opposing forces militarily and financially to fight against the democratically elected government by the masses? If citizens of any country are no longer happy with their government leaders, they need to vote out their government leaders out of office. It's possible that any government leader of any country, once they taste the state power, will not relinquish state power with ease without putting up a formidable fight. In a situation like that, then the AU or OAU and SADC are the credible bodies that can solve Africa's problems, and in the case of Syria, the EU or the Arab League can come very handy to solve the Syrian crisis, and if these above-mentioned credible bodies fail then the United Nations Security Council should be the last resort. I wonder sometimes who has the final say between the UN and the G7 countries about a political situation in any country that is in an endless war like Syria and CAR. It seems as if the UN will have a final say provided that the country in question is not rich in mineral deposits like gold, diamonds, and uranium. But if the country in question is rich in mineral resources like gold, diamond, and uranium, the West and its allies will just invade the country and turn the tables around and assemble an interim government structure and live their forces on the ground to monitor the situation and then come back to strike oil deals with the new government that is in place, just like the West did in the case of Iraq—kill Saddam Hussein then put the soldiers on the ground and then wait for frustrations and anger to subside then you can withdraw the troops completely from the ground and lift off the economic sanctions and open the economy up again. The day Pres. Robert Mugabe of Zimbabwe will be out of the Zimbabwean picture, I can bet my last dollar that there will be a political transformation in Zimbabwe. Everybody is banking on Pres. Robert Mugabe's health. That is why when the reports began to image that Pres. Robert Mugabe's health was drastically deteriorating, many people around the world who are anti-ZANU-PF were already begin to celebrate that at least there is now light at the end of the tunnel. There is a collective belief around the world that the Zimbabwean economic crisis as well as the political crisis that is hampering the foreign investment to flow into the economy is the result of a single person and should that person be out of the political equation, then the current political and economic problems will be solved diametrically. Let's just say there is some bit of truth in that statement. But we must also remember that the problems of Zimbabwe date back as far as to the Ian Smith era. Prior to the signing of the Lancaster House Agreement, there were economic sanctions that were in place, and they were imposed by the Great Britain because of Ian Smith's UDI. However, those economic sanctions were not severe to the extreme, since apartheid South Africa was very helpful in ensuring that the Ian Smith regime stayed afloat financially for some couple of years. The whole idea of supporting Ian Smith by the apartheid South African government was to ensure its draconian domination among black people and keep its political control of South Africa, which was also not threatened by the flames of fire due to the SOWETO uprising of June 16, 1976. It was abundantly clear to both the apartheid South African government and the Ian Smith government that the African nationalists, through the support of Russia and China, were going to wage one of the unprecedented political wars in the history of the sub-Saharan African region. I need to underscore a very valid point here and not to suggest that all the other points that I have mentioned were not valid. One of the things that I have learned in this drama of life is this: it's highly impossible to see your own personal mistakes. In other words, for you to see your own personal mistakes, you need to get somebody who can be brutally be honest with yourself and give you a fair and an honest view about yourself. I normally recommend political leaders who decide to take a decision to step down and leave politics to the young and energetic. If Muammar Gaddafi of Libya did take a decision to step down, probably he was going to be alive today. The former Liberian president Charles Taylor heeded the call and decided to step down; at least he is still alive today, though in prison, but at least he is alive. Remember what I have said: the West can't seek the United Nations' approval when they want to topple and dethrone a political leader who is anti-Western foreign policies. It does not make business and political sense to topple and dethrone a leader of a country that is in poverty. I think that is the main reason the West left Zimbabwe to "Uncle Bob." The West knew what they were doing when they imposed economic sanctions to the Zimbabwean government. The West knew very well that at the end of the day, the majority of the world's population would not blame the West, though it's the source of most Zimbabwean problems, but the whole world will eventually blame the regime of Pres. Robert Mugabe. When the masses are hungry, they become angry, and they will want to direct their frustrations and resentments toward another living human being. The economy of Zimbabwe is screaming, and that is exactly what the West had in mind when they concocted what Pres. Robert Mugabe of Zimbabwe calls "illegal economic sanctions." Most people from the West know nothing about the seriousness of economic sanctions and the ramifications of economic sanctions thereof; they read about economic sanctions in the *Oxford Advance Dictionary,* but in reality they have never seen and felt the pain of economic sanctions. Economic sanctions are real, and they are biting like a dog. I have heard people saying, if the economic sanctions that have been imposed by the West to the Zimbabwean government are illegal, why can't Pres. Robert Mugabe approach the International Criminal Court and press charges against the West for imposing illegal economic sanctions against the Zimbabwe government? As long as African leaders continue to dance to the political music of the West, they will be free from economic sanctions.

Chapter 10

THE WAR AGAINST ILLEGAL SUBSTANCE

The war against illegal substance is sometimes called the chemical warfare in South Africa. I will not concentrate on the impact and the role that these illegal substances play in Africa and the whole world. First thing first—there would not be a market for illegal substances if there were no clients for these illegal substances. The fact that there is market also means that there are people who are the final consumers for these illegal substances. Since there are final consumers, it also means that there is profit that is being made through smuggling and shipping illegal substances all over the world. Since we now know that there are final consumers, it also means that there are producers for these illegal substances. I have taken a considerable amount of time trying by all means to explain the main causes of poverty and the myth that a lot of people have about poverty. People believe that there is no need for all of us to be rich because there won't be enough roads to be driven in if all of us are rich and are driving our own cars. More often than not people who are advocating for poverty are people who failed to make it either in the business world or in the world of the academia. There is neither a challenge nor a goal to be achieved by people who are poor. The only thing that the majority of poor people think about is just a mere meal. Life is bigger than just a mere meal. I need to myself clear: there is a symbiotic relationship between poverty and illegal substance abuse. The supply of illegal substances is on a rampage in Africa and is claiming innocent lives of young people like never before. Africa is winning the war against the scourge of HIV/AIDS, but Africa is losing the war against illegal substance abuse. Poverty is the main source of illegal substance abuse. The main driver behind poverty is unemployment. If the leaders of the world can dismantle unemployment, therefore they can eliminate poverty, but unemployment and poverty alone are not the only causes of illegal substance abuse; this problem is much wider and deeper than just restricting it to unemployment and poverty. Any society that lacks strong and robust family values is likely to produce members of the community that are irresponsible and uncaring about the future. The more people are uncaring and irresponsible about the future more frequent than not will spend the entire of their lives seeking temporal pleasure, and that is what these illegal substances can provide—the short burst of excitement and the short burst of ecstasy that worsen the economic lives of its user afterward. Crime is another crucial factor that comes into play in the community that is riddled with heavy illegal substances supply. Unfortunately in South Africa and elsewhere in the world, communities that were poor already because of lack of basic services are the ones that are excessive users of illegal substances. The next factor that will come into the picture will be prostitution, which is deadly difficult to control and monitor, since it involves sex in between, which is sometimes called "the drug of choice." Imagine a situation where all these role players are involved, and the next thing you know, guns and women and innocent bodies lying in the pool of blood just because of drugs, sex, guns, and prostitution. Communities that are riddled with crime more frequent than not attribute the high rate of crime only to one factor: unemployment only. You will be making a big mistake if you only attribute the high rate of crime to unemployment and poverty only. The problem of substance abuse is bigger than that. Dysfunctional families are another crucial factor that is at play in most communities that are riddled with illegal substance abuse. There is a striking factor one needs to pay an undivided attention to. Most of these areas where there is a problem of illegal substance abuse are the very same areas where there were a lot political activities during the liberation struggle. Simply put, when the liberation struggle ended, the drug supply ensued thereafter. It's possible to draw a conclusion then that the majority of these areas, which were considered to be the hotbed for political activities, are very same areas that have become the hotbed for drug supply and drug abuse also. There is no nation in the world that can be able to perform mighty exploits if its youth that was supposed to perform these mighty exploits are drug addicts and are dying due to cocaine. There has never been a harsher sentence imposed by the courts to the convicted drugs smugglers to deter young aspiring drug smugglers to stop in their destructive path. It's possible that one of the contributing factors in this problem of illegal drug supply is unemployment. Whenever the world leaders want to solve the problem of unemployment, they need to solve first the old elephant in the room, which is inequality and lack of education. The biggest hindrance in the creation of sustainable employment is not only the lack of foreign investment only but also the lack of creativity and ingenuity. Students spend almost twelve years in class and are taught to study hard and acquire more qualifications in order to get high-paying jobs. Even though there are no high-paying jobs anymore because the world is in the financial crisis, we still teach students the same thing over and over again. As long as any economy of any country cannot produce new entrepreneurs who will dare to take an opportunity to create new jobs for the school leavers, then the school leavers are in trouble. There is a point in time where qualifications mean absolutely nothing, specifically in the economies that are not having new entrepreneurs. It's important to go to school and acquire good grades and get senior degrees from the university, but that is not enough in today's world of economic uncertainty. Education alone is no longer the key to success. That is what we were told when we were growing up—that education is the key to success, but we all learned that through the economic crisis that has engulfed most countries, that assertion was far-fetched and flimsy. Part of the Arab Spring was not merely political dissatisfaction but also economic dissatisfaction. What do you tell a young bright man who has just completed his degree in the university if there are no jobs in the market? Do you tell him to wait a little bit longer and things will get better in the near future? Most of the graduates think that they are entitled to a sustainable employment opportunity just because they have relevant qualifications from the university. The mind-set of entitlement is also entrenched in the minds of the poor. The same mind-set is also deeply entrenched in the minds of the university graduates. At least just for one moment the poor and the university graduates have something in common—entitlement mentality. The poor are entitled to social grants because they are not working and they don't have even degrees that can enable them to be employed, while the university graduates think that by the mere fact of having degrees from the prestigious university therefore it's a lottery ticket to a high-paying job with fat fringe benefits. The old ideas of good education and good salary are over. The world has changed dramatically from the dark ages to the information age. The arrival of technology has rendered many people who were once useful useless. There is more money that is made online right now than ever before, therefore the arrival of technology makes majority of people who are semiskilled redundant because there is no market for their skills. Simply put, people who are not highly skilled are not required anymore by the economy because there are no longer sufficient jobs for these kinds of people who are not highly skilled. The mass production of goods today takes place via the computer, therefore people who are not equipped and skilled enough are not able to function. Labor-intensive employment is very scarce to find, and as a result, there will be high unemployment rate in the near future because of technology that has replaced physical labor with the mouse. Though it's true that there are drugs of the rich, like cocaine and meth, and the drugs of the poor, but on average drugs are the food for the poor. The poor prostitute themselves to get money to buy drugs, and they do drugs because they prostitute themselves. There are many singers and soccer players and even men of the white cloth who died because of excessive use of drugs. The main problem with people who are using drugs is living in denial. Most athletes use drugs to boost their stamina and energy, while some use drugs as a way of life. There is no way where one can grind the supply of drugs to a screeching halt unless otherwise we know for sure where these drugs originate from and who the users are. Even pointing fingers at people would not help the scourge of drugs supply. For me to knit together a perfect picture about the movement of drugs, I need to establish the main causes why the majority of young stars and even old people use these illegal substances. While certain drugs are classified as illegal, others are classified as legal. Before I can get too deep into this subject of illegal drugs supply, let me just make mention of this crucial point. There are many social ills and financial pressure in the African society right now unlike before, and many people will do anything to numb their pains by at least taking something that will make them forget about the real situation that they are facing on a daily basis. Simply put, drugs are the shortest solution to a long-term problem. Economic problems are the major problem that the majority of people are faced with, and as the result of these economic problems, many people feel left out in the cold, and these people will eventually do anything necessary to numb their pain, like taking illegal substances. Economic crisis not only left many people unemployed but also left many people in prison during the economic crisis, even though I cannot say with certainty that the economic crisis is over, but understand the fact that economic crisis became very severe during 2007/8. From 2008 until 2014, the world economy has recovered. There were many TV shows during the economic crisis that was meant to help people who were in debt who couldn't service their debts anymore. I think that during the economic crisis, the very same financial experts who were debt counselors were also in debt themselves while providing financial counseling to the masses who were also in financial debt. The financial counselors who were in financial debt were providing financial counseling to people who were also in financial debt, and the blind was now leading the blind. I know of a lot of people who will tell almost everyone they know that they are rich financially without providing financial statements to support their claims. You are financially rich to the point that you can prove it with a financial statement, and you are not financially rich until the point of proving it with financial statements. During the financial crisis in 2007/8, the price of petroleum products was soaring rapidly in the twinkling of an eye. I think that the financial crisis is to blame for most of the Zimbabweans' problems. Though Zimbabwe was under economic sanctions already from the European Union and the West, the Zimbabwe economic sanctions would not have had a long-lasting impact had it not been for the economic crisis that the whole world was in. Imagine a situation where a country like Zimbabwe is under wave of economic sanctions, and to top it up, there is another wave of financial crisis that is attacking the very same countries that were supposed to rescue the sanctioned country from the economic sanctions that are already making the economy of Zimbabwe scream. During the financial crisis, the economy of Zimbabwe indeed screamed, and it was screaming very loudly to the point that you could tell what was happening in the economy of Zimbabwe while you were in South Africa. At that point in my mind, I never, not even in a thousand years, thought that I will visit a country like Zimbabwe where poverty is reigning supreme. The family disintegration that is permeating the whole world partly is because of the financial crisis. People who had made vows to love each other for better or for worse during the financial crisis were reneging from their vows that they have made before the God of heaven and the body of Christ, which is the church—because making a vow is damn too easy, but honoring your vow is another different story altogether. The divorce rate in South Africa shot up astronomically during the financial crisis of 2007/8. Those who could not divorce because of financial reasons were hiring a hit man to eliminate their spouse in order for the surviving spouse to inherit all the possessions without any opposing party. There are many married men who were eliminated during the financial crisis by their loving wives just because they could not bring money home anymore, and they were also a stumbling block to the new love that these very wives had found. There were fewer street kids in South Africa prior to the financial crisis than there are right now. Though I need to say that South Africa is a better place to live in now than before 1994, as Pres. Jacob Zuma said in his state of the nation address on February 13, 2014, there is still a mammoth task that lies ahead to be solved by South Africa. There were numerous complaints in 2013 by the residents of the El Dorado Park, south of Johannesburg. It was easy to acquire drugs in El Dorado Park like never before, and the youth was the most targeted by these drug lords. The complaints from the El Dorado Park community were so severe to the point that they even thought that the SAPS (South African Police Service) had deserted them. The call was made at the right time, and the president of South Africa Jacob Zuma descended to El Dorado Park. Let me make this point: all along there has been belief about the president of South Africa Jacob Zuma that he was accessible, but that statement had not yet been put into the test. The El Dorado Park community was the first in the line of many communities that have probably wished to be visited by the president of South Africa Jacob Zuma. The president of South Africa Jacob Zuma did visit the El Dorado Park community, proving the naysayers wrong that indeed he is an accessible person. Drugs in El Dorado Park were not only the only food that was available on the table, but it was very easy to get drugs in El Dorado Park. I remember seeing a picture in a newspaper where a teacher asked his students to complete a puzzle in words on the board in class. I remember vividly one student wrote "tik, cocaine, and whoonga." All the above words are the different names for drugs. Simply put, children from the El Dorado Park knew drug names with their hearts, and they could even spell the names of these drugs with their eyes closed. After the visit of the president of South Africa Jacob Zuma in El Dorado Park, there were visits by the police ransacking and searching pupils at schools.[1] The operation was successful, but the residents of El Dorado Park began complaining after the operation has ceased. Poppy Louw writes:

> *Things went well following the president's visit . . . but only for about three months. They soon went back to how they were. If anything, they may have gotten worse, said Dereleen James, one of the mothers who told Zuma of their experiences of living with drug-addicted children.*[2]

There are many parents who are paying less attention to this serious issue of drugs. These parents are normally concerned when the drug addiction has already done the work to the child, meaning that the child is already past beyond rehabilitation stage and the only thing that can stop that child to take drugs anymore is the coffin. An average man thinks that buying grocery and paying bills for his family is what is required from the man to gain respect from the wife and children. The responsibilities of being a parent are not only restricted to providing for the family financially only but also include monitoring the child until he is now a fully grown human being who can get a job and work and provide for a family of his own. In the process of raising this child, there will be serious storms that the child and the parent need to hold hands and walk together in thorns and thistles. Drugs-infested communities produce drug addicts and people who are dependent on government for their lives. There is nothing that one can expect from a drug-infested community except crimes and more crimes and guns. I have often asked myself many times this question: How come the majority of prisons all over the world are full to the rafter with black inmates than white inmates—even in countries where black people are few, but black people will be the one dominating in numbers in prison? I have an answer for that question: since the colonization of Africa until this day, Africa is still a violent continent, and this situation is attributed to the fact that the majority of African countries have been under the Western oppression for quite a long period of time, and God knows why it was so. In order for one to understand crime, poverty, and unemployment, one needs to understand the role and place of drugs in a society. Illegal substances can't just mushroom in a middle-class community and even rich community for that matter. These illegal substances find its way through communities that are already in the bottomless pit of poverty and attempt to close that vacuum that has been created by poverty and high rate of unemployment. There are drugs of the rich and there are drugs of the poor; even if that is still the case, however, there are very few rich people who are drug addicts compared to poor people who are drug addicts. Please, I know that there are rich and famous people who died because of drug abuse, but the point that I attempting to drive home here is this: the number of poor people who are drug addicts is higher than the number of rich people who are drug addicts. Rich people who are having a drug addiction problem can afford to go to the rehabilitation centers, while the poor people who are drug addicts cannot even afford a decent meal, let alone approach the drug rehabilitation center for help. Africa was once a continent of peace and tranquility, and even the concept of drugs and illegal substances did not even exist at that time. Globalization means that the whole world is connected through the single unbreakable umbilical cord. It therefore means that countries had to begin to trade legally and sometimes even illegally. Wherever there is legal trade in the world, there would be also illegal trade. The rhino poaching bears testament to that effect. In other words, there will be illegal trade coupled with contraband goods even in the near future as long as countries continue to trade legally and large companies decide to invest globally. Wherever in the world there are endless economic activities and companies are establishing new branches, there will be legal trade and there will be another economy called the underground economy. Let me give you a perfect picture. We all know by now that the government of Pres. Robert Mugabe has been screwed up by the imposition of economic sanctions by the West. And as a result of the economic collapse, there was massive exodus of people from Zimbabwe to South Africa in search for a better life and better working conditions. In other words, since there was this movement of people in high number, not only did it leave the economy of Zimbabwe weak and crippled, but it also means that there are many homes who don't have people to live in them in Zimbabwe. This picture creates another problem for the South African government because it meant that the South African government had to accommodate a considerable amount of people of whom some don't have requisite scarce skills that are required by the South African economy to grow. The net effect of accommodating a considerable amount of both legal and illegal migrants who lack requisite skills to grow the economy is this: these very people who now call South Africa home need to be fed, and they are likely to make love to each other and increase the population of South Africa, which is already very high. The next thing you know, some of them will be naturalized citizens by hook or by crook. Those who can't find jobs due to lack of requisite skills by the economy of South Africa will be forced to commit crimes in order to survive. The drug industry is a very lucrative industry, and it involves traveling all over the world, but the price that people pay for smuggling drugs is higher than the benefits that are made when you reach your destination with the consignment that is full of drugs. There are South African families today that are still reeling from the loss of their children through the smuggling of drugs. There are South African families whose children are kept abroad serving their prison sentences because of the crimes that they have committed in those countries. Thailand laws when it comes to smuggling drugs are simple and straightforward; when a suspect is convicted of a crime of smuggling drugs into Thailand or out of Thailand, that convict will be hanged by the Thailand government, period. There are some South Africans who have been hanged in Thailand because of trying to make quick bucks through smuggling drugs into Thailand. Africa is losing the war against illegal substances abuse, though Africa has made measured strides and measured advancement on other areas; but on the war against the distribution of illegal substances, Africa has not made significant advances. Writing a book is art at its best. One feels like he is talking to the whole universe through writing, and the universe somewhat will respond back to me in a positive way. There is no better present that one can be given than to be given an opportunity to be listened to by the whole world when you are talking. It's true that there are many people who have something to say about the economic problems that are going on in the world right now including the endless war that is going on in the Middle East. When you take stock of what the majority of people are going through on the planet, if all of us were to be given an opportunity by God to express our disappointments and the unfairness that we see happening in the world, I doubt that there would be even enough podium and platform to accommodate us all to express our grievances by the heavens. I have also learned that the most painful thing in the world is when your loved one is very sick because you become sick too. When a close member of your family is very sick, the moment you hear that, it makes you sick too simply because this close member of your family not only is a member of your family but is also your best friend. A best friend is somebody who will never turn her back on you, and a close friend is somebody who loves you even if you failed in life to achieve what the majority of people might see as significant achievements. Your best friend will always will be there for you. When I am praying, I get a sense that somewhere, somehow God is listening to my prayers, and not only does he listen to my prayers but also he answers my prayers in a positive way that not only a natural person can understand but also a spiritual person can understand. There are many good things that God has done for me, and there are many beautiful things that he will still do for me. Why could I have thought about writing a book, maybe let's say, in 2009? In 2009 the whole world was going through the global financial crisis, and probably there could have never been a perfect opportunity to write a book then than right now. But God said many times in his holy scriptures, Jeremiah 29 verse 11, that his plans are not like our plans. Many people in church normally read that scripture, and they think that they understand what it means. The fact of the matter is this: your plan of getting married and having your family are not like God's plan. It also means that the time that you have set for yourself to achieve certain things in your life might not be in God's plan, and therefore it makes your own plan useless and insignificant. Very few people take time to do an introspection and ask God about the plan about their lives, and all what the majority of people do is to follow the crowd. The fact that your siblings and your friends are registering a certain degree, that does not necessarily mean that you have to follow them and do the same. I have often asked myself this question: Why would a normal person spend a considerable amount of years in the university studying art and music? The main reason very few people don't study music and art is that simply they believe that there is no financial guarantees in music; no wonder the majority of people are studying degrees that are perceived to be a ticket to financial heaven. There is nothing until this point in time on this planet that is so healing and refreshing to me like when I listen to good music. When I was in Zimbabwe in one of the Nando's restaurants, I felt very relaxed and refreshed when I listened to the music that they were playing inside to the point that I even forgot that I was in Zimbabwe. The same thing happened when I was on my way to Bulawayo from Harare. I lay relaxed inside my seat in the bus watching the videos that they are playing on the monitor of the bus, which are soothing to the soul, and the next thing you know, I was in Bulawayo without even feeling the distance of the trip. Music is healing to my bones and medication to all my diseases. The same feeling that I get when I listen to soothing music is the same feeling that I get when I see the face of my mother. She just lights up my world, and I begin to feel that I have a person who loves me indeed on this planet. My relationship with my mother will live forever, just like God will live forever. Our relationship is not contractual but eternal. Our relationship is not based on material things, but it's based on spiritual things. There are very few people on this planet who love you because of who you are, but the majority of people who love you love you based on what you have, not because of who you are. In other words, you are likely to hear a woman say, "I am looking for a man who is rich." First of all, I don't know any man who is looking for a woman who is poor and broke. All men wish that they can marry a woman who has money in order for her to cover some of the bills in the house. The truth of the matter is there are very few women who are very rich and can agree to marry a man who has the mentality of being taken care of by them. Let me make my point simple and straightforward:

there is no man who is looking for a housewife, and there is no woman who is looking for a poor man too. Bear in mind the following that until this point I have never mentioned anything in relation to love. Why look for a rich woman if you are a man, and look for rich man if you are a woman without looking for love first? It seems as if in the twenty-first century the concept of love has diminished completely. Before you start looking for a rich man, make sure that you are rich if you're a woman, and before looking for a rich woman if you are a man, make sure that you are rich yourself. Since the whole world is still recovering from the global financial crisis of 2007/8, I wonder how many people can consider themselves to be out of the woods financially yet. The majority of countries in Asia are reeling from the financial crisis, and that is why there are endless protests that are going on all over the world as a result of the global financial crisis. Perhaps part of the unhappiness of a human being is caused by the lack of unrealistic goals that we are setting as a people. There are certain goals that can't be achieved in the absence of the other. Whenever you are setting goals, you need to take into consideration the time factor. Time is everything, and if you lose track of time, you might find yourself educated but miserable without any life partner. My friend Sunny boy used to say to me, "Time wasted can never be regained." It's important to master the movement of time. Drugs are the greatest time waster and dream buster. There is nothing so painful like finding out five years later that you have lost a considerable amount of time going up and down, but when you look at the results, you have achieved absolutely nothing. One of the greatest hindrances of success is lying to yourself and following the crowd. Year in and year out, there are many people who normally make New Year resolutions that they can't continue with until the end of the year. Many universities make a lot of money through what is called "university dropouts." A university dropout is somebody who starts a degree with oomph and energy in the beginning of the year, but before the year is over, this person has already changed his mind about the very same degree that he is registered for. What will normally happen is this: not only is this person going to lose the money that he has already paid to the university, but he will also lose time. There is no expensive commodity in the whole world like time. There are many people out there who feel that they have wasted time to the point that there is no turning back the clock of time. The fact of the matter is this: it does not matter what happened in the past—what matters most is what lies ahead. One of my colleagues is against this idea that life begins at forty, and he went on to say that people who normally say life begins at forty are people who have failed in life and they are trying to console themselves. Let me just say there is a bit of truth in that statement. But whining and complaining about what you should have done and did not do won't help the situation but will worsen the excruciating pain that is there already. Life does begin at forty if you are not forty years old right now. The fact of the matter is this: we have wasted time, all of us, in one way or the other. There is no living person who can profess with certainty and say that he has not wasted time in his life in one way or the other. We all have wasted our precious moments to shine sometimes in life. Since we all wasted some of our time, should we then keep on focusing our energy and effort on time wasted already rather than focusing on the time that is still on our hands? I suggest that we need to focus on time that is in our hands rather than time that has been lost already and we can't buy back. We can't change the past, but surely there is something that we can do about the present to at least change the future. The same is true even about what happened in Zimbabwe in the year 2000. There is no reason to mourn and cry about the farm invasion. What happened has happened, and the best thing that we Africans need to do right now is to focus on the future rather than to lament about what happened in the past. Poppy Louw writes:

> *"The English made a lot of money back then, a lot of money," he says with a sigh. "I think it is fair for we to get a bit of compensation for what all our people been through." A coalition of fourteen Caribbean states, including Jamaica, agrees with Thompson and is now mounting the first united campaign for reparations from Britain over its role in the Atlantic slave trade.*[3]

Jamaica was a colony of Britain, just like South Africa and Zimbabwe. The Western wealth that has been invested in the European Central Bank, International Monetary Fund, and World Bank was not earned by the West through hard work. It's wealth that was made by the West through the colonial era. The West made a considerable amount of wealth through the colonization of African and other parts of the world to the point that until this day, the West has not started tapping much on that original amount that was invested in these financial institutions like IMF, World Bank, and European Central Bank. It's possible that the majority of people will probably say there is no evidence to support the assertion that the West stole Africa's wealth. There is voluminous amount of historical evidence that pinpoints straight to the West and its oppressive and dictatorship style in Africa that indeed the West profited immensely in Africa through the colonization of Africa and its oppressive rules during the colonial era. The biggest problem with proving the crime that happened centuries ago it's the reliable historical evidence that is plausible to the court for the court to reach a conclusion. It's extremely painful and difficult for anybody who had been robbed before to see the robber continuing to walk free as if nothing wrong happened. It's even more painful and difficult to see the very same person who robbed you becoming the champion of human rights and supporting the idea of prosecuting people who have committed crimes against humanity. I am not using the West as a scapegoat to most African problems that are reaping the continent of Africa apart. It's true that some of the Western countries have come to the fore and admitted the inhuman atrocities that they have committed in the African continent with impunity. It's still the very same Western countries that even today are enjoying the very democracy that we are talking about in Africa. Most Africans until this day have not yet enjoyed the dividends of democracy and freedom. It's still the Western settlers even today who are enjoying the very same democracy and freedom that have been fought for very hard by the African nationalists. Simply put, most African people who were poor during the colonial era are likely to say even today that they are still poor even in this democratic dispensation. The majority of African people after the liberation of Africa have fallen back again into the ditch of poverty and unemployment simply because they are not politically connected. The West is now killing the African youth with illegal substances like cocaine and tik. The more the African youth is in drugs, the more economic and political problems we are going to have in Africa even in the near future. Africa is winning the war against HIV/AIDS but it is losing the war against illegal trafficking of illegal substances. There has never been a point in African history where the majority of young people were drinking alcohol like they do now. In fact it has been said by many African scholars that Africans love Heineken. Unfortunately, this Heineken is not even manufactured in the African continent by African companies, but it's manufactured for Africans by the Western companies who are based in Africa for African children to continue to live life without a purpose and direction. That is why there are few black scientists in Africa owing to the fact that the majority of the African youth who were supposed to be exploring these areas of study are either in the rehabilitation centers because of drug addictions or in the streets hustling and contemplating about the next fix. Mail & Guardian reports:

> *A UNODC map shows that heroin and cocaine also filter across Tanzania's border into Mozambique, Malawi, and Zambia. Some of it shifted onward to the United States and the Western Europe. The 2012 UNODC report said smaller quantities of heroin are moved by air, making use of both cargo and courier services.*[4]

There were less illegal drugs in Africa during the colonial era simply because there were no pubs and clubs; people were listening to music through the radio and hi-fi. At that time families would not even allow their children to go out and play at night. The family rules and culture were still intact. The arrival of democracy in Africa was ushered by not only family disintegration but also the abolishment of those African rules and values that were protecting children against impending danger. Democracy and freedom granted children many rights. Let me give you an example: a child is allowed to drop out of school without accounting to the government and even to the parents. In other words, a child has a right to do what he wants irrespective of the repercussions and the consequences of the action that the child might be taking. Family values and rules have been set aside in pursuit of the Western democracy. African democracy is patterned after the Western democracy. Unfortunately, there are no culture and values in the West. Children are allowed to own guns when they reach the age of eighteen years old in the West. First of all, why would a child own a gun at the age of eighteen instead of focusing on his studies and schoolwork. The arrival of what is called "house music" became the game changer among the African youth. Pubs and clubs began to spread like octopus in Africa, and in every corner and every street in big cities there is a pub or a club; there are even gay clubs and gay pubs. There are many of these clubs even in Pretoria, the capital city of South Africa. Pretoria is also called "the Heart of South Africa." I have seen the same thing unfolding before my very eyes when I was in Bulawayo, Zimbabwe. There was a tragic incident that happened in North West province in December 2012, where the youth of North West died in one of the pubs because of stampede. It became an eye-opener to most South Africans that the majority of our youth interpret enjoyment in a different and unique way. Enjoyment and fun do not necessarily mean that you should be in a place where there is loud music and big speakers that are toxic to your eardrums and even to your brains. You can also have fun and enjoyment even if you are seated at home with your parents while drinking soft drinks. Enjoyment and fun do not mean jumping up and down in the presence of loud music and being in the midst of cigarette smoke. Through these pubs and clubs, cocaine and heroin are found easily, since almost everybody wants to remain happy and stay in cloud nine for a long period of time. Alcohol and cigarette alone can't offer the same ecstasy and euphoria that these illegal substances are able to offer. No wonder in Africa there is a high rate of HIV/AIDS infection. The main reason behind this high rate HIV/AIDS infection is not only that the African governments are failing to curb and curtail the scourge of HIV/AIDS but that simply there are also a lot of pubs and clubs in Africa, and through these pubs and clubs, things do go down. In fact there are more pubs and clubs in Africa than there are schools and universities in Africa. Unprotected sex is prevalent among the youth, and more frequent than not it normally takes places through these pubs and clubs at night. When an average person is under the influence of alcohol, normally he loses control of his emotions, and bad things normally happen after that. If an average person is under the influence of illegal substances, things can get even worse. Through these clubs and pubs, HIV/AIDS spreads faster and easily through unprotected sex among the African youth because in those pubs and clubs everything goes. Pubs and clubs are the American concept of having fun; however, this concept of having fun somehow has found its way to Africa, and even drugs followed suit thereafter. The main problem with drugs industry is this: there are even politicians involved, and I am not talking about just an ordinary police official—I am talking about the Commissioners of police in some cases. There are police officials who are receiving double salaries, one from the drug lord's payroll and the other salary from the state payroll. What is abundantly clear to all most everyone is this: not only does the smuggling of drugs from one country to another is the quickest way to make money, but the dividends of this kind of business are humongous. People make more money quickly through the smuggling of drugs than in their secular jobs—and should I say tax-free hard cash. The same is also happening in the poaching of rhino horns. A poor person can wake up the next day filthy stinking rich without having exerted concerted effort. Average people, even those who are law-abiding citizens, have reached a stage where they now say, "It pays to be corrupt—by the way, everybody is corrupt." When justice can no longer take its cause and police commissioners have become corrupt, what should the average people who are the law-abiding citizens do? The law-abiding citizens eventually take the law into their own hands. Most people have realized that there is no longer justice in this world. They have come to the realization that the reason the majority people are behind bars is not that they have violated the law per se, but the main reason some people are behind bars is that simply they don't have the money to pay their way out of prison. I have just witnessed that in South Africa—that some people in prison are treated differently compared to others. Simply put, it all depends on what you have and who you know. If you know people in high places and you have money, you are likely to turn around your prison cell into something spectacular. While people are arrested and taken to prison for smuggling of drugs, the very same prison where they are going to serve their time in is the hotbed of drugs distribution. Africa is suffering from the unholy leprosy of corruption and from the leprosy of greed. People are not patient enough to stand on the queue anymore, and they want to jump everybody and go straight to the counter to do whatever they want to do; even if it's illegal, it does not matter anymore. Africans all over the continent have reasonable reason they commit crime and acts of corruption. Most Africans believe that they have been failed by the political system, and to make up for this shortfall that has been created by the colonial system, the best way is to steal. Some of these drug dealers are much respected people among their communities, and some of these drug lords are even serving in their church committees as elders and deacons. It's surprising that corrupt people will normally hide their evil acts through a holy house of God. Some even give a lot of money in their churches during the time of offering to deflect and divert the attention of the police and the public. Africans are struggling to lay hold of their moral compass that had been decimated and destroyed by the West. Some African scholars like Tafataona Mahoso will probably argue that Africans are not corrupt per se but they have been taught corruption by the West imperialists. I subscribe to that school of thought: African leaders are not corrupt per se but they have learned corruption from their Western masters. All freedom fighters had one thing in common during the African liberation struggle: they were fighting for political freedom and economic freedom, and unfortunately, they did not win the war, but they won the battle. They achieved what I call Pyrrhic victory. They lost the economic struggle and economic freedom; however, they settled for too little—political freedom. Economic freedom gives you economic power, and you can even hoodwink and pull some strings of strong politicians who have strong morals if you have economic power. With political freedom, you have a right to vote, but the fact of the matter is this: you are still going to remain poor and humble. You have political freedom to do window-shopping, but you don't have economic freedom to buy what you want. You are allowed to look, but you are not allowed even to touch, and that makes a lot of people to have depression and anxiety. Drug lords and drug cartels mastered the whole system by controlling everybody including the democratically elected officials by even loaning them money to prove to these democratically elected politicians that these drug lords and drug cartels are not only corrupt but also even generous. The business of illegal drugs supply is a lucrative business, and it's also dangerous. It involves prostitution, racketeering, and money laundering. For a long time in South Africa, there had been illegal mining of gold in most of the closed mines. These illegal mining activities had been taking place for quite a long period of time, and ordinary people will incorporate their own illegal corporation—meaning the group of people coming together and infiltrating the old mines where there are no mining activities taking place anymore and embarking on their mining activities without even being noticed by the authorities. Let me make this clear: there would not be illegal mining activities that are taking place under the belly of earth in Africa if there was no market for diamonds and gold. I remember vividly at one point when I was coming from Zimbabwe that a certain woman was arrested in the Beitbridge border with diamond stones in her possession. It simply attests to the fact that there are a lot of economic activities and financial transactions taking place illegally without even the African governments knowing about it. Africans have become impatient; they have come to the realization of the fact that there is no justice and fairness anymore. The rich become richer, and the poor become poorer, and the queue to financial success is very long, and I mean the legal queue to financial success will probably take a long time for an average person to reach the winning line financially. However, different scholars have different views about this matter; for example, Mr. Milkshake, a PhD student from the University of Kwazulu Natal, argued in favor of the net gain that the South African government is making through the migration of Zimbabweans from Zimbabwe to South Africa. The revelations that unfolded in South Africa in the mining industry about the illegal mining that is taking place underground have proven his claim otherwise. All along I have been accusing the West—that it has stolen Africa's wealth, and it seems as if right now Africans are now stealing from each other in order to survive. It had been apparently clear that not all foreign immigrants are coming to South Africa because of true and genuine economic and political reasons, but some of these foreign immigrants are in the business of corruption. They are not in South Africa to look for jobs, but they are in South Africa to push their illegal agenda of illegal mining of gold and diamonds. As always there wouldn't be illegal mining activities without an illegal market, and the big question: Who are these people behind illegal mining activities? I suggest that before illegal mining can take place underground in the belly of the earth, there are orders already that are waiting for the merchandise to be delivered in due time. The closer I get to understanding how the West corrupted and stole Africa's wealth, the more I begin to understand the damage that had been done in Africa by the West. I would not like to be an acquiescent and believe that the damage had been done, therefore what is the use of blaming the West? The Western agents are now infiltrating Africa, and they are now using Africans to steal from Africa. The rhino poachers are made up of both Africans and Chinese. It makes logical sense to conclude that the Chinese know nothing much about Africa, and they would not be poaching rhino horns if it was not for the help that they get from Africans themselves. Simply put, the West is now using poor Africans that are jobless and poor to provide them with information that is useful to commit acts of crime in Africa. The Western agents are also using young unemployed Africans to conduct their illegal mining activities in the belly of the earth in Africa. These unemployed African youth also bear the brunt of losing their lives in pursuit of gold of which they don't know its worth in the first place. The truth of the matter is this: just because the person can get into the belly of the earth and mine gold and diamonds, it does not necessarily mean that the very illegal miner understands the very price of the gold that he is mining. The price of gold and diamonds is not determined by the miners themselves, but it's determined by these Western agents who are sipping coffee in Sandton Square, while the illegal miners are breaking their spines trying by all means to navigate their way from the belly of the earth to the ground. At the end of the day, it's not the miner who has diamond and gold on his hand who will determine the price of the diamond and gold, but it is the guy who has been sipping coffee all day long in Sandton Square who has never been in the belly of the earth. The very illegal miners that are involved in illegal mining of gold actually have nothing to show for even after they have delivered the real material to their big bosses who are always sipping coffee in Sandton Square, while these illegal miners are in the belly of the earth risking their lives to support their children and wives. The biggest question is this: How do these illegal mining activities come about? Get this into your skull: when the West invaded Africa, the West had mineral deposits in mind. Simply put, the West was not exploring Africa as many Western scholars suggested. Even the same Cecil John Rhodes never invaded Zimbabwe for the mere fact of exploring Africa, but it was all about the minerals deposits from the beginning. As legal mining activities took place, it became very difficult back then to acquire enough manpower to sustain the workforce of these mines. The more gold and diamonds were mined, it became apparent that there were too much mineral deposits in the belly of the African soil, and the workforce could not cope with the demand for gold and diamonds. There was a growing need then to get more men on the ground to conduct the mining operation on behalf of the Western governments who had discovered the so-called Dark Continent, where the people of that continent were uncivilized and backward as some of these Western scholars suggested, like Hugh Marshall Hole, who wrote the book *Old Rhodesian Days*. This rationale that black people were backward and uncivilized breaks my heart into pieces. As more mines were discovered, that meant that the workforce in the mining sector had to be bolstered in the twinkling of an eye, and as a result, it became very easy to get a job if you are a man in the mine without any formal education. Let me be quite honest with you: I had three uncles who were working in the mines in Rustenburg, and out of these three uncles of mine, one died in the mine because of the rock that fell on him, though there were suspicions that witchcraft was at play in his death, but on the surface he died because of the rock that fell on him, period. I would not like to explore the witchcraft aspect of his death because it's probable that there was indeed witchcraft at play in his death. I know very well that in the court of law it's very difficult to prove the existence and validity of witchcraft. But the fact of the matter is this: witchcraft does exist and is alive in Africa. Out of these three uncles of mine, one as I said died in the mine, leaving behind a wife and children that are still at this moment mourning for the death of their father. I know that the West normally mistakes witchcraft to superstitions, something that is not even existing but only existing in your mind. Witchcraft exists to the point that you believe it, and it does not exist to the point that you don't believe it. Some of the things do exist irrespective of whether you believe them or not; they do exist just like demons exist even though you can't prove the existence of demons in the court of law, but you see the effects of demons to a person who is controlled by demons. There are certain things you don't need to be academical about in order to understand them. In other words, there are certain things that are understood better by elders, and these elders are not educated with PhD from a prestigious university. There is an aspect of African culture that is purely oral, and there is no information you can found about it in the library because it's purely based and rooted on secrecy and among elders only. There are certain things that I have just learned recently. I have learned that African elders are normally taught and trained not to tell children all the secrets including the secrets about the existence of witchcraft. But when a certain plague strikes a family, they will quickly tell you that this is not a normal disease that could be cured by the Western medicine but through the African doctors. Though the majority of us like people of my generation don't believe in things like witchcraft, the effects of it are visible and known by the elders every day. One of my uncles who was part of the trio who is still working in the mine normally phones me in the early hours of the morning to tell me, "We are on strike here, my nephew." I will normally say, "Uncle, what is the problem, man?" He will tell me all the problems that are in the mine. One of the trios of these uncles of mine decided to quit working after another rock fell on him, and he cheated death and served the mine with a resignation letter and bought taxis, and right now he owns taxis. There was no need for education then to get employment in the mining industry, and this situation remained liked that for a considerable amount of time. The main problem with the mining sector had been the fact that these mining companies have been cheating African governments by not paying company taxes that are due to the African governments.

> *Initial findings from the research on illicit capital flows from the continent done by the panel chaired by former president Thabo Mbeki indicate that most of the illicit outflows of capital from Africa are not as a result of corrupt politicians as popular wisdom has it, but by companies who evade taxes, under declare, inflate their costs, and other illegal ways of avoiding paying African countries what are due to them in rents. In fact the amounts taken out of the continent in this manner are much higher than what Africa receives in development aid.*[6]

Simply put, Africa was not supposed to be the begging continent and relying on foreign aid as it is still the case. Africa was supposed to be financially independent to the point that she can even feed her children and her people. There was no need for Africans to drown on the sea on their way to the island of Lampedusa because the African continent can't provide sustainable employment for its people and provide necessary infrastructural development without the financial assistance from the financial institutions like the World Bank and IMF. But unfortunately, until this point in time, most African countries are still on the queue begging for foreign aid from the West as if God made a mistake when he was creating Africa. We Africans reduce ourselves to the level of beggars because of the way we perceive ourselves. Very few of us Africans take time to master our own backyard, and very few of us do take time to master the mineral deposits that are buried in the belly of the African soil. The average demand for mining staff shot up due to the fact that there were many mines that they were being discovered in the process. There was now a need for a considerable amount of employees in the mines like never before; by the way, back then if you are a gentleman and you were working for one of the mining companies like Anglo American and De Beers, all the girls were yours in the village even if you didn't know how to write your name. The perception then that the majority of girls had was that a gentleman who is working in the mine is getting paid per fourteen nights and he is paid a lot of money. There was another theory about people who are working in the mines. There was a belief that mine workers were paid their salaries with a buckets because there was too much money in the mining sector to the point that an average person could not even manage to hold his salary with his bare hands, therefore the bucket came very handy. Some of these theories and myths about the mines were told by the miners themselves; I guess it was their tricks to get all the beautiful girls in the village. One gentleman was proposing to a lovely beautiful lady one day, and it happened that I was passing by. I heard this gentleman saying something that I have never heard any man before saying to a woman. He said, "Baby, when I see you, my heart melts." This lady that he was talking to froze like a chicken in the refrigerator as if she was struck by lightning. I passed them, but I believe that this gentleman might have unlocked the door to the heart of that lady. I don't know what happened after that, and it's possible that the lady did fall for his lies. That is exactly what the miners were saying when they arrive in the villages during Christmas. They will be telling people that they were getting paid a lot of money to the point that they were no longer using envelopes to receive their salaries but they were using buckets to receive their salaries. It's true that this was a myth that the miners were earning a lot of money. During the Marikana massacre of August 16, 2012, in South Africa, the lid on the salaries of miners was wide open, and we as the public were given an opportunity for the very first time to the lives of the miners, and it became abundantly clear for the first time that miners were not being paid a lot of money as they suggested in the previous years. There are two crucial points that are worth mentioning that the Zimbabwean crisis contributed into the South Africa economy. The Zimbabwean crisis caused by the "illegal economic sanctions of the West" noticed that the term "illegal economic sanctions" was coined by Zimbabwean president Robert Mugabe. The fact of the matter is this: the West imposed economic sanctions, not illegal sanctions as Pres. Robert Mugabe suggested. If the economic sanctions are illegal, he must approach the ICC (International Criminal Court), but I think the problem with approaching the ICC is he might not make it back home, since even him there are some charges that he might be compelled by the ICC to answer. Therefore, economic sanctions are not totally illegal; it depends on which side of the fence you stand on and case you stand on the side of the fence where there is justice and peace, not on the side of the fence where there are atrocities and heinous crimes. The Zimbabwean economic crisis brought to the South African education system mathematics, physics, and biology teachers. That is a positive part of the Zimbabwean economic crisis, and I need to make this point clear: not everybody in Zimbabwe is educated, and not everybody in Zimbabwe can do math, though the Zimbabwean literacy rate is higher compared to South Africa literacy rate; but we must remember that South Africa is a country of roughly 53 million people, while Zimbabwe is a country of roughly 14, 2 million people, and 5 million of these 14,2 million people are already dwelling in South Africa. And as long as the Zimbabwean economic fiasco remains as it is now, there are no possibilities that the Zimbabweans who are dwelling in South Africa are going to return home someday because some of them have already made South Africa a permanent home, and I don't have a problem with that. Besides the fact that the Zimbabwean economic crisis brought seasonal teachers in South Africa, most of whom studied math and Spanish in Cuba, the Zimbabwean economic crisis also brought enough workforce in South African economy. The South African economy is the fastest-growing economy in the world, and now and then South African government is working tirelessly to grow the economy even further. There are many projects that are under way in South Africa while this book is being written; for example, there is Mudupi Power Station that is under construction in Limpopo, and there is Kusile Power Station that is under construction right now in Mpumalanga province. It simply means that through these mega projects that were undertaken by the South African government, they need sufficient workforce to see these projects until the end. Those are not the only projects that are under way in South Africa at the moment. There are other EPWP (Expanded Public Works Programme) like the upgrading of the old roads because of the new bus system that is going to be unveiled. Therefore, even the Zimbabweans who are in South Africa have benefited immensely through these projects because some of the Zimbabweans have been employed in different sectors of the South African economy temporarily. It's important, though, to note that these EPWP are not there forever at some point in time; they will have to come to an end. The majority of these people will invariably be laid off, and some of course will have to get jobs in other sectors of the economy like in construction. We all know that there are two sides of any story even though it is a good story. The bad side of this story is this: the Zimbabwean economic crisis brought to South Africa what are so-called Zama Zama's gold prospectors. There has never been an illegal mining activity before like there are illegal mining activities right now in South Africa. These Zama Zamas are former mine employees, and some of them came as far as Marange in Zimbabwe. They brought not only their skills of how to mine gold and diamond but also their skills of how to navigate in the belly of the earth and evade some heavy rocks and make it to the ground with the precious stones. It's almost possible right now that in every mine right now where there are legal mining activities taking place, there are illegal mining activities that are taking place on the other side of the shafts. The revelations of the illegal mining drama that took place in Benoni, East of Johannesburg, bear testament to that. This is where forty miners were arrested during the month of January 2014, and two men lost their lives as a result of robbery in the belly of the earth.[7] When the rescue operation was over, there were still miners who were dead but still trapped by the rocks, and they could not be brought to the surface. This episode was aired through the South Africa media, and we were all taken aback about what is happening in our backyard without us knowing. Most of these miners were from Zimbabwe, and one of the relatives of the deceased wept bitterly in front of the cameras and said, "When I get home to (Zimbabwe), what will I tell my parents?" because they know that when Zimbabweans leave their home country and come to South Africa, they are not coming to open old shafts of the abandoned mines to search for the precious stones, but they are coming to South Africa to look for sustainable employment. It's ironic then that a person who comes to South Africa to look for sustainable employment could be found in the mine shaft dead, and it proves again that there is more to this than meets the eye. The word "Zama Zama" is a Zulu word; it means "to try," and I will assume then that these Zama Zamas are people who are hustling in the shafts to make a living through illegal mining activities. The truth of the matter is this: there has not been enough national and international attention dedicated to the illegal mining activities that are taking place in South Africa. And it begs the national question: What will happen underground if the mines are nationalized and if there are illegal mining activities happening right now? The day South African mines are going to be nationalized; everybody will loot for his family. One of the reasons why DRC is always in this constant war that does not seem to come to an end is the mineral deposits in Katanga province dubbed "the triangle of death." Not only are Zimbabwe's economic sanctions affecting South Africa positively in the educational sector due to the seasonal Zimbabwean teachers that are in South Africa teaching in South African schools, but there are negatives also that come with the Zimbabwean economic sanctions. Let me put it bluntly: South African government is losing money through the illegal mining activities that are taking place in the mines. When these gold prospectors lay hold of the precious stones from the South African soil, they sell them at street value and make money, and they don't pay tax to the government. The South African mineral deposits are meant to support the South African people and build the South African infrastructure. These precious mineral deposits are not meant to be looted as if South Africa is Marange or South Africa is Katanga province in the DRC. The net loss effect that the South African economy is experiencing is the result of the Zimbabwean economic sanctions. Due to the Zimbabwean economic sanctions, there had been upsurge in the piracy of DVD and CD. We all know that Africans love music, and I love music too, and even the late Nelson Mandela loved music, and Bishop Desmond Tutu loves music too. Africans in their nature are people of rhythm and music. African children start dancing while they are in their mother's womb. African women can tell before the birth of the child whether the child is alive or dead before birth. African children love music even before birth. The problem with music is this: it has become an expensive commodity. Since time immemorial, music was free and costless; but through capitalism and commerce, suddenly everything is money. During the slave trade era, "Negroes," African Americans as they are known today, were singing and dancing for their slave masters as gestures to quell their masters' anger and pain. That is why even today in the United States of America most musicians and comedians are African Americans, people who don't take life seriously all the time. The point that I am driving home here is this: most African Americans are not scientists, but they are musicians and comedians. The Zimbabweans who came to South Africa and who could not find an employment in mining sector or in the construction sector resorted into the underground economy—music piracy. Through the Internet you can copy any music video of any singer in the world and copy even the CD cover page. Through this music piracy, the majority of Zimbabweans are making a living, and they are killing the South African music industry and defrauding the South African government taxes that are due to it. The South African musicians like Mzwakhe Mbuli have been in the forefront of the campaign against the music piracy. Though the South African government is reaping the benefits in other sectors of the economy through the Zimbabwean economic sanctions, it is also losing millions of rands in taxes through the music piracy, and the South African police are not even up to the task. Just like the South African police can't police to the letter almost all mines to ensure that there are no illegal mining activities that are taking place, they can't police all the streets to ensure that there is no selling of fake and cheap DVDs on the streets of Pretoria and Johannesburg. The South African economy is losing almost millions of rands on a daily basis because of the underground economy, which consists of music piracy and illegal mining activities due to the so-called Zama Zamas. The South African national elections were around the corner, and all the political parties were out to meet the people and launch their manifestos, and that is usually in any democracy. One of my concerns about the launching of these manifestos by these political parties was this: they (political parties) will promise to move heaven and earth if they get the votes from the electorate and eradicate all our political and economic problems once and for all. While it's important to get the votes from the electorate, it's also important to make sure your political promises are not far from the truth. One of the greatest mistakes that normally happened in almost all the democratic states in this: politicians are not asked the fundamental question, which is, where will you get the money to bankroll all these promises that you made to us? The masses of our society will meet in sports ground and listen to one person speaking his mind and trying to solve all the problems of the masses should these masses give him their vote. One thing that I know about the South African politicians is this: once they are voted for by the electorate and become MP (members of parliament), they relocate to Cape Town even if they were staying in other provinces. While they are in Cape Town, it will be very difficult to get hold of some of these politicians, and most of them are likely to change even their starter pack after they have been voted for by the electorate. It's usual and normal that when your high school friend who used to play marbles with you all day long until sunset completes his grade twelve and gets admission to the prestigious university, not only will your friendship be over, but also he is likely to avoid your calls and cite academical reasons even though there aren't any. The point is he is no longer in the same level with you intellectually. I have noticed even with me some of my friends are obsessed with marriage and children, and they don't even bother to look at the state of the South African domestic politics, and all what they are worried about are promotions and adding more children to the current number of children that they have. As the South African politicians delivered manifestos after manifestos, which are full of promises on top of another unfulfilled bag of promises, we, the electorate, were told to listen attentively and vote for the future and vote for our political freedom. There is one manifesto that struck me to the core while reading it, and I was bound to question the rationale behind that political manifesto. One political party in its own political manifesto supported the idea of increasing the social grants across the board. There are almost six different types of social grants in South Africa at the moment, and they are: grant for older persons, disability grant, war veterans grant, care dependency grant, foster child grant, and child support grant.[8] The political party in question said that it will increase the current amount that is being received by the recipients of the above-mentioned grants by 100 percent. Let me expatiate extensively: a recipient for a grant for older persons right now is currently receiving R1, 300 per month, and should a grant for an older person be increased by 100 percent, it therefore means that the current recipient of a grant for an older person will receive up to R2,600 per month, almost R31,200 per annum. The one-million-dollar question is this: Where will the state get such a considerable amount of billions of rands to finance such a government program? There is great chasm between reality and fantasy, and it's possible that some of our politicians are not really mentally stable. It's quintessential of a mentally unstable person to make such absurd to the extreme promises. South Africa needs to reduce the number of people who are on SASSA payroll, and the best way to do this is the following: all social grants recipients need to be further reregistered to determine as to whether they are still alive or not.

We all know of people who are receiving money for children who are long dead and buried, further costing the state more billions of rands for people that are gone. It's true that some of the South African social grant recipients are not really South Africans by birth, but they are from Swaziland who only comes to South Africa to receive their social grants and cross the border back to Swaziland after receiving their social grants. I wonder why political parties would still flirt with the danger of distributing social grants as if they are doughnuts. Social grants are the main cause of Africa's intellectual bankruptcy. When the majority of people are fed without having to work for their income, they normally become complacent and lazy intellectually and even physically. The more African countries migrate from egalitarianism and meritocracy to welfare state; eventually they will run out of financial muscle to bankroll these social security programs. Social grants are an interim intervention to long historical problem of poverty, which had been caused by the West. By the way, most of the African countries don't have sufficient financial resources to bankroll social security programs, and as a result, they rely heavily on the World Bank and IMF, including the foreign aid, which is coming from the West, to finance programs like the social grants program. Welfare states are a ticking time bomb that is about to explode at any time. If we (Africans) cast our eyes across the sea, we can quickly see what is happening in socialist countries where everything is owned by the state, where the state is expected to be the largest contributor in the economy and largest employer at the same time. Almost all the socialist countries were in flames in the late 2013 and early 2014 because of the high rate of unemployment and high rate of crime. It's invariably inevitable that the success of any state will depend on the public-private partnership with the private sector. The rationale of disregarding the private sector and building a public sector–centered economy is extremely dangerous because the public sector is more frequent than not controlled and used as political mouthpiece and political machinery for political parties. When the public sector–centered economy collapses, everything falls apart, though I should mention the fact that the majority of these private companies are normally owned by the Western governments while based in Africa. There is an urgent need to ensure that while African countries are opening up their doors of economic trade with the West and engaging in this private-public partnership, there must still be robust rules and regulations to ensure that there is no further exploitation by the West just like before in the colonial era. It's logically sound and politically correct to suggest that Africa can't exist in isolation without the rest of the world in terms of economic trade. Africa needs to come into the party and forge economic trade relations with the rest of the world in order to lift the masses from the scourge of poverty that is ravaging the African continent. While Africa needs to open up its economic arms for more new economic trade partners, it's also important to bear in mind that African mineral resources' exploitation of Machiavellian proportion that happened through the colonial era should not be accepted and promoted in the near future. Africa has been robbed of its people and its mineral resource by the West. In fact the West and its allies have been pillaging Africa's mineral resources for quite a long period of time, and the people of Africa until this day have not gotten a clue about the exact amount of mineral resources that the West has extracted from the belly of the African soil. If there is one thing that makes me to toss and turn in the middle of the night is the mere fact that the current poverty that many African countries are experiencing was not even supposed to there in the first place had Africa remained politically free and economically free from the Western imperialist. There are Western settlers who believe that they were brought to Africa to fulfill a divine assignment—that is, to save the perishing souls of African people who were destined to burn in the flames of fire in hell, where the fire can't be quenched and the worms don't die. These Western scholars suggest that Africans, before the arrival of the West in Africa, didn't know God. Therefore, these Western settlers came to Africa not to steal, kill, and destroy, but they came for the divine assignment and divine appointment, which was to save Africans from self-destruction. It's common belief even among Africans themselves that they (African people) are not organized and they like fighting among themselves and killing each other for a mere meal. Therefore, the Western settlers had to come into the picture not because the Western settlers wanted to come and settle in Africa per se but because there was a divine assignment that they (Western settlers) had to fulfill, which was beyond their own wish and dream. The master plan for the Western settlers to come to Africa was not to exploit the mineral resource of Africa but to show the perishing African masses who did not even know the name God the way and to help them to taste the spiritual freedom that they were being deprived of because of worshipping foreign gods and idols. Hugh Marshal Hole writes:

> *The Matabele, in common with most Bantu natives, regarded deaths or diseases, whether of human being or cattle, not as due to natural causes, but as the result of illicit sorcery, and when*

any such event occurred looked to the wizards to discover and punish the authors.[8]

The birth and the death of a person have a significant meaning to Africans at large. Therefore, there should be serious questions that need to be asked if a person dies haphazardly without any serious sickness. Africans are generous in nature and are also humble in nature, and most Western settlers have mistaken this to mean dumb or incompetent. The way African children were brought up back in the day is not the same way most African children are brought up now. Death on its own leaves a gaping hole in an African family, unlike in the West where people are killing each other like flies. Most of the Western countries associated what is happening in Central African Republic with the rest of the African continent. African people are people of peace and music. The arrival of the West changed all of that, and in fact it is the West that stripped off African people their languages, their culture, and even their belief. The West is now setting rules and regulations for Africans as to how to worship and who to worship, and who is the devil and who is Christ. Africans knew God, and they knew the Trinity of heaven—God the Son and God the Father and God the Holy Spirit. Africans knew God in their own African way, not in the Western way. Africans knew very well the danger of manufacturing weapons of mass destruction that can destroy the world completely, and they did not even dare to manufacture such weapons, while the West was busy manufacturing the atomic bombs and killing its people in the name of democracy and political freedom. Absolute power should not be demonstrated by decimating and destroying the life of another person. Absolute power should be seen in saving lives and providing the masses with food and shelter, not with the supply of guns to one group to kill the other in the pursuit of total subjugation of the other group. In other words, there is no need to express your intellectual power by manufacturing weapons of mass destruction that should make the whole world fear your ingenuity to the point of thinking that should they have dissenting views with you, they will be put to rest. This is what is happening right now in the world. Most African countries are told by the West what to do in their own African countries, and failure to adhere to the rules and regulations that have been imposed by the West is economic sanctions. African leaders who are not going to take political orders from the West are branded dictators and are normally dragged all the way to the International Criminal Court (ICC) to answer for charges of human rights violation. Let me ask this question:

Is imposing economic sanctions to a small country like Zimbabwe that led to the death of many people because of HIV/AIDS not human rights violation? There is a double standard that is being applied in ICC when it comes to African leaders. One of the main reasons perhaps why Pres. Robert Mugabe of ZANU-PF did not vacate his position as the president of the Zimbabwean government was the fear that should he leave his position as the head of government, he will be dragged to the International Criminal Court (ICC) by the West. Though most of the political leaders of the West commit heinous crimes against humanity, they will never have to answer for their heinous crimes in the ICC simply because they are bankrolling the financial bills of the ICC. That is why most African leaders will stay in political power until they collapse in the government offices because of the fear that they will be dragged to Hague. This fear is real and genuine, though the majority of people have mistaken this fear for dictatorship and autocratic management style. Though I should state that some African leaders do like to stay in power even if their time to go home and play with the kids has come. This is simply because they have another kind of fear, the fear of the unknown. I believe that it could be the main reasons why Pres. Robert Mugabe of Zimbabwe stayed in power until this day simply because there is no one in Zimbabwe who is viewed as a qualified candidate to succeed Pres. Robert Mugabe should he step down, not out of his willing heart but due to medical problems that seem to trouble him now and then. The big question then is this: Who will succeed Pres. Robert Mugabe after he has vacated his political position as the state president of Zimbabwe and as the president of the ZANU-PF? Joice Mujuru who is currently a deputy president of the country could succeed Pres. Robert Mugabe, but another question that springs forth into mind is this: Are African countries ready to be led by women in government and in politics? There are few women in Africa who are leading their countries as presidents except the few like the Liberian president Ellen Johnson Sirleaf and the CAR president Catherine Samba-Panza. The majority of African countries are led by men not by women because women in general are seen to be weak and less intelligent than men, and though this is not a view that is expressed openly in public, but we all know that this is the view that is existing in the political corridors and in political circles of many political parties. South Africa is not likely either to have a female president soon, maybe in the near future, which I don't even see it happening. This does not to suggest that women can't lead a nation, but my own personal problem with women in general is this: women normally are emotionally fragile, and they are likened to a weaker vessel in the Bible, therefore a woman president is likely to fail to absorb a political heat when the political oven has been turned 360 degrees. I have seen the former prime minister of Thailand Yingluck Shinawatra crying in front of the TV cameras many times; instead of giving a political direction, she was sobbing. Political leaders have to be able to take the punches from the ordinary people and even from political analysts. It's absurdity to the extreme to see a political leader of a country crying in front of TV cameras just because the country that she is leading has been engulfed by political problems like protests and unemployment. A political leader must show character and political astute through difficult times and amid challenges and show leadership qualities. Most of the political leaders amid tough times, challenging period, normally go on holiday or decide to marry in the midst of a national turmoil. When Ukraine was in flames, which resulted in the death of twelve people, the then president of Ukraine Viktor Yanukovych went on a sick leave because of flu. Where was this flu all along when there was peace and stability in Ukraine? But as soon as Ukraine was engulfed in political problems, the honorable president Viktor Yanukovych became sick, and he became sick when his nation needed him most. I am not suggesting that a political leader of any country should not be sick in the midst of a national crisis, but it's also true that when you are running out of solutions in the midst of problems, you are likely to have flu attesting to the fact that you are even sick mentally because of mental problems. It's also true that the best way to avoid the masses is to suggest that you are sick, and they will let you off the hook. The then Ukraine president Viktor Yanukovych eventually made concessions to end the long and protracted protest that has claimed innocent lives of children and women. After making concessions with the oppositional party, he fled the country, and nobody knew then where he was. The Ukraine parliament issued a warrant of arrest for Viktor Yanukovych. Antoine Roger Lokongo writes:

> *China has already transferred some of its technologies to Africa-Hisense company in South Africa and oil extraction technology in Sudan. Indeed, "give a man a fish and you feed him for a day; teach a man to fish and you feed him for a life time" (Chinese proverb). History has proven that we Africans can believe and trust China. We trust China when China says that it is ready to cooperate that "we put Africans' interest first." As Chinese scholar Luo Jianbo writes, "Of course, it is well*

> *known that a nation's foreign policy always serves its national interest first. China is no exception. China never denies that its African policy aims to pursue its own strategic interest in Africa [nor that it has not made mistakes there]. However, one of the most outstanding features of China's African policy from the very beginning is its aspiration to promote a win-win South-South cooperation and the restoration of Asia and Africa's dignity.*[10]

Most of the African scholars don't see the Republic of China as a country that has a potential to recolonize Africa like the West did in the past. Most African scholars don't see a problem of taking the Marange diamonds and giving them to a Chinese company, but they have a big problem when Western companies take our mineral deposits and create sustainable employment opportunities. The China-Africa relationship is going stronger than before. Most African leaders think that they have found a real economic partner with China. The fact that China was helping Africa during the colonial era with military training and weapons, that should not be mistaken to mean that Africa has a bosom friend in China. What is abundantly clear even to the blind man is this: China wants to grow and bolster its economic power in Africa, and by ensuring that China bolsters and grows and entrenches its economic roots in Africa, it should pose for the picture with a smile while deep down China is not smiling. Have you ever been in the situation where you have to take a picture and the camera man says "cheese"? Please! That is what China is doing exactly to Africa. There is no way China can smile for the African picture without having evil and ulterior motives about Africa within. The rationale that Africa is a consuming continent not a producing continent is the basis for the China-Africa relations. Simply put, China knows for the fact that Africa until this day and age is still incapable to feed its people, let alone have a wherewithal to manufacture complex electronic and technological equipments. I don't see any difference between the West, Africa's former colonizer, and the Republic of China, though the majority of people might differ with me in this case. Africa is the hottest girl of the world, and everybody is looking for Africa's hand in marriage, if I may put it that way. That does not necessarily mean that Africa should not engage in bilateral trade agreements with China, but to put China on the pedestal is deadly dangerous. There is no way that China can come to Africa with pure heart and genuine motives. What glitters is not always gold. The fact that China has been helping African countries with military training and military weapons that should not necessarily mean that Africa should therefore pay back China with these bilateral trade agreements that include Marange diamond deals, like in the case of Zimbabwe. BRICS (Brazil, Russia, India, China, and South Africa) is the latest formation of the trading block that sought to increase and bolster the economies of these countries that form the BRICS block. BRICS also sought to make funds available for young entrepreneurs who will like to start businesses from scratch. Through the BRICS block, one can at least see the relevance and the importance of this BRICS block, unlike exposing African mineral deposits to the Chinese companies only to be economically exploited and cheated by China even further. Different people have different economic perspectives about China. It's not surprising that different people have different perspectives about China, and our divergence in understanding China should not be influenced by our narrow minds and stupidity. The fact that Africa does not trust the West anymore because of the diabolic history between the West and Africa influenced by what happened in the colonial era, that must not render Africa vulnerable and desperate to take everything with ease from anyone. Poverty and hunger can induce a person to make stupid decisions in the interim only to regret later in life. Just because Africa has been cheated and hoodwinked by the West, it should not therefore mean that Africa should be running to China crying for help like an orphan who is living in an orphanage home. If Africa displays its desperation to China, even if China had no ulterior motives to harm Africa, it will be left with no option but only to hit where it hurts most, which is in the stomach. One of the questions that I frequently ask myself is this: What will happen to most African countries the day China will decide to end these current trade agreements with African countries? Can Africa survive without China? But we all know that China can survive without Africa. The fact of the matter is this: Africa can't survive without China, and the day China will decide to end its trade relationship with Africa, there will be weeping and gnashing of teeth in many African countries, just like there is endless weeping and wailing in Zimbabwe. In fact the Zimbabweans have been spread all over the world because of poverty and economic sanctions that are ravaging the country. One of my friends from Zimbabwe who now resides in Johannesburg said to me, "I am afraid that Zimbabwe will be like Somalia." It's possible that his worst fears might be realized. The thing that I fear most has come upon me; those are the words of Job from the Holy Bible. With cash liquidity crisis further rubbing salt on the already bleeding wound, it's possible that the thing that my Zimbabwean friend from Johannesburg fears most might have come upon him little bit sooner than the whole world expected. To suggest that Zimbabwe's ailing economy has reached an irreparable stage is discouraging. That is like saying to an unbeliever, "You have committed many sins to the point that God can't forgive you of your sins anymore although you confess them." I still believe that there is still redemption and the forgiveness of sins for the Zimbabweans. There is still economic redemption for the people of Zimbabwe. I have said before that the people of the world must continue to offer prayers of supplication and thanksgiving to God for everything that is happening to the Zimbabwean people. I sometimes believe that perhaps it is the plan of the Almighty and specifically for African leaders and Africans in general for all of us to see how cruel and evil the West is. The West has been killing African people since time immemorial, and it continues to do so even in Zimbabwe to this day with its "illegal economic sanctions." It's possible that the Zimbabwean economic debacle also wanted to teach people of my generation that holding too much political power at the expense of the masses is unhealthy and perilous. It's also possible that the Zimbabwean economic debacle wanted to teach people of my generation that depending on foreign aid can be deadly dangerous sometimes for Africa. African countries must learn to diversify their economies rather than hoping and praying for the manna of the foreign aid that should come from the West. Gone are the days of relying and depending on single trading partner for African countries and depending on foreign aid and cheap blankets from the United Nations. I wonder whether or not the founders of the United Nations had Africa in mind because it looks to me as if the United Nations was created to save Africa from poverty and economic sickness. The founders of the United Nations knew exactly well that African leaders were going to screw up the African continent and plunged the majority of African people into the bottomless pit of poverty and hunger. Each and every country has its own sovereignty, and that sovereignty should be respected by the international community. It also means that the West even though it's the largest donor to many African countries, these African countries are still sovereign in a sense that they have their own laws and their own judiciary systems that govern and control them. Since each African country is a sovereign state, South Africa could not invade Zimbabwe and seek regime change through a war or coup d'état as the majority of Western leaders suggested. South African government understands very well the concept of the sovereignty. Though the former South African president Thabo Mbeki was accused of using quiet diplomacy in resolving the Zimbabwean political debacle, at least at the end there was a political solution that led to Zimbabwe to form unity government in 2009 after two hundred people died due to the political violence that was perpetuated by the election rerun. There is a statement that was uttered by Terry when we were driving from Chikurubi Prison and going back to Harare. He said to me, "Why did it take almost eight weeks to count the votes of the national elections of 2008, while it took almost two days to complete the counting of votes in the July 31, 2013, national elections?" The truth of the matter is this: I don't have an answer why it took two days to count the votes for July 31, 2013, whereas it took almost eight weeks to do the votes counting in 2008 in the election rerun. Let me just say, maybe in 2013 the ZEC (Zimbabwe Election Commission) was thoroughly prepared for the national election of July 31, 2013, and maybe there was a monumental rigging of the national election as the MDC-T supporters suggest. It's possible that the MDC-T lost the national elections that were held on July 31, 2013, free and fair and simply because of their own stupidity. There are lessons that the MDC-T needs to learn from the national election of July 31, 2013. I was in Zimbabwe prior to the national election, and I can tell you this: the security was deadly tight, and the police were indeed ready for any political fiasco and they were armed to teeth for any political misdemeanors. There was fear in Harare that there will be an impending violence should the ZANU-PF lose the national election. We all know what happened in 2008 with the election rerun—that the death toll went up to two hundred people. Each and every African country has its own laws and its own judiciary system. In the case of South Africa, there is a parliament and the provincial legislature. There is a constitutional court, which is the highest court in the land, in the case of South Africa. The president of South Africa makes an appointment out of his own discretion as the president of the Republic of South Africa, but his political appointment can still be nullified and reversed by the constitutional court of South Africa. This legal exercise where the president of South African appointment was challenged and nullified was witnessed in the case of Menzi Simelane, the then NDPP (National Director of Public Prosecution). The Democratic Alliance (DA) challenged the appointment of Menzi Simelane, citing the finding of the Ginwala Commission, which was instituted by the then president of South Africa Thabo Mbeki to find out whether or not the then NDPP (National Director of Public Prosecution) Vusi Pikoli was fit to hold public office. The point I am making is this: the decision of the state president in the case of the South

African legal system is not final and it can be challenged in the constitutional court. The president of Uganda Yoweri Museveni who has been in power for nearly three decades has done the unthinkable by signing into law the antigay law that could see "repeat homosexuality offenders be jailed for life," and the whole world was left with egg in the face when Yoweri Museveni signed that antigay bill into law. But if we, the whole world, were to respect the sovereignty of any African country, there would not be any problem about what happened in Uganda. The fact of the matter is this: Yoweri Museveni was cleaning his backyard, and what is the problem with that? There were all sorts of comments that were made about this antigay bill that was eventually signed into law by Pres. Yoweri Museveni of Uganda. Some Western countries suggested that they were going to cut off foreign aid that was meant for Uganda. In other words, Pres. Yoweri Museveni's government was going to lose a considerable amount of foreign aid by just signing into law the antigay bill. It simply means that for African countries to continue to receive the endless flow of foreign aid from the West, the leaders of these African countries must sign into law pro-gay laws, and foreign aid will flow to Africa nonstop. When the president of Uganda Yoweri Museveni was doing what is considered morally correct from the African point of view, he was threatened by cuts of foreign aid.

> *Yoweri Museveni's spokesperson, Tamale Mirundi, answered the US leader swiftly: "Uganda's relationship with the US was not built on homosexuality."*[11]

The relationship between the West and the rest of Africa was built on homosexuality. When the West has nothing to degrade and debase Africa with, it will just make an issue out of a tissue. Big countries must respect the sovereignty of other countries, whether small or big, including the national laws of the so-called small countries. Almost all Western media are quoting and overanalyzing what Yoweri Museveni said, and some of the quotations are sometimes manufactured to further label Africans as people who are backward and ignorant. It was reported that Pres. Yoweri Museveni said, "The main reason why women are turning into homosexuality is that they are starved sexually by their husbands," reported by a journalist who was based in Nigeria working for the Western media about a statement made by Pres. Yoweri Museveni in Uganda. The more African leaders are deviating from the Western moral standards, the more they are going to be punished severely as far as foreign aid is concerned. It simply means that the more any African country can copy and duplicate the Western laws and even go as far as practicing the Western laws in African soil, the more that African country is likely to receive more foreign aid from the West even from the Western donors. The relationship between Africa and the West has been built on a very shaky ground, and that ground on which this West-Africa relationship was built on is likely to crumble sooner rather than later. The crux of the matter is this: Africa is not free on its entirety. Just like a prisoner who has been given parole, he is not yet free even though he might walk and greet people; should he do anything wrong, he might wind up back into custody. The fact that African countries are politically free from the Western control does not necessarily mean that the West has completely let Africa off the hook diametrically. The West now and then peeps into its radar to see where Africa is heading economically and politically. It would not surprise me if one day Pres. Yoweri Museveni will be dragged all the way into the ICC (International Criminal Court) for the violation of human rights. When is the slave going to be free? The slave is free from his master when the slave master is no longer meddling in the social affairs of the slave. As long as the master slave keeps on helping the slave and providing for the slave, then this slave is not yet free. Many slaves like the help of their former master to the point that they (slaves) even ask their former master, "Whom should I marry?" The West is meddling in Africa's domestic affairs. The fact that the West is not happy with Pres. Yoweri Museveni of Uganda is clear testament that the West has Africa where it wants it to be. Can you imagine the West threatening Pres. Yoweri Museveni about cutting off foreign aid as if Pres. Yoweri Museveni was manufacturing the weapons of mass destruction? The West-Africa relationship is based on foreign aid and homosexuality. What the West considers being morally correct, even though the African leaders see it morally incorrect, they (African leaders) still need to nod their heads in agreement with the West in case they disagree; the conduit pipe of foreign aid could be cut off. It's like being in a relationship with a woman that is based on material. The day the material is gone then love will also fly out of the window. The relationship between the West and Africa is the slave-master relationship where Africa keeps on looking to its former master for help and this master keeps on feeding the former slave with foreign aid even with advice. There is a belief among most African scholars that China-Africa trade relationship is the way to go. I would like to give you an assignment from the day you bought this book until you depart from this planet: anytime you purchase any item in any grocery store, even clothes, you must look at the tag on that item where it was manufactured, and I hope what you will find what I have found. Most of the clothes that I wear were manufactured in China, not in Africa. Even though I call myself a proud South African living in Africa, surely that does not make me proud. There is nothing to be proud of when your underwear was manufactured in China and the computer that you are using was manufactured in China. I have nothing against China, but I believe that China-Africa trade relationship does not benefit Africa more than it benefits China.

> *A new study reveals, however, that perceptions of China in Africa differ from country to country. Done by the Pretoria-based Ethics Institute of South Africa (EthicsSA), it shows that of the countries questioned, South Africans are the most anti-Chinese. The results show that of the 1,056 Africans from fifteen countries surveyed, the majority were largely negative about Chinese businesspeople in Africa (43.3 percent were negative and 35.4 percent positive), the quality of Chinese products and services (55.9 percent negative), and the economic and social responsibility of Chinese business (40.1 percent and 45.7 percent negative, respectively). Perceptions of the environmental responsibility of Chinese business (53.9 percent negative) and their employment practices (46 percent negative) in Africa are also very bad. Labor practices are seen in a particular poor light. "There is a perception that Chinese companies do not treat their African staff with respect, do not provide decent working conditions, have little regard for health and safety conditions of their employees, and have little regard for basic workers' rights," the report states.*[12]

Africa needs foreign investment from China, but Africa does not need to be oppressed by China anymore just like in the colonial era. It is estimated that there are about one million Chinese living in Africa, and little is known about the number of Africans who are living in China. The fact that the number of Chinese living in African is increasing, it therefore means that the Chinese influence in Africa will increase, and at one point it will reach the level that will be uncontrollable. The Pharaoh of Egypt became concerned about the average number of the Israelites who were living in Egypt to the point that he decreed an order that all the Israeli sons should be killed in order to reduce their influence and the impending danger that was about to happen to Egypt. It's possible that Africa's hospitality to Chinese migrants can one day work against Africa's favor. All African countries must house and provide for migrants, but we must also be careful that the very migrants that we are housing in our countries can't turn their backs on us and stab us from behind. The King of Matabele, Lobengula, was generous man. But out of his generosity, he allowed Cecil John Rhodes to settle in Zimbabwe, and the next thing you know, Cecil John Rhodes was chasing King Lobengula around, taking what belonged to Lobengula and his people. Though the Shona people from Mashonaland even to this day are full of bitterness and resentment against King Lobengula because they believe that it is out of his sheer stupidity that brought Zimbabwe where it is economically and politically today. Many people don't study history, and because many people don't study history, they normally think that the mistakes that were made in the eighteenth century were purely made by people who were not educated, and we, the educated generation, can't repeat the same mistakes that were committed by our forefathers. When the African future generations read the history of my generation, I don't see the future generation include me as one of those people who were also dull just like my generation blame the past generation for the economic and political dilemmas we the African people find ourselves in. We the African people find ourselves in a very bad situation where we rely on the West for everything and for anything. The curriculum in many African schools still depicts that of the oppressor. Many of the African youth still believe that good education is the Western education, and since good education is the Western education, it means that good economic policies are Western economic policies. You will often hear African scholars normally praise and recite a speech that was written and delivered by either former president of the United States of America or the former prime minister of the Great Britain. Why praise your former master if you are a former slave? It's typical of slaves—they normally envy the master's behavior, and even after we Africans have been legally and impartially released from the colonial oppression, most of the African leaders have not found their political feet in terms of running and governing their countries. Most of the judiciary systems of many African countries still mirrored that of Great Britain. Even to this day and age more often than not you will hear judges quoting from the judgment that was delivered by the Great Britain court during the colonial era. When are we Africans going to be intellectually free? It seems as if there is nothing good that one can expect from Africans and that is why the West is taking the mineral resources of Africa out of Africa and using them for its benefit. Good education is Western education and bad education is African education. In fact a young African scholar who studied all his degrees in an African university is more often than not ridiculed by other African scholars who have studied their degrees in the West. Even to this day many African scholars who studied in the West believe that they are intellectually superior to African scholars who have studied in the African universities. That is why most of the African scholars who have received Western education don't really cut it in the African politics because of their myopic attitude and their lack of understanding of the grassroots politics. African scholars who received Western education are normally getting a thumping of their life in African politics because they can't identify themselves with the masses on the ground. That is why even in South Africa today most of the African scholars who are critics of South African government, even to the ANC itself, have received Western education. Then it begs this question: If these African scholars are the products of the Western education, why can't they enter the political arena in order to solve African problems once and for all, since they have received better education than African scholars who studied in African universities? There is a great difference between the structured environment and the unstructured environment. Scholars can function very well in a structured social setting, while in politics there is no consistent and structured social setting. That is why sometimes it's better to be led by an uneducated leader who can identify with the masses than to be led by an academic who is accustomed to a class and a structured social setting who can't even identify with the masses on the ground. The majority of African leaders are slowly and surely alienating themselves from the masses, and I have seen the exact same thing when I was in Zimbabwe. One of the main causes to this alien behavior to many African leaders is the power of money. While they were poor, many African leaders would visit the masses and can even go as far as educating the illiterate masses about the policies and visions of their political parties, including the necessity for the liberation struggle. Once the African liberation struggle was over and there was a power shift from the white elite few to the majority rule, the very same African leaders are no longer accessible, and they have turned from being ordinary people to becoming celebrities. The only time you can have an access to the African leaders is when they are looking for votes in order to continue to maintain their celebrity status life of flying in private jets and drinking expensive red wine at the expense of the masses. The deadliest addiction of them all is to be addicted to the state resources and state facilities. State facilities and state resources, you can't finish them. One of the reasons why the majority of African leaders don't want to vacate the state facilities and leave the state resources behind is that they think that someone else will come and utilize inappropriately the very same state facilities and state resources that they have been using for quite a long period of time. African leaders, just like the poor and the university students who think that they are entitled to a high-paying employment just because of a degree from the prestigious university, also think that they are entitled to the state facilities and state resources forever until the day they die. Politicians are also struggling to divorce the idea of living life without using the state resources and state facilities. That is why many politicians struggle to live their ordinary lives after their political career is over. When the South African national elections were done and dusted, some of the political leaders of the so-called small parties had to contend with the fact that they no longer had to go back to Cape Town and they had to join the masses looking for the secular jobs that are not even paying the same salary that is equal to what they had been receiving when they were members of the South African parliament. There is nothing permanent in politics. Even the very political friendships that you can establish actively in politics are not permanent. In politics your best friends can be your worst enemies in the twinkling of an eye. In South Africa I have witnessed this with my naked eyes. At one moment two leaders of political parties kissed in public to affirm their undying love of each other and their just political cause that they were embarking on. And before we know it, they were accusing each other again in public and ending the very same marriage that was sealed with a French kiss. Once you seal a marriage with a French kiss, that marriage will not last. I therefore suggest to the young couple that is going to get married soon: they must seal their marriage with an African kiss instead of a French kiss. A French kiss is a deal buster and the African kiss is a deal maker. There is nothing so painful than to be rejected by the very same people who once loved you and supported you, and that in politics is inevitable. There are no permanent friends in politics and there are no permanent enemies either. You just need to master the game of politics in order to stay in the game. In politics it does not necessarily mean that the good guys are always the winners; sometimes the bad guys are the winners. The theory that says, "You shall know the truth and the truth shall set you free," does not work in politics. The law of the jungle (eat or be eaten) is the only law that is being applied in politics. I prefer to work hard for my personal success rather than to be parachuted from rags to riches overnight by people. When you are an office bearer and you have been parachuted by people to the public office, you must always make the people happy even though you are not happy yourself. In other words, people who rely on votes to survive and for their financial success are slaves of the people. Politicians fall victims of being the slaves of the people just because of their insatiable addiction to state resources and state facilities. In democracy what the electorates want is more rights to destroy themselves without having to face the consequences of their actions, and they will give politicians votes to stay in the political office and fly all over the world using state resources and state facilities at the expense of the public. The responsibility of a political leader and a leader of a country is to give the electorate what they want even though it is immoral in the face of the Almighty, but as long as it is what the electorate wants, you must give it to them. Yoweri Museveni, the president of Uganda, will soon learn the dangers of not following the masses and what it can do to the Ugandan economy. The masses are on the self-destructive path in the name of democracy, and they want political leaders to endorse their destructive behavior in exchange of votes. The majority of African leaders have been bowing to this pressure of votes for fear of losing the luxury and the comfort of using the state resources and state facilities. The deadliest addiction of them all is to be addicted to something that belongs to the people and that you don't have control over it yourself. The West stole Africa's wealth, and right now it is stealing African mineral resources by using migrants who are also from SADC countries. The political instability accompanied by economic instability not only disrupts the normal lives of ordinary people but also disrupts the flow and the movement of money from one country to the other. In any country where there is political instability, there will be economic instability, and the lawlessness will reign supreme, and that is what has been happening in CAR. Whatever political gains and economic gains have been achieved through a democratic and peaceful process can be quickly be reversed by a war. Africans in their nature are peaceful people who love poems and music. African people are children of a single mother. Africa has become a violent continent over the years due to colonization and oppression from the West for quite a long period of time. Colonization has changed Africa's political profile and Africa's economic profile diametrically. There are very few people around the whole world who still believe that the continent of Africa can be one of the economic power houses that can even be ranked with the developed countries due to its political instability and economic instability. It's important to mention the fact that not all Africa countries are going through what CAR and Somalia are going through. South Africa has been very stable for a considerable amount of time, and that does not mean that South Africa does not have domestic problems of its own, but at least there is a political will and political urgency to maintain this political stability from the government of South Africa. Two of the crucial ingredients in ensuring that South Africa's political stability and economic stability are perennial will be political tolerance and political education about the results of the national elections. One of the greatest challenges about African democracy and African development has been a consistent failure by the political parties to accept the outcome of the national elections though they were fair and peaceful. Most of the African elections have been mirrored by vote rigging and corruption from the onset until the end. The main reason behind vote rigging, what they call "monumental rigging" in Zimbabwe, is that purely certain political leaders in the African continent have been in the public office for quite a long period of time. Even if their time has come to leave the public office, they just decide to stay until they die in the office. The late president of South Africa Nelson Mandela has taught many African leaders a lesson that they should practice now and then. The late president of South Africa Nelson Mandela only served his first term in government and resigned with dignity, leaving the rest of the work to the young and vibrant up-and-coming politicians. The other reason many African leaders normally stay in power for quite a long period of time is that simply while they are still young and full of vibe, they don't train and mentor young politicians who should succeed them if they vacate the political office. This reality of vacating the public office without having anyone to replace them that they can trust because they haven't trained him haunts them to the point of panicking. A good leader should train and equip his people and allow them an opportunity to assume the leadership roles and responsibility in his presence. A bad leader does not train anyone when he is gone; he leaves a leadership vacuum behind that can't be filled by anyone. The African youth have been also complaining about the economic blunder and the political blunder that has been happening under the leadership of some of the African political leaders. Most of the African leaders are only looking at the interests of their families and their friends, leaving the masses languishing in the bottomless pit of poverty. This culture by African leaders of making things easy for their relatives and friends that are in their close circle has been going on for quite some time, and it has reached an unacceptable level. There is no African country in the whole continent of Africa where you can't hear about the complaints of corruption and fraud. In fact Africa is a continent of fraud and corruption. I need to state that Africans are not corrupt in nature, but African leaders have contracted the virus of corruption and fraud from the West. It is the West that taught most of the African leaders' corruption, and it is the West that taught African leaders that the only way to stay in public office even if the ordinary people are sick and tired of you is to rig votes and win elections, and there is nothing that the ordinary people can do about it. The African Union (AU) has finally come to its senses and begun to realize that the marginalization of the African youth in major decision has a dire repercussion for the continent of Africa in the long run. AU summit resolutions:

> *"For the united and prosperous Africa, we need to prepare programs devoted to the youth education, especially in scientific and technical skills, in order to upgrade the continent's human resources," the chairperson stressed. In his view, educated and employed youths would have no inclination to engage in acts of violence and terrorism. "It is the youth who will lead development efforts of our continent. Though education is the key in preparation of the youth, we have an educational system which is not tailored to our needs in terms of employment and market."*[13]

The AU has realized that the majority of terrorist attacks that have been committed in many African countries are committed by the youth. If the majority of the African youths are found in schools and universities, they would not have enough time and even space to think about terrorist acts. It goes without saying then that as long as African leaders are not solving the African problem of youth unemployment and drug abuse, Africa will be forever the breeding ground for wars. There is no way a busy person who has a secular job can even think about indulging himself in drugs provided that there is something rewarding that keeps him busy and happy all the time. As long as the majority of the African youth are loitering the streets of Harare and the streets of Johannesburg, these young people become suitable candidates to be used by the drug lords and drug cartels to transport drugs consignment. In South Africa there has been a burning issue of youth wage subsidy, which was meant for the youth that was unemployed but had skills to be used by the economy. The youth wage subsidy idea never came to fruition until the writing of this book. No wonder, if the majority of the youth have nothing serious to do, they will normally engage in very diabolical criminal acts and eventually end up in jail and cost taxpayers' considerable amount of money and resources. The best way to keep the youth out of the streets and out of prisons is through sustainable employment opportunities and effective educational system that yields desired results in the long run. It's true that education is the key to success, and not only education alone can solve all African problems. Some of the African problems are structurally related rather than politically related. In other words, there is no need for a considerable amount of money to change all African problems; to put it differently, there is no need for a considerable amount of billions of US dollars to solve our African problems because they can't be solved by money as such. Let me give you a crystal-clear example: the land redistribution problem in South Africa can't be solved by a considerable amount of money, but it can be solved by expediency and collective concerted effort by all parties involved in seeking a long-lasting solution that is mutually beneficial. Surely South Africa is not Zimbabwe. Even though most of the South Africans don't know with certainty what happened exactly in Zimbabwe in 2000, we can all learn obviously from the costly political mistakes that have been made by the Zimbabwean government. Therefore, to solve some of Africa's problems, there is a need to change Africa's economies holistically, which have been designed by Africa's colonial master only to enrich the few elite and who are politically connected in high places, while the African masses are languishing in the bottomless pit of poverty eating crumbs that are falling from the rich man's table. We have witnessed the danger that comes with illegal mining in South Africa. We all have seen in South Africa how young people can be easily exploited and abused by those who have money in order to further enrich themselves at the expense of the youth who are unemployed and uneducated. The greatest danger in Africa right now is the majority of the youth who are unemployed and unskilled. Any African country has the majority of its population made up by the youth, and this very youth are not working and not even in education—that country is a magnet for terrorism. Young people who are not in employment and not in education are prone to commit crimes and acts of terrorism. In other words, African leaders have to take this matter of youth unemployment seriously because it's likely to be an instigator of many African problems to come in the near future. If you can go through the profile of the majority of the terrorists who were involved in Kenya, Westgate mall attack, in 2013, you can quickly get the perfect picture about the danger that the African youth can cause to a country if they are collectively determined to achieve a common objective. In other words, the rhino poaching that we Africans are whining and complaining about in Africa is also perpetuated by the African youth at some point. As long as African leaders are not united and together in the fight against drug abuse and drug trafficking in the African continent, Africa is likely to lose most of its young and bright minds because of the drug addictions and drug-related crimes. Philani Nombembe and Nashira Davids write:

> *Manenberg, on the Cape Flats, is dripping in blood. Young children at the neighborhood's fourteen schools are enduring hell. Gangsters are at it again—a drugs turf is at the heart of it. The news headlines are failing to accurately depict how most of the 52,866 residents have become hostages in their own homes. What also escapes the news is how children as young as nine are recruited by gangs and trained to shoot, using live targets.*[14]

Africa is winning the war against HIV/AIDS, and surely most African countries are going to win the war against rhino poaching and human trafficking. But it's also true that most of the African countries are losing the war against drug trafficking and the scourge of drugs that is ravaging the fragile African continent. The main problem with drug smuggling and drug addiction is the monetary element that is attached to drugs. It is now an open secret that the best way to a financial prosperity is the smuggling of drugs and rhino poaching. There are educated fellows who are quitting their secular jobs just to smuggle cocaine and to poach rhino horns just because it's easier to make quick bucks through rhino poaching and smuggling drugs than to follow the conventional wisdom of working hard and saving money and studying hard and acquiring postgraduate degrees in order to be promoted and get a better raise. This mantra of working hard is what parents have been preaching to their children, and the children are already sick of hearing it again and again from their middle-class parents. Children are no longer buying that old cliché from their parents because they know that they can get a financial breakthrough just like that in the twinkling of an eye through drugs smuggling and rhino poaching. The scourge of drugs in the Cape Flats is simply unbearable, and

I know children who left Cape Flats for Pretoria because of drug-related crimes in the Western Cape. Some people suggest that the reason there is a problem of drugs in the Cape Flats is the lack of political will from the political leadership in the Western Cape to end the problem of drugs. Until this day and age, the majority of people who are in prison right now are still blacks and coloreds in South Africa. The majority of these areas that are drug- infested are predominantly coloreds communities. I wouldn't want to stoop too low to further discuss the main reason the majority of coloreds communities are drug-infested communities. The same thing goes for the "hood," as they call it in the United States of America. The same is true with most locations in South Africa where the majority of black people are residing. There is one thing that is common among black people in the United States and even Africa, and that is poverty. The few that managed to escape the scourge of poverty, not only do they escape poverty completely but they also relocate and resettle among white community in order to muffle their children to be exposed to violent-riddled communities and drug-riddled communities. There is nothing wrong about protecting your children from impending danger, and that is the vital responsibility of a parent. The West is slowly but surely doing everything possible in the book to destroy and decimate African youth completely. The West knows it for a fact that if the majority of the African youth are in drugs and are in the streets, they can easily be manipulated, and they can even be employed to be illegal miners for the Western kingpins without even questioning the repercussion for their actions. There is no way the West can bring the African youth to extinction without the help of Africans to destroy completely the African youth. The point I am making is this: it takes two to tango. It takes the Western agents with the help of the African agents who are likely poor and unemployed to distribute drugs and kill the innocent lives of many young people who were going to be the future leaders of the African continent tomorrow. No wonder most African leaders decide to stay in power as long as they breathe. Though most of them are addicted to the state resources and state facilities, some of them are not addicted to state resources and state facilities; they have genuine comprehensive reasons why they are staying in power even if the time to go home and play with the kids has come. African leaders don't trust the African youth that they can still champion the course of the fallen heroes and fallen heroines. Most of the African leaders believe that the only things that the majority of African youth is obsessed with are drugs, booze, hot chicks, and sex. There is really nothing politically sound that the majority of the African youth can profess that can persuade and move the African leaders to relinquish their political position to the African youth. No wonder African countries, like Angola, Zimbabwe, and including Uganda, are stuck with the same old political leaders who are no longer creative and innovative as far as the economics and the politics of the day is concerned. The only thing that these African leaders can profess is the old cliché about the West—that the West has colonized Africa and took what rightfully belongs to Africa. Even though most of these African leaders had enough time and space to change the economic profile of their African countries, they didn't do anything substantial to change the economic profile of their countries. The only thing that these African leaders did was to enrich their families, including their friends who are in their close circles. There is no honor among thieves. Political relationships that are built upon patronage and cronyism are likely to crumble sooner rather than later. Marriage, which is also based on material gain and monetary gain, is as fragile as the political relationship, which is based on patronage and cronyism, which is what is happening in Africa today. There is nothing so painful as to discover later in life that the closest person whom you thought loves you with genuine love actually loved you because of your material wealth and material possession. More often than not you are likely to find out when the material possession and material wealth are gone and you are sick and bedridden. One of my friends came to me the other day and said something that left me emotionally traumatized. He said, "There is no love in marriage—it's only compromise and patience for one another." It's possible that his statement was purely based on his life experience and his own social environment. What is his reality is not my reality, and what is my reality is not his reality. It's important to listen to different people expressing their own opinions on a same subject who are not your peers. I have listened to different people about different political subjects, including the Zimbabwean economic debacle, and the more I listen to different people including Zimbabweans and non-Zimbabweans, the more I can quickly spot the level of ignorance and arrogance in their opinions. I have come across people who think that they possess the sole truth about what happened in Zimbabwe in the year 2000. Some of them are scholars who were not even in Zimbabwe when the farm invasion took place, yet they claim to possess the sole truth about the political sequence of events that led to the final moments of the farm invasion disaster. Their version of events is the only plausible version of events that should be adopted and recorded in the history books for the future generations to read.

CHAPTER 11

CASH LIQUIDITY CRISIS

The cash liquidity crisis is predominantly caused by political instability or political uncertainty, which is largely attributed to political mismanagement. Cash liquidity crisis in its nature means that there is insufficient cash in circulation, and as a result, businesses more often than not have difficulty in getting customers to buy products. The cash liquidity crisis also means that the banks don't have sufficient cash at their disposal. Zimbabwe is moving from the frying pan straight to the fire, and the West is largely responsible for the Zimbabwean cash liquidity crisis. After the GPA (Global Political Agreement), the Zimbabwean economy took a better shape due to political stability and conducive economic climate that came about as a result of the political certainty and political stability. The West became very ambitious about the Zimbabwean national elections that took place on July 31, 2013. There was a belief from the West, though not explicitly stated, that the national election results of July 31, 2013, will be in favor of the MDC-T. If, and that is the big if, the national elections of July 31, 2013, had been won by the MDC-T, it meant that the West has also won in its attempt to control and manipulate Zimbabwe just like it did in the past. Since things didn't go according to the MDC-T way, which is sponsored and supported by the West financially, it meant that the West had to come up with a new way to make the government of Pres. Robert Mugabe and ZANU-PF scream even louder than February 18, 2002, when the economic sanctions were introduced. The economic sanctions of February 18, 2002, still largely remain in place, though the EU (European Union) has lifted some of the economic sanctions from the total package of the economic sanctions that were imposed on February 18, 2002. But the majority of economic sanctions remain in place until this moment. Prior to the national election of July 31, 2013, there was economic stability largely attributed to the political stability. The big question then was this: what will happen should the ZANU-PF win the national elections of July 31, 2013? This is the question that the majority of people never wanted to answer because they largely believed that finally Pres. Robert Mugabe will be gone and never to return anymore into the Zimbabwean political stage. Pres. Robert Mugabe professed that should he lose the national elections of July 31, 2013, he will quit politics for good. The whole world was waiting for the Zimbabwean national election results with bated breath because there was a belief that the national election results will free Zimbabwe's economy from the illegal economic sanctions of the West. The unexpected happened; in fact what the majority of people were not anticipating will happen eventually happen: ZANU-PF won the national elections, and the fear crippled the potential foreign investors even and the financial institutions. After the national election results were announced, panic crept in, and the blood pressure of most people shot up immediately. People began to develop growing headaches that were unprecedented. The worst fear for most people became a reality. Pres. Robert Mugabe, with the brothers of farm invasions, is going to sit in the Zimbabwean government for another five long and hard years; poverty and power outages were going to be a normal way of living in Zimbabwe. During the Government of National Unity, there were economic problems even then; it will be unfair and unjust to suggest that during the Government of National Unity, everything was rosy. The difference between the Government of National Unity and post–Government of National Unity is this: political parties were working together during the Government of National Unity, and some of the ministries were headed by the MDC-T, and some ministries were headed by the ZANU-PF. There was political compromise from all political parties during the Government of National Unity. The Zimbabwean government during the Global Political Agreement era could even source money from different financial sources in order to keep the economy going. Though the civil servants didn't see the salary increments during the GPA, most of them were still receiving their salaries in time and being paid in US dollars at least by the Government of National Unity (GNU). Zimbabwe's civil servants were angry at the ministry of finance, which was headed by Tendai Biti from the MDC-T. Zimbabwe's civil servants believed that the Government of National Unity had money to increase their salaries, but the then minister of finance Tendai Biti chose not to increase their salaries intentionally and purposefully. There are insignificant decisions momentarily in politics that could have devastating ramifications in the near future if one does not take these insignificant decisions seriously. Simply put, most of the civil servants in Zimbabwe were already fed up with Tendai Biti and the MDC-T, and they had vowed that they will do everything in their power to make sure that the MDC-T does not return to government after July 31, 2013. Though that was not overtly stated by the civil servants, it was written all over their faces before the run-up to the national elections and even after the national elections. After I left Zimbabwe in September 2013, there were reports in the media that sixty elephants had died from cyanide poisoning in Hwange National Park.[1] The elephants' ivories were smuggled from Zimbabwe to Dubai and were estimated to be 447 kilograms. As long as economic sanctions remain in place, the worse is likely to fall upon the economy of Zimbabwe. There is no way in the world a person from Dubai can just come to Zimbabwe to poach ivory without having sufficient information about Hwange National Park. It's also impossible for the ordinary Zimbabweans to poison the elephants for ivory if they don't have a market to sell these ivories after they have been extracted from the elephants. What is apparently clear here is this: there is a syndicate among some Zimbabweans who are working closely with the Dubai poachers to ensure that after the elephants have been poisoned to death with cyanide, ivory gets extracted from the elephants meticulously and packaged properly and eventually airlifted to Dubai where there is a market and clients waiting for the ivory. Due to poverty and unemployment that had engulfed the economy of Zimbabwe, everybody is doing everything necessary to make sure that at least there is food on the table for the children. Even though it means embarking on an illegal trade of smuggling ivory out of Zimbabwe to Dubai, as long as the proceeds from that illegal business will put money in their pocket, that is enough for the day. What do you expect an ordinary person to do when there is permanent poverty and permanent corruption that are crippling a country like Zimbabwe apart? During any crisis, whether it's a political crisis or an economic crisis, even in war, people are compelled by the pressing circumstances to act in the defense of their families that they don't get hurt and at the same time to protect their families that they don't die because of hunger. During that period of uncertainty and mayhem, the law of the jungle will apply—eat or be eaten. It's true that the majority of elephants' ivories that are reported in the mainstream media are far less than the actual elephants' ivories that are being smuggled out of Zimbabwe day and night without the authorities knowing about it. The smuggling of elephants' ivories and rhino horns have been happening for a considerable amount of time before even the mainstream media knew about it. Smuggling of rhino and ivory gives poachers leverage compared to the average law-abiding citizens. The majority of the people survive through secular jobs, which largely come from the public sector and the private sector. These secular jobs don't even pay that much, meaning a person who is relying on a secular job will take a little bit longer to get the majority of things done quickly unless otherwise there is an external intervention to supplement his salary. In order for people to avoid starving their families to death, they would rather take the illegal route—let me call it "the elephants' ivories and rhino horns" route. We all know of families who were poor the previous week only to be filthy rich the following week in the twinkling of an eye. It seems as if ordinary people who are law-abiding citizens are also running out of patience with their national governments. People are fed up with listening to the old record of fighting corruption and prosecuting the perpetrators and their accomplice. The same thing that is happening in Zimbabwe is the same thing that is happening in South Africa. Ordinary people who are law-abiding citizens like me have waited patiently for far too long, and some of them are expressing their dissatisfaction through illegal means. There are people who like to draw national attention by protesting on the streets, but there are some who don't subscribe to the conventional thinking of believing that most of your problems will be solved by the ballot paper and the faint pen. They just take the ropes and get underground and get the job done, and the next thing you know, they have cars and properties and they are living in the posh suburbs of South Africa without even burning the tires on the streets protesting. These groups of people who believe in solving their financial problems without having to queue for the government grants are called "Zama Zamas" gold and diamond prospectors. They are doing it for themselves without the help of the national government—the pursuit of wealth at all costs. Even if the pursuit of wealth will cost one his precious gift of life, it really does not matter much to some people. It's important to pursue wealth at all costs, if that is possible, but I have a slightly different view than most people. Pursuing wealth at all costs even if the pursuit of the wealth and material can cost you the greatest gift of them all, which is life itself at the expense of wealth, material, and possessions, is dangerous. However, one should not just pray and bury his head on the sand and think that things will just happen without putting concerted effort. It's important to work hard to achieve your dreams legally not illegally. South African roads are jam-packed with cars, and some of these people who are causing the congestion on the South African national roads are rhino poachers who are driving big cars, which were bought from their ill-gotten wealth from their illegal business. If the South African government was to conduct lifestyle audit from all these people who are driving big cars, one will be shocked at the findings of the audit. The fact of the matter is this: most people in Africa are now living beyond and above their normal means, though they are earning very little in their secular jobs. One wonders, how can an employee who is earning R12,000 per month afford an apartment in the posh suburbs that is costing R2 million? That is exactly what is happening in most African countries—ordinary people are filthy rich, and they can't even account and disclose the original source of their wealth. Let me give you piece of a financial advice: not all people who are rich today can account and disclose their original sources of their wealth, and as a result, it will be very unwise for you to compete and compare yourself with a professional rhino poacher because rhino poachers make a considerable amount of money in the twinkling of an eye, while an average person has to rely on a paycheck that comes once a month at least. The cash liquidity crisis is upon the Zimbabweans, and it seems as if for the next five years things will become even worse economically, though there is political stability in the country. The West is laughing again just like in the year 2000 when the war veterans were invading the commercial farms. It's possible to win the battle and lose the war. What is the use of winning national elections if the very same people who voted for you will continue to live in abject poverty with no end in sight? African leaders have a huge responsibility on their shoulders; not only are they expected to lead their people and even their ailing economies, but they are also expected to make sure that the African people on the ground have sustainable jobs that will make meaningful contribution on their lives. The time for lame excuses and finger pointing is over. The West stole Africa's wealth, and even to this day there is no indication whatsoever that the West is keen and interested in acknowledging the damage that it has caused in the African continent. The West is not even ready to listen to the narrative that Africa is the richest continent in the whole world, and due to the Western interference in the African domestic affairs until this day, Africa, realistically speaking, answers to the Western powers. Most of the African leaders beam with excitement if they are visiting the West because they know for a fact that they will not come back home to the African soil empty-handed; at least they will get financial help in a form of foreign aid. The financial liquidity crisis in Zimbabwe has spilled over to South Africa, and the ramification of the cash liquidity crisis is astounding to me as the person who is constantly monitoring and following what is happening in Zimbabwe and the effect that the Zimbabwean economic sanctions have on the South African economy. When the majority of people are hungry, they will literally become angry and they will look for any sort of means to express their anger, including embarking on an illegal trade as long as they will get money in order to survive. Sometimes when people are not happy with the government of the day, they will just immigrate to the nearest country to look for greener pastures, and that is exactly what is happening in Zimbabwe. If you can take a tour to Beitbridge just to observe how many Zimbabweans are crossing the Beitbridge border each and every day to South Africa legally and illegally, you are likely to ask yourself many questions that can't even be answered. When I was on the way to South Africa from Bulawayo, I was told by several people in the bus that the Zimbabwean government would not issue passports to the Zimbabweans who wanted to immigrate to other countries like South Africa unless otherwise you pay the bribe to the officials to get your application form for the passport to be processed quickly. The rest of the people, especially those who don't have money for their application forms for the passport, would lie on the government offices unprocessed for quite a long period of time until the people get fed up with the government red tape and devise means to solve their dilemma illegally. Ordinary Zimbabweans became alive to the fact that their government was not entirely happy with the idea of processing the application forms for passport applicants with ease because that will render Zimbabwe as a ghost country with everybody leaving the country for South Africa legally. The best strategy that was employed by the government was to delay the issuing of passports and the processing of the application forms for passport applicants; this technique will at least deter the masses to come to South Africa legally. It's true that there are some Zimbabweans who still want to come to South Africa even at this point in time legally, but because of lack of passports, they are still trembling with fear that should they choose the illegal route, they might get arrested in South Africa and deported back to Zimbabwe with immediate effect. The Zimbabwean government system, to delay the processing of passport applications, could not deter the dreams and the aspirations of ordinary Zimbabweans to live a better life and to search for better living conditions elsewhere. The ordinary Zimbabweans began to jump the Beitbridge border illegally, specifically those who don't have necessary documents to enter South Africa legally, and those who don't have necessary documents to cross the Beitbridge border legally just devise means to get to South Africa illegally. Each and every crisis brings financial losses and financial gains with it. Most bus companies from South Africa were incorporated during the economic sanctions of February 18, 2002. Some of these bus companies were not existing prior to the economic sanctions of February 18, 2002, because there were few Zimbabweans who were emigrating Zimbabwe to South Africa to look for greener pastures, and as it has been said many times that once a upon a time Zimbabwe was the breadbasket of Southern Africa and the food exporter, but right now Zimbabwe is the basket case of the Southern Africa and only surviving through importing almost everything. There are medium-size transport companies that are still responsible for transporting Zimbabweans from the bushes of the Beitbridge border to the city of gold, Johannesburg. I remember vividly an incident that happened around 2010 when one Zimbabwean lady was transported from the bushes of Beitbridge to Johannesburg, the city of gold, though there is no gold anymore in Johannesburg because the West has stolen all the gold that was underground in the belly of Johannesburg, but even to this day Johannesburg is still called the city of gold as if there is gold everywhere lying on the street. The fact of the matter is this: Johannesburg is no longer the city of gold because there is no gold anymore in Johannesburg. The West has stolen all the gold that was once buried in the belly of Johannesburg. Get it to your skull: there is no longer a city of gold in South Africa. This mantra that Johannesburg is the city of gold is an ancient fairy tale. When this Zimbabwean lady was transported to South Africa from the bushes of Beitbridge, the transport arrangements were, once she gets to South Africa, she will meet some of her relatives in Johannesburg, and her relatives will be able to pay the bus fare to the bus driver for her. The moment the bus got to Johannesburg, none of her relatives apparently came to collect her and pay the bus fare for her, and the bus driver had to devise means to collect his money from the woman. The bus driver sold her on the spot. I remember him saying, "If you have R400 give me and I will give you a wife." The woman was sold for almost R400. The point of the matter is this: Zimbabwe's economic crisis never got the world's attention that it ought to get. There are many Zimbabweans who are still living in abject poverty because of the Zimbabwean economic crisis. Sometimes it's not easy to understand the extent and the gravity of a situation unless otherwise you are in it yourself. The world leaders have turned a blind eye on the Zimbabwean political and economic dilemma. When I was in Zimbabwe for the first time in my life, I developed anger and loathness within me, and I began to hate politics and the politicians themselves, and I didn't care about the imminent national elections that were about to take place in the country, and instead of me being scared of the government forces that were also roaming around the streets of Harare and trying to maintain order on the streets, I was conducting interviews even though the political climate warranted one to be politically quiet. When I was asleep at night alone in the hotel, I would sometimes become afraid and ask myself this question: What if the CIO (Central Intelligence Organization) officials are following me? The good thing about all those train of evil thoughts that were in mind is that none of them materialized. I have come to understand my faith better now unlike before. I have come to the understanding that the majority of people follow the mainstream media reports, and they believe what a single reporter reports without even daring to question the validity of the report. I am not implying that everything that is being reported in the mainstream media is a lie, but as a responsible person, it is vital that you conduct your independent research about things that are reported in the mainstream media. There more I read about the Zimbabwean political and economic chaos, the more I began to understand that sometimes most of the African problems will take a considerable amount of time to be solved than what it ought to take because of the information gap and information deficit that exists among Africans themselves. My driver who was driving me around in Bulawayo on my second trip shocked me to the extreme when he said to me, "I have never been in Cecil John Rhodes's grave." Here is a man who is almost in his fifties who was born and bred in Zimbabwe and he is almost ageing, but he does not understand the history of his country! Here I am coming all the way from South Africa, Pretoria, to Zimbabwe, Bulawayo, just to see the old grave of Cecil John Rhodes and understand the significant role that Cecil John Rhodes played in impoverishing Africa. There are many Africans who don't understand Africa like they ought to understand it, but for the moment, most of the African children don't understand where we Africans as people come from. If this generation, which is supposed to understand our history and even go further to write our African history, is busy on Face book and WhatsApp, who will then write our African history? Our African history will continue to be owned and written in the West. The African history becomes the African history from the Western perspective. Pres. Robert Mugabe turned ninety in February 2014, and he is even going stronger like never before, and his message on his birthday was this: "I am not resigning." There were multiple conflicting reports about his state of health, and some reports were even suggesting that during his birthday he was likely to announce his resignation from the national government. Baba Jukwa, the Richard Snowden of Zimbabwe, already went further to suggest that Pres. Robert Mugabe fainted inside the presidential compound, and they had to pour buckets and buckets of water to resuscitate him again to life. Although the state reports and state media rejected the reports, one can't ignore the fact that Pres. Robert Mugabe is no longer in good health; he looks very pale and fragile. Perhaps I need to take this moment and express my birthday wishes to Pres. Robert Mugabe: Happy birthday, Mr. President, and I hope that you will grow old and stay in power for another five years and, if it's possible, maybe serve another term in office—I mean, when the 2018 national elections come, I hope you will still be around, man. We all know that the majority of people are banking on the health of Pres. Robert Mugabe, and there is a belief in the corridors of the White House that when Pres. Robert Mugabe is gone, there will be political transitions in Zimbabwe, as the head of the house will be gone. Zöe Mahopo writes:

> *Our brothers, we have come to ask for your spirits from beneath this hole. Rise up and return home where your kin and ancestors are resting. Your life on earth has come to an end. Another life with the ancestors awaits.* [2]

South Africans woke up to the disturbing images of illegal miners who died on the Johannesburg old shafts, and the bodies of these illegal miners had begun to decompose. The total number of the miners who died that day was twenty, and almost the entire twenty illegal miners were from the West of Zimbabwe, and their bodies had to be transported back to their country of birth where a decent burial was going to be held. I need to tell the truth based on my experience from traveling between Zimbabwe and South Africa. It's extremely expensive to transport a dead body from South Africa to Zimbabwe, and the processes that should be followed on the Beitbridge border are complicated and convoluted. Dead people queue too if they get to the Beitbridge border. The fact that you are dead, that does not exonerate the deceased from the government red tape. There is a queue that has been specifically designated for the dead, and there is no living human being who should queue on that queue except the hearse that is transporting the deceased. I met two gentlemen on the Beitbridge border on my second trip to Zimbabwe in Zimbabwe's immigration office who was getting stamps for their passports. They were driving the hearse and they were from South Africa, and guess what! They were drunk, and I could smell alcohol from a distance! I can't blame them. I think driving a dead person is the most traumatizing experience ever, and what can one do if he finds himself in a situation where you have to drive a dead person for almost 1,070 kilometers? The siblings of the deceased miners blamed the whole situation to the economic conditions that are prevailing in Zimbabwe. When the West imposed economic sanctions to the Zimbabwean economy on February 18, 2002, it did not impose economic sanctions on the Zimbabwean economy alone but also imposed economic sanctions on the neighboring countries that are surrounding Zimbabwe, like Mozambique, Botswana, and South Africa. Though the majority of Zimbabweans prefer to immigrate to South Africa than immigrating to Botswana and Mozambique, Mozambique and Botswana also received some of the Zimbabweans at the end of the day. The fact of the matter is this: the country to which the influx of people will immigrate to will have to provide sustainable jobs and shelter for this influx of people who are coming from another country. The same is true with South Africa due to the mass exodus of people from Zimbabwe to South Africa. It means that the South African government should see to it that the little resource that it has set aside for its EPWP (Expanded Public Works Programme) should now be utilized to cater for the refugees that are now in South Africa. The twenty illegal miners who died in the old unused shafts in Johannesburg where they were mining the South African gold illegally, not the Zimbabwean gold, were also mining in South Africa's soil, not in Zimbabwe's soil. The point I making is this: the fact of the matter is, the Zimbabwean economic crisis, whether people agree with me or not, : it is costing the South African government billions and billions of rands. The South African president Jacob Zuma in his state of the nation address made it plain and simple that the South African mines employ more than five hundred thousand people, and the mines themselves contribute R20 billion rands in revenue to the national government, which in turn this money is utilized to fund the government projects and even to build the infrastructure. The more the illegal miners continue to steal the gold in the belly of the South African soil, the more the mines are losing millions of rands, and as a result, the less revenue the mines generate, the less tax they will pay to the national government, and eventually that will affect negatively the national government financially. The illegal mining of the South African gold is tantamount to what the Mozambicans were doing post the Mozambican war. The Mozambicans post–civil war began stealing the herd of cattle from the South Africans who are residing close to the Lebombo border. The argument that was put forward then by the Mozambicans is this: South Africans stole the herds of the cattle from the Mozambicans during the apartheid era. Now the Mozambicans claimed they were taking what belonged to them by stealing from the South Africans. There is no point in history where South Africans who are residing next to the Lebombo border once stole the herds of cattle from the Mozambicans. I wonder whether or not that will be the narrative that will be put forward by the Zimbabweans when they argue their case. The fact still remains: mining illegally from the South African soil by the illegal miners is tantamount to theft, and that is robbing the very same South Africans who were supposed to benefit immensely from these mineral deposits. There is no way and no point in history where the Zimbabweans, just like the Mozambicans, can claim that the main reason they are mining illegally in the South African soil is that purely South Africans stole their mineral resources during the apartheid era. Though Zimbabwe was colonized by Great Britain through its BSAC (Britain South Africa Company), South Africa itself was a colony of Great Britain, and bona fide South Africans, the Nguni people, didn't even see a dime of those proceeds, which were made during the colonial era either through the colonization of Zimbabwe or the colonization of South Africa itself as a country by Great Britain. The point I making is this: South Africans did not steal from the Zimbabweans when Mzilikazi left South Africa. He became a Zimbabwean permanently—meaning his citizenship changed diametrically from being a South African to a Zimbabwean. Whatever Mzilikazi did to the Shona people, he did it in his capacity as a Zimbabwean not as a South African. We all know that Mzilikazi was a cattle raider and he was stealing the herd of cattle from the Shonas, and that has been his life since birth. That is not a justifiable reason for the Zimbabweans and especially this current generation to illegally mine gold from the South African soil with impunity as if the South African soil is the Zimbabwean soil. King Mzilikazi did not conduct mining operations in Zimbabwe; he was purely stealing the herds of cattle from the Shonas only, not mining gold illegally. The cash liquidity crisis does not only mean that there is insufficient money in circulation, but it also means that the majority of companies are closing shop. When companies are closing shop, the workforce of the company in question should be retrenched, and some should be dismissed with immediate effect. The cycle of poverty gets perpetuated even further when the majority of people lose their secular jobs. It's very unfortunate that innocent children have to starve to death because of the sins of the past that have been committed by the West to the continent of Africa. There is a proverbial saying that I love dearly, which goes like this: "The more things change, the more they stay the same." This is true with the African story. Until this point in our African history, things have been changing, and most African countries are now politically independent, and guess what! The more African countries get independence from the West, the more they stay in poverty except the few ruling elites who are connected in high places. Political connectivity is the fastest train to financial freedom. It seems as if people who are going to follow the conventional wisdom of saving money and try to play by the rules are likely to stay in poverty for quite a long period of time, while the few elites are enjoying the dividends of financial freedom and political freedom. The majority of African people are stuck in the cul-de-sac of political freedom without financial freedom. There are few people who are beginning to wake up from the long sleep of political freedom. What would you do if I could give a candle without a box of matches? The fact of matter is this: you would still be in the dark and what do you think would happen if I gave you a candle with a box of matches? Surely you would light up the candle and stay in the light. Africa has been given the candle without the box of matches, and the West is running away with the box of matches until this day. The foreign aid and the doughnuts of loans from the IMF and the World Bank are temporary measures to keep the African light on, and that is not even permanent. Africa needs a permanent light, not the candle without a light. Political freedom is the candle, and financial freedom is the box of matches. Africa has the candle, but it does not have the box of matches. That is why most African countries, still to this day, play the Western music and study the Western culture in order to fit into the Western practices because of foreign aid and food parcels from the West. The greatest danger that is facing most of the African countries is the incessantly financial dependency to the West. When will it be when all African countries will be able to stand on their own financially and even politically? We all know now that as long as African countries in their domestic politics and even in the domestic financial affairs develop economic policies that are anti-Western agenda, these African countries are likely to struggle to secure any financial assistance from the IMF (International Monetary Fund) and the World

Bank. We all know that if any African country does not subscribe to the Western belief, like decriminalization of same-sex marriages, these African countries can even be branded as anti-democratic and anti–freedom of expression. The point I am making is this: as long as African countries continue to depend on the West for financial assistance, they won't have any option in the near future but to follow the Western practices and pass laws that support the Western agenda. As soon as the president of Uganda Yoweri Museveni passed the antigay bill, the West was on his neck and threatening to cut the foreign aid that was destined for Uganda. The one-million-dollar question that I have been asking myself all along is this: What will happen to African countries the day when the West will decide to cut off the foreign aid that was destined to Africa permanently? How will these African countries, which are foreign aid dependent, survive? The best people to answer that question are the African leaders. Our political freedom is a Pyrrhic victory, and the fact of the matter is this: Africa is not free politically and even financially. Most people will probably say, "We are free politically free because we have the right to vote for our own political leaders, and we are free because we have the right to choose where we want to stay, and we are free because we are no longer carrying a Dom pass as it used to be the case in South Africa during the apartheid era." Political freedom does not necessarily mean freedom of movement and freedom of choice; it goes wider than that. Political freedom means that African people who were robbed of their land by the West are given back their land without paying a dime of dollar. What is happening in Africa about the land is appalling and disgusting. Though I have said many times that this book is not about the Land Reform Program or Land Redistribution Program. There are certain things that just creep into your mind even though you know for a fact that you don't want to discuss them at length purely because you believe that you have dealt with them in depth in a particular chapter. In my last chapter, when I will write my summary, I will deal in depth with the land grab and the Land Restitution Program, as we call it in South Africa, as well as the Land Redistribution Program, as they call it in Zimbabwe. Though the Zimbabwean government cannot admit comprehensively that there is such a thing as a cash liquidity crisis, the fact of the matter is; there is a cash liquidity crisis on the ground. In 2009 the ZRB (Zimbabwe Reserve Bank) introduced what is known as the dollarization. The introduction of the dollarization meant that Zimbabwe will use the US dollar as their functional currency. The overall objective of the introduction of the US dollar was to stabilize the economy that was in tatters because of the political climate and the economic fiasco that was caused by the farm invasion of 2000. The dollarization did perform some magic for the Zimbabwean economy, but even then there were economic problems. There is one thing that I have been complaining about in the entire of my trip when I was in Zimbabwe—that is the high prices of goods and services. I remember at one point I had to pay ten dollars in Bulawayo to gain access to the museum. Ten US dollars according to South African currency is equivalent to one hundred rands. For me to visit the former Transvaal Museum, I have to pay just twenty rands, which is equivalent to two US dollars, if the foreign exchange rate is one dollar is equal to ten rands. I hope that you get the picture. Life is not easy in Zimbabwe not only for the Zimbabweans but also even for foreign visitors. I need to make this point crystal clear: I love Zimbabwe and I also love the Zimbabweans though I am not a Zimbabwean. If I didn't love Zimbabwe, I would not have wasted my money and visited an African country that I hate with passion. One of the things that make me love Zimbabwe and the Zimbabwean people is the respect that the majority of the Zimbabweans have toward the law and the law enforcer. I have noticed a great difference between the South African people's attitudes toward the South African law enforcers and the people of Zimbabwe toward the Zimbabwean law enforcers. In Zimbabwe a police officer can just get into the bus without even paying the bus fare and commute from one area to another, while in South Africa that is not the case; the law enforcers, if they are using the public transport like the taxi and the bus, will still have to fork out money to pay for bus fare. Though this assertion that the law enforcers don't pay the bus fare when they are commuting from one area to another in Zimbabwe has been disputed by many law enforcers, I have seen it with my naked eyes happening in Bulawayo in broad daylight. Sometimes lying to protect the image of your country can be detrimental in the long run to your reputation as a human being and is the microcosm of a person who has character flaws. I know a lot of people who have been lying to me to protect the image of their country in order to be respected and revered. The same is true with the Western countries and their citizens; they will be talking about the African poverty as if there is no poverty in their own countries. Let me oversimplify it for you: there is no country in the world that doesn't have domestic problems, including the so-called G7 countries. There are drug addicts and junkies in the so-called richest countries in the world. There are people who are sleeping on the streets even in the G7 countries. The fact that certain Western countries are advanced economically than most of the African countries does change the fact that there are domestic problems even in these Western countries. It's an inescapable reality that Western countries are more advanced technologically and economically than most of the African countries. But that does not negate the fact that African countries do have the potential to match pound for pound most of the Western countries if the West can repay Africa what was stolen from Africa during the colonial era. It's common knowledge that the skyscrapers that are in the West have been built by the African slaves, and the West didn't even pay a dime of a dollar to these African slaves. All the skyscrapers that are in the West have been built by my African forefathers and my African brothers who were held in captivity just like the children of Israel who were held in captivity in Egypt during Pharaoh's era. There is nothing that the West can claim to own except the fact that they have explored Africa because of hunger that was permeating Europe, North America, and Canada. After the July 31, 2013, Zimbabwe's national elections, ordinary investors who thought that the MDC-T was going to win the national election became very depressed and traumatized, including my driver Terry who thought at least once and for all MDC-T have managed to get rid of the "old man." Due to the fear and anxiety that were permeating the atmosphere through panic, people went to the banks to withdraw their monies and kept it in their safe at home, and some even went as far as withdrawing their monies from the banks and putting it under their beds in Zimbabwe. The fact of the matter is this: people knew exactly what the economic ramification was for the ZANU-PF to win the national elections. After the announcement of the national elections, there were disappointments and sadness among most people even in South Africa. There are people who went as far as saying, "Pres. Robert Mugabe rigged the elections," though there is no crystal-clear evidence to support that assertion except pieces of information that can't survive the legal scrutiny. Though from the surface it might be true that ZANU-PF hired an Israeli company and a Chinese company to rig the outcome of the national election in favor of ZANU-PF that does not change the fact that there are some people who voted for ZANU-PF of Pres. Robert Mugabe. I don't believe that there could be a wholesale rigging of national election results. What I can accept is this: there was rigging of the national election results to a certain acceptable degree to ensure that ZANU-PF secured a political victory, what the majority of people called "landslide victory." In response to the cash liquidity crisis question, the minister of finance Patrick Chinamasa said:

> *The banking sector is not sick. We have twenty-one banks, and of those, three had challenges of liquidity.*[3]

Let me accept the assertion that has been made by the finance minister Patrick Chinamasa. The fact of the matter is this: there is a cash liquidity crisis, and it's worth documenting it for the future generation. Sometimes mistakes should happen in order to teach the future generation not to repeat the same mistakes just like the past generation. Though three out of twenty banks are sick, the fact that remains is this: there is a cash liquidity crisis in Zimbabwe, and that is not deniable. My greatest concerns about the African liberation struggle are the following: many African liberation movements were not prepared and trained enough to run their economies post-liberation struggle. What is the use of being politically independent if you can't be financially independent? It seems as if most of the African countries are politically independent but financially dependent on the West, and the next question that warrants to be raised is this: Is political independence sufficient enough to ensure that there is financial independence? There is one cardinal sin that had been committed by "Mother Moscow," Russia. Mother Moscow, the capital city of Russia, played a pivotal role in ensuring that the majority of the African countries get their political independence either through the guerilla war or through the diplomatic process like CODESA in South Africa. The cardinal sin that had been committed by Russia is this: it (Russia) never trained the ex-combatants how to survive after the end of the African liberation struggle and how to run their economies in a modern era. Things are changing, and they are changing very fast. There is always a new product that is being introduced in the market now and then. Companies that were once regionally based are now globally based. Money moves faster than the speed of sound. Companies are incorporated and registered within a second, and some companies are dissolved and deregistered within a split of a second also. It therefore means that human beings are in this new search of a better life and a better business deals that can alter their life once and for all. The spirit of materialism and endless wealth is sweeping almost all families and all institutions whether private or public. Every now and when I go to church on Sunday, out of nowhere a preacher will page through the Holy Bible just to find a scripture that compels the congregation to give all what they have in the spirit of sacrificial giving. I am not ant-giving, and I believe that people should give in their churches for the betterment of the church, for the construction of the church building, and for paying salaries of people that are working in the church. The problem that all NGOs and NPOs have in common is the lack of financial disclosure. When you suggest that there should be financial disclosure, the leadership of the church is likely to get angry because they see financial disclosure to the very congregation that is giving money to the church as a sign of disrespect and dishonor. The government requires NGOs to provide all necessary documents for funding purposes and to even make available their previous audited financial statements for funding purposes. While NGOs like churches don't provide financial statements to their church members, now and then you will hear a minister of the word hammering on the same point about money and even going as far as blackmailing the congregation spiritually about not giving the tithe and even the sacrificial offering. I have been visiting different churches in South Africa, and I am extremely thrilled with the way some of the South African churches are handling their finances. In fact one church will put it on its website how much money it has made in the past six months and even laid it bare to its congregation the next project that the church will embark on. Financial disclosures not only give the congregation the crystal-clear picture about the finances of the church but also exonerate the church board and the finance committee of any financial wrongdoing. If you are dealing with money and the next thing people will see you driving a new car, people are likely to say that the car that you are driving was bought with their money I am paying tax in South Africa each and every month, and the South African government is deducting income tax from my salary. Even though that is money that was hard earned by me, the state just takes my money without even getting a concession from me in the name of income tax. As long as the state deducts money from my salary in the name of income tax, therefore the state is obliged to the people of South Africa to disclose and lay bare its financial affairs to the public as long as the state receives income taxes from the taxpayers. The point I am making is this: as long as the churches are continuing to receive the tithes from their congregations, then these churches are obliged to disclose their financial affairs to the very same congregations from which they receive the tithes. I know there are conflicting and multiple theories about this point. Some ministers of the word say, when you give your money to the church, don't dare to ask what church used your money for. By asking the church how it used your money that you have given wholeheartedly is tantamount to not giving at all and there won't be any blessing that you will receive from the Lord. In other words, give your money into the church basket, but don't ask how it is used because that is none of your business. Yours is to give and never ask any question, and it's the responsibility of the church to see to it how to use your money. I have great difficulties with this kind of assertion. I am from the financial disclosure school of thought, and I believe that if the congregation is giving money to the church, therefore the congregation is entitled to know how the funds of the church are utilized and what prompts the church to buy certain things and why certain things were bought and how much these equipments cost the church and how much is left in the church coffers at the moment. The majority of people would give gladly and happily so if they know how much their church is having in its financial coffer. Last on the issue of the church and the offering, as long as the church expects the congregation to offer tithes and offerings to the church, then the church itself has the moral responsibility to disclose the financial affairs of the church to the congregation. I know for a fact that this statement will not go down well with the majority of people because some of them have been profiting through robbing the congregation a considerable amounts of money by not disclosing the financial affairs of the church to the very same congregation that is giving its money week in and week out to the church. The fact that Russia didn't give sufficient financial training to the ex-combatants during the African liberation struggle is crystal clear in the way most African countries are failing decimally to run their economies. A good soldier does not always make a good manager, and just like in soccer, it does not mean that a good soccer player will automatically be a good coach in the near future. That has been a problem with many African countries after the African liberation struggle. Most of the African leaders who were in exile are now sitting presidents of most African countries and still bitter and angry because of the past memories of the African liberation struggle. The economic sanctions of February 18, 2002, not only hurt the economy of Zimbabwe only but also rendered the relationship between the West and Africa to be even sourer than ever before. There is a lack of trust between the West and Africa because of the long unhealthy historical trauma between the West and Africa. The question that comes to mind is this: Can the slave trust his master slave? The slave has all the rights to believe that the slave master has one thing in mind—that is to further oppress the slave like never before. Even though the slave master can exhibit a change of heart and a change of mind, the fact remains: the salve can't trust his master because of what happened in the past. Economic sanctions are the political tools of the West to compel any country that is rebellious like

Russia to the West to feel the heat. I regret to inform you that there are no longer G8 countries. What was known as the G7 countries in the past, that G8 club is nonexistent, and now there is a newly formed G7 countries. The G7 is now constituted by Britain, the United States, Germany, France, Italy, Canada, and Japan. All of the G7 countries made it clear that they are not supporting the Russian idea of annexing Crimea, which is part of Russia and part of Ukraine. The G7 countries then imposed economic sanctions to Russia. The cardinal sin that had been committed by Russia does not only emanate from the annexation of Crimea by Russia; it dates as far back as the eighteenth century. It will be inappropriate and even unwise to go back in time and give a long boring lecture about how the Soviet Union came about and the collapse of the Soviet Union. What I would like to do is to explain to you very briefly how Russia got itself in this hot water that it's currently in. Any country that is anti-Western and anti-Seven Sisters, which are the Western companies that are doing the dirty businesses for the West in the whole world under the notion of bilateral trade agreement, is likely to get economic sanctions imposed on it. The United Nations does not see the imposition of economic sanctions by the West as a violation of human rights. Though the same United Nations sees the funding of terrorist organization as a human rights violation, and any country and any person who is found to be financially supporting terrorists organizations will be arrested and prosecuted by the ICC (International Criminal Court). The G7 countries do not need an approval of the United Nations Security Council to impose economic sanctions to any country that is rebellious to the West just like Russia. I need to further make it clear that right now the economic sanctions that have been imposed to the Russian economy won't have a serious dent to the economy of Russia simply because they have been imposed on individuals who are pro–Vladimir Putin, and if the status quo remains, the G7 countries will impose the wholesale economic sanctions to Russia just like the Zimbabwean economic sanctions that were imposed on February 18, 2002. The big question then is, what is it that Russia did on the face of the West that invited such economic sanctions, which can sometimes wind up being full-scale economic sanctions if the Russian stance toward the annexation of Crimea does not change? There are myriad political misdemeanors that I can mention that compelled the West to impose the economic sanctions to Russia. Most of the Western cultural practices that are even allowed in most African countries are not allowed in Russia. Simply put, homosexuals were not even allowed to protest in the Russian streets, and if homosexuals can stage a protest, they will be arrested with an immediate effect in Russia. During the Sochi Olympics of 2013, there are protestors who were arrested because of advocating and protesting for antigay laws in Russia. The second cardinal sin that had been committed by Russia is its attempt by Russia to be a global superpower and to remain as the European regional superpower. The West and its G7 corrupt countries and its Seven Sisters want to control the whole world and run the whole show without being interrupted by Russia. The fact that Russia welcomed Edward Snowden and gave him a political asylum in Russia did not sit well with the Western countries because they saw that act as a sign of disrespect and as a sign of betrayal by Russia. What Vladimir Putin ought to have done was to arrest Richard Snowden and deport him back to the United States. The Russian president Vladimir Putin did the opposite. The third cardinal sin that had been committed by Russia's president Vladimir Putin was preventing the United States to decimate and dismantle Bashar al-Assad and his Syrian troops. The fact of the matter is this: there were no sufficient and reasonable reasons as to why the West wanted to decimate and destroy Syria diametrically, except the fact that the West wanted to display to the world its latest-acquired military equipment on the Syrian soil and on the Syrian people. I still hold the view that had it not been for the Russian intervention in the Syrian crisis, the West had long razed Damascus walls to the ground with its weapons of mass destruction that should only be possessed by the West and nobody else in the world. When the West began meddling in the Syrian politics and in the Syrian War by supporting the oppositional parties with financial resources and military equipments, it thought that it will remove Bashar al-Assad with ease just like the West did with Muammar Gaddafi of Libya, though there are conflicting political narratives as to who exactly removed the Libyan leader Muammar Gaddafi from power. The US narrative tells us that Muammar Gaddafi was removed by his Libyan people whom he had been oppressing for quite a long period of time. The narrative goes, Muammar Gaddafi was a tyrant and a dictator, and he was by large supporting terrorist organizations and countries that are anti-Western and anti-Western foreign policy. While Muammar Gaddafi was still alive, he made it known that he was supporting the political actions that have been taken by the brothers of farm invasion known as the war veterans of Zimbabwe. Muammar Gaddafi was paying his allegiance to the Somali pirates who were abducting and kidnapping people and seeking ransom in US dollars for their release. There are certain people who have died in the hands of the Somali pirates who could not afford the ransom that was required by the Somali pirates. The Somali pirates survive through the ransoms that they get from the relatives of those who have been kidnapped. Though the Somali pirates are the militia group and affiliated to the big terrorist organization like al-Qaeda, they don't function like al-Qaeda in its intents and purposes. The Somali pirates only want to control the sea, and simply because they have been defeated on the ground, they make the sea their only legitimate home and their only legitimate base. The Somali term for "pirate" is *burcad badeed*, which means "ocean robber," though the pirates themselves prefer to be called *badaaadinta badah,* or "savior of the sea."[4] In response to the Somali piracy and their actions of abducting and kidnapping innocent people and seeking heavy ransoms in return for their release for their victim, the late Libyan leader Muammar Gaddafi said the following:

> *It is a response to greedy Western nation who invade and exploit Somali's water illegally. It is not piracy, it is self-defense.*[5]

Assertions like these ones mentioned above made the late Libyan leader Muammar Gaddafi to be in the West death wish list. As soon as the West was through with Saddam Hussein, it was invariably crystal clear that the next project that the West had to undertake was to deepen its political control in the world and further enrich their Seven Sister companies, which were to destroy Muammar Gaddafi and take control of his massive oil tanks. The greatest cardinal sin that had been committed by Saddam Hussein when he came into office was to nationalize the Iraqi oil. What is the meaning of nationalization of the oil? What it means literally is this: there is what is known as the Seven Sisters, and these Seven Sisters are the petroleum companies that are based in the West, and the West continues its dominance and economic imperialism around the world through these petroleum companies. The moment Saddam Hussein nationalized the oil that meant literally that the Seven Sisters were supposed to leave Iraq, and the Western governments were unhappy to lose control over the Iraq economy just because of one man, Saddam Hussein, who decided to nationalize the oil. The invasion of Iraq and the ousting of Saddam Hussein from his political power opened the window of economic opportunity for the West to further send back to Iraq the Seven Sisters to further strike trade agreements with the Iraqi government that is pro-Western. The then prime minister of Iraq Nouri al-Maliki was taking his orders from the

West. As soon as the dictator and tyrant Saddam Hussein was gone and forgotten, the West lifted all the economic sanctions that were imposed on the Iraqi government during the Saddam Hussein era. The wars of the Middle East are perpetuated and influenced by oil. Now that all these political and economic obstacles that were hindering the economic success of the West were out of its way, the only political and economic obstacle that is remaining is Russia. The West was very unhappy about the Russian president Vladimir Putin's actions of shielding and protecting Richard Snowden. Moscow was seen by the West as meddling into the Western politics and seemed to stick its nose to political and economic problems, which were purely Western not even Russian. The bigger picture is not about the Russian invasion to Crimea, but it's about the West displaying to the whole world that Russia is not the European superpower as it claims to be. The main problem about imposing economic sanctions to Russia is this: the majority of countries in Europe depend heavily on Russia for fuel. If the West will impose wholesale economic sanctions on Russia, the economies of the majority of countries in Europe will scream. Russia is the key player in the European economy. I need to say this: though during the writing of this book the West and the G7 countries, which is the new club that had been incorporated on March 24, 2014, after Russia had been expelled from the G8, have not yet imposed the wholesale economic sanctions on Russia. The current economic sanctions that have been imposed on Russia have been targeting only individuals who are pro–Vladimir Putin government and individuals who supported the notion of annexation of Crimea. What the US president Barack Obama made clear during the EU and US meeting in Belgium, Brussels, is this: the diplomatic route was still wide open, and as soon as Russia de-escalates the annexation of Crimea, the economic sanctions would not be imposed to the Russian economy, and if Russia does not de-escalate the annexation of Crimea and continue in its current path of occupying Crimea permanently, then the wholesale economic sanctions will be imposed on the Russian government. There is an undeniable fact that even the members of the newly formed G7 countries acknowledge. If and only if the G7 countries will finally impose the wholesale economic sanctions on the Russian economy, most of the European countries will struggle with fuel. The US president Barak Obama made it abundantly clear that the United States is blessed with fuel; therefore, if Europe will need fuel, the United States will be glad to supply Europe with fuel. Let me just delve on the depth of speculation and prediction. Let's just say the G7 countries impose economic sanctions on

Russia, and in the whole of Europe there is a shortage of fuel, and since Europe has cut its ties with Russia, it will have to go back to the United States and buy fuel again from the Seven Sisters, and that will give the United States more political power and political control over Europe, since the whole of Europe will be dependent entirely on the United States for fuel. The one-million-dollar question is this: What is it that the United States stands to gain in this episode of economic sanctions on Russia? As soon as the economic sanctions have hit the Russian economy, everybody in Europe will scream, "Help us, USA." The Seven Sisters will come running to save the sinking economic ship of Europe with ease, and that will make Europe itself to be dependent on the United States in terms of fuel. As far as Ukraine is concerned, the IMF, which is another political vehicle that is controlled and manipulated by the West, had already set aside a financial package that will ensure that there is economic stability in Ukraine and the Ukrainians will hold democratic elections that are to be free and fair and entirely peaceful. As soon as the Ukrainians hold their national elections and elect a new president, then the IMF will come into the picture with the so-called rescue package. At the end of it all, the Ukraine government will be indebted to the IMF, which is the Western vehicle and a political instrument to control and manipulate the whole world. Ukraine had been saved by the West, and it goes without saying then that Ukraine will look up to the West not only for economic solutions but also for political solutions, and the West will be glad to offer such help in the time of need to the Ukrainians. The main reason I took a considerable amount of time to explain extensively and expansively the European debacle is the following: I want you to get the whole picture—politics is about power and money. We know for a fact that the Nigerian crisis is purely about the political power not about the Islamic laws, but it's about the power that comes with owning and controlling a vast amount of crude oil. The West does not love peace and stability because peace and stability are cheap and bring nothing with it, though civil wars bring a lot of economic gain and political power with it. If the West cannot manage to penetrate the heart of any political stable country through a war, it will stick its long nose through the domestic politics of that country in question. Each and every county has its own absolute powers and absolute rights to make its own choices about its domestic policies and its economic policies. We know that when it comes to African countries, there is no country in Africa that has the luxury to make its own political and economic decisions that are adverse to the Western agenda because that could cause the foreign aid pool to dry up. The classic example is Yoweri Museveni of Uganda. The moment he appended his signature to the antigay bill and signed in into law, the West told him straightforward that he no longer stands a chance to receive foreign aid, and in effect the foreign aid that was destined for Uganda was eventually diverted somewhere else where the political conditions and economic conditions condone and support homosexuality. The world has now come to this: you do what I deem right before my eyes and I will give you foreign aid and our relationship will be strengthened, and even if what I deemed right before my eyes might not be right according to your culture and religion, it does not matter to me because I have foreign aid and you don't have foreign aid and you need it to survive. The West makes the whole world go round just like money makes the whole world go round. What is the better way to destabilize a united country without supporting one ethnic group with military weapons to wage ethnic war with the other in order to confuse and divide this united country in between and then have an open door to loot all the natural resources through bilateral agreement and trade agreements? There are two types of investors in the West: the post-war investors and the prewar investors. All of them have the same thing in mind: they like war. The pre-war investors will stay in any African country as long as the national government does not meddle in their business; meaning as long as the national government allows these pre-war investors to steal from the people and conduct their mining operations and make gigantic profits in broad daylight with the support of the African government, there is no problem. If there is a regime change and a new political party comes into power that they don't like, they will pack their bags and fund the militia group and leave the country in flames and establish a new mining company somewhere where the government of that country will relax the tax laws in order for the pre-war investor to make more money and pay less in taxes. These are the pre-war investors, but they have the same thing in common with the post-war investors: they don't care much about the environmental effects that their business activities have on the environment and on ordinary people of the area where they conduct their business. All what they are concerned about is profit, and not just an ordinary profit but big, fat numbers. The post-war investors like war and they hate peace too. If they realize that a particular African country is rich in mineral resources but the government of the day is stiff and unreceptive to the international corporations, what they will do is to find a person in that particular country who can form an opposition party within a speed of lightning and support the leaders of that newly formed oppositional party with funds and ensure that he gets international publicity as soon as possible. I have already mentioned to you in the previous chapters that I have seen the house of Morgan Tsvangirai of MDC-T and I love it. That is why the national elections of Zimbabwe have never been free and fair since time immemorial; there has been corruption after corruption and election rigging after election rigging. In Zimbabwean politics, rigging the national election results is now a norm. It's no longer surprising even to the SADC, which observes that the national election results are not rigged due to the normalization of rigging. The post-war investors are dangerous investors because they can even pay to see blood dripping on the bodies of people. The post-war investors can go as far as acquiring military weapons for their militia group in order to defeat the government. This is exactly what is happening in the Syrian War. The post-war investors from the West have been trying all the tricks in the book just to get rid of Bashar al-Assad. The post-war investors have been shipping military arms and military equipment through Turkey just to make sure that the government of Bashar al-Assad is defeated, and when they could not defeat the government of Bashar al-Assad, they manufacture fake and unreliable pictures and reports that the government of Bashar al-Assad has been using scud missiles and chemical weapons, and realizing that Bashar al-Assad was stuck between a rock and a hard place, Vladimir Putin came into the picture to save the situation. I know it will sound stupid and absurd to the extreme sometimes, but ask yourself this question: What do you think could have happened had the United States gotten its way and begun bombing the already destroyed Syria? The old cliché "The boots won't hit the ground" would not have lasted for a long period of time. The fact of the matter is this: had the war started, the boots were going to hit the ground, and not only would the boots hit the ground but also the boots were going to stay in the ground for a very long period of time. The post-war investors make profits through the spilling of blood, and they love blood money and they also love blood diamonds. For each and every country that has been wrecked by a civil war, it normally takes a considerable amount of time and money to rebuild what had been destroyed by the war. It's easy to destroy than to build, just like it's easy to divorce than to marry. Rebuilding a country from scratch needs a considerable amount of financial injection and the post-war investors will come handy in a situation like that. The post-war investors have diversified business interests. They have a variety of business interests. They have business interest in Mining and they have business interest in IT (Information Technology) and they have business interest also in construction. Bear in mind that the business of construction is very wide: building low-cost houses, building of new roads and servicing the old roads, and building clinics and hospitals. The post-war investors have all sorts of interest just to make sure that they collect gigantic profits as soon as possible at the expense of the ordinary people. Both the post-war investors and pre-war investors have the same thing in common: they hate paying too much taxes, but they like amassing humongous profits and destroying the natural environment and the ecosystem with impunity. One of my concerns about the mining companies in Africa is this: they mine in Africa and amass a considerable amount of profits, and when there is no gold and diamonds on the ground, they close shop and pack and go, leaving behind a large amount of people unemployed and sick with TB (tuberculosis) and silicosis. They (both pre-war investors and post-war investors) don't take the social responsibility of the very land where they are conducting their mining operations. They don't invest even in their workforce, which has been working for them for a very long time. The qualitative characteristics of pre- and post-war investors are these: they don't care about anyone; what they are in Africa for is profits and nothing but profits only. They don't mind about environmental side effects. There must come a point in time where we realize as Africans that the majority of the Western investors don't have the African interests at heart; the only thing that they see out of African people is profits and more profits only. We the African people have been dancing for the Western music for a long period of time now. The time has come for Africa to rise up and start looking after its own political and economic affairs rather than depend and rely on the West even for the Face book and Twitter accounts. The cash liquidity crisis that the Zimbabwean economy was experiencing was as a result of the illegal economic sanctions that have been imposed by the West. There is lesson that I think the Russian people can quickly learn from Zimbabwe's economic sanctions, and it's worth saying that the fact that the West will impose economic sanctions does not necessarily mean that Russia will not export its goods to all the European countries. There are some European countries that will go behind the back of the European Union and even the West and its G7 countries to import products from Russia without even the EU's or the Western knowledge. Let me give you a practical example: there are countries in the world that are still supporting Zimbabwe financially, even though some of these countries are in Europe. When Pres. Robert Mugabe is sick, he normally goes to Malaysia and even sometimes to Dubai for his medical treatment owing to the fact that if a particular social and economic club in the world stage like the EU and the West imposes economic sanctions to one country simply because they hate the country concerned, it does not necessarily mean that the whole world will be against the sanctioned country. The economic sanctions of Zimbabwe are still in place, and they are biting the people of Zimbabwe and the economy of Zimbabwe; but you still have China and other countries in the Middle East, like Israeli, which are the closest friends of the United States doing business with the government of Zimbabwe, and you also have the Chinese government investing a considerable amount of money in the Zimbabwean economy. During the national elections, there were tablets that were sold at a very cheap price in Zimbabwe. I have not managed to purchase any of those tablets simply because they were sold out quickly. What I do know is this: if you were to buy those tablets, already in those tablets are ZANU-PF songs downloaded by the manufacturer. We all know that China is the manufacturer of those tablets, and they were used by the ZANU-PF in their national elections campaign of July 31, 2013. The point I am making is this: some of the very same countries that will present the united front on the face of the earth when the going gets tough will have no option but to bow down to the very same Russia to which they were casting stones to ask for assistance and help. I have learned that economic sanctions are very dangerous, and the effects of economic sanctions normally go a long way. When the West imposed economic sanctions on February 18, 2002, to the government of Zimbabwe, majority of Zimbabweans thought that life will continue to be business as usual. They realized very late that the economic sanctions have already destroyed their economy and made the food-exporting country to a food-importing country. I have already said that I had bought the aloe vera lotion in Zimbabwe that was manufactured in Tanzania, and I still have it in my closet, though I need to be honest—I rarely apply it on my skin. If the Zimbabwean economic sanctions are anything to go by, the people of Russia and their government were supposed to do anything in their power to avoid the West and its gangsters of the G7 countries to impose economic sanctions on Russia. Though sometimes we all have to go through the wilderness in order to reach the Promised Land, which is overflowing with milk and honey, but if it's possible to avoid the wilderness, just go straight to the Promised Land and avoid the unforgiving heat of the desert. The impending Russian economic sanctions are not wholly about Crimea; they are about the West flexing its economic muscles and proving to Russia that it is neither a regional superpower nor the future world superpower. The message that the West was sending to the Russian government is this: "If you are contemplating to be the world superpower, think again." The main problem with economic sanctions is the forever rising inflation to the point that even the economists will sometimes lose count. At one point in the Zimbabwean inflation, they saw the inflation souring to 283 million percent, and it's during this time that even if you were to rob the bank, you would not even afford a loaf of bread still. I remember my driver in Bulawayo John telling me that when you leave in the morning for work and the moment you take the second trip back home with the bus, the bus fare had increased already—meaning, prices of goods and services were shooting up in the twinkling of an eye. The one-million-dollar question is this: Are Russians ready for the economic sanctions that the West wants to wield toward the Russian people and the Russian economy, and where is the United Nations in all of these? Peta Thornycroft writes:

> *Zimbabwe may be struggling to pay its civil servants, but the first family's wedding date yesterday was a lavish extravagant in the grounds of the president Mugabe's home, one of the largest houses in sub-Saharan Africa.*[6]

African leaders have been accused of either enriching their families at the expense of the ordinary people who voted for them to the government leadership position or sometimes using state funds for their own personal affairs. As far as I know, there is no African leader who had not stood accused of misusing public funds for their own personal affairs. Bona Mugabe got married on March 1, 2014, to Simbarashe Chikore in Harare. Pres. Robert Mugabe has been moving from one party to another, and I don't think that is healthy for a person who is ninety years old. The exact amount of money that has been spent on Pres. Robert Mugabe's birthday party in February 2014 was an anecdotal US$1 million. And if the exchange rate between the South African rand and the US dollar is one dollar is to ten rands, then it means the exact amount that has been spent by the Zimbabwean government for the birthday party of Pres. Robert Mugabe is R10 million. There is nothing wrong when the president of a country, once in his lifetime, throws an extravagant birthday party specifically if there are resources by the state to cater for such birthday party. What the problem to me is spending considerable amount of money on an individual while the masses are starving to death of because of hunger and poverty. There should be a balance that should be struck in between. What matters more between hundreds of people who are starving due to hunger and poverty, and the birthday party that will only benefit one individual who is also old for that matter? Good leaders put the interest of their people first then their personal interests must follow after. The majority of African leaders put the interest of their friends and their families first, and then after everybody who is close to them has eaten, including their dogs, whatever is left on the table they give it to the masses for public consumption. There more I think about this, the more I can feel my blood pressure shooting up immediately. The cancer of cronyism and tribalism in Africa is spreading like swine flu and with no end in sight. The more I come to think of corruption and cronyism, the more I come to the realization as to how selfish and self-centered human beings have become. Greed and gluttony are two of the deadliest sins on the list of the deadliest sins. The cash liquidity crisis compelled the ZRB (Zimbabwe Reserve Bank) to introduce more foreign currencies compared to the foreign currencies that were already in circulation in Zimbabwe. There were two official currencies that are used in Zimbabwe: one, the US dollar that was introduced in 2009 during the Government of National Unity; and, second, the South African rand, which is largely used in Bulawayo, the second-largest city in Zimbabwe. The world "Bulawayo" means "the place of slaughter." The main reason Bulawayo is using the South Africa rand, unlike in Harare where the majority of people are using the US dollar, is that simply Bulawayo is very close to South Africa, unlike Harare, "the worst city on earth," as some Western media call it. Though I have been in Harare—clearly Harare is not like Pretoria or Johannesburg in terms of size—I should admit that I have enjoyed myself while I was in Harare. I have great difficulties with understanding my African brothers and sisters sometimes. I wonder why the majority of African people are not critical of African leaders even if they are involved in fraud and corruption. If you are critical of corrupt activities and state institutions and even ordinary people, they begin to act funny toward you, and you can even get arrested for a minor thing. The majority of young people in Africa just decided to take a backseat as far as corruption is concerned and as far as politics is concerned. If young people, the leaders of tomorrow, decide to spend a considerable amount of time on Face book, one wonders, how these young African people who were supposed to be empowering themselves with African history will lead their people to the future. It simply means that there will be a leadership vacuum in the near future in Africa. The majority of African leaders who are currently leading their countries come from the apartheid generation or Ian Smith generation. There is no African leader in the sub-Saharan region who is from the new generation except maybe the president of DRC Joseph Kabila who took over from his late father, Laurent Kabila, who was killed by his bodyguard. Mswati III, the king of Swaziland, is still in power after he took over the kingship from his father, Mswati II. But the crop of African leaders who is in power right now is very, very old and disgruntled. Most of the African leaders cannot offer anything new and fresh anymore except repeat what we already know and say what has been already said before. Africa, in order to move forward, needs a new breed of young leaders—political leaders who will shape the African continent for the better, not folks who are angry about the past and who spend too much time worried about the past instead of concentrating on the future. Yesterday is gone and there is nothing we can change about the past, but we have everything to live for in the future. There are multiple political narratives about the Zimbabwean economic situation to the point that even if you think you understand the Zimbabwean economic problems properly, with so many political narratives, you even begin to doubt the accuracy of your own political narrative. I have learned in my journey to Zimbabwe that there are honest people who can really, with all honesty, speak the truth, and I have seen also that there are people who will never profess the truth simply because they believe that by professing the truth is tantamount to espionage. As long as we Africans keep on protecting and preventing our political leaders to be held accountable, we will continue now and then to read about how corrupt our African leaders are from the Western media and from the Western sources. Truth be told, most Africans love their political leaders to the point that even if the said leader is corrupt and he steals public money to build a palace for himself and his family, they won't be able to see it. True love rebukes and corrects. When you love a person to the point that even if he makes mistakes you can't see his mistakes, then that is not true love. We Africans should love our political leaders to the point of death, and I don't mean it in a South African way where you will hear people say, "I will kill for my president"—I mean, love our political leaders wholeheartedly to the point that if they are stealing public funds, we should be bold enough to accompany them all the way to prison singing and chanting revolutionary songs. It's true that there is corruption in the West just like there is corruption in Africa, but most of the corrupt activities that are happening in Western governments don't get reported in the Western media. Since corruption by the Western governments don't get reported by the Western media, somewhere somehow it gives the whole world an impression that there is no corruption that is taking place in the West, which is also not true. There is corruption everywhere just like there is a problem of drugs everywhere. The main reason corruption is reported more often in Africa than in the West is simply because of the Western media. The Western media is used by the West as the political tool and political instrument to fight its political wars. Few African leaders take into consideration the influence and the impact that the Western media has in their domestic politics of the African continent. Take for example the case of Pres. Robert Mugabe, how he has been portrayed by the Western media. Every now and then when there is a report about Zimbabwe, you know it already before the report is over that there is nothing good that can be said about the people of Zimbabwe and there is nothing good that can be said about Zimbabwe as a country. My concern about the foreign media is this: it reports extensively about Africa and tells the whole world the African story, which is not true in its entirety. I have been in Zimbabwe, but I can't just assume to know everything about Zimbabwe simply because of those visits I have made to Zimbabwe. There are underlying issues that are not on the public domain that underpins certain actions that happen in the public domain. Most of what we ordinary people read about in the mainstream media is old news. When a true story happens, the mainstream media won't even report it. There are political leaders who are now dead because of the Western media, and they were prosecuted and found guilty in the court of public opinion. I never thought that the people of Zimbabwe loved Pres. Robert Mugabe as they do until I visited Zimbabwe. If I were to follow the Western media, I would have been fooled to believe that everybody in Zimbabwe hates Pres. Robert Mugabe with passion. But when the Western companies are abusing their employees and underpaying them or there is a corruption scandal that is happening in the Western governments, that does not gets full coverage in the Western media. All of what we know from the Western media is this: all African leaders are corrupt and there is nothing good that they are doing for their people except stealing the very same money that has been given to them by the West for infrastructural projects. This narrative is very dangerous and deceiving at some point, but not all Africans are blind and stupid enough to believe what is being reported by the Western media about the African leaders. If I were to be brutally honest, I have never watched any report about Africa in the Western media that tells a good African story. The only thing now and then that is being broadcasted to us Africans is how corrupt African leaders have become and how anti-progressive Pres. Yoweri Museveni of Uganda is by signing the antigay bill into law. When African leaders hold a different political view that is totally different compared to the view that is held by the West, those African leaders are likely to be branded “backward and anti-progressive.” It seems as if people who are progressive and educated are the people who are taking everything as it comes from the West at face value as long as that information is coming from the West and from the Western media. There are few Africans nowadays who are watching African programs, even their own country current affairs. Most Africans know a lot about the Western history, though they have never been in the West physically. The point I am making is this: What is it good for to know more about your oppressor than to know more about yourself? One of my colleagues told me that she is no longer watching wrestling with her children simply because her children, after watching wrestling together, start fighting among themselves, and that is exactly what is happening to most adults. As soon as the Western media files reports about corruption that is being committed by African leaders, we Africans believe the Western media and we start protesting without testing the validity and authenticity of what we are told by the Western media. The whole world was fooled in 2003 into believing that Saddam Hussein was in possession of weapons of mass destruction to the point that the majority of countries compelled Saddam Hussein to allow the UN inspectors in Iraq to verify whether or not he had the wherewithal to manufacture weapons of mass destruction. Even after Saddam Hussein had done everything possible and necessary to redeem himself and refute the notion that he was not manufacturing weapons of mass destruction, it was still not enough, and the line has already been drawn and he had to die just like Muammar Gaddafi of Libya. I wonder why the West did not take Pres. Robert Mugabe’s regime head-on and topple him just like they did with Saddam Hussein and Muammar Gaddafi of Libya, but I think partly because Zimbabwe is a small country; besides there is no oil in Zimbabwe. The West would not just invade a country like Zimbabwe, which they know very well they won’t get the return for their money. The main reason the West invaded Iraq and Libya was purely on the basis of a vast amount oil that these two countries possess. No oil, no war; and more oil, more wars. As long as there is no oil, there wouldn’t be wars in the world, and as long as some countries possess a vast amount of oil in their reserves, these countries are likely to control fuel prices and influence inflation of the world, and that is what the West is against. The

West does foresee a situation where there is another superpower in the world, and that is why the West will do everything in its power to make sure that it is stifling emerging countries economically that have the potential to be the superpower of the world, just like Russia and China in the near future. The West is doing everything possible to keep the Chinese influence in Africa under control. That is why I didn't believe the Western reports about Zimbabwe, and I took it upon myself to visit Zimbabwe to see the commercial farms that were once upon a time very productive and supported the whole world and that now lie in waste and underutilized. It's possible that the African nationalists who were fighting in the African liberation struggle didn't comprehend thoroughly the ramifications of their actions, and they didn't even understand that the West has already destroyed Africa and benefited immensely through the African mineral resources. I have come to the realization that the African problems can't be solved through the African dialogue, nor does it require an African solution. The old cliché that African problems require African solution is sheer madness. We know that most African countries are fighting within themselves in the war that is called "ethnic cleansing." The Rwandese killed each other in 1994 as if they were fighting for something that was worth fighting for. Instead of us Africans using our collective wisdom as Africans to defend and protect our sovereignty, most of the time we are attacking each other, even using the Western media. African problems that require undivided attention are poverty and high level of illiteracy. The remnants of colonization and the scars of apartheid in South Africa are indelible. The colonization of the spirit and the colonization of the mind are the worst forms of colonization compared to the colonization of the body. The main reason I say that is the following: the body can be liberated with ease, but it takes time and effort to liberate the mind and the spirit. That is why even to this day and age in South Africa and in many African countries, African people are still angry at what happened to them during the colonial era, and the indelible scars of the colonial era are there for everyone to see, while most of the Western folks who benefited immensely through the colonial era are become richer each and every day. When the African people suggest to the Western settlers who were enriched by the political system and the government system of the day, "Let's share the wealth in between us in order for all of us to be on the same financial altitude," most of the Western settlers just look the other way. What has triggered the farm invasion in Zimbabwe in 2000 was partly the problem of income inequality and the unfair distribution of wealth. The white commercial farmers, when they were confronted with the question of relinquishing to the black Zimbabweans their land that was taken from them forcefully in the past by Cecil John Rhodes and his British mafias, just went to the court to seek the legal protection. This naivety and stupidity by the white commercial farmers got them into a very serious trouble with the war veterans. I think those who are writing Africa's encyclopedia should nickname the war veterans of Zimbabwe "the brothers of destruction." There are historical problems that can't be solved by the high court just like the issue of land and the mineral resources. Historical problems need to be settled through Commission of Inquiry and parliamentary processes without involving the lawyers and the high court judges. The moment we Africans resort to the high court to seek legal remedies concerning a matter that has historical connection, then we are likely to replicate the same ugly scene and drama that happened in Zimbabwe where ordinary people became fed up and decide to solve a historical problem with a quick-fix solution that was appropriate and good on the face value but diabolical in the long run. But in the long run, they (Zimbabweans) have all come to understand that what happened in 2000 was a very serious mistake, and not only a serious mistake but also a costly mistake to the country and to the economy of Zimbabwe. There is one incident that I am very reluctant to talk about because it is heartbreaking to me and it epitomizes the exact situation on the ground. I was walking on the street of Bulawayo as usual, and a certain lady came to me and said, "Sir, I am looking for a job. Can you hire me to be your maid please?" I didn't respond. I just kept quiet and kept moving, and when I was reflecting in my hotel room on that day about the events of the day, somehow I began to understand the concept that "economic sanctions are illegal" and their effects are worse than the effects of weapons of mass destruction (WMD). There were many young people on the streets of Bulawayo whom I saw standing in a form of group, and you can quickly tell from a distance that these are young people who have been failed by the government of the day, and there is nothing that they can do about it except to stand on the streets and hope that somebody will come with some form of a job offer. I remember one morning getting out of my hotel room and standing on the balcony of my hotel room, getting a panorama view of Bulawayo, and within me, I asked myself many questions, and some of the questions that I asked myself were these: Why am I here? What am I doing? What if I get arrested? I remembered vividly asking this question: What if the majority of people won't believe what I will say or they will just criticize me from the moment they open the first page of my book? There are many questions that came to me while I was standing on that balcony, but I need to say that in the entire of my journey, I met amazing people. There are ordinary people who would not be silenced by the government of the day, and there are people who feel that it is better to tell a stranger their economic problems than tell somebody that they know. An average person will prefer to tell a stranger their problems than tell their siblings and even their acquaintances. That is why married men can spill the bins about their unhappiness in their marriages to prostitutes rather than tell their colleagues and family members. It's human nature that you feel better and secure with your dirty secrets if they are known by somebody who does not know much about you. One day I walked into a clothing shop in Pretoria, and while I was ready to pay, the cashier out of nowhere started telling me about the skeletons in her closet, and I just said, "I will pray for you, but you must also pray and that it will go away and you will forget about it." I am not at liberty to disclose what is it that she told me, but believe me, it was very heartbreaking, and she was heartbroken too.

INDIGENIZATION AND NATIONALIZATION

The Southern Times reports:

> *Africa can even rewrite the principles of a world economy that has grown fat on cheap resources sourced from Africa and elsewhere in the developing world. This makes the former South African president Thabo Mbeki's recent admonition to Africa not to let Zimbabwe fail in the implementation of its indigenization program. Because of the critical place Zimbabwe's example has for the future of Africa, it is crucial that we quote liberally here from a speech given on August 23, 2013. He said, "I think we should ask ourselves the question: Why is Zimbabwe such a major issue for some people? Zimbabwe is a small country by any standard; there is no particular reason Zimbabwe should matter to the New York Times, the London Guardian, and whoever else . . . why are they paying so much attention to Zimbabwe?" Mbeki answered the question himself by telling a story. "Toward the end of last year (2012)," he said, "they asked me to speak at a conference on Zimbabwe diamonds. So I went, and what surprised me about the conference held at Victoria*

> *Falls was that everybody and anybody who has anything to do with diamonds in the world was there, from America, from Israel, from India, from Brussels, everybody."*[7]

There are two fundamental economic issues that I need to look at right now partly because they are crucial in the Zimbabwean economic fiasco. I have asked Terry about the Marange diamond fields, which are owned by the government of Zimbabwe in conjunction with a Chinese company. When I was in Harare, before I took the bus the following day to Bulawayo, I hired a driver by the name of Terry. Through him I managed to solicit a considerable amount of information that I was looking for, though I need to say that the majority of information that Terry was giving me seemed as if he was giving the MDC-T version of events. It's better sometimes to get both sides of the story in order to make an independent judgment and thorough assessment. Through interacting with Terry, I have quickly learned to tell the difference when a person is telling me the ZANU-PF version of events or the MDC-T version of events, or the so-called the Zimbabwean political gospel according to ZANU PF or the Zimbabwean political gospel according to MDC-T. Terry made it clear to me when I asked him about the Marange diamond fields and indigenization. The concept of indigenization came with the ZANU-PF government, and the main reason the ZANU-PF government came up with this government policy was to enrich the ordinary people of Zimbabwe and to avoid the situation where the majority of the companies registered in Zimbabwe Stock Exchange are FOC (foreign-owned companies) but have deep roots in the economy of Zimbabwe. The indigenization program is the BEE (Broad Economic Empowerment) of Zimbabwe, though BEE was introduced by the former president of South Africa Thabo Mbeki in the case of South Africa, and its intentions and objectives were good, though at the end of the day it benefited those who were politically connected and those who have friends in high places. There were roughly four hundred companies in Zimbabwe prior to the economic collapse that led to the hyperinflation in the late 2002 after the imposition of economic sanctions by the West. All these four hundred companies were foreign-owned companies (FOC), meaning that they were owned by the Western settlers while they were based in Zimbabwe and operating in Zimbabwe. When Pres. Robert Mugabe began to experience too much nightmares and could not sleep at night, he allowed the war veterans to do as they wished, and mayhem followed. The Zimbabwe economy was metamorphosed in the twinkling of an eye, and the Land Redistribution Program became a land redistribution problem. All those four hundred companies, which were based in Zimbabwe, had to close shop and leave the country unceremoniously. That meant that the majority of the people were without work, and the Zimbabwean government kept on coming with its draconian laws that were stifling small businesses on the ground. Indigenization meant that if you are an investor and you incorporate your own company and get funding for your own company and then take the company that you have helped to create to Zimbabwe as the place of operation, the moment you reach the Zimbabwean soil, you must now take 51 percent shareholding and give it to the Zimbabwean government, and then you remain with the 49 percent shareholding, and what about the debt that you already incurred because of the funding that you have received? How can you pay back the borrowed capital with the 49 percent shareholding that you now have as the result of indigenization? This indigenization policy was a nightmare economic policy, and it managed and succeeded to bring the economy of Zimbabwe into a coma, which was already in the intensive care unit due to economic sanctions. Some have said already that the economy of Zimbabwe is an irreparable economy, though as an optimist I believe that the economic situation in Zimbabwe will get better through prayer and not forgetting serious fasting also. There point is indigenization policy was a zanufication program, and most of the people who are in favor of indigenization were suffering from the ZANU-PF syndrome, as one of my Zimbabwean friends puts it. There is no way in hell can a sophisticated investor inject a considerable amount of money in a company that will later be owned by the government. Whoever conceived the idea of indigenization needs to see a shrink and have his head thoroughly examined. The fact that a single person had his night filled with nightmares does not necessarily mean that everything should change the following day. Unplanned and not-thought-through economic decisions should not have been implemented without thorough and vigorous economic debate. We all know that in Africa some of the major economic decisions are not even discussed with ordinary people; the government just decides what it deemed fit for the people and imposes it to the people without people's consent. What I do know is this: sleeping with a woman, even if she is your wife, without her consent is rape, and sleeping with woman who is below the age of eighteen years is statutory rape; but when the African governments impose their unplanned and not-thought-through economic policies on their people without people's consent, it's not rape. Just like the BEE (Broad Economic Empowerment) failed decimally in South Africa and only enriched those who are politically connected in high places, so is the indigenization program in Zimbabwe. There are people who have benefited through the indigenization program in Zimbabwe; those are the people who are also connected in high places. Political connection is all what you need nowadays, and without political connection, you can kiss the government tender good-bye. The BEE (Black Economic Empowerment) was later changed in South Africa into the BBBEE (Broad-Based Black Economic Empowerment). The reason the South African government changed the BEE to BBBEE was after realizing that BEE was not broad-based benefiting the masses but benefiting the few black ruling elite. The same applies also in Zimbabwe; the majority of ordinary people didn't benefit through the indigenization program but only those who are connected to a certain political party. When you have political connection, "a boardroom issue becomes a bedroom issue." What it means is this: let's say your husband sits in the government tender board. It makes sense that whatever it is said on that tender board meeting you will get to know simply because you share a lot in common; besides, you share the most precious thing together, which is love. There is no way that with you as a wife, your husband who sits in government tender board (GTB) can't reveal some of the crucial information through your moments of intimacy while you are together. The boardroom issue more frequent than not is the bedroom issue, and it will remain like that for quite a long period of time whether we like it or not. The Marange diamond fields did not benefit the poor and the ordinary people, but it benefited the political heavyweights and the who's who in the zoo of Zimbabwe. Those who are critical and vocal against the government—that the indigenization policy and the farm invasion didn't benefit the ordinary people on the ground—were "persecuted by the prosecution," as they say in Zimbabwe. The game of politics is a dirty game.There are fundamental principles that govern the economy of any country, and when these fundamental principles that govern the economy of any country are disregarded and flouted, the country in question is likely to suffer the devastating effects economically. Political stability and the respect for the rule of law, though it might appear insignificant, play a crucial role in ensuring that the economy of a country takes a better shape. As long as there is no respect for the rule of law and everybody is doing everything and there is no law and order and government institutions are utilized as political weapons, then you can easily tell that something bad is about to happen. There are times when the government should be held accountable by the very same institutions that it has established. And when these government institutions that help to keep the checks and balances of government are criticized by the politicians, they lose focus and become weak and irrelevant. There are times when the national government will lose its footing, and if there is a strong independent institution, like the public protector in the case of South Africa, the government's mistakes can be picked it up and corrected with ease. Though I need to stress that independent institutions that don't answer to the executive of the country but answer only to parliament must also take into consideration that they are not a political party and part and parcel of the executive, but only a mere independent institution that is supposed to deepen and ensure that the constitution of the country does not get violated by the politicians, and the public funds are not used by politicians and government officials to build houses and swimming pools for themselves. But above all the same government institutions should make sure that they don't get caught up in the game of politics where they are selective in investigating a particular political party and quick to publish the findings, and on the other side they are very slow and move with a tortoise's pace to investigate a certain political party simply because they can't attract attention of the media and the attention of the public on the other cases. It's true and possible that some of the so-called independent institutions have become political parties on their own and some of them have become the courts of law on their own, though they don't have the jurisdiction and the power to be a court of law. Some of the so-called independent institutions have become the darling of the media, and they seek publicity and popularity with passion. The cash liquidity crisis is the microcosm of the economic problems that have engulfed the economy of Zimbabwe. If Zimbabwe was to be auctioned, China was going to be the highest bidder and China was going to buy Zimbabwe right away. Political problems and economic problems present us Africans with an opportunity to learn and grow, though some of the economic problems and political problems take time to be corrected and sorted out; but with collective wisdom and a clear plan that is realistic, they can be solved. There are two types of people in the world: the problem solvers and the problem makers. Most of the people are the problem makers without even knowing that they are the problem makers. The problem makers are people who prefer trial and error, and they like other people to use their suggestions and their opinions as if they are experts in their own field. The fact of the matter is this: some of the problem makes are old. Just because of them having a certain age, that does not make them an expert in a certain field, even in life itself. Some of the problem makers are in politics. They are problem-oriented and they like asking more questions without even coming up with solutions. Then there are the problem solvers or trouble shooters. These are the guys who see every problem as an opportunity to grow and learn more and develop new skills and knowledge. Quite frankly I don't see the Zimbabwean problems as the end of the world or as life under the bus. I see the Zimbabwean problems as the African problem that can be solved provided that certain political leaders accept the fact that there should be a time of acknowledging their mistakes of the past and moving on, never to repeat them anymore. Mistakes are part of life. Politicians too do make mistakes, but what matters most about a mistake are the actions that you take after you have made the mistake. Ignorance is the lack of knowledge, and arrogance is when you think you know too much to the point that you don't take into consideration the fact that as a human being you have shortcomings. The combination of ignorance and arrogance is deadly, specifically if you are a politician who is influencing the majority of people now and then. "Zimbabwe is not for sale." Such messages were normally flashed on our TV screens during the ZANU-PF rallies before the national elections of July 31, 2013. The message and the tone of this message is this: there are people who want to buy Zimbabwe and they are waiting in the corner somewhere with a stash of money in their pockets to buy Zimbabwe if an opportunity presents itself. What I do know, and it has become public knowledge and even the chickens know, that Zimbabwe is importing everything, and when I say everything I mean everything, including the toilet paper or tissue and Sunlight liquid soup. Just like DRC was importing everything during the 1998 war that saw the late president of DRC Laurent-Désiré Kabila got killed by his bodyguard, so is Zimbabwe. Please don't take it as joke that Zimbabwe is importing everything; what it means is this: there is a very serious problem in the economy of Zimbabwe. As long as this problem is not solved, things are about to get even worse than they already are. The idea that things can't get worse than they are now is not true. As long as there is nothing serious that is done by the African regional leaders in the sub-Saharan Africa, things are going to get even worse than they already are. We know these from the wave of problems that has been hitting hard on the economy of Zimbabwe to point where ordinary people realized that the best way to stay alive is to get out of the country and search for better opportunities somewhere outside the border of the country. What is it that ordinary people need to do when all hope is gone? What is it that ordinary people should do when they come to the realization that what they thought was a just and true cause actually was a costly mistake? It's one thing to fight a just and true cause, but to sustain the political gain from that just cause is a totally different story altogether. We all know that most of the African nationalists fought very hard during the African liberation struggle and they have done everything possible and necessary to overcome the Western enemy and the Western imperialism, but the one-million-dollar question is this: Have the political gains, which were accomplished through the armed struggle, been sustained up to this point, or we Africans just lost the war and won the battle? I have noticed something strange among most African countries after the attainment of their political independence from the West—they went into the sleeping mode and thought that all was well. Most of the African countries, after attaining their independence, thought that political freedom meant financial freedom, and they thought that the Western settlers who were in power for quite a long period of time were just going to give away their land and the companies that they own without a fight. The West still has a firm financial grip on Africa's economy. No wonder it's easy for the West to dispense economic sanctions to any country that is opposing its foreign policy. The West knows very well that Africa is not economically free, and Africa has not yet reached a stage where it can be self-sufficient to sustain itself economically. The grim economic picture of Africa relying on the West for foreign aid is likely to remain as it is, unless otherwise there is drastic change in Africa's economic policies and the way Africa sees itself as a continent.

> *The tragic cohabitation of capital flight and poverty in Africa's oil-rich countries is the result of occult management of natural resources and external borrowing by African governments on the one hand, and a global banking system plagued by perverse incentives as well as the primacy of myopic strategies interest on the part of the Western governments on the other hand. As corrupt African leaders accumulate wealth, the African people are saddled with debts and watch helplessly as their natural resources are depleted with little to show for in return. On the other side, Western bankers and governments turn a blind eye to the plunder of African resources and the illicit accumulation of wealth by the continent's elites.*[8]

It's shocking to the extreme if one takes a look at the houses that the majority of African leaders have built for themselves and their families and the money that they have in the Western banks. This painful picture about the African continent being in abject poverty while its leaders are living large with their families on the Western real estate is astounding. I can't wrap my mind around the notion that says that African leaders are "rich presidents of poor nations."[9] During the reign of Pres. François Bozizé of Central African Republic, there is one thing that happened on the day his presidential compound was invaded by the Seleka rebels. It was reported on the media that he took a stash of money that was in his house and fled the country to France. Ever since he left the country, the former president of Central African Republic has been residing in a hotel in France. The one-million-dollar is this: Why is Africa the only poverty-stricken continent in the world? The answer lies with African leaders. African leaders are the ones, with the help of their Western agents, who are siphoning the continent's wealth and riches that were meant to improve the lives of ordinary people on the ground. The main reason the majority of African countries will remain in poverty for quite a long period of time is that when financial resources come, they don't trickle down to the ordinary people on the ground, but they disappear in the hands of the government officials, just like in Malawi. The government of Joyce Banda was in hot water due to the embezzlement of public funds that was meant for building Malawian infrastructure, and Joyce Banda eventually lost the national elections in 2014 and lost her political career. It's startling to know the fact that public funds, which were meant for public use, are the very same public funds that get stolen by the government officials. Malawi is the classic example of how deep the root of corruption is in Africa. The Malawi Cash gate scandal puts Africa in a bad light on the world stage. There are things that can be bought with money, and there are things that can't be bought with money. We all know that trust is earned, and as things stand, the Malawi Cash gate scandal has diminished and destroyed that little public trust that the Malawian people had for their government. It will take time for the Malawian people to believe in their government any more, though with time people forget; but when one takes a look at the scourge of corruption in the African continent, one is convinced that Africa is not a poverty-stricken continent by design, but it's a poverty-stricken continent by mistake. What do you expect the ex-combatants to do when they see a considerable amount of millions of US dollars before them for the very first time? It makes no logical sense to put a considerable amount of money in the hands of people who are not accustomed to money. Money is a drug, and to some people it gives them the same effects as any other drug like cocaine and heroin. There are people who tremble and can even do the unthinkable if there is money before them. Both men and women are prone to corruption whether they are educated or uneducated. What has been abundantly clear after the end of the armed struggle is this: most of the former freedom fighters were given strategic positions in government just for the mere fact that they were in exile and fighting in the liberation struggle without formal qualification and knowledge of the same position that they are holding. Simply put, ex-combatants became CEOs (chief executive officers) of government parastatals without formal qualification owing to the long years that they have spent in the bush. There is no problem with appointing an ex-combatant on a municipal committee where there is no complex and challenging responsibilities that need to be performed by the ex-combatants. When one looks at the organogram of many companies in the African continent, it is startling to realize that the majority of these ex-combatants are listed as directors in many companies without having the competence and the knowledge of running these companies. Then it begs this question: What qualification does one need to have in order to be a director of a company? And the answer to that question is armed struggle credentials. The Zimbabwean cash liquidity crisis was partly because of the banks that are owned by former freedom fighters, which were given banking licenses under mysterious and suspicious circumstances. The element of comradeship and brotherhood can be dangerous sometimes. Most of these banks, which are owned by the former freedom fighters, are run comparatively badly in comparison to the banks that are Western owned. We should accept as Africans that we must not settle for mediocrity at the expense of excellence and quality just because of some stupid concept like indigenization in order to appease the African people. I share the same sentiments with most Africans that there should be transferring of wealth from those who benefited on Africa's wealth illegally in the past to the people of the African continent who have been struggling for quite a long period of time, though Africa's wealth should change hands between the Western settlers to the African people (the sons and daughters of the soil). The proper way to redress the imbalances of the past is to reverse the injustices of the past economically. What has happened in Africa until this point in time is the reversal of the injustices of the past through a commission like TRC (Truth and Reconciliation Commission), which was purely dealing with the atrocities that were committed by the whites against the blacks and blacks against the whites, and after that the chapter was closed. We need to open another TRC in Africa that will deal only with Africa's wealth that was stolen by the West and the reversal of that wealth to its rightful owners. As long as we continue to live life as if nothing wrong happened in the past that is affecting us now, racial hatred and racial tensions will not come to an end. The rich remain rich, and the poor remain poor. We all know that most of the wealth that Western settlers have, they never worked for it, but they attained their wealth through the exploitation of African people. Apartheid South Africa made sure that the Europeans were living in better living conditions and better working conditions at the expense of the black South African people. Until this day the chasm between the black child and the white child is wide and deep, and the situation will remain like that unless there is a political will between both the Western settlers and the black South Africans to come to the table via the TRC (Truth and Reconciliation Commission) to chart the way forward to share with the black South Africans the very wealth that these Western settlers have. The main problem with some of these Western settlers is that some of them have already squandered their wealth, and that is why they don't want to come to the negotiating table because they too are looking for help from the government, and that is a fact that we can't run away from. We Africans need to be very careful when we are dealing with the issue of wealth and land, though I will still deal with it in my last chapter. What has been abundantly clear from African liberation struggle is this: due to the international pressure and fear of economic sanctions and the wind of change that was blowing in the African continent at that time, there was a sense of urgency from the African nationalists to proclaim political victory to their people, though that political victory was Pyrrhic victory in a sense. The African nationalists made a lot of concessions economically to the West for them to get political freedom. The West didn't give Africa its economic liberation but gave Africa its political liberation knowing full well that political freedom is useless unless otherwise it is accompanied by economic freedom. At the end of it all, we are free as Africans, but we are unemployed; we are free as Africans, but we still remain where we were prior to the liberation struggle. Some Zimbabweans, I guess, say, "It was better during the Ian Smith era. He was oppressing us, but at least we had food to eat, but now with Pres. Robert Mugabe, we don't have even food to eat." Though I have never heard any Zimbabwean uttering such statement in public literally, I believe that some of them do think along those lines, but they can't utter such statements because of fear and trepidation of the CIO (Central Intelligence Organization). When we all thought that the Zimbabwean economy has hit rock bottom and it can't get worse than that, the unthinkable happened. There are two things that were eating the Zimbabwean economy with a speed of lightning: first, there was a cash liquidity crisis, which meant that certain parts of Zimbabwe banks were literally empty; I mean, there was nothing in the bank, no money, zilch. Second, the Zimbabwean government was failing to pay the civil servants' salaries in time, with some of the civil servants' salaries being delayed, and they were hoping and praying that at least a miracle was going to happen and they will be able to get their salaries. How do you explain that to your children that the government that you are working for can't pay your salary though you have been waking up early every morning and going to work for thirty-one days? How do you look at your children in the face and say, "Daddy has not received his salary yet?" I can't fathom and imagine the pain that the Zimbabwean children were going through coupled with the fact that already the Zimbabwean economy is a hyperinflationary economy. The biggest problem with the majority of African leaders is that they are living in denial. The fact of the matter is this: Zimbabwe is a sinking ship and is sinking very fast than most of the people think. When we patriotic Africans thought just like most of the people of the world thought—that at least the Zimbabwean economy is about to turn the corner economically—the worse just happened. There were also reports that the very same soldiers who have been maintaining law and order during the national elections of July 31, 2013, and even after the national elections were now short of food and were living in the barracks in Bulawayo. How can soldiers maintain law and order if they are hungry, and how can soldiers take orders from their generals if they are hungry? Who is going to save the Republic of Zimbabwe and its people? What do you do when all hope is gone, and what do you do when bad news is the only news available? The king of Israel in the Holy Bible once wrote that "a living dog is better than a dead lion." In the case of Zimbabwe, a dead lion is better than a living dog because at least the dead lion does not have to worry about tomorrow like the living dog, which is anxious and frustrated now and then about the cash liquidity crisis and about the salary that is not coming. There is one thing that the majority of people miss to comprehend specifically when a country goes through economic difficulties, and that is the death toll normally shoots up, and that was clearly epitomized from the twenty Zimbabwean illegal miners who died in South Africa in March 2014 and had to be transported to the west of Zimbabwe for burial. The whole world has turned a blind eye on Zimbabwe and its people, and the Western leaders are guilty of genocide due to the number of people who are dying each and every day due to Zimbabwe's economic sanctions. If I were to look at Zimbabwe's political conundrum holistically; the national elections of July 31, 2013, should not have occurred given the fact that the country was still bleeding from the economic and political wounds of 2009; but on second thought, that is how democracy works; there should be the national elections after every five years, and indeed elections were held. The national elections of July 31, 2013, should have been kept on hold until such time where the economy of the country was at the point where it could stand alone without teetering on the brink of collapsing, as is the case in this moment. It should be said that the only saving grace that kept the light on even to this day in the economy of Zimbabwe was the Government of National Unity. When the Government of National Unity came to an end, the worse began to happen. If it was possible, the Government of National Unity should have remained in place until such a time where the economic woes have normalized. There is an inescapable reality that we can't run away from. MDC-T and MDC-M have played a critical role in ensuring that the Zimbabwean economy normalizes when the GPA was signed in 2009. If it was not for the GNU (Government of National Unity), Zimbabwe should have been Somalia in 2009. The West stole Africa's wealth, and the West is continuing to kill innocent Zimbabwean children and women with hunger and starvation. The question that I am asking myself now and then is this: Do the people of the world see what I see and saw and what I saw in Zimbabwe? The more I pay undivided attention toward Zimbabwe's economic and political problems, the more I begin to tremble and shiver with fear. Is Africa the hopeless continent, and is Africa the Dark Continent? Zimbabwe's economic situation is the microcosm of the hopeless Africa and the Dark Continent. Though in essence Africa is not a hopeless continent, but when one looks at the problems that have engulfed Zimbabwe, it takes one's breath away. The majority of South Africans know nothing about what is happening in Zimbabwe, and most of them are ignorant and arrogant because they think that the main reason the Zimbabweans are suffering is that they keep on voting for Pres. Robert Mugabe wittingly. Most people don't understand the military-backed government and election rigging. When the national elections have been rigged, it means that the electorate has voted for the ANC, and the election results say that the DA has won the national election with two-thirds majority, and that is what exactly happened in Zimbabwe. When you ask the majority of Zimbabweans in the taxis and even in buses, they will tell you that they have voted for the MDC-T; but when the national election results were announced, they tell the opposite story. Ordinary Zimbabweans, whom I pity and I continue to pray for, are stuck between a wall and a rock. The brick wall is the cash liquidity crisis, and the rock is the salaries that the Zimbabwean government could not pay in time. When parents run out of ideas, children begin to cry incessantly. When the government runs of ideas, the ordinary people begin to get sick and die as the result of fear and trepidation. It will be surprising under this economic and political climate that the economy of Zimbabwe finds itself in to be able to distribute textbooks at schools in time and distribute medical supplies to hospitals around the country timeously. When the state has failed decimally to live to its expectation and to save the majority of people out of poverty, that state becomes irrelevant and useless. Some wish just like me that at least the GNU (Government of National Unity) should have remained intact at least a little bit longer. There were calls in 2014 that were suggesting that the Zimbabwean government should further cut the civil servants' salaries in order to keep up with the mounting debts that were eating a large chunk of the national budget. The Zimbabwean government has already lost a considerable amount of teachers due to the economic instability and political intolerance before, and if the current calls are anything to go by, it's highly likely that the government of Zimbabwe will lose further teachers in the near future to the South Africa education system. "Why wait until we die here?" are the famous words from the Holy Bible, and I know that deep down in the hearts and souls of most Zimbabweans, this scripture resonates well with them. There is a time when all hope is gone, and when that time has come, there is nothing that one can do to save himself except to move on with life. There is time in this life when the best solution that one can take is just to leave the situation that one is in rather than to try to solve it. There are problems that are worth solving, and there are problems that are not worth solving. There are marriages that are worth fighting for, and there are marriages that are not worth fighting for, and there are relationships that are worth fighting for, and there are relationships that are not worth fighting for. You just need to know which relationships are worth fighting for and which relationships are not worth fighting for. There are situations that can be salvaged, and there are situations that can't be salvaged due to their nature and their size. The Zimbabwean problems require collective wisdom and collective effort of the masses. There are times when the ordinary people of the land have to wake up and join their hands together in building their country. South Africans have that undying spirit in them; they can't retreat and surrender if they want to, but that South African spirit of not retreating and not surrendering has died down over the years because of money and power. The majority of the people in South Africa are no longer working together to fight what is just and fair. Now it's everybody for himself and God for us all. The Third Chimurenga has come and gone. Why wait here until we die? Is the attitude that the majority of Zimbabweans need to have. They need to work together as a collective and then as a united force. If it warrants new and fresh negotiation, let it be so at least if all attempts will manage to save the lives of the people on the ground, and if there is a need for a mediator, let the mediator be invited. One of the main problems with the so-called the mediator is this: he will come only just before the national elections, and when the results of the national elections have been announced and the national elections have been declared free and fair, then his responsibility is over; he forgets about the country in question. The mediator was supposed to act and function as an administrator and work with the democratic new elected government to see to it that the economic situation is turned around for the better. People's aspirations and people's dreams are realized. The administrator was supposed to make sure that the country does not reverse and revert into the ditch that the Zimbabwean economy is about to fall in again. The only time when the mediator was supposed to leave Zimbabwe was supposed to be after the economic situation has normalized, and when the Zimbabwean economy has managed to stand with both of its feet, then the administrator can leave thereafter. As things stand, the economic situation will get worse day by day until the economy is on its knees, and the people will be pinning all their hopes yet again on the coming national elections that should take place in 2018. From July 31, 2013, to July 2018, depending on which month the national election will be held, it is a very long time specifically if you are a Zimbabwean. An ordinary person can say five years is not that very long time. Trust me, five years is a very long time specifically if you are in a bad economic situation like most Zimbabweans find themselves in. The cash liquidity crisis is just the tip of the iceberg of myriad things that are about to fall on the people of Zimbabwe. There are times as an individual where you need to lower your expectations and lower your hopes and widen your room for disappointments specifically if disappointments are the order of the day. Though we Africans must remain positive and hopeful against all hopes, but after all we must have a room for disappointment. It will be sheer madness for any Zimbabwean to think that the current economic situation will get better in the twinkling of an eye; therefore to avoid further disappointments and unnecessary headaches, people need to lower their expectations and their dreams.

CHAPTER 12

THE VICIOUS CYCLE

The *Macmillan English Dictionary for Advanced Learners* describes the vicious cycle in this way: a process in which the existence of a problem causes other problems and this makes the original problem worse. We as African people will never learn enough to further liberate this young African generation if we are not learning from our African history. Accordingly most Africans don't know African history and don't even bother to study African history because it is viewed as irrelevant and useless to this modern time that we live in. I have satisfied myself in the process of writing this book that the problem about the Zimbabwean economic problems are not centered diametrically on a single person—Pres. Robert Mugabe. The Zimbabwean economic problems are much wider and deeper than that. It will be unfair and unjust to apportion the national problems to an individual as if Pres. Robert Mugabe is Zimbabwe and Zimbabwe is Pres. Robert Mugabe. He is Robert Mugabe, not Robert Zimbabwe for that matter. It's also true that most of the authors of African history have never lived and walked in the African soil. Most of them have studied about Africa on the Internet and made baseless and unfounded conclusions about the sequence of political events that they don't really comprehend thoroughly. History is in motion, and there is a new reality that is unfolding before our very eyes each and every day. Most people are trying to catch up with history and the historical events that have already happened in the past. Pres. Robert Mugabe is not solely the Zimbabwean problem as if, if he is out of the picture, then the whole economic puzzle of Zimbabwe will sort itself out within a minute. It is logically correct that he has a role and a place in the Zimbabwean economic problems that led to the current economic sanctions that are currently in place. It will be unfair and unjust to assume that the Zimbabwean economic problems on their entirety were orchestrated single-handedly by Pres. Robert Mugabe with the help of Grace Mugabe, his wife. History has never favored Pres. Robert Mugabe and never even painted him in a good light. Though he has been in prison for almost eleven years for his people, until this day he never got the well-deserved recognition as a hero, but he has been projected as a dictator. He has been described as the Osama Bin Laden of Africa, and some call him the Adolf Hitler of Zimbabwe. When the economy of Zimbabwe was booming and the people of Zimbabwe were doing very well economically and otherwise, Pres. Robert Mugabe was hailed as the true African leader as long as the land was still in the hands of the white commercial farmers. Pres. Robert Mugabe of Zimbabwe has received many honorary doctorate degrees from the Western universities as tokens of appreciation for his unique leadership style, which managed to unite the people of Zimbabwe who were battered and bruised by the colonization for quite a long period of time. As long as the land remained in the hands of the Western settlers, there were no problems in Zimbabwe. In fact very few South Africans knew where Zimbabwe was in the map of Africa. There was peace and tranquility in Zimbabwe before the farm invasion of 2000, which must have been written and talked about to the point that it's even very difficult as to whose political narrative to believe. The people of Zimbabwe point their fingers to the war veterans, and the war veterans point their fingers to the West, and the West point its fingers to Pres. Robert Mugabe as the president of the country who had all the powers and arsenal at his disposal to make sure that land invasion fiasco was curtailed and derailed to happen. Whatever the case may be about the farm invasion of 2000, the fact of the matter is this: Where to from here, and how do the Zimbabweans get out of the economic ditch that they have fallen in? The point of departure in solving any problem is the recognition that there is a problem, and all stakeholders involved need to understand their roles that they have played in instigating the problem to the surface. The blame game needs to stop if the economy of Zimbabwe is to be resuscitated to its original state that it was once in. I remember vividly when I was in the bus from Bulawayo to Beitbridge border when Jabulile said to me, "My grandparents were not buying maize meal here in Zimbabwe. We always had enough in the past." It's mind boggling to try and understand what went wrong, and that is not even relevant at this point in time. Zimbabwe held its democratic election in 1980, and Prime Minister Robert Mugabe became the first democratically elected prime minister, and he ruled the Zimbabwean people until this day. Though he is very sick and fragile, his people still love him. This is what I have seen in Zimbabwe, and ordinary people are not even allowed to denigrate him in public because of his stature and office that he holds. That was very surprising to me in comparison to what I have heard and read from the Western media. As far as I know, in each and every hotel I checked into there was a picture of Pres. Robert Mugabe on their reception, and that is a fact. It will be unfair and unjust to assume that there is a clause in the constitution of Zimbabwe that compels every hotel that I have checked into to put the picture of Pres. Robert Mugabe as a matter of order. The fact of the matter is this: there are Zimbabweans who love their president wholeheartedly to the point that they can even kill for him if the need arises. Unlike in South Africa, Pres. Jacob Zuma of the ANC as the president of South Africa is disrespected by the media and even denigrated even by the columnists that are writing trash on the newspaper now and then. In fact the average comedians in South Africa, when they have run out of jokes, will just come up with an impromptu joke about the president of South Africa, and the audience will be laughing. Freedom of expression has been more often than not violated many times against the president of South Africa, and his constitutional rights have been trampled upon many times on the print media and even on many radio stations. Much has been written about Pres. Jacob Zuma of South Africa that projects him as a bad person and who can't manage his financial affairs or his family affairs. The same goes for Pres. Robert Mugabe; much has been said about him and his family. I will try by all means to fuse together everything I have said into one chapter then I will make my conclusion and that will be sufficient for the day. My original hypothesis is the West stole Africa's wealth. All the wars that have taken place in the past and even the ones that are still going on right in the African continent have been sponsored by the West. The turmoil and political instability that are happening in Africa can be easily traced back to the West. It's common knowledge now that the West has destroyed the economy of Zimbabwe with its illegal economic sanctions just because the Zimbabweans took their land in 2000 from the white commercial farmers. I need to stress this point even further again: the main reason the economy of Zimbabwe is in shambles is that simply Pres. Robert Mugabe ceased dancing to the Western music. As long as any African leader will stop dancing to the Western music, what happened to Pres. Robert Mugabe is what the West will do to any African leader who does pay allegiance to the foreign policy of the West, and that is not a laughing matter, guys. The West can spill blood and impose economic sanctions to any country as long as that country is seeking economic and financial emancipation. The West is in the business of controlling and running the world, and all the mineral wealth of any country on the planet belongs to the West whether we agree or not. The reason South Africa froze like a chicken in the refrigerator when it comes to the land issue is that the South African government saw exactly what happened in Zimbabwe. The West means business, and it does not back off. The West has already ripped the Central African Republic apart, and all there is in Central African Republic are empty cases of bullets and mass graves of people. Its mind boggling why the West would commit so many atrocities on the face of the earth yet continue to claim to be the custodian of human rights while it is the human rights violator itself. What is the use of being politically free if you are not economically and financially free? The West has dispensed political freedom only to Africa. Until this day it has not yet allowed any African country to get economic freedom and financial freedom. Most of the African leaders are ambassadors of the West in the African continent. They take orders from the West where they get foreign aid and free food parcels. African leaders who are going to be hotheaded like Pres. Robert Mugabe of Zimbabwe and try some Mickey Mouse maneuvering tactics like taking back the land that is owned by the daughters and the sons of the West are going to be dealt with accordingly by the West just like Pres. Robert Mugabe. It appears as if Pres. Yoweri Museveni of Uganda is beginning to misbehave and he is defiling the order from his masters in the West. South Africa and other neighboring countries now know the ramifications of economic sanctions. Average people think that economic sanctions are just a paper exercise that will not translate into anything meaningful in real life. The fact of the matter is this: economic sanctions are like dying through suffocation because the body is being weakened slowly and there is nothing that the victim can do about it because the victim is powerless. Economic sanctions stretch from the freezing of assets that are in the USA and UK banks to the imposition of travel restrictions and cutting of foreign aid, which the majority of African countries can't live without. The sole purpose of economic sanctions is to suffocate the anti-Western leaders like Pres. Robert Mugabe of Zimbabwe until he screams for help. As long as you don't scream for Western help, then you will surely die a political and economic death. The number of people that have been killed by the West in Zimbabwe supersedes the number of 9/11 victims in hundredfold. When Saddam Hussein was refusing with his massive reserve of oil, the West accused him of aiding and sponsoring terrorists and toppled him just like that. The cardinal sin that had been committed by Saddam Hussein was refusing to dance to the Western music and to give away his massive reserve of oil to the Seven Sisters of the West. The Seven Sisters are the seven companies that call the shots on the petroleum industry of the world, and they all belong to the West. The imposition of economic sanctions on February 18, 2002, until 2014 is seriously affecting the people of Zimbabwe in a negative way. It has been thirteen years since those illegal economic sanctions have been imposed on Pres. Robert Mugabe's neck. As long he continues to be adamant and rebellious to his Western masters that he once served very well in the past, the economic sanctions will remain in place until the return of Jesus Christ. The West wants nothing but Pres. Robert Mugabe out of the picture because he is defeating the objectives and master plan of the West. As long as African leaders continue to take orders and instructions from the West, they are settled, so to speak. The West wants nothing to do with Pres. Robert Mugabe because of his disrespect and disloyalty to his former Western masters. Pres. Hassan Rouhani of Iran has come back to the West to ask for the forgiveness of sins from his former leaders, and he has already professed to the Western masters that he is a prodigal son who is asking for forgiveness. The West is willing to forgive as long as you are going to give them more oil for free now, since you are the former troublesome son. The tit-for-tat fight between the West and Pres. Robert Mugabe will soon come to an end as his personal health is taking its toll on him. The West is monitoring Pres. Robert Mugabe's medical condition as if he is in the ICU of the West. Vladimir Putin of Russia has been on the radar of the West for quite some time, and eventually the West has caught him through the Crimea debacle. There is nothing serious that the Russian president has committed that can warrant economic sanctions and eventually suffocate the Russian economy. There is one thing that I have learned in my trip to Zimbabwe, and it's this: it takes a considerable amount of time to bounce back from the economic collapse by the sanctioned country to the economic upswing specifically if you have been economically sanctioned by the West. The longer economic sanctions remain in place, the longer you are likely to die from economic suffocation. It's common knowledge now that the Western media had already professed that the economy of Zimbabwe has been damaged beyond repair. Simply put, Zimbabwe is a failed state and is about to be the Somalia of the sub-Saharan African region. I don't believe that Zimbabwe is a failed state and the economy of

Zimbabwe is irreparable. Though there are serious and drastic adjustments that the government of Zimbabwe should embark upon in order to turn the economic situation around, I believe that there is still glimpse of light at the end of the economic tunnel.

LAND

It's common knowledge that when the Western settlers came to Africa, they didn't carry land on their ships, and the question that springs into mind is this: How come these folks are owning a vast tracts of land in our own country of birth, though we know for a fact that they didn't carry with them land from the West? The answer to this question is simple and straightforward: the Western settlers, through their oppressive and corrupt Western agents, stole the very land that they now own from the African indigenous people using guns and dogs to evacuate the masses of the natives in land that they were given by God. The issues of land grab forcefully have been a thorn in the butt of many African countries until this day. This quagmire of land has not been given sufficient attention it deserves. During the 1979 Lancaster House Agreement, the issue of land was not addressed properly and thoroughly. Due to political and international pressure that the African nationalists were under, they had less choices and less time to think through the ramifications and the consequences of conceding that the land reform will take place after ten years. The Patriotic Front of Zimbabwe signed on the dotted line, literally selling the very land it has been fighting for, for quite a long period of time in the bush with the Ian Smith regime. The Patriotic Front was led by Robert Mugabe of ZANU and the late Joshua Nkomo of ZAPU, and the Patriotic Front did not fathom the deal that they have signed that; it literally meant that they were still keeping the land in the hands of the white commercial farms.[1] The African nationalists were under pressure from the ordinary people on the ground who have been working for the white commercial farmers for quite a long period of time without earning a meaningful salary to support their families. The ordinary people on the ground from Zimbabwe misinterpreted and miscalculated the meaning of political freedom and political independence. The mere fact that you are politically free does not mean in all material respect that you are actually free in the true sense of the word. The Southern Times reports:

> *Brethren, you must understand that imperialism knows how to invent lies that sound very good because there is no such thing as political freedom existing as a stand-alone from economic power. Freedom is a holistic entity. It is achieved as is and not in compartments; you are either free or you are not, and there's nothing in between. A prisoner who is in solitary confinement, eating crumbs and sleeping on the floor with no blanket, and a prisoner who has a nutritious menu, a good mattress, and even time for television and gym are both prisoners; yes, the one might have better conditions to live under, but they are both prisoners nonetheless.*[2]

The fact of the matter is this: the nationalists missed out on the golden opportunity to reverse the injustices and atrocities of the past through the Lancaster House Agreement in 1979, and they could not get the job done. The African nationalists were intellectually exhausted from the long protracted intellectual marathon that they were running with the West. The African nationalists finally got extremely tired of running the intellectual marathon with the West and eventually signed the Land Reform Program, which will only take place after ten years, and the West would fund the Zimbabwean Land Redistribution Program. The African nationalists signed on the dotted line, and just like King Lobengula signed on the dotted line and sold the land and the mineral resources of Zimbabwe to the British mafia Cecil John Rhodes, so are the African nationalists. I wonder whether or not the nationalists had read how Cecil John Rhodes stole the land from King Lobengula, the Matebele king who got angry and went to die in a place that is still unknown even to this day. The fact of the matter is this: when King (Inkosi) Lobengula signed on that dotted line, hoodwinked and compelled by Charles Rudd and his group of British mafias, little did the King Lobengula know that the West had already begun its project of annexing Africa one point at a time. The next thing you know, King Lobengula was running helter-skelter like a headless chicken running away from the Pioneer Column of Cecil John Rhodes. Had the African nationalists read the Zimbabwean history thoroughly, they would have vehemently refused to sign on the dotted line, but just like King Lobengula of the Matebele people, unfortunately, the African nationalists committed the same mistake. The more things change, the more they stay the same, and some people don't learn from the mistakes of others. The main reason we Africans should read history thoroughly is so that we can't repeat the same mistakes that have been committed by the previous generations in the past. The less time we Africans spend visiting our history books, the more we are likely to eat the very same forbidden fruit that Adam of the old ate and suffer the punishment from God. The point I making is this: there is nothing new under the sun; everything that will happen in the future is what has happened in the past. The present comes from the past, and the future comes from the present. People who are ignorant to what happened in the past are likely to apportion blame to the wrong people, accusing the wrong people for all the wrong reasons. The same is true about people who are blaming Pres. Jacob Zuma of South Africa and Pres. Robert Mugabe of Zimbabwe. When Cecil John Rhodes annexed Zimbabwe, Pres. Robert Mugabe was not even conceived in his mother's womb yet, and just like when Jan Van Riebeeck arrived in Cape Town on April 6, 1652, Pres. Jacob Zuma of South Africa was not born yet. Instead of focusing on the enemy, which is the West, many Africans are now pointing fingers on the same political leaders who have spent a considerable amount of years in exile and in prison for the same free unpolluted oxygen that the majority of Africans are freely inhaling. Do not hate the player; hate the game. Most Africans, due to lack of understanding, hate the game and the player at the same time. What Pres. Robert Mugabe could not do through his feeble and weak parliamentarians for a very long time, "the brothers of destruction" did it within a few minutes. What is it that could have sparked this flare of fire that has been burning uncontrollably for a very long time underground from the war veterans' hearts? The answer to this question is this: poverty. The fact that Zimbabwe got its political independence and not its economic independence earlier than South Africa meant actually nothing, practically speaking. The majority of land was still held by the white commercial farmers. The majority of peasants were still working as peasants in the commercial farmers of the whites. The problem about time is this: time is everything, and the time had come when the ordinary people could no longer cope with despicable inequality between the native people and the white people, knowing full well that the very same white commercial farmers were rich not simply because they worked hard but they were rich out of stealing. There is nothing wrong about taking back what was taken from you illegally, but the way you take it back might land you in another very serious trouble if you are not careful. There is nothing wrong with what the "the brothers of destruction" did, except taking the very same land that they have spent a considerable amount of years in the bush fighting for, but the way they took the land leaves a lot to be desired. Though there are many books written about this subject, some of the books suggest that the land that was taken from the white commercial farmers has been used effectively and efficiently and has benefited almost three hundred thousand families who were landless. The truth of the matter is this: that is a red lie. There is nothing in actual fact that suggests that the land that was taken by the "brothers of destruction" from the white commercial farmers has changed the lives of the ordinary Zimbabweans for the better. The fact of the matter is this: the lives of many Zimbabweans have been changed from bad to worse. Zimbabweans are the burden to the South African government, and that is not a xenophobic assertion; it is the truth and nothing but the truth. One parliamentarian once said because of the multitude of foreigners in South Africa, we South Africans are no longer enjoying our political freedom very well. The war veterans, bear in mind, fought in the Second Chimurenga, and they have scars all over their bodies to prove that they were in a Bush War. There are conflicting narratives as to why the war veterans decided to go on rampage and started taking the farms out of adrenalin and passion. One political narrative that is very plausible suggests that the Movement for Democratic Change (MDC) was formed in 2000. The multitudes of white commercial farmers, instead of giving away the very same land that was given to them by the government of Cecil John Rhodes and Ian Smith, decided to get into the sheets with the newly formed MDC, which is still today led by Morgan Tsvangirai. The rationale and the main reason the multitudes of white commercial farmers got into bed with the MDC-T was that they wanted political protection, and they wanted to oust Pres. Robert Mugabe with "the brothers of destruction" through a legitimate political process. Zimbabwe was teetering on the brink of a civil war. The war veterans were very poor, and the government of Pres. Robert Mugabe was in a very serious financial trouble, and the political popularity of ZANU-PF was dwindling very fast, and corruption had found its way into the DNA of Zimbabwean government officials. The peasants, since they were working for the white commercial farmers, were told that they needed to join the newly formed MDC-T, and gladly so they joined the MDC-T in order to keep their jobs. Political events unfolded with the speed of lightning. Before people know it, the war veterans had taken a vast tract of land from the white commercial farmers, and some who resisted were killed in broad daylight. The majority of South Africans knew nothing about Pres. Robert Mugabe, and they knew nothing even about the war veterans. In effect the national curriculum in the South

African schools does not cover extensively and expansively the Zimbabwean history. The grade twelve pupils of that time were still reading *Julius Caesar* written by William Shakespeare. What followed then was the economic catastrophe we Africans still see in Zimbabwe even to this day; it's illegal economic sanctions that are biting even the innocent monkeys in the bush. We all know that monkeys like food, and when there is no food, monkeys will also emigrate. When the economic sanctions were imposed on February 18, 2002, some of the monkeys were also experiencing some tough times, and they had no choice but to immigrate to South Africa without following the long protracted agonizing process that the normal human beings go through in the Beitbridge border. The economy of Zimbabwe has not yet hit rock bottom, yet the worst is still to come until the whole economy is on its knees. The next five years from 2014 to 2018 will be the longest years for the people of Zimbabwe that they have ever seen in their lives. The ordinary people of Zimbabwe will need a breakthrough prayer coupled with dry fasting in the mountains; I hope that Zimbabwe's economic debacle can be saved through a divine intervention. Pres. Robert Mugabe could not do much about the adverse effects of the economic sanctions that have been imposed by the West in the economy of Zimbabwe. What he was also worried about it is his political power that was also in serious trouble from the MDC-T. There have been factions even in his political party just like there have been splitter parties just like in the ANC of South Africa. Pres. Robert Mugabe has always emerged a victor in any national elections by hook or by crook. Until this day he is still in charge, though sick and weak, but he is still in charge. I have asked myself a very simple question, which is, would they still be in the economic fiasco and mess that the people of Zimbabwe are currently in had Joshua Nkomo won the national election in 1980? Most people suggest that Joshua Nkomo was more savvy and tactful, unlike Pres. Robert Mugabe, who sometimes acts and then thinks about his actions later. He would not have allowed the "the brothers of destruction" to take the farms in a hostile way as they did in 2000. The land issue was a matter of life and death, and it is even to this day. When I was in Zimbabwe for the first time, I looked at the vast tract of land that remains underutilized and lies in waste. Part of me thought that these lands need to be privatized to the South African government for better use. The cliché that says the rationale behind farm invasion was to resettle the landless community is a sheer madness. There is a vast tract of land in Zimbabwe, even to this day, that remains unoccupied by the very same landless communities which it was meant for.

RAINBOW NATION

After the release of Nelson Mandela in 1990, there was a sense of relief among many South Africans that apartheid will be buried once and for all. The oppressive regime of the time will finally get a decent burial through the national elections on April 27, 1994. I will not provide you with another long, tedious South African history, though it's important for the young generation. I think it's very irrelevant for the purpose of my discussion. I am sparing you the drudgery of reading South African history. The Reconstruction Development Programme (RDP) was the document of the ANC that spells out in detail how the ANC government will transform the economy of South Africa in favor of the previously oppressed masses if it wins the national democratic elections that was to be held on April 27, 1994. There is one common denominator between the Zimbabwean sequence of political events and the South African sequence of political events. The two countries are inextricably connected in more ways than one, and this political and economic interconnectedness is likely to remain as it is for a very long period of time. The classic example is this: during the Ian Smith government, Great Britain imposed economic sanctions to Rhodesia after Prime Minister Ian Douglas Smith has announced his UDI (Unilateral Declaration of Independence). Apartheid South Africa was supporting the regime of Ian Smith financially and militarily. The only thing that kept the Rhodesian government of Ian Douglas Smith from drowning in the sea of economic sanctions was apartheid South Africa. Pres. Nelson Mandela had a daunting task before him after being democratically elected, and that was to unite the broken nation that had been ravaged and divided by Hendrik Verwoerd's apartheid laws. South Africa was bleeding profusely from inside out. A multitude of families had lost their loved ones through the liberation struggle, affirming the notion that freedom is not free. Common sense and logical approach dictated that the nation had to go through the period of mourning and the period of forgiveness. There was no better man to lead the South African nation to that moment of mourning coupled with the moment of healing of the nation from its bleeding wounds that have been caused by the apartheid forces than Nelson Mandela himself. Pres. Nelson Mandela instituted the TRC (Truth and Reconciliation Commission), which was chaired by Bishop Desmond Tutu. It went too smooth, and the whole world learned a pivotal lesson: that it's possible to forgive your enemy and live next to him again. It's of significance to state it fair and clear that the TRC was dealing purely with the atrocities that have been committed by the apartheid forces to the multitude of black people. Some of them were abducted at night and shot at point-blank range by the apartheid forces. What is surprising to me even to this day is that some of the apartheid agents who were working for the apartheid governments then are still working for this democratically elected government, and that is astounding to me! The TRC never sought to deal with the land issue, and that could have been a better moment and better time to deal with the land issue then, since all role players were mostly alive. But the teething problem that was confronted by South African young democracy was that the majority of former apartheid forces had massive ammunition at their disposal, and they were ready to strike had their land that they stole from native people was going to be taken away from them by the ANC democratically elected government. The best way to deal with a problem is to confront it head-on. The deferral and delaying tactics make the problem even bigger and complicated to solve later. The land question was not on people's mind in South Africa. The multitude of people in South African including the former freedom fighters are struggling to wrap their heads around the millions of rands they had received from their BEE deals. Time waits for no man. While the majority of South Africans were eating their BEE pie, the West, through its sons and daughters, were buying more land from the municipalities and building more real estates. The next thing we know, the majority of the land in South Africa just like before is still even today held by the Western sons and daughters, and the multitudes of black people are where they were before 1994, which is in squatter camps and in matchbox houses. Poverty reigns supreme in squatter camps. AIDS/HIV also reigns supreme in squatter camps and in rural areas. During the state of the national address in 2012, Pres. Jacob Zuma alluded to the fact that the willing-buyer-willing-seller principle was no longer effective, since the state had only managed to repossess 2 percent of the land. Let me put that statement into context. It means since the dawn of democracy until in 2012, South Africa had only managed to repossess only 2 percent of its land from the Western settlers who took the land from the native people illegally. If South Africa only managed to repossess only 2 percent of the land in 2012 since the dawn of democracy, it means it will take South Africa more than 980 years to repossess 98 percent of the land from the Western settlers, and almost everybody who is alive today will be dead by then. There is a serious problem that the majority of South Africans are turning a blind eye on. The Chinese are in South Africa and they are buying South African land

and they are getting title deeds for the land when they buy land. We all know that China has just relaxed its one-child policy, and most of the Chinese couples do want to have more than one child, which is not allowed in China. The South African government does not have prescripts and laws that prevent and prohibit married couples to have more than once child. In effect, in South Africa, the more children you have, the more money you make through the child grants, and that is a fact. Most of the real estates in South Africa are not owned by native people, but they are owned by foreigners. Most of the Western settlers shielded their land via the game reserves and game farms instead of taking all their monkeys to Kruger National Park and give the land to the landless people. The Western settlers would rather keep the land just for rhinos and a few monkeys than to give it to the black people. The multitudes of black people are still building shacks on top of other shacks in Alexandra because of the insufficiency of the land. The 'born-frees' of South Africa are now in the university; they will wake up to this reality of land after they have completed their studies and joined the working class. The 'born-frees' will soon discover that the CODESA talks were riddled with blunders and errors because winners were literally losers. The born-frees will be confronted with the ugly reality that the majority of Zimbabwean war veterans were confronted with back in 2000. As long as the multitudes of people are renting flats and paying mortgage bonds to the Western banks, then South Africans are politically free but not economically free. What is the use of political freedom without economic freedom? I have to restrict myself sometimes; I will have to address that issue separately and give it sufficient attention and consideration it deserves. Pres. Thabo Mbeki succeeded Pres. Nelson Mandela, having taught many leaders of the world that you must resign from the state while the nation still loves you. That is what Nelson Mandela taught the whole world, including African leaders in the African continent. African leaders must desist and cease overstaying their welcome in government. Most African leaders can't let go of power and prestige of being in a leadership position for a long period of time. African leaders are addicted to state resources and state facilities; that is why they would rather leave the state facilities and state resources in a coffin than leave the states facilities and state resources ceremoniously through relinquishing their position ceremoniously. During Pres. Nelson Mandela's tenure, there was too much movement in the government of South Africa given the fact that the then deputy president Thabo Mbeki was going to succeed a world icon and a renowned political leader, the true father of the South African democracy. Pres. Thabo Mbeki is a scholar of rare breed. He never mimicked Pres. Nelson Mandela's style of leading, but he had to find his own mojo in government and establish himself as the president of South Africa. After the Polokwane watershed policy conference, which was held in 2007, the ANC NEC sent Pres. Thabo Mbeki to the retirement village unceremoniously in 2008. Though he still wanted to serve his country with humility and dignity, he resigned with humility and dignity, and the land question was still hanging in the air as is still the case. The majority of South Africans are still obsessed with gold, diamonds, and platinum. Very few South Africans are paying attention to the issue of land, and that is why the multitude of South Africans, specifically those that are residing in the big cities, are still renting apartments and flats and further enriching the Western settlers who are rich already from stealing from Africans. Since there was a vacuum in government because of the sudden resignation of Pres. Thabo Mbeki, the ANC had to swear in the deputy president of the ANC, Kgalema Petrus Motlanthe, to parliament, and he eventually became the interim president of South Africa. It's important and significant to contextualize the preceding political events that led to the unceremoniously recalling of Pres. Thabo Mbeki in 2008. Had Pres. Thabo Mbeki emerged as victor in the Polokwane Policy Conference in 2007, he would have still continued as the state president of South Africa, and he would not have been recalled unceremoniously as it was the case. The main problem ensued prior to the policy conference in Polokwane in 2007. Prior to the policy conference in Polokwane, there were factions and frictions within the ANC, and these frictions and factions were perpetuated and fueled by the ANCYL. Truth be told, Julius Malema resembled the true character of Nelson Mandela, and that is my own assessment. South African politics had reached a stalemate. The South African population was no longer looking forward to the prime-time news. When Julius Malema emerged as victor in April 2008 in the Mangaung conference, suddenly there was an eruption and the politics of South Africa awake from its sleeping mode.[3] Julius Malema breathed in life to the South Africa politics. To this day the majority of South Africans love Julius Malema, but they hate his politics. There were two camps in the Polokwane Policy Conference: the Zuma camp and the Mbeki camp. And all of the members of these camps are members of the ANC, but when it comes to voting for the president of the ANC, the delegates voted according to their own camps, just like in the recent policy conference in Mangaung in 2013. Again, Pres. Jacob Zuma's camp smacked the deputy president of South Africa Kgalema Petrus

Motlanthe's camp in the face. There was a statement that was made by the expelled president of the ANCYL Julius Malema after the Polokwane policy conference—that "if the National Executive Committee (NEC) of the ANC is not recalling *Thabo*, we will recall them." Africans are people of respect and humility. African tradition and African culture do not permit a child to call an elderly person with his name because that is a sign of disrespect and lack of home training. The ANC NEC indeed heeded to the call of the ANCYL. The ANC NEC struggled to conjure up an appropriate logical reason why they recalled the president of South Africa Thabo Mbeki as if he was the president of the members of the ANC only. The president of South Africa is still a member of the ANC, but he is also the president of the South African people, those that voted for the ANC and even those that did not vote for the ANC. Therefore, logic and common sense dictate that when the president of South Africa is recalled, the South African people should be given a well-thought reasonable reasons why the president of the country was recalled. What we South Africans have heard from the mainstream media was only the half-cocked, invalid, and illogical reason that there was a political assessment of his tenure as the president of South Africa, and the ANC was not satisfied with him, hence he was recalled. I should register my political stance on this matter: I am not a member of any political party, and I am not a disgruntled member of the former president Thabo Mbeki's camp. To comprehend a political event properly, one needs to place that political event in its contextual form and contextual period in order to understand the circumstances and the political climate within that political event. During this political period, the ANC as the governing party was going through its own period of trial and tribulation, and there were multiple conflicting political narratives around this political period. The ANC was going through an agonizing transitional period of leadership. The era for Pres. Thabo Mbeki had come to an end, though the majority of people could not foresee this happening, and it's possible that Pres. Thabo Mbeki himself still wanted to be the president of the ANC and thought his political life has come to an end. A wise man will always change his ways. From a vantage point, there was no reasonable reason for former president Thabo Mbeki to challenge Jacob Zuma in the Polokwane Policy Conference because Pres. Jacob Zuma had the support of the ANCYL, which was headed by the expelled ANCYL president Julius Malema. It's important to comprehend that I am not discussing the politics of the ANC and the politics of the ANCYL. It will be unfair and unjust to skip this critical piece of information and quickly jump to the issue of nationalization of mines and expropriation of land without compensation without tracing back the historical background of the ANC and the historical background of the ANCYL. I have nothing against the ANC, and I have nothing against the expelled ANCYL president Julius Malema. The South African media loved the expelled ANCYL president Julius Malema, and the youth of South Africa loved him too. In effect the expelled ANCYL president Julius Malema was more popular and more famous more than Coca-Cola at one point. There was a brewing national pressure that was exerted on the expelled ANCYL president Julius Malema to say something new. After the departure of former president Thabo Mbeki to his political retirement village, some called it self-imposed political wilderness. There was a deepening void and vacuum in South African politics. Pres. Robert Mugabe and ZANU-PF were suffocating and screaming louder from the economic sanctions that have been imposed by the West to the economy of Zimbabwe. There are many instances where the government of Zimbabwe requested the South African government to mediate on its behalf for the economic sanctions to be lifted off by the West. One thousand seven hundred people were dying per week in Zimbabwe because of AIDS/HIV.[4] The West was killing Zimbabweans with starvation and hunger, just like Bashar al-Assad was killing the Syrian people with hunger and starvation. As much as the West is quick and fast to spot terrorists, the biggest terrorist organizations in the whole world are in the West. NATO killed Muammar Gaddafi of Libya in conjunction with sex jihadists and the fundamentalists of the West. There have never been calls of nationalization of mines and expropriation of land without compensation prior to the 2007 Polokwane policy conference. The issue of disbandment of the Scorpion took center stage in Polokwane, and it is this Polokwane policy conference where the "Scorpion" died its own political death, and it was given a decent political burial. The main problem with Scorpion was that it was giving former freedom fighters and black entrepreneurs a tough time, and they could not enjoy their BEE pie without being disturbed by the Scorpion; the Scorpion was a thorn in the flesh. Most members of the Scorpion were working for apartheid government, and they were never compelled to take retirement packages after the collapse of apartheid system, and they could not stomach the feeling seeing a black person driving an expensive car. Most members of the Scorpion were very bitter and disgruntled at the very ANC that was the governing party, and they were out there, guns blazing, to prove that a black person is corrupt from the womb and he is not even fit to govern a country. Most members of the ANC thought that Pres. Thabo Mbeki had the power and the arsenal at his disposal to disband the Scorpion. Some believed that in turn he was using the Scorpion to silence his political rivals within the ANC. During the Scorpion era, most members of the ANC, specifically those that now belong to the Zuma camp, were incarcerated one way or the other. Most members of the Zuma camp prior to the Polokwane policy conference were not angry at Pres. Thabo Mbeki as a person, but they were angry at the Scorpion and they thought that he was very reluctant to dissolve and disband it. Judge Sisi Kampepe's report was not made public yet, and it was used by the then president Thabo Mbeki to disband the Scorpion legally, though the decision of disbanding the Scorpion had already been taken in Polokwane to disband it. Former president Thabo Mbeki was merely enforcing the political decision that was taken in Polokwane Policy Conference to do what the ANC wanted because whatever the ANC wants the ANC will always get. The expelled ANCYL president Julius Malema, a.k.a. JUJU, was not central and key to the issue of the disbandment of the Scorpion. The expelled ANCYL president Julius Malema could not have been vocal and central to the issue of disbandment of the Scorpion owing to the fact he was busy chewing his own BEE pie from the Limpopo departments. The best way to muzzle a politician in South African politics is to give him a BEE pie; he will not even have time and space to think about critical issues that are affecting the country. The political dust settled in South Africa, and it was business as usual. Pres. Jacob Zuma became the president of the ANC in 2009 and the darling of the tripartite alliance (ANC, COSATU, and SACP). Both the ANCYL president Julius Malema and the ANC president Jacob Zuma have been singing from the same political hymn book, and the BEE pies were still warm and intact. There are two crucial political events that happened during this period. The expelled president of the ANCYL Julius Malema began to lose his BEE contracts. Almost everything that he did as an individual was closely examined and monitored. The type of watch he was wearing on his wrist was closely monitored by those who were against him within the ANC due to political slumbering and political boredom, since there was no crucial national issue that the majority of politicians can toss and turn about in the middle of the night. The expelled ANCYL president Julius Malema removed from the archives of the ANC the most crucial document of the ANC and started reading it. The freedom charter speaks about the land of milky and honey that the people of South Africa will enjoy after entering the Promised Land. I have already discussed the content of the freedom charter in detail, and I am not going to repeat it here. While the expelled ANCYL president Julius Malema was busy digesting and dissecting the wording of the freedom charter, the multitudes of Zimbabweans were crossing the Beitbridge border illegally and legally; some of them were perishing in the hands of the crocodiles in the Limpopo River. The day the expelled ANCYL leadership completed studying the freedom charter, it made a shocking announcement: nationalization of mines and expropriation of land without compensation. Most of the people in the ANC NEC and even in the tripartite alliance were very shocked about such calls. Since the ANC NEC conjured up most of the government policies, it's possible to draw an inference that suggests that the expelled ANCYL president Julius Malema thought that the BEE pie was not good enough. In fact he was not satisfied with the BEE pie and he wanted the whole chocolate factory instead of just a mere chocolate to himself. The more money you get, the more money you want. The fact of the matter is this: South Africans knew very well who the ANCYL president Julius Malema was during this period. At one point the ANC misdiagnosed his misdemeanor and sent him to an anger management course, which he gladly undertook and came back better. He also gained a considerable amount of popularity during this period, and at one point he was hospitalized due to flu and was eventually released from the hospital. Though the ANC made it crystal clear that the issue of nationalization of mines and expropriation of land without compensation was not an ANC policy, and the then minister of mineral and energy Susan Shabangu made it crystal clear further that there won't be nationalization of mines even in her lifetime.[5] That statement made the ANCYL very sick to the extreme. There were ministers in the South African government that the ANCYL were not taking seriously when they were speaking about nationalization of mines and expropriation of land without compensation. The Limpopo provincial departments became bankrupt and they made headlines. The national government had to put five departments under administration. The premier of the Limpopo Province Cassel Mathale was compelled to resign by the ANC NEC, and he gladly resigned. The ANCYL in the Limpopo Province was also disbanded.

THE ZIMBABWEAN WAR VETERANS AND THE ANCYL

The ANCYL was like the war veterans under Pres. Robert Mugabe; they will do what they want at any time without even taking time to think about the ramifications of their actions in the long term. On April 3, 2010, the ANCYL leadership visited Zimbabwe of Robert Mugabe and saw the very same farm invasion fiasco that I also saw and the very farms that now lie in waste. The Youth Brigade of ZANU-PF gave the expelled ANCYL president a herd of cattle as a gift. While the expelled ANCYL president was in Zimbabwe, he made calls that South Africans needed to seize land and mines just like the Zimbabweans did in 2000.[6] In 2010 the expelled ANCYL leadership members were very young politically to have understood the complexity and the long-term effects of farm invasion. In 2009 when Zimbabwe fell into a ditch, former president Thabo Mbeki was tasked by SADC to pull out Zimbabwe from the ditch that in had fallen into. The dollarization was introduced in 2009 after the signing of the global political agreement (GPA) in Harare. If you thoroughly comprehend economic sanctions and their ramifications, you could avoid them in any possible way. Most of the South Africans don't understand economic sanctions, and that does not mean that South Africa has never been under economic sanctions in the past. The Zimbabwean economic sanctions are totally different from the set of economic sanctions that was imposed on South Africa in the past. The world is the global village. In the past countries were not united as they are nowadays. Some have argued that if the ANC was to continue allowing the expelled ANCYL president Julius Malema with his nationalization of mines and expropriation of land without compensation, the foreign investors were going to exit the South African economy within a split of a second. It's imperative at this stage to understand that South African politics have been shaped and influenced by the arrival of the ANCYL president Julius Malema, and there is no way one can attempt to give fair blow-by-blow account of South African politics without including the expelled ANCYL president Julius Malema. At one point in the South African politics and even in the South Africa print media, the expelled ANCYL president Julius Malema was the most famous politician in South Africa. In fact the expelled ANCYL president Julius Malema was the most popular politician more than the state president of South Africa, Jacob Zuma. It's important to understand the African liberation struggle and its overall objective. It has been argued by many political analysts that the majority of African liberation movements who were in the forefront of African liberation struggle did not have a comprehensive and detailed economic plan as to how they will change and overhaul the economy in favor of the masses. It's partly true that African liberation movements did not have a detailed and thorough plan that was talking about the fundamental issues that are related to equal redistribution of wealth and land redistribution. Most of the African liberation movements, once they got hold of political power, became corrupted by the same political power that they fought hard for to attain. The main reason these African liberation movements became corrupt is simply the sudden money and wealth they had to handle after the attainment of the political liberation that they were not used to in the past. It's an open secret that the majority of the African liberation movements have been in the bush for quite a long period of time, and they have been denied access to clean water and basic things like decent meal and decent sleep. All what the former freedom fighters were accustomed to were harsh social conditions, which were very inhabitable and unsafe for a normal human being to live in. While an average human being was enjoying life and enjoying the luxury of decent meal and a decent shower, the guerillas were starving to death in the bush to the point of eating cockroaches and frogs. We are told by the former freedom fighters that they were suffering in the bush fighting for political emancipation of the masses. It's possible also that some of the political narratives that are given by the former freedom fighters about the tough and harsh social conditions that they have experienced in the bush are amplified and embellished in order to fit their political version of events. When these freedom fighters had to come out of the bush and now had to build their economies and lead their people and their governments, they took that opportunity to make up for the loss they have suffered while they were in exile and in the bush. The former freedom fighters, when they were supposed to provide a detailed and comprehensive plan as to how to overhaul the economic disparities that only benefited the few to now benefit the rest of the people, began to get married and were even stealing from the state coffers from the same people whom they were fighting for, for a very long time in the bush. There are many former freedom fighters even in South Africa who are now having criminal records not because of political crimes that have been committed during the apartheid era but because of stealing from the state coffers from the very same people that they claim to love and sacrifice their youth for. It's true that the majority of African liberation movements were caught flat-footed when they entered the political negotiations to end the Western power of colonization in Africa. Those African countries that attained their political liberation first were also struggling to maintain democracy and peace in their countries. The classic example is Zimbabwe. When the Lancaster House Agreement was signed, many Africans in the continent of Africa thought that finally the people of Zimbabwe were now going to live a better life compared to the life that they were living under Ian Douglas Smith's regime, but little did they know that things were going to turn for the worse. Let me exclude economic sanctions for a little bit. The Catholic Commission for Justice and Peace in Zimbabwe and Legal Resources Foundation published its report through a book called *Gukurahundi*. While I was in Bulawayo from Cecil John Rhodes's grave for the first time in Zimbabwe, I remember vividly when I was talking to Jacob, my driver, about this concept of Gukurahundi. I asked Jacob, "What is this Gukurahundi?" He said it was rain that was washing away the chaff of the previous harvest, though this concept does not literally mean that. It means more than just rain that washes away the chaff of the last harvest. It actually meant cleaning the dirt. Zimbabwe had just attained its political liberation, and the economic sanctions that were imposed by Great Britain to Prime Minister Ian Douglas Smith's government were lifted, and the people expected everything to be normal. The ZANU won national election in 1980, and Prime Minister Robert Mugabe was at the helm of government and he was still angry and traumatized by the political treatment he received at the hands of Prime Minister Ian Douglas Smith's forces that were funded and supported by the apartheid South Africa. Ian Douglas Smith, through imprisoning Robert Mugabe and Joshua Nkomo for almost eleven years, still haunted the mind of Robert Mugabe even after he was released from prison and now at the helm of government. Most African former freedom fighters, after their release from prison, were suffering from posttraumatic stress disorder (PTSD), and they did not receive the necessary psychological assistance that should be given to political prisoners who were detained and incarcerated for political reasons. Due to the lack of the psychological assistance, the anger and bitterness that these political prisoners were exposed to while they were in the prison of Ian Douglas Smith, even after the signing of the Lancaster House Agreement, were still deep down in the center of their hearts. Their spirits were still in prison, though they were out of prison physically. This became very evident in Gukurahundi in Matabeleland. There are many books that have been written about Gukurahundi, and as a result, I will not give a blow-by-blow account of what happened in Bulawayo in 1980s. The point that I want to drive home is this: though there are genuine and reasonable reasons why Gukurahundi had to take place, above all the very same political leaders who were at the helm of government had not received necessary psychological treatment that they ought to have received, and had they received psychological treatment, the carnage that happened in Bulawayo could not have happened. The Catholic Commission for Justice and Peace in Zimbabwe and Legal Resources Foundation writes:

> *In 1981 there was an outbreak of violence at Entumbane that spilled over to Ntabazinduna and Connemara in the Midlands; more than three hundred died. The Zimbabwean government instituted a commission of inquiry, and the report findings of that commission were literally suppressed.*[7]

In 1982 there were weapons that were discovered in Matabeleland, and on that very same year there was an abortive attack on the Prime Minister Mugabe's residence. It became abundantly clear that the Bush War was not over and because the ex-combatants of ZIPRA still had arms at their disposal. The 5 Brigade was trained by the North Koreans. When the 5 Brigade completed their training, they were released to Matabeleland. The next thing you know, there was carnage in Matabeleland. It was black people killing other black people at the hands of the democratically elected government. And this has been the story of almost all African countries. After attaining political independence, the said country will inevitably degenerate to a war, either ethnical violence or secretarial violence, and that is what is happening even to this day in the Middle East. African leaders who were part of the African liberation struggle were not competent and equipped enough to run their countries and lift the multitudes of people out of poverty. But most African leaders have been busy killing the very same people whom they claim they love and have spent their youth in the bush just to ensure that the same people receive political freedom and economic freedom. The main problem with African leaders, once they taste the state power, is they want to hold on to the state power even if they have nothing to offer politically and otherwise, but they would rather stay in power with nothing new to offer rather than relinquish their political positions to the young ones. It's public knowledge that the majority of African leaders are corrupt and greedy to the extreme. The main reason the majority of African countries are retrogressing than progressing is the African leaders that are on the helm of African governments. Even if the IMF and the World Bank can release a considerable amount of funds that are meant to improve the lives of ordinary people on the ground, these funds don't trickle down to the ordinary people on the ground but they evaporate on the tables of African leaders. Malawi is the classic example of how money can evaporate in the hands of officials with no one to account for it. All over Africa there are voices that are crying day and night, crying about corruption and maladministration. In fact in South Africa most oppositional political parties have centered their political campaigns on corruption and maladministration. It's the consequence of poor planning and poor political strategy to center a political campaign on fighting corruption and maladministration only. While a political party should campaign and weaken its political opponents with political rhetoric of fighting corruption and maladministration at the same time, it should take an opportunity to give the electorate its detailed and comprehensive plan as to how it will change and overhaul the lives of ordinary people on the ground should it happen that it wins the national elections. But most of the political parties, specifically those that are in oppositions to the ANC, are vomiting the same old political rhetoric of fighting corruption and maladministration even if some of the leaders of these political parties are already having corruption charges hanging over their heads. They still continue on the same path of trying to convince the electorate that should they be in government, they will fight against corruption and maladministration. Political parties that don't have a clear, detailed and comprehensive political plan as to how to overhaul the economy will now and then reiterate the old cliché of fighting against corruption and maladministration, though this strategy does not yield effective results on the polls. Quite frankly some of the political parties that were on their political campaign using the political strategy of fighting corruption and maladministration never make it to parliament, and in fact some of these political parties died their political death after the national elections. I often see something strange in the South African politics. There will be many political parties prior to the national elections, and after the national elections, all these small political parties disappear on the surface, to emerge again on the next national elections. Why fight if you know you will not win, and why campaign if you don't have a political message to convey to the electorate? It's possible that the masses, in the case of South Africa, might not be happy with the current status quo, and that is possibly the case, but there is no political party at the moment in South Africa that is ready and prepared to take over the political power from the ANC and move the country forward simply because most of these political parties can't even craft their own unique political message to lure and entice the electorate, and what they did was leave everything in the hands of the ANC to have another feast on May 7, 2014. The ANCYL had a valid point about the nationalization of mines and expropriation of land without compensation. The question that perhaps one could ask is this: Were South Africans ready at that time to hear the concept of nationalization of mines and expropriation of land without compensation? What was abundantly clear before the ANCYL raised the issue of nationalization of mines and expropriation of land without compensation was that the multitudes of people, specifically those who are politically connected, had their tables full with the BEE pie, and as a result, it would have been very difficult for them to leave behind their tables full of the BEE pie and pursue a just course that sought to benefit the majority of people who are not even politically connected. It's public knowledge in all African countries that people who were not in exile during the African liberation struggle deserve the social grants and the disability grants and all sorts of social grants and the free food parcels. The former freedom fighters deserve the BEE pie only, and that has been the case in South Africa and even in Zimbabwe, Angola, and DRC. The trickle-down effect is nonexistent in Africa. The rich becomes richer, and the poor becomes poorer, and that is the order of the day. Unless one has very serious political connection and political network, one can't advance financially in this life. Politics is everything now in Africa, and it is the only place where everything is happening. The total difference between the ANCYL of Julius Malema with the ANCYL of Malusi Gigaba and the ANCYL of Fikile Mbalula was the quick economic transformation that it sought. The ANCYL of Julius Malema was radical and hasty and it wanted things to done within a split of a second, and in the process it lost patience and political respect. It's possible to raise a valid point, but how you raise your point is another issue altogether. The ANCYL of Julius Malema lost the most precious moment in the South African history, and that moment was to alter the lives of the multitudes of the youth who are unemployed and uneducated. Its common knowledge now in South Africa that there are three million young people who are unemployed and uneducated and the ANCYL was representing these voiceless voices. There are certain precious moments that life will give to you as an individual, and when you miss these precious moments, you will never get them anymore until you go six feet down. The ANCYL will never get those precious moments that were given to them by the ANC and the multitudes of the youth of South Africa that they were representing. Maybe the ANCYL was trying to pull some publicity stunt by suggesting that there should be nationalization of mines and expropriation of land without compensations. At one point the ANCYL led the "the economic freedom in our lifetime" protest to the Union building to submit the memorandum to the South African government, which was largely dominated by members of the ANC. It's like suing your biological father for not buying you Christmas presents, while you are staying in his house and eating his food each and every day. The ANCYL was submitting the memorandum to the very same government ministers whom they were sharing meeting with in Luthuli House now and then. Why would you embarrass your father in public if you have an opportunity to voice out your concerns inside the house at home one-on-one, in private? The ANCYL was embarrassing the ANC, and indeed the ANC was not happy about it. Since that time henceforth, the leaders of the ANCYL and the ANC NEC could not sing from the same hymn book. The leaders of that "economic freedom in our lifetime" march were none other the expelled ANCYL leadership. The economic freedom in our lifetime march was successful except for the fact that the ANCYL leadership was expelled from the ANCYL and even from the ANC itself. Those who had qualifications moved back to the line to look for employment, and those who did not have qualifications had to find means to survive in the economic jungle. The South African Land Redistribution Program has been in motion for quite a long period of time. Since the government of the ANC in 1994 until this day and age, there are still land claims that have not been processed yet, and those that have been processed, the majority of these claimants never opted to be resettle in the land of their forefathers, but they opted for money. Selling your land for money is a bad investment decision in the long run. Some black communities have entered into some worrisome deals with the same white commercial farmers who once owned the land single-handedly for quite a long period of time, profited from it, and made a considerable amount of money, to now share the land with the white commercial farmers in exchange of money that is only received once a year. I am not going to expand too much on this issue because it's very sensitive and it involves community leaders who are now rich in the twinkling of an eye by influencing their communities to accept money at the exchange of their fertile land. It's understandable that some people would not want to opt for the expropriation of land without compensation simply because they think that opting for the expropriation of land without compensation policy will bring the whole economy of South Africa to its knees. The fact of the matter is this: multitudes of people in South Africa do not own the land that they reside in, but they are renting apartments and houses on the land that they don't own. The municipalities are selling the land under the pretext of property development. In fact once the land has been sold to the property developer, that very land does not belong to the community that once settled there at all, but it belongs to the Anglo-Saxons. I should state it clearly even here that I don't have a personal problem with the Europeans. But why would you sell the land of the black community to the Europeans under the pretext of development? Black people in South Africa need to be given land next to the cities and be given title deeds in order for them to be able to build houses for themselves instead of giving black people RDP houses that make people even poorer. There are more black people today who are living on real estate that they don't own than at any time in the South African history. If you are living in a real estate today, that very land that your house was built on is not yours but for the property developer. Then you have the stratum of young people who can afford to build houses for themselves, but because of the dearth of land, they are just renting apartments that are owned by the Europeans and further enriching the very same people who have been enriched by the colonial system. As long as the land issue is not properly addressed and the multitudes of the young South Africans who have just completed their university degrees are entering the employment stratum, they will soon realize that the political freedom that they think they have in essence is like the old Zimbabwean dollar that was withdrawn from circulation in 2009. What is the use of political freedom without economic freedom, and what is the use of political freedom without financial freedom? As long as the majority of the youths in South Africa are renting houses in the real estate which is owned by western settlers, then our political freedom is like faith without works, which is dead faith. Our political freedom is a Pyrrhic victory. Most African countries are free politically, but even to this day they are relying on the foreign aid because of their political stupidity. I have yet to see an African country that will send its young scientists and astronauts into space, and I have yet see an Africa country that does not rely on foreign aid, and I have yet to see an African country that will not prostitute its mineral resources to the West because of lack of refineries in Africa. It's possible that the multitudes of African people have also accepted and embraced the status quo that perhaps we Africans are better off with our mineral resources in the hands of the West simply because we don't have refineries and are not even ready yet to run our economies. The main problem with such a school of thought is this: we African people have become reluctant and aloof to what is happening in our economies and not even interested in further understanding the very same mineral resources that are in our own backyard. It's true that even in South Africa there are mines that are owned wholly by black South Africans, and they are thriving those mines under the leadership of black management, but that is not enough. The majority of the mines in South Africa are not owned by black South Africans, but they are owned by the Western companies. The same is true with property in all the big cities, Cape Town, Durban, Johannesburg, and Pretoria. In fact the government of South African is renting some of its offices from the Western-owned property companies. I know a lot of buildings that are used by the South African government that are not even owned by the South African government but are owned by the Western settlers. The one-million-dollar question is this: When will Africa be financially free from the shackles of the West? Financial freedom is not the same thing as political freedom. The West cheated Africa by giving African leaders political power without economic power. Political power and political freedom give you enough time and space to make a lot of noise, but the very same political power does not put food on the table and does not pay the bills either. From the vantage point, the issue of cxpropriation of land without compensation and nationalization of mines in South Africa has died its political death. The failure of Pres. Robert Mugabe's government to handle the Land Redistribution Program with success had economic sanctions imposed on the Zimbabwean economy, which terrified countries like South Africa to further embark on its Fast-Track Land Redistribution Program as it ought to do. Everything now is just moving at a snail's pace because of what happened in Zimbabwe 2000. South Africa attained its political freedom in 1994, while Zimbabwe attained its political freedom in 1980. If South Africa was supposed to learn about Land Redistribution Program and nationalization of mines, it should have learned from the government of Pres. Robert Mugabe. Pres. Robert Mugabe of Zimbabwe was even blamed by South Africans for the political mess that happened in 2000 and the current economic sanctions that are in place and biting like never before. It seems as if the economy of Zimbabwe is yet to hit rock bottom, while the majority of people were saying, "It can't get worse than this." They were actually wrong because the worst is yet to come with calls of bringing back the Zimbabwean dollar that saw the economy of Zimbabwe failing to pay salaries of its civil servants in time. Africa is in the vicious cycle, and some of the African people do apportion the whole blame to their African leaders. Some Africans even blame the very idea of political independence, arguing the fact that it was better than under colonial powers because they had jobs and they could manage to feed their families, unlike now under this democratic political dispensation where they can't even find jobs and feed their families. African leaders have been very quiet for a very long time about the Western foreign policy simply because they know very well that should they develop an opposite stance against the Western foreign policy, they will lose a considerable amount in foreign aid. There are very few African leaders who have condemned the West about intervening in Uganda's domestic affairs. Whatever the Ugandan president Yoweri Museveni is doing, he is doing it in his own country to his own people. It does not mean that if the West condones same-sex marriages, then everybody in the world must now dance to the Western music. Africans are people of culture and rhythm. Africans are people of respect and God-fearing people. What is considered as an abomination in the Holy Bible is what Africans considered as abomination also. Africans even to this day and age find themselves in a political vicious cycle. We Africans who are living in the continent of Africa asked ourselves many questions without clear and straightforward answers. We are told even to this day that HIV/AIDS rate infection is high in Africa than anywhere in the world. We are told that Africa is the poorest continent in the world, yet we know very well that most of Western companies are based in Africa. There has never been a point in history where there was perennial peace and tranquility except during the colonial era in Africa. Ever since Africa has attained its political independence, Africans are living in the constant fear of death either by military weapons or by starvation. I have yet to see an African country that is financially liberated to the point that it will not require foreign aid and borrow funds from the World Bank and IMF. The ANCYL raised valid issues that were pertaining the economy, but the way the ANCYL raised those issues was problematic, just like the way the war veterans had raised the same issues in Zimbabwe that were pertaining the economy. The main problem with the ANCYL was hooliganism and radicalism. There is a great difference between being radical with respect to the elders and being radical without respect to the elders. The ANCYL lacked political respect of the ANC structures and constitution. The ANCYL had fashioned their way of life and their philosophy of life after the war veterans of Zimbabwe. The fact that the ANCYL was fashioning and patterning its modus operandi after the Zimbabwean war veterans was a very serious problem. There were calls even in the media that the ANC NEC was afraid of the ANCYL, and the foreign investors were terrified to the extreme. Let me put it differently: the expelled ANCYL president

Julius Malema had the potential to be the future president of South Africa, and even pensioners knew that. Since the ANCYL of Julius Malema has been visiting Zimbabwe constantly, it began to worry the ANC, though that could not be expressed publicly. The fact of the matter is, had the ANC failed to deal with the ANCYL properly like many people, I hold the very same view that perhaps South Africa would have been in economic shambles today. It's imperative to thoroughly comprehend political transformation and economic transformation. While political transformation is the only legal vehicle to effect economic transformation, ordinary people on the ground should not be allowed to suffer unnecessary. There are many ways to kill the cat, and if there are many ways to kill the cat, the choice lies with the killer. There are many ways that could have been used by the ANCYL that could not have gotten it in a very serious trouble with the ANC and finally lead their leadership to be expelled from the ANC. The ANCYL had an ample amount of opportunities at their disposal to raise those relevant and pertinent issues either in the policy conference of the ANC, unlike going to the media and trying to pull some political publicity stunt. The fact remains: most of the African leaders even to this day are still holding the begging bowl and facing it straight to the face of the West. The West somehow has accepted and assimilated the idea that Africa is a continent of orphans living in an orphanage home, and the only person who should look after these African orphans who are living in an orphanage home is the West. I have seen the same thing even in the CAR war. France took it upon itself to intervene in the CAR war before the African Union can intervene. The West, when it comes to African domestic affairs, does not need even United Nations Security Council resolution to act in African domestic affairs simply because the West owns and controls Africa. At one point the former France president Nicolas Sarkozy argued that the former president of South Africa Thabo Mbeki did not understand Africa. This view that Africans do not understand Africa is widely held in the West. The West attributes this view to the way African leaders behave toward the Western countries. Most of the African leaders have nothing strategic to offer except carrying the begging bowl as the symbol of poverty and backwardness all the way to the West. The poverty mentality is also prevalent in many African leaders even if their countries are rich in terms of mineral resources, but they will still carry the begging bowl wherever they go as a result of living in abject poverty. The West now and then takes economic advantage of Africa due to this attitude and behavior that is constantly displayed by African leaders. The one-million-dollar question is, where to from here? Are we ever going to have the ANCYL that will shake the political foundation that the very ruling party of South Africa stood on? The answer to that question is this: there will never ever be any other ANCYL that will surpass or match the ANCYL of Julius Malema in terms of radicalism and militancy. The ANCYL of Julius Malema was in a political class of its own. The ANCYL of Julius Malema had a considerable amount of potential to be either a strong force of change or a destructive force within the ANC. Had the potential of the ANCYL of Julius Malema been managed, harnessed, and controlled properly, there is no doubt that the ANCYL of Julius Malema was going to be a strong force of change. It's important to give a child leeway and freedom to grow and experience life on his own. The main reason you need to give a child freedom and latitude to experience life on his own without exerting too much pressure on the child is that simply you want the child to be responsible and account for his own actions. The greatest mistake that the majority of parents are doing is leaving the child to grow very fast without applying parental control to the child. The ANCYL was a child of the ANC, and this child was showing signs of growing very fast. There is no doubt that the ANC was very happy to hear the ANCYL of Julius Malema voicing the concerns of the South African youth. Though I will not say whether or not the ANC was happy with the ANCYL in conjunction with the National Youth Development Agency (NYDA) by organizing the so-called kissing party, where all the young people of different countries had to converge in South Africa to discuss political issues that are pertaining the youth. The organizers of the conference had good intentions in mind, but the outcome of the conference was "a kiss." Instead of the African youth deliberating on issues that are pertaining the African youth, all what happened was a kiss after a kiss. It's astounding that there are still young people in this day and age that are very promiscuous while knowing very well that the HIV/AIDS rate infection is very high specifically in Africa. In essence the ANCYL was given too much time and space to breathe by the ANC and in the process it began to take advantage of the ANC itself. It's common knowledge that the ANCYL knew the skeletons that the very ANC NEC members had in their closets. Whether its ANC NEC members had children out of wedlock or were arrested for drinking and driving, the ANCYL knew all of that very well. The ANCYL became disobedient and unruly toward the ANC even to the ministers that were deployed by the ANC to the government. At one point the ANCYL accused a government minister who has been deployed by the ANC to the national government of using "fake accent." Some of the government ministers were accused of drinking "too much red wine." The misdemeanors of the ANCYL were endless. The day the ANCYL misdemeanors came to an end is the day the ANC National Disciplinary Committee of Appeal (NDCA) dismissed the ANCYL leadership; some were given lighter sentences, and some were fired right then and there. It's imperative, though, to record in the South African history books the rationale that the ANCYL had and the objectives that it sought to achieve. Though it could not achieve its objectives that it planned, which was to redress the imbalances of the past using the political force and militancy, there still remains an opportunity not only in South Africa but also in the whole of Africa to redress the imbalances of the past without plunging the multitudes of people into the abyss of abject poverty and to ensure that there are no economic sanctions that are incurred in the process. It seems as if the West even to this day is keeping the economic sanctions intact in the economy of Zimbabwe to frighten African countries—that should African leaders misbehave and begin to question the foreign policies of the West in Africa, the same fate that Pres. Robert Mugabe had faced is the same fate that African leaders will face, specifically those that stand on the way of the foreign policy of the West. As long as the West is given enough space and time to continue to milk the African sheep until blood comes out, there is no problem. The main problem will be when African leaders begin to question the Western foreign policy concerning the African mineral resources that are used by the West to enrich the Europeans and Americans, impoverishing the African people. It's common knowledge that most of the African youth can't afford a white wedding simply because of the astronomical cost of a white wedding. Most of the diamond rings that are exchanged in these white wedding come from Africa but cut and polished in the West and they are sold back to the African continent at a very high price. No wonder the majority of African children are born out of wedlock because of the astronomical cost of carrying a white wedding. The West stole Africa's wealth, and that is why most Africans are living in abject poverty because of the Western imperialism in Africa. The China-Africa trade relations will not benefit Africa diametrically, but it will benefit China in the end. It's common knowledge that China seeks to increase its dominance and its influence in Africa by ensuring that it finds a market for all its products that are manufactured in China. Unlike many people who see China as the bosom friend of Africa and good trading partner, I see China's presence in Africa as another economic imperialist in the making. Africa is the playing ground of Asia now, and it has been a playing ground of the West in the past. I have already said that the very computer that I am using right now has been manufactured in China. I wonder how many African products that are used in Africa today were manufactured in Africa, including the Marange diamonds that now and then are ferried to China to be polished and then sold in the Dubai market. The fact of the matter is this: China does not have good intentions about Africa, and the next thing you know; African children will be forced to study Mandarin as the second language in schools in order to streamline the trade relations with China. I wonder whether or not Chinese children will be studying IsiZulu and Swahili to streamline the trade relations with Africa.

THE MINERAL-RICH CONTINENT

It's common knowledge that Africa is the poorest continent on the face of the earth, and if the African continent would not have been colonized, there was nothing precious to take home at the end of the day by the colonizers. Colonization of Africa came about simply because of the mineral wealth and mineral resources that the African continent possesses. Africa is the richest continent on the face of the earth in terms of mineral resources and mineral deposits but is the poorest continent in the world in terms of per capita income and wealth. The richest men on the face of the earth are all from the West except the few who are politically connected, who are in Africa, and who are not even in the top ten on the list if the richest people. It's common knowledge now that DRC is very rich in mineral deposits, but the same rich DRC is forever in an endless civil war that is ripping the country apart. Africa is also known as the Persian Gulf of mineral resources. This begs the following question: If Africa is so rich in mineral resources, why is it that the African people are in abject poverty? Is it sufficient enough to just merely conclude that the main reason the majority of African countries are rich in mineral resources but still remain in poverty is purely the corruption that is ripping the African continent apart? Though one should accept that there are multiple solutions to this problem, it will be unfair and unjust to carelessly conclude that the main reason the majority of African countries are still in the state of humiliating abject poverty is corruption. There is corruption even in the West, but corruption itself does not deter and derail foreign investments. There is a political puzzle and there is an economic puzzle. When Africa attained its political independence, the political puzzle was solved then and there; but the economic puzzle was not solved, and that is why the majority of African countries are still poor though politically liberated. In effect most of the African countries degenerated to the civil wars after attaining their political independence and the further lack of understanding that political freedom alone can't engender economic freedom. Ordinary people will still have to eat, and children will need to go to school without a robust economic strategy that can generate perennial employment opportunities. Ordinary people who were happy for the attainment of political freedom are likely to turn their backs on their own political leaders. There comes a point in time where ordinary people run of patience and respect, where they are no longer interested in listening to the lofty long political speeches that are meant to appease the heart. The question is this: What will the African leaders do when the African people who voted for these African leaders turn their backs on them because of poverty and starvation? The Arab Spring is the classic example of what ordinary people are capable of doing once they reach the breaking point. Whenever there is a conflict whether in the African continent or even in the Middle East, uninvited so, the West jumps inside the ongoing conflict without even understanding the political dynamics and geopolitics of the problem. Political conflicts don't just emerge out of nowhere; they have an origin and a base where they start. The Rwandan Genocide of 1994 was caused by the Belgians by dividing the Rwandese in between through height, size, and ethnicity. The West watched at a distance as Rwandese were killing each other through what was called ethnical cleansing. The same is true with CAR even to this day. There is no way there could be peace and tranquility in Africa if there is a considerable amount of guns floating around carelessly in the hands of militia groups. The best way to put civil war to an end, even sectarian violence, is to cease the supply of military weapons to the militia groups. I don't care whether these militia groups call themselves Christians or Muslims, but the UN troops that were in CAR were just failing to cease the supply of military weapons between the two warring functions. The Republic of Zimbabwe was celebrating its thirty-four years of political independence in April 2014.[8] While in the celebration mood, the Zimbabweans also need to think about the bleak future that still lies ahead. It's public knowledge now that the government of ZANU-PF was struggling to elicit financial resources to pay the civil servants' salaries in time. There were even calls to downsize the civil servants in order to keep the wage bill of the civil servants low. One would not expect the people of

Zimbabwe to celebrate and forget about the national problems that lie ahead, though it's important to celebrate minor achievements in life, but celebrating far too long can also be detrimental to your objective view about the future. Part of the African problems was celebrating far too long after attaining political independence. It began to dawn late on most African leaders that Africa was not actually politically liberated because it was not economically liberated. The political deals were already signed, and the marriage was already sealed by the black pen. South Africa went through the same process through the CODESA talks, and Zimbabwe went through the same process through the Lancaster talks. Political deals were reached just to avoid a civil war but plunging a considerable amount of people in perennial poverty. To this day and age we Africans are still belligerent about the colonial problems that should have been solved in the past. The West is eventful in conducting researches in its laboratories with financial resources that have been stolen from Africa, while here in Africa we are busy fighting one another and killing one another. Let me pause and ponder for a minute. My overall objective of writing this book is to find out the exact amount of wealth that the West has stolen from Africa. It's a baseless and useless accusation to suggest that the West has stolen Africa's wealth without having empirical evidence to substantiate my assertion. It's one thing to come up with a hypothesis, but proving it is another story altogether. It's also very difficult to draw a plausible inference whether or not one has indeed provided sufficient plausible information to substantiate his hypothesis. My overall objective now is not to introduce any new information but to reiterate everything that I have said before but providing you with a better and clearer picture of what I am talking about. I will not go back to the beginning to talk about the first trip to Zimbabwe and the places that I have visited. What I want to focus on for a minute is the sequence of events that led to the farm invasion of 2000 and the economic sanctions of February 18, 2002. While Zimbabwe was celebrating its thirty-four years of political independence in April 2014, it was also celebrating thirteen years of illegal economic sanctions that are still in place, and they are biting like never before, and they have been imposed by the West, culminating from the farm invasion of 2000. What made the war veterans of Zimbabwe take the farms without following the legal process of government and the legislation process? There are multiple political narratives to this question to the point that finding a definitive solution means opening a very long, winding discussion, which is dominated by contradictions and conflicting political views. I have interviewed

Zimbabweans who told me straight to my face that the reason why the multitudes of Zimbabweans are suffering is because of the government. It is very unfortunate and unfair that you can blame an old man and his government for almost all the economic problems that the Zimbabwean economy is currently facing. There is one thing that Terry said while I was in Zimbabwe; I remember it vividly. He said, “Robert Mugabe is old, and his ministers are taking advantage of his age. That is why they are stealing before his very eyes because of his poor eyesight.” The health of Pres. Robert Mugabe has sharply deteriorated, and it’s highly probable that he will not complete his political tenure in government if the same medical condition prevails as things stand right now. The point that Terry was making is this: due to the deteriorating medical condition of Pres. Robert Mugabe, he is no longer vigilant and alert as he used to be in the past. His ministers in government also know that his eyesight is very poor, and they can even conclude unscrupulous deals before his very eyes and he won’t see a thing. That is why Pres. Robert Mugabe reads about corrupt activities that his ministers are embroiled in on the print media just like everybody. There are countless books written about Zimbabwe and the sequence of political events that led to the farm invasion of 2000 and the economic sanctions that were imposed on February 18, 2002. I am not going even to bother myself to lambast the works that have been published by other authors. Frankly speaking, it bothers me now and then to read that the Land Redistribution Program was a success and Zimbabwe managed to resettle three hundred thousand families that were landless. If Zimbabwean Land Redistribution Program was a success, why is it that Zimbabwe right now is importing everything including toothpaste? There is a great difference between fantasy and reality. The majority of Africans are living in the world of fantasy, where reality is nonexistent. I wish to share the same view with many experts, specifically those that are very sympathetic to the people of Zimbabwe, even those who claim to be products of the Pan-Africanism school of thought. The truth of the matter is this: the Zimbabwean Land Redistribution Program became the land redistribution problem and plunged a considerable amount of people into the bottomless pit of poverty. That is why in South Africa today the issue of nationalization of mines and expropriation land without compensation has been given a decent political burial, never ever to be resurrected due to what was witnessed in Zimbabwe in 2000. When the ANCYL attempted to bring the issue of nationalization of mines and expropriation of land without compensation to the political table, it was decimated and dismantled. Pres.

Robert Mugabe and his Zimbabwe have placed Africa in a very bad light on the face of the earth. The fact that Zimbabwe failed decimally to handle the Land Redistribution Program is the main reason the majority of South Africans are still residing in squatter camps of Alexandra Township and Diepsloot. People are living like pigs in some parts of Africa using what is so-called the bucket system. That is why when the shack dwellers of Cape Town were sick and tired of the bucket system, they launched a "poo campaign," where they barricaded the roads with human waste. The so-called poo campaign stretched further even to the Cape Town International Airport. One can make a simple deduction from the poo campaign—that it was about service delivery. There is no government in the world that can attempt to address the issue of delivering basic services to its people without addressing the fundamental issue of Land Redistribution Program, and that is where Zimbabwe should have set a good example for South Africa. When Dali Tambo, the son of the late president of the ANC Oliver Tambo, asked Pres. Robert Mugabe of Zimbabwe on the TV program called *The People of the South* how South Africa should deal with its Land Redistribution Program, Pres. Robert Mugabe responded by saying South Africa should do it in their own way. He jokingly said, "I can't see people of Soweto going back to the farms to play in the mud." The truth of the matter is this: there is no way in hell can you attempt to solve the problems of inequality, poverty, and unemployment without solving the problem of land. Majority of South Africans, even those that are living in posh suburbs like Morningside in Sandton, do not have title deeds for the very land that they are living on. There is no way you can lift the majority of people out of poverty by building for them RDP houses far away from the city where everything is happening. The fact of the matter is this: we Africans were not supposed to vote for a particular political party in order for us to get clean water and decent roads. One of my friends from Tanzania said to me, "South African roads are nice," unlike the Tanzania roads. We were not supposed to vote for a political party to construct "nice roads," if I may put it like that. Water is life, and it is a fundamental human right for all people to have access to clean water. We all know that there are many people in Africa even to this day and age who do not have access to water and electricity just because of the cancer of corruption that is crippling most African governments, whether it's Malawi, Angola, or DRC—the list is endless and not excluding South Africa. Corruption is everywhere; even in the West there is corruption.

In *Old Rhodesian Days*, Hugh Marshall Hole writes,

> *So when Rhodes began coolly to talk about sending up an expedition to occupy this region of thrilling possibilities, and when, simultaneously, Boers, Belgians, Portuguese, and Germans were seen to be casting avaricious glances in the same direction, a wave of enthusiasm seized upon young Englishmen at home and in the South African colonies, and a keen competition to take part in the enterprise.*[9]

The place of thrilling possibilities that Hole talked about is none other than Zimbabwe, and there was a belief that in Zimbabwe there were too much gold and diamonds to the point that even King Solomon of Israel had a mine in Zimbabwe. That is why when Zimbabwe was under King Lobengula, the son of Mzilikazi, there was a belief that King Lobengula was filthy rich with diamonds and gold, and that turned out to be false later. There is part of African history that when you read it you just become sick in the stomach. The Western scholars in all their writings have projected a black person as a person who does not value things like land and mineral resources. That is why there is an assertion that says, even if the West did not colonize Africa, what is it that Africans could have done with the gold and diamonds that were in the belly of the African soil because Africans are backward in their nature and Africans don't value land and mineral deposits? When Cecil John Rhodes arrived in Zimbabwe with his Pioneer Column after he cheated the Matabele King Lobengula, he went further to search for King Solomon's mine, which was believed to be brimming with gold and diamonds. When the Afrikaners came to South Africa, they annexed the land and started farming on the very same land where the native South African people were residing and stole their herds of cattle, including the eggs that have been laid by their chickens. My maternal grandfather said to me, "When the apartheid government evicted us in our land, they shot our donkeys and stole our chickens and the eggs of our chickens." The same thing that the Afrikaners were doing in South Africa is the same thing that the British were doing to the native Zimbabweans: compelling native people to be crammed into an inhabitable residential area where there is no water and electricity and the soil is even infertile. All over Africa, black people having been living under appalling living conditions. In the case of Zimbabwe, the living conditions of ordinary people have now further degenerated into something dreadful.

King Solomon's gold mine, which Cecil John Rhodes was pursuing in Zimbabwe, was nowhere to be found, and he eventually settled for the vast amount of arable land. When I was in Zimbabwe for the second time, casting my eyes on the vast of amount of arable land that is underutilized, greed and lust took the better of me. I began to comprehend thoroughly the cliché that says, Zimbabwe was at one point the breadbasket of Southern Africa and exporting everything, unlike now when it is the basket case of Southern Africa importing even the powder soap. From the vantage point, the white commercial farmers can attest that they once lived in the land of milk and honey, referring to Zimbabwe and their commercial farms. It's possible that the war veterans also coveted the living conditions of the white commercial farmers, and the respect they commanded from their peasants. There is one big question that has been asked by many scholars about the farm invasion of 2000: If the Zimbabwe war veterans were former freedom fighters, which fought in the Second Chimurenga of 1966–1979? Why is it that during the farm invasion of 2000, some of the people who were involved in the farm invasion were in their youth? The logical explanation that one can give is this: it's possible that the war veterans could not manage to take the farms from the white commercial farmers alone owing to the fact that some of the war veterans were very old enough and could not run. Consequently the war veterans employed the service of their children, who were neither born during the 1966–1979 nor even involved in the Second Chimurenga because of their age. If we are to follow this logic, then the whole blame now shifts from the war veterans to the ZANU-PF Youth Brigade. It's possible that the majority of scholars missed the whole point. In effect the farm invasion of 2000 was prearranged by the war veterans, but the definite act of invading the farms was not carried by the war veterans alone; the war veterans employed the ZANU-PF Youth Brigade. It's public knowledge that the farm invasion of 2000 is a broad and diverse issue, and with the greatest respect of all, I have not in any way covered the farm invasion fiasco thoroughly and diametrically above all. This book is neither about the farm invasion of 2000 nor about the Lancaster House Agreement. Africa is the continent of coups and countercoups, and that is what I want to deal with right now. Before I deal with the African coups and countercoups, let me make this crucial point about Pres. Robert Mugabe.

Guy Arnold writes:

> *The conference came to the verge of collapse in October but continued on a knife-edge with Mugabe especially distrustful of the British proposals. On December 11, Lord Soames, who had been appointed as the governor of Rhodesia for the transition to independence, flew to Salisburg. On December 14, Edson Zvobgo, for ZANU-PF, had said no to Carrington, and Mugabe was on his way to catch a flight to New York to reject the cease-fire and drum up support to continue the war when he was recalled to take a phone call from Pres. Samora Machel of Mozambique. Machel told him bluntly to sign and indicated that if he didn't, all he could expect in Mozambique would be political asylum. By this time the country was suffering from the Rhodesia raids, damaged communications, and food shortages, and it needed the war to come to an end.*[10]

There is a statement that was made by Pres. Robert Mugabe of Zimbabwe in his interview with Dali Tambo, the son of the late president of the ANC Oliver Tambo, when he said that the Zimbabwean story has not been properly and accurately written. Though those are not his exact words, what he meant was that the African history has never until this point in time favored the African nationalists and has never been construed in a way that projects the African nationalists as true African heroes. If there is a person in the whole of African history whose name has been tarnished beyond repair and who lost the world's respect, he is Pres. Robert Mugabe of Zimbabwe. Most of the people who blame him lack the political understanding of the Zimbabwean political conundrum. There is a great difference between running a kiosk and running a country; the two are not the same. It takes brave men to put their lives on the line for the love of their people and for the love of their country. It's public knowledge now that Pres. Robert Mugabe and the Patriotic Front in Lancaster did not agree to the Lancaster House Agreement, but Pres. Robert Mugabe was coerced into signing the Lancaster House Agreement by Samora Machel because the war was no longer tenable. What got Samora Machel killed was the incessant political support that he was providing to the ANC of Nelson Mandela and the ZANU of Robert Mugabe, and Mozambique was the battleground of all battlegrounds. The ANC of South Africa and the ZANU-PF of Zimbabwe both owe their existence to the people of

Mozambique. Had it not been for Samora Machel, the political freedom of the people of South Africa and the people of Zimbabwe could not have been attained soon, though people like Samora Machel are not predominantly featured in many history books owing to the fact that the majority of Africans don't read and understand African history as they should. That is why many African scholars don't more often than not quote Samora Machel or Julius Nyerere when they speak because they find that demeaning and debasing. They would rather quote Pres. Ronald Reagan and Winston Churchill Sr., whom they never met. African scholars don't want to be associated with African leaders owing to the fact that most of the African leaders have been labeled as dictators by Western scholars. Any African who will gladly allow the West to embezzle African resources while true and native Africans are suffering will be the darling of the West and will now and then be invited by the Western leaders to its gallery dinners. African leaders who are critical of the West like Pres. Robert Mugabe of Zimbabwe, their names have been soiled and tarnished beyond repair. The fact of the matter is this: there is nothing that the West expects from Pres. Robert Mugabe except hearing news that he is gone. The West is watching Pres. Robert Mugabe's medical condition closely like a sick patient in the intensive care unit (ICU). One wonders what will happen to Zimbabwe when the health of Pres. Robert Mugabe fails him diametrically. What is abundantly clear at this stage is this: the Lancaster House Agreement was signed, though all parties that were involved in the negotiation process were not entirely satisfied with the proposals that were tabled by Great Britain, and in fact Pres. Robert Mugabe was purely coerced by Samora Machel of Mozambique into signing the Lancaster House Agreement. Samora Machel died in Mbuzini, South Africa, in 1986. Pres. Robert Mugabe is still alive and is taking all the blame for the farm invasion of 2000 and the illegal economic sanctions of February 18, 2002. It's imperative to understand why Pres. Robert Mugabe said the economic sanctions are illegal. They are illegal because Britain reneged to its original agreement that they will fund the Land Redistribution Program. When Britain reneged on continuing to fund the Land Redistribution Program, which they originally agreed upon in 1979, that was the last straw that broke the camel's back, and the political volcano erupted in Zimbabwe. The war veterans became like wild young lions, which were uncontrollable; neither the government nor the military could stop them from their dreadful act of invading the farms. It was a dreadful act because some of the white commercial farmers who were resisting the farm invasion were killed point-blank in broad daylight. South Africans and the South African government are bearing the brunt of the Zimbabwean political mess. We South African have been taught the spirit of *Ubuntu*; we have learned to treat the Zimbabweans as our fellow brothers and sisters from another mother. Some Zimbabweans have made South Africa their permanent home, and they are not even contemplating the thought of going back to Zimbabwe, where they belong. It will be unfair and unjust then to rely on the Western media and expect a fair and just reporting about African leaders like Pres. Robert Mugabe. All what the Western media does is to continue to disseminate the Western propaganda that Pres. Robert Mugabe of Zimbabwe has been at the helm of Zimbabwean government from 1980 until 2014. What is the problem if Pres. Robert Mugabe is still the president of Zimbabwe from 1980 until 2014? There is one assertion that was made by Pres. Robert Mugabe prior to the national elections of July 31, 2013—that if he loses elections, he will quit politics. That assertion was doing rounds all over Pretoria, and in fact there were placards carrying those words: "If I lose elections, I will quit politics." Those words were not even true to the core. There is no way Pres. Robert Mugabe was going to lose the national election. I personally think that, that statement was meant to project Pres. Robert Mugabe as somebody who is not power hungry and consumed by greed. The truth of the matter is this: if ZANU-PF lost the national elections of July 31, 2013, I don't think that certainly Pres. Robert Mugabe was going to quit politics and pack his bags and go to the retirement village forever. Whatever the intention of that statement was, indeed it managed to achieve its objective, which was to portray Pres. Robert Mugabe as a person who listens to the people and who subscribes to the principles and dogma of democracy and freedom. The cliché "the will of the people" sometimes is used incorrectly to justify and conceal the true feelings of the people from the ground. What is happening on the ground is not the will of the majority of the people, and they don't even share the same views with the very same people who normally say, "The people have spoken." The sole purpose of the West about Africa is wealth and nothing else. The West does not contemplate a war-free Africa. As long as Africa is endowed with mineral deposits, the West will do anything in its power to ensure that it destabilizes the continent of Africa now and then in order to continue the prowling of mineral resources in Africa. Africa is the river overflowing of human blood from the wars that do not seem to come to an end.

AFRICA, THE CONTINENT OF COUP D'ÉTAT

Some of the African leaders who are in power today were never voted for by their people, but instead they have employed coups to ascend to the echelons of political power. We Africans also know that some of the African leaders, once they ascend to political position, settle in political power for far too long. It's a common political tactic and political weapon in Africa to seize power from your political opponent through a coup. In fact there are many political leaders in Africa even to this day who are in power that were not voted for by the masses. Why does a coup work? Political coups normally employ the services of mercenaries. There are mercenaries all over the world. In fact the most dangerous mercenaries are in the West, since coups are the political weapons of the West. When François Bozizé, who was ousted by a coup, came to power in Central African Republic, he employed the service of the mercenaries. Though after he was ousted, he cried foul that the Seleka rebels are a group of mercenaries. When the Seleka rebels had managed to get rid of Pres. François Bozizé, Michel Djotodia became the interim president of CAR without being voted in by the masses. CAR erupted in flames, and until this point the UN forces, in conjunction with the African forces, are still trying to put out the flames of fire. Ferocious crimes have been committed against the people of CAR simply because of coups. It's astounding that some African leaders will fight tooth and nail just to hold on to political power and state resources.

> *On September 1, 1969, when King Idris was undergoing medical treatment in Turkey, the Free Officers Movement that had founded Gaddafi as a student at Benghazi military college mounted a bloodless coup to oust the old kingdom. In September Gaddafi became chairman of the Revolutionary Command Council to inaugurate a new era of Libya.*[11]

Muammar Gaddafi came to power through a coup, and he stayed in power as long as he wanted until NATO and the Western extremists and the Western fundamentalists ousted him in 2011 through a Western-orchestrated coup. Though the West denies this, it's a known fact that the people of Libya could not just start a revolution against their leader Muammar Gaddafi without the aid from the West. The bone of contention in Libya is vast amount of oil reserves that are buried in the Libyan soil, and the West can't stomach that. The ousting of Muammar Gaddafi had to be prearranged and projected to the world as if ordinary people of Libya were fed up with the Gaddafi regime that was oppressing its people and corrupt to the core. There are many theories about Muammar Gaddafi that are not even true. They originated and emanated from the West to underpin the ousting of Gaddafi by the coup. The coups are the order of the day in Africa. When the DRC War was under way, there were reports that the six thousand Zimbabwean troops that were dispatched to DRC in 1998 were planning to oust Pres. Robert Mugabe with a coup[12]—though some of the people whom I have interviewed declined that there was such a plan to oust Pres. Robert Mugabe in 1998 with a coup. When Patrice Lumumba died, Joseph Mobutu Sese Seko seized power with his own coup and ruled DRC by theft. Since the coup of Joseph Mobutu in DRC, Africa has been a fertile ground for coup d'état after coup d'état. In fact in DRC it's an acceptable norm to ascend to political power via a coup d'état just like in CAR. Laurent Kabila launched his own coup to oust Joseph Mobutu, and DRC erupted all sorts of mercenaries from all over the world to descend to the shores of DRC. It is estimated that at one point there were seven hundred mercenaries in DRC who were employed just to carry out the coups. Laurent Kabila, the father of Robert Kabila, who is the current president of DRC, felt that the military heat was mounting. He began to cry for help; the M23 was closing in on him. The composition of M23 itself was a multitude of different groups whose single objective is to control the mineral-rich province of Katanga, "the triangle of death" as they call it. The M23 is not only made up of former DRC soldiers who were mistreated. The M23 was made up of Rwandese who were promised mineral resources in case they succeeded in ousting Pres. Laurent Kabila. Eventually Laurent Kabila was shot in the ass by his bodyguard and died a peaceful death, and his son Joseph Kabila became the president of DRC. Coups are not an African phenomenon but a Western phenomenon. As long as Africa is endowed with mineral resources and the West can't get its dirty hands on them, the West will do anything possible to destabilize this beautiful African continent of our forefathers. The West will never classify mercenaries as terrorists, though they resemble terrorist groups in totality. The fact that mercenaries are employed for a specific assignment and they are there just to carry out their act of killing only, that renders mercenary groups user-friendly and useful in coups. The mercenary groups were supposed to be classified as terrorist groups, and all their assets were supposed to be frozen. The reason most of the mercenary groups are not classified as terrorists is that the majority of these mercenary groups are emanating from the West. The classic case is the example of mercenaries who were arrested in the Harare International Airport who were heading to Equatorial Guinea. Those mercenaries came from diverse nationalities; some of them were from Britain, and some of them were from Africa. After they have been arrested in Zimbabwe, they were transported to the Chikurubi Prison, and they were given brown khakis as the prisoners' uniform. Some of those mercenaries, because of the Chikurubi Prison's appalling living conditions, were eventually released sick and dying. Some of those mercenaries were given parole, and they went to the West to enjoy life as if nothing had happened. They were not even classified as terrorists. As much the West is very grim on terrorists and sex jihadists, the same attitude and treatment that the jihadists and terrorists are experiencing is the same unfriendly treatment that the mercenaries should be subjected to. The truth of the matter is this: the West can't take a grim stance toward mercenary groups simply because mercenaries are the Western political instrument. There is no way the West can manage to continue incessantly to destabilize the African continent without the use of the mercenary groups. The United Nations Security Council does not even bother itself about mercenary groups because they are the Western political instruments to destabilize the mineral-rich African continent. Since the ousting of Muammar Gaddafi of Libya until the end of the 2014, there was no political stability and social peace in Libya. The old cliché that Muammar Gaddafi was a dictator and ousting him will bring peace and prosperity to the lives of the ordinary people of Libya is a dream that has not yet materialized. The Western mercenaries who were employed by the West to oust Bashar al-Assad failed decimally to get the job done, and the West became very furious because the mercenaries could not stand the military heat of the Syrian forces, which had the blessing of the Russian president Vladimir Putin. After the West realized that it could not oust Bashar al-Assad through the usage of mercenary groups, it turned back its focus to the Russian president Vladimir Putin. The Geneva Convention 2 did not yield any practical tangible results. The Geneva Convention 2 was designed to invariably establish a transitional government, which was going to prepare the ground for the national elections to take place and then oust the Syrian president Bashar al-Assad. The Syrian project failed, and the Geneva Convention project 2 failed, and the West had reached a political cul-de-sac. When you fail to kick the ball, at least kick the nearest object, and the nearest object was Ukraine. The West has quickly came up with a financial rescue package via the IMF to ensure that the economy of Ukraine was resuscitated immediately while the West was making sure that the incoming leadership of Ukraine will invariably depend and look to the West in times of political troubles and possibly from potential military intimidation from Russia. The fact of the matter is this: at least the West lost on the Syrian project, but now it has the Ukraine project doing wonders for it. The Syrian project required a considerable amount of military power, but the Ukraine project required the utilization of IMF only. It's public knowledge now that Russia was supplying Ukraine with a considerable amount of fuel. If the umbilical cord that binds Ukraine and Russia together has been cut off, how will Ukraine survive without Russia? The only possible and logical way for Ukraine to survive will be to look up to the West for fuel and all the petroleum products. Not only is Africa the continent of coups and countercoups, but the mercenary groups are also used by the West even in the Middle East. Kwame Nkrumah of Ghana was also ousted through a coup. The ANC of South Africa has also survived many coups that were meant to kidnap its leaders and then seize political power, and this is public knowledge in South Africa. There are instances where the Luthuli House in Johannesburg, the headquarters of the ANC, fire just ignited out of nowhere and burned the couch from the reception area. It's logically sound and politically correct that most of the African leaders stay in power until they are on a wheelchair. Let's face it, at least there is political stability in African countries where the leaders of those African countries have been in power for quite a long period of time. The president of Zimbabwe Robert Mugabe did not ascend to political power through a coup, but he was voted for by his people. He is in political power until this day not because of the help of some mercenary groups but because of the will of the people. If you hate Pres. Robert Mugabe, unfortunately the people of Zimbabwe love him, and there is nothing that the West can do about it. There is nothing that we South Africans can do about. This reality confronted me when I was in Zimbabwe. Most hotels in Zimbabwe have the face of His Majesty, Robert Mugabe, in their reception, and that is a fact that can't be changed. What is real to you becomes your reality. Horizon is experience. The benefit that comes with traveling is that your old horizon becomes fused with the new horizon, and now you have the expanded horizon. When a con man is telling you lies, you can tell on the spot if your horizon has been expanded. The more you are restricted to one area with the same group of friends; you are likely to believe what they are telling you even if what they are saying is a lie. The same is true about politics. I know of many news networks that can never expose the vile and wicked scheme about the Western plan toward African mineral resources. Some of these news networks are funded by the West and are used to gather information that can be used by the West to further steal Africa's mineral resources. If something meager happens in Africa, the whole world will know about it. If a humongous financial scandal breaks out in the West, it will take time and days for the Western media to report about it. There are many African American prisoners who are doing time in the US prisons just because of the color of their skins not because they have committed crime, yet there are many white Americans who are walking free just because of the color of their skin. These are the facts of life and they are swept under the carpet, and life continues as normal as if nothing wrong is happening. It still astounds me even to this day why many black people are in detention centers all over the world even in the so-called developed countries. The majority of people doing time in prison are blacks even in South Africa to this day. It's possible that black people are prone to violent crimes comprehensibly because of their social background. It's highly impossible that a normal child who was raised in a warm and loving environment can just become violent out of nowhere. The more there is political violence in Africa because of coups and countercoups, it's more logically sound to draw an inference that the majority of children that are raised in hostile social environments become hostile and impatient when they grow up; just like sexual abused children, more frequent than not they become promiscuous when they are adults. That does not give you the license to have sex with anyone just because you were sexually abused. The point is, if a necessary psychological intervention is not given to such children; they replicate and perpetuate the same behavior that they have been victims off over and over again. Africans have been traumatized by colonization and slavery, and very few Africans have healed from the oppressions of the past. With all these coups and countercoups going on all over Africa, even those who were on the path of the healing process have relapsed to the same conditions they were in, in the past. Violence breeds violence. It's an inescapable reality that children who are born in politically violent countries can't grow up to be responsible and loving parents when they are adults. This is true even in the case of South Africa and any other African country. Charity begins at home, the old saying goes. It's important for young Africans to be taught about the African history at school. This will not only help the young African intellectuals to become better future African leaders tomorrow, but also help these young African intellectuals to understand why this beautiful African continent of our forefathers has been suffering for many years at the hands of the West. The sole purpose of the West about Africa is to keep the continent of Africa behind technologically and otherwise so that Africa and its people will continue to carry the begging bowl while the West is pouring foreign aid in the bowl. I have tossed and turned about the title of this book, but I have to come to this painful conclusion that indeed the West stole African's wealth. I can discuss land and mineral resource issue until the cows come home, and the fact is the West has cheated Africa and invested the proceeds of its crime in the IMF and World Bank. The very same foreign aid that is given to many African countries is the same money that has been stolen from the African continent during the years of colonization. The skyscrapers that are in the West have been built by the African slaves free of charge, and the West didn't pay a cent for it. The same goes for the farms and the land. The West during the slave trade made a killing. I have often observed even in South Africa whether it's a road construction or a construction of a skyscraper. The white folks will be standing doing absolutely nothing, while the black folks will have to contend with the scorching sun up there in the air, laying brick after another brick, and in the end, the white folks take credit for the job well done, and the black person's name it not even mentioned. I have watched big bridges been constructed; the black person will have to do the hard job and the dangerous job for that matter. At the end of the construction, he is dismissed as if he was not important in the first place. Most of the African Americans, when they were shipped to the United States from the Gorée Island in Senegal, will work in the farm of the slave master and watch the children be paid with food only. Sometimes the slave master will require sex from the slave if he is tired with his wife. When the slave master is angry, it was the responsibility of the slave to sing until the slave master becomes happy; that is why most African Americans are not scientists, but they are clowns, rappers. There are very few African Americans who are scientists just because they were not allowed to go to school and they were supposed to work in the farms for their slave masters. This painful picture about the African slaves cuts across the world. The same thing has been happening in South Africa. I have already said that my grandmother was working for a white family in a small town called Komatipoort. She was not paid enough because in those days maids were given leftovers. When that white family my grandmother was working for was through with their lunch, she will collect the remnants of their food and put it inside the plastics and come home with it. We knew that every day when my grandmother comes from work, she would not come empty-handed, but she will be coming with leftovers of rice. While I was young, I could not comprehend the impact of eating leftovers had on my psyche when I was growing up. I had mistaken the act of being given leftovers by your employer as a token of love. It's only now when I am old and matured that I begin to understand that the act of being given leftovers by your employer is a sign of disrespect and a sign of mockery, and its mental exploitation of an extreme proportion. This is what was happening to black maids who were working in the kitchen of Western settlers, but to the black people who were working in the farms, they were given a bag full of beans and five kilograms of maize mealie. If you are lucky or if your boss loves you, he might give you his old stinking clothes. Most of the peasants were very happy with these bags of beans and the five kilograms of maize meal. In fact most of the peasants will go all-out bragging, saying that "my boss loves me." The West has been stealing from Africa since the colonial era, and there are many Africans who died at the hands of the Western settlers who can't be accounted for even to this day. The livestock and land of Africans were taken by the barrel of the gun, and when these issues are raised, the West threatens African leaders with economic sanctions that will kill a considerable amount of people. The West has no business in imposing economic sanctions to Pres. Robert Mugabe just because he took the land from the white commercial farmers. It's true that during the farm invasion, there were horrible mistakes that were also committed by the regime of Pres. Robert Mugabe; but above all, the crux of the matter is this: the West reneged from its initial agreements of providing the funds to purchase the land from the white commercial farmers, which were agreed upon in Lancaster in 1979. Africa will never be on an equal footing with the West economically and otherwise, unless otherwise the West can cancel all the debts of all African countries that are owed by the African countries to the IMF and World Bank and admit that the wealth that was stolen from the African continent during colonization was indeed invested in the IMF, World Bank, and European Central Bank. It should not be just admitting that the wealth that had been invested in the World Bank, IMF, and European Central Bank had been stolen from the African continent only, but half of that wealth should be given to African people to share it among themselves in order to be on an equal footing with the Western countries and the Western people. Until and unless what I have suggested above happened, African people must still expect to live life as second-class citizens, while the African wealth and mineral resources continue to enrich the West and its people at the expense of the poor African people. The Western infrastructure, roads, and universities are of high quality compared to the same infrastructure, roads, and universities in the African continent. We know very well that Africa is the continent of corruption and fraud, but sometimes these concepts are often used to conceal the real issues. It's also true that African leaders are corrupt, but there are African leaders who are not corrupt to the core. It's unfortunate that we use the blanket approach when we are talking about African leaders as if the Western leaders are not corrupt. In fact the Western leaders are more corrupt than the African leaders. The Western leaders taught the African leaders corruption and how to use the military power in order to stay in power by force even if the ordinary people on the ground don't want you anymore. It's the Western leaders who taught African leaders how to rig the election results; in effect the West is an expert when it comes to election results rigging. Unfortunately we only hear one side of the story; we don't get to hear both sides of the story. Morgan Tsvangirai of MDC-M cried foul when he lost the national elections of July 31, 2013, to Pres. Robert Mugabe of ZANU-PF. Morgan Tsvangirai complained about what he called "monumental rigging." Pres. Robert Mugabe said the following: people who can't accept the outcome of the national elections must go and hang themselves. Africa is the continent of coups and countercoups. Political violence makes it easier for the Western agents to loot the mineral resources in Africa. The more there is political violence, the more looting takes place. A house that is divided will not stand, Jesus said, but a house that is united can stand against the strong winds and floods. The West has studied Africa for many years as to how to destabilize the African continent and then loot its mineral resources while the African people are busy killing each other without any reasonable reason. If you were to ask why the majority of African countries are embroiled in civil wars, the response that you will get will be hilarious to the extreme. If you were to ask the Rwandese why they were killing each other in 1994, you will probably realize that they were hypnotized by the West. The same thing happened in South Africa in Kwazulu Natal, and in this case it was the Zulus killing other Zulus just because of political affiliation, which was even hilarious to the extreme.

CHAPTER 13

THE FUTURE

Doing the same thing over again and again and expecting different results is sheer madness. It's abundantly clear that there is nothing that will change in the future if there is no change in present. The future is as a result of the present. It's public knowledge now that Africa's past was littered with pain and agony, and there are few things that we Africans can boast about concerning the past. However, we have to learn and understand the mistakes of the past in order to understand the present and the very future that we have already in mind. Africa can no longer expect different results economically and politically if it is going to use the same economic model over and over again. Africa has been robbed by the West, and we all know that. What is it that the future holds for Africa, and are things going to change for the better compared to what they are already right in now in Africa? I don't have the crystal ball, but when one analyzes the political predicament that the majority of African countries find themselves in, it's possible to predict the unpredictable. When I ask my colleagues and my friends about the Zimbabwean economic trajectory, all of them said that the worst is yet to come and Zimbabwe might end up just like Somalia. It has been said before that expecting death is worse than death itself. For Zimbabweans to live their lives expecting that the worst is yet to come is just worse than death itself. It's also not fair and just to raise too much hope about the future, knowing full well that in the present things are not getting better. The ANCYL of Julius Malema proposed at one point what they called "leadership generational mix." There are different times and different seasons that confront different generations. The generations of Pres. Robert Mugabe and the late president Nelson Mandela were confronted with the political problems of their time, and they had to stand up and be counted among the people of their time in order to fight what they believed was right and appropriate for that time. The current African generation is facing different political and economic problems, and the question that arises then is this: is it appropriate to keep the same political leaders in the forefront simply because they have fought in African liberation struggle even though African liberation struggle is over? It would be unfair and unjust to suggest that we don't need the political wisdom of our old African leaders, while we should accept that African leaders of the previous generation still have a role to play in African political debate. It's also true that we Africans should accept that there is a need for the introduction of a new set of political leaders who will carry on the baton to the future. The main reason until this day why the majority of African leaders are probably hesitant to relinquish their political position is the fact that the majority of African youth are not involved politically in the domestic affairs of their countries. The African youth behave like African Americans who are obsessed with rap music and comedy. Most of the African youth are not aware about their African history, and the only thing that they are worried about is their Face book status and their Twitter accounts. When African leaders who fought in the African liberation struggle observe this societal behavior, they draw an inference that says that the youths of Africa are not ready to pursue the second phase of African economic liberation struggle, which is meant to reverse and redress the economic imbalances of the past. African leaders have only managed to get their countries out of political slavery and oppression, but they could not manage to take their countries forward to the land of milk and honey, and they could not be blamed for that. Different generations will be faced with different sets of political and economic challenges. The challenges of the past African generations were partially solved by the African leaders, and the remaining part of the economic problems that could not be solved by the previous African generation should be solved by this current African generation, which is addicted to social networks. If this African generation is stuck on its Face book page and on Twitter accounts, not even studying the African history, then the current African political and economic problems, which were supposed to be solved by this current African generation, will be solved by the future generation. It will be unfair and unjust to put upon the future African generation a considerable amount of pressure to solve political and economic problems that could have been solved by this current African generation. The generation of the late president Nelson Mandela had their own successes and their own failures also. Our current African generation at least can build on what the generation of the late president Nelson Mandela accomplished and move forward. The issue of land in South Africa has not been solved yet, and it remains hanging in the balance, and it's the responsibility of the South African generation to approach the issue of land head-on and solve it once and for all. The mining crisis in Africa has not been solved by the past African leaders, and it's the responsibility of this current African generation to solve the mining crisis once and for all. The farm invasion issue, which brought the economy of Zimbabwe to its knees, has not been solved, and it's the responsibility of the current Zimbabwe's generation to solve it once and for all. The multitudes of people in South Africa have not tasted the fruits of political freedom let alone economic freedom. Should I say multitudes of people in the African continent don't even know what political freedom is? Political freedom and economic freedom can't be compartmentalized; in other words, a person can't claim to be politically free unless otherwise that person is economically free also. Political freedom and economic freedom go together, and the other can't exist in the absence of the other. The grave mistake that had been committed by African leaders in the past is they confused political freedom for economic freedom. African leaders thought that political freedom automatically breeds economic freedom. This illusion is the main cause for many African crises that are ripping the African continent apart. It's possible and logically sound that in any political negotiation, there are issues that need urgent attention and there are issues that can be deferred to the future. It's dangerous in any form of negotiations to defer hard-pressing economic and political critical issues to the future that were supposed to be dealt with in the present just to reach a quick consensus and move on. That is exactly what happened during African political negotiations that brought about the political peace and democracy. There was too much emphasis on the political freedom at the expense of economic freedom. The issue of political freedom is only resurfacing now because of the poverty that is ravaging the majority of Africans. The question that needs to be posed to our African leaders is this: Guys, did you get the job done? It's possible that they will scramble for a very long and convoluted response, but the fact of the matter is this: African leaders failed decimally to salvage the continent from the shackles of the West. The economic grip that the West has on Africa now has even deepened than what it was in the past. The West has more economic power in Africa now than at any other time in African history.

That is why poverty in the African continent is the order of the day. Africans are always on the run because of the political wars that are ravaging the African continent. Political freedom is the Pyrrhic victory without economic freedom. Most of the African countries, after attaining their political independence, degenerated to the civil wars. There are very few African countries that have managed to usher in the democratic dispensation in a peaceful and harmonious way. The majority of African countries are still struggling even to put together government institutions that can bring services to their people. It's astounding that even to this day there are wars that are going on in the African continent even after Africa is politically independent from the West. It's logically sound and highly probable to conclude that the majority of African countries were too immature to be politically independent, and they were not even prepared and ready for the political power that was given to them. As much as there are highs of money, there are also highs of political freedom. The highs of money come about when a poor person suddenly has a considerable amount of money because of the shocks of life that happened to him or her. This person is likely to misuse and abuse the very same money that he has. The classic example is the prodigal son who squandered his wealth with prostitutes, and then next thing you know he was very poor. After the long and winding African political negotiation, which brought about the political freedom that the majority of African countries are enjoying, there was a sudden wave of happiness that was sweeping the African continent. Its public knowledge that Africans love singing and dancing. From Zimbabwe to South Africa people were dancing on the streets of Harare, Pretoria, and Maputo after Africa has attained its political independence from the West. When one African country attained its political independence, other African countries, though they were still in political oppression, rejoiced with those who were free, believing that one day the very same political freedom that other Africans were enjoying in other African countries will suddenly come to them. When Zimbabwe became a democratic country in 1980 after Prime Minister Robert Mugabe won the national elections, other African countries were happy also. When black South Africans went to the polling stations for the first time to vote for their political freedom, there was happiness brewing in the streets of Bulawayo. There is a picture that makes me tremble and gives me goose bumps. That picture was taken in Zimbabwe, Harare. This picture was shot in 1993 after the release of the president Nelson Mandela in 1990. He embarked on the African campaign to get the support from other African counties. When the late president Nelson Mandela got to Zimbabwe, the people were waiting for him and there was no other person who could walk with him around and demonstrate him to the people except Pres. Robert Mugabe. Africans are the children of the same mother. We Africans are all connected in one way or the other. That is why when I was in Zimbabwe, I could not feel any different, and I was not even afraid at least in my second trip. African history can make you cry sometimes. That picture where Pres. Robert Mugabe and late president Nelson Mandela were both holding their feasts in the air and the people of Zimbabwe were dancing and shouting, until this day, is still vivid in mind. Africans, whether they are from Central African Republic, West Africa, or East Africa, are still brothers and sisters. They see each other as one big family. The West does not like unity and togetherness. It's the responsibility of the West to divide the African people in between in order for the West to find its way to the African continent and be able to steal African mineral resources. The *modus operandi* of the West since time immemorial has been to supply one group with military weapons for free, and then the war will ensue between two ethnic groups that have been living together peacefully for quite a long period of time, and looting of mineral resources will take place while African people will be busy killing each other like dogs. This is the *modus operandi* that the West has been using in Africa to destabilize the African continent for quite a long period of time. Where to from here? Is the one-million-dollar question that multitudes of the African people are frequently asking themselves. I have established that the reason African people are in abject poverty is not because they were born in a poverty-stricken continent. They were born in mineral-resources-rich continent. Unfortunately, the very same wealth that was meant for African people by the Almighty was stolen by the West. African poverty is not divine, but it's a man-made poverty. In effect the way the Western citizens live in the West is the way African people were supposed to be living their lives in the African continent. The world-class infrastructure, roads, health system, and quality education are what African people were supposed to be enjoying. Due to the Western greed and insatiable envy, that is why in Africa until this day we Africans are still talking about children who are still attending school under the trees and helping themselves in a bush where they are exposed to snakes. Africans are still murmuring about the lack of basic services like water and electricity. Africans are still lagging behind in terms of technology and innovation. African children, even to this day, are still studying the Western history as if history began in the West. After 1994 in South

Africa, the class of grade twelve in 2001 was still studying *Julius Caesar* written by William Shakespeare. Political freedom has not yet borne the envisaged political fruits in the African continent. The fact of the matter is this: there are few meaningful political changes that have taken place in the African continent since the African political independence. The laws have not changed much because we Africans are still having the same judges who were appointed by the previous political regimes except in the case of Zimbabwe, but in many African countries the same judiciary systems that hanged and killed a considerable amount of innocent African people are still used even today. The same judges who were killing black people who were fighting against the corrupt political system are still holding the same position they were holding during the apartheid era even in the case of South Africa. There are still the churches of the poor and the churches of the rich even in South Africa and elsewhere in the African continent. There is still the cemetery of the poor and the cemetery of the rich, and the schools for the black people and underprivileged and the school for the white people and privileged. This I have seen with my naked eye unless otherwise my eyes are deceiving me, but I have been having the very same eyes for quite a long period of time, and I have come to the point of believing my eyes. The future looks bright, but we can influence the future to look even brighter. The fact that the previous generations of Nelson Mandela, Kenneth Kaunda, Robert Mugabe, and Kwame Nkrumah could not get the job done, that should not deter this generation to forge with the struggle of economic emancipation.

The Southern Times reports:

> *Africa is known for its abundant resources. It is richly endowed with variety of natural resources including oil, diamonds, gold, iron, cobalt, uranium, copper, bauxite, silver petroleum, and cocoa beans, woods, and tropical fruits. A good number of these rich natural resources–endowed countries are found in the Southern African Development Community region. To show that the continent is resources endowed, five countries dominate Africa's upstream oil production. Together they account for 85 percent of the continent's oil production and are, in order of decreasing output, Nigeria, Libya, Algeria, Egypt, and Angola. Other oil-producing countries are Gabon, Congo,*

Cameroon, Tunisia, Equatorial Guinea, the Democratic Republic of the Congo, and Cote d'Ivoire.[1]

It's public knowledge that Africa is the richest continent in the world, but it's also public knowledge that the multitudes of African people are living in appalling living conditions that are not suitable for a normal human being to live under. It's an open secret now that the African continent is the richest continent in the world in terms of mineral resource. It's also an open secret that this African-rich continent has seen much bloodshed in the whole of the world unlike any other continent on the face of the earth. It's a slap on the face of African people to tell them to their face and say Africa is the richest continent in the whole world in terms of mineral resources. Though Africa is the richest continent in the whole world in terms mineral resources from the natural resource perspective, Africans are the poorest people in the world from the poverty point of view. African leaders are still stuck with the begging bowl, causing traffic jam on their way to the United Nations and the Western countries. The West until this day knows very well that Africa deserves foreign aid and donations. The argument that Africa is the richest continent in the world is neither relevant nor worthy to be raised anymore. The one-million-dollar question is this: If Africa is the richest continent on the face of the earth, why are the majority of Africans still living in abject poverty? We all know the answer to that question. The main reason the majority of Africans are still living in abject poverty is that simply the West gave Africa political freedom and withheld economic freedom. The African nationalists did not see that coming. The African nationalists were obsessed with political freedom without understanding what they were getting the African people into. There are two ways to political freedom coupled with economic freedom, which are the shortest route and the longest route. The shortest route is easy simply because it defers to the future the issue of economic freedom, downplaying the significance of economic freedom and leaving everything in the hands of the African gods and to happenstance. This shortest route is very superficial because it does not even bother to look at the root cause of colonization; it simply addresses the issue of the symptoms, leaving behind the root cause of the problems unaddressed. The chief advantage of this shortest route is that it brings to an end civil wars and infighting, but it does not change dramatically the economic injustices of the past. It still leaves those who benefited through the colonial system more wealthy than ever before, and those that were poor even poorer and the only saving grace are the social grants and free food parcels from the United Nations World Food Programme. The longest route to political freedom is long and winding, and it's based on good faith and mutual understanding. It addresses the root cause of the problems, not leaving anything to happenstance and to the African gods and the future. The longest route to political freedom and economic freedom is what most African nationalists did not opt for; they opted for the superficial political freedom, which was not entirely transparent and overt. The wealth that the West had amassed then before the African emancipation has accumulated a considerable amount in interest in the World Bank and IMF, and the very same wealth is still used today to lend to many African countries as loans for their African infrastructural programs. The future will look ever brighter for Africa if the West can come to its senses one day and admit and disclose the considerable amount of wealth that has been stolen from the African continent. Until and unless the West recognizes that it has contributed to the abject poverty that the multitudes of African people are living under, the Westerners will still live longer than the African people. The fact of the matter is this: the Westerners have a long life span than ordinary African people because of their habitable living conditions. African people have a short life span due to the appalling living conditions that they are living under. There is information deficit and leadership vacuum in Africa attributed to the lack of skills and knowledge as to how to run national institutions effectively and efficiently. Meanwhile in the West there is abundance of everything: world-class infrastructure, quality education, and good health system.The future looks bright, but the future can be influenced to look even brighter if the unjust imbalances of the past can be addressed fairly and honestly, unlike what happened. I need to say, though, that for many Zimbabweans, they will need serious prayers and fasting because for the next five years life will be a little bit difficult. Many Zimbabweans are now accustomed to appalling living conditions and they have absorbed a considerable amount of pain since the economic sanctions of February 18, 2002. But that is not enough, and they are not out of the woods yet, though; even if for them the future looks bright and can even look brighter, they need to be apply a bit of patience perhaps for the last time. The day economic sanctions will be lifted off from the Zimbabwean economy; everybody in the whole world will be flocking to Zimbabwe to look for investment opportunities. The truth of the matter is this: things are about to happen in the economy of Zimbabwe, and I don't mean that things will change tomorrow literally, but they will change eventually. I suggest that for one to be in a better economic position, one should not shy away from the idea of dual citizenship. The reason I am suggesting that is simply the day the West will come to its senses and realize just as Bashar al-Assad had been killing children with hunger and scud missiles, the West also has been killing the innocent children, women, and men with hungers in Zimbabwe. In fact the West has committed more atrocities in Africa than Adolf Hitler of Germany. There is one thing that will happen in Zimbabwe the day economic sanctions will be lifted off: there will be stampede in the Beitbridge border because everybody will be heading to Zimbabwe for investment opportunities. Even those who have never entertained the thought of going to Zimbabwe will be in the Beitbridge border queuing to gain access to Zimbabwe. There are few Chinese living in Zimbabwe right now, but wait until the economic sanctions have been lifted off—you will see the locomotion that will be caused by Chinese in Zimbabwe. Chinese are already causing stampede and conjecture in South Africa. Everybody will be faking and tailoring a very complicated and convoluted story just to get the Zimbabwean citizenship. Meanwhile, since the economic sanctions are biting the Zimbabwean people, they are biting them alone; but the day these economic sanctions will be lifted off, even the Zimbabweans who left their home country to reside in the United States of America and in the United Kingdom will come back running to Zimbabwe to reap the harvest of free international economic trade. It's true even in the case of South Africa. While black South Africans were bearing the brunt of the ruthless force of the apartheid system, the population of South Africa was very low and manageable. In effect it was very hard to come across black non-South Africans walking in the street of Pretoria during the apartheid era because apartheid was eating black South Africans alone, and after the fall of apartheid, which was biting black people alone, South African population has grown in leaps and bounds. In fact South African population is growing at a very disturbing rate. There are more foreigners right now in South Africa than ever before. There are multitudes of migrants on the queue day in and day out queuing for political asylum even though there is no war in their countries of birth for these asylum seekers. These immigrants are chasing the next big thing that is about to happen. The same thing that is happening in South Africa right now is what exactly will happen in Zimbabwe the day the economic sanctions will be lifted off on the Zimbabwean economy by the West. The future of Zimbabwe looks bright, but it will look even brighter if there could be a political will to acknowledge that the current economic stalemate has been created by partly the West and current Zimbabwean government with its impractical economic policies. There is no way in the world where the Zimbabwean government will ever attract foreign investments to the economy if it continues with its unfriendly economic policies to the foreign investors. The indigenization policy has run the economy of Zimbabwe to the ground, and the government should solely be blamed for indigenization. There is nowhere in the world where you can incorporate a company and source funding only to be told by the government that you need to give away the 51 percent and remain with the 49 percent. It's imperative to bear in mind that even if you are giving away the 51percent to the government and remain with the 49 percent, the company will still have to pay company tax and pay the salaries to the employees. If the company start-up capital was financed through loan from a financial institution, that loan still needs to be paid back with interests. Because of the half-baked economic policy, the Zimbabwean government lost a considerable amount of foreign investments as a result of indigenization policy. The Zimbabwean economy crumbled, coupled with the biting economic sanctions that have been imposed by the West on February 18, 20002. The future looks bright for the people of Zimbabwe, but they will still need to be patient a little bit because Rome was not built in one day; therefore, even if the economic sanctions can be lifted off from the economy of Zimbabwe, that will not necessarily mean the economy will be turned around within a week. One of the possible solutions that the government of Zimbabwe should be contemplating about seriously is downsizing the Zimbabwe Republic Police (ZRP). There is a low level of crimes in Zimbabwe. In fact many people in Zimbabwe are afraid of breaking the law because of the inhospitable living conditions in prison. Therefore, in a country like Zimbabwe, which is facing harsh economic conditions, it makes no logical sense to continue with humongous police force, since there is no potential of crime in the country to occur. When there is nothing to steal, people steals nothing. When there is something to steal, then people will steal because there is something that they can steal. The Zimbabwean indigenization policy is exactly the same as the South African BEE policy, which has enriched the few politically connected elites. The Black Economic Empowerment (BEE) was not even broad based, but it was elites based; rather than trickling down to the people on the ground, it ended enriching the few and the who's who in the political zoo of South Africa. The rationale about BEE was good, but the implementation was sheer madness. Until this day in South Africa there are still South Africans who are profiting considerably from the BEE policy. These are the people who will fight tooth and nail to make sure that the BEE policy remains in place because they have benefited immensely from it, and they still stand a chance even to benefit more even in the near future. Africa can be a competitive global player provided that the West acknowledges the mistakes of the past and compensates the African countries that were impoverished by the West. The foreign aid does not help any African country to be economically competitive, but what foreign aid does is ; it further plunges African countries in the bottomless pit of poverty. There is no country that should claim to be politically free unless otherwise it is economically free. It's public knowledge that social grants recipients are not using the social grants to buy food but to buy booze and drugs. As long as African people will live their lives depending on their national governments, then we Africans must accept that one way or the other the African governments must have sufficient financial resources in order to keep their people happy by providing them with the social grants incessantly. Its public knowledge that the reason the Zimbabwean government had economic sanctions imposed by the West into the Zimbabwean economy is the farm invasion fiasco of 2000. There is still a vast tract of land that is lying underutilized in Zimbabwe simply because there was not an effective structure that was responsible to redistribute the land to the legitimate beneficiaries. Let me put it differently: there is a multitude of farm occupants who were not legitimate land beneficiaries. When the economic sanctions have been lifted off from the economy of Zimbabwe, if one day the West will come to its senses, the illegitimate occupants of the land must be relocated and be given a hospitable land where they can live side by side with others. The current few farm occupants in Zimbabwe know absolutely nothing about farming except practicing what Bajabulile calls "selfish-farming." Why would a person who is untrained and unskilled about farming be allowed to occupy fifty hectares of land but only use one hectare and underutilize the rest of forty-nine hectares of land? That is exactly what is happening in Zimbabwe. The multitude of people currently dwelling in those few farms, which are not even productive, is incompetent and unskilled as far as farming is concerned. If these farm occupants were skilled and trained as far as farming is concerned, then Zimbabwe was not supposed to be the basket case of Southern Africa, but it was supposed to be breadbasket of Southern Africa as it was previously known. The Zimbabwe economy was not supposed to importing everything including toothpaste from South Africa, as is the case at this moment, if the farm occupants were trained and skilled on how to run the farms. The fact of the matter is this: whether we like or not, the farm invasion was the greatest mess of all time. The West is laughing at Africa, saying, "Now that we gave you your land, why are you starving and dying of hunger?" Failure to plan is planning to fail, and it's better to plan first and then take an action later rather than to take an action without understanding the ramifications of your action. That is what exactly happened in Zimbabwe; people were fooled that they can reverse the economic injustices of the past within a short space of time. The next thing you know, the rest of the people are now suffering due to few political leaders who were thoughtless and paranoid. The future looks bright, and the future can even look brighter for the people of Zimbabwe if the economic sanctions can be lifted off from the Zimbabwean economy by the West. The expropriation of land without compensation is moving at a snail's pace, and I know for a fact that the municipalities won't stop selling the South African land to the Europeans under the pretext of development and urbanization. It's astounding to me to hear people saying that there is still a considerable amount of land in South Africa that is still in the hands of the Westerners because South African municipalities are selling land each and every day to the Anglo-Saxons. There are more real estate's that are still under construction in South Africa, and there will be more real estate even in the near future. Let me put it bluntly: when you are residing in a real estate, you are paying administrative fees to the owner of the land until you go six feet under. It therefore means that a person who is residing in a real estate is a tenant forever even though the very same house that this person owns has been funded by the bank, but the land that the house was built on is owned by another person via a registered company. Let me simplify it for you: when you are living under a chief, literally the land that you have built your house on belongs to the chief even though the house that you have built might belong to you and the furniture that you own might be registered in your name. But the fact remains: the tribal chief owns the land, though he might not come anytime of the day to observe and inspect how you are living your life, but he still owns the land literally. Those who are living under the tribal chief know it very well that should they misbehave or be accused of being involved in witchcraft, they will be evicted by the tribal chief and the tribal council. The point that I am making is this: you don't own the real estate because that is not your real estate; you are just a tenant who should continue to pay administrative fees to keep the real estate clean. Do you know that banks don't approve a mortgage loan for a person who is going to build a house in a village? It's because the banks know very well that people who are residing under a tribal chief don't own the land that they live in but the land belongs to their tribal chief. Meanwhile, the banks approve a personal loan for a person who is going to build a house in a village even though the loan recipient is going to build a house in a land that is owned by a tribal chief. The point is that I am making is this: the personal loan has nothing to do with the tribal chief and his land, but it has everything to do with the loan recipient. The poverty cycle will remain intact as long as the multitudes of people are still living in the real estate's that they don't own and don't even have title deeds to the land that they live in. There is a difference between owning the land and owning a house in a land of someone. Many people confuse owning the house with owning the land. Villagers do not own the land; the land is owned by the tribal chief. People who are residing in the real estate own their mortgage bond houses, which have been financed through the bank, but they don't own the land because the real estate is someone's land, and that land was bought from the municipality for residential purposes. The classic example of what I am talking about happened in Durban, South Africa, where the real estate residents went to the local municipality to complain only to be told by the municipality that they need to solve their problems with the owner of the real estate not with the municipality. Once the municipality has sold the land to the property developer, the land does not belong to the municipality anymore, but it belongs to the property developer/real estate owner. The real estate residents are the tenants in the land of the real estate owner. Even though they have financed their mortgage bond via the bank, the land that they have built their house on belongs to the property developer, and that is the truth and the only truth. It's possible that if you are reading this and you are residing in a real estate, your blood pressure will shoot up, but at least you know now that the land that your house was built on is not yours—but at least the house is yours. When the apartheid government evicted black people in the fertile land of South Africa, they bulldozed black people to the mountainous areas where there were no rivers and roads but only rocks and snakes. The apartheid government took that fertile land and conducted farming and constructed factories and game reserves. There is a considerable amount of land concealed through what they call nature conservation at the expense of living and breathing people. Who is more important between a human being and a rhino? If a person is more important than a rhino, why is it that the preference is given to the rhinos compared to the normal people of South Africa? In South Africa some of the animals are living a better life compared to the normal human beings. The so-called game reserves was the strategy by the apartheid government to make sure that black people stay as far as possible from the city and from the white folks. That is why even to this day in South Africa there is a vast tract of land that is occupied by the rhinos at the expense of black people who are overcrowded in Alexandra and Diepsloot. It's important to acknowledge and accept that African economic and political problems did not emerge out of nowhere; they have their own origin and their source in the West. African problems, economic and otherwise, can't be blamed squarely on corruption and the lack of leadership only; they are intertwined and connected to what is happening in the West. The theory that says that Africans are blaming everyone except themselves is sheer madness.

The Southern Times reports:

> *According to the EU, under the Tenth European Development Fund (2008–2013) the bloc committed approximately €12 billion for African countries. The EU also argues that it remains the most important donor for Africa. African countries received close to €24 billion of Official Development Aid (OAD) from the EU for the period 2007–2012. Other top donors to Africa are the United States of America and the World Bank. European places a particular high priority on Africa within their development agenda as demonstrated by the share of aid to Africa as part of their total aid budget. The top-ten donors by share of aid to Africa include only European countries, topped by Ireland (with 81 percent of its total aid to Africa) and followed by Belgium (77 percent), Portugal (73 percent), and France (63 percent). Among other cocktails building dependency, the EU has proposed to make available €1 billion for a Pan-African Programme (PAP), as part of the Instrument for Development Co-operation.*[3]

There is no amount of foreign aid that can reverse the imbalances of the past in the African continent. The main problem with foreign aid is this: it does not solve the long-term problems of poverty and unemployment, but it is a short-term solution for a long-term problem. Unfortunately, most African leaders have became accustomed to the Western foreign aid to the point that they have assimilated the idea that says the best way out of poverty is more foreign aid and more foreign donations. Africa has been received foreign aid for quite a long period of time now, but when one takes a closer look at the impact of the foreign aid, the outcome is the unholy corruption and fraud that now have become the new cancer of Africa. There is no amount of foreign aid that can cure the economic problems of Africa. Instead of the foreign aid solving the economic problems that most African countries are faced with, foreign aid creates wars and division among many African countries. The DRC War ended in November, 2014. There were too much foreign donations to the point that some of the officials had to doctor the crime statistics just to get the foreign aid from the United Nations. When a country depends heavily on foreign aid, it's a clear indication of intellectual laziness and intellectual bankruptcy, meaning that people of that country are not doing anything constructively and are doing everything destructively. Some African countries have been experiencing a considerable amount of intellectual bankruptcy as a result of heavy dependency on the foreign aid. The moment a considerable amount of people begins to look up to the heavens for manna, it renders them to be incapable of thinking and being creative. For African countries who rely heavily on foreign aid, their citizens normally are more inclined to laziness and intellectual fatigue simply because they think that the government will take care of them, therefore they are not supposed to think and be able to do things for themselves because the government will take care of them anyway. The same mentality is prevailing in South Africa with the majority of people who are receiving the social grants from the national government. Social grants recipients have come to accept that they are the responsibility of the government, and as a result, they are not supposed to do anything for themselves because the big brother will take care of them, which is the government. The same thing is happening in a family where there is a big brother who is working; the younger siblings turn out to be stress-free because the big brother will pay the bills and buy food for all of them. They further go on to the point where they even think that the big brother is their biological father while they are all siblings. Its public knowledge that the lazy mind breeds evil ideas the more people are given free food parcels that hinder their minds to be inquisitive and creative. Human beings were not designed to be static and do the same thing over and over again. They were designed to be inquisitive and creative, and what social grants and free food parcels do is they further perpetuate the colonial misconception that Africans are not smart enough when it comes to technology and science. When the mind of a person is hassle-free and problem-free, therefore there is no need for that particular person to think critically, since there is no problem to solve. Social problems and economic problems compel ordinary people to think and search for solutions. The classic example is this: I have witnessed when the majority of black people were given sugarcane farms by the South African government as the result of their land that was taken from them by the apartheid government, the majority of people after their farm's harvest had a lot of money that they never thought in their lifetime they will ever have. The children of these black farmers became lazy academically because their parents had money from their farms. Most of the children whose parents had sugarcane farms did not complete their grade twelve, and as a result, they decided to quit schooling and began making babies as if there was no tomorrow. That is exactly what happens when the majority of people begin to see their government as the big brother who supposed to take care of them because he is working and he is the only one who is working in the family. The dependency syndrome and the entitlement syndrome are destroying the African youth bit by bit. The same goes for the social grants; they are not helping ordinary people to become economically active, but they create a welfare state. South Africa is a developmental state, so is Africa. Citizens of the developmental state must be creative and innovative and not rely on the national government for survival. Foreign aid just like social grants is detrimental to the creativity of Africans. Take a look at Malawi, since it is a foreign-aid-dependent country. Instead of corruption to come down in Malawi, corruption is soaring like never before. In fact Malawi will go down in the history books as the only African country that was dependent on foreign aid yet continuing nonstop on its path of unholy corruption and maladministration. The Malawian case study shows the whole world that the problems of poverty and unemployment can't be solved entirely by throwing a considerable amount of money at poverty and unemployment and close your eyes hoping that a miracle will take place automatically. Money does not solve the problems of poverty and unemployment, but it creates another problem, which is the problem of corruption and fraud, which is the new cancer for Africa. The West up to this far is the largest contributor of foreign aid to many African countries. It's public knowledge that the West colonized Africa and amassed a considerable amount of wealth during the colonial era. Even to this day the West is firmly entrenched in the African continent, stealing legally in broad daylight via its multinational corporations. The African economic outlook doesn't reflect and symbolize the continent that is free from the colonial oppression, but it paints a grim picture about people who are in dire need of foreign aid and social grants. Africa's literacy level is worse compared to that of the West. The top-ten universities in the world are from the West. It seems as if there is absolutely nothing that is going well with Africa except the social grants and foreign aid that are distributed to the African people. There are few African countries that are even financially able to distribute social grants to its people. The Zimbabwean government can't afford to pay its civil servants' salaries in time. Where can it get money to distribute social grants to its people? There are no social grants in Zimbabwe. That does not mean that the people on the ground don't need social grants given the current economic crisis. Perhaps social grants were going to help families that are languishing in the bottomless pit of poverty. The main problem with foreign aid just like with social grants is that the beneficiaries of social grants begin to develop a new weird behavior. The South African population prior to the distribution of social grants was very low, and after the distribution of social grants it shot up just like that. The main reason the South African population shot up astronomically is that simply the teenagers who are supposed to be focusing on their studies started paying too much attention to their sexual needs and their sexual desires because of the child grant reward that is associated with making a baby. It's a South African phenomenon that the more babies you make, the more money you make through the child grants—as if it means that those who are lazy to make babies won't get paid, and those who will do their nation proud by making more babies out of wedlock will be rewarded with child grants. Foreign aid is killing innovation and creativity of many African countries, just like social grants are propelling more high schools teenagers in South Africa to have children out of wedlock, exacerbating the scourge of poverty even further. I am aware that the majority of people will say foreign aid and social grants are two different things and the two cannot be linked and contrasted with each other. How many countries work for foreign aid, and how many families work for social grants? The answer is there is no country in the world that should work to receive foreign aid, and the same goes for the social grants; there is no family that is expected to work to receive social grants. In fact the social grants recipients hate working with passion. The question that they frequently asked is this: Why should I wake up in the morning and subject myself to the cold winter while I am getting paid to stay warm inside the blankets? This attitude is only possessed by social grants recipients. I decided to visit the SASSA offices here in South Africa. I was very shocked to see that the longest queue was the queue of new candidates who were going to register for the child grants. One lady who was on the queue was accompanied by the father of the baby who appeared to me to be a teenager as well. The term "social grant" in South Africa is frequently used interchangeably with the word "child grant." In other words, a person can talk about social grant as if he is referring to the disability grant or indigent grant, whereas he is talking about the child grant. In my case, when I am talking about child grant, I mean the child grant and not the indigent grant, which is received by people who are considered poor. When I am referring to the child grant, I am not referring to the old-age pension or disability pension. It's true that in any community there will be children who will be born with mental deformities and who will be born with physical disabilities. Where I live in Pretoria, there is a woman that I always come across pushing a pram with her physically disabled child, and that child is not just physically disabled but also needs constant medical treatment from doctors. Such cases should be taken care of by the national government by providing the social grants, which is specifically called disability grant. Then you have teenagers who were supposed to be focusing their energy on their schoolwork, but they focus the whole of their energy on their sexual needs, determined to make new sexual discoveries. Child grants are received by the high school teenagers who are trying to prove and affirm their endless love for one another by making a baby while at school. The more teenagers have too much time at their disposal; the only thing that is likely to come into their minds is love and more love. The idle mind breeds more evil ideas than the busy mind. The youths that are in school studying are better than the youths that are always loitering on the streets doing absolutely nothing. The youths are the future of any county, and if a country is neglecting its youth, it is likely to find itself in a very serious trouble. It's only now that the majority of people begin to fathom the danger of not having young people in employment and in education. The youth that are loitering around the streets are likely to cause the revolution and the African Spring just like the Arab Spring. The farm invasion of 2000 in Zimbabwe was the Zimbabwean uprising by the youth of Zimbabwe. The main reason countries like Belgium, France, and Portugal are on the forefront of dispersing foreign aid to Africa is that these countries know very well that the abject poverty that the majority of African people are living under in Africa was caused by them through the colonial era. It's Belgium that colonized DRC and Congo. It's Belgium that was responsible for the killing of almost eight hundred thousand people in Rwanda. The Belgium government started dividing Hutus and Tutsis by giving them tags that they were supposed to carry around. The Belgians' tactics made wonders and magic during the Rwandan Genocide of 1994 because that is how people were identified. Differently put, Belgium was responsible for the death of eight hundred thousand people in Rwanda in 1994, since it is Belgium that colonized Rwanda not the opposite. It is Belgium that has been stealing the mineral resources of DRC and Congo. The mineral-rich DRC became the pie of the West, and everybody in the West was vying for the slice of the DRC and Congo pie. DRC was known for its mercenary's attraction. There were more mercenary groups in the DRC than anywhere else in the African continent. Pres. Thabo Mbeki, as soon as he took over from Nelson Mandela, had to diffuse the war that was in the DRC that was ripping the DRC apart. That is why Belgium is pouring a considerable amount of US dollars via foreign aid because it's quite conversant with its atrocities that it has committed in the African continent. It is also Belgium that taught Joseph Mobutu Sese Seko how to be corrupt and steal and stay in power. Mobutu Sese Seko was Belgium's puppet, and the Belgians loved him because he was taking orders from Brussels. Mr. Silverton once said to me Mobutu was drinking water from France while living in DRC and he built himself a mansion with gold. African leaders love to live a lavish lifestyle, while their people whom they are leading are languishing in abject poverty. When Belgium couldn't contaminate the mind of Patrice Lumumba, they decided to kill him. There are many atrocities that have been committed by the Belgians in the African continent that were not reported adequately. There are many atrocities that have been committed, even in Burundi that have not been reported on adequately. That is why the West is guilty of war crimes, and it was not even once taken to the ICC for the atrocities that have been committed in DRC and Congo. The International Criminal Court was meant for African leaders who are rebellious to their Western masters. There is no way you will ever see a Western leader prosecuted and convicted by the ICC as if Western leaders are immune to corruption and war crimes. The ICC is yet to open the case about the death of Saddam Hussein and the perpetrators of crime that was committed by the West to the Iraqi people. The ICC is the kangaroo court of the West. Portugal colonized Mozambique and Angola. The Mozambican war was the most brutal war of them all. While I was a little boy, the survivors of the Mozambican war arrived in South Africa for the very first time. They told us horrible stories about the war. There were multiple players in the Mozambican war. There are many innocent people who died in the Mozambican war without any reasonable reasons. To this day there are still amputees in Mozambique as a result of the war. Once upon a time Mother Africa was a quiet continent beaming with peace and tranquility, and there came the West with terrorists and mercenaries, and until this day, the large part of the African continent is forever in a war that does not seem to come to an end. While these African wars were ongoing, the West was amassing wealth, and that's how the African wealth that had been looted from the African continent and invested in the European Central Bank and the IMF and World Bank and this African wealth generated a considerable amount of interest, and that interest is now being donated back to the African continent gratuitously as if the West loves Africa.There is no way that the West can suddenly be very wealthy without having stolen this wealth somewhere. Colonization was not purely about political oppression; it was also about siphoning the wealth from Africa to the West. If one looks at the colonial project from the vantage point and single out the wealth aspect in between, that person will miss the key clues. Colonization was not just purely about oppressing African people politically; it was also about making sure that the West gathers as much wealth as possible for its future generation by the Western powers for the future Western generation. Indeed the Western generations are enjoying the fruits of the colonial project. Africans are still starving and languishing in abject poverty simply because our forefathers were defeated and enslaved by the West, and that is why Africans are still stuck forever with foreign aid from the same people who colonized it. The main reason Portugal, just like France, is pumping in a considerable amount of foreign aid to the African continent is that; Portugal colonized three African countries, which are Mozambique, Angola, and Portuguese Guinea. It's public knowledge that Angola is rich in oil, but the ordinary people on the ground from Angola are still lamenting about the scourge of poverty. The one-million-dollar that we Africans from the African continent should ask ourselves is this: Through the colonial project, which was the master plan for the West to enrich itself at the expense of the African people, how much wealth did the West manage to siphoned out of the African continent through its colonial project, and can this wealth be quantified in terms of numbers? There are very few people who take time to pause and ponder these Africans issues. Mother Africa has been robbed, and until and unless these colonial injustices of the past are not solved once and for all, African people will continue to die, and the African problems of poverty and unemployment will never come to an end soon. This foreign aid that is forever given to the African countries numb African people from the pain that they were cheated their wealth by the West. After it has been established how much wealth was extracted from the African continent by the West, then the West has to come to the negotiation table where the issue of compensation should be discussed once and for all. Until and unless such exercise is embarked on, African problems will never come to an end. There will be forever inequality and racism. It's the West that introduced racism in Africa, where the poor of certain skin pigmentation are treated differently compared to certain group people of a certain skin color. Africans from the African continent are still in the receiving end of racism. Racism has not yet ended in Africa until this point in time. Black people are still mistreated even after the dawn of democracy. France, just like Portugal and Belgium, has profited immensely through its own colonial project and amassed a considerable amount of wealth and invested this wealth in the European Central Bank, IMF, and World Bank, since this has been the strategy of the West. The rationale behind the colonial project was this: colonize your subject and loot as much wealth as you can and then invest the wealth in a recognized international financial institution like the World Bank and IMF in order to protect and prevent this wealth to be questioned either where it came from or how they made it. The G7 club made its wealth through the colonial project, and even though the United States of America can vehemently deny that it did not colonize Africa, the fact of the matter is this: it bought the slaves in Africa at a very cheap price and profited extensively out of the slavery project. Slaves are not paid a salary, and slaves don't have rights. The only thing that slaves needed then was food and food only. It's France that colonized the Central African Republic, and no wonders France feels that it has a moral obligation to make sure that there is safety and peace in Central African Republic. The cardinal sin that has been committed by the West in many Africa countries was underdevelopment. Its one thing to colonize a country, but it's another thing to keep its people poor while you are taking away their mineral resources to the West to build world-class infrastructure while the African people are plunged in squatter camps like pigs. Mozambique until this day is still very poor with no world-class infrastructure, and the same is true with CAR. I have seen underdevelopment also in Zimbabwe. The public urinary in Zimbabwe is a mess. Every time the bus pulled over and the driver of the bus will instruct us to go to the toilet, one was always thinking about the fungus that he might contract through the unhygienic public urinary in Zimbabwe. It's logically sound that without a considerable amount of infrastructure investment, most of the African countries will remain where they are economically. For the future of Africa and for the sake of the future generations of Africa, it's imperative that the current African leaders must take time and a moment to ponder, investing immensely on Africa's infrastructure instead of thinking about foreign aid that is forever diminishing. South Africa's future looks very bright, and it is going to look even brighter if the cancer of unholy corruption and fraud can be cured once and for all. The main reason South Africa's future looks bright is that the current South African government has paid respect to the fact that the only way to lift the majority of people out of the ditch of poverty is expanded infrastructure program, though in South Africa it is called EPWP (Expanded Public Works Programme). When I was in Zimbabwe on my second trip, something bad happened. It was Saturday morning, and I just finished my trip for the day that included visiting Heroes' Acre, where the heroes of Zimbabwe are buried. It does not necessarily mean that all people who have been buried in Heroes' Acre are heroes in the literal sense of the word. But it means that their political contributions have impacted the lives of the ordinary people in Zimbabwe. There are people in Zimbabwe who have contributed immensely in the history of Zimbabwe, but they were not buried in Heroes' Acre. It does not necessarily mean, by no means, that their political contribution to the political struggle was not recognized and therefore insignificant. If all the people who fought in the Zimbabwean armed struggle had to be buried in Heroes' Acre, then there would not be enough space in Heroes' Acre left to be used as a burial site. I think people like Terry take the issue of being buried in Heroes' Acre very seriously. In South Africa there is Freedom Park, and it has the same symbolic feature in the South African history just like Heroes' Acre in the history of Zimbabwe. In the case of South Africa, Freedom Park is not used as a burial site just like in the case of Zimbabwe. In effect, that Saturday morning as I turned on the TV—I vividly recall it was after twelve in the afternoon—and there were disturbing pictures that were shown on the screen. Al-Shabaab, which is an affiliate to al-Qaeda, the proverbial terrorist group, had the Westgate mall under siege. The stalemate continued all day long, and I suddenly lost interest in the story. I thought the moment I get into South Africa, I will focus on this story and pay undivided attention to it. There are things that are worth pursuing in life and there are things that are not worth pursuing. There is information that I need and there is information that I don't need, just like there are relationships that I need and there are relationships that I don't need. It's futile to try and read everything because at the end of the day you will not even recall what you read and there is no relevance of what you read to your life. I love reading for leisure, don't get me wrong, but I find it useless when you have a humongous project before you that you can divert your focus on other things like following the Westgate mall story, though my prayers went to the victims of the Westgate mall. If I had to focus on the Westgate mall, I would have been confused and terrified because of the nature of that event. One thing that became abundantly clear to me during the Westgate mall siege is that there are terrorists in the West just like there are terrorists in Africa. But in general, Africans are not terrorists in their nature, and the main problem is the African youth have bought into this theory that the moment you die fighting in the holy war, you are going straight to heaven and Allah is going to prepare a place for you. This is a very serious problem, and it needs serious attention. Religion was not meant to kill people, but it was meant to make sure that people live together in harmony. It's surprising to me that some of the political battles have now found their way into the house of God and are now part of the sermons on a Sunday. The same thing is also happening in South Africa, where churches are involved in the politics of the country. Please don't get me wrong, and it's important to participate in the domestic political affairs of your country, but the house of God must remain as the house of God, not as a place to hold political rallies and store weapons just like what has happened in a mosque in Kenya. Many people confuse politics with Christianity, and they suggest that the two can coexist. The fact of the matter is this: the two can't coexist; you are either a Christian or a politician. Most of the politicians in South Africa are in the National Assembly in Parliament or in the provincial legislature or even in the municipalities. Politicians must just stick to politics, and pastors must just stick to prayer, fasting, and reading the word of God and leave the politics to the politicians. There is a tendency among politicians to move around from one church to another to look for prayers during their election campaigns, and after they have won their national elections, they are not even coming back to the same churches that helped them to win the national elections, but they invite the musicians of the world and gather people into the stadiums where liquor and wine are for free, and then next thing you know, when these political celebrations are over the following morning, you will find condoms on the ground to reflect the fact that it was not just about political celebration. It was more than just a political celebration, and perhaps we should accept that people celebrate in many different ways, sometimes sexually. The point that I making is this: politicians must not exploit the house of God when they are looking for votes, and the ministers of the word must not allow politicians to speak politics in the house of God, for God is holy and his house must be holy. If politicians want to canvass for the national elections, they must just gather people in the stadium to hold their political rally and canvass because Jesus was not a politician. My overall idea about writing this book is not to instigate discrimination and violence against a certain group of people, specifically the Western settlers, but my overall intention is to ensure that the current African youth understand African history from the perspective of the African youth. My main concern that has been a very serious concern throughout my entire journey has been this: African history has not been written by Africans. The majority of historical books about the African history have been written by people who were involved in the African liberation struggle physically and the danger about reading a book written by someone who was involved in the African liberation struggle is this: former freedom fighters provide their own political narrative that fits and suits their own political agenda. That is why if the former freedom fighters were to be asked what the overall objective of the African liberation struggle was, very few will be able to tell you straightaway what was the overall objective of the African liberation struggle. The worst-case scenario about reading books that have been written by former freedom fighters is that they are likely to paint a rosy picture about themselves, portraying themselves as if the African liberation struggle could not have been achieved if it was not for their own brave political contribution. The other problem with reading political books that have been written by former freedom fighters is this: they are likely to give a political narrative that is far-fetched and humanly impossible given the nature of the armed struggle. The last problem why one needs to be very carefully when reading political books that have been written by former freedom fighter is that they are likely to place themselves in the center of the African liberation struggle where everything was happening and nothing happened that was crucial that they could not see. That is why people like me took time and space to go back in time to find out about the past and the sequence of events as they have unfolded. The less history is written, the more people forget about their political heroes and about their political journey that they have traveled as a nation to be where they are today. It will be unfortunate and unfair then to suggest that African nationalists did not do their part in ensuring that the African people are politically liberated. Though the African nationalists did what they could back then, it should be acceptable to this African generation that the armed struggle might be over, but we have another struggle that is staring us in the face, and that struggle is the economic struggle. We can shy away from the economic struggle just like the African nationalists did and focus solely on the political freedom at the expense of economic freedom, or we can confront the economic struggle head-on just like the African nationalists did with the political freedom. It's important that our African people need to be taught that in democracy there are still laws that will still need to be observed. It does not mean that once we are in a democratic dispensation, everything in every sense of the word is free. This is a political misconception. The fact that most of the African countries are free politically, it does not therefore mean that everything will be free, so to speak. Ordinary people will still have to look for employment, and they will still have to wake up early in the morning and go to work and earn a salary and pay the bills. Even in a democratic country, you will still have to pay for water and electricity and garbage collection. The notion that we are politically free and as a result we should get everything free is highly incorrect and uncalled for. There is too much looting in Africa, and at some point it's the Africans of the continent who are stealing from their national governments. I have witnessed it by crossing the Beitbridge border that there is a lot of corruption that is going on in these African borders, and ordinary African people are continually ripping their governments apart through corruption and fraud. I need to take this time to explain myself clear lest some people misinterpret my theory. It's public knowledge that the West stole Africa's wealth, and had it not been for the West, Africans who are in the continent of Africa would be living a far better life than the current lives that they are living right now. Some of the African people of the continent have decided to leave the African continent to ply their trades somewhere in the West because of the economic conditions that are prevailing in the West. I don't see these kinds of actions helping the African continent to be able to rise again and stand on its political and economic feet. When you migrate to the West and things don't work out in the West, please make sure that you don't come to the African continent. The future looks bright here in Africa, and the future will look even brighter if the African people can work together to fight the problems of poverty and unemployment that are ravaging the African people. We are always astounded by images from the Western media about Africans who are dying on their way to the island of Lampedusa. Some of these African migrants have a wrong perception about the West; they watch too much TV and they believe everything that they see on TV. The Western media always projects the West as heaven on earth. One thing that we can't run away from is this: there is poverty and unemployment even in the West. The theory that says everything is rosy in the West is perilous, and that is what makes the majority of Africans to be squeezed into one unsafe vessel sailing all the way to the island of Lampedusa only to find out that their dreams that they have about the West are a pipe dream. I am not implying that when an individual is convinced that he should migrate to the West because of reasonable reason, then that individual should forbidden to migrate to the West. But what is critical is this: there will be forever a difference between Westerns and Africans. It is the Western ideology that all Africans are thieves and they are intellectually inferior compared to the Westerners. That is why most African American superstars are not making it in the media but they are making it in the music industry simply because they are speaking what they call "African American Vernacular English." Simply put, this is English that is spoken by African Americans who were working in the farms because of lack of education and lack of higher-order thinking. This is still true today. Most African Americans who are living in the hood are speaking AAVE because of poor education and lack of higher-order thinking. A black person is at home whenever he is in Africa and nowhere else in the whole world. There are many South Africans who left South Africa for greener pastures in Europe, and when things could not work out in the West, they come back running to the very same country that they were running away from. It's like being married to a woman who is always talking about leaving you and going back to her parents' house. It's better to get rid of that person now than to wait for that painful day when she will finally say, "I was always telling you that I will leave one day. Now I am finally leaving." Expecting death is worse than death itself. Africans who are always chasing the next big thing can't be entrusted with the responsibility of building their country from scratch because these are people who are always on the run for a better life. Even if they get a better life, they won't even recognize it because they have been on the run forever. Imagine this situation, during the apartheid era in South Africa, if the late president Nelson Mandela just took his family and left South Africa for good to resettle in the West, running away from the scourge of apartheid that was biting black South Africans alive, what do you think could have happened to the people of South Africa? Political problems present us with a rare opportunity to be able to stand out and be counted among the few. Cowards during a crisis normally run away simply because they have nothing to offer on the table. Cowards talk about the problem and do nothing about the problem. There is no country on the face of the planet that does not have political and economic problems. In effect problems are the part of life, and life would not be complete enough if there were no problems. The same goes with loving a person. While you might love a person wholeheartedly and with all the fiber of your being, it's important to remember that you still have to love yourself. The reasons why the majority of people are committing suicide now and then is that they don't love themselves enough to keep themselves alive. There is no logical reason for you to kill yourself just because somebody cheated on you. In fact, the main reason someone would cheat on you is to make you aware that you don't mean much to him or her. I was in Bulawayo in the afternoon and I was waiting in the bus terminal for the bus that was going to South Africa. I was extremely exhausted, and the only thing that I was thinking about is to get into the bus and find a seat for myself. I was hoping this time, unlike before, I will sit next to a young lady in order for us to have a fruitful political dialogue, and please don't get me wrong—if you have to travel from Bulawayo to South Africa seated next to a pensioner, you will feel like the journey is long and endless. Fortunately, as I have said before, this time around things are going according to my plan. I took my seat inside the bus after I have packed my only bag inside the luggage trailer and went straight to my seat. I was heading home to South Africa and I was going to see my mother. A young lady came straight to my seat and sat just next to me. She was young and skinny and she was speaking Ndebele. She started asking me what I was doing in Zimbabwe and where I was coming from. I refused to divulge my personal information. You will never know—maybe she is an undercover agent for the CIO. I saw that she was very bored by the fact that I was very reluctant to give away any personal information about my trip. There are few people who travel to research for books. Writers normally Google information on the Internet and start writing without knowing what they are talking about in reality. There are many people here in South Africa who can talk about Zimbabwe as if they have been in Zimbabwe. These are the kinds of people who rely on the Western media that killed Saddam Hussein and the very same media that suggested that Saddam Hussein was manufacturing the weapons of mass destruction. And when the weapons of mass destruction could not be found, the same Western media did not come back to report to the people of the world that they reported lies and Saddam Hussein is dead. The cardinal sin that has been committed by Saddam Hussein was to nationalize oil and get rid of the Western companies that were profiting immensely in Iraq. The cardinal sin that has been committed by Pres. Robert Mugabe of Zimbabwe was taking the land from the white commercial farmers, and he is still paying for it. The last straw that broke the camel's back is when Britain cut off the payments to the Zimbabwean government, citing that the Land Redistribution Program was agreed upon with the previous administration and they have nothing to do with the promises that were made by the previous administration. The economic sanctions fell on Pres. Robert Mugabe's head, and the people of Zimbabwe and started starving. The population of Zimbabwe has dwindled drastically, and there are fewer Zimbabweans who are living in Zimbabwe right now than the number of Zimbabweans who are living in South Africa. Let me put it differently: there are more Zimbabweans who are living in South Africa right now than Zimbabweans who are living in the Republic of Zimbabwe. Bajabulile's uncle was a war veteran, and he also got the share of the pie, farm pie, and he is now residing in his own farm in Bulawayo and continuing with his own "selfish farming." Selfish farming is when you have fifty hectares of land but you are using only one hectare of land for agricultural activities and the rest of the farm is underutilized and the land lies in waste. That is the painful African story and the painful Zimbabwean story. Bajabulile kept me cool like a cucumber all night long, and the next thing you know, we are in Beitbridge border, and that is the border that separates South Africa from Pres. Robert Mugabe, and that is the border that separates Julius Malema from Pres. Robert Mugabe, and should I say that is the border that separates Zimbabwean war veterans from South Africa. Sometimes the Beitbridge border can be very congested with trucks trying to cross the border to Zimbabwe and Zambia and the DRC. On this night it was very quiet, and we did not spend too much time on the border, and the moment I crossed the border, I called my mother to assure her that I was already in South Africa, the Saudi Arabia of mineral resources. I could not even feel the distance between the Beitbridge and the heart of South Africa, Pretoria. I have often wondered why the Zimbabweans love Pretoria, and Nigerians too they love Pretoria with passion. The Congolese love Sandton and Johannesburg with passion. There are more Congolese in Johannesburg and Sandton than there are Congolese in DRC. The moment I arrived in Pretoria, it was 3:00 a.m. It was still dark, and there were few people walking around, and I went straight to my place and I opened the door. As usual I have to pray and thank God for keeping me alive in the whole of my journey and making me travel such a long distance without experiencing any accident. There are many things that could have happened to me while I was in Zimbabwe, specifically traveling a country that I have no prior knowledge of. The only thing that I knew about Zimbabwe was that there was no political tolerance and you are not supposed to make debasing public comments about the president Robert Mugabe because that shows disrespect to the senior citizens of the country and you might pay a heavy price for that. I have learned in the process of my journey to learn to respect and obey laws of other countries including their political structures. If there is one person whom I will never forget in the entire of my journey that is Terry. I hope you know Terry by now. He is now owning his own taxi in Harare and he is no longer driving trucks from DRC to South Africa because he got sick and nearly died on his way to DRC. I hope that one day I will meet again with Terry to discuss the politics of Zimbabwe. Terry knows what votes rigging at firsthand. I always remember his punching line: "Do you know why ZANU-PF did not celebrate their national elections victory until now? It's because they rigged the national election." I always remember that line vividly in my mind until this day. According to Terry's version of events, people who are buried in Heroes' Acre are not heroes; they are just Pres. Robert Mugabe loyalists. People who are critical of Pres. Robert Mugabe are not going to get the luxury of being buried in Heroes' Acre. It became apparently clear to me that it's a national status to be buried in Heroes' Acre. People who were buried in Heroes' Acre have a national role and a place in the Zimbabwean history. With all due respect, it appeared to me that if Terry was given an opportunity to choose between being buried in his own village and being buried in Heroes' Acre, he probably would love to be buried in Heroes' Acre because of the significance of the place. Unfortunately, Terry can never be buried in Heroes' Acre simply because he is critical of Pres. Robert Mugabe. There are many nightmares I had about going to Zimbabwe for my second trip. At one point I dreamed of being incarcerated in Zimbabwe and, the moment I woke up, and I began to reconsider my decision of going back to the Republic of Zimbabwe. My main problem was this: since I have not covered key and central areas for this book, what will I write about then? I can't just lie and talk about a place that I have never visited in my life. There is a great difference between talking about the farms without having seen the farms and talking the about the farms after you have seen the farms. In fact it's easier to talk about something that you have seen physically than to talk about something that you have not seen with your naked eye. Most Africans don't know much about Africa let alone read about the very continent that they live in. I have seen this when I was in Zimbabwe. The African youth buy books that talk about the American history. First of all, you are not an America and you are not living in America. Why not read books that talk about your forefathers rather than buy books that talk about people that you have never met people that don't have even an iota of connection with you? In fact these are the people who colonized our forefathers and threw them in prison for their land and their chickens. The Western settlers are the same people who evicted our forefathers in the fertile land that God has given our ancestors for free. The South African youth must now brace themselves to fork out hefty prices to acquire a piece of land in the land of their forefathers. Something that you were supposed to be given for free right now you have to pay for it just because of colonization. Some young people decide to stay with their parents after getting married. I personally don't condone the idea of getting married and continuing to stay with your parents while you have your wife and your children. It's better to move out and establish your own home somewhere. I need to reiterate my assertions that the West stole Africa's wealth, and had it not been for the West, most African people were going be living a better life today compared to the current social and economic life that they are currently living in the African continent. In fact there are more wars now in Africa than at any other time in the history of the African continent; there are still Western mercenary groups that are planning to ply their trade in the African continent just to keep the African continent economically unstable. The more the African continent makes two steps forward economically, unfortunately it takes six steps backward either through corruption or through the civil war that is ravaging the continent. The African people of the continent of Africa are sick and tired of the endless wars. The West is responsible for the wars that are taking place in the CAR and South Sudan. The West is responsible for the illegal economic sanctions that have been imposed in the economy of Zimbabwe and killing of people like flies. It's the West that killed Muammar Gaddafi of Libya, and there was no one who was arrested for it, and it's also the West that is responsible for the mayhem that is going on in Syria in order to dethrone Bashar al-Assad and throne their favorite candidate who will give the West more oil and more mineral resources. It's the West that was responsible for the Arab Spring. The West loves chaos and confusion, and the only thing that the West seeks is mayhem and bloodbath. Through this confusion and chaos, looting can then take place in broad daylight. Most African leaders have to buy into the Western foreign policy of colonizing the whole world through technology. The fact of the matter is this: the majority of electronic appliances and electronically equipments that are used in Africa today are either from China or from the West. Until this day and age there is no African country that is able to manufacture its own aircrafts. Most of the airplanes that are used in Africa have been bought from the West. The Boeing 747 that are always flying in and out of Africa was not manufactured in Africa, but they are Western imports. We as African people still need to go back to the political mirror and take a serious look at ourselves. The fact that we are solely dependent on the imports from the West for everything is not healthy for our future generation, and it's even not healthy for our current generation. The reason the majority of African youth can never be creative is that simply there are too much social grants that are distributed to the African youth time and again. The more people are given things for free, the more their cognitive level becomes weak and useless. Then next thing you know, you have people who can't think, but the only thing that they can think about is to look upon the government for everything, and the government becomes the big brother who should take care of them for almost every day of their lives. The future looks bright for Africa, but the future can also look even brighter if the African people can be given what belongs to them—that is, their wealth that was stolen from them through the multinational corporations by the West. For the future to look even brighter, the economic deadlock that is currently happening in the Zimbabwe should be ended, and the best way to end the economic stalemate is to lift off the illegal economic sanctions from the Zimbabwean economy. The Zimbabwean economic sanctions don't make life difficult for the Zimbabwean people only, but they also make life very difficult for the neighboring countries like South Africa and Botswana. Since the imposition of economic sanctions, the economy of Zimbabwe has been in a vegetative state, and it's likely to remain like that for a considerable amount of time unless there is divine intervention. What will happen to the number of people who are currently living in Zimbabwe? Well, it means that the Zimbabweans that are currently living in Zimbabwe will need to stop thinking with their heads and start thinking with their stomachs, and logic dictates that when there is no food in the land, you must migrate where there is food. There are reliable reports that suggest that Pres. Robert Mugabe, the leader of the Zimbabwean people, has also taken a salary cut simply because of the economic challenges that are currently facing the economy of Zimbabwe. South Africa can only do so much; there is no way that the South African government can be able to maintain the momentum of providing the Zimbabwean people with help forever. There will come a time where the South Africa bank will break in between if the Zimbabwean crisis does not get the serious attentions that it deserves. Africans are children of a single mother. What is happening in DRC affects us in South Africa whether we like it or not. Many Africans see South Africa as the country of hopes and dreams, and unfortunately South Africa has its own economic and political problems also. It's not going to be possible for South Africa to be able to look after all the African migrants from the African continent without getting financial help from somewhere. The fact of the matter is this: when there is instability in the continent of Africa, that affects the whole of the continent, not only the country concerned only. The moment the spate of wars continues unabated, that reverses the political gains that have been made already and affects adversely the very substandard infrastructure that is not even there in the first place. That is my journey and that is my story. Let me paraphrase what Paul Rususebagina said: what happens in Mozambique spills over to Zimbabwe, and what happens in Zimbabwe spills over to South Africa. The South African government and the South African people are always in the receiving end of what is happening in the West Africa and also in Central Africa. I firmly believe that the West stole Africa's wealth, and that is not wishful thinking because there is a considerable amount of evidence to support my hypothesis. I have demonstrated from the beginning of this book that there is no other agenda that the West has toward Africa except running the African continent bankrupt either through selling them African people to the West and making them slaves or paying them nothing while they work night and day enriching the West, and I have also demonstrated that the West is using foreign aid to blind African leaders to the fact that the very same foreign aid that is given to the African countries is the same money that was stolen from the African continent through the colonial era through the Western companies that are based in Africa. The African continent has political freedom without economic freedom. The only thing that most African leaders are good at is they are good at carrying the begging bowl now and then to the West. The West is responsible to make sure that the African begging bowl is filled to the brim with foreign aid and free food parcels. The African continent is not the Dark Continent and the African continent is not even the hopeless continent. The African continent was cheated its mineral resources by the West. I hope that there will come a day and a time where the West will come to its senses and realize the evil deeds that it has committed against the African people. Justice must be done even if the heavens fall, as they say in the movie *Find Me Guilty*. That is my journey and that is my story, and I have enjoyed telling this African story, and I hope that other young African people will continue to tell their own African stories instead of updating their status on Face book and Twitter accounts. The African continent needs the African youth that will manage to redress the imbalances of the past—the African youth that will understand that life does not begin on Face book and Twitter, but life begins in Africa, and the Garden of Eden was in Africa. That is why up until this day this African continent has been the subject of bloodbath and endless wars. There is no other continent in the whole world that has suffered immensely like the African continent. There is no other pleasure that surpasses the pleasure of talking to many people within a short space of time. I believe that through this book I managed to talk to the multitudes of people within a short space of time. That is my story and that is my journey. God bless Mother Africa and God bless her mineral resources.

CONCLUSION

Multiple perspectives engender multiple realities, and multiple realities divide and destroy a united nation. It is these multiple perspectives and multiple realities that I sought to harmonize and unite in order to make sure that at least there is a single acceptable political version of events. There is no single reliable political narrative about what happened in Africa during the time of colonization. It's common knowledge that the majority of African natives were not educated back then in the stone age, therefore the pain and the suffering that have been inflicted to them by the West went undocumented and unregistered in the history books. It therefore means that there are multiple incidences where the African natives were abused and misused. Whether or not it's about being abused and misused by their colonizers, those incidences were never documented and registered in the history books in order to see the light of the day. I never sought to dig the old graves and reopen the political wounds that have already healed to some African people. What I sought to bring to light is the current political problems that the majority of African countries find themselves in and the causes of these economic and political challenges. Its public knowledge that Africa was colonized by the West and the West was not colonized by Africa. It's public knowledge that the West during its colonial project did not seek to sustain it through cheap labor, but it sought to sustain it through killing people that were against colonization and political oppression. Colonization is over and slavery is over, but the remnants of colonization still remain with the African people up until this point. Just like the remnants of the apartheid still remain with many South Africans until this point, so is the damage that has been caused by Ian Smith to the people of Zimbabwe. Prior to my visit to Zimbabwe, I was under the impression that the Zimbabwean infrastructure was that of the West, and

I was taken aback when I got to Zimbabwe to see the already dilapidated buildings. Most of the African countries are still underdeveloped, and they will need a considerable amount of financial resources to build the world-class infrastructure that was not even there in the first place. Africa's colonizers were not only cruel and greedy but also evil and destructive. There are no African countries that have world-class infrastructure that they can boast about and continue to relish which has been left behind by the African colonizers. When the African liberation movements took over from their colonial masters, they did nothing to improve the lives of the ordinary people except stole from the very people that they claim to empower and develop economically. The infrastructure collapse is visible all over Africa. The French colonized Central African Republic. When the French were fed up with the mineral resources that they have extracted from the CAR, they just left the bottomless pit on the ground and they did nothing positive and constructive to the development of the people of CAR and to the infrastructure of CAR. The same is true with Portugal in Mozambique. There is nothing that the Mozambican people can hold on to after the civil wars, which ripped the country apart. The things that are left behind are poverty, unemployment, and diseases. It's important to register this point because Africa's colonizers often blame the government of the African nationalists that they are responsible for Africa's dearth of infrastructure and underdevelopment. There is nothing that the African liberation movements could have done differently economically and politically, since most of the African liberation movements have only discovered that the infrastructure that has been left behind by Africa's colonizers had collapsed. Most of the African liberation movements spent too much time in the bush. Even after the African armed struggle was over, they were not mentally out of the bush, though they were out of the bush physically. Let me put it differently: since most of the African liberation movements spent a considerable amount of time in the bush owing to the African armed struggle that was fought in the bush, it became very difficult for African liberation movements to readjust their political and economic ambitions to what was happening on the ground. There are pressing needs for African liberation movements to conduct a thorough introspection as to whether or not they achieved what they sought to achieve economically and politically through the armed struggle, and what is it that can be done now to make up for the shortfall? It's public knowledge now that Africans are still languishing in poverty and they don't even live longer because of poverty that is ravaging the continent of Africa. It's also public knowledge that the infrastructure system that is available in most African countries is appalling if not pathetic. If you visit some of the African countries, you are likely to ask yourself this question: How do these people survive here in these bad living conditions? I think that is why African Americans hate Africa with passion, though they are black and they are from Africa, because when they look at the African infrastructure compared to that of the West, Africa's infrastructure is bad if not pathetic. The fact of the matter is this: though the African Americans hate the continent of Africa with passion, even some of the African people that are dwelling in the continent of Africa, the fact remains that Africa is the only home for Africans. That is why now and then African Americans are always associated with crime and violence in the United States because of the continent of Africa where they are originally from. Hating where you come from does not change anything. I have learned to love the continent of Africa with its economic and political problems. The best way to love yourself is to love the social environment where you are living. It does not therefore mean that Africans of the continent of Africa should be content and be satisfied with the present economic and political problems that are facing the African continent. But for the sake of long life and to avoid unnecessary stress that is killing people all over the world, it's better to accept the social environment where you are living and accept yourself the way you are. I have said many times that political problems present this African generation with an opportunity to learn and grow. Problems are meant to strengthen and improve our problem solving skills, and not meant to destroy us completely. It's through solving political and economic problems where one becomes a leader of his people and the leader of a nation. My point is running away from one country to another because of economic and political problems do not help either. There is no country in the world that does not have political and economic problems. No country in the world is immune from economic and political problems. My overall objective of narrowing down this multiplicity of perspectives that engender multiple realities is because of the divergent of political narratives that are now and then confusing and misleading especially to the youth of my generation. Times are changing, and the nature of politics is changing also. Though times are changing and politics is changing, political problems don't change. The problems of unemployment and landlessness are the primeval problems that have not yet been solved up until this day and age. Though times have changed, the problems that were faced by the previous African generations are still the same problems that are facing the current

African generation. Nothing is new in Africa. The African people have come to the point of realization of accepting the status quo as the norm. I am an optimistic person. I don't believe that we Africans should wail and weep all night long as if things are not going to change in the near future. Africa will rise one day and Africa we will be the superpower of the world one day. Though this dream seems like a pipe dream, it will come to pass one day. Inferiority complex can limit one's potential to see his dream turning into reality. It is inferiority complex that I think the majority of Africans are suffering from that is limiting Africa's potential to grow in leaps and bounds. That is why in this day and age Africa is the only continent that is foreign aid dependent. In fact Africa is the foreign-aid-dependent continent. There is no other continent on the face of the earth that is dependent on the Western foreign aid like the African continent. Africans have assimilated the idea of foreign aid as the only solution to the African economic and political problems. The main reason corruption and fraud in Africa are spreading like Mozambican mosquitoes are the foreign aid that is coming from the West. It's also true that the West is using foreign aid to contain Africa's potential to grow in leaps and bounds. It's of paramount importance that I reemphasize that the main reason I wrote this book was to inform and educate the young African generation about Africa's past while focusing on the future. It's of pivotal importance to reemphasize that my main objective of writing this book was not to reopen the old graves and old wounds of some of the Zimbabwean people who have already healed because of the troubling past of the Zimbabwean history. It will be unfair and unjust to provide a considerable amount of information about the farm invasion and then leave this thorny issue hanging in the air without providing necessary conclusion that it deserves. It's public knowledge that there is a considerable amount of land in Zimbabwe that lies underutilized until this point. It's also common knowledge that the Zimbabwean government is under severe financial stress whether it's a lack of financial muscles to pay the civil servants in time or to craft a holistic plan to ensure that the vast tract of land that lies underutilized is used to the benefit for the ordinary Zimbabweans. The economic sanctions have brought the economy of Zimbabwe to its knees, and there is no doubt about that. It's also true that the farm invasion is the instigator of the economic sanctions of February 18, 2002, though the farm invasion occurred before the economic sanctions were imposed. It's unfair and unjust to deal with farm invasion and the economic sanctions separately as if the two issues are not related. The fact of the matter is this: there would not have been economic sanctions, whether they are called illegal economic sanctions or legal economic sanctions, if it was not for the farm invasion of 2000.

Dumisani Muleya, the editor of the *Zimbabwe Independent,* writes:

> *Whenever Mugabe and his government have been unable to or unwilling to do something, they have a pretext sanctions. Just about everything that can or has gone wrong in Zimbabwe in recent years is dishonestly explained in terms of sanctions. That is why Mugabe and his loyalists now claim the economy has been ruined by sanctions, even if everybody, including themselves, actually knows it's mainly their corrupt and incompetent regime that has destroyed the economy.*[1]

It's public knowledge that due to the economic sanctions and the farm invasion of 2000 there are horrible stories that took place in Zimbabwe whether it's about the Marange diamond fields or the cancer of corruption in the Zimbabwean government without Pres. Robert Mugabe being privy to the acts of corruption. Nevertheless, it will be unfair and unjust to draw an inference that says the economic collapse of Zimbabwe came about as a result of the corrupt and incompetent regime that was running the economy. There is a symbiotic relationship between the economic sanctions that were imposed on February 18, 2002, and the farm invasion of 2000, just as there is a symbiotic relationship between the economy of Zimbabwe and the regime that is currently heading the government of Zimbabwe. There is nothing that the government of Zimbabwe can do differently to lift the economic sanctions from the economy of Zimbabwe except to relinquish political power and allow the West to do as it wishes in Zimbabwe. The point is as long as the government of ZANU-PF stays in power, the economic sanctions will also remain in place. It was in the grand plan of the West that once the economic sanctions were in place in Zimbabwe, the people of Zimbabwe and the economy of Zimbabwe were going to scream to the point that even the people of Zimbabwe would eventually blame Pres. Robert Mugabe and his regime because of hunger and poverty. Economic sanctions were designed to bring Zimbabwean political regime to its knees until the point that the regime that is in charge of the Zimbabwean government would kneel down to the West and ask for forgiveness of sins. Economic sanctions have been designed to destroy the people's hope about life and about the future. Economic sanctions have been designed to suffocate the economy and the lives of the ordinary people until there is a political solution and political transformation. One of the reasons why the economy of Zimbabwe was hit hard by the economic sanctions is not only the unwillingness and the corruption by the Zimbabwean government officials but also the problem of Land Redistribution Program, what I call land redistribution problem. It's important not to lose sight of the crucial chain of political events, wherein I think the majority of people during the course of time normally become relaxed and forget the source of the problems and focus purely on the problem itself without attempting to understand and address the source of the problem. Africa's problems have been caused by the West, whether the majority of Africans that are in the continent of Africa and even those that are not in the continent of Africa agree or disagree with this notion. The West has its economic grip in Africa's economy, and there is nothing that the majority of African leaders can do about it. Most of the African leaders know it deep down from the center of their hearts that Africa's problems didn't originate from the African continent, but they originated from the West, and should the African leaders dare to attempt to reverse the injustice of the past by seeking reparation from the West, the West could just simply impose economic sanctions indiscriminately to any Africa country that seeks reparation from the West. During the Mau Mau insurgence in Kenya, when Mau Mau victims complained to the West that they were tortured during the colonial era by the Western forces, as a result they are now crippled and paralyzed because of the pain and suffering sustained during the colonial era. They were given compensation to buy their silence. At least there were no economic sanctions that were imposed to Kenya. It's important to notice that it's not the Kenyan government that was seeking reparation from the West, but it was the Mau Mau victims. Opposite is the case in the scenario of Zimbabwe. The regime of Pres. Robert Mugabe sought Britain and the United States of America to honor and fund the Land Redistribution Program, which was agreed upon in the Lancaster House Agreement in 1979. The United States and Britain knew it very well from the onset that they were not going to stick to their promise of funding the Land Redistribution Program. What the United States and Great Britain planned to do during the course of time was to seek the regime change that will never ever reopen the history books and read the Lancaster House Agreement promises and the lies that were written in it. Through the Lancaster House Agreement, the United States and Britain managed to end the war and to lift the economic sanctions that were imposed by Britain to Ian Smith regime and to restore peace and tranquility in Zimbabwe. Through the Lancaster House Agreement, the African nationalists were parachuted to the highest echelons of government. Since the Zimbabwean nationalists were from the bush and had been denied natural pleasure for a considerable amount of time, when the Zimbabwe nationalists went to head the government, they forgot their overall objective of the political armed struggle, and the Zimbabwean nationalists began to befriend the West and started wining and dining with the West in the spirit of reconciliation and unity. As long as the land in Zimbabwe was held by the few and privileged, there was nothing wrong. But as soon as the war veterans began to wake up and smell the coffee that the Lancaster House Agreement was a trap, it was a little too late. The United States and Britain were on their destructive path to oust the government of Pres. Robert Mugabe and ZANU-PF and the same African nationalists that they have entered into the Lancaster House Agreement with by funding a new political party. It's public knowledge that the West will go an extra mile if they seek a regime change. The West can either form a new political party and fund it and change the current regime that is heading the government or oust the government through a coup. When I come to think of the Zimbabwean government and the tenure of Pres. Robert Mugabe of Zimbabwe, he should count himself lucky among the majority of African leaders. If I cast my eyes wide open to the northern part of Africa, I once asked myself this question: How come Pres. Robert Mugabe managed to stay in power for such a long period of time without having being ousted by the West? The West can oust any political leader of any country as long as that leader is refusing to take orders from the West. It baffles my mind as to how the West became extremely enraged by the fact that the president of Uganda Yoweri Museveni signed into law the antigay bill. The West was enraged at the president of Uganda Yoweri Museveni as if the guy was planning to manufacture weapons of mass destruction. When the late Libyan leader Muammar Gaddafi was ousted from political power and eventually killed and buried, the world thought that Libya was going to be a peaceful country headed by the regime that will be pro-Western and that will continue to sell oil to the West at a low price, while the West at the same time is continuing to kill Zimbabweans with hunger and diseases. Since the death of Muammar Gaddafi, Libya is the most unstable African country in the African continent, though Libya is rich in oil. There is no doubt in my mind that as soon as Libya degenerated into a war, economic opportunities will dwindle and there will be massive capital flight as a result of political instability and economic instability. It's imperative to comprehend thoroughly that political stability in Africa opens the window of economic opportunities, and political instability shuts down this window of economic opportunities. The West is quite aware that for the African continent to remain as a begging continent, it should remain locked up in endless wars because wars bring about political instability and engender economic instability. Africa will remain where it is economic if there is no long-lasting political stability. I would not have done justice to the issue of land if I don't address it now in my conclusion, though it's imperative to mention that this book is not about land but it's about Africa's wealth that was stolen by the West. However, there is a symbiotic relationship between land and economic freedom. South African natives whose land was dispossessed by the apartheid government have not until this point received their land back in totality. Zimbabweans from whom their land was taken by the Ian Smith government until this day and age have not yet gotten back their land in totality. South African Land Redistribution Program is moving at snail's pace, and what has been abundantly clear in the process is the fact that some South Africans communities, due to pressure and poverty, have entered into weird deals, like receiving coupons rather than getting their land. Though I have addressed the land issue and saw the land crisis, it's imperative to make mention that until this point in time, this issue of land will forever haunt many Africans even in the near future until and unless it's properly addressed. The one-million-dollar question is this: Are we Africans of the continent of Africa politically and economically free if we have not yet received our land back that was taken from us by Western settlers? The answer is a resounding no. We Africans will be politically and economically free if we will receive back the land that was stolen from us and not sell our land through coupons and vouchers of R30, 000. The freedom charter of the ANC, which the ANCYL of Julius Malema heavy relied upon in its economic policy of the nationalization of mines and expropriation of land without compensation, echoed the principles of sharing the land. The land shall be shared among those who work it.[5] The issue of land in South Africa still remains a big problem, and the main reason the majority of South Africans are not even bored paying undivided attention to the issue of land is that they are worried about the next big tender that might be advertised in the *Tender Bulletin*. The Zimbabweans, however, got their land back, and there is nothing that they did about their land simply because they got the land ill-prepared and ill-trained to cultivate the land. It's important to strike a very delicate balance between communal land and land for farming. It will be sheer madness to take the land that is feeding a considerable amount of people and resettle communities without an acceptable alternative. Let me put it differently: land that is used for farming purposes should not be taken and be given to communities for communal reasons unless proper and adequate measures have been put in place to continue the supply of food. I suggest that there was a misunderstanding between the ANCYL of Julius Malema and the ANC itself about the issue of land; without any shadow of a doubt, this misunderstanding did play itself out in the public domain. The ANCYL of Julius Malema seemed to be suggesting that South African land should be expropriated without compensation from the white commercial farmers who got their land illegally through apartheid government. It's public knowledge that the majority of South African land is still owned by the Anglo-Saxons, and the majority of black people are plunged up together in the townships and villages where there are no newspapers and running water let alone the issue of clinics and hospitals. Just like the Zimbabwean Land Redistribution Program, it became the land redistribution problem, so is the South Africa Land Restitution Program has become the land restitution problem. I need to make one thing simply clear and straightforward: there is no logical basis and logical reasoning to expropriate land from white commercial farmers and give it to the black people if they have not yet been trained to cultivate the land to the benefit of the country. Logical reasoning and political sanity are required in order to put the issue of land to bed. It's excruciatingly painful to see a black community dwelling in an uninhabitable area where there is no water, electricity, and tarred roads because of the deeds of the apartheid government. It's excruciatingly painful to see the Zimbabweans sleeping on the streets of Pretoria and inside the Methodist church in Johannesburg because of the Land Redistribution Program. The ANCYL of Julius Malema seemed to be advocating for the fast track of expropriation of land without compensation regardless of proper and structured program to cultivate the land after it has been expropriated from the white commercial farmers. Let me put it differently: farmland and communal land should be differentiated. There is no logical and reasonable basis to seize land from the white commercial farmers and then give it to the black community if that black community is not properly trained to cultivate the land to the benefit of the masses. That is the same mistake that the war veterans, "the brothers of destruction," made. There was no government plan and program that was put in place to cultivate the land after the fast track of land reform has taken place. The same mistake that the war veterans of Zimbabwe made was the same mistake that the ANCYL of Julius Malema was committing. When the ANCYL realized that its economic policy could not be integrated to the policy of the ANC to become part and parcel of the government economic policy, it became rebellious and bitter toward the ANC itself. I have addressed this issue before, but due to its sensitivity and its paramount importance, it warrants sufficient attention. Land is wealth whether we Africans like it or not. The Zimbabwean war veterans got tired of Pres. Robert Mugabe's Land Redistribution Program, which was slow and yielding no practical solutions to the economic problems and to the landless hence the farm invasion took place. The argument that suggests that the main reason the Zimbabwean war veterans took the land from the white commercial farmers is that they were poor and illiterate owing to the fact the only thing that they knew were machine guns and the war, holds no water whatsoever. What could have happened then had the ANC heeded the call of the ANCYL? It's inevitable and public knowledge that had the ANC heeded the call of the ANCYL, economic sanctions were going to fall on the South African economy and the majority of people were going to be plunged into the bottomless pit of poverty. The question is this: How do I know that had the ANC heeded the call of expropriation of land without compensation, the international community was going to impose economic sanctions to the economy of South Africa? The answer to that question is look at Zimbabwe, what happened to it after its fast track of land reform coupled with violence. Africans are prone to violence even if there is no need to act violent sometimes. I remembered vividly while I was in the university, at one point, students embarked on what was called "peaceful protest." The fact of the matter is this: there is nothing called peaceful protest in Africa. During our so-called peaceful protest, a certain gentleman by the name of Martin took the stage and said, "This is a peaceful march, but we must put a little bit of spices on this march." Indeed the students heeded his call and put in a little bit of spices, and mayhem followed and the police came; as they say, the rest is history. There is no way the fast track of expropriation of land without compensation would have occurred under the leadership of the ANCYL without a little bit of spices, and the spice is violence. To prove that indeed the ANCYL could not have managed the expropriation of land without compensation without some bit of spices, when the ANC had rejected the economic policy of the ANCYL to form part and parcel of the ANC policy and later to become the government policy, the ANCYL began to sing a song that incited violence, like "Shoot the farmer." The ANCYL lost its precious moment in the history of South Africa to redress the imbalances of the past due to its hasty and impatient approach to political issues. The vision and mission was good, but the execution was bad. It was good economic policy executed in a bad way, and until this day in South Africa the issue of nationalization of mines and expropriation of land without compensation has died its slow political death. The large junk of the South African wealth still remains in the hands of the few and those who are politically connected in high places and the rest of the people are still stuck in the bucket system until the end of time. Most of the African liberation movements, once they assume government, normally reject and forget the very same core economic and political principles that they were advocating for during the armed struggle. These African liberation movements began to realize that there is a great difference between being in government and having to look after the nation and being an oppositional party. The fact of the matter is most political parties, when they win national election, don't even dare to implement the same economic policies that they were advocating for once they assume power in government. This practice is not an African phenomenon, but it is practiced all over the world. Politics then becomes a game of promises and lies. It's of vital importance to differentiate between an economic policy that was properly planned and that can be properly implemented and an economic policy that is half- baked and sought to be used as an economic tool to score political points. It's better to craft an economic policy that will be implementable and will yield long-lasting economic benefits to the people than to craft an economic policy out of anger and rage, which will thrust a considerable amount of people to the bottomless pit of poverty. Harold Greene, a Pan-African activist based in Los Angeles, writes:

> *Despite the continuous racist and hominem attacks against Pres. Robert Mugabe, coupled with economic sanctions in an attempt to destroy Zimbabwe's land reform agenda, land reform in Zimbabwe is moving along with considerable degree of success. As evidenced in a host of books and reports published in recent years, most notably Zimbabwe's Fast Track Land Reform by Prosper B. Matondi and Zimbabwe Takes Its Land Back by Joseph Hanlon, Zimbabwe's land reform, in spite of its tumultuous and long-overdue start, has resulted in hundreds of*

> *thousands of black Zimbabweans becoming new and successful farmers. These reports dispel the racist myths about farming and food shortage due to failing black farms.*[2]

I have great difficulties with Harold Greene's assertion simply because I have been in Zimbabwe and I have conducted a considerable amount of interviews prior to the national election of July 31, 2013, and post–national election of July 31, 2013. Surely the views that Harold Greene expresses are based on his own understanding of Zimbabwe's Fast-Track Land Reform. I vehemently reject the assertion that says that "land reform, in spite of its tumultuous and long-overdue start, has resulted in hundreds of thousands of black Zimbabweans becoming new and successful black farmers." It's imperative to add new knowledge to the old knowledge. While it's imperative to add new knowledge to the old knowledge, we Africans of the continent of Africa should write our African stories and African history and be brutally honest with ourselves in our own writing. It's useless and it adds no value in continuing to praise our own African leaders even if they blatantly failed simply because we will appear as traitors or sell-outs to the West if we criticize them publicly. That is why most Africa scholars have divorced themselves from the politics of the African continent and channeled the entire of their efforts to the politics of the West because of the lack of honesty and fairness among African writers. There is no monopoly of knowledge and monopoly of understanding. It continues to baffle me even to this day as to why we Africans of the continent continue to praise our African leaders and praise their half-baked economic policy even if we Africans from the continent of African can clearly see that these economic policies have failed drastically and have achieved nothing tangible but plunged in a considerable amount of people into the bottomless pit of poverty. If Zimbabwe's Fast-Track Land Reform has been successful, then how come five million Zimbabweans immigrated to South Africa, and as I write this book they are selling fake CDs on the streets of Pretoria? If Zimbabwe's Fast-Track Land Reform has been successful, how come even to this day and age there is still a considerable amount of vast tract of land that lies underutilized in Zimbabwe? The truth of the matter is this: Zimbabwe is in very precarious positions than even before right now. Poverty and unemployment still reign supreme in Zimbabwe. When the GPA was still in place, at least the government could even afford to pay the civil servants on time. Post-GPA its prayers and fasting that will save the Zimbabwean people from the impending destruction from poverty. The West stole Africa's wealth and left Africa in a prison of poverty and hopelessness. The fact is she (Mother Africa) is still in economic bondage. She might be politically free, but she is not economically free from the bondage of the West. The West gave Africa a raw deal. The land, gold, diamonds, and all precious metals are continuing to benefit the West at the expense of the African people. The book written by Prof. Joseph Hanlon *Zimbabwe Takes Its Land Back* has been used more frequent than not by the proponents of Fast-Track Land Reform, and the same book has been criticized vehemently by the critics of Zimbabwe's Fast-Track Land Reform. The same book has been quoted by Harold Greene, who is based in Los Angeles, as evidence to support the notion that Zimbabwe's Fast-Track Land Reform was a success. Tony Hawkins, the professor of economics at the Graduate School of Management at the University of Zimbabwe, who is a critic of Joseph Hanlon, writes:

> *The fact that thirteen years after the Land Reform Program, the same men and women—in politics, business, government, and the security services—are using precisely the same language condoning if not glorifying such conduct. Hanlon et al. has demonstrated that in their view, the ends justify the means. In the process, they ignored 60 percent of the Zimbabwe population that live in poverty and the 50 percent (minimum) formally unemployed while simultaneously demonstrating their ignorance of the crucial role of strong institutions in the development process.*[3]

It's surprising to me as a South African that there are Zimbabweans who see Zimbabwe's Land Reform Program as a success, while there are those who see Zimbabwe's Land Reform Program as a mess. From the South African standpoint, if the Zimbabwe Land Reform Program was a success as the proponents of Zimbabwe's Land Reform Program claim, how come there are more than five million Zimbabweans in the streets of Pretoria and Johannesburg selling fake CDs trying to make a living? How come there are more than two thousand Zimbabwean teachers teaching in the South Africa schools? There is no province out of the nine provinces of South Africa (Kwazulu Natal, Mpumalanga, Limpopo, Free State, Northern Cape, Eastern Cape, North West, Western Cape, and Gauteng) where there are no Zimbabwe's teachers. That is the main reason the ANCYL could not get its economic policy, expropriation of land without compensation, and nationalization of mines to be the policy of the ANC, and had it been adopted by the ANC, it was going to be the South African government policy. It's inevitable that the ANC had monitored closely what had happened in Zimbabwe's Land Reform Program, and fear and trepidation consumed the ANC including the people of South Africa. Zimbabwe's land reform fiasco had grinded to a screeching halt the South African Land Restitution Program, though many South Africans might hold an opposite view about this matter. Zimbabwe's Land Reform Program was the cause for the xenophobic attacks that took place in 2008 and 2009 in many locations of South Africa, and it's also true that the political instability of the West African region was also a compounding factor. Human beings are not immune to political mistakes, and political leaders are not exonerated from this category. It goes without saying then that mistakes happened in Zimbabwe's Land Reform Program, and pointing fingers at one another and playing the blame game cannot even further add anything to the stale debate of Land Reform Program. The main question that the majority of the African people should ask themselves is this: Are we Africans ready to govern and take charge of the African continent, and do our African leaders know what they are doing, or are they just fiddling in the dark and experimenting with the lives of innocent people? I have asked one Zimbabwean who is based in Johannesburg about his take on the issue of land reform, and he puts the whole land reform saga on the shoulders of the Zimbabwean government, and I also understood his line of thinking simply because he is a Ndebele not a Shona. I have noticed a great chasm between Shonas and Ndebeles and their political views about the Zimbabweans politics, and I have also noticed some Zimbabweans' aloofness toward the Zimbabwean domestic politics. The fact of the matter is this: if truth be told, the majority of the Shonas were in support of Zimbabwe's land reform, and I should also mention the fact that not all Shonas are members of the ZANU-PF, but in general Shonas were in favor of the Land Reform Program. Mr. Milkshake, who is a PhD student in the University of Kwazulu Natal, despite his level of education, is a staunch supporter of Zimbabwe's Land Reform Program, and he blames the West for not providing funding to the Zimbabwean government for the purchasing of land from the white commercial farms, and he sees nothing wrong with what the Zimbabwean government did. Mr. Brown, who is a Shona also from Zimbabwe, normally blames the Zimbabwean government about the Land Reform Program, but he does not express his dissenting views publicly in the presence of Mr. Milkshake, though they are both Shonas because of the fear and trepidation to be seen as a traitor by Mr. Milkshake. The question that springs forth to mind many times is this: Has Africans of the African continent learned a valuable lesson from Zimbabwe's Land Reform Program, or is it just business as usual? It will be unfair and unjust to stoop too low to the point where the whole Zimbabwe's economic and political problems are squarely placed on the shoulders of Pres. Robert Mugabe as if he is the messiah who supposed to save the perishing souls of the masses. My argument is this: though he was a leader of the Zimbabwean people who took them out of the political captivity and economic captivity of Ian Smith and apartheid laws, he still leading them even right now through this valley of death that the Zimbabwean people are going through. It is unfair and unjust then to conclude that had it not been for the bad leadership of Pres. Robert Mugabe, the people of Zimbabwe would be living a better life than the life that they are currently living. It's also possible that along the way Pres. Robert Mugabe got tired of leading his people, since there is a leadership bankruptcy in the African continent and in Zimbabwe for that matter, and he had to stay even if his time to vacate his leadership position had come. Good leaders don't overstay their welcome in their leadership position. While they are in their prime of their leadership, they coach and mentor other young up-and-coming leaders. That is exactly what the late president of South Africa Nelson Mandela did. The former president of South Africa Thabo Mbeki is a product of the mentorship that was provided by both the late Nelson Mandela and the late Oliver Tambo. It's politically correct and politically true that had it not been for the leadership and the mentorship of the late president Nelson Mandela and the late ANC president Oliver Tambo that was provided to former president Thabo Mbeki, he would have fought tooth and nail when the ANC recalled him in 2008. Due to the entrenched political and leadership values that former president Thabo Mbeki acquired through the mentorship of Oliver Tambo and Nelson Mandela, he became a truly South African son and a servant of his people. However, opposite is the case in Zimbabwe. The mentorship program was nonexistent then, and it is still nonexistent even at this point in time. It's common knowledge now that Pres. Robert Mugabe is old and fragile, yet the succession debate is still not yet open. The South African Land Redistribution Program has been moving at a snail's pace and sometimes not even moving at all. Due to this snail's pace and tortoise movement of the South African Land Redistribution Program, it is sometimes confusing because it is sometimes called Land Redistribution Program, and the minute one grasps the concept of Land Redistribution Program, the government changes it to Land Redistribution for Agricultural Development. One of the reasons why the Land Reform Program took a very long time to be completed in South Africa is the constitutional constraints that are espoused in the constitution of South Africa. The constitution of any country is good to the point that it expedites the process of service delivery to the people. However, the constitution of any country is not good to the point that it grinds to a screeching halt the process of service delivery to the people. What is the use of the constitution if people are landless just because there are constitutional clauses and precepts that should be fulfilled before land can be distributed to the people? When the apartheid government dispossessed the land from my grandparents, there was no constitution that was followed; it was only guns and bullets and dogs that the apartheid government used. I am by no means suggesting that it should be tooth for a tooth and eye for an eye. It's of fundamental importance to register this point for the future generation that the constitution of South Africa is good enough to the point that it expedites the process of delivering essential services to the people of South Africa. If the South African constitution is not assisting in expediting the process of delivering the essential services to the ordinary people, then it warrants an overhaul. There are political parties that have been formed in South Africa merely to protect the South African constitution as if the South African constitution is the document that has been imported from heaven. The fact of the matter is this: the South African constitution is the product of the South African people, and I see no reason and logical soundness whatsoever to form a political party to protect and shield a document that has been assembled by the South African people. I should also say that there had been a wave of madness at one point in South Africa where ordinary people were using the South African constitution in an inappropriate way to justify their misdemeanors and theft. The freedom of expression, which is also contained in the bill of rights, sometimes is inappropriately and incorrectly used to settle political scores in the mainstream media under the pretext of exercising the freedom of expression. There are three spheres of government in South Africa: the national government, the provincial government, and the local government. Without going into details, these three spheres of government should work in harmony and not in silos. It's common knowledge now that these three spheres of government more often than not sometimes fight among each other for hegemony and power. The same is true with the judiciary system.

The main reason Zimbabwe's Land Reform Program was not easy to be implemented is that the high court orders were overlooked, and the state men and state women became law to themselves, and mayhem erupted. Let me make this point crystal clear: there is no need for a judiciary system to hold government in ransom as if the judiciary system and judiciary officers have been voted for by the electorate. The executive has all the power to govern and run the country because it's the executive that has been voted by the electorate not the judiciary officers. Separation of power is a very critical aspect to comprehend thoroughly in order to deal once and for all with the issue of South African land reform thoroughly. What is abundantly clear to all Africans is this: even after the end of the African liberation struggle, there has not been sufficient and adequate measures in place to ensure that the issue of land is addressed once and for all. There is a leadership vacuum in many African countries attributed to the fact that African leaders are addicted to power and glamour. It's common knowledge that if you are a political leader of any African country, you earn a celebrity status and you get incessantly media attention. That is what makes African leaders feel as if they are now demigods and should be worshipped by the masses. The very same African leaders that have been voted for by the electorate are now detached and isolated from the very masses that they claim to lead and serve.

The Southern Times reports:

> *In his memoirs, The Great Betrayal, Rhodesian last Prime Minister Ian Douglas Smith speaks of receiving "an interesting briefing" in 1976. The briefing was from Rhodesia Security Council and was about "the communist plan for Africa, as part of their overall scheme for world domination." Smith said a map was produced that showed the "communists had firmly established themselves in a number of countries in North Africa, methodically moving on to new ground once a base had been secured." He wrote, "The ultimate target was South Africa, which was not only the industrial giant of Africa, but was one of the mostly richly mineralized parts of the world. It was a few years later that I was pleased to receive a report that the United States had been alerted to this development and, as a result, their Congress Committee on Strategic Minerals and Mining had sent a mission to investigate." After visiting*

> *Zaire (now the DRC), Zambia, Rhodesia (now Zimbabwe), and South Africa, they produced a commendable report and in most expressive language termed the area "the Persian Gulf of strategic minerals of our earth."*[4]

There is ample amount of evidence to compel the West to the International Criminal Court for the theft and looting that happened in Africa. Not only had the West conspired among itself to bankrupt Africa, but also the African leaders who were seen to be standing in the way for the West were eliminated on the spot. The West stole Africa's wealth, and the stealing is now happening under our watch and there is nothing that the current African leaders can do about it. Because these African leaders have allowed the Western companies to have a deep and firm grip on Africa's economy to the point that grinding the process to a screeching halt simply means that the multitude of innocent men and women must lose their jobs. Africa is politically free on paper, but in practice, Africa is still in the economic slavery from the West. African leaders were given political power by the West, and the West remained with economic power, and that is a raw deal. It's like giving a person a car with an empty fuel tank; Africa is the car and the fuel is the West. We all know that there is nothing that a motorist can do with a car that is with an empty fuel tank. For the car to move, it needs fuel, and if there is no fuel, then there is no movement, and the one who owns fuel owns the world. That is why the West does not want to lose control of oil-rich countries. The Nigerian crisis is the oil crisis, and the Iraqi crisis is the oil crisis, just like the Syrian crisis is the oil crisis. Everywhere in the world where there is oil there is spilling of blood and the West loves it because it will eventually have a firm grip on the oil. When Saddam Hussein was still the president of Iraq, he never allowed the West to deepen its ugly economic grip on his oil, and the West eliminated Saddam Hussein because he was a hindrance to the oil project. The DRC War doesn't come to an end completely; it just paused temporarily, only to resume later. The Congolese are now immune from the pain that is inflicted by the war. In fact the Congolese have accepted the war as their way of life, just like the Zimbabweans have learned to embrace economic sanctions as their way of life. The same is true also in Libya; the killing of Muammar Gaddafi turned Libya into a valley of death, where there is no rule of law and government institutions have collapsed diametrically. The West hates Africa's peace and prosperity. The West rejoices and jubilates when Africans are fighting among each other like dogs fighting for a bone of meat. African leaders have great difficulties in condemning the Western cruel actions against Iraq or Syria because should African leaders blame the West on violent crimes committed against the Syrian people and Iraqi people, these African leaders are likely to lose foreign aid for their countries and their people will starve. When the president of Uganda Yoweri Museveni decided to sign into law the antigay bill, the West made its intention known that it will withhold foreign aid that was meant for the government of Yoweri Museveni. Foreign aid that is given to African countries is inextricably linked to homosexuality, in other words, African leaders like Pres. Robert Mugabe of Zimbabwe, even if Zimbabwe was not under economic sanctions, Zimbabwe would not make a killing through foreign aid because of the Zimbabwean government stance toward homosexuality. Legalization of homosexuality according to the Western gospel is a clear indication of advancement of democracy. I have a very big problem with such line of thinking. The rationale that in democracy everything is free—you do as you want and you love whomever you want to love whether male or female—is problematic. The land issue in South Africa and in Zimbabwe is a political issue, and it will require concerted effort to solve it once and for all at least for the future generation. It's common knowledge that African poverty is a generational poverty, just like the land issue is now a generation problem. If the current Zimbabwean government can put the issue of land to bed, then it will not have to be dealt with by future Zimbabwean generation. If South African land reform can't be solved diametrically by the current South African government, then it will have to be dealt with by the future generation. My main problem with the future generation is this: a lot will change in the future to the point that it will be very difficult in the near future for the future generation to pursue an old political problem that should have been solved in the past by the current African leaders. This book only pays undivided attention only to Zimbabwe and South Africa, and that does not necessarily mean that African countries that have not been covered in this book have registered success as far as land reform is concerned. Jon Swaine writes:

> *A coalition of fourteen Caribbean states, including Jamaica, agrees with Thompson and is now mounting the first united campaign for reparations from Britain over its role in the Atlantic slave trade. The group is ready to sue in the courts and has hired Leigh Day, the London Law firm that last year won £20 million for Kenyans tortured during the Mau*

> *Mau rebellion of the 1950s. This month it will unveil a list of demands for Britain, France, and Netherlands, including funds likely to total billions, an apology, and assurance that slavery will never be repeated. Prof. Verene Shepherd, the chairman of Jamaica's reparations committee, said British colonizers have "disfigured the Caribbean" and that their descendants must now pay to repair the damage. "If you commit a crime against humanity, you are bound to make amends."*

He went on to say,

> *From the mid-eighteenth century, British merchants shipped more than three million people from West Africa to America, taking the lead in a slave trade pioneered by the Dutch and Portuguese. About £4 trillion was extracted from the region in unpaid labor alone, according to researchers at the University of Birmingham, and the vast profits went to financing the construction of the modern Britain.*[5]

I have already said before that the skyscrapers that are in the West have been built by African slaves with the proceeds that have been extracted in the African soil. The West stole Africa's wealth, and now the West is stealing oil from the Middle East. It's not wishful thinking or an impromptu idea that I have just pulled out of the air. I knew what I was talking about from the beginning of this book. I know very well that some people will say, "But African leaders are also corrupt." Africa's future generation will have more financial challenges than the current African generation is facing. It's possible that in the near future the West will have new set of political leaders that will not buy into the idea of distributing foreign aid and food parcels to Africa. When these new Western leaders take office, they will not even recognize the injustices of the past that were committed against the African people by the West. Africa then will be in a very big trouble then than it is now. At least even if the current African leaders have failed in many aspects they are still managing to get foreign aid from the West including the cheap blankets from the United Nations World Food Programme. The future African leaders will be cut off from the supply of foreign aid, and the West will say, "We have given Africa too much foreign aid and food parcels. It's time that Africa learns to be economically independent." These words will come from the future Western leaders who will not buy into the theory of foreign aid and food parcels. When Tony Blair became the prime minister of Britain, he discontinued the funding of the Land Reform Program, which has been agreed upon in the Lancaster House Agreement in 1979. The Zimbabweans gave Tony Blair a new name; they call him "Tony B. Liar." Whether the former Britain prime minister is Tony B. Liar or Tony Blair, that does not change the fact that he discontinued the funding of Land Reform Program, and when Pres. Robert Mugabe and "the brothers of destruction," known as the Zimbabwe war veterans, invaded the white commercial farms and seized them, the economic sanction ax fell on the Zimbabwe economy, and the people started dying like flies, and those who could not afford to die because of hunger and poverty jumped to the Beitbridge border illegally to South Africa. When I was in Limpopo Province, I was told that one summer in 2008, two Zimbabweans crossed the Beitbridge border illegally and walked all night long to South Africa. They were tired and dehydrated. In the morning they found themselves in one of the villages, and they could not proceed with their journey to Johannesburg, since they were hungry and tired. They entered into a certain house and asked for water and food, and before they were given water and the food that they have requested, they both fainted. There are many sad stories about the Zimbabweans that they have encountered in their long journey to South Africa as their Promised Land and the land of milky and honey. All of these have been caused by the West, not by Pres. Robert Mugabe and "the brothers of destruction," Zimbabwe's war veterans. The future African generation will have to still contend with studying at the university with student loans simply because of poverty and unemployment. The future African generation will still have to contend with working for a slave wage just like in the case of the South African mining sector. The bosses of the mines are making a killing, while the miners can't even afford to pay the university fees for their children let alone dwell in a decent house where there is running water. It breaks my heart apart to see an African man drilling stones in the belly of the earth all day long only to be pay peanuts for monkeys, while the investors are sipping wine in the West and smoking the Cuban cigar and saying, "Africa is a hopeless continent," while receiving a considerable amount of profits from their investment in Africa. If Africa is a hopeless continent, why do you come to Africa to invest your blood money? There is another impending danger that I also see. The future African generation will have to work hard to pay back those foreign loans that have been taken by the current African leaders to build African infrastructure including the foreign loans that disappeared in the hands of African leaders. The future African generation will still have to contend with cleaning the mess that had been created by the current African generation. The West has corrupted Africa and the African people. It is the West that has introduced fast food, drugs, and prostitution. Once upon a time in Africa, there was peace and tranquility, and then came the West to disturb that prevailing peace and tranquility that was in Africa. When reading the Holy Bible, it is said, "And God rested on the seventh day." God rested in Africa on that seventh day. He would not have rested in the West, where there is too much drugs, guns, drones, fast food, and homosexuality. He rested in Africa, in the place of peace and tranquility. That peace and tranquility is gone, and Africa is forever in a war with itself fighting for the mineral resources that only benefit the West only not the African people. The future African generation still has to contend with infrastructure collapse that has been left behind by the current African leaders. It's common knowledge that African leaders borrow loans from the World Bank and IMF for infrastructural projects and eventually squander these loans by building their own expensive glass swimming pools and buying private jets for their families and their friends. The future African generation has to pay back those gigantic loans with hefty interest on top to the World Bank and IMF. The future African generation has to still contend with buying land from the Westerners, which has been stolen from the African people through guns, bullets, and dogs. The future African generation still has to contend with buying cars through the Western banks and making the Western investors richer than they are already. I have a very serious problem with the way things are happening in Africa. The West colonized Africa; whether they are British colonizers or French colonizers or Portuguese colonizers, it does not matter because at the end of the day, the West breathed together. Therefore, it does not matter whether Zimbabwe was colonized by Britain or Mozambique was colonized by Portugal. The fact is both Mozambique and Zimbabwe were the Western colonies, period. The West gave African nationalists political freedom and withheld the economic freedom due to the blindness owing to the fact that most African nationalists were not that long-sighted in their thinking. They settled for political freedom without economic freedom, which is what they should have pursued at all costs. The West until this day and age has a firm grip on Africa's economy. This is another problem that the African future generation should deal with. African liberation movements have done absolutely nothing to redress and reverse the economic imbalances of the past. Though they might get emotional and throw tantrum on the media about their economic achievements, the fact is the large chunk of African wealth is still at the hands of the white minority and the black capitalists who are claiming to be socialists and communists during the day while they are raving capitalists at night. It's painful to see Africans suffering the way they are suffering in the African continent knowing full well deep down that it was not supposed to be so had the peace talks that the African nationalists negotiated with the West covered the issue of reparations and reversal of Africa's wealth. When I say the West stole Africa's wealth, I don't necessarily mean mineral deposits only. The list that constitutes Africa's wealth is endless. The word "wealth" has been used to cover a variety of things that could be classified under wealth, whether it's mineral deposits, gold, diamonds, chrome, oil, platinum, and the list is endless. All of these precious metals and minerals resources are now in the hands of the West. My overall objective was not to incite violence against the West and wage wars against the West, but my overall objective was to bring to bear the blow-by-blow political account of events as they occurred in the past. It's true that the West colonized Africa and corrupted the African leaders by introducing them to the idea of foreign aid and social grants, and until this day and age, social grants are seen as the best mechanism to curb the scourge of poverty even if it is glaringly clear even to the blind man that social grants are the greatest contributor to the scourge of poverty that is ravaging the African continent. The number of social grant recipients in the case of South Africa is growing in leaps and bounds, and there's no end in sight that such upward trend will ever change. I have dealt with social grants in the chapter "The Poverty Cycle." If nothing is seriously done by the African leaders to put to an end to the poverty cycle that is ravaging the African continent, sooner or later the very same electorate that voted for these African leaders in power will soon turn against them. The same is true also in the Arab world. Part and parcel of the Arab Spring was simply because the Arab youth was sick and tired of seeing their political leaders getting richer at the expense of the ordinary people on the ground; the Arab youth revolted. It's true that the Arab Spring might have ended, but the end of the Arab Spring does not necessarily mean that the Arab Spring is over; it can reincarnate in a different form and fashion. The West was loving the Arab Spring; that is why the West jumped into the fire that was already burning and made huge financial injection to the Egyptian government in order to hijack the whole Arab Spring to look like it originated from the West. At the end of the Arab Spring, the winner was not the Egyptian people in the case of Egypt, but the West. There is one political line that I happened to love a lot, and this line is used by most US senators, and it goes like this: "America is with you." When the US senators are sent to Ukraine to monitor the situation on the ground, the US senators will deliver their long boring speeches and eventually say, "People of Ukraine, America is with you." The future African generation has to still deal with Chinese imports, which by then would have proliferated into hundredfold in the African continent. If the African leaders don't wake up from their sleep, they will sooner or later find out that China has deepened its firm economic grip on Africa's economy. Europe and the North America have had their share of the African pie, and now China and Russia want the very same African pie that the West is relishing. The West does not have a problem to throw money in Africa provided that there are long-lasting economic gains that will advance the lives of the Western future generation, while most African leaders don't look at the long-term effects of the current relationships that they have established with the West. George W. Bush, the former president of the United States of America, in his book titled *Decision Points,* writes:

> *The passage of time allows passions to cool, results to clarify, and scholars to compare different approaches.*[6]

Through the passage of time indeed passions of many African scholars have cooled down, and many Africans have never even dared to bother themselves about the source and the origin of the African problems. That is why I took it upon myself to research and find the real truth behind Africa's poverty and the African economic problems. It's logically unsound to attempt to predict and project the future without understanding the past and the present. I don't have the crystal ball, therefore I can't tell whether Pres. Robert Mugabe will complete his term of office as the president of Zimbabwe, but it is an inescapable reality that his health has deteriorated badly in recent months due to an eye operation.

THE WINDOW OF OPPORTUNITY

The window of opportunity has opened for many countries that had a bad relationship with the West. In the year 2013 and 2014 the world saw for the very first time the United States of America and Iranian supreme leader Ayatollah Ali Khamenei sending their delegations to resolve the long standoff between these two countries. Economic sanctions have been biting the Iranians for quite a long period of time, and the West was relentless to continue with the economic sanctions it has imposed to Iranian people unless otherwise the Iranian people show a change of heart and a change of political action. The Geneva talks between the Iranian delegation and the US delegation were meeting in good faith. The prime minister of Israel Benjamin Netanyahu was panicking and warning the United States that Iran is still on its path to develop chemical weapons, which it will later use to attack Israel. The political standpoint of Prime Minister Benjamin Netanyahu was that the United States must not buy into being hoodwinked by Iranians and ease the economic sanctions. In fact Prime Minister Benjamin Netanyahu was calling for more economic sanctions to the Iranian economy. The war between Benjamin Netanyahu of Israel and the youth of Iran became so bad that it even went to the social media because of comments that Benjamin Netanyahu made about the Iranian youth in which he said the Iranian youth will also like to wear jeans. The Iranian youth posted their pictures on Face book showing pictures of them wearing jeans, invalidating the statement that they will like to wear jeans as a result of lack of democracy. There were demands that were made by the US delegation in Geneva and there were demands that were also made by the Iranian delegation. At the end of the first Geneva talks between the USA and Iran, the Iranian delegation had struck a deal with the USA, and part of the deal meant that the Iranian government will limit the uranium enrichment by only 5 percent (over 80 percent is needed to make a nuclear weapon). This low level was sufficiently only for power generation. Iran is to stop enriching to 20 percent, the level needed for medical isotopes.[7] The Geneva Convention agreement was only a temporary measure between the P5+1 and the Iranian government. The Iranian government had come to the realization that economic sanctions are the cancer to its economy and trade relations with the West. It's common knowledge that the Geneva Convention agreement was going to be reviewed now and then. The point I am driving home about the Iranian deal with P5+1 is this: it is the window of opportunity for Iran to be allowed re-enter into the world's mainstream economy. Economic sanctions can sideline a country and even its people, though there are economic experts who will beg to differ with me. I have heard arguments in favor of economic sanctions, and I have also heard arguments that are against economic sanctions. The underlying point that is made by people who are in favor of economic sanctions is that economic sanctions will force the sanctioned country to look for new economic partners elsewhere and perhaps diversify its economy. There is some bit of truth in that statement. I likened Economic sanctions to leprosy, and there is no person who will wish to establish a relationship with a person who has leprosy. And then the next question will be, where will you get these economic partners that the proponents of economic sanctions are talking about? The truth of the matter is this: when you have leprosy, even your loving spouse will eventually run away from you, and that is what economic sanctions do to the economy of a country that is under economic sanctions even to the ordinary people on the ground. I have said before that there is an anecdotal five million Zimbabweans who are living in South Africa, and some of them have been absorbed by the South African economy due to the relevant skills and expertise that they possess to grow the South African economy. Therefore, as a result of economic sanctions that are eating the economy bit by bit, some of these Zimbabweans opted to establish small businesses, and some of them are selling fake CDs and vegetables on the streets of Pretoria. Therefore, economic sanctions are not good in their nature simply because they were not meant to make the economy of a sanctioned country to flourish, but they were meant to stifle the economy of the sanctioned country. That has been the overall rationale and objective behind the economic sanctions. The question that I want to pose into this last part of this book is the following: the world is witnessing the negotiations between the Iran and the P5+1, which are aimed at ending the economic sanctions, and what about ending the Zimbabwe's economic sanctions? Is Zimbabwe different from Iran? Before I answer that question, let me throw another question into the mix. How much Zimbabwean assets were frozen abroad due to economic sanctions? It's public knowledge that Iran, due to the Geneva Agreement between the Iranian government and the P5+1, will be paid US$100 billion from its assets, which were held abroad. The Zimbabwean economic sanctions are now thirteen years old on February 18, 2014. Let me put it differently: for a Zimbabwean child who was born on February 18, 2002, the only thing that this Zimbabwean child knows is economic sanctions; therefore this child has never lived life in a country that was economic sanction–free. I don't understand why the P5+1 can convene a meeting alone without including Zimbabwe, since the economy of Zimbabwe is still under economic sanctions just like Iran. Perhaps the West is still angry at the ZANU-PF victory of July 31, 2013, national elections. It's possible that had the MDC-T won the national of election, which were held on July 31, 2013, economic sanctions were going to be lifted by the West. It therefore gives rise to another problem now. It simply means that Zimbabwe's economic sanctions are not a political punishment for the ZANU-PF-led government, but it's a political instrument that sought to weaken and eventually bring to its knees the ZANU-PF regime and finally influence the people of Zimbabwe to turn against their own liberation movement that liberated them from the shackles of the Rhodesian laws of oppression. Now if that is the purpose of the economic sanctions, then the West has failed in its attempt to achieve its political and economic objectives in Zimbabwe. It's unfair and unjust that this window of opportunity is not open to the Zimbabwean government but it's only open to the people of Iran. The world has also witnessed the intervention of the West in the Syrian War. Though I have covered the Syrian War extensively and expansively, it's important that I give credit where credit is due. The West lowered its expectation for the government of Bashar al-Assad that it should only disclose its stockpile of chemical weapons and then give them to the hands of the international community for destruction. I have said before that had it not been for Vladimir Putin of Russia, Syria, Damascus, was going to be a ghost town or the Somali of the Middle East. If Zimbabwe's economic sanctions remain in place for the next four years, then Harare, as it has been said that it is the worst city on the earth, will ultimately be the ghost town of Zimbabwe.Garikai Chengu writes:

> *When Europeans came to Africa toward the turn of the fifteenth century, they found a prosperous civilization of enormous wealth. Agriculture and cattle rearing, pottery, ironwork, fisheries, salt mining, gold refining and ornament making, weaving, hunting, and long-distance trading were all well advanced at a time when Europe was still relatively backward.*

Garikai Chengu went on to talk about what he called Mugabeism—a model for African liberation:

> *Mugabeism is an ideology that appreciates that the only way to allow Africa to surpass its former glory is to undergo the three stages of any African revolution: political, agrarian, and economic.*[8]

Though I agree with the views that have been shared by Garikai Chengu about the three stages that an African revolution should undergo, African revolution until this day and age has not yet reached its intended objective, and the main reason African revolution has not yet reached its intended objective is simply the African liberation movements which stopped the agrarian and economic aspect of the African revolution. In the case of Zimbabweans, I can bear testament to this: agrarian and the economic revolution has cost the Zimbabwean people dearly. I will not go back to what I have already said to substantiate my point. The fact of the matter is this: the world has seen and learned how cruel the West is. The Western imperialists would rather kill for mineral resources from Africa rather than give away its economic grip for Africa's economy. The West feeds itself through African poverty, and chasing the West away from Africa simply means that the West will starve to death just like before it colonized Africa, and that is what the West will not allow to happen. The Zimbabwean government was supposed to do anything in its power to seize this precious moment in history, which is presented by the window of opportunity, and renegotiate with the West for economic sanctions to be lifted off. The stalemate and standoff between the West and Zimbabwe's government perhaps are the main causes why economic sanctions debate cannot be reopened with the West.

THE FUTURE

Political mistakes have been made by African liberation movements by embracing political freedom at the expense of economic freedom. My overall objective to write this book was to share the political light and perhaps assist the current African generation, which is stuck on its gadgets and social networks. I am by no way and means implying that this book should be used to settle political scores and political differences. I hope that the overall objective of this book has been achieved, which is partly to educate and inform the African generation where the African liberation movements went horribly wrong. It's understandable that the African liberation struggle stretched too long and lasted longer than the ordinary people anticipated including the freedom fighters, and fatigue in the process crept in. Hope dwindled in the process of hopeless, and dreams became shattered, and people turned to blame the very course that they have dedicated and sacrificed for all of their lives. That is exactly what happened during Africa's liberation struggle. African liberation movements were left with no exception but only to accept the political victory, which was based on ulterior motives from Africa's colonizers. The West has never given

Africa genuine political freedom coupled with economic freedom, but what the West did was to create a spiritual economic and political prison, which we Africans live in; we can't see it, taste it, or feel because it's spiritual. The fact of the matter is this: Africans are not politically free until this day and age, and I am not going to bother myself to attempt to talk about economic freedom because we all know in Africa that the West will never ever allow Africa to be free economically because economic freedom will destroy the very economic and political prison that the West has put Africa into. The West can't fathom a situation where Africa's mineral resources are used and owned by Africans to the benefit of the African people. That is why the West is happy to see African countries fighting among themselves and African nations fight each other simply because that brings political instability and will eventually engender economic instability. As long as the African continent will forever be in endless infighting with its people, there won't be political stability and economic opportunities that should end and decimate the scourge of poverty. Let me take this opportunity to reflect and make final remarks. There is nothing on the face of the earth that does not have an end. Therefore if a thing has its beginning, it has to have its end. There is too much information that I have gathered in the process of doing my research, and not all the information that I have gathered could find its way into this book. However, I have tried by all means to slice, cut, chop, and change indigestible information to the point where it was digestible and could fit into this book. This book is a candid and honest work that can be relied upon because the author of this book is not a political member of any political party and does not even support any political agenda of any political party. I hope that through this book you will get a better understanding of the African continent and perhaps understand the gravity of political mistakes that were made by the African liberation movements and the machinations of the West in the colonization of Africa. If the Berlin, Germany, conference resolved to the colonization of the African continent, then the Berlin, Germany, conference should be blamed for the colonization of Africa and the poverty that many African people find themselves in. The West stole Africa's wealth, and the whole world now knows it.

God bless Mother Africa and her mineral resources.

ACKNOWLEDGMENT

There is nothing so delighting like setting a goal for yourself and eventually seeing that goal becoming a reality. When I started this project, I had many hiccups on the way that prevented me to finish this project on time. I would like to take this opportunity to express my sincere gratitude to my mentor and my friend Mr. Letsoalo for encouraging me to continue with this project even at a time when the odds were against me. We took almost five months discussing about writing this book. I vividly remember Mr. Letsoalo's words—that I must be ready to be criticized, since the subject of Africa's wealth is a very sensitive subject. I should also highlight the fact that the main reason for writing this book is not to incite violence but to bring to bear the fundamental mistakes that have been committed in the past by the nationalists in the pursuit of a long-term solution via the short route. There are Africans that are living inside the continent of Africa, and those Africans who are in Diaspora will find this book relevant and will resonate with them very well. I hope that the people of Zimbabwe one day will enjoy those olden days when Zimbabwe was known as the breadbasket of Southern Africa. There is nothing so terrifying than to get into another country that is politically unstable before the national election. I went to Zimbabwe before the national elections of the July 31, 2013. There wasn't international media at that point in time. The international media came after I left Zimbabwe, and they went on to cover the national elections from the beginning until the end. The people of Zimbabwe made themselves proud, though there were dissatisfaction and complaints about the outcome of the national election results, but at the end of the day there was no political violence that was reported on the media. There is no way that the MDC-T will ever accept defeat simply because it had pinned all its hopes on this national elections, hoping that at least finally

Pres. Robert Mugabe will be sent to the retirement village once and for all. When the MDC-T failed diametrically to send Pres. Robert Mugabe to the retirement village, they complained about what they call "monumental rigging." I would also like to take this opportunity to express my sincere gratitude to the University of South Africa Library for lending me a variety of books that I have used in the process of completing this project. I am also indebted to the Gauteng Department of Education (GDE) Library for Educators in Pretoria for lending me books. There is one person that I will never forget in the entire of my journey, and that is Terry, the driver who was driving me around in Harare, the capital city of Zimbabwe. We went together in Heroes' Acre and we went together even in the notorious prison of Zimbabwe Chikurubi Prison. Pres. Robert Mugabe's health has deteriorated dramatically since July 31, 2013. It would not surprise many people if he does not complete his tenure in office as the president of the country due to his forever deteriorating medical condition. Mr. Silverton does not hold the same view that is shared by many people. He believes that Pres. Robert Mugabe will live to finish his political term in office. Personally I believe that Pres. Robert Mugabe will not complete his political term in office as the president of Zimbabwe. Quite frankly it does not have any grave bearing to the politics of Zimbabwe, since the national elections have been held already even if Pres. Robert Mugabe can step down from the political office without completing his term in office. That is my story, and that is my journey. The West stole Africa's wealth, and I have proven it with both objective evidence and circumstantial evidence. God bless Mother Africa and God bless her mineral resources.

REFERENCES

Chapter 1: Pyrrhic Victory

[1] *The Holy Bible: New King James Bible*, copyright ©1982 by Thomas Nelson Inc., Nashville, Tennessee, USA. Genesis 1 verse 1–2. p. 1.

[2] Mandela, Nelson: *LONG WALK to FREEDOM*, first published in Great Britain in 1994 by Little, Brown and Company. p. 583.

[3] Feiler, Bruce: *Walking the Bible*, published in 2001 by William Morrow an imprint of Harper Collins Publishers. p.162.

[4] Ibid., p. 162.

[5] Ibid., p. 163.

[6] Maylam Paul: *A History of the African People of South Africa: From the Early Iron Age to the 1970s.*

[7] Ibid.

[8] Ibid.

[9] Ibid.

[10] Ibid.

[11] *Path of Blood*, Becker, P., Penguin Books, London, (1979).

[12] www.geni.com.

[13] www.govt.co.za.

[14] www.geni.com.

[15] Ibid.

[16] Ibid.

[17] Ibid.

[18] www.thehda.co.za/upload/image/unpan005172pdf. 1996. p. 8–9.

Chapter 2: The Fatal Error of Trial and Error

[1] www.*Sunday Times*.co.za.

[2] www.maropeng.co.za.

[3] *The Holy Bible: New King James Bible*, copyright ©1982 by Thomas Nelson Inc., Nashville, Tennessee, USA. Genesis 1 verse 1–2. p. 1.

[4] Towns, Elmer L., *Bible Answers for almost All Your Questions* published in Nashville 2003, Tennesee, by Thomas Nelson Inc.

[5] The *Sunday Mail*, 16–22 June 2013.

[6] Hlumelo Biko, *The Great African Society: A Plan for a Nation Gone Astray*, published in 2013 by Jonathan Ball Publishers (pty) Ltd.

[7] The guide through IFRS, Part B 2, 2012. IFRS Foundation. Official pronouncements issued at July 2012 with extensive cross-references and other annotations.

[8] Koenderman, Tony, *Sanctions*, first published in 1982 by Jonathan Ball publishers.

[9] Ibid.

[10] www.govt.co.za.

[11] www.thezimbabwean.org.

Chapter 3: Justice

[1] www.wikepedia.com.

[2] Hill, Geoff. *The Battle for Zimbabwe: The Final Countdown*, 2003. p. 52.

[3] Harman, Nicholas and Nkomo, Joshua, *The Story of My Life* (autobiography), 1984: ISBN 0-413-54500-8, ISBN 978-0-413-54500-8.

[4] "Ranking of the World's Diamonds by Estimated 2013 Production" Kitco August 2, 2013.

[5] "Marange may not be the world's largest diamond producer for much longer," Mining.com, February 10, 2014.

[6] The *Zimbabwean Gazette* 19–25 September 2013.

[7] The *Standard* September 15–21 2013.

[8] Hutson, H. P. W. Major General, *Rhodesia: Ending an Era*.

[9] Ibid.

[10] Mandela, Nelson: *LONG WALK to FREEDOM*, first published in Great Britain in 1994 by Little, Brown and Company, p. 127–128.

[11] Koenderman, Tony, *Sanctions*, first published in 1982 by Jonathan Ball publishers. p. 50.

[12] Ibid.

[13] www.unwfp.org.
[14] Ibid, p. 163.
[15] Ibid, p. 164.
[16] Ibid.
[17] Ibid.
[18] Guy Arnold, *Africa: A Modern History*, published in Great Britain in 2005 by Atlantic Books.
[19] Meredith, op. cit, p. 149.
[20] *Mail & Guardian* June 21 to 27, 2013.

Chapter 4: Lifetime Error

[1] Anthea Jeffery, *Conflict at the Crossroads in Bophuthatswana.*
[2] *Southern Times* 1 Sunday December 2013.
[3] Brown Richard and Christopher Saunders, *Africa South of the Sahara.*
[4] New Zimbabwe 05/07/2013 by staff reporter.
[5] The *Southern Times* Sunday, 29 September 2013.
[6] Chikane Frank, *Eight Days in September*, Publisher: Pan Macmillan South Africa
[7] *Sunday Times* 2 June 2013.
[8] www.guro.com.
[9] *Sunday Times* 4 April 2010.
[10] Ibid.
[11] Ibid.
[12] www.anc.org.
[13] Koenderman, Tony, *Sanctions,* first published in 1982 by Jonathan Ball Publishers, p. 88.
[14] Mandela, Nelson: *LONG WALK to FREEDOM*, first published in Great Britain in 1994 by Little, Brown and Company, p. 196.
[15] Ibid. p. 197.

Chapter 5: The Land Crisis

[1] *Sunday Mail in Depth* September 22–28 2013.
[2] *Mail & Guardian* September 6 to 12 2013.
[3] Http://www.zambuko.com/mbirapage/resources.
[4] Chung, Fay, *Re-living the Second Chimurenga*; Kaarsholm, preben (2006).
[5] Mandela, Nelson: *LONG WALK to FREEDOM*, first published in Great Britain

in 1994 by Little, Brown and Company, p. 35.

[6] Spengane Yamkela Fortune, *Southern Times* 1 Sunday September 2013, p. 13.

[7] *Sunday Times* August 25 2013.

[8] Becker, P., *Path of Blood*, Penguin Books, London (1979).

[9] *Herald* Barry, David, "The Past Is the Future." Published by Weaver Press, 5 September 2005.

[10] Brown Richard and Christopher Saunders, *Africa South of the Sahara*.

[11] Hamouchene Hamza, The *Southern Times* Sunday 13 October 2013.

[12] Guchu Wonder, The *Southern Times* Sunday 4 August 2013.

[13] Ibid.

[14] Ibid.

[15] Ibid.

[16] Hoile, David, *Mozambique Resistance and Freedom: A Case for Reassessment*, published by Taylor & Francis Ltd.

[17] Hoile David, *Mozambique 1962–1993: A Political Chronology*, published by Mozambique Institute (October 1994).

[18] Ibid.

[19] Preston, Mathew. *Ending the Civil War: Rhodesia and Lebanon in Perspective.*

[20] Chung, Fay, *Re-living the Second Chimurenga* ; Kaarsholm, preben (2006).

[21] Faber and Faber, *The Struggle for Zimbabwe*. Boston.

[22] Galbraith, J. S., *The Early Years of the British South Africa Company* (1974).

[23] Slinn, P. 9 (1971). *Commercial Concessions and Politics during the Colonial Period: The Role of the British South African Company in Northern Rhodesia 1890–1964.* Pp. 367, 374.

[24] Raftopous, Brian and Savage, Tyrone, *Zimbabwe Injustice and Political Reconciliation*. Published by Weaver Press, September 5, 2000.

[25] Guy Arnold, *Africa: A Modern History*, published in Great Britain in 2005 by Atlantic Books, p. 903.

[26] Zunga, Luke, *Farm Invasions in Zimbabwe*, published in 2003.

[27] The *Guardian*, UK "Land Redistribution Is not Robbery, but a Necessity."

[28] *Online News Hour*—"Land Redistribution in the Southern Africa: Zimbabwe Program." Pbs.org. Retrieved 2012-11-20.

[29] Ibid. p. 4.

[30] Ibid. p. 5.

Chapter 6: The End of an Era

[1] Putin, Vladimir, The *New York Times*, 11 September 2013, p. 6.

[2] www.govt.za.
[3] *Sunday Times* 8 December 2013.
[4] Habib, Adam, *Sunday Times* 15 December 2013.
[5] Netshitenzhe, Joel, *Sunday Times* 8 December 2013.
[6] The *Southern Times* 20 October 2013.
[7] Mahoso, Tafataona, The *Sunday Mail in Depth* September 22–28 2013.
[8] Mandela, Nelson: *LONG WALK to FREEDOM*, first published in Great Britain in 1994 by Little, Brown and Company. p. 438.
[9] Ibid, 464.

Chapter 7: The Poverty Cycle

[1] Obama, Barack, *Dreams from My Father*, 2004, Crown Publisher. p. 22.
[2] www.competition commission.org.
[3] Froese Udo, The *Southern Times* 4 Sunday August 2013.
[4] Zaba, Faith, *Zimbabwe Independent* September 20 to 26 2013.
[5] Mbeki, Thabo, The *Southern Sun* Sunday, 10 November 2013.
[6] Njini, Felix, The *Southern Times* Sunday 13 October 2013.
[7] Guy Arnold, *Africa: A Modern History*, published in Great Britain in 2005 by Atlantic Books.
[8] *Hutchinson Encyclopedia*, "Cycle of Poverty."
[9] www.statssa.gov.za.
[10] www.moneyweb.co.za.
[11] Berry Ruth, The *New Zealand Herald*, 12 July 2006.
[12] http://media.nzherald.co.n/webcontinet/document/pdf/living-standatrds-2004.
[13] Trump, Donald J. and Kiyosaki, Robert, *Why We Want You to be Rich: Two Men, One Message*. Originally in USA in 2006 by Rich Press in 2006.
[14] Ruby K. Payne, *The Framework of Understanding Poverty*.
[15] Sachs Jeffrey. *The End of poverty*, 2005, p. 20.
[16] Ravallion, Martin, Chen, Shaohua, and Sangraula, Prem "Dollar a Day," The *World Bank Economic Review*, 23, 2, 2009, pp. 163–168.
[17] "Indicators of Poverty." Retrieved 2008-02-14.
[18] Banda Mabvuto, *Mail & Guardian* October 18 to 24 2013.
[19] Cabeche, Aristides, *Mail and Guardian* October 18 to 24 2013.
[20] *Mail & Guardian* August 8 to 15 2013.
[21] Manuel, Trevor, The *Southern Times* Sunday, 1 December 2013.
[22] Ibid.
[23] Bush, George W. *Decision Points*, first published in the United States by Crown

Publishers in 2010. p. 335.

[24] Shingirai, Philip, The *Southern Times* Sunday, 2 February 2014.

[25] Gates, Bill and Melinda, *Mail & Guardian* January 24 to 30 2014.

Chapter 8: Reflect

[1] Rusesabagina, Paul with Zoellner, Tom, *An Ordinary Man: THE TRUE STORY BEHIND HOTEL RWANDA.* first published in Great Britain in 2006 by Bloomsbury Publishing Plc. p. 25.

[2] "Rwanda: How the Genocide Happened," BBC, April 1, 2004, which gives an estimate of eight hundred thousand, and OAU sets inquiry into Rwandan Genocide, *Africa Recovery*, vol. 12.

[3] Ibid p. xi.

[4] *Mail & Guardian* January 10 to 16 2014.

[5] Mabasa Sasa and Tichaona Zindoga, The *Southern Times* Sunday, 10 November 2013.

[6] Tebele, Mpho, The *Southern Times* Sunday 6 to 12 December 2013.

[7] Kay, Joseph, The *Southern Times* Sunday, 4 August 2013.

[8] Ibid.

Chapter 9: The Plundering of Wealth

[1] Guy Arnold, *Africa: A Modern History*, published in Great Britain in 2005 by Atlantic Books.

[2] Ibid.

[3] "Iran-Iraq War (1980–1988-The History Beat –SearchBeat.com." history.searchbeat.com. Retrieved 5 October 2013.

[4] Malone, Andrew, The *Sunday Independent*, June 15, 2014, p. 11.

[5] Steyn, Lisa, *Mail & Guardian* June 27 to July 3, 2014, p. 1 of Business column.

[6] Sauti Lazarus, The *Southern Times*, 25 May 2014, p. 13.

[7] Ibid.

[8] www.Aljazeera.com.

[9] *City Press* 12 January 2014.

[10] Rusesabagina, Paul with Zoellner, Tom, *An Ordinary Man: THE TRUE STORY BEHIND HOTEL RWANDA.* first published in Great Britain in 2006 by Bloomsbury Publishing Plc. p. 25.

[11] Hengeveld, Maria, The *Southern Times* Sunday, 25 August 2013

[12] Masote Mamello, *City Press* 12 January 2014.
[13] Bush, George W. *Decision Points*, first published in the United States by Crown Publishers in 2010. P. 270.
[14] Ibid, p. 262.
[15] Ibid, p. 351
[16] Ibid
[17] Walter, Rodney, *How Europe Underdeveloped Africa*. Washington DC, Harvard University Press, 1981.
[18] www.NEWS24 NEWS.

Chapter 10: The War against Illegal Substance

[1] www.timeslive.co.za
[2] Ibid.
[3] The *Times* Monday February 17 /2014.
[4] Majani, Florence, The *Mail & Guardian* August 30 to September 2013.
[5] Sowetan, February 17, 2014.
[6] The *Southern Times* Sunday, 23 February 2014.
[7] Ibid.
[8] The *Sunday Independent* February 23, 2014.
[9] Ibid.
[10] Lokongo Antoine Roger, The *Southern Times* Sunday, 16 February 2014.
[11] Butagira Tabu, *Mail & Guardian* February 21 to 27, 2014.
[12] Ibid.
[13] The *Southern Times* Sunday, 16 February 2014.
[14] Davids Nashira and Nombembe Philani, The *Times* Wednesday February 26, 2014.

Chapter 11: Cash Liquidity Crisis

[1] Mazire Itai, The *Sunday Mail* September 22–28, 2013.
[2] Mahopo Zöe, Sowetan Monday March 10, 2014.
[3] The Voice of America Tuesday, March 25, 2014.
[4] www.wikipedia.com.
[5] Ibid.
[6] The *Sunday Independent* March 2, 2014, by Peta Thorny croft.
[7] The *Southern Times* Sunday, 30 March 2014 by Baffour Ankomah.

[8] http://www.blommberg.com/apps/news.

[9] Ibid.

Chapter 12: The Vicious Cycle

[1] Preston, Mathew (2004). *Ending Civil War; Rhodesia and Lebanon in Perspective.* London: Taurus. p. 25. ISBN 1850435790.

[2] Spengane Fortune, The *Southern Times*, Sunday 1 September 2013.

[3] *Mail & Guardian* (Johannesburg, South Africa). Retrieved 3 November 2009.

[4] Brown Richard and Christopher Saunders, *Africa South of the Sahara* 2005.

[5] www.News24. 28 February 2012.

[6] Dlamini Jacobs, *Business Day* 19 November 2009.

[7] Catholic Commission for Justice and Peace and the Legal Resources Foundation in Harare *Breaking the Silence*: *Building True Peace* in Zimbabwe in 1997.

[8] The *Southern Times* Sunday, 20 April 2014.

[9] Hugh Marshall Hole, *Old Rhodesian Days*, published by London News in 1896 30 May, p. 2.

[10] Guy Arnold, *Africa: A Modern History*, published in Great Brtain in 2005 by Atlantic Books, p. 521.

[11] Ibid, p. 186.

Chapter 13: The Future

[1] Sauti Lazurus, *Southern Times* Sunday, 2 February 2014.

[2] Ibid.

[3] Shingirai, Philip, The *Southern Times* Sunday, 2 February 2014.

Conclusion

[1] Muleya Dumisane, The *Sunday Independent*, 23 February 2014.

[2] Greene Harold, The *Southern Times* Sunday, 9 March 2014, p. 12.

[3] Hawkins, Tony, Politicsweb, 28 June 2014, p. 4.

[4] Mabasa Sasa, The *Southern Times*, Sunday, 18 August 2013, p. 3.

[5] Swaine, Jon, The *Southern Times*, Sunday 9 March 2014, p. 13.

[6] Bush, George W. *Decision Points*, first published in the United States by Crown Publishers in 2010.

[7] Margolis, Eric, The *Southern Times*, Sunday, 15 December 2013, p. 15.

[8] Garikai Chengu, The *Southern Times*, Sunday 2 March 2014, p. 23.

Made in the USA
Columbia, SC
27 November 2021

49842945R00381